T0214378

Lecture Notes in Computer Science 8961

Commenced Publication in 1973
Founding and Former Series Editors:
Gerhard Goos, Juris Hartmanis, and Jan van Leeuwen

Editorial Board

More information about this series at http://www.springer.com/series/7407

Marian Gheorghe · Grzegorz Rozenberg
Arto Salomaa · Petr Sosík · Claudio Zandron (Eds.)

Membrane Computing

15th International Conference, CMC 2014
Prague, Czech Republic, August 20–22, 2014
Revised Selected Papers

 Springer

Editors

Marian Gheorghe
Department of Computer Science
University of Sheffield
Sheffield
United Kingdom

Grzegorz Rozenberg
Leiden Inst. Advanced Computer Science
Leiden University
Leiden
The Netherlands

Arto Salomaa
Turku Center for Computer Science
Turku
Finland

Petr Sosík
Dept. Mathematics & Computer Science
Silesian University
Opava
Czech Republic

Claudio Zandron
DISCO
University of Milan-Bicocca
Milan
Italy

ISSN 0302-9743
Lecture Notes in Computer Science
ISBN 978-3-319-14369-9
DOI 10.1007/978-3-319-14370-5

ISSN 1611-3349 (electronic)

ISBN 978-3-319-14370-5 (eBook)

Library of Congress Control Number: 2014958974

LNCS Sublibrary: SL1 – Theoretical Computer Science and General Issues

Springer Cham Heidelberg New York Dordrecht London

Printed on acid-free paper

Springer International Publishing AG Switzerland is part of Springer Science+Business Media
(www.springer.com)

Preface

This volume contains a selection of papers presented at the 15th International Conference on Membrane Computing (CMC 15), held in Prague, Czech Republic, during August 20–22, 2014 (*http://cmc15.slu.cz/*).

The CMC series was initiated by Gheorghe Păun as the Workshop on Multiset Processing in the year 2000. Then two workshops on Membrane Computing were organized in Curtea de Argeş, Romania, in 2001 and 2002. A selection of papers from each of these three meetings was published as volume 2235 of the Lecture Notes in Computer Science series, as a special issue of Fundamenta Informaticae (volume 49, numbers 1–3, 2002), and as volume 2597 of Lecture Notes in Computer Science, respectively. The next six workshops took place in Tarragona, Spain (in July 2003), Milan, Italy (in June 2004), Vienna, Austria (in July 2005), Leiden, The Netherlands (in July 2006), Thessaloniki, Greece (in June 2007), and Edinburgh, UK (in July 2008), with the proceedings published in Lecture Notes in Computer Science as volumes 2933, 3365, 3850, 4361, 4860, and 5391, respectively. The 10th workshop returned to Curtea de Argeş in August 2009 (LNCS volume 5957).

From the year 2010, the series of meetings on membrane computing continued as the Conference on Membrane Computing with the 2010, 2011, 2012, and 2013 editions held in Jena, Germany (LNCS volume 6501), Fontainebleau, France (LNCS volume 7184), Budapest, Hungary (LNCS volume 7762), and Chişinău, Republic of Moldova (LNCS volume 8340), respectively. Nowadays a Steering Committee takes care of the continuation of the CMC series which is organized under the auspices of the European Molecular Computing Consortium (EMCC). A regional version of CMC, the Asian Conference on Membrane Computing, ACMC, started with 2012 edition in Wuhan, China and continued with 2013 and 2014 editions held in Chengdu, China and Coimbatore, India.

CMC 15 was organized by the Institute of Computer Science of the Faculty of Philosophy and Science, Silesian University in Opava, in collaboration with the Action M Agency, Prague. A special session was dedicated to the memory of Prof. Yurii Rogozhin, the main organizer of the CMC 14, a world-class mathematician and computer scientist and, last but not least, a dear friend of many participants of the CMC series.

Invited lectures were given by Luděk Cienciala (Czech Republic), Erzsébet Csuhaj-Varjú (Hungary), Mario J. Pérez Jiménez (Spain), Jiří Wiedermann (Czech Republic), and Claudio Zandron (Italy). Based on the votes of the CMC 15 participants, the Best Paper Award for this year's CMC Conference was given to Alberto Leporati, Luca Manzoni, Giancarlo Mauri, Antonio E. Porreca, and Claudio Zandron for their paper "Simulating Elementary Active Membranes with an Application to the P Conjecture."

In addition to the texts of the invited talks, this volume contains 19 papers out of the 24 presented at the Conference and two papers selected from the 22 presented at the

ACMC 2014. Each paper was subject to at least two referee reports for the Conferences and of an additional one for this volume.

The editors warmly thank the Program Committee, the invited speakers, the authors of the papers, the reviewers, and all the participants for their contributions to the success of CMC 15.

November 2014

Marian Gheorghe
Grzegorz Rozenberg
Arto Salomaa
Petr Sosík
Claudio Zandron

Organization

Steering Committee

Gabriel Ciobanu	Iaşi, Romania
Erzsébet Csuhaj-Varjú	Budapest, Hungary
Rudolf Freund	Vienna, Austria
Marian Gheorghe (Chair)	Sheffield, UK
Vincenzo Manca	Verona, Italy
Maurice Margenstern	Metz, France
Giancarlo Mauri	Milan, Italy
Linqiang Pan	Wuhan, China
Gheorghe Păun	Bucharest, Romania/Seville, Spain
Mario J. Pérez-Jiménez	Seville, Spain
Petr Sosík	Opava, Czech Republic
Sergey Verlan	Paris, France

Organizing Committee

Petr Sosík (Co-chair)	Opava, Czech Republic
Petr Čermák (Co-chair)	Opava, Czech Republic
Luděk Cienciala	Opava, Czech Republic
Miroslav Langer	Opava, Czech Republic
Šárka Vavrečková	Opava, Czech Republic
Štěpánka Tůmová	Opava, Czech Republic
Hana Černíková	Opava, Czech Republic

Program Committee

Artiom Alhazov	Chişinău, Moldova
Luděk Cienciala	Opava, Czech Republic
Gabriel Ciobanu	Iaşi, Romania
Erzsébet Csuhaj-Varjú	Budapest, Hungary
Giuditta Franco	Verona, Italy
Rudolf Freund	Vienna, Austria
Marian Gheorghe (Co-chair)	Sheffield, UK
Thomas Hinze	Cottbus, Germany
Florentin Ipate	Bucharest, Romania
Shankara Narayanan Krishna	Bombay, India
Alberto Leporati	Milan, Italy
Vincenzo Manca	Verona, Italy
Maurice Margenstern	Metz, France
Giancarlo Mauri	Milan, Italy

P Systems:
A Formal Approach to Social Networks
(Abstract)

Erzsébet Csuhaj-Varjú[1], Marian Gheorghe[2], and György Vaszil[3]

[1] Department of Algorithms and Their Applications, Faculty of Informatics
Eötvös Loránd University, Pázmány Péter sétány 1/c, 1117 Budapest, Hungary
csuhaj@inf.elte.hu
[2] Department of Computer Science, University of Sheffield
Regent Court, 211 Portobello, Sheffield S1 4DP, United Kingdom
m.gheorghe@sheffield.ac.uk
[3] Department of Computer Science, Faculty of Informatics
University of Debrecen, PO Box 12, 4010 Debrecen, Hungary
vaszil.gyorgy@inf.unideb.hu

One of the major challenges for membrane computing is to find applications of the obtained theoretical results in different scientific areas. Concepts and methods in P systems theory have been so far successfully employed in some other areas of computer science and in modeling several biological phenomena, but except applications in linguistics and natural language processing, only a limited amount of attention has been paid to using membrane systems as formal tools in social sciences.

One of the few steps in this direction was made in [12] where P systems were proposed to model social networks, an area of contemporary computer science and practice which is rapidly growing, involving methods and approaches from a multitude of research areas.

Roughly speaking, social networks are communities of individuals connected through a communication network and interested in some common social phenomena or activities. When formalizing these networks, their special features, as interpersonal relationships between individuals, are expected to appear in the syntactic model. In various formalisms related to the study of social phenomena, these relationships are defined as information-carrying connections. Two basic types of them are *strong* and *weak ties*. Weak ties are responsible for the embeddedness and structure of social networks and for the communication within these systems [16]. There are other measures that characterize connections between nodes (agents). *Centrality* gives an indication of the social power of a node and the strength of its connections. It relies on other measures, *betweenness* or *closeness degrees*. Betweenness is the degree of connectivity between a node and the nodes that have a significant number of neighbors (direct connections). Closeness measures the distance between a node and all the other nodes in the network, degree counts the number of connections. For more details on these concepts and for some other measures of connections existing in social networks the reader is advised to consult [25].

Research supported in part by the Hungarian Scientific Research Fund, "OTKA", project K75952.

To describe communities of agents interacting with each other and with their dynamically changing environment, purely syntactic models have already been used. Examples from formal language theory are the framework of eco-grammar systems, launched in [10] and networks of (parallel) language processors describing populations of agents by rewriting systems in [8,14]. Multi-agent systems in terms of formal language theory and membrane computing were discussed in [5], [6], [4], and [17].

P systems, especially tissue P systems, can also be considered as collections of agents (individuals) communicating with each other: the compartments or nodes with the multisets of objects represent the individuals and the rules of the system describe the communication/interaction between the components. In the case of population P systems, see [7], the established communication links may dynamically change. Notice that the objects can also be considered as information pieces. In this case a node represents a loosely organized community of agents.

In [12] new classes of P systems capturing communication aspects in social networks were introduced and various research topics related to connections between P systems theory and the theory of social interactions and networks were initiated. They are called *population P systems governed by communication* (pgcP systems, for short). In this case, in addition to the multisets of standard objects which are called cellular objects, so-called communication objects are present in the network. The transition takes place by rewriting and communication of the cellular objects and recording the performed communication. The transitions are governed by communication, i.e., rules can be performed only if some predicates on the multisets of communication symbols associated to the links are satisfied. Whenever communication takes place, the number of communication symbols associated to the link increases.

It is easy to see that the model provides various possibilities to study the behavior of the nodes: *ordinary* or *popular* nodes - those that host individuals and allow communication between them; *new-born* nodes - those that are dynamically created and linked to the existing network; *non-visible* or *extinct* nodes - the nodes that are no longer connected to the network or have disappeared; nodes with one way communication, only allowing information to go into, *blackholes* or allowing only to exit from, *whiteholes*. Some of these aspects have been already discussed in membrane computing: for example, population P systems allow nodes to be dynamically connected and disconnected [7]. We can also take into account connections between nodes and look at the *volume of communication* - the amount of (new) information generated or sent-received by various nodes or groups of nodes; *frequency of communicated messages* - the number of communication steps related to the evolution (computation) steps; *communication motifs* - patterns of communication identified throughout the network evolution.

In [12] we have focused on communication in these networks. In order to characterize it, and the fact that the strength of connections might evolve in time by either increasing or decreasing the frequency of communication, we introduced some sort of symbols that act in this respect, called complementary communication symbols. The customary (or positive) symbols strengthen a connection, whereas the complementary (negative) ones weaken it.

The idea of complementary alphabets is not new in the field of natural computing. It is a core idea of *DNA computing*, and the concept of related notions have been discussed in membrane computing as well [1], [2], [3], [20], [19].

In [12] some further concepts regarding some specific types of pgcP systems have also been defined, and some preliminary results for *deterministic* and *non-cooperative* pgcP systems, based on tools of Lindenmayer systems (D0L systems), have been presented. Among others, we described the growth of the communication volume, the frequency, and the intensity of communication on the links.

In our talk we discussed pgcP systems and presented a preview of open problems and possible research directions. For example, important questions are how the different types of predicates for communication affect the volume and the intensity of communication and the types of communication motifs in the network. Description of other *concepts and measures* from social networks like *leaders and clusters emergence* in terms of pgcP systems would also be of interest.

References

1. A. Alhazov, B. Aman, R. Freund, Gh. Păun. Matter and Anti-Matter in Membrane Systems. In: *BWMC12* (L.F. Macías, M.A. Martínez-del-Amor, Gh. Păun, A. Riscos-Núñez, L. Valencia-Cabrera, eds.), Fénix Editora, 1–26, 2014.
2. B. Aman, G. Ciobanu. Turing completeness using three mobile membranes. In *Unconventional Computing 2009*, Lecture Notes in Computer Science, 5715, 42–55, 2009.
3. B. Aman, G. Ciobanu. Mutual mobile membranes systems with surface objects. In *7-th Brainstorming Week of Membrane Computing*, 29–39, 2009.
4. G. Bel-Enguix. A Multi-agent Model for Simulating the Impact of Social Structure in Linguistic Convergence. In *ICAART(2)* (J. Filipe et. al, Eds.), INSTICC Press, 367–372, 2009.
5. G. Bel-Enguix, M. A. Grando, M. D. Jiménez López. A Grammatical Framework for Modelling Multi-Agent Dialogues. In *PRIMA 2006* (Z.-Z. Shi, R. Sadananda, Eds.), LNAI 4088, Springer Verlag, Berlin Heidelberg, 10–21, 2009.
6. G. Bel-Enguix, M. D. Jiménez López. Membranes as Multi-agent Systems: an Application for Dialogue Modelling. In *IFIP PPAI 2006* (J.K. Debenham, Ed.), Springer, 31–40, 2006.
7. F. Bernardini, M. Gheorghe. Population P systems. *Intern J of Universal Comp Sci*, 10, 509–539, 2004.
8. E. Csuhaj-Varjú. Networks of Language Processors. *EATCS Bulletin* 63, 120–134, 1997.
9. E. Csuhaj-Varjú. Computing by networks of Watson-Crick D0L systems. In *Proc. Algebraic Systems, Formal Languages and Computation* (M. Ito, Ed.) RIMS Kokyuroku 1166, August 2000, Research Institute for Mathematical Sciences, Kyoto University, Kyoto, 43–51, 2000.
10. E. Csuhaj-Varjú, J. Kelemen, A. Kelemenová, Gh. Păun. Eco-Grammar Systems: A Grammatical Framework for Studying Lifelike Interactions. *Artificial Life*, 3(3), 1–28, 1997.
11. E. Csuhaj-Varjú, V. Mitrana. Evolutionary systems: a language generating device inspired by evolving communities of cells. *Acta Informatica*, 36(11), 913–926, 2000.
12. E. Csuhaj-Varjú, M. Gheorghe, M. Oswald, Gy. Vaszil. P systems for Social Networks. In *BWMC9* (M.A. Martínez-del-Amor, Gh. Păun, I. Pérez-Hurtado, F.J. Romero-Campero, L. Valencia-Cabrera, eds.), Fénix Editora, 113–124, 2011.
13. E. Csuhaj-Varjú, A. Salomaa. Networks of Watson-Crick D0L systems. In *Words, Languages & Combinatorics III. Proceedings of the International Colloquium, Kyoto, Japan, March 14-21, 2000.* (M. Ito, T. Imaoka, Eds.), World Scientific Publishing Co., Singapore, 134–149, 2003.
14. E. Csuhaj-Varjú, A. Salomaa. Networks of Parallel Language Processors. In *New Trends in Formal Languages. Control, Cooperation, and Combinatorics* (Gh. Păun, A. Salomaa, Eds.), LNCS 1218, Springer Verlag, Berlin Heidelberg, 299-318, 1997.

15. E. Csuhaj-Varjú, Gy. Vaszil. P automata or purely communicating accepting P systems. In *Membrane Computing*, LNCS 2579, Springer Verlag, Berlin Heidelberg, 219–233, 2003.
16. M.D. Granovetter. The Impact of Social Structures on Economic Development. Journal of Economic Perspectives, 19, 33–50, 2004.
17. M. D. Jiménez López. Agents in Formal Language Theory: An Overview. In *Highlights in Practical Applications of Agents and Multiagent Systems. 9th International Conference on Practical Applications of Agents and Multiagent Systems* (J. Bajo Pérez et. al, Eds.) Advances in Intelligent and Soft Computing 89, Springer, 283–290, 2011.
18. M. Minsky. *Finite and Infinite Machines*. Prentice Hall, Englewood Cliffs, New Jersey, 1967.
19. Gh. Păun. *Membrane computing. An Introduction*. Springer, 2002.
20. L. Pan, Gh. Păun. Spiking neural P systems with anti-spikes, *Int J Computers Comms Control*, 4, 273–282, 2009.
21. Gh. Păun. Computing with Membranes. *J. of Comput. Syst. Sci.*, 61, 108–143, 2000.
22. Gh. Păun, G. Rozenberg, A. Salomaa. *DNA Computing - New Computing Paradigms*. Springer Verlag, 1998.
23. G. Rozenberg, A. Salomaa. (Eds). *Handbook of Formal Languages I-III*. Springer, 1997.
24. Gh. Păun, G. Rozenberg, A. Salomaa. (Eds). *The Handbook of Membrane Computing*. Oxford University Press, 2009.
25. S. Wasserman, K. Faust. *Social Networks Analysis: Methods and Applications*. Cambridge University Press, 1994.

Inconspicuous Appeal
of Amorphous Computing Systems
(Invited Talk)

Jiří Wiedermann

Institute of Computer Science, Academy of Sciences of the Czech Republic,
Pod Vodárenskou věží 2, 182 07 Prague 8, Czech Republic
jiri.wiedermann@cs.cas.cz

Abstract. Amorphous computing systems typically consist of myriads of tiny simple processors that are randomly distributed at fixed positions or move randomly in a confined volume. The processors are "embodied" meaning that each of them has its own source of energy, has a "body" equipped with various sensors and communication means and has a computational control part. Initially, the processors have no identifiers and from the technological reasons, in the interest of their maximal simplicity, their computational, communication, sensory and locomotion (if any) parts are reduced to an absolute minimum. The processors communicate wirelessly, e.g., in an airborne medium they communicate via a short-range radio, acoustically or optically and in a waterborne medium via molecular communication. In the extreme cases the computational part of the processors can be simplified down to probabilistic finite state automata or even combinatorial circuits and the system as a whole can still be made universally programmable. From the theoretical point of view the structure and the properties of the amorphous systems qualify them among the simplest (non-uniform) universal computational devices. From the practical viewpoint, once technology will enable a mass production of the required processors a host of new applications so far inaccessible to classical approaches to computing will follow.

Extended Abstract: The history of amorphous computing systems began by the end of the twentieth century, mainly as an engineering endeavor (cf. [1], [2], [4], [5], [6], or [13]). Namely, in those days the progress in constructing the micro-electro-mechanical systems (MEMS) has enabled to think of devices integrating a central data processing unit (the microprocessor) and several components that interact with the surroundings such as micro-sensors, wireless communication unit, and the energy source in a small unit. These parts can possibly be complemented by micro-actuators and locomotive means. The resulting device can be viewed as an embodied computational unit. Note that such a unit possesses all the necessary parts characterizing autonomous embodied robots.

MEMS devices generally range in size from 20 micrometres (20×10^{-6} m) to a millimetre (i.e. 0.02 to 1.0 mm). Current ideas about nano-electro-mechanical systems (NEMS) and nano-technology consider such systems at a nano-scale (10^{-9} m).

The driving force behind the respective development has mainly been a vision of huge amounts of the respective "micro-robots" engaged in various application tasks

This work was partially supported by RVO 67985807 and the GA ČR grant No. P202/10/1333.

requiring local computation, local sensing, local actions and wireless communication among the randomly distributed units of the system. The joint idea has been that using local communication, the respective devices could self–organize in order to perform a coordinated action none of the elements alone was able to realize.

It is obvious that the resulting system of locally communicating units has no fixed architecture what is reflected by the term "amorphous computing systems".

The application range of amorphous computing systems is tremendous, covering practically all areas of life. For instance, when spread around, they can be used for surveillance of regions, buildings, road traffic, natural environments like oceans, deserts, inaccessible mountains, alien planets, etc. (cf. [3], [5], [6], [12], [13], and [14]). They can monitor various parameters, like temperature, precipitation, movements of persons and/or their life function, traffic density, presence of chemical compounds, seismicity, winds, water flow, life manifestation, etc., etc. The respective measurements are transmitted and collected in a base station for further processing. In medical sciences, nano-sized devices can even enter living bodies in order to monitor their interior organs and suppress undesirable phenomena. In futuristic applications amorphous computing systems can perform genetic manipulations at the cell level to strengthen the immune system, to heal up injuries, to cure heart or brain strokes, etc. (cf. [7]). The latter ideas are inspired by the existing bacteria that represent a template for such systems in nature.

Amorphous computing systems communicating via radio can be seen as an extreme case of wireless sensory networks. From the latter networks they differ in several important aspects. First, they are considered under severe restriction on resources, such as energy, memory and computational speed. Second, in order to simplify their mass production the computational and communication hardware is reduced to a minimum which seems to be necessary to maintain the required functionality and scalability of the network. Among the respective requirements the absence of node identifiers, practical non-existence of embedded communication software and asynchronicity of processors is assumed. Specific probabilistic protocols, entirely differing from those used in the wireless sensory networks, must be developed allowing reliable message delivery among the processors of amorphous computing systems. Last but not least, amorphous computing systems must be much more robust than the wireless sensory networks. This is due to the increased probability of their nodes' loss caused by their (perhaps temporal) inaccessibility, failure or damage, low reliability of a single inter-processor communication and quite general assumptions concerning their placement or movement (cf. [10], [11], [16], [18]).

Waterborn amorphous computing systems usually work on different principles than the radio-driven systems since radio waves do not travel well through good electrical conductors like salt water and similar liquids. Therefore, the former systems communicate with the help of the signal molecules that spread around via Brownian motion [16]. In some cases the decisions of nano-machines are based on so–called quorum sensing [18], i.e., on the density of signal molecules in the environment. This calls for a completely different design of the communication and control mechanisms that has no counterpart in the domain of classical distributed computing.

The inconspicuous appeal of amorphous computing systems consists in their immense variety of forms, in the possibility of their adaptation to particular characteristics of their operational environment, in their extreme simplicity and, last but not least, in their wide applicability to problems that cannot be solved by classical computational means. All these properties are supported by the computational universality of the underlying systems.

So far, the prevailing focus of research in amorphous computing systems has mostly been focused towards engineering or technological aspects of such systems almost completely ignoring theoretical questions related to their computational power and efficiency. Obviously, without knowing their theoretical limits, one cannot have a complete picture of the potential abilities and limitations of such systems. This was the starting point of the project of the present author and his (then) PhD student L. Petrů (cf. his PhD thesis [8]) devoted to studies of theoretical issues in amorphous computing initiated in 2004. Since that time various models of amorphous systems have been investigated.

The aim of the present talk is to give a brief overview of the developments in the corresponding research as performed within our amorphous computing research project. In the talk we present the main design ideas behind the respective models, point to the main problems to be solved, indicate their solution, and present the main results. The models will be approached roughly in the order of their increased generality (cf. [19], [20], [21]).

We start with the simplest model of amorphous cellular automata [8] and will continue with more elaborated asynchronous stationary amorphous computing systems [9], [17]. Then we turn our attention towards the so-called flying amorphous computing systems with mobile processors (cf. [10] and [11]). Finally, we describe molecularly communicating nano-machines that orchestrate their activities either by a molecular analogue of radio broadcast [16] or via quorum sensing [18]. Interestingly, in the latter case the nano-machines must be endowed by the self-reproduction ability.

The main result of our investigations is the proof of the computational universality of the amorphous computing systems considered above. This points to the versatility of such systems in various computational or robotic applications (cf. [15], [17]).

We conclude by stressing that the amorphous computing systems offer a radically new concept in information technology that has the potential to revolutionize the way we communicate and exchange information.

References

1. H. Abelson, et al. Amorphous Computing. MIT Artificial Intelligence Laboratory Memo No. 1665, Aug. 1999
2. H. Abelson, D. Allen, D. Coore, Ch. Hanson, G. Homsy, T. F. Knight, Jr., R. Nagpal, E. Rauch, G. J. Sussman, R. Weiss. Amorphous Computing. Communications of the ACM, Volume 43, No. 5, pp. 74–82, May 2000
3. D. K. Arvind, K. J. Wong: Speckled Computing Ű A Disruptive Technology for Network Information Appliances. Proc. IEEE International Symposium on Consumer Electronics (ISCE'04), 2004, pp. 219-223
4. D. Coore: Introduction to Amorphous Computing. Unconventional Programming Paradigms: International Workshop 2004, LNCS Volume 3566, pp. 99–109, Aug. 2005
5. J. M. Kahn, R. H. Katz, K. S. J. Pister. Next century challenges: mobile networking for "Smart Dust". In: Proceedings of the 5th Annual ACM/IEEE International Conference on Mobile Computing and Networking, MobiCom '99, ACM, pp. 271–278, Aug. 1999

6. J. M. Kahn, R. H. Katz, K. S. J. Pister. Emerging Challenges: Mobile Networking for Smart Dust. Journal of Communications and Networks, Volume 2, pp. 188–196, 2000

7. Kurzweil, R.: The Singularity is Near. Viking Books, 652 pages, 2005

8. L. Petrů: Universality in Amorphous Computing. PhD Disseration Thesis. Dept. of Math. and Physics, Charles University, Prague, 2009

9. L. Petrů, J. Wiedermann: A Model of an Amorphous Computer and Its Communication Protocol. In: Proc SOFSEM 2007: Theory and Practice of Computer Science. LNCS Volume 4362, Springer, pp. 446–455, July 2007

10. L. Petrů, J. Wiedermann: A Universal Flying Amorphous Computer. In: Proc. Unconventional Computation, 10th International Conference, UC'2011, LNCS, Vol. 6714, 2011, pp. 189-200

11. L. Petrů, J. Wiedermann: A Robust Universal Flying Amorphous Computer. In: C. Calude, R. Freivalds, K. Iwama (Eds.), Jozef Gruska Festschrift, LNCS, 2014, to appear

12. M. J. Sailor, J. R. Link: Smart dust: nanostructured devices in a grain of sand, Chemical Communications, Vol. 11, p. 1375, 2005

13. S. C. Shah, F. H. Chandio, M. Park: Speckled Computing: Evolution and Challenges. Proc. IEEE International Conference on Future Networks, 2009, pp. 181-185

14. B. Warneke, M. Last, B. Liebowitz, K. S. J. Pister: Smart Dust: Ccommunicating with a Cubic-Millimeter Computer. Computer, Volume: 34, Issue: 1, pp. 44–51, Jan. 2001

15. J. Wiedermann, L. Petrů: Computability in Amorphous Structures. In: Proc. CiE 2007, Computation and Logic in the Real World. LNCS Volume 4497, Springer, pp. 781–790, July 2007

16. J. Wiedermann, L. Petrů: Communicating Mobile Nano-Machines and Their Computational Power. In: Third International ICST Conference, NanoNet 2008, Boston, MA, USA, September 14-16, 2008, Revised Selected Papers, LNICST Vol. 3, Part 2, Springer, pp. 123-130, 2009.

17. J. Wiedermann, L. Petrů: On the Universal Computing Power of Amorphous Computing Systems. Theory of Computing Systems 46:4 (2009), 995-1010, www.springerlink.com/content/k2x6266k78274m05/fulltext.pdf

18. Wiedermann, J.: Nanomachine Computing by Quorum Sensing. In: J. Kelemen and A. Kelemenová (Eds.): Paun Festschrift, LNCS 6610, p. 203-215, 2011

19. Wiedermann, J.: Amorphous Computing: A Research Agenda for the Near Future. Natural Computing, 2012, Vol. 11, No. 1, p. 59-63.

20. Wiedermann, J.: Computability and Non-computability Issues in Amorphous Computing. In Baeten, J.C.M., Ball, T., de Boer, F.S. (ed.). Theoretical Computer Science. Berlin: Springer, 2012, p. 1-9.

21. Wiedermann, J.: The many forms of amorphous computational systems. In: H. Zenil (Ed.): A Computable Universe. Understanding Computation and Exploring Nature As Computation, p. 243-256, Singapore: World Scientific, 2013

Contents

Invited Papers

From P Colonies to 2D P Colonies
and Simulations of Multiagent Systems

Luděk Cienciala[(✉)] and Lucie Ciencialová

Institute of Computer Science and Research Institute of the IT4Innovations
Centre of Excellence, Silesian University in Opava, Opava, Czech Republic
{ludek.cienciala,lucie.ciencialova}@fpf.slu.cz

Abstract. P colonies were introduced in 2004 as an abstract computing device evolved from membrane systems – a biologically motivated
computational massive parallel model – composed of independent single
membrane agents, reactively acting and evolving in a shared environment.

Different variants of the P colonies were derived from original model
since that time. What is shown in this paper is not only a list of these
variants, but also finding connections between the results related to the
computational power.

1   Introduction

P colonies (introduced in [17])are a class of abstract computation devices based
on one-membrane agents acting in a shared environment. They belongs to a
family of models inspired by biology and biochemistry of cells called P systems
introduced in [19] by Gheorghe Păun in 2000.

Each agent is represented by a collection of objects embedded in a membrane
and by a set of programs for processing these objects. The number of objects
placed inside each agent is unchangeable and it is called the capacity of P colony.
The computational abilities in particular depend on the capacity of P colony, on
the number of agents and on the type of processing rules in the programs.

The rules used in programs are rewriting $a \rightarrow b$, communication $c \leftrightarrow d$ or
checking r_1/r_2. Using rewriting rule agent evolves object a to object b. Both
objects have to be placed inside this agent. Using rewriting rule agent change
its state. If the communication rule $c \leftrightarrow d$ is applicable, the object c must
be contained inside the agent and there is at least one copy of object d in
the environment. By applying communication rule the object c moves to the
environment and one object d comes to the agent. We can say, that agent took
information d from the environment and left information c in the environment.
The checking rule is not really new type of rules but checking rule can be obtained
by putting together two rules of previous types. This provides a pair of rules and
the order determines a priority among them.

Computational power of such a kind of devices with or without using checking
rules has been a point of interest of lots of research papers (e.g. [9,12,14]) and
it was shown, that they are computationally complete.

© Springer International Publishing Switzerland 2014
M. Gheorghe et al. (Eds.): CMC 2014, LNCS 8961, pp. 3–19, 2014.
DOI: 10.1007/978-3-319-14370-5_1

The environment is a communication channel for agents and storage place for objects. It plays strategic role in synchronization of works of single agents during computation. The environment has become the most changing / extending part of P colonies.

In the eco-P colonies ([1,7]) the static environment was replaced by the evolving one using 0L-scheme. The input tape was add to P colony in the model called Pcol automaton ([6]). The last model derived from P colony uses environment resembling cellular automata and it is called 2D P colony ([10]). The environment is changed to a form of a 2D grid of square cells. The agents are located in this grid and their view is limited to the cells that immediately surround them. Based on the contents of these cells, the agents decide their future locations. This formal model seems to be suitable for e.g. simulations of artificial and natural multiagent systems.

In the paper we describe the individual models, compare them from different viewpoints and we outline the development of models from the original model of P colonies to 2D P colonies.

Throughout the paper we assume that the reader is familiar with the basics of the formal language theory.

2   Preliminaries

We briefly summarize denotations used in the present paper.

We use NRE to denote the family of the recursively enumerable sets of non-negative integers and N to denote the set of non-negative integers.

A register machine (see [18]) is the construct $M = (m, H, l_0, l_h, P)$ where:

- m is the number of registers,
- H is the set of instruction labels,
- l_0 is the start label,
- l_h is the final label,
- P is a finite set of instructions injectively labelled with the elements from the set H.

The instruction of the register machine are of the following forms:

$l_1 : (ADD(r), l_2, l_3)$ Add 1 to the content of the register r and proceed to the instruction (labelled with) l_2 or l_3.

$l_1 : (SUB(r), l_2, l_3)$ If the register r stores the value different from zero, then subtract 1 from its content and go to instruction l_2, otherwise proceed to instruction l_3.

$l_h : HALT$ Halt the machine. The final label l_h is only assigned to this instruction.

Without loss of generality, one can assume that in each ADD-instruction $l_1 : (ADD(r), l_2, l_3)$ and in each SUB-instruction $l_1 : (SUB(r), l_2, l_3)$ the labels l_1, l_2, l_3 are mutually distinct.

The register machine M computes a set $N(M)$ of numbers in the following way: it starts with all registers empty (hence storing the number zero) with the instruction labelled l_0 and it proceeds to apply the instructions as indicated by the labels (and made possible by the contents of registers). If it reaches the halt instruction, then the number stored at that time in the register 1 is said to be computed by M and hence it is introduced in $N(M)$. (Because of the nondeterminism in choosing the continuation of the computation in the case of ADD-instructions, $N(M)$ can be an infinite set.) It is known (see e.g. [18]) that in this way we compute all Turing computable sets.

3   P Colonies — Basic Model

P colonies were introduced in 2004 (see [17]) as an abstract computing device formed by synthesis of grammar systems – colonies (see) of simple formal grammars and membrane systems – so-called P systems, models related to the field of bio-inspired computing. The P colony is composed of independent single membrane agents, reactively acting and evolving in a shared environment.

Each agent is represented by a collection of objects embedded in a membrane. The number of objects inside each agent is constant during the computation. With each agent is associated a set of simple programs. Each program is composed of the rules which can be of two types. The first type of rules, called the evolution rules, are of the form $a \rightarrow b$. It means that the object a inside the agent is rewritten (evolved) to the object b. The second type of rules, called the communication rules, are of the form $c \leftrightarrow d$. If the communication rule is performed, the object c inside the agent and the object d outside the agent swap their places. Thus after executing the rule, the object d appears inside the agent and the object c is placed outside the agent.

If the checking rule r_1/r_2 is performed, then the rule r_1 has higher priority to be executed over the rule r_2. It means that the agent checks whether the rule r_1 is applicable. If the rule can be executed, then it is compulsory for the agent to use it. If the rule r_1 cannot be applied, then the agent uses the rule r_2. The program determines the activity of the agent. The agent can change the content of itself or of the environment.

The environment contains several copies of the basic environmental object denoted by e. The environmental object e appears in arbitrary large number of copies in the environment.

This interaction between agents is the key factor of the P colony function. In each moment each object inside the agent is affected by execution of the program.

For more information about P systems see [21] or [22].

Definition 1. *The P colony of the capacity k is a construct*
$$\Pi = (A, e, f, V_E, B_1, \ldots, B_n), \text{ where}$$

- *A is an alphabet of the colony, its elements are called objects;*
- *$e \in A$ is the basic object of the colony;*
- *$f \in A$ is the final object of the colony;*
- *V_E is a multiset over $A - \{e\}$, it determines the initial state (content) of the environment;*
- *B_i, $1 \le i \le n$, are agents, each agent is a construct $B_i = (O_i, P_i)$, where*

- O_i is a multiset over A, it determines the initial state (content) of the agent, $|O_i| = k$;
- $P_i = \{p_{i,1}, \ldots, p_{i,k_i}\}$ is a finite multiset of programs, where each program contains exactly k rules, which are in one of the following forms each:
  * $a \rightarrow b$, called the evolution rule;
  * $c \leftrightarrow d$, called the communication rule;
  * r_1/r_2, called the checking rule; r_1, r_2 are the evolution rules or the communication rules.

The initial configuration of a P colony is an $(n+1)$-tuple of strings of objects present in the P colony at the beginning of the computation. It is given by the multiset O_i for $1 \leq i \leq n$ and by the set V_E. Formally, the configuration of the P colony Π is given by $(w_1, \ldots, w_n, w_E)$, where $|w_i| = k$, $1 \leq i \leq n$, w_i represents all the objects placed inside the i-th agent, and $w_E \in (A - \{e\})^*$ represents all the objects in the environment different from the object e.

At each step of the computation, the contents of the environment and of the agents change in the following manner: In the maximally parallel derivation mode, each agent which can use any of its programs should use one (non-deterministically chosen), whereas in the sequential derivation mode, one agent uses one of its programs at a time (non-deterministically chosen). If the number of applicable programs for one agent is higher than one, then the agent nondeterministically chooses one of the programs.

A sequence of transitions is called a computation. A computation is said to be halting, if a configuration is reached where no program can be applied any more. With a halting computation we associate a result which is given as the number of copies of the objects f present in the environment in the halting configuration.

Because of the non-determinism in choosing the programs, starting from the initial configuration we obtain several computations, hence, with a P colony we can associate a set of numbers, denoted by $N(\Pi)$, computed by all possible halting computations of given P colony.

In the original model (see [17]) the number of object inside each agent is set to two. Therefore the programs were formed from only two rules. Moreover the initial configuration was defined as $(n + 1)$-tuple $(ee, \ldots, ee, \varepsilon)$ so the P colony is at the beginning of the computation "empty", without an input information.

The number of agents in a given P colony is called the degree of Π; the maximal number of programs of an agent of Π is called the height of Π and the number of the objects inside an agent is called the capacity of Π. The family of all sets of numbers $N(\Pi)$ computed as above by P colonies of capacity at most $c \geq 0$, degree at most $n \geq 0$ and height at most $h \geq 0$ (using checking programs, i.e., priorities on the communication rules in the programs) working in the sequential mode is denoted by $NPCOL_{seq}K(c, n, h)$; whereas the corresponding families of P colonies working in the maximally parallel way are denoted by $NPCOL_{par}K(c, n, h)$. If one of the parameters n;h is not bounded, then we replace it with $*$. If only P colonies using programs without priorities are taken into account, we omit the parameter K.

4 The Variants of the P Colonies

We start this section with P colonies from the original model – with P colonies with capacity two. The programs of these P colonies are formed from two rules. The first rule must be evolution and the second one is communication or checking rule(consisting from two communication rules). This variant of P colonies is called *restricted* P colonies. If we speak about the family of all sets of numbers computed by restricted P colonies with priorities, we note this fact in notation by R placed before parentheses with parameters - $NPCOL_{par}KR(c, n, h)$ or $NPCOL_{seq}KR(c, n, h)$. Naturally, if the restricted P colonies are without priorities we omit parameter K.

For restricted P colonies following results are known from the literature:

- $NPCOL_{par}KR(2, *, 5) = NRE$ in [11,17],
- $NPCOL_{par}R(2, *, 5) = NRE$ in [14],
- $NPCOL_{par}K(2, *, 4) = NRE$ in [13],
- $NPCOL_{par}KR(2, 1, *) = NRE$ in [14],
- $NPCOL_{par}R(2, 2, *) = NRE$ in [9].

On previous list the reader can see that family of sets of natural numbers computed by restricted P colonies with or without use of checking rules having at most 5 programs associated with agent equals to *NRE*. If we remove the restriction on the type of rules in programs P colonies needs only at most 4 programs associated with agent to obtain computational completeness. The difference in last two results demonstrates the power of checking rules and power of synchronized cooperation. To generate *NRE* the restricted P colony needs only one agent if the agent can use checking rules and two agents if they cannot use checking rules.

If each program in the P colony is formed from the rules of the same type (for the P colony with capacity 2 it means program is formed from two evolution, two communication or two checking programs) we can call the P colony *homogeneous*. The checking rules used in the homogeneous P colony are formed from the same type of rules too.

- $NPCOL_{par}KH(2, *, 4) = NRE$ in [4],
- $NPCOL_{par}KH(2, 1, *) = NRE$ in [4].

Now we can proceed to the P colonies with capacity one. It means that there is only one object inside each agent and each program is formed from only one rule.

- $NPCOL_{par}K(1, *, 7) = NRE$ in [9],
- $NPCOL_{par}KH(1, *, 6) = NRE$ in [4],
- $NPCOL_{par}K(1, 4, *) = NRE$ in [9],
- $NPCOL_{par}(1, 6, *) = NRE$ in [8].

One more interesting result dealing with P colonies with capacity 3 we can find in the papers [13] and [2].

- $NPCOL_{par}K(3,*,3) = NRE$ in [13],
- $NPCOL_{par}H(3,2,*) = NRE$ in [2].

In the table 1 the reader can find summarized list of results related to P colonies.

Table 1. Computational complete classes of P colonies

n.	mode of comp.	capacity	degree	height	checking rules / restricted programs / homogeneous programs		
1.	par	1	*	7	K		in [9]
2.	par	1	*	6	K	H	in [4]
3.	par	1	4	*	K		in [9]
4.	par	1	6	*			in [8]
5.	seq	2	*	5	K	R	in [14]
6.	par	2	*	5		R	in [14]
7.	par	2	*	4	K		in [13]
8.	par	2	*	4	K	H	in [4]
9.	seq/par	2	1	*	K	R	in [14]
10.	par	2	2	*		R	in [9]
11.	seq/par	2	1	*	K	H	in [4]
12.	par	2	23	5	K	R	in [12]
13.	par	2	22	6	K	R	in [12]
14.	par	2	22	5	K		in [12]
15.	par	2	1	142	K	R	in [12]
16.	par	2	35	8			in [12]
17.	par	2	57	8		R	in [12]
18.	par	3	35	7			in [12]
19.	seq/par	3	*	3	K		in [13] and [16]
20.	par	3	2	*		H	in [2]

5   Eco-P Colonies

In [7] new types of programs for P colonies with two objects inside each agent were introduced. The first of them is deletion program — $\langle a_{in}; bc \to d \rangle$, using this program agent consumes one object (a) from the environment and transforms two objects (b, c) inside agent into new one (d). The second type of programs is insertion type, the insertion program is in the form $\langle a_{out}; b \to cd \rangle$. By executing it agent sends to the environment one object (a) and from the second object (b) agent generates new two objects (c, d).

The environment is static in the basic model, it can be changed only by activity of agents. Eco-P colonies are constructed as an natural extension of P colonies with dynamically evolving environment, the evolution is independent from activity of agents. The mechanism of evolution in the environment is based on $0L$ scheme. $0L$ scheme is a pair (Σ, P), where Σ is the alphabet of $0L$ scheme and P is the set of context free rules, it fulfils following condition $\forall a \in \Sigma \ \exists \alpha \in \Sigma^*$ such that $(a \to \alpha) \in P$. For $w_1, w_2 \in \Sigma^*$ we write $w_1 \Rightarrow w_2$ if $w_1 = a_1 a_1 \ldots a_n, w_2 = \alpha_2 \alpha_2 \ldots \alpha_n$, for $a_i \to \alpha_i \in P, 1 \leq i \leq n$.

Definition 2. *The eco-P colony is structure*
$$\Pi = (A, e, f, V_E, D_E, B_1, \ldots, B_n), \ where$$

- *A is the alphabet of the colony, its elements are called objects,*
- *e is the basic (environmental) object of the colony, $e \in A$,*
- *f is final object of the colony, $f \in A$,*
- *V_E is the initial content of the environment, $V_E \in (A - \{e\})^\circ$,*
- *D_E is $0L$ scheme (A, P_E), where P_E is the set of context free rules,*
- *B_i, $1 \leq i \leq n$, are the agents, every agent is the structure $B_i = (O_i, P_i)$, where O_i is the multiset over A, it defines the initial state (content) of the agent B_i and $|O_i| = 2$ and $P_i = \{p_{i,1}, \ldots, p_{i,k_i}\}$ is the finite set of programs of two types:*
  (1) generating $\langle a \to bc, d \ out \rangle$ - the program is applicable if agent contents objects a and d. Object a is used for generation of new content of the agent and object d agent sends to the environment.
  (2) consuming $\langle ab \to c, d \ in \rangle$ - the program is applicable if the agent contents objects a and b. These objects are evolved to one new object c and object d the agent imports from the environment.

Every agent has only one type of programs. The agent with generating programs is called **sender** *and the agent with consuming programs is called* **consumer**.

The computation of eco-P colonies is maximally parallel.
We denote $NEPCOL_{x,y,z}(n, h)$ the family of the sets computing by eco-P colonies such that:

- x can be formed by two symbols: s, c. s — if there is agent sender in eco-P colony, c — if there is agent consumer in eco-P colony,
- $y = passive$ if the rules of $0L$ scheme are of type $a \to a$ only,
- $y = active$ if the set of rules of $0L$ scheme disposes of at least one rule of another type than $a \to a$,
- $z = ini$ if the environment or agents contain objects different from e, otherwise we eliminate this notation,
- the degree of eco-P colony is at most n and
- the height is at most h.

The eco-P colonies with two agents (senders and consumers) with passive environment ($0L$ scheme contains the rule of type $a \to a$ only) are computationally complete. If there is active environment the eco-P colony can be computationally complete with two agents consumers and initial content of environment different from e.

- $NEPCOL_{sc,passive}(2, *) = NRE$ in [2],
- $NEPCOL_{c,active,ini}(2, *) = NRE$ in [1].

6 PCol Automata

In reference to finite automaton we extend P colony by an input tape and change the generating device to the accepting one. The agents of the P colony are working according to actually read symbol from the input tape. To do this they have rules which can "read" the input tape, we call them tape or T-rules. The other rules are called non-tape or N-rules. The input symbol is said to be read if at least one agent follow it (use corresponding T-rule).

Now we recall definition of a PCol automaton.

Definition 3. *A PCol automaton of capacity k and with n agents, $k, n \geq 1$, is a construct $\Pi = (V, e, w_E, (w_1, P_1), \ldots, (w_n, P_n), F)$ where*

- *V is an alphabet, the alphabet of the PCol automaton, its elements are called objects;*
- *$e \in V$ is the environmental object of the automaton; $w_E \in (V - \{e\})^*$ is a string representing the multiset of objects different from e which is found in the environment initially;*
- *$(w_i, P_i), 1 \leq i \leq n$, is the i-th agent; and*
- *F is a set of accepting configurations of the PCol automaton.*
  For each agent, (w_i, P_i), $1 \leq i \leq n$,
  - *w_i is a multiset over V, it determines the initial contents of the agent*
  - *P_i is a set of programs, where every program is formed from k rules of the following types:*
    - *tape rules of the form $a \xrightarrow{T} b$, or $a \xleftrightarrow{T} b$, called rewriting tape rules and communication tape rules, respectively; or*
    - *nontape rules of the form $a \rightarrow b$, or $c \leftrightarrow d$, called rewriting (nontape) rules and communication (nontape) rules, respectively.*

For each i, $1 \leq i \leq n$, the set of tape programs (shortly T-programs) is denoted by P_i^T, they are formed from one tape rule and $k - 1$ nontape rules, the set of nontape programs (shortly N-programs) which contain only nontape rules, is denoted by P_i^N, thus, $P_i = P_i^T \cup P_i^N$, $P_i^T \cap P_i^N = \emptyset$.

For each i, $1 \leq i \leq n$, the set of tape programs (shortly T-programs) is denoted by P_i^T, they are formed from one tape rule and $k - 1$ nontape rules, the set of nontape programs (shortly N-programs) which contain only nontape rules, is denoted by P_i^N, thus, $P_i = P_i^T \cup P_i^N$, $P_i^T \cap P_i^N = \emptyset$.

The computation starts in the initial configuration with the input word placed on the input tape. For configuration $(w_E, w_1, \ldots, w_n)$ and input symbol a we can construct the sets of applicable programs $\mathcal{P}$. To pass from one configuration to another we define following transitions:

- *t-transition $\Rightarrow_t^a$:* If exists at least one set of applicable programs $P \in \mathcal{P}$ such that every $p \in P$ is T-program with T-rule in the form $x \xrightarrow{T} a$ or $x \xleftrightarrow{T} a, x \in A$ and the set P is maximal.

- *n-transition* $\Rightarrow_n$: If exists at least one set of applicable program $P \in \mathcal{P}$ such that every $p_i \in P$ is N-program and the set P is maximal.
- *tmin-transition* $\Rightarrow^a_{tmin}$: If exists at least one set of applicable program $P \in \mathcal{P}$ such that there is at least one T-program in P and it is in a form $x \xrightarrow{T} a$ or $x \xleftrightarrow{T} a, x \in A$, it can contain N-programs too and the set P is maximal.
- *tmax-transition* $\Rightarrow^a_{tmax}$: If exists at least one set of applicable program $P \in \mathcal{P}$ such that P contain as many T-programs (they are in a form $x \xrightarrow{T} a$ or $x \xleftrightarrow{T} a, x \in A$) as it is possible, P can contain N-programs too, and the set P is maximal.

PCol automaton works in t (tmax, tmin) *mode* of computation if it uses only t- (tmax-, tmin-) transitions. It works in nt (ntmax or ntmin) mode if it uses t- (tmax- or tmin-) transitions and if there isn't any set of applicable programs formed from T-programs it can use n-transition. PCol automaton works in init mode if it does only t-transitions and after reading all the input symbols it uses n-transitions.

If PCol automaton works in t, tmax or tmin mode, it reads one input symbol in every step of computation. Consequently, the length of computation equals to the length of the input string.

Computation ends by reaching final state computation is terminated after reading the last input symbol if it does not halt before. It is successful if the whole input tape is read and PCol automaton reaches configuration in F.

Let us designate $M = \{t, nt, tmax, ntmax, tmin, ntmin, init\}$. The *language accepted by a PCol automaton* Π as above is defined as the set of strings which can be read during a successful computation:

$$L(\Pi, mode) = \{\, w \in V^* | (w; w_E, w_1, \ldots, w_n) \text{ can be transformed by } \Pi \text{ into } (\varepsilon; v_E, v_1, \ldots, v_n) \in F \text{ with a computation in mode } mode \in M\}.$$

Let $\mathcal{L}(PColA, mode)$ denote the class of languages accepted by PCol automata in the computational mode $mode \in M$, and let RE denote the class of recursively enumerable languages.

For every regular language L there exists PCol automaton working in t-mode having only 1 agent accepting all words from L(in [6]. There is context-free language, which can be accepted by PCol automaton with only 1 agent and working in t-mode. The family of languages accepted by PCol automata with one agent working in *t*-mode is subset of context-sensitive languages. It is open question if the subset is proper. Unlike other variants of P colonies this model working in t-mode is not computationally complete.

In [6] the authors showed that class of languages accepted by PCol automata working in nt, ntmin or ntmax mode equals to the class of recursively enumerable languages.

- $\mathcal{L}(PColA, nt) = RE$ in [6],
- $\mathcal{L}(PColA, ntmin) = RE$ in [6],
- $\mathcal{L}(PColA, ntmax) = RE$ in [6],
- $\mathcal{L}(PColA, init) = NRE$ in [2].

7 The Agents Placed on the Tape — APCol Systems

In the paper [3] the authors make one step further in combining properties of P colonies and automata. While in the case of PCol automata the behaviour of the system is influenced both by the string to be processed and the environment consisting of multisets of symbols, in the case of Automaton-like P colonies or APCol systems, for short, the whole environment is a string. The interaction between the agents in the P colony and the environment is realized by exchanging symbols between the objects of the agents and the environment (communication rules), and the states of the agents may change both via communication and evolution; the latter one is an application of a rewriting rule to an object. The distinguished symbol, e (in the previous models the environmental symbol) have a special role: whenever it is introduced in the string by communication, the corresponding input symbol is erased. An evolution rule is of the form $a \rightarrow b$. It means that object a inside of the agent is rewritten (evolved) to the object b. The second type of rules, called a communication rule, is in the form $c \leftrightarrow d$. When this rule is performed, the object c inside the agent and a symbol d in the string are exchanged, so, we can say that the agent rewrites symbol d to symbol c in the input string. If $c = e$, then the agent erases d from the input string and if $d = e$, symbol c is inserted into the string.

The computation in APCol systems starts with an input string, representing the environment, and with each agents having only symbols e in its state. Every computational step means a maximally parallel action of the active agents. Only one agent can act on one symbol. The computation ends if the input string is reduced to the empty word, there are no more applicable programs in the system, and meantime at least one of the agents is in so-called final state.

Definition 4. *An Automaton-like P colony (an APCol system, for short) is a construct*

$$\Pi = (O, e, A_1, \ldots, A_n), \text{ where}$$

- *O is an alphabet; its elements are called the objects,*
- *$e \in O$, called the basic object,*
- *A_i, $1 \leq i \leq n$, are agents. Each agent is a triplet $A_i = (\omega_i, P_i, F_i)$, where*
  - *ω_i is a multiset over O, describing the initial state (content) of the agent, $|\omega_i| = 2$,*
  - *$P_i = \{p_{i,1}, \ldots, p_{i,k_i}\}$ is a finite set of programs associated with the agent, where each program is a pair of rules. Each rule is in one of the following forms:*
    - *$a \rightarrow b$, where $a, b \in O$, called an evolution rule,*
    - *$c \leftrightarrow d$, where $c, d \in O$, called a communication rule,*
  - *$F_i \subseteq O^*$ is a finite set of final states (contents) of agent A_i.*

In the following we explain the work of an Automaton-like P colony; to help the easier reading we provide only the necessary formal details.

During the work of the APCol system, the agents perform programs. Since both rules in a program can be communication rules, an agent can work with two objects in the string in one step of the computation. In the case of program $\langle a \leftrightarrow b; c \leftrightarrow d \rangle$, a substring bd of the input string is replaced by string ac. If the program is of the form $\langle c \leftrightarrow d; a \leftrightarrow b \rangle$, then a substring db of the input string is replaced by string ca. This means that the agent can act only in one place in the one step of the computation and what happens to the string depends both on the order of the rules in the program and on the interacting objects. In particular, we have the following types of programs with two communication rules:

- $\langle a \leftrightarrow b; c \leftrightarrow e \rangle$ - b in the string is replaced by ac,
- $\langle c \leftrightarrow e; a \leftrightarrow b \rangle$ - b in the string is replaced by ca,
- $\langle a \leftrightarrow e; c \leftrightarrow e \rangle$ - ac is inserted in a non-deterministically chosen place in the string,
- $\langle e \leftrightarrow b; e \leftrightarrow d \rangle$ - bd is erased from the string,
- $\langle e \leftrightarrow d; e \leftrightarrow b \rangle$ - db is erased from the string,
- $\langle e \leftrightarrow e; e \leftrightarrow d \rangle$; $\langle e \leftrightarrow e; c \leftrightarrow d \rangle$, ...- these programs can be replaced by programs of type $\langle e \rightarrow e; c \leftrightarrow d \rangle$.

At the beginning of the computation of the APCol system the environment is given by a string ω of objects which are different from e. This string represents the initial state of the environment. Consequently, an initial configuration of the Automaton-like P colony is an $(n + 1)$-tuple $c = (\omega; \omega_1, \ldots, \omega_n)$ where w is the initial state of the environment and the other n components are multisets of strings of objects, given in the form of strings, the initial states the of agents.

A configuration of an Automaton-like P colony Π is given by $(w; w_1, \ldots, w_n)$, where $|w_i| = 2$, $1 \leq i \leq n$, w_i represents all the objects placed inside the i-th agent and $w \in (O - \{e\})^*$ is the string to be processed.

At each step of the (parallel) computation every agent attempts to find one of its programs to use. If the number of applicable programs is higher than one, the agent non-deterministically chooses one of them. At one step of computation, the maximal possible number of agents have to be active, i.e., have to perform a program.

By applying programs, the Automaton-like P colony passes from one configuration to another configuration. A sequence of configurations started from the initial configuration is called a computation. A configuration is halting if the APCol system has no applicable program. A computation is called accepting if and only if at least one agent is in final state and the string to be processed is ε. Hence, the string w is accepted by the Automaton-like P colony Π if there exists a computation by Π such that it starts in the initial configuration $(\omega; w_1, \ldots, \omega_n)$ and the computation ends by halting in the configuration $(\varepsilon; w_1, \ldots, w_n)$, where at least one of $w_i \in F_i$ for $1 \leq i \leq n$.

Let Σ be an alphabet, $L \subseteq \Sigma^*$ be a recursively enumerable language. Let $L' = S \cdot L \cdot E$, where $S, E \notin \Sigma$. Then there exists an Automaton-like P colony Π with two agents such that $L' = L(\Pi)$ holds.

8   2D P Colonies

The last modification of basic model of the P colonies has capacity two – there are two objects inside each agent. As in the original model the agents are equipped by the sets of the programs formed from rules – communication and evolution. The main change is in the environment. The authors of the paper [10] put the agents to the 2D grid of cells and they give the agent possibility to move – motion rule. The direction of the movement of the agent is determined by the content of cells surrounding the cell in which the agent is placed.

The program can contain at most one motion rule. To achieve the greatest simplicity in agent behaviour, we set another condition. If the agent will move, it cannot communicate with the environment. So if the program contains a movement rule, then the second rule is the evolution rule.

Definition 5. *The 2D P colony is a construct*
$$\Pi = (A, e, Env, B_1, \ldots, B_k, f), k \geq 1, \text{ where}$$

- *A is an alphabet of the colony, its elements are called objects,*
- *$e \in A$ is the basic environmental object of the colony,*
- *Env is a pair $(m \times n, w_E)$, where $m \times n, m, n \in N$ is the size of the environment and w_E is the initial contents of environment, it is a matrix of size $m \times n$ of multisets of objects over $A - \{e\}$.*
- *B_i, $1 \leq i \leq k$, are agents, each agent is a construct $B_i = (O_i, P_i, [o, p])$, $0 \leq o \leq m$, $0 \leq p \leq n$, where*
  - *O_i is a multiset over A, it determines the initial state (contents) of the agent, $|O_i| = 2$,*
  - *$P_i = \{p_{i,1}, \ldots, p_{i,l_i}\}$, $l \geq 1, 1 \leq i \leq k$ is a finite set of programs, where each program contains exactly 2 rules, which are in one of the following forms each:*
    - *$a \rightarrow b$, called the evolution rule,*
    - *$c \leftrightarrow d$, called the communication rule,*
    - *$[a_{q,r}] \rightarrow s, 0 \leq q, r \leq 2, s \in \{\Leftarrow, \Rightarrow, \Uparrow, \Downarrow\}$, called the motion rule;*
- *$f \in A$ is the final object of the colony.*

A configuration of the 2D P colony is given by the state of the environment - matrix of type $m \times n$ with multisets of objects over $A - \{e\}$ as its elements, and by the state of all agents - pairs of objects from alphabet A and the coordinates of the agents. An initial configuration is given by the definition of the 2D P colony.

A computational step consists of three parts. The first part lies in determining the applicable set of programs according to the actual configuration of the P colony. There are programs belonging to all agents in this set of programs. In the second part we have to choose one program corresponding to each agent from the set of applicable programs. There is no collision between the communication rules belonging to different programs. The third part is the execution of the chosen programs.

A change of the configuration is triggered by the execution of programs and it involves changing the state of the environment, contents and placement of the agents.

A computation is nondeterministic and maximally parallel. The computation ends by halting when no agent has an applicable program.

The result of the computation is the number of copies of the final object placed in the environment at the end of the computation.

The reason for the introduction of 2D P colonies is not the study of their computational power but monitoring of their behaviour during the computation.

For example there exists 2D P colony simulating a kind of cellular automata – Conway's Game of Life([15]). Following example shows the pattern called beacon (see fig. 1).

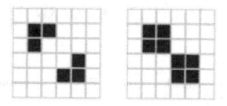

Fig. 1. Pattern beacon changes in two consequential steps

Let Π_2 be 2D P colony defined as follows: $\Pi_2 = (A, e, Env, B_1, \ldots, B_{16}, f)$, where

- $A = \{e, f, D, S, Z, M, O, L, N\}$,
- $e \in A$ is the basic environmental object of the colony,
- $Env = (6 \times 6, w_E)$,
- $w_E = \begin{bmatrix} D & D & D & D & D & D \\ D & S & S & D & D & D \\ D & S & S & D & D & D \\ D & D & D & S & S & D \\ D & D & D & S & S & D \\ D & D & D & D & D & D \end{bmatrix}$,
- $B_1 = (ee, P_1, [1, 1])$, $B_2 = (ee, P_2, [1, 2])$, ..., $B_{16} = (ee, P_{16}, [4, 4])$,
- $f \in A$ is the final object of the colony.

The states of the automata are stored inside the cells (D - dead automaton, S - live automaton). There is only one kind of agent in this 2D P colony, so there are sixteen identical agents located in the matrix 4×4 of inner cells (see fig. 2).

To simulate one step of the cellular automata, all agents move one step forward and rewrite one of their objects e to object M (automaton will be dead) or to object O (automaton will be live). The following steps are for downward movement and for refreshing the state of an automaton - i.e., the replacement of the object in the cell for an object in the agent to change the state of the automaton.

The next 2D P colny was defined to simulate the colony of the ants. The ant is moving in the environment (nondeterministically) and searching for the food. When it founds a food source the ant take one piece of food and carry it to the

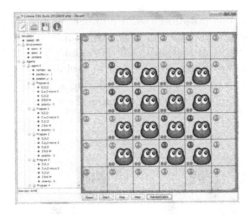

Fig. 2. The configuration of the 2D P colony simulating beacon

home-cell. The ant carrying food puts the object – tag to every cell the ant goes through. If the searching ant comes across the cell with object – tag, it follows the path to the food source.

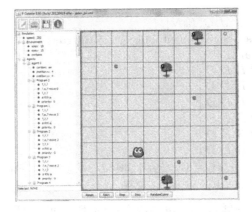

Fig. 3. The configuration of 2D P colony with one agent – ant and three nonreachable cells – trees

The problem occurs when agent following the path reaches empty food source. The agent stays locked at the end of the path. The solution lays on distributing the programs to *the priority levels*. To every program the authors add the natural number which determine the priority of the use of the program. Then the agent ant has program to erase the path. This program has lower priority than program for carrying the piece of the food to the home–cell.

This type of P colonies seams to be suitable to simulate multiagent systems. In the paper [5] the authors presented hydrological modelling flow of liquid over

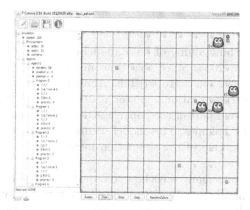

Fig. 4. The configuration of 2D P colony with four agents – ants carrying the food to the home–cell

the earth's surface using 2D P colonies. Based on the entered data - the slope surface, a source of fluid and quantity - we simulate the fluid distribution in the environment.

The issue of the flow of liquid over the Earth's surface is studied by experts from two areas - hydrology and geoinformatics. Both of these disciplines work closely together on the issue of the so-called "surface runoff". Surface runoff is the water flow that occurs when the soil is saturated to full capacity and excess water from rain, meltwater, or other sources flows over the land.

The environment can contain objects representing slope of terrain, type of cover and soil. Agents represent the units of water and their programs determine behaviour of water running over the surface. We can assume that the soil is already saturated thus the main factor of overland flow is the slope of the field. The type of terrain and soil is not implemented yet.

Agents in 2D P colonies have capacity of 2. It means that an agent contains two objects. Each of the objects inside the agent carries the information about the state of the agent. The first object has information about the activity of the agent. It is the information that the agent "flows" down the terrain or it is inactive (belonging to the rainfall that have not fall or it stops in sinks). The second object stores information about the previous direction of flow. This information can further modify the way of the agent as inertia.

The are some advantages and disadvantages of 2D P colonies for modelling surface runoff. The first disadvantage is the "calibration" of the model. This procedure gives us the answer to the questions: What amount of water one agent represents? What time corresponds to two computational steps? Answer to the first question is given by rainfall per unit of time. How long one time unit takes is given by the average speed of water – we must take into account resolution of map and roughness of terrain. The main advantage is simplicity and transparency of the definition of the agent.

9 Conclusion

We recalled idea and functioning of basic model of P colonies. This model was introduced in [16] in 2005. Since this time many papers and studies about the model and its variations were written. Almost all the reports are focused on determination of computational power of more or less restricted variants of P colonies. The second part of the paper was dedicated to the extension of the P colonies called 2D P colonies. This model seams to be suitable for simulations of multiagent systems. One of the simulation introduced in [5] is simulation of surface runoff.

In the future, it seems many ways how to improve model of the 2D P colonies. One way is assign the number to objects in addition to the type. This number will indicate the value of the parameter that the object represents. Another possibility is to extend the environment with mechanism which is able to change the object in the environment independently from the activity of the agents.

Remark 1. Article has been made in connection with project IT4Innovations Centre of Excellence, reg. no. CZ.1.05/1.1.00/02.0070.

Research was also supported by project OPVK no. CZ.1.07/2.2.00/28.0014 and by projects SGS/24/2013 and SGS/6/2014.

References

1. Cienciala, L., Ciencialová, L.: Eco-P colonies. In: Păun, Gh., Pérez-Jiménez, M.J., Riscos-Núñez, A. (eds.) Pre-Proceedings of the 10th Workshop on Membrane Computing, Curtea de Arges, Romania, pp. 201–209 (2009)
2. Cienciala, L., Ciencialová, L.: P colonies and their extensions. In: Kelemen, J., Kelemenová, A. (eds.) Computation, Cooperation, and Life. LNCS, vol. 6610, pp. 158–169. Springer, Heidelberg (2011)
3. Cienciala, L., Ciencialová, L., Csuhaj-Varj, E.: P Colonies Processing Strings. Fundamenta Informaticae **134**, 51–65 (2014)
4. Cienciala, L., Ciencialová, L., Kelemenová, A.: Homogeneous P colonies. Computing and Informatics **27**, 481–496 (2008)
5. Cienciala, L., Ciencialová, L., Langer, M.: Modelling of Surface Runoff Using 2D P Colonies. In: Alhazov, A., Cojocaru, S., Gheorghe, M., Rogozhin, Yu., Rozenberg, G., Salomaa, A. (eds.) CMC 2013. LNCS, vol. 8340, pp. 101–116. Springer, Heidelberg (2014)
6. Ciencialová, L., Cienciala, L., Csuhaj-Varjú, E., Vaszil, Gy.: PCol Automata: Recognizing Strings with P Colonies. Report of Eight Brainstorming week on membrane computing, Sevilla, Spain, pp. 65–76 (2010)
7. Ciencialová, L., Csuhaj-Varjú, E., Kelemenová, A., Vaszil, Gy.: On Very Simple P Colonies. In: Proceeding of the Seventh Brainstorming Week on Membrane Computing, vol. I, Sevilla, Spain, pp. 97–108 (2009)
8. Ciencialová, L., Csuhaj-Varjú, E., Kelemenová, A., Vaszil, Gy.: Variants of P Colonies with Very Simple Cell Structure. Int. J. of Computers, Communications & Control **IV**(3), 224–233 (2009)

9. Cienciala, L., Ciencialová, L., Kelemenová, A.: On the number of agents in P colonies. In: Eleftherakis, G., Kefalas, P., Păun, Gh., Rozenberg, G., Salomaa, A. (eds.) WMC 2007. LNCS, vol. 4860, pp. 193–208. Springer, Heidelberg (2007)
10. Cienciala, L., Ciencialová, L., Perdek, M.: 2D P colonies. In: Csuhaj-Varjú, E., Gheorghe, M., Rozenberg, G., Salomaa, A., Vaszil, Gy. (eds.) CMC 2012. LNCS, vol. 7762, pp. 161–172. Springer, Heidelberg (2013)
11. Csuhaj-Varjú, E., Kelemen, J., Kelemenová, A., Păun, Gh., Vaszil, Gy.: Cells in environment: P colonies. Multiple-valued Logic and Soft Computing 12(3–4), 201–215 (2006)
12. Csuhaj-Varjú, E., Margenstern, M., Vaszil, Gy.: P colonies with a bounded number of cells and programs. In: Hoogeboom, H.J., Păun, Gh., Rozenberg, G., Salomaa, A. (eds.) WMC 2006. LNCS, vol. 4361, pp. 352–366. Springer, Heidelberg (2006)
13. Csuhaj-Varjú, E., Kelemen, J., Kelemenová, A., Păun, Gh.: Computing with cells in environment: P colonies. Journal of Multi-Valued Logic and Soft Computing 12, 201–215 (2006)
14. Freund, R., Oswald, M.: P colonies working in the maximally parallel and in the sequential mode. In: Ciobanu, G., Păun, Gh. (eds.) Pre-Proceedings of the 1st International Workshop on Theory and Application of P Systems, Timisoara, Romania, pp. 49–56 (2005)
15. Gardner, M.: Mathematical Games - The fantastic combinations of John Conway's new solitaire game "life". Scientific American 223, 120–123 (1970). ISBN 0-89454-001-7 (Archived from the original on June 03, 2009) (Retrieved June 26, 2011)
16. Kelemen, J., Kelemenová, A.: On P colonies, a biochemically inspired model of computation. In: Proc. of the 6th International Symposium of Hungarian Researchers on Computational Intelligence, Budapest TECH, Hungary, pp. 40–56 (2005)
17. Kelemen, J., Kelemenová, A., Păun, Gh.: Preview of P colonies: A biochemically inspired computing model. In: Bedau, M., et al. (eds.) Workshop and Tutorial Proceedings, Ninth International Conference on the Simulation and Synthesis of Living Systems, ALIFE IX, Boston, Mass, pp. 82–86 (2004)
18. Minsky, M.L.: Computation: Finite and Infinite Machines. Prentice Hall, Englewood Cliffs (1967)
19. Păun, Gh.: Computing with membranes. Journal of Computer and System Sciences 61, 108–143 (2000)
20. Păun, Gh.: Membrane computing: An introduction. Springer, Berlin (2002)
21. Păun, Gh., Rozenberg, G., Salomaa, A.: The Oxford Handbook of Membrane Computing. Oxford University Press (2009)
22. P systems web page. http://ppage.psystems.eu (online: October 15, 2014)

A Bioinspired Computing Approach to Model Complex Systems

Mario J. Pérez-Jiménez[✉]

Research Group on Natural Computing,
Department of Computer Science and Artificial Intelligence,
University of Sevilla, Seville, Spain
marper@us.es

Abstract. The use of models is intrinsic to any scientific activity. In particular, formal/mathematical models provide a relevant tool for scientific investigation. This paper presents a new Membrane Computing based computational paradigm as a framework for modelling processes and real-life phenomena. P systems, devices in Membrane Computing, are not used as a computing paradigm, but rather as a formalism for describing the behaviour of the system to be modelled. They offer an approach to the development of models for biological systems that meets the requirements of a good modelling framework: relevance, understandability, extensibility and computability.

Keywords: Membrane Computing · Multienvironment P systems · Multicompartimental P systems · Population Dynamics P systems

1 Introduction

Scientists regularly use abstractions with the aim to describe and understand the reality they are examining. Computational modelling is the process of representing real world problems in mathematical terms in an attempt to find solutions to their associated complex systems. A formal model is an abstraction of the real-world onto a mathematical/computational domain that highlights some key features while ignoring others that are assumed to be secondary. A formal model should not be considered as representation of the truth, but instead as a statement of our current knowledge of the phenomenon under research.

It is desirable for a model to fulfill four properties: *relevance, understandability, extensibility* and *computability* [19]. A formal model must be relevant capturing the key features while ignoring others assumed to be secondary. The abstract formalism used should adecquately match the informal concepts and ideas from the investigated phenomenon. Mathematical models should also be extensible to higher level of organizations, like tissues, organs, organisms, etc, in the case of cellular systems. Finally, a formal model should be able to be implemented in a computer so that we can run simulations to study the dynamics of the system in different scenarios, as well as the qualitative and quantitative reasoning about its properties.

© Springer International Publishing Switzerland 2014
M. Gheorghe et al. (Eds.): CMC 2014, LNCS 8961, pp. 20–34, 2014.
DOI: 10.1007/978-3-319-14370-5_2

One of the main objectives of any model is to provide a predictive capability, that is, the possibility to make guesses in terms of plausible hypotheses related to the dynamics of the observed phenomenon in different scenarios that are of interest to experts.

Cellular systems and population biology often depend on many parameters related to the observed behaviours. Since they define the dynamics of the system, parameters must satisfy some conditions, which can be referred to as the invariants of the associated behaviour. Some of these invariants can be expressed by rules and can be obtained by carrying out experiments, while others cannot be measured or they are very expensive to estimate. Therefore, before simulations can be performed in order to make predictions, we need to *calibrate* our model. Several parameters values are tested by calibration and the results corresponding to the state parameters are compared with the observed/expected behaviour of the system for the same state parameters. In some cases, the design of the model has to be reconsidered [15].

Nowadays ordinary/partial differential equations (ODEs/PDEs) constitute the most widely used approach in modelling complex systems. Nevertheless, in some cases such as molecular interaction networks in cellular systems, any model described by means of a system of ODEs/PDEs is based on two assumptions: (a) cells are assumed to be well stirred and homogeneous volumes so that concentrations do not change with respect to space; and (b) chemical concentrations vary continuously over time in a deterministic way. This assumption is valid if the number of molecules specified in the reaction volume are sufficiently large and reactions are fast.

Membrane Computing is an emergent branch of Natural Computing introduced by G. Paun at the end of 1998. This new computing paradigm starts from the assumption that processes taking place in the compartmental structure of a living cell can be interpreted as computations. In contrast to differential equations, P systems explicitly correspond to the discrete character of the components of a complex system and use rewriting/evolution rules on multisets of objects which represent the variables of the system. The inherent stochasticity, external noise and uncertainty in cellular systems is captured by using stochastic or probabilistic strategies. A general bioinspired computing modelling framework, called *multienvironment P systems* is introduced.

The paper is structured as follows. First, the framework of multienvironment P systems is defined in a formal way. Section 3 is devoted to multicompartmental P systems, the stochastic approach. Besides, four case studies at cellular level are presented in this Section. Population dynamics P systems, the probabilistic approach, are studied in Section 4 and three case studies related to real ecosystems are described. Finally, some conclusions are drawn.

2   Multienvironment P System

A *multienvironment P system* of degree (m, n, q) taking T time units is a tuple

$$(G, \Gamma, \Sigma, \mu, T, \Pi_1, \ldots, \Pi_n, \mathcal{R}, E_1, \ldots, E_m, \mathcal{R}_E)$$

where:

- $G = (V, S)$ is a directed graph. Let $V = \{e_1, \ldots, e_m\}$ whose elements are called environments;
- Γ is the working alphabet and $\Sigma \subsetneq \Gamma$.
- μ is a rooted tree with q nodes.
- T is a natural number that represents the simulation time of the system;
- $\Pi_k = (\Gamma, \mu, \mathcal{M}_{1,k}, \ldots, \mathcal{M}_{q,k}, \mathcal{R})$, $1 \leq k \leq n$, is a basic P system of degree q, and $\mathcal{R}$ is a finite set of rules of the type $u[v]_i^\alpha \longrightarrow u'[v']_i^\beta$.
- $E_j \in M_f(\Sigma)$, $1 \leq j \leq m$.
- $\mathcal{R}_E$ is a finite set of communication rules among environments of the following forms $(x)_{e_j} \longrightarrow (y_1)_{e_{j_1}} \cdots (y_h)_{e_{j_h}}$ and $(\Pi_k)_{e_j} \longrightarrow (\Pi_k)_{e_{j'}}$.
- No rules from $\mathcal{R}$ and $\mathcal{R}_E$ compete for objects.
- Each rule of the system has associated a computable function whose domain is $\{0, \ldots, T\}$.

A multienvironment P system can be viewed as a finite set of environments and a finite set of P systems, such that: (a) the links between environments are given by the arcs taken from a directed graph; (b) each P system has the same working alphabet, the same membrane structure and the same evolution rules; and (c) each environment contains several P systems, where each evolution rule has associated a computable function and each one of them has an initial multiset which depends on the environment; and (d) there is a finite set of rules among the environments. Furthermore, inside the environments, only objects from a distinguished alphabet can exist.

It is worth pointing out that this bioinspired computational approach has some qualitative advantages with respect to ordinary/partial differential equations approach:

- They use a language closer to experts than differential equations.
- They are not affected by the usual constraints present when defining differential equations based models.
- They are modular, that is, once an initial version of the model is designed, adding modifications is relatively easy. On the one hand, small changes in the system entails small changes in the model. On the other hand, when using differential equations most times we have to start from scratch.

3   Stochastic Approach: Multicompartmental P Systems

A multienvironment P system of degree (m, n, q) taking T time units, is said to be stochastic if:

(a) the computable functions associated with the rules of the P systems are *propensities*: they are computed from *stochastic constants* by applying the law of mass-action law (the reaction rate depends proportionally on the product of the concentrations of the reactants), and the stochastic constants are obtained from the kinetic constants in an easy way [18]; these rules depend on time but not on the environment;

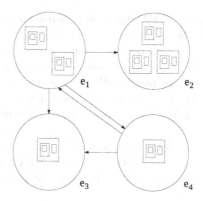

Fig. 1. A multienvironment extended P system

(b) at the initial moment, the P systems $\Pi_1, \ldots, \Pi_n$ are ramdomness distributed between the m environments; for instance, as in the picture.

These kind of P systems are called *multicompartmental P systems*.

The dynamics of these systems is captured by either the *multicompartmental Gillespie's algorithm* [18] or the *deterministic waiting time algorithm* [2]. Gillespie's algorithm [10–13] provides an exact method for the stochastic simulation of systems of bio-chemical reactions; the validity of the method is rigorously proved and it has been already successfully used to simulate biochemical processes and it is based on the inversion method of Monte Carlo theory. The deterministic waiting time algorithm is based on the fact that in vivo chemical reactions take place in parallel in a asynchronous manner. The time taken for the formation of each molecule, called waiting time, is calculated and the rule (reaction) with the least waiting time is applied, changing the concentration in their respective compartments. Each time there is a change in the concentration of a molecule in any compartment, the waiting time for reactions "using" that molecule needs to be recalculated for the compartment.

Infobiotics workbench is a computational framework implementing a synergy among multicompartmental stochastic simulations, formal model analysis and structural/parameter model optimisation for computational systems and synthetic biology (http://www.infobiotics.org/index.html)

In this section some practical examples of multicompartmental P systems applications for modelling cellular systems are presented.

3.1   Apoptosis Mediated by FAS Protein

The FAS-induced apoptotic signalling pathway was shown to be one of the most relevant processes for understanding and combating cancer, AIDS and neurodegenrative diseases such as Parkinson's disease, Alkzheimer, etc.

Two pathways activated by FAS have been identified [23], and are referred to as type I (*death receptor pathway*) and type II (*mitochondrial pathway*), where caspases play a crucial role for both the initiation and execution of apoptosis (*programmed cell death*). The pathways diverge after activation of initiator caspases and converge at the end by activating executor caspases. In the type I pathway, initiator caspases activate executor caspases directly. In the type II pathway, a more complicated cascade is activated involving the disruption of mitochondrial membrane potential.

We have designed a multicompartmental P system with only one environment that consists of 53 objects and 99 evolution rules (see [2] for details) in order to study when a cell chooses the mitochondrial pathway or the death receptor pathway to produce apoptosis.

A *Java* simulator has been implemented and it accepts as input a *Systems Biology Markup Language* (SBML) file containing the rules to be simulated and initial concentrations for the molecules in the system. We used the *Cell Designer* package to generate the SBML source file for the reactions (Cell Designer is a structured diagram editor for drawing gene-regulatory and biochemical networks). The simulator engine mimics the biological cell and it is designed in a modular way so that it can use different strategies for different pathways if needed. The specific strategy, based on the deterministic waiting time algorithm, will be executed depending on the initial concentrations of various objects present in the system. A simulator designed in *Scilab*, a scientific software package for numerical computations providing a powerful open computing environment for engineering and scientific applications [23], using the multicompartmental Gillespie algorithm has been also considered [2].

The consistency between the framework and the experimental results in the paper [14] validates our model. We have stated that our discrete methods handle low levels of molecules in a different way that ODE/PDE techniques. To further investigate the differences between discrete and ODE/PDE methods, we have chosen to focus on one rule from the FAS-mediated pathway (a transformation)

Multicompartmental P systems constitute an alternative to ordinary/partial differential equations methods. We have argued that the discrete nature of our technique might be better for simulating the evolution of systems involving low numbers of molecules.

3.2   Gene Regulation Systems in Lac Operon in E. coli

In most bacteria, gene expression is highly regulated in order to produce the necessary proteinic machinery to respond to environmental changes. Therefore, at a given time, a bacterial cell synthesises only those proteins necessary for its survival under the particular conditions of that time.

Many of the genes in Escherichia coli (E. coli) are expressed constitutively; that is, they are always turned on. Others, however, are active only when their products are needed by the cell, so their expression must be regulated. The most direct way to control the expression of a gene is to regulate its rate of transcription. Adding a new substrate to the culture medium may induce the formation of new enzymes capable of metabolising that substrate. An example of this phenomenon happens when we take a culture of E. coli that is feeding on glucose and transfer some of the cells to a medium containing lactose instead. In this case a revealing sequence of events takes place.

A multicompartmental P system modelling the gene expression control in the Lac Operon has been designed (see [20] for details). Specifically, the system has only one environment, the total number of symbols in the working alphabet is 51 and there are 55 evolution rules. The novelty of this design is that the objects can be symbols or strings over the alphabet. In this context, finite multisets of strings within membranes represent the genetic information encoded in DNA and RNA. The central dogma of molecular cell biology states that genetic information is stored in the DNA. This information is transcribed into mRNA which in turn is translated into proteins. It is worth pointing out that transcription and translation have been modelled as rewriting and concurrent processes on strings.

Using the Multicompartmental Gillepie's Algorithm and a simulator developed in *Scilab*, we have studied the behaviour of the system for different environmental conditions to see how the system is able to sense the presence of different substrate (glucose and lactose).

The delay between the sensing of the signal and the expression of different genes is not explicitly modelled but emerges as a consequence of the formulation of our approach. Our results agree well with experimental observations and results obtained by using other approaches.

3.3 Quorum Sensing in Vibrio Fischeri

Bacteria are generally considered to be independent unicellular organisms. Nevertheless, in some circumstances bacteria exhibit coordinated behaviour which allows an entire population of bacteria to regulate the expression of specific genes depending on the size of the population. This phenomenon is called *quorum sensing*, that is, a cell density dependent gene regulation system. It was first investigated in the marine bacterium *Vibrio Fischeri*. The bacteria colonise specialised light organs in the squid which cause it to become luminescent. Vibrio Fischeri only causes luminescence when colonising the light organs and do not emit light when in the planktonic free-living state. Luminescence in the squid is involved in the attraction of prey, camouflage and communication between different individuals.

Bacteria colonies behave like multicellular organisms. Each bacterium must be able to sense and communicate with other units in the colony to express some specific genes in a coordinated way. The cooperative activities carried out by members of the colony generate a *social intelligence* [17].

In this case, we have designed a multicompartmental P system of degree $(25, n, 1)$, with 25 environments containing each of them an ordinary P system only having the skin membrane (see [21] for details) This model has been represented in the *Systems Biology Markup Language* using *Cell Designer* [9].

The emergent behaviour of the system has been studied for three colonies of different size (10, 100 and 3000 bacteria) to examine how bacteria can sense the number of individuals in the colony and produce light only when such number is big enough.

Our simulations show that Vibrio fischeri has a quorum sensing system where a single bacterium can guess that the size of the population is big enough and start to produce light. This bacterium starts to massively produce signals, but if the signal does not accumulate in the environment it means that the guess was wrong and it switches off the system. In contrast, if the signal does accumulate in the environment meaning that the number of bacteria in the colony is big enough, a recruitment process takes place that causes the entire population of bacteria to become luminescent. Let us stress that this emergent behaviour is a result of local interactions in the environments between different simple agents, the bacteria, which are only able to produce and receive molecular signals. These results agree well with in vitro observations.

4   Probabilistic Approach: Population Dynamics P Systems (PDP Systems)

A multienvironment functional P system with active membranes of degree (q, m, n) taking T time units, is said to be probabilistic if:

(a) the computable functions associated with the rules of the systems are *probability functions* verifying some conditions (these rules depend on the environment but not on the time, they are constant functions);

(b) the total number of P systems Π_k is equal to the number of environments: each environment contains one P system; and

(c) the rules among environments are only of the form: $(x)_{e_j} \longrightarrow (y_1)_{e_{j_1}} \cdots (y_h)_{e_{j_h}}$

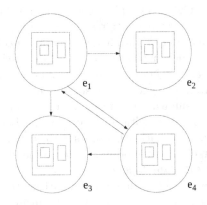

Fig. 2. A Population Dynamics P system

This kind of P systems are called *Population Dynamics P systems* [5]. The dynamics/semantics of these systems is captured by *ad hoc* algorithms such as *Binomial block based simulation algorithm* (BBB) [1], *Direct Non Deterministic distribution with Probabilities algorithm* (DNDP) [7] and *Direct distribution based on Consistent Blocks algorithm* (DCBA) [16], among others.

The BBB algorithm follows a strategy based on the binomial distribution and blocks of rules with the same left-hand side. In general, each simulation step is divided into two main stages: *selection* and *execution*. In the first one, the algorithm decides which rules will be applied, and the number of applications for each one (taking into account their left-hand sides and the available objects in the current configuration). In the second stage, the selected rules are applied, consuming the multisets of the rules' left-hand sides and adding the multisets of the rules' right-hand sides the selected number of times, and possibly changing the polarization of membranes.

The DNDP algorithm performs a non-deterministic distribution of objects along the rules, but considering the probabilities. The algorithm is split into two phases, selection and execution. This time, selection phase is divided into two micro-phases: selection phase 1 (consistency) and selection phase 2 (maximality). Together with an initialization phase, it has a total of four phases. The first selection phase calculates a multiset of consistent applicable rules. This is performed by looping the rules in a random order, and applying each one (if consistent with the already selected rules) using the binomial distribution according to the probabilities. The second selection phase eventually increases the multiplicity of some of the rules in the previous multiset to assure maximal application, obtaining a multiset of maximally consistent applicable rules. Again, there is a loop over the remaining rules, checking the maximality condition. Although the DNDP algorithm achieves better results than its predecessor (BBB), the behaviour still produces some distortion in many situations (it is biased towards the rules with the highest probabilities).

The DCBA algorithm is based on the idea of proportionally distributing the amount of objects along the rule blocks. A proportional calculus is made in such a way that rules requesting for more objects are penalized. However, this calculation can be adapted to the biological semantics to be captured by the model. Probabilities are applied to rule blocks locally. The simulation algorithm consists on two phases, selection and execution. But this time, selection is split into three micro-phases: phase 1 (distribution), phase 2 (maximality), and phase 3 (probabilities). Selection phase 1 uses a distribution table, where rows represent objects inside regions, and columns are rule blocks. A normalized distribution of the objects is performed over the rows. Phase 2 iterates the remaining rule blocks assuring maximality, and phase 3, once rule blocks have been selected, calculates multinomial distributions for each one (according to the selected number for it, and the probabilities of the corresponding rules). DCBA is able to reproduce the desired semantics for the model of PDP systems. However, its efficient implementation is a challenge (the distribution table can be very large).

P-Lingua (http://www.p-lingua.org/wiki/index.php/Main_Page) is a programming language for Membrane Computing which aims to be a standard to define P systems, in particular, population dynamics P systems. MeCoSim (http://www.p-lingua.org/mecosim/) is a visual environment to model, simulate, analyse and verify solutions based on P systems, by defining custom apps for virtual experimentation under different scenarios.

In what follows some practical examples of PDP systems applications for modelling real ecosystems are presented.

4.1 Bearded Vulture

The Bearded Vulture is a cliff-nesting and territorial large scavenger distributed in mountains ranges in Eurasia and Africa. This is one of the rarest raptors in Europe (150 breeding pairs in 2007). This endangered species feeds almost exclusively on bone remains of wild and domestic ungulates. Its main food source is bone remains of dead small and medium-sized animals.

The ecosystem to be modelled is in the Pyrenean and Prepyrenean mountains of Catalonia (NE Spain) and it is composed of 13 species: (a) three avian scavengers (Bearded vulture,the Egyptian vulture and the Griffon vulture as predator species); (b) six wild ungulates (Pyrenean Chamois, Red deer, Fallow deer, Roe deer, Mouflon and Wild boar); and (c) four domestic ungulates (sheep, cow, goat and horse) that are found in an extensive or semi-extensive regime providing carrion for the avian scavengers and considered as prey species. Prey species are herbivores and their remains form the primary food resource for the avian scavengers in the study area.

In order to model this real ecosystem, a population dynamics P system with two environments containing each of them an ordinary P system of degree 2 has been considered (see [3] for details). The model addresses:

(a) the population dynamics previously mentioned;
(b) the interactions among the 13 species;
(c) the presence of two zones in the study area;
(d) the communication protocol between the two areas; and
(e) the ecosystem maximum load capacity for each of the areas.

The algorithmic scheme of the proposed model is shown in Figure 3 and it is structured following a series of modules which are run sequentially corresponding to the passing of 1 year in the ecosystem.

We have studied the dynamics of the ecosystem modifying the initial conditions in order to analyse how the ecosystem would evolve if different biological factors were modified either by nature or through human intervention. We have designed a population dynamics P system with only one environment and 49 types of rules. For each type of animal the number of biological parameters are related to reproduction, mortality, feeding and other general processes of the species itself. We have shown the robustness of the model with respect to a modified order of application of the different processes modules.

MeCoSim software has been used for the execution of the model. The population trend of the three scavenger species and the six wild ungulates has been obtained by

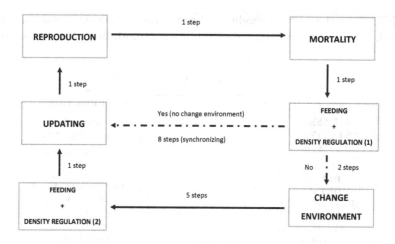

Fig. 3. Algorithmic scheme of the Bearded vulture model [3]

the model with respect to data recovered by direct censuses from 1994 to 2008. The model has been experimentally validated with data experimentally obtained corresponding to the years from 1994 to 2008 (the input being the number of animals in 1994) covering a period of 14 years.

4.2 Pyrenean Chamois

Pyrenean Chamois (*Rupicapra p. pyrenaica*) is an ungulate species inhabiting the Catalan Pyrenees. It is of great interest, not only from a hunting standpoint, but also naturalistic and touristic. In recent years, several diseases have caused a drastic decrease in the number of individuals. In particular, the disease associated to a pestivirus is having a very important impact on a social and economic scale in the Pyrenees. Since they provide significant economic contributions in the area and constitutes an important food resource for obligate and facultative scavengers, it is very interesting to provide a model in order to facilitate the management of their ecosystems.

We have given the first computational model of a real ecosystem from the Catalan Pyrenees involving the Pyrenean Chamois. Specifically we have designed a population dynamics P system model [6] which consists of four environments containing each of them an ordinary P system of degree 11. The system uses 47 types of rules and considers four separated areas in the Catalan Pyrenees where the species lives. Weather conditions, especially in winter (particularly the thickness of the snow layer), influences the values of biological parameters of the Pyrenean Chamois species[8]. Causes of death for this species include: natural death, hunting and diseases. Only Pestivirus infection has been taken into account.

The algorithmic scheme of the proposed model is shown in Figure 4. The algorithm has been sequenced, but all animals evolve in parallel. The processes to be modelled will be the weather conditions (snow), reproduction, regulation of density, food, natural mortality, hunting mortality and mortality due to a disease.

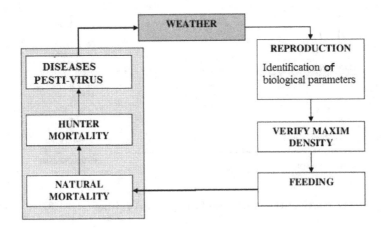

Fig. 4. Algorithmic scheme of the Pyrenean Chamois model [6]

We have shown the robustness of the model with respect to the order of application of different rules.

There are experimental data available from 1988 on, although censuses where not carried out annually so that, experimental series is not a continuous one. Using the censuses in 1988 as input for the model, 22 years have been simulated repeating the process 50 times for each of the years simulated. In general, the model behaves well in all cases.

4.3   Zebra Mussel

The Zebra Mussel (*Dreissena polymorpha*) is a long known invasive species in Middle East, Europe or even Northern USA rivers and fresh water lakes. This species provokes serious ecological and socioeconomic impacts. It is an agent of radical ecologic change, threatening colonized ecosystems in the short and half terms by modifying certain water and sediments parameters, causing the displacement of autochthonous species.

In Spain, its colonization began in Ebro river, in the summer of 2001 [22], threatening not only the infrastructure of several reservoirs but also tourism and the ecological sustainability of the affected ecosystems.

The ecosystem to be modelled is very complex as a consequence of the combined effect of different features: the biological cycle of Zebra Mussels, the heterogeneity of the physical environment, the size of the reservoir, and its water turnover. Thus, the variations in the level of water can be considered negligible. As a result, the application of conventional techniques for modelling may be unfeasible.

In order to study the population dynamics of the Zebra Mussel in the fluvial reservoir of Riba-roja, the following factors have been considered:

(1) The basic biological processes of the species, determined by the thermal conditions and the substrate suitability in the reservoir;
(2) the features of the special habitat under study, that is, an artificial reservoir with water currents and eddies, and changes in water renewal depending on the depth and time of year, according to the reservoir management for hydropower and characteristics of incoming water;
(3) the possibility of external larvae entering from an upstream reservoir and the transfer of individuals to the reservoir by boats.

The algorithmic scheme of the proposed model is shown in Figure 5. Each individual may initiate the loop at different times. The processes sequenced in the figure are run in parallel in an area at the same time. The processes are out of sync between areas. The passing of a year is represented by running the loop twice.

A population dynamics P system based model for the Zebra Mussel at the Ribarroja reservoir (Spain) has been presented [4]. The system consists of 17 environments containing each of them an ordinary P system of degree 40. The system uses 55 types of rules. The main goal of this model is to provide a management tool to aid in the decision-making process, with the aim of controlling (eradicating or decreasing) the population of these invasive mussels.

Three different scenarios have been studied:

– The first set of simulations is addressed to determine the effect of the current water flow on the reservoir.
– The goal of the second set of simulations is to obtain a water flow (water turnover) that allows the elimination of the Zebra Mussel in the reservoir, keeping the other conditions constant.
– The last set of simulations aimed to test one of the main hypotheses concerning the invasion of the Zebra Mussels in the reservoir. It studies the effect of the external introduction of larvae considering the current hydrological regime.

The software tool MeCoSim has been used to design the simulator interface. Input values (i.e., parameters and value variables of the model) are introduced directly into the interface of the simulator. In order to study the behaviour of the model in a specific scenario, we simply need to change the input values in this interface.

The results obtained by the simulation of the presented model under the given scenarios are consistent with those published by other authors and observed by the experts responsible for the monitoring and management of the population of Zebra Mussels in the reservoir of Riba-roja.

5   Conclusions

In this paper, a general bioinspired computing modelling framework, called multienvironment P systems, is introduced. The framework is based on Membrane Computing and two approaches are described: stochastic approach which is usually applied to model *micro*-level systems (such as signalling pathways, gene expression

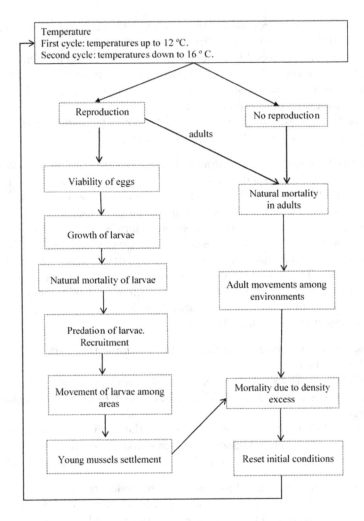

Fig. 5. Algorithmic scheme of the Zebra Mussel model [4]

control, bacteria colonies, etc.), and the probabilistic approach which is normally used for *macro*-level modelling (such as real ecosystems). Stochastic multienviron-ment P systems are called multicompartmental P systems, and probabilistic mul-tienvironment P systems are called population dynamics P systems. The dynamics of multicompartmental P systems is captured by either the multicompartmental Gillespie's algorithm or the deterministic waiting time algorithm. The dynamics of the population dynamics P systems is captured by *ad hoc* algorithm such as bino-mial block based simulation algorithm (BBB), direct non Deterministic distribu-tion with probabilies algorithm (DNDP), the direct distribution based on consis-tent blocks algorithm (DCBA).

Several case studies are presented in order to illustrate the bioinspired computing modelling framework. Specifically, three cases for multicompartmental P systems (apoptosis mediated by FAS protein, gene regulation system in Lac Operon in E. coli and quorum sensing in Vibrio Fischeri) and three cases for population dynamics P systems (real ecosystems related to bearded vulture, Pyrenean Chamois and Zebra Mussel).

Acknowledgements. The author wishes to acknowledge the support of the project TIN2012–37434 of the Ministerio de Economía y Competitividad of Spain, co–financed by FEDER funds.

References

1. Cardona, M., Colomer, M.A., Margalida, A., Palau, A., Pérez-Hurtado, I., Pérez-Jiménez, M.J., Sanuy, D.: A computational modeling for real ecosystems based on P systems. Natural Computing **10**(1), 39–53 (2011)
2. Cheruku, S., Păun, A., Romero, F.J., Pérez-Jiménez, M.J., Ibarra, O.H.: Simulating FAS-induced apoptosis by using P systems. Progress in Natural Science **17**(4), 424–431 (2007)
3. Colomer, M.A., Margalida, A., Sanuy, D., Pérez-Jiménez, M.J.: A bio-inspired computing model as a new tool for modeling ecosystems: The avian scavengers as a case study. Ecological modelling **222**(1), 33–47 (2011)
4. Colomer, M.A., Margalida, A., Valencia, L., Palau, A.: Application of a computational model for complex fluvial ecosystems: The population dynamics of zebra mussel Dreissena polymorpha as a case study. Ecological Complexity **20**, 116–126 (2014)
5. Colomer, M.A., Margalida, A., Pérez-Jiménez, M.J.: Population Dynamics P System (PDP) Models: A Standardized Protocol for Describing and Applying Novel Bio-Inspired Computing Tools. PLOS ONE **8**(4), e60698 (2013). doi:10.1371/journal.pone.0060698
6. Colomer, M.A., Lavín, S., Marco, I., Margalida, A., Pérez-Hurtado, I., Pérez-Jiménez, M.J., Sanuy, D., Serrano, E., Valencia-Cabrera, L.: Modeling population growth of Pyrenean chamois (Rupicapra p. pyrenaica) by using P-systems. In: Gheorghe, M., Hinze, T., Păun, Gh., Rozenberg, G., Salomaa, A. (eds.) CMC 2010. LNCS, vol. 6501, pp. 144–159. Springer, Heidelberg (2011)
7. Colomer, M.A., Pérez-Hurtado, I., Pérez-Jiménez, M.J., Riscos, A.: Comparing simulation algorithms for multienvironment probabilistic P system over a standard virtual ecosystem. Natural Computing **11**, 369–379 (2012)
8. Crampe, J.P., Gaillard, J.M., Loison, A.: L'enneigement hivernal: un facteur de variation du recrutement chez l'isard (Rupicapra pyrenaica pyrenaica). Canadian Journal of Zoology **80**, 306–1312 (2002)
9. Funahashi, A., Morohashi, M., Kitano, H.: Cell Designer: a Process Diagram Editor for Gene-regulatory and Biochemical Networks. Biosilico **1**, 159–162 (2003)
10. Gillespie, D.T.: A General Method for Numerically Simulating the Stochastic Time Evolution of Coupled Chemical Reactions. Journal of Computational Physics **22**, 403–434 (1976)
11. Gillespie, D.T.: Exact Stochastic Simulation of Coupled Chemical Reactions. The Journal of Physical Chemistry **81**(25), 2340–2361 (1977)

12. Gillespie, D.T.: Approximate Accelerated Stochastic Simulation of Chemically Reacting Systems. Journal of Chemical Physics **115**(4), 1716–1733 (2001)
13. Gillespie, D.T.: Improved Leap-size Selection for Accelerated Stochastic Simulation. Journal of Chemical Physics **119**(16), 8229–8234 (2003)
14. Hua, F., Cornejo, M., Cardone, M., Stokes, C., Lauffenburger, D.: Effects of Bcl-2 Levels on FAS Signaling-Induced Caspase-3 Activation: Molecular Genetic Tests of Computational Model Predictions. The Journal of Immunology **175**(2), 985–995 (2005). (and correction **175**(9), 6235–6237 (2005))
15. Jørgensen, S.E.: Ecological Modelling. An introduction. WIT Press, Southampton (2009)
16. Martínez-del-Amor, M.A., et al.: DCBA: Simulating population dynamics P systems with proportional object distribution. In: Csuhaj-Varjú, E., Gheorghe, M., Rozenberg, G., Salomaa, A., Vaszil, Gy. (eds.) CMC 2012. LNCS, vol. 7762, pp. 257–276. Springer, Heidelberg (2013)
17. Nunes de Castro, L., Silveira, R., Pasti, R., Dourado, R., Szabo, A., Gomes, D.: The Grand Challenges in Natural Computing Research: The Quest for a New Science. International Journal of Natural Computing Research **2**(4), 17–30 (2011)
18. Pérez-Jímenez, M.J., Romero-Campero, F.J.: P Systems, a New Computational Modelling Tool for Systems Biology. In: Priami, C., Plotkin, G. (eds.) Transactions on Computational Systems Biology VI. LNCS (LNBI), vol. 4220, pp. 176–197. Springer, Heidelberg (2006)
19. Regev, A., Shapiro, E.: The π-calculus as an abstraction for biomolecular systems. In: Ciobanu, G., Rozenberg, G. (eds.) Modelling in Molecular Biology. Springer, Berlin (2004)
20. Romero, F.J., Pérez-Jiménez, M.J.: Modelling gene expression control using P systems: The Lac Operon, a case study. BioSystems **91**(3), 438–457 (2008)
21. Romero, F.J., Pérez-Jiménez, M.J.: A model of the Quorum Sensing System in Vibrio Fischeri using P systems. Artificial Life **14**(1), 95–109 (2008)
22. Ruíz Altaba, C., Jiménez, P.J., López, M.A.: El temido mejillón cebra empieza a invadir los ríos españoles desde el curso bajo del río Ebro. Quercus **188**, 50–51 (2001)
23. Scaffidi, C., Fulda, S., Srinivasan, A., Friesen, C., Li, F., Tomaselli, K.J., Debatin, K.M., Krammer, P.H., Peter, M.E.: Two CD95 (APO-1/Fas) signaling pathways. The Embo Journal **17**, 1675–1687 (1998)
24. ISI web page. http://esi-topics.com/erf/october2003.html
25. SciLab Web Site. http://scilabsoft.inria.fr/
26. P Systems Modelling Framework Web Site. http://www.dcs.shef.ac.uk/~marian/PSystemMF.htm

P Systems with Active Membranes Working in Sublinear Space

Claudio Zandron$^{(\boxtimes)}$, Alberto Leporati, Luca Manzoni, Giancarlo Mauri, and Antonio E. Porreca

Dipartimento di Informatica, Sistemistica e Comunicazione,
Università degli Studi di Milano-Bicocca, Viale Sarca 336/14, 20126 Milano, Italy
{zandron,leporati,luca.manzoni,mauri,porreca}@disco.unimib.it

Abstract. P systems with active membranes are a variant of P systems where the membranes can be created during the computation by division of existing ones. Using this feature, one can create an exponential number of membranes in a polynomial time, and use them in parallel to solve computationally hard problems, such as problems in **NP** or even in **PSPACE**. This possibility raises many interesting questions concerning the trade–off between time and space needed to solve various classes of computational problems by means of membrane systems. In this paper we concentrate on P systems with active membranes working in sublinear space, with a survey on recent research results concerning such systems.

1 Introduction

P systems with active membranes have been introduced in [7] as a variant of P systems where the membranes play an active role in the computation: an electrical charge, that can be positive (+), neutral (0), or negative (−), is associated with each membrane; the application of the evolution rules can be controlled by means of these electrical charges. Moreover, new membranes can be created during the computation by division of existing ones. A very interesting feature of such systems is that, using these operations, one can create an exponential number of membranes in polynomial time, and use them in parallel to solve computationally hard problems, such as problems in **NP** or even in **PSPACE**.

This possibility raises many interesting questions concerning the trade–off between time and space needed to solve various classes of computational problems by means of membrane systems. In order to clarify such relations, a definition of space complexity for P systems has been proposed [9], on the basis of an hypothetical implementation of P systems by means of real biochemical materials: every single object and every single membrane requires some constant physical space. Research on the space complexity of P systems with active membranes has shown that these devices, when using a polynomial amount of space, exactly characterize the complexity class **PSPACE** [10], [11]. The result has then been generalized, showing that any Turing machine working in space $\Omega(n)$ can be simulated with a polynomial space overhead [1].

© Springer International Publishing Switzerland 2014
M. Gheorghe et al. (Eds.): CMC 2014, LNCS 8961, pp. 35–47, 2014.
DOI: 10.1007/978-3-319-14370-5_3

In this paper we concentrate on P systems with active membranes that work in *sublinear* space, with a survey on recent research results. The first natural approach, when considering the use of sublinear space in the framework of membrane systems, is to compare logarithmic space P systems Turing machines using the same amount of space. In Section 3 we present a result from [13] showing that **DLOGTIME**–uniform P systems with active membranes, using a logarithmic amount of space, are able to simulate logarithmic-space deterministic Turing machines, and thus to solve all problems in the class **L**.

In [3] it is pointed out that, while logarithmic-space Turing machines can only generate a polynomial number of distinct configurations, P systems working in logarithmic space have *exponentially* many potential ones, and thus they can be exploited to solve computational problems that are harder than those in **L**. In particular, polynomial-space Turing machines can be simulated by means of P systems with active membranes using only logarithmic auxiliary space, thus obtaining a characterization of **PSPACE**.

We present then a result concerning P systems using only a *constant* amount of space; it turned out [4] that, quite surprisingly, a constant amount of space is sufficient (and trivially necessary) to solve all problems in **PSPACE**. This result challenges our intuition of space, formalized in the definition of space complexity for P systems adopted so far. Thus, a more accurate estimate of the space required by a configuration of a P system was proposed. Using the new space definition, all the results involving at least a polynomial amount of space, according to the first definition, still hold. The difference appears only when P systems with severely tight bounds on the amount of space used during computations are considered.

Finally we present a result, also from [4], that highlights the importance of rewriting input symbols for P systems when a sub-logarithmic number of membrane labels is used. Under this last condition, if we only allow the use of rules that move the input objects in the membrane hierarchy (i.e. send-in, send-out, and dissolution rules), then it is even impossible to correctly distinguish two input strings of the same length (unless the ordering of the symbols is not taken into account), even when no bound on the amount of space is present. In other words, P systems having such limitations and accepting (resp., rejecting) a long enough string x also accept (resp., reject) any other string obtained by swapping two symbols of x.

2 Basic Notions

For a comprehensive introduction to P systems we refer the reader to *The Oxford Handbook of Membrane Computing* [8]. The definition of space complexity for P systems can be found in [9].

In order to consider sublinear space in the framework of P systems, we need to define a meaningful notion of sublinear space inspired by sublinear space definition for Turing machines: we consider two distinct alphabets, an *INPUT* alphabet and a *WORK* alphabet, in the definition of a P system. The input objects cannot be rewritten and do not contribute to the size of the configuration of a P system. The size of a configuration is defined as the sum of the number of membranes in the current membrane structure and the total number of working objects they contain. We recall here the basic definitions related to P systems with active membranes with an input alphabet [13]:

Definition 1. *A P system with (elementary) active membranes having initial degree $d \geq 1$ is a tuple $\Pi = (\Gamma, \Delta, \Lambda, \mu, w_{h_1}, \dots, w_{h_d}, R)$, where:*

- *Γ is an alphabet, i.e., a finite non-empty set of symbols, usually called* objects;
- *Δ is another alphabet, disjoint from Γ, called the* input *alphabet;*
- *Λ is a finite set of labels for the membranes;*
- *μ is a membrane structure (i.e., a rooted unordered* tree, *usually represented by nested brackets) consisting of d membranes labelled by elements of Λ in a one-to-one way;*
- *$w_{h_1}, \dots, w_{h_d}$, with $h_1, \dots, h_d \in \Lambda$, are strings over Γ describing the initial multisets of objects placed in the d regions of μ;*
- *R is a finite set of rules over $\Gamma \cup \Delta$.*

Each membrane possesses, besides its label and position in μ, another attribute called *electrical charge*, which can be either neutral (0), positive ($+$) or negative ($-$) and is always neutral before the beginning of the computation.

A description of the available kinds of rule follows. This description differs from the original definition [7] only in that new input objects may not be created during the computation.

- *Object evolution rules*, of the form $[a \to w]_h^\alpha$
  They can be applied inside a membrane labelled by h, having charge α and containing an occurrence of the object a; the object a is rewritten into the multiset w (i.e., a is removed from the multiset in h and replaced by the objects in w). At most one input object $b \in \Delta$ may appear in w, and only if it also appears on the left-hand side of the rule (i.e., if $b = a$).
- *Send-in communication rules*, of the form $a\,[\,]_h^\alpha \to [b]_h^\beta$
  They can be applied to a membrane labelled by h, having charge α and such that the external region contains an occurrence of the object a; the object a is sent into h becoming b and, simultaneously, the charge of h is changed to β. If $b \in \Delta$ then $a = b$ must hold.
- *Send-out communication rules*, of the form $[a]_h^\alpha \to [\,]_h^\beta\, b$
  They can be applied to a membrane labelled by h, having charge α and containing an occurrence of the object a; the object a is sent out from h to the outside region becoming b and, simultaneously, the charge of h is changed to β. If $b \in \Delta$ then $a = b$ must hold.
- *Dissolution rules*, of the form $[a]_h^\alpha \to b$
  They can be applied to a membrane labelled by h, having charge α and containing an occurrence of the object a; the membrane h is dissolved and its contents are left in the surrounding region unaltered, except that an occurrence of a becomes b. If $b \in \Delta$ then $a = b$ must hold.

- *Elementary division rules*, of the form $[a]_h^\alpha \rightarrow [b]_h^\beta [c]_h^\gamma$
  They can be applied to a membrane labelled by h, having charge α, containing an occurrence of the object a but having no other membrane inside (an *elementary membrane*); the membrane is divided into two membranes having label h and charges β and γ; the object a is replaced, respectively, by b and c while the other objects in the initial multiset are copied to both membranes. If $b \in \Delta$ (resp., $c \in \Delta$) then $a = b$ and $c \notin \Delta$ (resp., $a = c$ and $b \notin \Delta$) must hold.

Each instantaneous configuration of a P system with active membranes is described by the current membrane structure, including the electrical charges, together with the multisets located in the corresponding regions. A computation step changes the current configuration according to the following set of principles:

- Each object and membrane can be subject to at most one rule per step, except for object evolution rules (inside each membrane several evolution rules can be applied simultaneously).
- The application of rules is *maximally parallel*: each object appearing on the left-hand side of evolution, communication, dissolution or elementary division rules must be subject to exactly one of them (unless the current charge of the membrane prohibits it). The same principle applies to each membrane that can be involved in communication, dissolution, or elementary division rules. In other words, the only objects and membranes that do not evolve are those associated with no rule, or only to rules that are not applicable due to the electrical charges.
- When several conflicting rules can be applied at the same time, a nondeterministic choice is performed; this implies that, in general, multiple possible configurations can be reached after a computation step.
- In each computation step, all the chosen rules are applied simultaneously (in an atomic way). However, in order to clarify the operational semantics, each computation step is conventionally described as a sequence of micro-steps as follows. First, all evolution rules are applied inside the elementary membranes, followed by all communication, dissolution and division rules involving the membranes themselves; this process is then repeated to the membranes containing them, and so on towards the root (outermost membrane). In other words, the membranes evolve only after their internal configuration has been updated. For instance, before a membrane division occurs, all chosen object evolution rules must be applied inside it; this way, the objects that are duplicated during the division are already the final ones.
- The outermost membrane cannot be divided or dissolved, and any object sent out from it cannot re-enter the system again.

A *halting computation* of the P system Π is a finite sequence of configurations $\mathcal{C} = (\mathcal{C}_0, \ldots, \mathcal{C}_k)$, where $\mathcal{C}_0$ is the initial configuration, every $\mathcal{C}_{i+1}$ is reachable from $\mathcal{C}_i$ via a single computation step, and no rules of Π are applicable in $\mathcal{C}_k$. A *non-halting* computation $\mathcal{C} = (\mathcal{C}_i : i \in \mathbb{N})$ consists of infinitely many configurations, again starting from the initial one and generated by successive computation steps, where the applicable rules are never exhausted.

P systems can be used as language *recognisers* (see, e.g. [2]) by employing two distinguished objects **yes** and **no**; exactly one of these must be sent out from the outermost membrane, and only in the last step of each computation, in order to signal acceptance or rejection, respectively; we also assume that all computations are halting. If all computations starting from the same initial configuration are accepting, or all are rejecting, the P system is said to be *confluent*. If this is not necessarily the case, then we have a *non-confluent* P system, and the overall result is established as for nondeterministic Turing machines: it is acceptance iff an accepting computation exists. Unless otherwise specified, the P systems in this paper are to be considered confluent.

In order to solve decision problems (i.e., decide languages over an alphabet Σ), we use *families* of recogniser P systems $\boldsymbol{\Pi} = \{\Pi_x : x \in \Sigma^*\}$. Each input x is associated with a P system Π_x that decides the membership of x in the language $L \subseteq \Sigma^*$ by accepting or rejecting. The mapping $x \mapsto \Pi_x$ must be efficiently computable for each input length [6].

Definition 2. *Let $\mathcal{E}$ and $\mathcal{F}$ be classes of functions. A family of P systems $\boldsymbol{\Pi} = \{\Pi_x : x \in \Sigma^*\}$ is said to be (E, F)-uniform if and only if*

- *There exists a function $f \in F$ such that $f(1^n) = \Pi_n$, i.e., mapping the unary representation of each natural number to an encoding of the P system processing all inputs of length n, and defining a specific membrane as the input membrane.*
- *There exists a function $e \in E$ mapping each string $x \in \Sigma^*$ to a multiset $e(x) = w_x$ (represented as a string) over the input alphabet of Π_n, where $n = |x|$.*
- *For each $x \in \Sigma^*$ we have $\Pi_x = \Pi_n(w_x)$, i.e., Π_x is Π_n with the multiset encoding x placed inside the input membrane.*

Generally, the above mentioned classes of functions $\mathcal{E}$ and $\mathcal{F}$ are complexity classes; in the most common uniformity condition $\mathcal{E}$ and $\mathcal{F}$ denote polynomial-time computable functions.

Any explicit encoding of Π_x is allowed as output of the construction, as long as the number of membranes and objects represented by it does not exceed the length of the whole description, and the rules are listed one by one. This restriction is enforced in order to mimic a (hypothetical) realistic process of construction of the P systems, where membranes and objects are presumably placed in a constant amount during each construction step, and require actual physical space proportional to their number; see also [6] for further details on the encoding of P systems.

Finally, we describe how space complexity for families of recogniser P systems is measured, and the related complexity classes [9, 13].

Definition 3. *Let $\mathcal{C}$ be a configuration of a recogniser P system Π. The size $|\mathcal{C}|$ of $\mathcal{C}$ is defined as the sum of the number of membranes in the current membrane* structure and the total number of objects from Γ (i.e, the non-input objects) they contain. If $\mathcal{C} = (\mathcal{C}_0, \ldots, \mathcal{C}_k)$ is a computation of Π, then the space required by $\mathcal{C}$ is defined as

$$|\mathcal{C}| = \max\{|\mathcal{C}_0|, \ldots, |\mathcal{C}_k|\}.$$

The space required by Π itself is then obtained by computing the space required by all computations of Π and taking the supremum:

$$|\Pi| = \sup\{|\mathcal{C}| : \mathcal{C} \text{ is a computation of } \Pi\}.$$

Finally, let $\boldsymbol{\Pi} = \{\Pi_x : x \in \Sigma^\star\}$ be a family of recogniser P systems, and let $s: \mathbb{N} \to \mathbb{N}$. We say that $\boldsymbol{\Pi}$ operates within space bound s iff $|\Pi_x| \leq s(|x|)$ for each $x \in \Sigma^\star$.

By (E, F)-**MCSPACE**$_{\mathcal{D}}(f(n))$ we denote the class of languages which can be decided by (E, F)-uniform families of confluent P systems of type $\mathcal{D}$ (in the following we will mainly refer to P systems with active membranes, and we denote this by setting $\mathcal{D} = \mathcal{AM}$), where each $\Pi_x \in \boldsymbol{\Pi}$ operates within space bound $f(|x|)$. The class of problems solvable in (E, F)-logarithmic (resp. polynomial) space is denoted by (E, F)-**LMCSPACE**$_{\mathcal{D}}$ (resp. (E, F)-**PMCSPACE**$_{\mathcal{D}}$).

3   Simulating Logarithmic–Space Turing Machines

In this section we recall a result from [13] showing that P systems with active membranes, using a logarithmic amount of space, are able to simulate logarithmic-space deterministic Turing machines, and thus to solve all problems in the class **L**.

In order to consider such systems, we need to define a uniformity condition for the families of P systems that is weaker than the usual **P** uniformity, to avoid the possibility to solve a problem directly by using the Turing machine that builds the P systems we use to compute. One such possibility is to consider **DLOGTIME**-uniformity, defined on the basis of **DLOGTIME** Turing machines [5]. We refer the reader to [13] for formal definitions.

The efficient simulation of logarithmic space Turing machines (or other equivalent models) has to face two main problems: we cannot use a polynomial number of working objects (to avoid violating the logarithmic space condition) and we cannot use a polynomial number of rewriting rules (to avoid violating the uniformity condition). It has been shown in [13] that such problems can be avoided by a simulation that uses membrane polarization both to communicate objects through membranes as well as to store some information.

Theorem 1. *Let M be a deterministic Turing machine with an input tape (of length n) and a work tape of length $O(\log n)$. Then, there exists a $(\mathbf{DLT}, \mathbf{DLT})$-uniform family $\boldsymbol{\Pi}$ of confluent recogniser P systems with active membranes working in logarithmic space such that $L(M) = L(\boldsymbol{\Pi})$.*

Proof. (sketch) Consider a Turing machine M working in logarithmic space. The P system Π_n that simulates M on input of length n is composed of:

- A skin membrane containing a *state object* object $q_{i,w}$ to indicate that M is currently in state q and its tape heads are on the i-th and w-th symbols of the input and work tape, respectively.
- $O(\log n)$ nested membranes (INPUT tape membranes) containing, in the innermost one, the input symbols of M, and $O(\log(n))$ membranes to store the work tape of M (WORK tape membranes).
- Two sets of membranes, whose size depend on the dimensions of the input and the working alphabet of M (SYMBOL membranes), respectively.

To simulate a computation step of M, the state object enters the INPUT membranes, storing the bits corresponding to the actual position of the INPUT head of M in their polarizations. Only one object (corresponding to the INPUT symbol actually read) can travel to the outermost membrane. Then, the state object identifies the symbol actually under the WORK head (using the WORK tape membranes) and proceeds to simulate the transition of M using the SYMBOLS membranes.

Each P system Π_x (simulating each $M(x)$ such that $|x| = n$) only requires $O(\log|x|)$ membranes and objects besides the input objects; moreover, the family Π is $(\mathbf{DLT}, \mathbf{DLT})$-uniform. The time required by the simulation is $O\big(n \cdot t(n)\big)$, where $t(n)$ is the maximum number of steps performed by M on inputs of length n.   □

An immediate corollary of Theorem 1 is that the class of problems solved by logarithmic-space Turing machines is contained in the class of problems solved by $(\mathbf{DLT}, \mathbf{DLT})$-uniform, logarithmic-space P systems with active membranes.

Corollary 1. $\mathbf{L} \subseteq (\mathbf{DLT}, \mathbf{DLT})\text{-}\mathbf{LMCSPACE}_{\mathcal{AM}}.$ □

4   Simulating Polynomial-Space Turing Machines

The result presented in the previous section only represents a lower bound for the power of logarithmic-space P systems; as a matter of fact, already in [13] it was conjectured that it could be improved, as P systems working in logarithmic space have an *exponential* number of different configurations, which could possibly be used to efficiently solve harder problems than those in the class $\mathbf{L}$. It turned out [3] that this is the case, and that polynomial-space deterministic Turing machines can be simulated by means of P systems with active membranes using only logarithmic auxiliary space, thus characterising **PSPACE**.

The simulation was based on two key ideas. First, input objects (of the form τ_i) are distributed, during the computation, in various substructures. Apart from an initial phase, the value of τ is disregarded: the symbol σ written on the i-th tape cell of the Turing machine being simulated can be inferred from the label of the substructure that contains τ_i. The second idea is applied when querying the symbol under the tape head: the position i of the head is written in binary in the electrical charges of the membranes composing the substructure where the object τ_i is placed, so that the only input object having the correct subscript can leave the substructure corresponding to the sought symbol, and reach the skin membrane. The depth of each substructure is logarithmic, thus allowing to represent a polynomial number of possible head positions. As a result, we can simulate any polynomial space computation of a deterministic Turing machine with only a logarithmic number of symbols (plus a polynomial number of read-only input symbols) and membranes.

Theorem 2. *Let M be a single-tape deterministic Turing machine working in polynomial space $s(n)$ and time $t(n)$. Then, there exists an $(\mathbf{L}, \mathbf{L})$-uniform family Π of P systems with active membranes using object evolution and communication rules that simulates M in space $O(\log n)$ and time $O(t(n)s(n))$.*

Proof. (sketch) Let $x \in \Sigma^n$ be an input string, and let $m = \lceil \log s(n) \rceil$ be the minimum number of bits needed in order to represent the tape cell indices $0, \ldots, s(n) - 1$ in binary notation. The P system Π_n, associated with the input length n, has a membrane structure consisting of an external skin membrane that contains, for each symbol of the tape alphabet of M, the following set of membranes, linearly nested and listed from the outside in:

- a *symbol-membrane*;
- a *query-membrane*;
- for each $j \in \{0, \ldots, m - 1\}$, a membrane labelled by j_σ.

An arbitrary configuration of M on input x is encoded by a configuration of Π_x as follows:

- the outermost membrane contains the *state-object* q_i, (where q is the current state of M, and i is the current tape head position);
- if membrane $(m - 1)_\sigma$ contains the input object τ_i, then the i-th tape cell of M contains the symbol σ.

The symbol written on the i-th tape cell of M can be inferred from the label of the substructure which contains the corresponding input symbol τ_i. Notice that a logarithmic depth membrane structure allows to represent a polynomial number of possible head positions.

The state-object q_i queries each membrane substructure, by encoding in binary the tape position i on the electrical charges of the membranes. Only the symbol whose subscript is i can reach the skin membrane and be used to conclude the simulation of a computation step.

The family Π described above is $(\mathbf{L}, \mathbf{L})$-uniform, and each P system Π_x uses only a logarithmic number of membranes and a constant number of objects per configuration, besides the input objects, which are never rewritten. Π_x works in space $O(\log n)$ and in time $O(t(n)s(n))$. □

As a consequence, we have the following:

Theorem 3. *For each class $\mathcal{D} \subseteq \mathcal{AM}$ of P systems with active membranes using object evolution and communication among their rules we have*

$$(\mathbf{L}, \mathbf{L})\text{-}\mathbf{LMCSPACE}_{\mathcal{D}} = (\mathbf{L}, \mathbf{L})\text{-}\mathbf{PMCSPACE}_{\mathcal{D}} = \mathbf{PSPACE}.$$

Proof. The inclusion **PSPACE** $\subseteq$ **(L, L)-LMCSPACE**$_\mathcal{D}$ follows immediately from Theorem 2. By definition, the class **(L, L)-LMCSPACE**$_\mathcal{D}$ is included in **(L, L)-PMCSPACE**$_\mathcal{D}$. Finally, to prove the inclusion of **(L, L)-PMCSPACE**$_\mathcal{D}$ in **PSPACE** it suffices to simulate P systems by means of Turing machines, which can be carried out with just a polynomial space overhead, as shown in [1, 10]. □

This was the first case where the space complexity of P systems and that of Turing machines differ by an exponential amount. Since, as previously said, **PSPACE** had already been proved to be characterised by *polynomial*-space P systems, these results also highlight a gap in the hierarchy of space complexity classes for P systems: super-polynomial space is required in order to exceed the computational power of logarithmic space.

5   Constant–Space P Systems

After considering P systems with active membranes working in logarithmic space, a natural question arises concerning the power of such systems using only a constant amount of space. Surprisingly it turned out that constant space is sufficient to simulate polynomial-space bounded deterministic Turing machines, as proved in [4]:

Theorem 4. **(L, L)-MCSPACE**$_{\mathcal{AM}}(O(1)) =$ **PSPACE**.

Proof. (sketch) Let $L \in$ **PSPACE**, and let M be a Turing machine deciding L in space $p(n)$. We can construct a family of P systems $\boldsymbol{\Pi} = \{\Pi_x : x \in \Sigma^\star\}$ such that $L(\boldsymbol{\Pi}) = L$ by letting $F(1^n) = \Pi_n$, where Π_n is the P system simulating M on inputs of length n, and

$$E(x_0 \cdots x_{n-1}) = x_{1,1} \cdots x_{n-1,n-1} \sqcup_n \cdots \sqcup_{p(n)-1},$$

i.e. by padding the input string x with $p(n) - n$ blank symbols $\sqcup$ before indexing the result with the positions of the symbols on the tape.

The simulation relies on two main ideas. As in the previous proof of Theorem 2, input objects of the form τ_i are distributed in substructures, and the symbol written on the i-th tape cell of M can be inferred from the label of the substructure where the corresponding input symbol τ_i is placed. The second idea is that it is possible to "read" a subscript of an input object τ_i without rewriting it and by using only a constant number of additional objects and membranes: in particular, a timer object is used to change the charge of a membrane after a requested amount of steps. Any other object that was counting together with the timer is able to observe the charge of the membrane, and thus obtain the designed value.

Since at each computation step only a constant number of working objects and membranes are present, then the simulation requires, according to definition 3, a constant amount of space. Moreover, both F and E can be computed in logarithmic space by Turing machines, since they only require adding subscripts having a logarithmic number of bits to rules or strings having a fixed structure, and the membrane structure is fixed for all Π_n. This proves the inclusion of **PSPACE** in $(\mathbf{L}, \mathbf{L})\text{-}\mathbf{MCSPACE}_{\mathcal{AM}}(O(1))$, while the reverse inclusion is proved in [10]. $\qquad\qquad\qquad\qquad\qquad\qquad\qquad\qquad\qquad\qquad\qquad\qquad$ □

6   Rethinking the Definition of Space

The result of Theorem 4 shows that all problems in **PSPACE** can be solved by constant-space P systems with active membranes. This rises some natural questions about the definition of space complexity for P systems adopted until now [9]. Does counting each non-input object and each membrane as unitary space really capture an intuitive notion of the amount of space used by a P system during a computation? Is it fair to allow a polynomial padding of the input string when encoding it as a multiset?

In [4], it was highlighted that the constant number of non-input objects appearing in each configuration of the simulation actually encode $\Theta(\log n)$ bits of information, since they are taken from an alphabet Γ of polynomial size. According to the original definition of space recalled in Section 2, each of these objects would only require unitary space, whereas the binary representation of the subscript i requires $\log p(n) = \Theta(\log n)$ bits. It may be argued that this amount of information needs a proportional amount of physical storage space. Similarly, each membrane label contains $\Theta(\log |\Lambda|)$ bits of information, which must also have a physical counterpart.

The information stored in the *positions* of the objects within the membrane structure is also not taken into account by Definition 3. However, the information on the location of the objects is part of the system and it is *not* stored elsewhere, exactly as the information on the location of the tape head in a Turing machine, which is not counted as space.

Due to the above considerations, in [4] an alternative definition of space was proposed:

Definition 4. *Let $\mathcal{C}$ be a configuration of a P system Π. The size $|\mathcal{C}|$ of $\mathcal{C}$ is defined as the number of membranes in the current membrane structure multiplied by $\log |\Lambda|$, plus the total number of objects from Γ (i.e, the non-input objects) they contain multiplied by $\log |\Gamma|$.*

Adopting this stricter definition does not significantly change space complexity results involving polynomial or larger upper bounds, i.e., the complexity classes $\mathbf{PMCSPACE}_{\mathcal{AM}}$, $\mathbf{EXPMCSPACE}_{\mathcal{AM}}$, and larger ones remain unchanged.

As for padding the input string, one may argue that this operation provides the P system with some "free" storage, since input objects are not counted by Definition 3. The proof of Theorem 4 exploits the ability to encode an input string of length n as a polynomially larger multiset in a substantial way, as allowed by the most common uniformity conditions, including **P** and **LOGSPACE**-uniformity, but also weaker ones such as $\mathbf{AC}^0$ or **DLOGTIME**-uniformity.

The simulation described in the previous section would require logarithmic space according to Definition 4. Also the space bounds of the simulation of polynomial-space Turing machines by means of logarithmic-space P systems with active membranes described in Section 4 also increase to $\Theta(\log n \log \log n)$, since in that case each configuration of the P systems contains $\Theta(\log n)$ membranes with distinct labels and $O(1)$ non-input objects. Both simulations would be limited to *linear*-space Turing machines, rather than polynomial-space ones, if input padding were disallowed.

7   Computing Without Rewriting Input Objects

In this section we present another result from [4] showing that if input objects are only moved around the membrane structure (without rewriting them into other objects), then evolution rules involving the input objects are essential in order to perform a simulation of a Turing machine using less than a logarithmic number of membrane labels. In fact, if only non-rewriting send-in, send-out, and dissolution rules are applied to input symbols, and the number of membrane labels is $o(\log n)$, then it is even impossible to correctly distinguish two input strings of the same length. This happens independently of the space used by the P systems, as long as the function E encoding the input $x \in \Sigma^\star$ as a multiset w_x is "simple":

Definition 5. *Let A be an alphabet containing Σ, and let*

$$s \colon A^\star \to \{\sigma_i : \sigma \in A, i \in \mathbb{N}\}^\star$$

be the function defined by $s(x_0 \cdots x_{n-1}) = x_{0,0} \cdots x_{n-1,n-1}$, i.e. the function subscripting each symbol with its position in the string.

An encoding E of $\Sigma^\star$ is "simple" if there exists a function $g \colon \mathbb{N} \to A^\star$ such that $E(x) = s(x \cdot g(|x|))$ for all $x \in \Sigma^\star$, i.e. $E(x)$ is the original input string x, concatenated with a string depending only on the length of x, and indexed with the positions of its symbols.

Notice that the encoding employed in Theorem 4 is indeed simple.

When the encoding is simple and the input alphabet is at least binary, P systems with the limitations described above accepting (resp., rejecting) a long enough string x also accept (resp., reject) another string obtained by swapping two symbols of x.

Theorem 5. *Let Π be a family of $(\mathcal{E}, \mathcal{F})$-uniform, possibly non-confluent recogniser P systems with active membranes, where $\mathcal{F}$ is unrestricted, and $\mathcal{E}$ is a class of simple encodings. Suppose that the only rules involving input symbols are send-in, send-out and membrane dissolution, that these rules never rewrite the input symbols, and that the family uses $o(\log n)$ membrane labels. Then, there exists $n_0 \in \mathbb{N}$ such that, for each string $x = x_0 \cdots x_{n-1} \in \Sigma^\star$ with $|x| = n \geq n_0$, there exist $i < j < n$ such that x can be written as $u \cdot x_i \cdot v \cdot x_j \cdot w$ with $u, v, w \in \Sigma^\star$, and $x \in L(\Pi)$ if and only if $u \cdot x_j \cdot v \cdot x_i \cdot w \in L(\Pi)$.*

Proof. (sketch) Let Π be a family of P systems as defined in the statement of the theorem, let $F \in \mathcal{F}$ be its "family" function, and let

$$F(1^n) = \Pi_n = (\Gamma, \Delta, \Lambda, \mu, w_{h_1}, \ldots, w_{h_d}, R).$$

Assume that the objects in Δ are subject, in R, only to rules of type send-in, send-out, and dissolution not rewriting them. On the other hand, we impose no restriction on rules involving objects in Γ. If we consider the possible rules applicable to a fixed object $a \in \Delta$ and respecting the imposed restrictions, we notice that there are $21|\Lambda|$ possible rules per input object and hence $2^{21|\Lambda|}$ possible sets of rules involving each input object. Since the encoding of the input string is simple, each input object has the form σ_i for some $\sigma \in A$; hence, for each position i in the input multiset there are $\left(2^{21|\Lambda|}\right)^{|A|} = 2^{21|\Lambda||A|}$ possible sets of rules.

A necessary condition to distinguish two input objects $a, b \in \Delta$ is that the set of rules involving b cannot be simply obtained by replacing a with b in the set of rules involving a (i.e. their sets of rules are not isomorphic); otherwise, replacing a with b in the input multiset would not change the result of the computation of Π_x. In particular, this holds for the first n input objects $x_{0,0}, \ldots, x_{n-1,n-1}$, obtained by indexing $x = x_0 \cdots x_{n-1} \in \Sigma^n$. In order to be able to distinguish these n input objects it is thus necessary that

$$2^{21|\Lambda||\Sigma|} \geq n$$

that is, that the sets of rules associated with the first n objects are pairwise non-isomorphic. This means that

$$|\Lambda| \geq \frac{\log n}{21|\Sigma|}$$

However, since $|\Lambda|$ is $o(\log n)$, the inequality does not hold for large enough n. Instead, there exists n_0 such that, for each $n \geq n_0$, there are two indistinguishable positions i and j with $0 \leq i < j < n$: for each $x = u \cdot x_i \cdot v \cdot x_j \cdot w \in \Sigma^n$, either x and $u \cdot x_j \cdot v \cdot x_i \cdot w$ are both accepted, or they are both rejected.   □

8   Final Remarks

In this paper we survey recent results concerning P systems with active membranes working in sublinear space. We showed that such systems characterize **PSPACE** either when using logarithmic space, as well as when using only a constant amount of space.

A new definition of space has thus been proposed, which considers also the number of bits necessary to encode the non-input objects and the labels of the membranes. While the new definition does not change any result involving an amount of space which is polynomial or larger, it changes the result for sublinear space. In particular, according to the new definition the simulation used to prove that constant space P systems with active membranes characterize **PSPACE** would now require logarithmic space.

We also recalled a result showing that rewriting input objects is essential when less than a logarithmic number of membrane labels is present; in this case, it is not possible to distinguishing two different input strings when the input objects are only moved around in the membrane structure, even when no restrictions on the amount of space are present.

Acknowledgments. This work was partially supported by Università degli Studi di Milano-Bicocca, Fondo d'Ateneo (FAR) 2013: "Complessità computazionale in modelli di calcolo bioispirati: Sistemi a membrane e sistemi a reazioni".

References

1. Alhazov, A., Leporati, A., Mauri, G., Porreca, A.E., Zandron, C.: Space complexity equivalence of P systems with active membranes and Turing machines. Theoretical Computer Science **529**, 69–81 (2014)
2. Csuhaj-Varju, E., Oswald, M.: Vaszil, Gy.: P automata, Handbook of Membrane Computing. In: Păun, Gh. et al. (ed.) pp. 144–167. Oxford University Press (2010)
3. Leporati, A., Mauri, G., Porreca, A.E., Zandron, C.: A Gap in the space hierarchy of P systems with active membranes. Journal of Automata, Languages and Combinatorics **19**(1–4), 173–184 (2014)
4. Leporati, A., Manzoni, L., Mauri, G., Porreca, A.E., Zandron, C.: Constant-space P systems with Active Membranes, Fundamenta Informaticae (to appear)
5. Mix Barrington, D.A., Immerman, N., Straubing, H.: On uniformity within NC^1. Journal of Computer and System Sciences **41**(3), 274–306 (1990)
6. Murphy, N., Woods, D.: The computational power of membrane systems under tight uniformity conditions. Natural Computing **10**(1), 613–632 (2011)
7. Păun, Gh.: P systems with active membranes: Attacking NP-complete problems. J. of Automata, Languages and Combinatorics **6**(1), 75–90 (2001)
8. Păun, Gh., Rozenberg, G., Salomaa, A. (eds.) Handbook of Membrane Computing. Oxford University Press (2010)
9. Porreca, A.E., Leporati, A., Mauri, G., Zandron, C.: Introducing a space complexity measure for P systems. Int. J. of Comp., Comm. & Control **4**(3), 301–310 (2009)
10. Porreca, A.E., Leporati, A., Mauri, G., Zandron, C.: P Systems with Active Membranes: Trading Time for Space. Natural Computing **10**(1), 167–182 (2011)
11. Porreca, A.E., Leporati, A., Mauri, G., Zandron, C.: P systems with active membranes working in polynomial space. Int. J. Found. Comp. Sc. **22**(1), 65–73 (2011)
12. Porreca, A.E., Mauri, G., Zandron, C.: Complexity classes for membrane systems. RAIRO-Theor. Inform. and Applic. **40**(2), 141–162 (2006)
13. Porreca, A.E., Leporati, A., Mauri, G., Zandron, C.: Sublinear-Space P systems with Active Membranes. In: Csuhaj-Varjú, E., Gheorghe, M., Rozenberg, G., Salomaa, A., Vaszil, Gy. (eds.) CMC 2012. LNCS, vol. 7762, pp. 342–357. Springer, Heidelberg (2013)

Regular Papers

Membrane Computing Inspired Approach for Executing Scientific Workflow in the Cloud

Tanveer Ahmed, Rohit Verma$^{(\boxtimes)}$, Miroojin Bakshi, and Abhishek Srivastava

Indian Instititue of Technology Indore, Indore, India
{phd12120101,phd12110101,cse1200105,asrivastava}@iiti.ac.in

Abstract. The continuous expansion and appreciation of the service oriented architecture is due to the standards of loose-coupling and platform independence. Service-Oriented Architecture is the most commonly and effectively realized through web services, and their temporal collaboration commonly referred to as web service composition. In the present scenario, the most popular variant of composition is service orchestration. Orchestration is achieved through a centralized *'heavyweight'* engine, the orchestrating agent, that makes the deployment configuration a massive *'choke-point'*. The issue achieves significance when data and compute intensive scientific applications rely on such a centralized scheme. Lately, a lot of research efforts are put in to deploy a scientific application on the cloud, thereby provisioning resources *elastically* at runtime. In this paper, we aim at eliminating this central 'choke' point by presenting a model inspired from *'Membrane Computing'* that executes a scientific workflow in a decentralized manner. The benefit of this paradigm comes from the natural process of autonomy, where each cell provision resources and execute process-steps on its own. The approach is devised keeping in mind, the feasibility of deployment on a cloud based infrastructure. To validate the model, a prototype is developed and real scientific workflows are executed in-house (with-in the Intranet). Moreover, the entire prototype is also deployed on a virtualized platform with software defined networking, thereby studying the effects of a low bandwidth environment, and dynamic provisioning of resources.

Keywords: Scientific Workflows · Service Oriented Architecture · Membrane Computing

1 Introduction

Service oriented architecture has now become a multipurpose paradigm executing business processes and helping compute intensive scientific applications [2]. It's success can largely be attributed to advancements in the field of cloud computing. The technological advancements, notwithstanding, the paradigm relies on a centralized solution to orchestrate either a business process or data intensive scientific applications as the case may be. The orchestrator, by virtue of its inherent centralized nature is a single point of failure and suffers from the issues of scalability, reliability, fault tolerance, security, and privacy [4].

© Springer International Publishing Switzerland 2014
M. Gheorghe et al. (Eds.): CMC 2014, LNCS 8961, pp. 51–65, 2014.
DOI: 10.1007/978-3-319-14370-5_4

It is well known fact that a scientific workflow is resource intensive, whereas a business workflow is control oriented. A scientific workflow is well exemplified by the Large Synoptic Survey Telescope[1] experiment aimed to recursively explore and take images of the sky for a period of 10 years and expected to generate data (300MB/s) in the order of exabytes (both raw and pruned). To rely on a centralized architecture in this context, is a potential processing and communication bottleneck. Moreover, the failure of an orchestrator or the hosted platform (cloud's Infrastructure as a Service), causes a cascaded chain reaction, making the entire hierarchy of deployed services moot. The issue is evident by the failure of Amazon in 2011, 2012, and 2013. A decentralized setup, on the other hand, achieves a reduction in failures and enables quick recovery. Considering the example of Astro-Grid science (calculating Redshift) presented in [1], a reduction of 43.47% (data transfer) was achieved by enacting a workflow using a decentralized architecture. Hence, in the context of scientific applications, we believe a fault tolerant decentralized solution towards workflow execution should be the way forward.

With the advent of cloud computing, concepts such as *Elastic Computing*, *federation of clouds*, and *Mobile Cloud Computing*, are just around the corner. In respect to the scientific workflows, the benefit of decentralization comes in the context of Elastic Computing. Consider, a compute intensive workitem is processing huge volumes of data. If a centralized orchestrator is handling this task, then the orchestrator is responsible for gathering resources, provision them into the existing workflow, perform migrations at remote locations and several others resulting in an un-necessary burden on the controlling authority. Moreover, a centralized engine foster a lot of infrastructure, development, maintainence and operational costs. Therefore, for certain scientific experiments limited by budget constraints, the decentralized architecture is an ideal candidate.

Bell *et al.* [3] states "the rapidity with which any given discipline advances is likely to depend on how well the community acquires the necessary expertise in database, '*workflow management*', visualization, and cloud computing technologies". Taking this line of reasoning as a benchmark for the proposed work, we propose a decentralized solution to execute a scientific workflow via membrane computing approach. We take inspiration from biology to design a workflow management model that execute services, realizing the *process-steps* or *workitems*, in a decentralized manner. We use the elementary principles of membrane computing to model the execution of a workflow. The choice of this type of an architecture comes with the benefit that it provides a natural and an intuitive method to model workflows, pass parameters and elastically increase or decrease resources at runtime. We consider each membrane as a service capable of executing a scientific workitem. The membranes are self capable of discovering other resources (or services) on their own. Each service is provided with *evolutionary rules* (Membrane terminology), it is through these rules the services evolve, allocate & provision extra resources, and execute their respective tasks in a cost-efficient manner.

Substantial literature focuses on achieving scientific workflow execution over the cloud [1], [2], [9], [11], [12]. However, most of these rely on the hosted platform

---

[1] http://www.lsst.org/lsst/science

(or the orchestrator) to elastically increase or decrease resources at runtime, or don't focus on elasticity at all. Therefore, our objective is to introduce '*autonomy*' in resource provisioning by the work-items themselves.

To the best of our knowledge, this is the first endeavour to explore the possibility of executing a workflow via Membrane Computing. To demonstrate the viability of the same in actual deployment, we have developed a prototype with 'real' services. We execute real scientific workflows collected from myexperiment[2], and deploy the prototype on a virtualized platform (XENServer) to test the validity of the proposed work. During validation, the services exchange data and parameters via a stable storage. The stable storage itself was offered as a service, thereby affirming to the standards of Service-Oriented Architecture. Moreover, using Software Defined Networking, we study the effects of limited bandwidth capabilities during execution.

The contribution of this paper is two-fold:

1) A novel membrane inspired approach for decentralizing workflow execution, with autonomous provisioning of computing resources

2) A proof of concept, via actual deployment and execution of scientific workflows.

The rest of the paper is organized as follows: Section 2 presents a brief introduction to membrane computing. Membrane Inspired Scientific Workflow execution is discussed in Section 3. Results are discussed in Section 4, Related Work is presented in Section 5. We conclude with Future Work in Section 6.

For the purpose of clarification, a scientific workflow is called a workflow throughout this paper. A resource is analogous to a service instantiated on a Virtual Machine.

2   Membrane Computing Paradigm

Before beginning the discussion of Membrane Inspired workflow management, we present a small discussion on the Membrane Computing paradigm.

Membrane computing takes its inspiration from a living cell. A living cell is encapsulated by a membrane that separate its internals from the external environment. The cell encloses multiple natural artifacts, e.g. nucleus, golgi apparatus, molecules, vesicles etc. The cytoplasm holds charged ions, whose movement (either inwards or outwards) is controlled by the presence of certain type of proteins. Using chemical receptors, the membrane allows a selective passage of molecules and achieves cell-to-cell signaling.

The pioneering work in the area of membrane computing was proposed in [6]. The author proposed, the basic structure of a membrane consist of several separate sub-membranes. The membranes consist of the delimiting region, called multiset, where several different objects are placed. The evolution, manipulation, and transformation of objects is accomplished via evolutionary rules. The objects are transferred from one membrane to another membrane, causing transitions and carrying out the intended tasks. The execution rules are chosen in a

---

[2] http://myexperiment.org

non-deterministic manner, thereby presenting an illusion of having infinite parallel computing capability. The application of these rules is conditional i.e. a rule is invoked if certain reaction conditions are applicable. The rules as explained in [6] are of the form $a \longrightarrow b$, where a and b represent multisets of objects. Since the data and objects are transferred from one membrane to another, the author proposed the notion of 'target indications'. Using target indications, the objects are retained, transferred and consumed. It can be deduced that using these rules the multiset can be written very easily. An example of a rule applied towards object evolution is demonstrated below.

Consider a rule of the form *(ij)* $\longrightarrow$ *(i,here) (i,out) (j,in) (j,out)*. In this example, a copy of i and j is consumed and two copies of i and j are produced. One copy of i is retained within the same membrane (the 'here' indicator), while the other one moves out to the surrounding environment (the 'out' indicator). Out of the two copies of j produced, one goes to the surrounding environment and the other moves inwards toward the inner membrane(s). There exists catalytic rules demonstrating the applicability only in the presence of a certain type of an object, e.g. $cb \longrightarrow cv$, where c is the catalyst. Also, there are non co-operating rules, e.g. $a \longrightarrow b$, membrane dissolving rules, e.g. $j \longrightarrow o\delta$, where δ denotes the membrane dissolving action. It should noted here, the author [6] deliberately points out that the membrane dissolving rule cannot be applied to the skin membrane (for obvious reasons). Further, there are communication rules, symport and antiport, demonstrating how membranes communicate. As outlined earlier, in the real world the membranes communicate via protein channels. Therefore, the protein channel and the molecules are the agents of communication in membrane computing. The *'symport rules'* allows for the passage of molecules in one way. On the other hand, the *'antiport rules'* allow for a two way communication via molecules. We have primarily used membranes with *'symport' and 'antiport' rules* in this paper.

There also exists membrane division and merging rules. A membrane division rule is of the form $[_1 a]_1 \longrightarrow [_2 b]_2 [_3 c]_3$ (a membrane is denoted as '[ ]', [6]), while a membrane merging rule is of the form $[_2 e]_2 [_3 f]_3 \longrightarrow [_1 d]_1$. Further, there exists endocytosis rules, exocytosis rules, gemmation rules etc. The rules are applied locally in each membrane in a non-deterministic, maximally parallel manner, thereby causing *transitions* in the system.

In this paper, we try to use these elementary concepts to achieve a decentralized workflow execution. Based on the discussion so far, it is understood that this paradigm has a natural orientation, and can solve any type of computation problem (e.g. Satisfiability [14], Traveling Salesman Problem [16] etc). It is due to this feature, it has received a lot of attention in literature, right from the moment of its inception. It can be deduced that the membrane computing paradigm allows a natural metaphor and an intuitive mechanism to model the complex behavior of scientific workflows. As discussed previously the paradigm allows communication rules (symport and antiport), membrane dissolving rules, membrane division and merging rules etc. Using these rules, scientific workflow constructs and functionality can be managed with little efforts. Further, applying the evolutionary rules, a workflow itself can be modified dynamically (via endocytosis, exocytosis, gemmation etc.).

3   Membrane Inspired Scientific Workflow Execution

In the proposed work, a membrane is considered as a service capable of realizing a single 'workitem' or a '*process-step*'. Each membrane has its fluid (local memory) capable of storing the contextual information and local data (or molecules). The contextual information includes the load-indicator parameters, the inner membranes (the successor workitems), the outer membranes (the predecessor workitems), the resource pool etc (discussed below). The membranes communicate via the 'symport' rules to pass control to the subsequent membrane. The objects and data are passed via the multiset. The data is equivalent to the proteins capable of penetrating the membrane structure. The membranes do not pass data directly, but rather direct the subsequent membranes to read from the stable storage location (implemented as a scalable distributed shared memory). In the following text, a *service* is called a '*membrane*' for the rest of the paper.

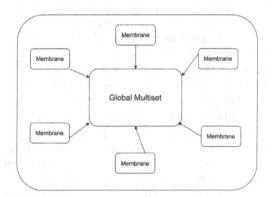

Fig. 1. Membrane Architecture

Before proceeding any further, we must outline the basic architecture utilized to achieve a decentralized execution. Fig. 1 represents the overall design used while executing a workflow. The outermost membrane represents the skin membrane, the inner membranes demonstrates the individual workitems. As visible, all membranes pass data and parameters to the global multiset. Each membrane operates on the objects available in the multiset locally. Hence, there is no need of a central controlling authority. After completing an execution, the membrane dissolves and leaves the transformed objects in the multiset. This procedure is followed till the objects are pushed out to the surrounding i.e. the execution of a workflow has completed. In the membrane computing model, we focus on the property of elastically provisioning resources, by the membranes themselves using cell division rules. An example of cell division rules was outlined previously. Using such type of division rules, the membrane is instantly divided, and the load is dynamically shared between the parent membrane and the newly born child membranes. It should be pointed out here that the provisioning of resources is done autonomously (i.e. by a membrane itself), thereby the need of the cloud service provider to locate and provision resources is removed completely. While provisioning extra resources (resource elasticity property), or in membrane terminology, when a parent membrane is dynamically divided into child membranes, the child membranes also read and write to the same multiset. In this way, a membrane is self capable of finding and provisioning resources into existing workflow.

During execution, when a membrane is dynamically divided, the load has to be shared between parent and child membranes. Since the provisioning of resources, or rather, the membrane division process is autonomous (no orchestrator), therefore one might think that the division process will take some time. However, in the results section we prove that the division process, rather than slowing things down, actually speeds up the process.

To dynamically divide a membrane, a *load-indicator* is instantiated with each membrane. When a threshold value is reached, for either the response time, the throughput, the queue size etc., the membrane division rule is invoked and the parent membrane is divided into multiple child membranes. Whenever, the load-indicator sensed the load has reduced, the membrane merging rule was invoked and the extra provisioned resources were released.

In the proposed model, the multiset is considered as a stable, semantically distributed shared memory offered as a service. Semantic space allow an inherent capability for parallel processing and a distributed stable data management platform. This type of platform allows huge volumes of data to be stored in a semantic format, with event-driven and asynchronous mode of communication. Such type of a storage schema allows a simple Application Programming Interface (API) to read and write to a persistent storage. The APIs to access the protocol are exposed as a web service (SOAP & RESTful APIs). The data center allows the query to specified in GData, OpenSearch, XQuery/XPath over HTTP, SPARQL etc. Since, the discussion of semantic spaces is out of scope for this paper, we direct the interested reader to [7], [8].

To demonstrate the procedure used in the membrane computing model to execute a workflow is explained with the help of an example. A simple workflow with four activities in BPMN (Business Process Management Notation) [15] format is demonstrated in Fig. 2. The equivalent representation using membranes is shown in the same Figure. The rules to execute the workflow are shown in Fig. 3. The rules here do not include any division behavior, rather they specify the execution procedure from a global point of view. It should be pointed out here that the elastic behavior or the cell division rules are specified locally to each membrane.

In this Figure, a, b, c, d, e, f are multisets of objects. The execution begins when membrane one performs a transition, and writes the transformed data to the multiset (Rule 1). Further, using Rule 1 the membrane dissolved (the δ indicator)

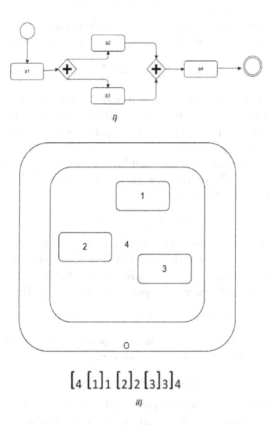

Fig. 2. A Simple Workflow & Membrane Representation

$$[_1a]_1 \longrightarrow [_2b,in]_2 \ [_3c,in]_3 \ \delta$$
$$[_2b]_2 \longrightarrow [_4d,in]_4 \ \delta$$
$$[_3c]_3 \longrightarrow [_4e,in]_4 \ \delta$$
$$[_4de]_4 \longrightarrow [_of,out]_o \ \delta$$

Fig. 3. Execution Rules

and let membranes two and three access the multiset to read the objects b and c respectively. A similar procedure is followed for all the execution rules. The last rule demonstrates the completion of transition activities, and the system halts. In the proposed work, we have used the notion of the *dependency operator*, enabling a sense of determinism during execution. In this paper, we propose the use of dependency operator as $\xrightarrow{\quad (Details) \quad}_{Dependency}$, where Dependency represents the type of dependency (data or control) and details demonstrate the list of dependent membranes. It is a known fact that the membranes at same level execute their rules in a non-deterministic manner. However, owing to control dependencies, certain membranes have to be restricted from execution. In such scenarios, the proposed operator provides a certain level of determinism and restrict few of the membranes from execution. For example, consider the following dependency rule:

$$[_1[_{S_1}a]_{S_1}[_{S_2}b]_{S_2}[_{S_3}c]_{S_3}]_1 \xrightarrow[Control]{S_2,S_3} [_1[_{S_1}a]_{S_1}]_1\delta \tag{1}$$

In this rule, the dependency is control and the membrane list contains $\{S_2, S_3\}$. The rule implies that prior to the execution of S_1, or, in other words, prior to the application of this rule, both S_2 and S_3 must dissolve (or S_2 and S_3 must have completed their resp. tasks).

It was outlined previously, the membranes are self sufficient to procure resources on their own. To accomplish this functionality, cell division rules are utilized. For example, consider a rule

$$[_1a]_1 \longrightarrow [_{1.1}a]_{1.1}[_{1.2}a]_{1.2}$$

In this example, membrane one is divided into two halves, each having the same processing functionality and capability. The division process is carried out using symport rules, involving the membrane and the load-indicator. As soon the membrane divided, the execution procedure and order became

$$[_{1.1}a]_{1.1}[_{1.2}a]_{1.2} \longrightarrow [_2b,\ in]_2\ [_3c,\ in]_3\ \delta$$

If, in the middle of a transaction, the provisioned resources have to be released, then cell merging rules are invoked, e.g.

$$[_{1.1}a]_{1.1}[_{1.2}a]_{1.2} \longrightarrow [_1a]_1$$

Hence, by applying the division rules and the merging rules, resources can be provisioned and released. The specification and application of these rules is dependent on each individual membrane, there is no authority that controls the division and merging process. The membranes are self-sufficient and self-capable of invoking division rules and merging rules independently. During real world experimentation, we have also used the same procedure to execute the scientific workflows.

In the membrane computing model, a specific role is assigned to each membrane. Moreover, the membranes are assigned a unique name and an identifier. Membranes assigned to the same role can execute the same functionality. In the *Future Internet*, the issue of reliability is inevitable, therefore redundant membranes should be kept as back-up in case one fails during execution. Next, while executing a workflow there are certain input and output dependencies that must be resolved before proceeding. In the proposed work, these dependencies are specified in an XML format thereby providing a straightforward mapping to a machine readable format. Since, a lot of work [1], [5], [13] has been done to resolve dependencies and automate the execution of traditional workflows, therefore we rely on those procedures to proceed with the execution.

Now, to begin with the execution, a workflow is specified to the multiset. Every participating membrane reads its corresponding dependencies (a low level locking mechanism). In the experiments, we used an XML schema as shown

Listing 1.1. ResourcePool

```
<ResourcePool>
<Resource>
<Address>
http://10.200.40.139/Traffic/Diverte/node1
</Address>
<Endpoint>
.

.

</Endpoint>
</Resource>
<Resource>
<Address>
http://10.200.40.132/Traffic/Diverte/node2
</Address>
<Endpoint>
.

.

</Endpoint>
</Resource>
</ResourcePool>
```

in 1.1. It should be noted that our motive is *'not'* to introduce a new *description language*. The schema is not limited and was constructed using the principles of domain specific languages. Therefore, any type of workflow can be mapped to a machine readable and executable format, thereby presenting a language independent interface. In that case, each membrane must be equipped to handle any type of description. A question arises here: How do membranes understand these specifications? To interpret these constructs, each membrane is equipped with a local interpreter. Hence, an extra layer is added to the membranes to correctly interpret the workflow description (either XML or normal rules).

4   Results

4.1   Experimental Setup

In order to evaluate the proposed work, and to check the viability in actual deployment scenarios, we have conducted experiments with multiple workflows collected from myexperiment.org. The execution of these workflows was achieved in 1) Inside the Institute's Intranet 2)Virtual Machines within the Computing Lab of the Institute. The configuration of each machine in the Intranet is i5 Processor with 4 GB RAM, whereas the resource pool had multiple machines, each having Quad-Core processors with 8GBs and 16GBs of RAM. The distributed shared memory, MozartSpaces[3], was deployed as a RESTful service. The application container for the services was Apache Tomcat v7.0.41. The experiments

---

[3] http://www.mozartspaces.org/

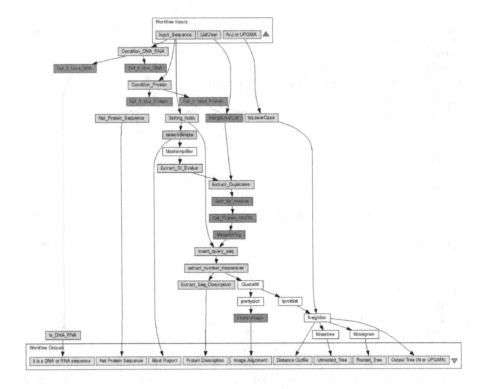

Fig. 4. One of the Workflows for Experimentation

were conducted specifically keeping in mind the capability to provision resources independently, specifically we concentrate on Infrastructure as a Service.

To study the effect of a low bandwidth environment, the networking capabilities of each Virtual Machine (VM) was constrained. In this paper, one of our motive was to test the model's performance and feasibility to execute a decentralized scientific workflow under duress with limited bandwith capabilities. We discuss the behavior of the model in the next subsection.

4.2   Execution Efficiency

As outlined previously, we have chosen workflows from myexperiment. The workflows are uploaded by the people in the research community, and spans different fields viz. Bio-Informatics, Protein Sequence Analysis, nucleotide and protein sequence analysis. Each workflow was executed multiple times. A total of 13, 28, and 18 services were developed for workflow I[4], II[5], and III[6].

---

[4] http://www.myexperiment.org/workflows/244.html

[5] http://www.myexperiment.org/workflows/124.html

[6] http://www.myexperiment.org/workflows/1477.html

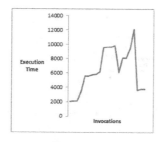

Fig. 5. Execution Time WF-I No Constraints

During the experiments, it was assumed that each of the discrete workitems are realized by a web service. In Fig. 5, we have shown the execution time of the workflow I, with no constraints on the bandwidth capabilities. As visible, the execution time of the workflow started at a normal pace. But, when the invocations increased linearly, the execution time followed. The moment, the load-indicator (*of each individual membrane*) sensed duress, a new resource or a Virtual Machine (VM) was provisioned from the resource pool. The newly provisioned resource was made aware of the stable storage location and access methodology.

After provisioning resources, the execution time experienced a sudden drop. This is clearly visible in Fig. 5. It should be noted here that in the experiments, each workitem (or membrane) provisioned resources on its own. The first reduction in the execution time is due to the fact that only a few membranes provisioned an extra resource. Therefore, the drop is not that much steep. However, a sudden decrement in the execution time at the end of the graph indicate multiple VMs were provisioned to complete the workflow. We invoked the same workflow multiple times (in regular intervals), in the move to analyze the behavior of autonomously provisioning resources. It should be noted here, when the membranes provisioned extra resources, it happened when the load indicator sensed duress for the *new* incoming request. The already existing requests were not dynamically *migrated* (live migration). In business terminology, the SLAs (Service Level Agreements) were violated for the new requests only, there is no need to provision resources for non-SLA violating requests (*principles of cost elasticity*).

The same procedure was followed to execute workflows II and III. The result demonstrating the execution time for workflow II is shown in Figure 6. As visible, the execution time dropped the moment the load indicator sensed an increment in the load of the individual membrane. Hence, looking at the execution results for workflows I and II, it can be said that though the membranes provisioned resources autonomously, but the execution efficiency was never compromised. The results demonstrate the feasibility of the membrane computing paradigm towards executing scientific workflows without requiring a centralized controller, or without pre-defined arrangements with the cloud service provider (Infrastructure as a Service).

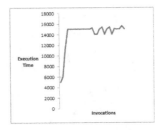

Fig. 6. Execution Time WF-III No Constraints

In the experiments conducted so far, the bandwidth of each VM was not limited. During experimentation, we limited the bandwidth of each VM deployed to 2KBytes/s. This was done to evaluate the feasibility of the prototype in real world scenarios. The resulting graph for the execution time is shown in Fig. 7 (workflow I). As demonstrated in the Figure, the provisioning of extra resources resulted the same sudden drop in the execution time. However, in this case the execution time increased. This effect is due to the fact that the bandwidth is limited and each individual membrane required some time to receive the data dependencies. Moreover, it was observed that there were instances when the request was dropped due to severe congestion.

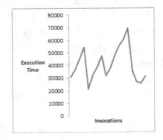

Fig. 7. Execution Time WF-I Limited Bandwidth

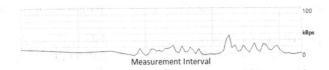

Fig. 8. Network Performance Limited Bandwidth

In Figure 8, we have shown the snapshot of the network perfromance of one of the VMs chosen at random. It can be seen from the Figure that the network capabilities witnessed its peak during execution. It is at that instant, the new incoming requests were dropped. Further, the performace showed that whenever the load increased beyond the threshold limit, new VMs were provisioned to balance the load.

5 Related Work

In literature, there are lot of techniques available to execute a workflow, either centrally or decentrally. In the decentralized scenario, the services share data and parameters either by passing messages directly or indirectly. However, only a few are in the context of dynamically provisioning resources for scientific workflows with actual deployment.

Nature inspired metaphors have caught some attention lately. Based on these approaches we found two interesting metaphors for workflow enactment: 1) Chemistry Metaphor 2) Physics Metaphor. A decentralized framework to execute workitems, is proposed in [5], [2]. Fernandez et al. [2] propose executing a workflow using the chemical paradigm. Similar to our work, the authors used a decentralized environment, however, they used a centralized shared memory (hence, the authors suffered from scalability issues). Moreover, they kept the services fixed to execute the workitems, with no provision of dynamic adaptations. Further, the issues of elasticity is not addressed. A similar method to achieve orchestration and choreography is proposed in [5]. The author used the same chemistry model to achieve orchestration and choreography. Next, the work in physics, focus achieving *motion co-ordination*, using the notion of '*Computational Fields*' [17]. However, the focus is distributed motion co-ordination, not scientific workflow execution. A similar technique to synchronize the motion of 'Unmanned aerial system (UAS)' is proposed in [18]. The author has used the notion of physics inspired co-fields to accomplish this functionality. A similar physics inspired technique is proposed in [10]. The authors also focus achieving a decentralized service composition in dynamic environments. However, the focus is not scientific workflow execution.

A cloud based middleware is proposed in [11]. It is a platform proposed to elastically provision resources at run time. However, the main focus of [11] is not scientific workflow execution in a decentralized environment. In [9], a comparison between the resource consumption between a high performance computing machine and a cloud based environment is presented. The cloud experiments are conducted on Amazon's EC2. The author found, the resources provisioned from the cloud were not that powerful as compared to a traditional high performance computing machine. They found, though executing scientific workflow was acceptable, however the data transfer costs were high. This is one of the factors we will be focusing in the future works. How to find an optimal balance between resource and cost elasticity? [12] introduces the concept of scheduling data intensive scientific workflows in a cloud based environment with virtual clusters. The scheduling is based on the 'iterative ordinal optimization' algorithm. The application of the algorithm produces a significantly lower processing overhead involved in scheduling the workflows. In this paper, we also achieved a decentralized workflow execution based on observable virtual clusters.

6   Conclusions and Future Work

In this paper, we introduced the membrane computing paradigm towards realizing a scientific workflow. The membranes acted independently, with a global perspective, and provisioned resources autonomously. We validated our approach over real services, on real virtualization platform within the computer labs of our institute. We were able to demonstrate that the proposed methodology was effective in provisioning resources autonomously at run-time, thereby validating the technique for an actual deployment. Future work in this direction includes work to extend the methodology for incorporating mobile devices. Further, we are looking towards deploying the services on a grid based facility, while provisioning resources from a public cloud. Finally, we propose to study the effects of cost elasticity on resource provisioning.

Acknowledgement. The authors would like to thank fellow Ph. D students, to help with the technical issues faced during experimentation, and figuring out with the technicalities of Membrane Computing. We would also like to thank the people in the research community, for sharing their scientific workflows.

References

1. Barker, A., Walton, C.D., Robertson, D.: Choreographing web services. IEEE Transactions on Services Computing **2**(2), 152–166 (2009)
2. Fernandez H., Tedeschi C., Priol T.: A Chemistry Inspired Workflow Management System for Decentralizing Workflow Execution. IEEE Transactions on Services Computing. doi:10.1109/TSC.2013.27 (pre-print)
3. Bell, G., Hey, T., Szalay, A.: Beyond the data deluge. Science **323**(5919), 1297–1298 (2009)
4. Alonso, G., Agrawal, D., Abbadi, A.E., Mohan, C.: Functionality and limitations of current workflow management systems. IEEE Expert **12**(5), 105–111 (1997)
5. Wang C., Pazat J.: A Chemistry-Inspired Middleware for Self-Adaptive Service Orchestration and Choreography. In: 2013 13th IEEE/ACM International Symposium on Cluster, Cloud and Grid Computing (CCGrid), pp. 426–433. IEEE (2013)
6. Paun, G.: Computing with membranes. Journal of Computer and System Sciences **61**(1), 108–143 (2000)
7. Wang, X., Dong, J.S., Chin, C., Hettiarachchi, S.R., Zhang, D.: Semantic space: An infrastructure for smart spaces. Computing **1**(2), 67–74 (2002)
8. Zhuge, H.: Semantic grid: Scientific issues, infrastructure, and methodology. Communications of the ACM **48**(4), 117–119 (2005)
9. Juve G., Deelman E., Vahi K., Mehta G., Berriman B., Berman B.P., Maechling P.: Scientific workflow applications on Amazon EC2. In: 2009 5th IEEE International Conference on E-Science Workshops, pp. 59–66. IEEE (2009)
10. Ahmed T., and Srivastava A.: Minimizing Waiting Time for Service Composition: A Frictional Approach. In: 2013 IEEE 20th International Conference on Web Services (ICWS), pp. 268–275. IEEE (2013)
11. Calheiros, R.N., Vecchiola, C., Karunamoorthy, D., Buyya, R.: The Aneka platform and QoS-driven resource provisioning for elastic applications on hybrid Clouds. Future Generation Computer Systems **28**(6), 861–870 (2012)

12. Zhang F., Cao J., Hwang K., Wu C.: Ordinal Optimized Scheduling of Scientific Workflows in Elastic Compute Clouds. In: 2011 IEEE Third International Conference on Cloud Computing Technology and Science (CloudCom), pp. 9–17. IEEE (2011)

13. Zaha, J.M., Barros, A., Dumas, M., ter Hofstede, A.: Let's dance: A language for service behavior modeling. In: Meersman, R., Tari, Z. (eds.) OTM 2006. LNCS, vol. 4275, pp. 145–162. Springer, Heidelberg (2006)

14. Cecili, J.M., Garca, J.M., Guerrero, G.D., Martnez-del-Amor, M., Hurtado, I.P., Prez-Jimnez, M.: Simulating a P system based efficient solution to SAT by using GPUs. The Journal of Logic and Algebraic Programming **79**(6), 317–325 (2010)

15. White, S.A.: Introduction to BPMN. IBM Cooperation **2**(0), 0 (2004)

16. Nishida T.Y.: An approximate algorithm for NP-complete optimization problems exploiting P systems. In: Proc. Brainstorming Workshop on Uncertainty in Membrane Computing, pp. 185–192 (2004)

17. Mamei M., Zambonelli F., Leonardi L.: Distributed motion coordination with co-fields: A case study in urban traffic management. In: The Sixth International Symposium on Autonomous Decentralized Systems, 2003, ISADS 2003, pp. 63–70. IEEE (2003)

18. Reza, H., Ogaard, K.: Modeling UAS swarm system using conceptual and dynamic architectural modeling concepts. In: Andrews, S., Polovina, S., Hill, R., Akhgar, B. (eds.) ICCS-ConceptStruct 2011. LNCS, vol. 6828, pp. 331–338. Springer, Heidelberg (2011)

P Systems with Anti-Matter

Artiom Alhazov[1], Bogdan Aman[2], and Rudolf Freund[3](✉)

[1] Institute of Mathematics and Computer Science, Academy of Sciences of Moldova,
Academiei 5, MD-2028 Chişinău, Moldova
artiom@math.md

[2] Institute of Computer Science, Romanian Academy, Iași, Romania
bogdan.aman@iit.academiaromana-is.ro

[3] Faculty of Informatics, Vienna University of Technology,
Favoritenstr. 9, 1040 Vienna, Austria
rudi@emcc.at

Abstract. The concept of a matter object being annihilated when meeting its corresponding anti-matter object is investigated in the context of P systems. Computational completeness can be obtained with using only non-cooperative rules besides these matter/anti-matter annihilation rules if these annihilation rules have priority over the other rules. Without this priority condition, in addition catalytic rules with one single catalyst are needed to get computational completeness. Even deterministic systems are obtained in the accepting case. Allowing anti-matter objects as input and/or output, we even get a computationally complete computing model for computations on integer numbers. Interpreting sequences of symbols taken in from and/or sent out to the environment as strings, we get a model for computations on strings, which can even be interpreted as representations of elements of a group based on a computable finite presentation.

1 Introduction

Membrane systems as introduced in [16] and usually called *P systems* can be considered as distributed multiset rewriting systems, where all objects – if possible – evolve in parallel in the membrane regions and may be communicated through the membranes. Overviews on this emerging field of research can be found in the monograph [17] and the handbook of membrane systems [18]; for actual news and results we refer to the P systems webpage [20]. Computational completeness (computing any partial recursive relation on non-negative integers) can be obtained with using cooperative rules or with catalytic rules (eventually) together with non-cooperative rules. In this paper, we use another concept to avoid cooperative rules in general: for any object a *(matter)*, we consider its anti-object *(anti-matter)* a^- as well as the corresponding *annihilation rule* $aa^- \to \lambda$, which is assumed to exist in all membranes; this annihilation rule could be assumed to remove a pair a, a^- in zero time, but here we use these annihilation rules as special non-cooperative rules having priority over all other

M. Gheorghe et al. (Eds.): CMC 2014, LNCS 8961, pp. 66–85, 2014.
DOI: 10.1007/978-3-319-14370-5_5

rules in the sense of weak priority (e.g., see [2], i.e., other rules then also may be applied if objects cannot be bound by some annihilation rule any more). The idea of anti-matter has already been considered in another special variant of P systems with motivation coming from modeling neural activities, which are known as spiking neural P systems; for example, spiking neural P systems with anti-matter *(anti-spikes)* were already investigated in [15]. Moreover, in [6] the power of anti-matter for solving NP-complete problems is exhibited.

As expected (for example, compare with the Geffert normal forms, see [19]), the annihilation rules are rather powerful. Yet it is still surprising that using matter/anti-matter annihilation rules as the only non-cooperative rules, with the annihilation rules having priority, we already get computational completeness without using any catalyst; without giving the annihilation rules priority, we need one single catalyst. Even more surprising is the result that with priorities we obtain *deterministic* systems in the case of accepting P systems. Allowing anti-matter objects as input and/or output, we even get a computationally complete computing model for computations on integer numbers. Finally, by interpreting sequences of symbols taken in from and/or sent out to the environment as strings, we also consider P systems with anti-matter as computing/accepting/generating devices for string languages or even for languages over a group based on a computable finite presentation.

2   Prerequisites

The set of integers is denoted by $\mathbb{Z}$, and the set of non-negative integers by $\mathbb{N}$. Given an alphabet V, a finite non-empty set of abstract symbols, the free monoid generated by V under the operation of concatenation is denoted by V^*. The elements of V^* are called strings, the empty string is denoted by λ, and $V^* \backslash \{\lambda\}$ is denoted by V^+. For an arbitrary alphabet $V = \{a_1, \ldots, a_n\}$, the number of occurrences of a symbol a_i in a string x is denoted by $|x|_{a_i}$, while the length of a string x is denoted by $|x| = \sum_{a_i \in V} |x|_{a_i}$. The Parikh vector associated with x with respect to $a_1, \ldots, a_n$ is $(|x|_{a_1}, \ldots, |x|_{a_n})$. The Parikh image of an arbitrary language L over $\{a_1, \ldots, a_n\}$ is the set of all Parikh vectors of strings in L, and is denoted by $Ps(L)$. For a family of languages FL, the family of Parikh images of languages in FL is denoted by $PsFL$, while for families of languages over a one-letter (d-letter) alphabet, the corresponding families of sets of (vectors of) non-negative integers are denoted by NFL (N^dFL).

A (finite) multiset over a (finite) alphabet $V = \{a_1, \ldots, a_n\}$, is a mapping $f : V \to \mathbb{N}$ and can be represented by $\langle a_1^{f(a_1)}, \ldots, a_n^{f(a_n)} \rangle$ or by any string x for which $(|x|_{a_1}, \ldots, |x|_{a_n}) = (f(a_1), \ldots, f(a_n))$. In the following we will not distinguish between a vector $(m_1, \ldots, m_n)$, a multiset $\langle a_1^{m_1}, \ldots, a_n^{m_n} \rangle$ or a string x having $(|x|_{a_1}, \ldots, |x|_{a_n}) = (m_1, \ldots, m_n)$. Fixing the sequence of symbols $a_1, \ldots, a_n$ in an alphabet V in advance, the representation of the multiset $\langle a_1^{m_1}, \ldots, a_n^{m_n} \rangle$ by the string $a_1^{m_1} \ldots a_n^{m_n}$ is unique. The set of all finite multisets over an alphabet V is denoted by V°.

The family of regular and recursively enumerable string languages is denoted by *REG* and *RE*, respectively. For more details of formal language theory the reader is referred to the monographs and handbooks in this area as [5] and [19].

Register Machines. A *register machine* is a tuple $M = (m, B, l_0, l_h, P)$, where m is the number of registers, B is a set of labels, $l_0 \in B$ is the initial label, $l_h \in B$ is the final label, and P is the set of instructions bijectively labeled by elements of B. The instructions of M can be of the following forms:

- $l_1 : (ADD(j), l_2, l_3)$, with $l_1 \in B \backslash \{l_h\}$, $l_2, l_3 \in B$, $1 \leq j \leq m$.
  Increases the value of register j by one, followed by a non-deterministic jump to instruction l_2 or l_3. This instruction is usually called *increment*.
- $l_1 : (SUB(j), l_2, l_3)$, with $l_1 \in B \backslash \{l_h\}$, $l_2, l_3 \in B$, $1 \leq j \leq m$.
  If the value of register j is zero then jump to instruction l_3; otherwise, the value of register j is decreased by one, followed by a jump to instruction l_2. The two cases of this instruction are usually called *zero-test* and *decrement*, respectively.
- $l_h : HALT$. Stops the execution of the register machine.

A *configuration* of a register machine is described by the contents of each register and by the value of the current label, which indicates the next instruction to be executed. Computations start by executing the instruction l_0 of P, and terminate with reaching the HALT-instruction l_h.

In order to deal with strings, this basic model of register machines can be extended by instructions for reading from an input tape and writing to an output tape containing strings over an input alphabet T_{in} and an output alphabet T_{out}, respectively:

- $l_1 : (read(a), l_2)$, with $l_1 \in B \setminus \{l_h\}$, $l_2 \in B$, $a \in T_{in}$.
  Reads the symbol a from the input tape and jumps to instruction l_2.
- $l_1 : (write(a), l_2)$, with $l_1 \in B \setminus \{l_h\}$, $l_2 \in B$, $a \in T_{out}$.
  Writes the symbol a on the output tape and jumps to instruction l_2.

3   P Systems

The basic ingredients of a (cell-like) P system are the membrane structure, the multisets of objects placed in the membrane regions, and the evolution rules. The *membrane structure* is a hierarchical arrangement of membranes, in which the space between a membrane and the immediately inner membranes defines a *region/compartment*. The outermost membrane is called the *skin membrane*, the region outside is the *environment*. Each membrane can be labeled, and the label (from a set *Lab*) will identify both the membrane and its region; the skin membrane is identified by (the label) 1. The membrane structure can be represented by an expression of correctly nested labeled parentheses, and also by a rooted tree (with the label of a membrane in each node and the skin in the root). The *multisets of objects* are placed in the compartments of the membrane structure and usually represented by strings.

The *evolution rules* are multiset rewriting rules of the form $u \rightarrow v$, where $u \in O^\circ$ and $v = (b_1, tar_1) \ldots (b_k, tar_k)$ with $b_i \in O^\circ$ and $tar_i \in \{here, out, in\}$ or $tar_i \in \{here, out\} \cup \{in_j \mid j \in Lab\}$, $1 \leq i \leq k$. Using such a rule means "consuming" the objects of u and "producing" the objects from $b_1, \ldots, b_k$ of v, where the target *here* means that the objects remain in the same region where the rule is applied, *out* means that they are sent out of the respective membrane (in this way, objects can also be sent to the environment, when the rule is applied in the skin region), *in* means that they are sent to one of the immediately inner membranes, chosen in a non-deterministic way, and in_j means that they are sent into the specified inner membrane. In general, the target indication *here* is omitted.

Formally, a (cell-like) P system is a construct

$$\Pi = (O, \mu, w_1, \ldots, w_m, R_1, \ldots, R_m, l_{in}, l_{out})$$

where O is the alphabet of objects, μ is the membrane structure (with m membranes), $w_1, \ldots, w_m$ are multisets of objects present in the m regions of μ at the beginning of a computation, $R_1, \ldots, R_m$ are finite sets of evolution rules, associated with the regions of μ, l_{in} is the label of the membrane region where the inputs are put at the beginning of a computation, and l_{out} indicates the region from which the outputs are taken; l_{out}/l_{in} being 0 indicates that the output/input is taken from the environment.

If a rule $u \rightarrow v$ has $|u| > 1$, then it is called *cooperative* (abbreviated *coo*); otherwise, it is called *non-cooperative* (abbreviated *ncoo*). In *catalytic P systems* non-cooperative as well as *catalytic rules* of the form $ca \rightarrow cv$ are used, where c is a *catalyst* – a special object that never evolves and never passes through a membrane, but it just assists object a to evolve to the multiset v. In a *purely catalytic P system* only catalytic rules are allowed. In both catalytic and purely catalytic P systems, in their description O is replaced by O, C in order to specify those objects from O that are the catalysts in the set C.

The evolution rules are used in the non-deterministic maximally parallel way, i.e., in any computation step of Π a multiset of rules is chosen from the sets $R_1, \ldots, R_m$ in such a way that no further rule can be added to it so that the obtained multiset would still be applicable to the existing objects in the membrane regions $1, \ldots, m$. A *configuration* of a system is given by the membranes and the objects present in the compartments of the system. Starting from a given *initial configuration* and applying evolution rules as described above, we get *transitions* among configurations; a sequence of transitions forms a *computation*. A computation is *halting* if it reaches a configuration where no rule can be applied any more.

In the *generative case*, a halting computation has associated a result, in the form of the number of objects present in membrane l_{out} in the halting configuration (l_{in} can be omitted). In the *accepting case*, for $l_{in} \neq 0$, we accept all (vectors of) non-negative integers whose input, given as the corresponding numbers of objects in membrane l_{in}, leads to a halting computation (l_{out} can be omitted). For the input being taken from the environment, i.e., for $l_{in} = 0$, we need an additional target indication *come*; $(a, come)$ means that the object a is taken into the skin from the environment (all objects there are assumed to be available in an unbounded number). The multiset of all objects taken from the environment during a halting computation then is the multiset accepted by this accepting P system, which in this case we shall call a *P automaton* [4]. The set of non-negative integers and the set of (Parikh) vectors of non-negative integers generated/accepted/accepted in the automaton way as results of halting computations in Π are denoted by $N_\delta(\Pi)$ and $Ps_\delta(\Pi)$, respectively, with $\delta \in \{gen, acc, aut\}$.

A P system Π can also be considered as a system computing a partial recursive function (in the deterministic case) or even a partial recursive relation (in the non-deterministic case), with the input being given in a membrane region $l_{in} \neq 0$ as in the accepting case or being taken from the environment as in the automaton case. The corresponding functions/relations computed by halting computations in Π are denoted by $ZY_\alpha(\Pi)$, $Z \in \{Fun, Rel\}$, $Y \in \{N, Ps\}$, $\alpha \in \{acc, aut\}$.

Computational completeness for (generating) catalytic P systems can be achieved when using two catalysts or with three catalysts in purely catalytic P systems, and the same number of catalysts is needed for P automata; in accepting P systems, the number of catalysts increases with the number of components in the vectors of natural numbers to be analyzed [8]. It is a long-time open problem how to characterize the families of sets of (vectors of) natural numbers generated by (purely) catalytic P systems with only one (two) catalysts. Using additional control mechanisms as, for example, priorities or promoters/inhibitors, P systems with only one (two) catalyst(s) can be shown to be computationally complete, e.g., see Chapter 4 in [18]. Last year several other variants of control mechanisms have been shown to lead to computational completeness in (purely) catalytic P systems using only one (two) catalyst(s), see [7], [10], and [11]. In this paper we are going to investigate the power of using matter/antimatter annihilation rules – with the astonishing result, that no catalysts are needed any more in case the annihilation rules have weak priority over the other rules.

The families of sets $Y_\delta(\Pi)$, $Y \in \{N, Ps\}$, $\delta \in \{gen, acc, aut\}$, computed by (purely) catalytic P systems with at most m membranes and at most k catalysts are denoted by $Y_\delta OP_m(cat_k)$ ($Y_\delta OP_m(pcat_k)$). The following characterizations are known:

Theorem 1. *For any* $m \geq 1$, $d \geq 1$, $\gamma \in \{gen, aut\}$,

$$Ps_{acc}OP_m(cat_{d+2}) = Ps_{acc}OP_m(pcat_{d+3}) = N^d RE \quad and$$
$$Ps_\gamma OP_m(cat_2) = Ps_\gamma OP_m(pcat_3) = PsRE.$$

4   Using Matter and Anti-Matter

This concept to be used in (catalytic) P systems is a direct generalization of the idea of anti-spikes from spiking neural P systems (see [15]): for each object a we introduce the anti-matter object a^-. We can look at these anti-matter objects a^- as objects of their own or else we may extend the notion of a (finite) multiset over the (finite) alphabet V, $V = \{a_1, \cdots, a_n\}$, as a mapping $f : V \longrightarrow \mathbb{N}$ to a mapping $f : V \longrightarrow \mathbb{Z}$ now also allowing negative values. In a usual way, such an extended multiset on $\mathbb{Z}$ is represented by $\left\langle a_1^{f(a_1)}, \cdots, a_n^{f(a_n)} \right\rangle$. A unique string representation for such an extended multiset is obtained by assigning a string over the (ordered) alphabet $\langle a_1, a_1^-, \cdots, a_n, a_n^- \rangle$ as $a_1{}^{f(a_1)} \cdots a_n{}^{f(a_n)}$ such that $(a_i)^{-m}$, $m > 0$, is represented by $(a_i^-)^m$, $1 \le i \le n$. Any other string having the same Parikh vector with respect to the (ordered) alphabet $\langle a_1, a_1^-, \cdots, a_n, a_n^- \rangle$ can be used for representing the multiset given by f as well.

As in spiking neural P systems with anti-spikes, also in cell-like P systems we might consider the annihilation of matter and anti-matter objects to happen in zero-time or in an intermediate step between normal derivation steps in the maximally parallel mode. Whenever related matter a and anti-matter a^- meet, they annihilate each other, as, for example, in an extended multiset on $\mathbb{Z}$ matter a and anti-matter a^- cannot exist at the same moment, hence, also not in a string representing an extended multiset on $\mathbb{Z}$.

Yet in this paper we consider both objects and anti-objects to be handled by usual evolution rules; the annihilation of matter and anti-matter objects then corresponds to an application of the (non-context-free!) rule $aa^- \to \lambda$. In contrast to the case described above, now in an instantaneous description of a configuration of a P system both matter and anti-matter objects may appear. When working with context-free or catalytic rules over an (ordered) alphabet $\langle a_1, a_1^-, \cdots, a_n, a_n^- \rangle$, we may give the matter/anti-matter annihilation rules weak priority over all other rules – in order to not have matter a and anti-matter a^- in some configuration at the same moment and let them "survive" for longer.

We now consider catalytic P systems extended by also allowing for annihilation rules $aa^- \to \lambda$, with these rules having weak priority over all other rules, i.e., other rules can only be applied if no annihilation rule could still bind the corresponding objects. The families of sets $Y_\delta(\Pi)$, $Y \in \{N, Ps\}$, $\delta \in \{gen, acc, aut\}$, and the families of functions/relations $ZY_\alpha(\Pi)$, $Z \in \{Fun, Rel\}$, $\alpha \in \{acc, aut\}$, computed by such extended P systems with at most m membranes and k catalysts are denoted by

$$Y_\delta OP_m(cat(k), antim/pri) \quad \text{and} \quad ZY_\alpha OP_m(cat(k), antim/pri);$$

we omit $/pri$ for the families without priorities.

The matter/anti-matter annihilation rules are so powerful that we only need the minimum number of catalysts, i.e., **zero**!

Theorem 2. *For any $n \ge 1$, $k \ge 0$, $Y \in \{N, Ps\}$, $\delta \in \{gen, acc, aut\}$, $\alpha \in \{acc, aut\}$, and $Z \in \{Fun, Rel\}$,*

$$Y_\delta OP_n(cat(k), antim/pri) = YRE \quad and$$
$$ZY_\alpha OP_n(cat(k), antim/pri) = ZYRE.$$

Proof. Let $M = (m, B, l_0, l_h, P)$ be a register machine. We now construct a one-membrane P system Π which simulates M:

$$\Pi = (O, [\ ]_1, l_0, R_1, l_{in}, 1) \text{ with}$$
$$O = \{a_r, a_r^- \mid 1 \le r \le m\} \cup \{l, l' \mid l \in B\} \cup \{\#, \#^-\}.$$

Initially the skin membrane only contains the object l_0. The contents of register r is represented by the number of copies of the object a_r, $1 \le r \le m$, and for each matter object a_r we also consider the corresponding anti-matter object a_r^-. The instructions of M are simulated by the following rules in R_1:

- $l_1 : (ADD(j), l_2, l_3)$, with $l_1 \in B \setminus \{l_h\}$, $l_2, l_3 \in B$, $1 \le j \le m$.
  Simulated by the rules

$$l_1 \to a_r l_2 \text{ and } l_1 \to a_r l_3.$$

- $l_1 : (SUB(r), l_2, l_3)$, with $l_1 \in B \setminus \{l_h\}$, $l_2, l_3 \in B$, $1 \le r \le m$.
  As rules common for all simulations of SUB-instructions, we have

$$a_r^- \to \#^-, \ 1 \le r \le m,$$

and the annihilation rules

$$a_r a_r^- \to \lambda, \ 1 \le r \le m, \text{ and } \#\#^- \to \lambda$$

as well as the trap rules

$$\#^- \to \#\# \text{ and } \# \to \#\#;$$

these last two rules lead the system into an infinite computation whenever a trap symbol is left without being annihilated.
The *zero test* for instruction l_1 is simulated by the rules

$$l_1 \to l_1' a_r^- \text{ and } l_1' \to \# l_3.$$

The symbol $\#$ generated by the second rule $l_1' \to \# l_3$ can only be eliminated if the anti-matter a_r^- generated by the first rule $l_1 \to l_1' a_r^-$ is not annihilated by a_r, i.e., only if register r is empty.
The *decrement case* for instruction l_1 is simulated by the rule

$$l_1 \to l_2 a_r^-.$$

The anti-matter a_r^- either correctly annihilates one matter a_r thus decrementing the register r or else traps an incorrect guess by forcing the symbol a_r^- to evolve to $\#^-$ and then to $\#\#$ in the next two steps in case register r is empty.

- $l_h : HALT$. Simulated by $l_h \to \lambda$.
  When the computation in M halts, the object l_h is removed, and no further rules can be applied provided the simulation has been carried out correctly, i.e., if no trap symbols $\#$ are present in this situation. The remaining objects in the system represent the result computed by M.   □

Without this priority of the annihilation rules, the construction is not working, hence, a characterization of the families $Y_\delta OP_n\,(ncoo, antim)$ as well as $ZY_\alpha OP_n\,(ncoo, antim)$ remains as an open problem. Yet in addition using catalytic rules with one catalyst again allows us to obtain computational completeness:

Theorem 3. *For any $n \geq 1$, $k \geq 1$, $Y \in \{N, Ps\}$, $\delta \in \{gen, acc, aut\}$, $\alpha \in \{acc, aut\}$, and $Z \in \{Fun, Rel\}$,*

$$Y_\delta OP_n\,(cat(k), antim) = YRE \qquad and$$
$$ZY_\alpha OP_n\,(cat(k), antim) = ZYRE.$$

Proof. We again consider a register machine $M = (m, B, l_0, l_h, P)$ as in the previous proof, and construct the catalytic P system

$$\Pi = (O, \{c\}, [\ ]_1, cl_0, R_1, l_{in}, 0) \text{ with}$$
$$O = \{a_r, a_r{}^- \mid 1 \leq r \leq m\} \cup \{l, l', l'' \mid l \in B\} \cup \{\#, \#^-, d\},$$

with the single catalyst c in the skin membrane. The results now are sent to the environment, in order not to have to count the catalyst in the skin membrane; for that purpose, we simply use the rule $a_i \rightarrow (a_i, out)$ for the output symbols a_i (we assume that output registers of M are only incremented).

For each ADD-instruction $l_1 : (ADD\,(j)\,, l_2, l_3)$ in P, we again take the rules

$$l_1 \rightarrow a_r l_2 \text{ and } l_1 \rightarrow a_r l_3.$$

For each SUB-instruction $l_1 : (SUB\,(r)\,, l_2, l_3)$, we now consider the four rules

$$l_1 \rightarrow l_2 a_r{}^-,$$
$$l_1 \rightarrow l_1'' d a_r{}^-,$$
$$l_1'' \rightarrow l_1', \text{ and}$$
$$l_1' \rightarrow \# l_3.$$

As rules common for all SUB-instructions, we again add the matter/antimatter annihilation rules

$$a_r a_r{}^- \rightarrow \lambda \text{ and } \#\#^- \rightarrow \lambda$$

as well as the trap rules

$$\# \rightarrow \#\# \text{ and } \#^- \rightarrow \#\#,$$

but in addition, also

$$d \rightarrow \#\#$$

as well as the catalytic rules

$$cd \rightarrow c \text{ and } ca_r{}^- \rightarrow c\#^-, \, 1 \leq r \leq m.$$

The decrement case is simulated as in the previous proof, by using the rule $l_1 \rightarrow l_2 a_r{}^-$ and then applying the annihilation rule $a_r a_r{}^- \rightarrow \lambda$. The zero-test now is initiated with the rule $l_i \rightarrow l''_i d a_r^-$ thus introducing the (dummy) symbol d which keeps the catalyst busy for one step, where the catalytic rule $cd \rightarrow c$ has to be applied in order to avoid the application of the trap rule $d \rightarrow \#\#$. If register r is empty, then a_r^- cannot be annihilated and therefore evolves to $\#^-$ in the third step by the application of the catalytic rule $ca_r^- \rightarrow c\#^-$, which symbol $\#^-$ afterwards annihilates the symbol $\#$ generated by the rule $l'_i \rightarrow \#l_k$ in the same step; if register r is not empty, a_r^- is annihilated by some copy of a_r already in the first step, hence, the trap symbol $\#$ generated by the rule $l'_i \rightarrow \#l_k$ does not find its anti-matter $\#^-$ and therefore evolves to $\#\#$, thus leading to an infinite computation. Although the annihilation rule $a_r a_r^- \rightarrow \lambda$ now does not have priority over the catalytic rule $ca_r^- \rightarrow c\#^-$, maximal parallelism enforces $a_r a_r^- \rightarrow \lambda$ to be applied, if possible, already in the first step instead of $ca_r^- \rightarrow c\#^-$, as in a successful derivation the catalyst c first has to eliminate the dummy symbol d.

The rule $l_h \rightarrow \lambda$ is applied at the end of a successful simulation of the instructions of the register machine M, and the computation halts if no trap symbol $\#$ is present; the symbols sent out to the environment during the computation represent the result of this halting computation.   □

In the accepting case, with priorities, we can even simulate the actions of a deterministic register machine in a deterministic way, i.e., for each configuration of the system, there can be at most one multiset of rules applicable to it.

Theorem 4. *For any $n \geq 1$, $k \geq 0$, and $Y \in \{N, Ps\}$,*

$$Y_{detacc}OP_n\left(cat(k), antim/pri\right) = YRE \quad and$$
$$FunY_{detacc}OP_n\left(cat(k), antim/pri\right) = FunYRE.$$

Proof. We only need to show how the SUB-instructions of a register machine $M = (m, B, l_0, l_h, P)$ can be simulated in a deterministic way without introducing a trap symbol and therefore causing infinite loops by them:

For every register r, let $B_-(r) = \{l \mid l : (SUB(r), l', l'') \in P\}$, and the rule

$$a_r^- \rightarrow \prod_{l \in B_-(r)} \tilde{l}^- \ \prod_{l \in B_-(r)} \hat{l};$$

moreover, we take the annihilation rules $a_r a_r^- \rightarrow \lambda$ as well as $\hat{l}\hat{l}^- \rightarrow \lambda$ and $\tilde{l}\tilde{l}^- \rightarrow \lambda$ for all $l \in B_-(r)$.

Any SUB-instruction $l_1 : (SUB(r), l_2, l_3)$, with $l_1 \in B_-(r)$, $l_2, l_3 \in B$, $1 \leq r \leq m$, is simulated by the rules

$$l_1 \rightarrow \bar{l}_1 a_r^-,$$
$$\bar{l}_1 \rightarrow \hat{l}_1^- \prod_{l \in B_-(r) \setminus \{l_1\}} \tilde{l},$$
$$\hat{l}_1^- \rightarrow l_2 \prod_{l \in B_-(r) \setminus \{l_1\}} \tilde{l}^-, \text{ and}$$
$$\tilde{l}_1^- \rightarrow l_3 \prod_{l \in B_-(r) \setminus \{l_1\}} \hat{l}^-.$$

The symbol $\hat{l}_1^-$ generated by the second rule is eliminated again and replaced by $\tilde{l}_1^-$ if a_r^- is not annihilated (which indicates that the register is empty).   □

5   When Matter/Anti-Matter Annihilation Generates Energy

The matter/anti-matter annihilation may also be assumed to result in the generation of a specific amount of "energy", which is also well motivated by physics. In the definitions of these systems, the matter/anti-matter annihilation rules $a_r a_r^- \to \lambda$ are replaced by $a_r a_r^- \to e$ where e is a symbol denoting this special amount of energy.

The family of sets $Y_\delta(\Pi)$, $Y \in \{N, Ps\}$, $\delta \in \{gen, acc, aut\}$, and the set of functions/relations $ZY_\alpha(\Pi)$, $Z \in \{Fun, Rel\}$, $\alpha \in \{acc, aut\}$, computed by such P systems with at most m membranes and k catalysts is denoted by $Y_\delta OP_m(cat(k), antimen/pri)$ and $ZY_\alpha OP_m(cat(k), antimen/pri)$; we omit $/pri$ for the families without priorities.

The following results are immediate consequences of the corresponding Theorems 2 and 4 – in both cases, each matter/anti-matter annihilation rule $xx^- \to \lambda$ is replaced by $xx^- \to e$ where e is this symbol denoting a special amount of energy, and, in addition, we add the rule $e \to \lambda$:

Corollary 1. *For any $n \geq 1$, $k \geq 0$, $Y \in \{N, Ps\}$, $\delta \in \{gen, acc, aut\}$, $\alpha \in \{acc, aut\}$, and $Z \in \{Fun, Rel\}$,*

$$Y_\delta OP_n(cat(k), antimen/pri) = YRE \text{ and}$$
$$ZY_\alpha OP_n(cat(k), antimen/pri) = ZYRE.$$

Corollary 2. *For any $n \geq 1$, $k \geq 0$, and $Y \in \{N, Ps\}$,*

$$Y_{detacc} OP_n(cat(k), antimen/pri) = YRE \text{ and}$$
$$FunY_{detacc} OP_n(cat(k), antimen/pri) = FunYRE.$$

But we can even show more, i.e., omitting the rule $e \to \lambda$ and leaving the amount of energy represented by the number of copies of e in the system, the energy inside the system at the end of a successful computation is a direct measure for the number of SUB-instructions simulated by the P system or even a measure for the number of all instructions which were simulated.

Corollary 3. *The construction in the proof of Theorem 2 can be adapted in such a way that the simulation of each instruction of the register machine M takes exactly three steps (including the annihilation rules), and moreover, the number of energy objects e at the end of a successful computation exactly equals the number of instructions of M simulated by the corresponding P system.*

Proof. Let $M = (m, B, l_0, l_h, P)$ be a register machine. Following the construction given in the proof of Theorem 2, the instructions of M now can be simulated as follows:

- $l_1 : (ADD\,(j)\,, l_2, l_3)$, with $l_1 \in B \setminus \{l_h\}$, $l_2, l_3 \in B$, $1 \leq j \leq m$.
  Simulated by the rules

$$l_1 \rightarrow l_1{}',$$
$$l_1{}' \rightarrow l_1{}'',$$
$$l_1{}'' \rightarrow ea_r l_2,$$
$$l_1{}'' \rightarrow ea_r l_3.$$

- $l_1 : (SUB\,(r)\,, l_2, l_3)$, with $l_1 \in B \setminus \{l_h\}$, $l_2, l_3 \in B$, $1 \leq r \leq m$.
  As rules common for all simulations of SUB-instructions, we have

$$a_r{}^- \rightarrow \#^-, 1 \leq r \leq m,$$
$$a_r a_r{}^- \rightarrow e, 1 \leq r \leq m,$$
$$\#\#^- \rightarrow e,$$
$$\#^- \rightarrow \#\#,$$
$$\# \rightarrow \#\#.$$

The *zero test* for instruction l_1 is simulated by the rules

$$l_1 \rightarrow l_1{}'a_r{}^-,$$
$$l_1{}' \rightarrow \#l_1{}'', \text{ and}$$
$$l_1{}'' \rightarrow l_3;$$

the symbol $\#$ generated by the second rule $l_1{}' \rightarrow \#l_1{}''$ can only be eliminated if the anti-matter $a_r{}^-$ generated by the first rule $l_1 \rightarrow l_1{}'a_r{}^-$ is not
annihilated by a_r, i.e., only if register r is empty; e is generated by $\#\#^- \rightarrow e$.
The *decrement case* for instruction l_1 is simulated by the rules

$$l_1 \rightarrow \tilde{l}_1 a_r{}^-,$$
$$\tilde{l}_1 \rightarrow \tilde{l}_1{}',$$
$$\tilde{l}_1{}' \rightarrow l_2;$$

here, e is generated by $a_r a_r{}^- \rightarrow e$.

- $l_h : HALT$. Simulated by the rules

$$l_h \rightarrow l_h{}',$$
$$l_h{}' \rightarrow l_h{}'',$$
$$l_h{}'' \rightarrow e.$$

In each case, exactly one symbol e is generated during each cycle of three
steps simulating an instruction of M. □

Remark 1. Let M be a register machine and

$$RS(M) = \{(n, m) \mid n \in L(M), n \text{ is computed by } M \text{ in } m \text{ steps}\}.$$

Then, according to [3], RS is recursive. Hence, although $L(M)$ may not be
recursive, $RS(M)$ is recursive in any case.

Now let $L \in NRE$ and $L = L\,(M)$ for a register machine M. Following the
construction given in the proof of Corollary 3, we can construct a P system with
energy Π such that $Ps\,(\Pi) = RS(M)$.

6   Computing with Integers

As already discussed in Section 4, given an alphabet $V = \{a_1, \cdots, a_d\}$ we may extend the notion of a (finite) multiset over V as a mapping $f : V \longrightarrow \mathbb{N}$ to a mapping $f : V \longrightarrow \mathbb{Z}$ now also allowing negative values, with a unique string representation for such an extended multiset being obtained by assigning a string over the (ordered) alphabet $\langle a_1, a_1^{-}, \cdots, a_d, a_d^{-} \rangle$ as $a_1{}^{f(a_1)} \cdots a_d{}^{f(a_d)}$ such that $(a_i)^{-m}$, $m > 0$, is represented by $(a_i^{-})^{m}$, $1 \leq i \leq d$. Besides this canonical representation of f by the string $a_1{}^{f(a_1)} \cdots a_d{}^{f(a_d)}$, any other string having the same Parikh vector with respect to the (ordered) alphabet $\langle a_1, a_1^{-}, \cdots, a_d, a_d^{-} \rangle$ can be used for representing the multiset given by f as well. According to these definitions, matter and related anti-matter cannot be present in the same string or multiset over the alphabet $\{a_1, a_1^{-}, \cdots, a_d, a_d^{-}\}$. Obviously, their is a one-to-one correspondence between vectors from $\mathbb{Z}^d$ and the corresponding Parikh vectors over $\langle a_1, a_1^{-}, \cdots, a_d, a_d^{-} \rangle$, which can also be viewed as vectors over $\mathbb{Z}^{2d}$: for any of these vectors $v = (v_1, v_2, \cdots, v_{2d-1}, v_{2d})$, we have either $v_{2i-1} = 0$ or $v_{2i} = 0$ (or both), for all $1 \leq i \leq d$.

In order to specify that now we are dealing with d-dimensional vectors of integer numbers, we use the notation $Ps^{\mathbb{Z}^d}$: the families of sets of integer numbers $Ps_{\delta}^{\mathbb{Z}^d} (\Pi)$, $\delta \in \{gen, acc, aut\}$, and the families of functions/relations $ZPs_{\alpha}^{\mathbb{Z}^d} (\Pi)$, $Z \in \{Fun, Rel\}$, $\alpha \in \{acc, aut\}$, computed by such P systems with at most m membranes and k catalysts are denoted by $Ps_{\delta}^{\mathbb{Z}^d} OP_m (cat(k), antim/pri)$ and $ZPs_{\alpha}^{\mathbb{Z}^d} OP_m (cat(k), antim/pri)$; we omit $/pri$ for the families without priorities. Moreover, the family of recursively enumerable sets of integer numbers is denoted by $Ps^{\mathbb{Z}^d} RE$, the corresponding families of functions/relations by $ZPs^{\mathbb{Z}^d} RE$.

Theorem 5. *For any $d \geq 1$ we have that:*

- for any $n \geq 1$, $k \geq 0$, $\delta \in \{gen, acc, aut\}$, $\alpha \in \{acc, aut\}$, and $Z \in \{Fun, Rel\}$,

$$Ps_{\delta}^{\mathbb{Z}^d} OP_n (cat(k), antim/pri) = Ps^{\mathbb{Z}^d} RE \quad and$$
$$ZPs_{\alpha}^{\mathbb{Z}^d} OP_n (cat(k), antim/pri) = ZPs^{\mathbb{Z}^d} RE;$$

- for any $n \geq 1$, and $k \geq 0$,

$$Ps_{detacc}^{\mathbb{Z}^d} OP_n (cat(k), antim/pri) = Ps^{\mathbb{Z}^d} RE \quad and$$
$$FunPs_{detacc}^{\mathbb{Z}^d} OP_n (cat(k), antim/pri) = FunPs^{\mathbb{Z}^d} RE.$$

Proof. As we have shown in Section 4, all variants of P systems with anti-matter mentioned in the theorem are computationally complete when dealing with multisets over any arbitrary alphabet, being able to simulate the actions of a register machine. Hence, as any d-dimensional vector of integer numbers can be represented by a $2d$-dimensional vector of non-negative integers, which can be processed in the usual way by register machines and thus simulated by all the variants of P systems with anti-matter mentioned in the theorem, we only have to solve the technical detail how to get this $2d$-dimensional vector of non-negative integers from a given d-dimensional vector of integer numbers represented by symbols over the (ordered) alphabet $\langle a_1, a_1^-, \cdots, a_d, a_d^- \rangle$: given the input in an input membrane $\neq 0$, we there just make a first step using in parallel the non-cooperative rules $a_i \rightarrow [a_i, +]$ and $a_i^- \rightarrow [a_i, -]$, $1 \leq i \leq d$. Then the multisets over these symbols can be handled in the usual way, now both of them having the corresponding anti-matter objects $[a_i, +]^-$ and $[a_i, -]^-$. In a similar way, we can take the input from the environment by using rules of the form $q \rightarrow p\, (a_i, come)\, [a_i, +]$ or $q \rightarrow p\, (a_i^-, come)\, [a_i, -]$ where q, p represent states of the register machine. The symbols a_i and a_i^- then are not needed any more and can be eliminated by the rules $a_i \rightarrow \lambda$ and $a_i^- \rightarrow \lambda$. The remaining computations in the respective P system then can be carried out by simulating the actions of a register machine.   □

7   Computing with Languages

P systems with anti-matter, as most of the computationally complete variants of P systems, can also be considered as language generating devices – the objects sent out can be concatenated to strings over a given alphabet, and the objects taken in during a halting computation can be assumed to form a string. For sake of simplicity, we may assume that in each computation step, at most one symbol is sent out or taken in; otherwise, as usual, e.g., see [4], we may take any permutation of the symbols sent out or taken in to be part of a string to be considered as output or input, respectively. Obviously, according to this method of getting an input string, for the accepting case only the automaton variant is to be considered now, as otherwise we would have to take an encoding of the input string by a multiset.

7.1   Languages over Strings

Let V be a finite alphabet. The set of strings (over V) generated or accepted (in the sense of automata) by a P system with anti-matter Π is denoted by $L_\delta^V(\Pi)$, $\delta \in \{gen, aut\}$, the function/relation computed by Π is denoted by $ZL_{aut}^V(\Pi)$, $Z \in \{Fun, Rel\}$. The families of sets $L_\delta^V(\Pi)$, $\delta \in \{gen, aut\}$, and the families of functions/relations $ZL_{aut}^V(\Pi)$, $Z \in \{Fun, Rel\}$, computed by such P systems with at most m membranes and k catalysts are denoted by $L_\delta^V OP_m\,(cat(k), antim/pri)$ and $ZL_{aut}^V OP_m\,(cat(k), antim/pri)$, respectively.

We omit $/pri$ for the families without priorities; $cat\,(0)$ is used as a synonym for $ncoo$. If the alphabet is arbitrary, we omit the superscript V in these notations. Moreover, the family of languages over V in RE is denoted by RE^V, the corresponding family of functions/relations by ZRE^V.

The use of anti-matter and of matter/anti-matter annihilation rules (having priority over other rules) allows us to give a simple example how to generate an even non-context-free string language:

Example 1. Consider the P system with anti-matter

$$\Pi = (O, [\ ]_1, q_1, R_1, 1) \text{ where}$$
$$O = \{a, b, c\} \cup \{b^-, c^-\} \cup \{q_1, q_2, q_3\},$$
$$R_1 = \{q_1 \rightarrow q_2, q_2 \rightarrow q_3, q_3 \rightarrow \lambda, q_1 \rightarrow q_1 (a, come) b^- c^-\}$$
$$\cup \{q_2 \rightarrow q_2 (b, come), q_3 \rightarrow q_3 (c, come)\}$$
$$\cup \{a \rightarrow \lambda\} \cup \{x \rightarrow x, x^- \rightarrow x^-, xx^- \rightarrow \lambda \mid x \in \{b, c\}\}.$$

The reader may easily verify that

$$L_{aut}^{\{a,b,c\}} (\Pi) = \{a^n b^n c^n \mid n \geq 0\}.$$

For each symbol a taken in with state q_1 (which is eliminated in the next step by $a \rightarrow \lambda$) using the rule $q_1 \rightarrow q_1 (a, come) b^- c^-$, an anti-matter object for both b and c is generated. The anti-matter objects b^- are eliminated in state q_2, and afterwards the anti-matter objects c^- are eliminated in state q_3. The computation only halts (with empty skin membrane) after having used the rule $q_3 \rightarrow \lambda$ if and only if an equal number of objects a, b, and c has been taken in, as otherwise, the rules $x \rightarrow x$ or $x^- \rightarrow x^-$, $x \in \{b, c\}$, keep the system in an infinite loop if too many x or not enough x have been taken in, respectively. Observe that this system also works if we do not require priority of the annihilation rules, but then, for each successful computation accepting the string $a^n b^n c^n$, $n \geq 1$, there exist infinite computations where we use one of the rules $x^- \rightarrow x^-$ again and again instead of letting x^- being annihilated by $xx^- \rightarrow \lambda$. Hence, we may say that

$$\{a^n b^n c^n \mid n \geq 0\} \in L_{aut}^{\{a,b,c\}} OP_1 (ncoo).$$

Theorem 6. *For any arbitrary alphabet V we have that:*

– for any $n \geq 1$, $k \geq 0$, $\delta \in \{gen, aut\}$, and $Z \in \{Fun, Rel\}$,

$$L_{\delta}^V OP_n (cat(k), antim/pri) = RE^V \text{ and}$$
$$ZL_{aut}^V OP_n (cat(k), antim/pri) = ZRE^V;$$

– for any $n \geq 1$, $k \geq 1$, $\delta \in \{gen, aut\}$, and $Z \in \{Fun, Rel\}$,

$$L_{\delta}^V OP_n (cat(k), antim) = RE^V \text{ and}$$
$$ZL_{aut}^V OP_n (cat(k), antim) = ZRE^V.$$

Proof. As we have shown in Section 4, all variants of P systems with anti-matter mentioned in the theorem are computationally complete when dealing with multisets, being able to simulate the actions of a register machine. Hence, by well-known techniques, input symbols composing an input string can be encoded as numbers in an input register and thus as a multiset in the simulating P system with anti-matter. In the same way, the results of a computation in the P system can be decoded from the multiset representing the output register of the underlying register machine. An input symbol $a \in V$ is taken in by rules of the form $q \rightarrow p (a, come)$ where q, p represent states of the register machine, and sent out by rules of the form $q \rightarrow p (a, out)$; these rules correspond with the register machine instructions $q : (read(a), p)$ and $q : (write(a), p)$. $\square$

7.2 Languages over Computable Finite Presentations of Groups

Strings may be used in a wider sense as representations of group elements. In order to establish these more general results, we first need some definitions and examples from group theory, e.g., see [12].

Groups and Group Presentations. Let $G = (G', \circ)$ be a group with group operation $\circ$. As is well-known, the group axioms are

- *closure*: for any $a, b \in G'$, $a \circ b \in G'$,
- *associativity*: for any $a, b, c \in G'$, $(a \circ b) \circ c = a \circ (b \circ c)$,
- *identity*: there exists a (unique) element $e \in G'$, called the *identity*, such that $e \circ a = a \circ e = a$ for all $a \in G'$, and
- *invertibility*: for any $a \in G'$, there exists a (unique) element a^{-1}, called the *inverse* of a, such that $a \circ a^{-1} = a^{-1} \circ a = e$.

Moreover, the group is called *commutative*, if for any $a, b \in G'$, $a \circ b = b \circ a$. In the following, we will not distinguish between G' and G if the group operation is obvious from the context.

For any element $b \in G'$, the order of b is the smallest number $n \in \mathbb{N}$ such that $b^n = e$ provided such an n exists, and then we write $ord(b) = n$; if no such n exists, $\{b^n \mid n \geq 1\}$ is an infinite subset of G' and we write $ord(b) = \infty$.

For any set B, B^{-1} is defined as the set of symbols representing the inverses of the elements of B, i.e., $B^{-1} = \{b^{-1} \mid b \in B\}$. We now consider the strings in $(B \cup B^{-1})^*$ and two strings as different unless their equality follows from the group axioms, i.e., for any $a, b, c \in (B \cup B^{-1})^*$, $a \circ b \circ b^{-1} \circ c = a \circ c$; using these reductions, we obtain a set of irreducible strings from those in $(B \cup B^{-1})^*$, the set of which we denote by $I(B)$. Then the *free group* generated by B is $F(B) = (I(B), \circ)$ with the elements being the irreducible strings over $B \cup B^{-1}$ and the group operation to be interpreted as the usual string concatenation, yet, obviously, if we concatenate two elements from $I(B)$, the resulting string eventually has to be reduced again. The identity in $F(B)$ is the empty string.

In general, B (not containing the identity) is called a *generator* of the group G if every element a from G can be written as a finite product/sum of elements from B, i.e., $a = b_1 \circ \cdots \circ b_m$ for $b_1, \ldots, b_m \in B$. In this paper, we restrict ourselves to finitely presented groups, i.e., having a finite presentation $\langle B \mid R \rangle$ with B being a finite generator set and moreover, R being a finite set of relations among these generators. In a similar way as in the definition of the free group generated by B, we here consider the strings in B^* to be reduced according to the group axioms and the relations given in R. Informally, the group $G = \langle B \mid R \rangle$ is the largest one generated by B subject only to the group axioms and the relations in R. Formally, we will restrict ourselves to relations of the form $b_1 \circ \cdots \circ b_m = c^{-1}$ with $b_1, \ldots, b_m, c \in B$, which equivalently may be written as $b_1 \circ \cdots \circ b_m \circ c = e$; hence, instead of such relations we may specify R by strings over B yielding the group identity, i.e., instead of $b_1 \circ \cdots \circ b_m = c^{-1}$ we take $b_1 \circ \cdots \circ b_m \circ c$ (these strings then are called *relators*).

Example 2. The free group $F(B) = (I(B), \circ)$ can be written as $\langle B \mid \emptyset \rangle$ (or even simpler as $\langle B \rangle$) because it has no restricting relations.

Example 3. The *cyclic group* of order n has the presentation $\langle \{a\} \mid \{a^n\} \rangle$ (or, omitting the set brackets, written as $\langle a \mid a^n \rangle$); it is also known as $\mathbb{Z}_n$ or as the quotient group $\mathbb{Z}/\mathbb{Z}_n$.

Example 4. $\mathbb{Z}$ is a special case of an Abelian group generated by (1) and its inverse (-1), i.e., $\mathbb{Z}$ is the free group generated by (1). $\mathbb{Z}^d$ is an Abelian group generated by the unit vectors $(0, ..., 1, ..., 0)$ and their inverses $(0, ..., -1, ..., 0)$. It is well known that every finitely generated Abelian group is a direct sum of a torsion group and a free Abelian group where the torsion group may be written as a direct sum of finitely many groups of the form $\mathbb{Z}/p^k\mathbb{Z}$ for p being a prime, and the free Abelian group is a direct sum of finitely many copies of $\mathbb{Z}$.

Example 5. A very well-known example for a non-Abelian group is the hexagonal group with the finite presentation $\langle a, b, c \mid a^2, b^2, c^2 \rangle$. All three generators a, b, c are self-inverse.

Remark 2. Unfortunately, given a finite presentation of a group $\langle B \mid R \rangle$, in general it is not even decidable whether the group presented in that way is finite or infinite. Hence, in this paper we restrict ourselves to infinite groups where the word equivalence problem $u = v$ is decidable, or equivalently, there is a decision procedure telling us whether, given two strings u and v, $u \circ v^{-1} = e$. In that case, we call $\langle B \mid R \rangle$ a *recursive* or *computable* finite group presentation.

As a first example we now consider the set ("language") of all one-dimensional vectors:

Example 6. Consider the P system

$$\Pi = (\{q_0, q_+, q_-, q_h\}, [\ ]_1, q_0, R_1, 1) \text{ where}$$
$$R_1 = \{q_0 \to q_h, q_+ \to q_h, q_- \to q_h\}$$
$$\cup \{q_0 \to (+1)q_+, q_+ \to (+1)q_+, q_0 \to (-1)q_-, q_- \to (-1)q_-\}.$$

In order to generate the empty string, corresponding with the zero-vector (0), we simply apply $q_0 \to q_h$. We may also choose to generate a positive or a negative vector, i.e., we start with $q_0 \to (+1)q_+$ or $q_0 \to (-1)q_-$, respectively. After $n-1$ applications of the rules $q_+ \to (+1)q_+$ and $q_- \to (-1)q_-$ as well as of the final rule $q_+ \to q_h$ or $q_- \to q_h$, respectively, we have sent out a string representing the unique irreducible representation of the vector $(+n)$ or $(-n)$, respectively.

Remark 3. The reader may easily verify that, given any finitely generated Abelian group, such a regular P system exists which generates all strings representing the (unique, with respect to a complete order on the positive generators) irreducible representations of the group elements. For non-commutative groups with relators, such trivial representations are not possible.

If we do not require irreducibility of the string sent out to the environment, then of course, for any finitely generated group, we can generate representations of all its elements very easily:

Example 7. Given a finite presentation of a group $\langle B \mid R \rangle$, with $B^- = B$, consider the P system

$$\Pi = (\{q_0\}, [\ ]_1, q_0, R_1, 1) \text{ where}$$
$$R_1 = \{q_0 \to \lambda\} \cup \{q_0 \to g q_0 \mid g \in B\}.$$

Most of the strings sent out now will not be reduced.

Remark 4. In general, as long as we have given the group by a computable finite presentation, for a mechanism having the full power of Turing computability, we can require that the "strings" sent out to the environment are irreducible ones. Hence, for a given recursively enumerable set L of elements over the computable finite presentation $\langle B \mid R \rangle$ of a group, such a mechanism can generate the irreducible string representations of the elements in L. Thus, the results collected in the following theorem are obvious consequences of the results stated in Theorem 6.

Let $\langle B \mid R \rangle$ be the computable finite presentation of a group G. The set of string representations (of elements of this group with respect to this finite presentation $\langle B \mid R \rangle$) generated or accepted (in the sense of automata) by a P system with anti-matter Π is denoted by $L_\delta^{\langle B \mid R \rangle}(\Pi)$, $\delta \in \{gen, aut\}$. The families of sets $L_\delta^{\langle B \mid R \rangle}(\Pi)$, $\delta \in \{gen, aut\}$ computed by such P systems with at most m membranes and k catalysts are denoted by $L_\delta^{\langle B \mid R \rangle} OP_m(cat(k), antim/pri)$. We omit $/pri$ for the families without priorities. The family of recursively enumerable sets of elements over the computable finite presentation $\langle B \mid R \rangle$ of a group is denoted by $RE^{\langle B \mid R \rangle}$. If the (computable finite) group (presentation) may be an arbitrary one, we omit the superscript $\langle B \mid R \rangle$ in these notations.

Let $\langle B \mid R \rangle$ and $\langle B' \mid R' \rangle$ be the computable finite presentations of two groups G and G', respectively; the function/relation from G to G' (with respect to these finite presentations $\langle B \mid R \rangle$ and $\langle B' \mid R' \rangle$) computed by a P system with anti-matter Π is denoted by $ZL_{aut}^{(\langle B \mid R \rangle, \langle B' \mid R' \rangle)}(\Pi)$, $Z \in \{Fun, Rel\}$; the families of such functions/relations $ZL_{aut}^{(\langle B \mid R \rangle, \langle B' \mid R' \rangle)}(\Pi)$ computed by P systems with anti-matter and at most m membranes and k catalysts are denoted by $ZL_{aut}^{(\langle B \mid R \rangle, \langle B' \mid R' \rangle)} OP_m(cat(k), antim/pri)$. We omit $/pri$ for the families without priorities. If the computable finite group presentations may be arbitrary ones, we omit the superscript $(\langle B \mid R \rangle, \langle B' \mid R' \rangle)$ in these notations. The families of recursively enumerable functions/relations from G to G' (with respect to the finite presentations $\langle B \mid R \rangle$ and $\langle B' \mid R' \rangle$) are denoted by $ZRE^{(\langle B \mid R \rangle, \langle B' \mid R' \rangle)}$, $Z \in \{Fun, Rel\}$.

Theorem 7. *Let $\langle B \mid R \rangle$ and $\langle B' \mid R' \rangle$ be the computable finite presentations of two groups G and G', respectively. Then we have that:*

– *for any $n \geq 1$, $k \geq 0$, $\delta \in \{gen, aut\}$, and $Z \in \{Fun, Rel\}$,*

$$L_\delta^{\langle B|R \rangle} OP_n\left(cat(k), antim/pri\right) = RE^{\langle B|R \rangle} \ and$$
$$ZL_{aut}^{(\langle B|R \rangle, \langle B'|R' \rangle)} OP_n\left(cat(k), antim/pri\right) = ZRE^{(\langle B|R \rangle, \langle B'|R' \rangle)};$$

– *for any $n \geq 1$, $k \geq 1$, $\delta \in \{gen, aut\}$, and $Z \in \{Fun, Rel\}$,*

$$L_\delta^{\langle B|R \rangle} OP_n\left(cat(k), antim\right) = RE^{\langle B|R \rangle} \ and$$
$$ZL_{aut}^{(\langle B|R \rangle, \langle B'|R' \rangle)} OP_n\left(cat(k), antim\right) = ZRE^{(\langle B|R \rangle, \langle B'|R' \rangle)}.$$

Proof. As for string languages, all computations can be carried out by simulating register machines, hence, again the results from Section 4 apply. Moreover, as already mentioned in Remark 4, the additional computations can also be carried out in this way, as $\langle B \mid R \rangle$ and $\langle B' \mid R' \rangle$ are computable. □

Remark 5. Let us mention that the results obtained in Theorem 7 for arbitrary computable finite presentations $\langle B \mid R \rangle$ of a group can also be applied to the infinite Abelian groups $\mathbb{Z}^d$ with their canonical group presentations by the unit vectors $(0, ..., 1, ..., 0)$ and their inverses $(0, ..., -1, ..., 0)$. Keeping in mind that there is a one-to-one correspondence between the representation of a vector in $\mathbb{Z}^n$ by a multiset of symbols and the corresponding string representing this multiset, most of the results shown in Theorem 5 are special cases of the respective results stated in Theorem 7.

8 Summary

We have shown that only non-cooperative rules together with matter/anti-matter annihilation rules are needed to obtain computational completeness in P systems working in the maximally parallel derivation mode if annihilation rules have weak priority; without priorities, one catalyst is needed. In the case of accepting P systems we are able to get even deterministic systems. Allowing anti-matter objects as input and/or output, we obtain a computationally complete computing model for computations on integer numbers. Interpreting sequences of symbols taken in from and/or sent out to the environment, we get a model for computations on strings, where strings can even be interpreted as representations of elements of a group based on a computable finite presentation.

There may be a lot of other interesting models of P systems allowing for introducing anti-matter objects and matter/anti-matter annihilation rules. Several problems remain open even for the models presented here, for example, can we avoid both catalysts and priorities. Moreover, the variants of P systems with anti-matter computing on sets of integer numbers and on languages of strings, even considered as representations of elements of a group based on a computable finite presentation, deserve more detailed investigations.

Acknowledgements. The authors gratefully acknowledge the inspiring ideas and discussions with Gheorghe Păun on the topics exhibited in this paper; even more results on P systems with anti-matter can be found in [1]. Artiom Alhazov acknowledges project STCU-5384 *Models of high performance computations based on biological and quantum approaches* awarded by the Science and Technology Center in the Ukraine.

References

1. Alhazov, A., Aman, B., Freund, R., Păun, Gh.: Matter and Anti-Matter in Membrane Systems. In: Macías-Ramos, L.F., Martínez-del-Amor, M.Á., Păun, Gh., Riscos-Núñez, A., Valencia-Cabrera, L. (eds.) Proceedings of the Twelfth Brainstorming Week on Membrane Computing, pp. 1–26. Fénix Editora, Sevilla (2014)
2. Alhazov, A., Sburlan, D.: Static Sorting P Systems. In: Ciobanu, G., Păun, Gh., Pérez-Jiménez, M.J. (eds.) Applications of Membrane Computing. Natural Computing Series, pp. 215–252. Springer (2005)
3. Cavaliere, M., Freund, R., Leitsch, A., Păun, Gh.: Event-Related Outputs of Computations in P Systems. Journal of Automata, Languages and Combinatorics **11**(3), 263–278 (2006)
4. Csuhaj-Varjú, E., Vaszil, Gy.: P Automata or Purely Communicating Accepting P Systems. In: Păun, Gh., Rozenberg, G., Salomaa, A., Zandron, C. (eds.) WMC-CdeA 2002. LNCS, vol. 2597, pp. 219–233. Springer, Heidelberg (2003)
5. Dassow, J., Păun, Gh.: Regulated Rewriting in Formal Language Theory. Springer (1989)
6. Díaz-Pernil, D., Peña-Cantillana, F., Gutiérrez-Naranjo, M.A.: Antimatter as a Frontier of Tractability in Membrane Computing. In: Macías-Ramos, L.F., Martínez-del-Amor, M.Á., Păun, Gh., Riscos-Núñez, A., Valencia-Cabrera, L. (eds.) Proceedings of the Twelfth Brainstorming Week on Membrane Computing, pp. 155–168. Fénix Editora, Sevilla (2014)
7. Freund, R.: Purely Catalytic P Systems: Two Catalysts Can Be Sufficient for Computational Completeness. In: Alhazov, A., Cojocaru, S., Gheorghe, M., Rogozhin, Yu. (eds.) CMC14 Proceedings - The 14th International Conference on Membrane Computing, pp. 153–166. Institute of Mathematics and Computer Science, Academy of Sciences of Moldova (2013)
8. Freund, R., Kari, L., Oswald, M., Sosík, P.: Computationally Universal P Systems without Priorities: Two Catalysts Are Sufficient. Theoretical Computer Science **330**, 251–266 (2005)
9. Freund, R., Oswald, M.: A Small Universal Antiport P System with Forbidden Context. In: Leung, H., Pighizzini, G. (eds.) 8th International Workshop on Descriptional Complexity of Formal Systems - DCFS 2006. Las Curces, New Mexico, USA, June 21–23. Proceedings DCFS, pp. 259–266. New Mexico State University, Las Cruces (2006)
10. Freund, R., Oswald, M., Păun, Gh.: Catalytic and Purely Catalytic P Systems and P Automata: Control Mechanisms for Obtaining Computational Completeness. Fundamenta Informaticae **136**, 59–84 (2015)
11. Freund, R., Păun, Gh.: How to Obtain Computational Completeness in P Systems with One Catalyst. In: Neary, T., Cook, M. (eds.) Proceedings Machines, Computations and Universality 2013, MCU 2013, Zürich, Switzerland, September 9–11. EPTCS, vol. 128, pp. 47–61 (2013)
12. Holt, D.F., Eick, B., O'Brien, E.A.: Handbook of Computational Group Theory. CRC Press (2005)

13. Korec, I.: Small Universal Register Machines. Theoretical Computer Science **168**, 267–301 (1996)
14. Minsky, M.L.: Computation: Finite and Infinite Machines. Prentice Hall, Englewood Cliffs (1967)
15. Pan, L., Păun, Gh.: Spiking Neural P Systems with Anti-Matter. International Journal of Computers, Communications & Control 4(3), 273–282 (2009)
16. Păun, Gh.: Computing with Membranes. Journal of Computer and System Sciences **61**(1), 108–143 (2000) (and Turku Center for Computer Science-TUCS Report 208, November 1998, www.tucs.fi)
17. Păun, Gh.: Membrane Computing: An Introduction. Springer (2002)
18. Păun, Gh., Rozenberg, G., Salomaa, A. (eds.): The Oxford Handbook of Membrane Computing. Oxford University Press (2010)
19. Rozenberg, G., Salomaa, A. (eds.): Handbook of Formal Languages, 3 vol. Springer (1997)
20. The P Systems Website: www.ppage.psystems.eu

Priorities, Promoters and Inhibitors in Deterministic Non-cooperative P Systems

Artiom Alhazov[1] and Rudolf Freund[2($\boxtimes$)]

[1] Institute of Mathematics and Computer Science,
Academy of Sciences of Moldova,
Academiei 5, MD-2028 Chişinău, Moldova
artiom@math.md

[2] Faculty of Informatics, Vienna University of Technology,
Favoritenstr. 9, 1040 Vienna, Austria
rudi@emcc.at

Abstract. Membrane systems (with symbol objects) are distributed controlled multiset processing systems. Non-cooperative P systems with either promoters or inhibitors (of weight not restricted to one) are known to be computationally complete. Since recently, it is known that the power of the deterministic subclass of such systems is subregular. We present new results on the weight (one and two) of promoters and inhibitors, as well as characterizing the systems with priorities only.

1 Introduction

The most famous membrane computing model where determinism is a criterion of universality versus decidability is the model of catalytic P systems, see [3] and [6].

It is also known that non-cooperative rewriting P systems with either promoters or inhibitors are computationally complete, [2]. Moreover, the proof satisfies some additional properties:

- Either promoters of weight 2 or inhibitors of weight 2 are enough.

- The system is non-deterministic, but it restores the previous configuration if the guess is wrong, which leads to correct simulations with probability 1.

Recently, in [1] we have shown that computational completeness cannot be achieved by deterministic non-cooperative systems with promoters, inhibitors, and priorities (in the maximally parallel or the asynchronous mode, unlike the sequential mode), and characterized the corresponding classes:

$$
\begin{aligned}
NFIN \cup coNFIN &= N_{deta}OP_1^{asyn}\left(ncoo, pro_{1,*}, inh_{1,*}\right) \\
&= N_{deta}OP_1^{maxpar}\left(ncoo, pro_{1,*}\right) \\
&= N_{deta}OP_1^{maxpar}\left(ncoo, inh_{1,*}\right) \\
&= N_{deta}OP_1^{asyn}\left(ncoo, (pro_{*,*}, inh_{*,*})_*, pri\right) \\
&= N_{deta}OP_1^{maxpar}\left(ncoo, (pro_{*,*}, inh_{*,*})_*, pri\right), \text{ but} \\
NRE &= N_{deta}OP_1^{sequ}\left(ncoo, pro_{1,1}, inh_{1,1}\right).
\end{aligned}
$$

M. Gheorghe et al. (Eds.): CMC 2014, LNCS 8961, pp. 86–98, 2014.
DOI: 10.1007/978-3-319-14370-5_6

A few interesting questions have been left open. For instance, what is the power of P systems, e.g., in the maximally parallel mode, when we only use priorities, or when we restrict the weight of the promoting/inhibiting multisets. These are the questions we address in this paper.

2 Definitions

An *alphabet* is a finite non-empty set V of abstract *symbols*. The free monoid generated by V under the operation of concatenation is denoted by V^*; the *empty string* is denoted by λ, and $V^* \setminus \{\lambda\}$ is denoted by V^+. The set of non-negative integers is denoted by $\mathbb{N}$; $\mathbb{N}_k$ denotes the set of the non-negative integers $\geq k$. A set S of non-negative integers is called *co-finite* if $\mathbb{N} \setminus S$ is finite. The family of all finite (co-finite) sets of non-negative integers is denoted by $NFIN$ ($coNFIN$, respectively). The family of all recursively enumerable sets of non-negative integers is denoted by NRE. In the following, we will use $\subseteq$ both for the subset as well as the submultiset relation.

Since flattening the membrane structure of a membrane system preserves both determinism and the model, in the following we restrict ourselves to consider membrane systems as one-region multiset rewriting systems.

A *(one-region) membrane system (P system)* is a tuple

$$\Pi = (O, \Sigma, w, R'),$$

where O is a finite alphabet, $\Sigma \subseteq O$ is the input sub-alphabet, $w \in O^*$ is a string representing the initial multiset, and R' is a set of rules of the form $r : u \to v$, $u \in O^+$, $v \in O^*$.

A configuration of the system Π is represented by a multiset of objects from O contained in the region, the set of all configurations over O is denoted by $\mathbb{C}(O)$. A rule $r : u \to v$ is applicable if the current configuration contains the multiset specified by u. Furthermore, applicability may be controlled by *context conditions*, specified by pairs of sets of multisets.

Definition 1. *Let P_i, Q_i be (finite) sets of multisets over O, $1 \leq i \leq m$. A rule with context conditions $(r, (P_1, Q_1), \cdots, (P_m, Q_m))$ is applicable to a configuration C if r is applicable, and there exists some $j \in \{1, \cdots, m\}$ for which*

- *there exists some $p \in P_j$ such that $p \subseteq C$ and*
- *$q \not\subseteq C$ for all $q \in Q_j$.*

In words, context conditions are satisfied if there exists a pair of sets of multisets (called *promoter set* and *inhibitor set*, respectively), such that at least one multiset in the promoter set is a submultiset of the current configuration, and no multiset in the inhibitor set is a submultiset of the current configuration.

Note 1. The definition above is taken from [1]. As it will be shown in Remark 2, without restricting generality, every set P_j may be assumed to be a singleton. The meaning of a **set** of promoters may be defined differently, replacing "there exists some $p \in P_j$" by "for all $p \in P_j$" in the definition above. This alternative definition corresponds to definitions of sets as permitting context in string rewriting models, yet, such a promoter set would be equivalent to a singleton promoter which is a union of this set, so (unless we stress the descriptional complexity) also in this case we do not need to deal with multi-element promoters. In the rest of the paper we assume the first interpretation, as in the definition above, noting that this variation does **not** influence results from [1] or those in this paper.

Definition 2. *A P system with context conditions and priorities on the rules is a construct*

$$\Pi = (O, \Sigma, w, R', R, >),$$

where (O, Σ, w, R') is a (one-region) P system as defined above, R is a set of rules with context conditions and $>$ is a priority relation on the rules in R; if rule r' has priority over rule r, denoted by $r' > r$, then r cannot be applied if r' is applicable.

Throughout the paper, we will use the word *control* to mean that at least one of these features is allowed (context conditions or promoters or inhibitors only and eventually priorities).

In the *sequential mode* (*sequ*), a computation step consists in the non-deterministic application of one applicable rule r, replacing its left-hand side ($lhs(r)$) by its right-hand side ($rhs(r)$). In the *maximally parallel mode* (*maxpar*), multiple applicable rules may be chosen in a non-deterministic way to be applied in parallel to the underlying configuration to disjoint submultisets, possibly leaving some objects idle, under the condition that no further rule is applicable to them (i.e., no supermultiset of the chosen multiset is applicable to the same configuration). Maximal parallelism is the most common computation mode in membrane computing, also see Definition 4.8 in [5]. In the *asynchronous mode* (*asyn*), any positive number of applicable rules may be chosen in a non-deterministic way to be applied in parallel to disjoint submultisets in the underlying configuration. The computation step between two configurations C and C' is denoted by $C \Rightarrow C'$, thus yielding the binary relation $\Rightarrow: \mathbb{C}(O) \times \mathbb{C}(O)$. A computation halts when there are no rules applicable to the current configuration (*halting configuration*) in the corresponding mode.

The computation of a *generating* P system starts with w, and its result is $|x|$ if it halts; an *accepting* system starts with wx, $x \in \Sigma^*$, and we say that $|x|$ is its results – is accepted – if it halts. The set of numbers generated/accepted by a P system working in the mode α is the set of results of its computations for all $x \in \Sigma^*$ and denoted by $N_g^\alpha(\Pi)$ and $N_a^\alpha(\Pi)$, respectively. A (one-region) P system with context conditions and priorities on the rules with rules of type β working in the mode α is said to be of type $OP_1^\alpha(\beta, (pro_{k,l}, inh_{k',l'})_d, pri)$; d denotes the maximal number m in the rules with context conditions $(r, (P_1, Q_1), \cdots, (P_m, Q_m))$; k and k' denote the maximum number of promoters/inhibitors in the P_i and Q_i, respectively; l and l' indicate the maximum of weights of promoters and inhibitors, respectively. If any of these numbers k, k', l, l' is not bounded, we replace it by $*$. As types of rules we are going to distinguish between cooperative ($\beta = coo$) and non-cooperative ones (i.e., the left-hand side of each rule is a single object; $\beta = ncoo$). The family of sets of numbers generated/accepted P systems of that type is denoted by $N_\delta OP_1^\alpha (\beta, (pro_{k,l}, inh_{k',l'})_d, pri)$ with $\delta = g$ for the generating and $\delta = a$ for the accepting case;

In the case of accepting systems, we also consider the idea of determinism, which means that in each step of any computation at most one (multiset of) rule(s) is applicable; in this case, we write *deta* for δ.

In the literature, we find a lot of restricted variants of P systems with context conditions and priorities on the rules, e.g., we may omit the priorities or the context conditions completely. If in a rule $(r, (P_1, Q_1), \cdots, (P_m, Q_m))$ we have $m = 1$, we say that $(r, (P_1, Q_1))$ is a rule with a *simple context condition*, and we omit the inner parentheses in the notation. Moreover, context conditions only using promoters are denoted by $r|_{p_1, \cdots, p_n}$, meaning $(r, \{p_1, \cdots, p_n\}, \emptyset)$, or, equivalently, $(r, (p_1, \emptyset), \cdots, (p_n, \emptyset))$; context conditions only using inhibitors are denoted by $r|_{\neg q_1, \cdots, \neg q_n}$, meaning $(r, \lambda, \{q_1, \cdots, q_n\})$, or $r|_{\neg\{q_1, \cdots, q_n\}}$. Likewise, a rule with both promoters and inhibitors can be specified as a rule with a simple context condition, i.e., $r|_{p_1, \cdots, p_n, \neg q_1, \cdots, \neg q_n}$ stands for $(r, \{p_1, \cdots, p_n\}, \{q_1, \cdots, q_n\})$. Finally, promoters and inhibitors of weight one are called *atomic*.

Remark 1. If we do not consider determinism, then (the effect of) the rule $(r, (P_1, Q_1), \cdots, (P_m, Q_m))$ is equivalent to (the effect of) the collection of rules $\{(r, P_j, Q_j) \mid 1 \le j \le m\}$, no matter in which mode the P system is working (obviously, the priority relation has to be adapted accordingly, too).

Remark 2. Let $(r, \{p_1, \cdots, p_n\}, Q)$ be a rule with a simple context condition; then we claim that (the effect of) this rule is equivalent to (the effect of) the collection of rules

$$\{(r, \{p_j\}, Q \cup \{p_k \mid 1 \le k < j\}) \mid 1 \le j \le m\}$$

even in the the case of a deterministic P system: If the first promoter is chosen to make the rule r applicable, we do not care about the other promoters; if the second promoter is chosen to make the rule r applicable, we do not allow p_1 to appear in the configuration, but do not care about the other promoters p_3 to p_m; in general, when promoter p_j is chosen to make the rule r applicable, we do not allow p_1 to p_{j-1} to appear in the configuration, but do not care about the other promoters p_{j+1} to p_m; finally, we have the rule $\{(r, \{p_m\}, Q \cup \{p_k \mid 1 \le k < m\})\}$. If adding $\{p_k \mid 1 \le k < j\}$ to Q has the effect of prohibiting the promoter p_j from enabling the rule r to be applied, this makes no harm as in this case one of the promoters p_k, $1 \le k < j$, must have the possibility for enabling r to be applied. By construction, the domains of the new context conditions now are disjoint, so this transformation does not create (new) non-determinism. In a similar way, this transformation may be performed on context conditions which are not simple. Therefore, without restricting generality, the set of promoters may be assumed to be a singleton. In this case, we may omit the braces of the multiset notation for the promoter multiset and write (r, p, Q).

Remark 3. As in a P system $(O, \Sigma, w, R', R, >)$ the set of rules R' can easily be deduced from the set of rules with context conditions R, we omit R' in the description of the P system. Moreover, for systems having only rules with a simple context condition, we omit d in the description of the families of sets of numbers and simply write

$$N_\delta O P_1^\alpha \left(\beta, pro_{k,l}, inh_{k',l'}, pri \right).$$

Moreover, each control mechanism not used can be omitted, e.g., if no priorities and only promoters are used, we only write $N_\delta O P_1^\alpha \left(\beta, pro_{k,l} \right)$.

3 Results

In this section we first recall several results from [1] and then we establish our new results, first for deterministic P systems with non-cooperative rules and only priorities as control mechanism, and then we characterize systems using promoters or inhibitors of weight 2.

3.1 Recent Results

We first recall from [1] the *bounding* operation over multisets, with a parameter $k \in \mathbb{N}$ as follows:

$$\text{for } u \in O^*, \ b_k(u) = v \text{ with } |v|_a = \min(|u|_a, k) \text{ for all } a \in O.$$

The mapping b_k "crops" the multisets by removing copies of every object a present in more than k copies until exactly k remain. For two multisets u, u', $b_k(u) = b_k(u')$ if for every $a \in O$, either $|u|_a = |u'|_a < k$, or $|u|_a \geq k$ and $|u'|_a \geq k$. Mapping b_k induces an equivalence relation, mapping O^* into $(k+1)^{|O|}$ equivalence classes. Each equivalence class corresponds to specifying, for each $a \in O^*$, whether no copy, one copy, or $\cdots k - 1$ copies, or "k copies or more" are present. We denote the range of b_k by $\{0, \cdots, k\}^O$.

Lemma 1. *[1] Context conditions are equivalent to predicates defined on boundings.*

Theorem 1. *[1] Priorities are subsumed by conditional contexts.*

Remark 4. It is worth to note, see also [4], that if no other control is used, the priorities can be mapped to sets of atomic inhibitors. Indeed, a rule is inhibited precisely by the left side of each higher priority rule. This is straightforward in case when the priority relation is assumed to be a partial order.

If this is not the case, then both the semantics of computations in P systems and the reduction of priorities to inhibitors is a bit more complicated, but the claim still holds.

Fix an arbitrary deterministic controlled non-cooperative P system. Take k as the maximal size of all multisets in all context conditions. Then, the bounding does not influence applicability of rules, and $b_k(u)$ is halting if and only if u is halting. We recall that bounding induces equivalence classes preserved by any computation.

Lemma 2. *[1] Assume $u \to x$ and $v \to y$. Then $b_k(u) = b_k(v)$ implies $b_k(x) = b_k(y)$.*

Corollary 1. *[1] If $b_k(u) = b_k(v)$, then u is accepted if and only if v is accepted.*

Finally, the "at most $NFIN \cup coNFIN$" part of characterizing

$$N_{deta}OP_1^{maxpar}\left(ncoo, (pro_{*,*}, inh_{*,*})_*, pri\right)$$

(the main theorem of [1]) is shown with the following argument:

> Each equivalence class induced by bounding is completely accepted or completely rejected. If no infinite equivalence class is accepted, then the accepted set is finite (containing numbers not exceeding $(k-1) \cdot |O|$). If at least one infinite equivalence class is accepted, then the rejected set is finite (containing numbers not exceeding $(k-1) \cdot |O|$).

3.2   Deterministic Non-cooperative P Systems with Priorities Only

We start with an example showing how an object t can be rewritten in a deterministic way depending on the presence or absence of an object a.

Example 1. Consider the following deterministic P system with priorities on its non-cooperative rules:

$\Pi = (\{a, A, A', t, t', t_+, t_-\}, \{a\}, tA, R, >)$, where
$R = \{1 : t \to t', \ 2 : a \to \lambda, \ 3 : A \to A', \ 4 : t' \to t_+, \ 5 : t' \to t_-, \ 6 : A' \to \lambda\}$,
$> = \{a \to \lambda > A \to A', \ A \to A' > t' \to t_-, \ A' \to \lambda > t' \to t_+\}$.

Indeed, object t waits for one step by becoming t', while A will change to A' or wait, depending on the presence of a. Then, object t' becomes either t_+ or t_-, depending on whether A or A' is present. Notice, e.g., how adding either rule $t_+ \to t_+$ or rule $t_- \to t_-$ leads to a system accepting $\{0\}$ or $\mathbb{N} \setminus \{0\}$. Of course, accepting only zero could be done instead by a trivial one-rule system with the rule $a \rightarrow a$, but this example is important because such a deciding subsystem can be used, with suitable delays, as a building block for checking combinations of presence/absence of multiple symbols.

We now proceed with characterizing systems with priorities only. As it will be clear immediately below, the upper bound and its proof is analogous to systems with (sets of) atomic promoters and/or atomic inhibitors.

Theorem 2. *The following inclusions hold:*

$$N_{deta}OP_1^{maxpar}\,(ncoo, pri) \subseteq \{\mathbb{N}_k, \mathbb{N}_k \cup \{0\} \mid k \geq 0\} \cup \{\{0\}, \emptyset\}.$$
$$N_{deta}OP_1^{maxpar}\,(ncoo, (pro_{*,1}, inh_{*,1})_*) \subseteq \{\mathbb{N}_k, \mathbb{N}_k \cup \{0\} \mid k \geq 0\} \cup \{\{0\}, \emptyset\}.$$

Proof. It follows from Remark 4 that the priorities can be replaced by sets of atomic inhibitors, therefore we have

$$N_{deta}OP_1^{maxpar}\,(ncoo, pri) \subseteq N_{deta}OP_1^{maxpar}\,(ncoo, (inh_{*,1}))\,.$$

Hence, it suffices to prove the second claim of the theorem. Consider an arbitrary P system Π of type $OP_1^{maxpar}\,(ncoo, (pro_{*,1}, inh_{*,1})_*)$. It follows from Corollary 1, see also a comment after it, that Π accepts a union of some equivalence classes induced by bounding b_1 (i.e., checking presence/absence). Here it is important to recall that adding a fixed initial configuration to the input does not split equivalence classes, so in the rest of the proof, whenever convenient, we may assume that the initial configuration mentioned above is empty; this will simplify the explanation. Bounding b_1 maps configurations into multisets with multiplicity at most one, i.e., essentially sets: $b_1(w)$ contains symbol $a \in O$ if and only if a is present in w.

Clearly, $b_1(w) = \lambda$ if and only if $w = \lambda$. This equivalence class, if accepted, contributes $\{0\}$ to the result. If, however, $b_1(w) \neq \lambda$, then $|b_1(w)| > 0$ different symbols are present in w, in arbitrary multiplicities of least one. Hence, any of such equivalence classes, if accepted, contributes $\mathbb{N}_{|b_1(w)|}$ to the result (note that, by definition of an equivalence class, $|b_1(w)|$ is the same for all representatives w). If no infinite class is accepted, then Π accepts either $\{0\}$ or $\emptyset$. Otherwise, notice that all infinite equivalence classes are comparable with respect to inclusion:

Let $k = \min\{|b_1(w)| \mid \Pi$ accepts $w, w \neq \lambda\}$. Then there exists an accepted input w with $|b_1(w)| = k$, and the equivalence class of w is accepted, yielding $\mathbb{N}_k$. However, by the minimality of k, all accepted positive numbers are already in $\mathbb{N}_k$. Therefore, if Π accepts an infinite set of numbers, then it is either $\mathbb{N}_k$ or $\mathbb{N}_k \cup \{0\}$. The family of all these sets is

$$F_{pri} = \{\mathbb{N}_k, \mathbb{N}_k \cup \{0\} \mid k \geq 0\} \cup \{\{0\}, \emptyset\}.$$

Hence, we conclude $N_{deta}OP_1^{maxpar}\,(ncoo, pri) \subseteq F_{pri}$. □

The following theorem shows the converse inclusion for the case of priorities.

Theorem 3. $N_{deta}OP_1^{maxpar}(ncoo, pri) \supseteq \{\mathbb{N}_k, \mathbb{N}_k \cup \{0\} \mid k \geq 0\} \cup \{\{0\}, \emptyset\}$.

Proof. We proceed with the converse inclusion. Let $\Pi_0 = (\{a, t\}, \{a\}, t, R, >)$, then $R = \{t \to t\}$ and the empty relation $>$ yield $\emptyset$. To accept $\{0\}$, it is enough to instead set $R = \{a \to a\}$ and again take the empty relation $>$.

Now suppose we want to accept $\mathbb{N}_k$. It suffices to count that we have at least one of each of the objects $a_1, \cdots, a_k$ (we recall that we need to accept *at least one* input of size j for each $j \geq k$, and to reject the input if $j < k$). To accept $\mathbb{N}_k \cup \{0\}$ instead, we may perform a simultaneous check for the absence of all input symbols.

Using the idea from Example 1, we now construct the system

$$\Pi_1 = (O, \Sigma = \{a_{i,0} \mid 1 \leq i \leq k\}, tA_{0,0} \cdots A_{k,0}, R, >), \text{ where}$$
$$O = \{a_{i,j} \mid 1 \leq i \leq k, \ 0 \leq j \leq i+1\} \cup \{A_{i,j} \mid 0 \leq i \leq k, \ 0 \leq j \leq i+2\}$$
$$\quad \cup \{t, z, p\} \cup \{t_i \mid 0 \leq i \leq k+1\},$$
$$R = R_a \cup R_A \cup R_t,$$
$$R_a = \{a_{i,j} \to a_{i,j+1} \mid 1 \leq i \leq k, \ 0 \leq j \leq i\},$$
$$R_A = \{A_{i,j} \to A_{i,j+1} \mid 1 \leq i \leq k, \ 0 \leq j \leq i+1\},$$
$$R_t = \{t \to t_0, \ t_0 \to z, \ t_0 \to t_1, \ p \to p\} \cup \{t_i \to t_{i+1}, \ t_i \to p \mid 1 \leq i \leq k\},$$
$$> = \{a_{i,0} \to a_{i,1} > A_{0,0} \to A_{0,1} \mid 1 \leq i \leq k\}$$
$$\quad \cup \{A_{0,0} \to A_{0,1} > t_0 \to z, \ A_{0,1} \to A_{0,2} > t_0 \to t_1\}$$
$$\quad \cup \{a_{i,i} \to a_{i,i+1} > A_{i,i} \to A_{i,i+1} \mid 1 \leq i \leq k\}$$
$$\quad \cup \{A_{i,i} \to A_{i,i+1} > t_i \to p, \ A_{i,i+1} \to A_{i,i+2} > t_i \to t_{i+1} \mid 1 \leq i \leq k\}.$$

Such a system accepts exactly $\mathbb{N}_k \cup \{0\}$. Indeed, after the first step, $A_{0,1}$ is present if all input symbols were absent, otherwise $A_{0,0}$ is still present instead. For any i, $1 \leq i \leq k$, after step $1 + i$, object $A_{i,i}$ is present if input symbol $a_{i,0}$ was present in the input, and otherwise $A_{i,i+1}$ is present instead. These "decision symbols" are used by t_i, $0 \leq i \leq k$, to build the "presence picture". We recall that it suffices to accept when all input symbols are present, or when none is present. In the second case, t_0 becomes z, and the computation only continues by rules from R_A, leading to halting. Now let us assume that the first s of the input symbols are present, $s < k$. Then, t_0 becomes $t_1 \cdots, t_s$, yet at the end the absence of t_{s+1} causes t_s to change into p, leading to an infinite computation. But if all input symbols are present, then finally the computation halts with t_{k+1}.

It remains to notice that accepting $\mathbb{N}_k$, $k \geq 1$, can be done by simply adding the rule $z \to z$. □

3.3   Deterministic Non-cooperative P Systems with Promoters or Inhibitors of Weight 2

We start from examples, illustrating the deterministic choice of rewriting p, depending on whether object a is absent, occurs exactly once, or occurs multiple times.

Example 2. Symbols A, B are primed if input is present (multiple input symbols are present). Then primed and unprimed symbols form mutually exclusive conditions.

$$\Pi = (O = \{p, p', p'', p_>, p_1, p_0, A, B, a\}, \Sigma = \{a\}, pAB, R), \text{ where}$$
$$R = \{1 : p \to p', \ 2 : A \to A'|_a, \ 3 : B \to B'|_{aa},$$
$$4 : p' \to p_>|_{B'}, \ 5 : p' \to p''|_B, \ 6 : p'' \to p_1|_{A'}, \ 7 : p'' \to p_0|_A\}.$$

Example 3. Notice that if we replace all promoters by inhibitors with the *same* context, the effect of blocking rules will be reversed, but the result will be the same. Indeed, the role of A' and B' will switch from "found a" and "found aa", respectively, to "not found a" and "not found aa", respectively.

$$R = \{1 : p \to p', \ 2 : A \to A'|_{\neg a}, \ 3 : B \to B'|_{\neg aa},$$
$$4 : p' \to p_>|_{\neg B'}, \ 5 : p' \to p''|_{\neg B}, \ 6 : p'' \to p_1|_{\neg A'}, \ 7 : p'' \to p_0|_{\neg A}\}.$$

We now proceed with characterizing systems with context of weight two. Notice that we already know that their power does not exceed $NFIN \cup coNFIN$.

Theorem 4. *The following characterizations hold:*

$$NFIN \cup coNFIN = N_{deta}OP_1^{maxpar}(ncoo, pro_{1,2})$$
$$= N_{deta}OP_1^{maxpar}(ncoo, inh_{1,2}).$$

Proof. We use the technique from Example 2 for all input symbols and combine the extracted information. Consider an arbitrary finite set M, and let $\max(M) = n$. We will use the following strategy: to accept a number $j \in M$, we will accept an input multiset with exactly j symbols appearing once, and nothing else. To accept the complement of M, we split it into sets $M'' = \{j \mid j > n\}$ and $M' = \{j \mid j \leq n, \ j \notin M\}$. While M' is treated in a similar way as M, it only remains to accept M'', which is covered by equivalence classes when all symbols are present, and at least one is present more than once.

$$\Pi = (O, \Sigma = \{a_i \mid 1 \leq i \leq n\}, tA_1 \cdots A_n B_1 \cdots B_n, R), \text{ where}$$
$$O = \{t_{i,j}, T_{i,j}, t'_{i,j}, T'_{i,j} \mid 1 \leq i \leq n+1, \ 0 \leq j \leq n\}$$
$$\cup \{A_i, A'_i, B_i, B'_i \mid 1 \leq i \leq n\} \cup \{t, \#\},$$
$$R = \{t_{i,j} \to T_{i+1,j+1}|_{B'_i}, \ T_{i,j} \to T_{i+1,j+1}|_{B'_i}, \ t_{i,j} \to t'_{i,j}|_{B_i}, \ T_{i,j} \to T'_{i,j}|_{B_i},$$
$$t'_{i,j} \to t_{i+1,j+1}|_{A'_i}, \ T'_{i,j} \to T_{i+1,j+1}|_{A'_i}, \ t'_{i,j} \to t_{i+1,j}|_{A_i}, \ T'_{i,j} \to T_{i+1,j}|_{A_i}$$
$$\mid 1 \leq i \leq n, 0 \leq j < n\}$$
$$\cup \{A_i \to A'_i|_{a_i}, \ B_i \to B'_i|_{a_i a_i} \mid 1 \leq i \leq n\} \cup \{t \to t_{1,0}, \ \# \to \#\}$$
$$\cup \{T_{n+1,j} \to \# \mid 1 \leq i \leq n\} \cup \{t_{n+1,j} \to \# \mid j \notin M\}.$$

The meaning of $T_{n+1,j}$ is that exactly j input symbols are present, and at least one of them is present multiple times. The meaning of $t_{n+1,j}$ is that the input consisted of exactly j different symbols. This is how an arbitrary finite set is accepted. To accept the complement of M, we replace $j \notin M$ by $j \in M$ and remove rule $T_{n+1,j} \to \#$. Therefore, deterministic P systems with promoters of weight two accept exactly $NFIN \cup coNFIN$.

For the inhibitor counterpart, notice that the computation of the number of different symbols present, as well as checking if any symbol is present multiple times, stays correct by simply changing promoters to the inhibitors with the same condition, just like in Example 3. Rules processing objects $t_{n+1,j}$ and $T_{n+1,j}$ will have an opposite effect, accepting the complement of the set accepted by the system with promoters, again yielding $NFIN \cup coNFIN$.   □

It is still open whether only inhibitors in the rules or only promoters in the rules are sufficient to yield $NFIN \cup coNFIN$ with the asynchronous mode, too.

3.4 Deterministic Non-cooperative P Systems with Atomic Promoters or Inhibitors

We now consider the systems as in the previous subsection, except now the weight of promoters/inhibitors is bounded by 1 instead of 2. In Subsection 3.2 the upper bound was already established for the power of such systems. In the following, we show that this upper bound is actually an equality.

Consider examples 2 and 3. We simplify them by removing rules with promoters/inhibitors of weight 2, which are no longer allowed. As expected, now these P systems produce p_0 and p_1 out of p, depending on whether any symbols a are present in the input. In fact, a few more symbols may be renamed and removed, leading to the same result already with four rules:

Example 4. Symbol A is primed if input is present, i.e., if at least one copy of the symbol a is present. Then primed and unprimed symbols form mutually exclusive conditions.

$$\Pi = (O = \{p, p', p_1, p_0, A, A', a\}, \Sigma = \{a\}, pA, R), \text{ where}$$
$$R = \{1 : p \to p', \ 2 : A \to A'|_a, \ 6' : p' \to p_1|_{A'}, \ 7 : p' \to p_0|_A\}.$$

In a similar way as in previous examples, we may replace all promoters by inhibitors with the *same* context; the effect of blocking rules will be reversed, but the result will be the same. Indeed, the role of A' will switch from "found a" to "not found a".

$$R' = \{1 : p \to p', \ 2 : A \to A'|_{\neg a}, \ 6' : p' \to p_1|_{\neg A'}, \ 7' : p' \to p_0|_{\neg A}\}.$$

To prove the characterization for P systems with (sets of) atomic promoters and/or inhibitors, we need to put together checking for all input symbols.

Theorem 5. *The following equalities hold:*

$$\{\mathbb{N}_k, \mathbb{N}_k \cup \{0\} \mid k \geq 0\} \cup \{\{0\}, \emptyset\} = N_{deta}OP_1^{maxpar}\,(ncoo, pro_{1,1})$$
$$= N_{deta}OP_1^{maxpar}\,(ncoo, inh_{1,1})\,.$$

Proof. The following construction is based on the main idea described in Example 4.

$$\Pi = (O, \Sigma = \{a_i \mid 1 \leq i \leq k\}, t, R), \text{ where}$$
$$O = \{t_i, z_i \mid 1 \leq i \leq k+1\} \cup \{t, \#\}$$
$$\cup \{A_i, A_i' \mid 1 \leq i \leq k\},$$
$$R = \{t \to t_1, \ t_1 \to t_2|_{A_1'}, \ t_1 \to z_2|_{A_1}, \ \# \to \#\}$$
$$\cup \{A_i \to A_i'|_{a_i} \mid 1 \leq i \leq k\}$$
$$\cup \{t_i \to t_{i+1}|_{A_i'}, \ t_i \to \#|_{A_i} \mid 2 \leq i \leq k\}$$
$$\cup \{z_i \to \#|_{A_i'}, \ z_i \to z_{i+1}|_{A_i} \mid 2 \leq i \leq k\}.$$

Starting with t, the system first changes each object A_i into A_i' provided at least one copy of the symbol a_i is present. In the second step, the system checks the presence of the first symbol a_1; in case at least one copy is present, in the following it checks for the presence of all other symbols, too, with using the objects t_j, whereas otherwise it checks if the input is zero, i.e., the objects z_j check that no symbol a_j is present. The meaning of t_{j+1} is that the input checked so far contained at least one copy of the first j symbols, whereas z_j indicates that up to a_j all symbols so far were missing. If either t_{k+1} or z_{k+1} are reached, the system halts and accepts. Hence, the P system constructed above accepts exactly those inputs where all input symbols are present or zero, i.e., $\mathbb{N}_k \cup \{0\}$. In order to only accept $\mathbb{N}_k$, the objects z_j and all related rules have to be omitted, and moreover, we have to add the trap rule $t_1 \to \#|_{A_1}$, i.e., to expand the range of the trap rules $t_i \to \#|_{A_i}$ from $2 \leq i \leq k$ to $1 \leq i \leq k$.

In a similar way as in the proof of Theorem 4, the same result for inhibitors is obtained by turning all promoters in Π into inhibitors, just negating them. The role of the object A_i' will thus be reversed from presence to absence of the corresponding object a_i in the input, and using them as inhibitors instead of promoters results in accepting the same set as the system with promoters.

The finite cases are trivial: the empty set is accepted by the system $(O = \{a, t\}, \Sigma = \{a\}, t, R = \{t \to t\})$, and the singleton $\{0\}$ is accepted by the system $(O = \{a\}, \Sigma = \{a\}, \lambda, R = \{a \to a\})$.

Therefore, deterministic P systems with singleton atomic promoters or inhibitors of weight one accept exactly all the sets in the family $\{\mathbb{N}_k, \mathbb{N}_k \cup \{0\} \mid k \geq 0\} \cup \{\{0\}, \emptyset\}$. □

This construction is like a simpler version of the one in Theorem 4, but the result is no longer closed with respect to the complement, even though deciding between presence and absence looks symmetric. This may be attributed to the following reason: for any k, we may reject all numbers smaller than k by verifying that k different symbols are present in the input. However, we cannot even accept any finite set containing 1, since if a one-symbol input is accepted, then also any larger number of copies of it has to be accepted.

Finally, we put together the upper bounds from Theorem 2 and the lower bounds from Theorems 3 and 5, thus obtaining the following corollary.

Corollary 2. *The following characterizations hold:*

$$\{\mathbb{N}_k, \mathbb{N}_k \cup \{0\} \mid k \geq 0\} \cup \{\{0\}, \emptyset\} = N_{deta}OP_1^{maxpar}\left(ncoo, pro_{1,1}\right)$$
$$= N_{deta}OP_1^{maxpar}\left(ncoo, inh_{1,1}\right)$$
$$= N_{deta}OP_1^{maxpar}\left(ncoo, (pro_{*,1}, inh_{*,1})_*\right)$$
$$= N_{deta}OP_1^{maxpar}\left(ncoo, pri\right).$$

4   Conclusion

We have shown characterizations of deterministic non-cooperative P systems with inhibitors of weight 2, with promoters of weight 2, and with priorities only. The first two cases did not reduce the accepting power with respect to (unrestricted cardinality of promoter/inhibitor sets and) unrestricted weight of promoters/inhibitors.

Moreover, we have shown that P systems with (sets of or singleton) atomic promoters and/or inhibitors have exactly the same power as P systems with priorities only.

Acknowledgements. Artiom Alhazov acknowledges project STCU-5384 *Models of high performance computations based on biological and quantum approaches* awarded by the Science and Technology Center in the Ukraine.

References

1. Alhazov, A., Freund, R.: Asynchronous and Maximally Parallel Deterministic Controlled Non-cooperative P Systems Characterize *NFIN* and *coNFIN*. In: Martínez-del-Amor, M.Á., Păun, Gh., Pérez-Hurtado, I., Romero-Campero, F.J. (eds.) The Tenth Brainstorming Week in Membrane Computing, vol. 1, pp. 25–34. Fénix Editora, Sevilla (2012), and in: Csuhaj-Varjú, E., Gheorghe, M., Rozenberg, G., Salomaa, A., Vaszil, Gy. (eds.) CMC 2012. LNCS, vol. 7762, pp. 101–111. Springer, Heidelberg (2013)
2. Alhazov, A., Sburlan, D.: Ultimately Confluent Rewriting Systems. Parallel Multiset–Rewriting with Permitting or Forbidding Contexts. In: Mauri, G., Păun, Gh., Pérez-Jímenez, M.J., Rozenberg, G., Salomaa, A. (eds.) WMC 2004. LNCS, vol. 3365, pp. 178–189. Springer, Heidelberg (2005)
3. Freund, R., Kari, L., Oswald, M., Sosík, P.: Computationally Universal P Systems without Priorities: Two Catalysts are Sufficient. Theoretical Computer Science **330**(2), 251–266 (2005)

4. Freund, R., Kogler, M., Oswald, M.: A General Framework for Regulated Rewriting Based on the Applicability of Rules. In: Kelemen, J., Kelemenová, A. (eds.) Computation, Cooperation, and Life. LNCS, vol. 6610, pp. 35–53. Springer, Heidelberg (2011)
5. Freund, R., Verlan, S.: A Formal Framework for Static (Tissue) P Systems. In: Eleftherakis, G., Kefalas, P., Păun, Gh., Rozenberg, G., Salomaa, A. (eds.) WMC 2007. LNCS, vol. 4860, pp. 271–284. Springer, Heidelberg (2007)
6. Ibarra, O.H., Yen, H.-C.: Deterministic Catalytic Systems are Not Universal. Theoretical Computer Science **363**, 149–161 (2006)
7. Minsky, M.L.: Finite and Infinite Machines. Prentice Hall, New Jersey (1967)
8. Păun, Gh.: Membrane Computing: An Introduction. Springer (2002)
9. Păun, Gh., Rozenberg, G., Salomaa, A.: The Oxford Handbook of Membrane Computing. Oxford University Press (2010)
10. Rozenberg, G., Salomaa, A. (eds.): Handbook of Formal Languages, 3 vol. Springer (1997)
11. P systems webpage: http://ppage.psystems.eu

P Systems with Toxic Objects

Artiom Alhazov[1] and Rudolf Freund[2]([⊠])

[1] Institute of Mathematics and Computer Science,
Academy of Sciences of Moldova,
Academiei 5, MD-2028 Chişinău, Moldova
artiom@math.md
[2] Faculty of Informatics, Vienna University of Technology,
Favoritenstr. 9, 1040 Vienna, Austria
rudi@emcc.at

Abstract. We introduce the new concept of toxic objects, objects that must not stay idle as otherwise the computation is abandoned without yielding a result. P systems of many kinds using toxic objects allow for smaller descriptional complexity, especially for smaller numbers of rules, as trap rules can be avoided. Besides presenting a number of tiny P systems generating or accepting non-semilinear sets of (vectors of) natural numbers with very small numbers of rules, we also improve the results for catalytic and purely catalytic P systems: 14 rules for generating a non-semilinear vector set and 29 rules for generating a non-semilinear number set are sufficient when allowing only the minimal number of two and three catalysts, respectively; moreover, with using toxic objects, these numbers can be reduced to 11 and 17. Yet only 23 rules – without using toxic objects – are needed if we allow for using more catalysts, i.e., five for catalytic P systems and seven catalysts for purely catalytic P systems.

1 Introduction

P systems using non-cooperative rules without any additional control have the behavior of $E0L$ systems, but when only taking the results at halting means that the objects evolve in a context-free manner, generating $PsCF$, which is known (by Parikh's theorem) to coincide with $PsREG$, i.e., with the family of semilinear sets. In the accepting setup, P systems using non-cooperative rules without any additional control are even weaker, accepting all multisets over some subalphabet, or nothing, see [1].

In [2] we were interested in P systems able to generate or accept non-semilinear sets of natural numbers or at least sets of vectors of natural numbers, yet with as small ingredients as possible for different variants of P systems. Our main focus was on the descriptional complexity of these P systems, i.e., on how small the total number of rules may be, depending on the specific features of particular models of P systems. As most of the models of P systems can be shown to be computationally complete based on a simulation of the actions of

© Springer International Publishing Switzerland 2014
M. Gheorghe et al. (Eds.): CMC 2014, LNCS 8961, pp. 99–125, 2014.
DOI: 10.1007/978-3-319-14370-5_7

a register machine, even simple examples often turn out to be somehow more complicated than the general proof.

As an example of special interest we consider the case of (purely) catalytic P systems. Ideas how to find good examples of catalytic P systems generating a non-semilinear set of numbers were discussed intensively during the Fourteenth International Conference on Membrane Computing (CMC 2013) in Chişinău, especially by Petr Sosík and Rudolf Freund, based on a draft by Petr Sosík, and most of them finally being included in his paper [21]. Some new observations just found recently allowed us to reduce the number of rules again in a considerable way, see Section 4.6. Using the concept of toxic objects allows for saving a lot more rules. As a second interesting example we consider P systems with target selection and give another example which shows how toxic objects may help to save a lot of rules.

In this paper, we also focus on the new concept of *toxic objects* (first mentioned in [2]) which allows us to "kill" a computation branch if we cannot find a multiset of rules covering all occurrences of toxic objects which then somehow become "lethal" by killing such a computation. For all the proof techniques using a trap symbol # to "kill" a computation by introducing the trap symbol # with a non-cooperative rule $a \rightarrow \#$ or with a catalytic rule $ca \rightarrow c\#$, the concept of toxic objects allows us to save most of these rules, thus improving the descriptional complexity of the underlying P systems.

The rest of the paper is organized as follows: We first recall the basic definitions from formal language theory as well as the definitions for the most important variants of P systems considered later. Then we present examples for variants of P systems generating or accepting a non-semilinear set of natural numbers or of vectors of natural numbers with only a few rules, especially for the maximally parallel derivation mode, explained in more detail in [2]. As a specific example for a variant of P systems where the use of toxic objects allows for saving a lot of rules we consider P systems with label selection. Then, for the catalytic and purely catalytic P systems, we improve previous results established in [21] and [22].

2   Definitions

In this section we first recall the basic notions from formal language theory needed in this paper and then the definitions of the basic variants of P systems considered in the following sections. For more details in formal language theory we refer the reader to the standard monographs and textbooks as [19] and for the area of regulated rewriting to [8]. All the main definitions and results for P systems can be found in [16] and [17]; only specific notations and models not yet to be found there will be explained in more detail in this paper, especially the new idea of *"toxic objects"*, which will be explained and studied in Section 4. For actual informations and new developments in the area of membrane computing we refer to the P systems webpage [23].

2.1 Prerequisites

The set of non-negative integers (*natural numbers*) is denoted by $\mathbb{N}$. An *alphabet* V is a finite non-empty set of abstract *symbols*. Given V, the free monoid generated by V under the operation of concatenation is denoted by V^*; the elements of V^* are called strings, and the *empty string* is denoted by λ; $V^* \setminus \{\lambda\}$ is denoted by V^+. Let $\{a_1, \cdots, a_n\}$ be an arbitrary alphabet; the number of occurrences of a symbol a_i in a string x is denoted by $|x|_{a_i}$; the *Parikh vector* associated with x with respect to $a_1, \cdots, a_n$ is $\left(|x|_{a_1}, \cdots, |x|_{a_n}\right)$. The *Parikh image* of a language L over $\{a_1, \cdots, a_n\}$ is the set of all Parikh vectors of strings in L, and we denote it by $Ps(L)$. For a family of languages FL, the family of Parikh images of languages in FL is denoted by $PsFL$; for families of languages over a one-letter alphabet, the corresponding sets of non-negative integers are denoted by NFL; for an alphabet V containing exactly d objects, the corresponding sets of Parikh vectors with d components is denoted by $N^d FL$, i.e., we replace Ps by N^d.

A (finite) *multiset* over the (finite) alphabet V, $V = \{a_1, \cdots, a_n\}$, is a mapping $f : V \longrightarrow \mathbb{N}$ and represented by $\langle f(a_1), a_1 \rangle \cdots \langle f(a_n), a_n \rangle$ or by any string x the Parikh vector of which with respect to $a_1, \cdots, a_n$ is $(f(a_1), \cdots, f(a_n))$. In the following we will not distinguish between a vector $(m_1, \cdots, m_n)$, its representation by a multiset $\langle m_1, a_1 \rangle \cdots \langle m_n, a_n \rangle$ or its representation by a string x having the Parikh vector $\left(|x|_{a_1}, \cdots, |x|_{a_n}\right) = (m_1, \cdots, m_n)$. Fixing the sequence of symbols $a_1, \cdots, a_n$ in the alphabet V in advance, the representation of the multiset $\langle m_1, a_1 \rangle \cdots \langle m_n, a_n \rangle$ by the string $a_1^{m_1} \cdots a_n^{m_n}$ is unique. The family of regular, context-free, and recursively enumerable string languages is denoted by REG, CF, and RE, respectively.

ET0L Systems. An *ET0L* system is a construct $G = (V, T, w, P_1, \cdots, P_m)$ where $m \geq 1$, V is an alphabet, $T \subseteq V$ is the terminal alphabet, $w \in V^*$ is the *axiom*, and the P_i, $1 \leq i \leq m$, are finite sets (*tables*) of non-cooperative rules over V. In a derivation step in G, all the symbols present in the current sentential form are rewritten using one table. The language generated by G, denoted by $L(G)$, consists of all terminal strings $w \in T^*$ which can be generated by a derivation in G starting from the axiom w. The family of languages generated by *ET0L* systems and by *ET0L* systems with at most k tables is denoted by $ET0L$ and ET_k0L, respectively.

Register Machines. A *register machine* is a tuple $M = (m, B, l_0, l_h, P)$, where m is the number of registers, P is the set of instructions bijectively labeled by elements of B, $l_0 \in B$ is the initial label, and $l_h \in B$ is the final label. The instructions of M can be of the following forms:

- $l_1 : (ADD(j), l_2, l_3)$, with $l_1 \in B \setminus \{l_h\}$, $l_2, l_3 \in B$, $1 \leq j \leq m$.
  Increase the value of register j by one, and non-deterministically jump to instruction l_2 or l_3. This instruction is usually called *increment*.

- $l_1 : (SUB(j), l_2, l_3)$, with $l_1 \in B \setminus \{l_h\}$, $l_2, l_3 \in B$, $1 \le j \le m$.
  If the value of register j is zero then jump to instruction l_3, otherwise decrease the value of register j by one and jump to instruction l_2. The two cases of this instruction are usually called *zero-test* and *decrement*, respectively.
- $l_h : HALT$. Stop the execution of the register machine.

A *configuration* of a register machine is described by the contents of each register and by the value of the current label, which indicates the next instruction to be executed. Computations start by executing the first instruction of P (labeled with l_0), and terminate with reaching the $HALT$-instruction.

Register machines provide a simple universal computational model, for example, see [14]. In the following, we shall call a specific model of P systems *computationally complete* or *universal* if and only if for any register machine M we can effectively construct an equivalent P system Π of that type simulating M and yielding the same results.

Non-semilinear Sets of Numbers and of Vectors of Numbers. In most of the examples described in the following sections, we will use (variants) of the set of natural numbers

$$\{2^n \mid n \ge 0\} = N\left(\left\{a^{2^n} \mid n \ge 0\right\}\right)$$

and the set of (two-dimensional) vectors of natural numbers

$$\{(n, m) \mid n \ge 1, n \le m \le 2^n\} = Ps\left(\{(a^n b^m) \mid n \ge 1, n \le m \le 2^n\}\right),$$

which both are known to not be semilinear.

2.2 P Systems

The ingredients of the basic variants of (cell-like) P systems are the membrane structure, the objects placed in the membrane regions, and the evolution rules. The *membrane structure* is a hierarchical arrangement of membranes. Each membrane defines a *region/compartment*, the space between the membrane and the immediately inner membranes; the outermost membrane is called the *skin membrane*, the region outside is the *environment*, also indicated by (the label) 0. Each membrane can be labeled, and the label (from a set *Lab*) will identify both the membrane and its region. The membrane structure can be represented by a rooted tree (with the label of a membrane in each node and the skin in the root), but also by an expression of correctly nested labeled parentheses. The *objects* (multisets) are placed in the compartments of the membrane structure and usually represented by strings, with the multiplicity of a symbol corresponding to the number of occurrences of that symbol in the string. The basic *evolution rules* are multiset rewriting rules of the form $u \to v$, where u is a multiset of objects from a given set O and $v = (b_1, tar_1) \dots (b_k, tar_k)$ with $b_i \in O$ and $tar_i \in \{here, out, in\}$ or $tar_i \in \{here, out\} \cup \{in_j \mid j \in Lab\}$, $1 \le i \le k$. Using such a rule means "consuming" the objects of u and "producing" the objects $b_1, \ldots, b_k$ of v; the *target indications here*, *out*, and *in* mean that an object with the target *here* remains in the same region where the rule is applied, an object with the target *out* is sent out of the respective membrane (in this way, objects can also be sent to the environment, when the rule is applied in the skin region), while an object with the target *in* is sent to one of the immediately inner membranes, non-deterministically chosen, whereas with in_j this inner membrane can be specified directly. In general, we may omit the target indication *here*.

Yet there are a lot of other variants of rules we shall consider later; for example, if on the right-hand side of a rule we add the symbol δ, the surrounding membrane is dissolved whenever at least one such rule is applied, at the same moment all objects inside this membrane (the objects of this membrane region together with the whole inner membrane structure) are released to the surrounding membrane, and the rules assigned to the dissolved membrane region get lost. Another option is to add *promoters* $p_1, \ldots, p_m \in O^+$ and *inhibitors* $q_1, \ldots, q_n \in O^+$ to a rule and write $u \to v|_{p_1, \ldots, p_m, \neg q_1, \ldots, \neg q_n}$, which rule then is only applicable if the current contents of the membrane region includes any of the promoter multisets, but none of the inhibitor multisets; in most cases promoters and inhibitors are rather taken to be singleton objects than multisets. Further variants of P systems will be defined later.

Formally, a (cell-like) *P system* is a construct

$$\Pi = (O, \mu, w_1, \ldots, w_m, R_1, \ldots, R_m, f)$$

where O is the alphabet of *objects*, μ is the *membrane structure* (with m membranes), $w_1, \ldots, w_m$ are multisets of objects present in the m regions of μ at the beginning of a computation, $R_1, \ldots, R_m$ are finite sets of *evolution rules*, associated with the membrane regions of μ, and f is the label of the membrane region from which the outputs are taken/the inputs are put in ($f = 0$ indicates that the output/input is taken from the environment).

If a rule $u \to v$ has at least two objects in u, then it is called *cooperative*, otherwise it is called *non-cooperative*. In *catalytic P systems* we use non-cooperative as well as *catalytic rules* which are of the form $ca \to cv$, where c is a special object which never evolves and never passes through a membrane (both these restrictions can be relaxed), but it just assists object a to evolve to the multiset v. In a *purely catalytic P system* we only allow catalytic rules. For a catalytic as well as for a purely catalytic P system Π, in the description of Π we replace "O" by "O, C" in order to specify those objects from O which are the catalysts in the set C. As already explained above, cooperative and non-cooperative as well as catalytic rules can be extended by adding promoters and/or inhibitors, thus yielding rules of the form $u \to v|_{p_1, \ldots, p_m, \neg q_1, \ldots, \neg q_n}$.

All the rules defined so far can be used in different derivation modes: in the *sequential* mode (*sequ*), we apply exactly one rule in every derivation step; in the *asynchronous* mode (*asyn*), an arbitrary number of rules is applied in parallel; in the *maximally parallel* (*maxpar*) derivation mode, in any computation step of Π we choose a multiset of rules from the sets $R_1, \ldots, R_m$ in a non-deterministic way such that no further rule can be added to it so that the obtained multiset would still be applicable to the existing objects in the membrane regions $1, \ldots, m$.

The membranes and the objects present in the compartments of a system at a given time form a *configuration*; starting from a given *initial configuration* and using the rules as explained above, we get *transitions* among configurations; a sequence of transitions forms a *computation* (we often also say *derivation*). A computation is *halting* if and only if it reaches a configuration where no rule can be applied any more. With a halting computation we associate a *result generated* by this computation, in the form of the number of objects present in membrane f in the halting configuration. The set of multisets obtained as results of halting computations in Π working in the derivation mode $\delta \in \{sequ, asyn, maxpar\}$ is denoted by $mL_{gen,\delta}(\Pi)$, the set of natural numbers obtained by just counting the number of objects in the multisets of $mL_{gen,\delta}(\Pi)$ by $N_{gen,\delta}(\Pi)$, and the set of (Parikh) vectors obtained from the multisets in $mL_{gen,\delta}(\Pi)$ by $Ps_{gen,\delta}(\Pi)$.

Yet we may also start with some additional input multiset w_{input} over an *input alphabet* Σ in membrane f, i.e., in total we there have $w_f w_{input}$ in the initial configuration, and *accept* this input w_{input} if and only if there exists a halting computation with this input; the set of multisets accepted by halting computations in

$$\Pi = (O, \Sigma, \mu, w_1, \ldots, w_m, R_1, \ldots, R_m, f)$$

working in the derivation mode δ is denoted by $mL_{acc,\delta}(\Pi)$, the corresponding sets of natural numbers and of (Parikh) vectors are denoted by $N_{acc,\delta}(\Pi)$ and $Ps_{acc,\delta}(\Pi)$, respectively.

The family of sets $Y_{\gamma,\delta}(\Pi)$, $Y \in \{N, Ps\}$, $\gamma \in \{gen, acc\}$ computed by P systems with at most m membranes working in the derivation mode δ and with rules of type X is denoted by $Y_{\gamma,\delta}OP_m(X)$.

For example, it is well known (for example, see [15]) that for any $m \geq 1$, for the types of non-cooperative (*ncoo*) and cooperative (*coo*) rules we have

$$NREG = N_{gen,maxpar}OP_m(ncoo) \subset N_{gen,maxpar}OP_m(coo) = NRE.$$

For $\gamma \in \{gen, acc\}$ and $\delta \in \{sequ, asyn, maxpar\}$, the family of sets $Y_{\gamma,\delta}(\Pi)$, $Y \in \{N, Ps\}$, computed by (purely) catalytic P systems with at most m membranes and at most k catalysts is denoted by $Y_{\gamma,\delta}OP_m(cat_k)$ and $Y_{\gamma,\delta}OP_m(pcat_k)$, respectively; from [10] we know that, with the results being sent to the environment (which means taking $f = 0$), we have

$$Y_{gen,maxpar}OP_1(cat_2) = Y_{gen,maxpar}OP_1(pcat_3) = YRE.$$

If we allow a catalyst c to switch between two different states c and $\bar{c}$, we call c a *bi-stable catalyst*; in that way we obtain *P systems with bi-stable catalysts*. For $\gamma \in \{gen, acc\}$ and $\delta \in \{sequ, asyn, maxpar\}$, the family of sets $Y_{\gamma,\delta}(\Pi)$, $Y \in \{N, Ps\}$, computed by (purely) catalytic P systems with bistable catalysts with at most m membranes and at most k catalysts is denoted by $Y_{\gamma,\delta}OP_m(2cat_k)$

and $Y_{\gamma,\delta}OP_m\,(p2cat_k)$, respectively. We note that in the generative case we do not count the catalysts in the output membrane region.

For all the variants of P systems of type X, we may consider to label all the rules in the sets $R_1, \ldots, R_m$ in a one-to-one manner by labels from a set H and to take a set W containing subsets of H. Then a *P system with label selection* is a construct

$$\Pi = (O, \mu, w_1, \ldots, w_m, R_1, \ldots, R_m, H, W, f)$$

where $\Pi' = (O, \mu, w_1, \ldots, w_m, R_1, \ldots, R_m, f)$ is a P system as defined above, H is a set of labels for the rules in the sets $R_1, \ldots, R_m$, and $W \subseteq 2^H$. In any transition step in Π we first select a set of labels $U \in W$ and then apply a non-empty multiset R of rules such that all the labels of these rules in R are in U (and in the case of maximal parallelism, the set R cannot be extended by any further rule with a label from U so that the obtained multiset of rules would still be applicable to the objects existing in the membrane regions $1, \ldots, m$). The families of sets $Y(\Pi)$, $Y \in \{N, Ps\}$, computed by P systems with label selection with at most m membranes and rules of type X as well as $card\,(W) \leq k$ are denoted by $Y_{\gamma,\delta}OP_m\,(X, ls_k)$, for any $\gamma \in \{gen, acc\}$ and $\delta \in \{sequ, asyn, maxpar\}$.

For all variants of P systems using rules of some type X, we may consider systems containing only rules of the form $u \to v$ where $u \in O$ and $v = (b_1, tar) \ldots (b_k, tar)$ with $b_i \in O$ and $tar \in \{here, out, in\}$ or $tar \in \{here, out\} \cup \{in_j \mid j \in H\}$, $1 \leq i \leq k$, i.e., in each rule there is only one target for all objects b_i; if catalytic rules are considered, then we request the rules to be of the form $ca \to c\,(b_1, tar) \ldots (b_k, tar)$. For a rule $u \to (b_1, tar) \ldots (b_k, tar)$ we then write $u \to (b_1, \ldots, b_k; tar)$, for a rule $ca \to c\,(b_1, tar) \ldots (b_k, tar)$ we write $ca \to c(b_1, \ldots, b_k; tar)$.

A *P system with target selection* contains only these forms of rules; moreover, in each computation step, for each membrane region i we choose a multiset of rules from R_i having the same target indication tar; for different membrane regions these targets may be different; moreover, the total multiset obtained in this way must not be empty. The families of sets $Y_{\gamma,\delta}\,(\Pi)$, $Y \in \{N, Ps\}$, computed by P systems with target selection with at most m membranes and rules of type X are denoted by $Y_{\gamma,\delta}OP_m\,(X, ts)$, for any $\gamma \in \{gen, acc\}$ and $\delta \in \{sequ, asyn, maxpar\}$.

Remark 1. P systems with target selection were first defined in [11], but there the chosen multiset of rules for each R_i had to be non-empty if possible. In this paper, we only require the total multiset of rules, obtained by choosing multisets of rules in each R_i with the results going to a chosen target membrane, to be non-empty. Yet as in [11] we assume that when choosing the target *in* all objects are sent to just one selected inner membrane.

We may extend rules of the form $u \to (b_1, \ldots, b_k; tar)$ to rules of the form $u \to (b_1, \ldots, b_k; Tar)$ where Tar is a finite set of targets, thus obtaining *P systems with target agreement*. In each computation step, for each membrane we first choose a target tar and then a multiset of rules of the form $u \to (b_1, \ldots, b_k; Tar)$

with $tar \in Tar$ – again, for different membranes these targets may be different. The families of sets $Y_{\gamma,\delta}(\Pi)$, $Y \in \{N, Ps\}$, computed by P systems with target agreement with at most m membranes and rules of type X are denoted by $Y_{\gamma,\delta}OP_m(X, ta)$, for any $\gamma \in \{gen, acc\}$ and $\delta \in \{sequ, asyn, maxpar\}$.

P systems with target agreement have the same computational power as P systems with target selection, as proved in the following theorem, yet they allow for a more compact description of rules as we will see in Subsection 3.2.

Theorem 1. *For any type of rules X, any $\gamma \in \{gen, acc\}$, any derivation mode $\delta \in \{sequ, asyn, maxpar\}$, any $Y \in \{N, Ps\}$, and any $m \in \mathbb{N}$, we have*

$$Y_{\gamma,\delta}OP_m(X, ta) = Y_{\gamma,\delta}OP_m(X, ts).$$

Proof. Given a P system with *target selection*

$$\Pi = (O, \mu, w_1, \ldots, w_m, R_1, \ldots, R_m, f)$$

we can also interpret Π as a P system

$$\Pi' = (O, \mu, w_1, \ldots, w_m, R'_1, \ldots, R'_m, f)$$

with *target agreement* by replacing each rule $u \to (b_1, \ldots, b_k; tar)$ in any of the sets R_i, $1 \leq i \leq m$, by the corresponding rule $u \to (b_1, \ldots, b_k; \{tar\})$ in R'_i; for catalytic rules, this means replacing $ca \to c(b_1, \ldots, b_k; tar)$ by $ca \to c(b_1, \ldots, b_k; \{tar\})$ in R'_i. Obviously, $Y_{\gamma,\delta}(\Pi) = Y_{\gamma,\delta}(\Pi')$.

On the other hand, given a P system

$$\Pi' = (O, \mu, w_1, \ldots, w_m, R'_1, \ldots, R'_m, f)$$

with *target agreement* we immediately get the corresponding P system with *target selection*

$$\Pi = (O, \mu, w_1, \ldots, w_m, R_1, \ldots, R_m, f)$$

such that $Y_{\gamma,\delta}(\Pi) = Y_{\gamma,\delta}(\Pi')$: for each rule $u \to (b_1, \ldots, b_k; Tar) \in R'_i$ or $ca \to c(b_1, \ldots, b_k; Tar) \in R'_i$ we take all the rules $u \to (b_1, \ldots, b_k; tar)$ or $ca \to c(b_1, \ldots, b_k; tar)$ with $tar \in Tar$ into R_i. □

Whereas for most of the other variants considered in this paper the so-called *flattening* procedure (for more details see [11]) allows for finding equivalent systems with only one membrane, for P systems with target selection or target agreement the membrane structure usually plays an essential rôle.

For any of the families of (vectors of) natural numbers $Y_{\gamma,\delta}OP_m(X)$ we will add subscript k at the end to indicate that only systems with at most k rules are considered, i.e., we write $Y_{\gamma,\delta}OP_m(X)_k$. If any of the finite parameters like m and k is unbounded, we replace it by $*$ or even simply omit it.

3   Examples for P Systems with a Small Number of Rules

In this section, we give examples for P systems with a very small number of rules accepting or generating a non-semilinear set (of vectors) of natural numbers. In [2], most of the examples comprised in the following table were elaborated in detail; for the models not defined above and the examples for these models, we refer the reader to this paper.

Table 1. Examples for using n rules in specific models of P systems

n	models
1	– deterministic cooperative rules, accepting numbers with a special (non-standard) halting and accepting condition
	– non-cooperative rules with target agreement, generating numbers
2	– non-cooperative rules with target selection, generating numbers
	– non-cooperative rules with label selection, generating numbers
	– non-cooperative rules with tables, generating numbers
	– non-cooperative rules with membrane dissolution, generating numbers
	– non-cooperative rules in active membranes with two polarizations, generating numbers
	– non-cooperative rules with one inhibitor, generating numbers
3	– non-deterministic cooperative rules, accepting numbers
	– symport/antiport rules of weight ≤ 2 and size ≤ 4, accepting numbers
	– non-cooperative rules with one promoter, generating numbers
4	– purely catalytic rules with one bi-stable catalyst, generating vectors
	– symport/antiport rules of weight ≤ 2 and size ≤ 3, accepting numbers
5	– non-cooperative rules with promoters/inhibitors, generating numbers
9	– [purely] catalytic rules with one bi-stable catalyst and toxic objects, generating numbers
11	– (purely) catalytic rules with two (three) catalysts and toxic objects, generating vectors
12	– [purely] catalytic rules with one bi-stable catalyst, generating numbers
14	– (purely) catalytic rules with two (three) catalysts, generating vectors
17	– (purely) catalytic rules with two (three) catalysts and toxic objects, generating numbers
23	– (purely) catalytic rules with five (seven) catalysts, generating numbers
29	– (purely) catalytic rules with two (three), generating numbers

3.1   Accepting P Systems

Consider the P system

$$\Pi_1 = (O = \{a, s\}, \Sigma = \{a\}, \mu = [\ ]_1, w_1 = \lambda, R_1, f = 1) \text{ where}$$
$$R_1 = \{aa \to a, \ a \to s, \ ss \to ss\}.$$

In each derivation step, Π_1 halves (part of) the objects a, renaming the rest of objects a into s. If more than one s is produced, an infinite computation is forced due to the rule $ss \to ss$. The only way to produce not more than one s is to always have even multiplicity of objects a until it reaches the last one; hence, we conclude $mL_{acc,maxpar}(\Pi_1) = \{a^{2^n} \mid n \geq 0\} \cup \{\lambda\}$.

This accepting P system Π_1 has 3 cooperative rules, i.e., we have

$$\{2^n \mid n \geq 0\} \cup \{0\} \in N_{acc,maxpar}OP_1(coo)_3.$$

It is well-known that P systems with cooperative rules are computationally complete. The smallest known universal one has 23 rules, see [6].

3.2 Generating by Doubling in the Maximally Parallel Mode

This section contains models of P systems with "mass influence", where something can simultaneously affect (directly or indirectly) an unbounded number of copies of specific objects (e.g., target agreement, target selection, label selection, tables, membrane dissolution). In that way we obtain tiny P systems using massive parallelism for repeated doubling, and using one of the effects mentioned above to halt.

P Systems with Target Agreement or Target Selection. We first consider the case of *target agreement* which allows for the smallest descriptional complexity with only one rule:

$$\Pi_2 = (O = \{a\}, \mu = [\,]_1, w_1 = a, R_1, f = 0) \text{ with}$$
$$R_1 = \{a \to (aa, \{here, out\})\}.$$

Π_2 doubles the number of objects each turn that the objects stay in the skin membrane by choosing the target *here*. At some moment, all objects agree in the target destination *out* thus moving all objects a into the environment where no rule can be applied any more. At any moment of the computation, all objects simultaneously must agree in the same destination, effectively choosing between continuing the doubling or halting.

If we resolve the rule $a \to (aa, \{here, out\})$ into its two corresponding rules $a \to (aa, here)$ and $a \to (aa, out)$, we immediately get the P system with *target selection*

$$\Pi_3 = (O = \{a\}, \mu = [\;]_1, w_1 = a, R_1, f = 0) \text{ with}$$
$$R_1 = \{a \to (aa, here), a \to (aa, out)\}.$$

In sum, we therefore infer

$$\{2^n \mid n \geq 1\} \in N_{gen,maxpar}OP_1(ncoo, ta)_1 \cap N_{gen,maxpar}OP_1(ncoo, ts)_2.$$

P Systems with Tables. The following P system with tables of rules (*tabled P system*) needs only 2 rules and is closely related to the P system with target selection described above.

$$\Pi_4 = (O = \{a\}, \mu = [\;]_1, w_1 = b, R_1, f = 0) \text{ with}$$
$$R_1 = \{T_1 = \{a \to aa, here\}, T_2 = \{a \to a, out\}\}.$$

Π_4 doubles the multiplicity of objects a each step as long as it uses table T_1. At any time, if after $n \geq 0$ such steps the second table T_2 is chosen, all objects a are sent out to the environment and the computation halts, having generated a^{2^n}.

We also note that the second table (and thus the table feature) is not needed under a specific variant of halting called *unconditional halting* which resembles the L systems (Lindenmayer systems) mode of taking the result; P systems using non-cooperative rules and taking the results after each computation step (i.e., with unconditional halting) were considered in [7] and shown to characterize *PsET0L*.

In sum, we have obtained

$$\{2^n \mid n \geq 0\} \in N_{gen,maxpar}OP_1\,(ncoo, table_2)_2 \cap N_{gen-u,maxpar}OP_1\,(ncoo)_1\,,$$

where $gen - u$ indicates that we take the results generated in the output membrane after every computation step (i.e., with unconditional halting) and $table_2$ indicates that we are using 2 tables.

P Systems with Label Selection. Instead of selecting different targets, in the P system with label selection

$$\Pi_5 = (O = \{a\}, \mu = [\ ]_1, w_1 = a, R_1, H = \{1, 2\}, W = \{\{1\}, \{2\}\}, f = 0) \text{ with}$$
$$R_1 = \{1 : a \to (aa, here), 2 : a \to (aa, out)\},$$

we select different labels to be able to choose when to send out all objects from the skin membrane to the environment; hence, we have

$$\{2^n \mid n \geq 1\} \in N_{gen,maxpar}OP_1\,(ncoo, ls_2)_2\,.$$

We will return to this model of P systems with label selection later when considering catalytic rules only.

3.3 P Systems with Membrane Dissolution

When using only non-cooperative rules we cannot obtain computational completeness with the additional feature of membrane dissolution; yet, in [9] an infinite hierarchy with respect to the number of membranes was established using membrane dissolution in a linear membrane structure. Now consider

$$\Pi_6 = (O = \{a\}, \mu = [\ [\ ]_2\ ]_1, w_1 = \lambda, w_2 = a, R_1 = \emptyset, R_2, f = 1)$$

where $R_2 = \{a \to aa,\ a \to aa\delta\}$. Π_6 doubles the number of objects each turn when only using the rule $a \to aa$ until at some moment the inner membrane may be dissolved by, at least for one a, using the dissolution rule $a \to aa\delta$, thus stopping the computation. This generative system has 2 non-cooperative rules and membrane dissolution and computes $mL_{gen,maxpar}(\Pi_6) = \{a^{2^n} \mid n \geq 0\}$, i.e.,

$$\{2^n \mid n \geq 0\} \in N_{gen,maxpar}OP_2\,(ncoo, \delta)_2\,.$$

4   P Systems with Catalysts

P systems with catalysts were already considered in the originating papers for membrane systems, see [15]. In [10], two (three) catalysts were shown to be sufficient for getting computational completeness with (purely) catalytic P systems. Whether or not one (two) catalyst(s) might already be enough to obtain computational completeness, is still one of the most challenging open problems in the area of P systems. We only know that purely catalytic P systems (working in the maximally parallel mode) with only one catalyst simply correspond to sequential P systems with only one membrane, hence, to multiset rewriting systems with context-free rules, and therefore can only generate linear sets.

Using additional control mechanisms as, for example, priorities or promoters/inhibitors, P systems with only one catalyst can be shown to be computationally complete, e.g., see Chapter 4 of [17]. On the other hand, additional features for the catalyst may be taken into account; for example, we may use bi-stable catalysts (catalysts switching between two different states) as will be considered next.

4.1   Generating a Non-semilinear Number Set with One Bi-Stable Catalyst

Throughout the rest of the paper, we will focus on the generative case, which – in general – is more difficult.

$$\Pi_7 = (O, C = \{c, \bar{c}\}, \mu = [\ ]_1, w_1 = \bar{c}pa, R_1, f = 1) \text{ where}$$
$$O = \{c, \bar{c}\} \cup \{a, b\} \cup \{p, q, s, t\} \cup \{\#\},$$
$$R_1 = \{ca \rightarrow \bar{c}bb,\ s \rightarrow t,\ \bar{c}t \rightarrow cs,\ ct \rightarrow \bar{c}p,\ t \rightarrow \#,\ \# \rightarrow \#,$$
$$\bar{c}b \rightarrow ca,\ p \rightarrow q,\ cq \rightarrow \bar{c}p,\ \bar{c}q \rightarrow cs,\ \bar{c}p \rightarrow \bar{c},\ q \rightarrow \#\}.$$

Π_7 works in two phases. In phase 1, in addition to the bi-stable catalyst toggling between c and $\bar{c}$, a state object is present, toggling between s and t. Every two steps, one a is replaced by bb with c changing to $\bar{c}$ while s changes to t; then $\bar{c}t$ are reset to cs. If objects a are no longer present, c is idle for one step, and then ct change to $\bar{c}p$, entering phase 2.

In phase 2, the state object toggles between p and q. Every two steps, one b is renamed into a with $\bar{c}$ changing to c while p changes to q; then cq are reset to $\bar{c}p$. If objects b are no longer present, then either $\bar{c}$ erases p thus causing the system to halt or else $\bar{c}$ is idle for one step and in the succeeding step $\bar{c}q$ change to cs thus returning to phase 1.

In both phases, if the bi-stable catalyst "chooses" a "wrong" rule, then either t or q are left to themselves, forcing the system to use $t \rightarrow \#$ or $q \rightarrow \#$, thus entering an infinite computation, so this computation does not lead to a result any more. Hence, in sum we obtain $mL_{gen,maxpar}(\Pi_7) = \{a^{2^n} \mid n \geq 0\}$.

Π_7 is a purely catalytic P system with only one bi-stable catalyst and 12 rules, hence, we have

$$\{2^n \mid n \geq 0\} \in N_{gen,maxpar}OP_1\,(2cat_1)_{12}.$$

The computational completeness of P systems with one bi-stable catalyst working in the maximally parallel mode was established in [3].

4.2   P Systems with Toxic Objects – a Special Variant of Halting for Avoiding the Trap Symbol

Throughout this section, a main part of the constructions (which is inevitable for proving computational completeness, too) is the introduction of the trap symbol # in case the derivation goes the wrong way and by the rule $\# \rightarrow \#$ (or $c\# \rightarrow c\#$ with a catalyst c) guaranteeing the derivation never to halt. Yet most of these rules can be avoided if we apply a specific *new halting strategy* allowing the system to halt without yielding a result. This somehow corresponds to the case of a Turing machine halting its computation in a non-final state, and as for Turing machines, where each such computation halting in a non-final state can be transformed into an infinite computation, in P systems usually the trap rules perform this task to yield an infinite computation.

This specific *new halting strategy* allowing the system to halt without yielding a result can be defined in various ways, e.g., with a special symbol (like the trap symbol) appearing in the configuration. As our main goal now is to save as many rules as possible, we want to stop one step earlier, i.e., before the trap symbol would be introduced. Hence, we specify a specific subset of *toxic* objects O_{tox}; the P system is only allowed to continue a computation from a configuration C by using an applicable multiset of rules covering all copies of objects from O_{tox} occurring in C; moreover, if there exists no multiset of applicable rules covering all toxic objects, the whole computation having yielded the configuration C is abandoned, i.e., no results can be obtained from this computation.

This idea somehow resembles the strategy of using priorities with having the rules involving the objects from O_{tox} having priority over other rules. Yet this strategy is both weaker and stronger compared with the strategy of priority on rules: on one hand, we can only specify priorities with respect to the objects from O_{tox}; on the other hand, if not all copies of *toxic* objects from O_{tox} can be covered by any multiset of rules, we stop without getting a result, whereas in the case of priorities any multiset of rules respecting the priority relation can be used to continue the computation.

For any variant of P systems, we add the set of *toxic* objects O_{tox} and in the specification of the families of sets of (vectors of) numbers generated/accepted by P systems with toxic objects using rules of type X we add the subscript tox to O, thus obtaining the families $Y_{\gamma, maxpar} O_{tox} P_m (X)$, for any $\gamma \in \{gen, acc\}$ and $m \geq 1$.

Hence, for the P system with one bi-stable catalyst Π_7 elaborated in the preceding subsection, we obtain the corresponding P system Π_8 with toxic objects

$$\Pi_8 = (O, C = \{c, \bar{c}\}, O_{tox}, \mu = [\ ]_1, w_1 = \bar{c}pa, R_1, f = 1) \text{ where}$$
$$O = \{c, \bar{c}\} \cup \{a, b\} \cup \{p, q, s, t\},$$
$$O_{tox} = \{q, t\},$$
$$R_1 = \{ca \rightarrow \bar{c}bb,\ s \rightarrow t,\ \bar{c}t \rightarrow cs,\ ct \rightarrow \bar{c}p,$$
$$\bar{c}b \rightarrow ca,\ p \rightarrow q,\ cq \rightarrow \bar{c}p,\ \bar{c}q \rightarrow cs,\ \bar{c}p \rightarrow \bar{c}\}.$$

According to the arguments established in the preceding subsection, we immediately infer $mL_{gen,maxpar}(\Pi_8) = \{a^{2^n} \mid n \geq 0\}$. This system now does not need more than 9 rules, and therefore we have

$$\{2^n \mid n \geq 0\} \in N_{gen,maxpar}O_{tox}P_1\,(2cat_1)_9\,.$$

4.3   General Results for (Purely) Catalytic P Systems with Toxic Objects

Looking closer into the computational completeness proofs for catalytic P systems given in [10], we see that the only non-cooperative rules used in the proofs given there are rules involving the trap symbol. When going to purely catalytic P systems, we realize that all rules involving the trap symbol can be assigned to one additional catalyst; for example, to generate any recursively enumerable set of natural numbers we need two catalysts for catalytic P systems and three catalysts for purely catalytic P systems.

As the proof of the basic result

$$PsRE = Ps_{gen,maxpar}OP_1(cat_2) = Ps_{gen,maxpar}OP_1(pcat_3)$$

also is the basis of the construction for the (purely) catalytic P system elaborated in Subsection 4.6, we first recall the main ideas for the simulations of ADD- and SUB-instructions of a register machine $M = (d, B, l_0, h, R)$.

For every instruction label $j \in B$ of the register machine to be simulated two symbols are used to keep the two main catalysts c_1, c_2 busy, starting with $p_j\tilde{p}_j$. At the end, for the halting label h we use the two rules $c_1 p_h \rightarrow c_1$ and $c_2\tilde{p}_h \rightarrow c_2$ to stop the derivation in case the simulation has succeeded to be correct. The number n_r stored in register r is represented by n_r copies of the symbol a_r.

Each ADD-instruction $j : (ADD(r), k, l)$, for $r \in \{1, 2, \ldots, d\}$, can easily be simulated by the rules $c_1 p_j \rightarrow c_1 a_r p_k \tilde{p}_k$, $c_1 p_j \rightarrow c_1 a_r p_l \tilde{p}_l$, and $c_2 \tilde{p}_j \rightarrow c_2$.

Each SUB-instruction $j : (SUB(r), k, l)$, only necessary to be considered for $r \in 1, 2$, is simulated in four steps as shown in the table listed below:

Simulation of the SUB-instruction $j : (SUB(r), k, l)$ if	
register r is not empty	register r is empty
$c_r p_j \rightarrow c_r \hat{p}_j \hat{p}_j'$	$c_r p_j \rightarrow c_r \bar{p}_j \bar{p}_j' \bar{p}_j''$
$c_{3-r}\tilde{p}_j \rightarrow c_{3-r}$	$c_{3-r}\tilde{p}_j \rightarrow c_{3-r}$
$c_r a_r \rightarrow c_r a_r'$	$c_r \bar{p}_j \rightarrow c_r$
$c_{3-r}\hat{p}_j \rightarrow c_{3-r}$	$c_{3-r}\bar{p}_j'' \rightarrow c_{3-r}p_j''$
$c_r a_r' \rightarrow c_r a_r''$	
$c_{3-r}\hat{p}_j' \rightarrow c_{3-r}\hat{p}_j''$	$c_{3-r}p_j'' \rightarrow c_{3-r}p_j'$
$c_r \hat{p}_j'' \rightarrow c_r p_k \tilde{p}_k$	$c_r p_j' \rightarrow c_r p_l \tilde{p}_l$
$c_{3-r}a_r'' \rightarrow c_{3-r}$	$c_{3-r}\bar{p}_j' \rightarrow c_{3-r}$

In addition, we take the rule $c_r \hat{p}_j' \rightarrow c_r \#$ and special trap rules to guarantee that in case the guess whether the contents of register r is empty or not was wrong, the derivation enters an infinite loop with the rule $\# \to \#$ in the catalytic case or $c_3\# \to c_3\#$ in the purely catalytic case. These objects x for which we have such trap rules $x \to \#$ in the catalytic case or $c_3x \to c_3\#$ in the purely catalytic case, are a_1', a_1'', a_2', a_2'' and, for every label j of a SUB-instruction $j : (SUB(r), k, l)$, the objects $p_j, p_j', p_j'', \hat{p}_j, \hat{p}_j'', \tilde{p}_j, \bar{p}_j, \bar{p}_j''$, and for every label j of an ADD-instruction $j : (ADD(r), k, l)$ the objects $p_j, \tilde{p}_j$ as well as the objects $p_h, \tilde{p}_h$ for the HALT-instruction. We should like to mention that these trap rules for the objects $p_j, \tilde{p}_j$ coming from the ADD-instructions $j : (ADD(r), k, l)$ and the objects $p_h, \tilde{p}_h$ for the HALT-instruction were forgotten to be included in the proof of the special Corollary 8 in [10], whereas in the more general Theorem 4, due to writing down the range of the trap rules in a different way, these trap rules for the symbols indicating an ADD-instruction and the HALT-instruction were included correctly.

The construction shown above strictly follows the proof elaborated in [10]; yet we observe that many symbols are just needed to keep one of the two catalysts busy for one step with being erased or else having to evolve to the trap symbol. Hence, every symbol x for which we only have a rule $c_i x \to c_i \lambda$, $i \in \{1, 2\}$, can be replaced by just one symbol d_i. In addition, for p_j we now always use c_1 and for $\tilde{p}_j$ (which in fact now is replaced by d_2) we now always use c_2. Finally, we can also replace all symbols $\bar{p}_j'$ by just one variable $\hat{d}_{3-r}$.

In that way, we obtain the following tables of rules for the simulation of ADD-instructions and SUB-instructions:

Simulation of the ADD-instruction $j : (ADD(r), k, l)$
$c_1 p_j \to c_1 a_r p_k d_2$, $c_1 p_j \to c_1 a_r p_k d_2$; $c_2 d_2 \to c_2$.

The table for a SUB-instruction now contains several identical entries:

Simulation of the SUB-instruction $j : (SUB(r), k, l)$ if

register r is not empty	register r is empty
$c_1 p_j \to c_1 d_{3-r} \hat{p}_j'$	$c_1 p_j \to c_1 d_r \hat{d}_{3-r} \bar{p}_j''$
$c_2 d_2 \to c_2$	$c_2 d_2 \to c_2$
$c_r a_r \to c_r a_r'$	$c_r d_r \to c_r$
$c_{3-r} d_{3-r} \to c_{3-r}$	$c_{3-r} \bar{p}_j'' \to c_{3-r} p_j''$
$c_r a_r' \to c_r d_{3-r}$	
$c_{3-r} \hat{p}_j' \to c_{3-r} \hat{p}_j''$	$c_{3-r} p_j'' \to c_{3-r} p_j'$
$c_r \hat{p}_j'' \to c_r p_k d_2$	$c_r p_j' \to c_r p_l d_2$
$c_{3-r} d_{3-r} \to c_{3-r}$	$c_{3-r} \hat{d}_{3-r} \to c_{3-r}$

The zero-test case now can be reduced considerably to only two steps:

$c_1 p_j \to c_1 \bar{p}_j$
$c_2 d_2 \to c_2$
c_r remains idle
$c_{3-r} \bar{p}_j \to c_{3-r} p_l d_2$

Moreover, we still have the rule $c_r \hat{p}_j' \to c_r \#$ for checking the correct simulation of the decrement case. For x being an element of the following set, we take the trap rules $c_3 x \rightarrow c_3 \#$ in the purely catalytic case and the corresponding rules $x \rightarrow \#$ in the catalytic case:

$$\{\#, d_1, d_2, c_1', c_2'\} \cup \{p_j \mid j : (ADD(a), k, l)\} \cup \{p_j, \hat{p}_j'', \bar{p}_j \mid j : (SUB(a), k, l)\}$$

In the case of catalytic P systems, the only non-cooperative rules are these trap rules, and in the case of purely catalytic P systems, the trap rules, and only those, are associated with the third catalyst c_3. If we take exactly those objects for which such a trap rule exists as *toxic objects* and omit all trap rules, then we immediately infer the following computational completeness result, where O_{tox} indicates that we are using toxic objects:

Theorem 2. $PsRE = PsO_{tox}P_{gen,maxpar}(cat_2) = PsO_{tox}P_{gen,maxpar}(pcat_2).$

In general, for all the results elaborated in [10] we obtain similar results: when using toxic objects, then the construction for obtaining the results for catalytic and purely catalytic P systems coincide, as for example in the preceding theorem, where in both cases we only need two catalysts (which number currently is assumed to be the minimal one). Moreover, the simulation becomes somehow deterministic, as only the correct simulation paths survive; in that sense, deterministic register machines can be simulated by *deterministic* (purely) catalytic P systems with toxic objects.

4.4   Generating a Non-semilinear Vector Set with a (Purely) Catalytic P System

We now construct (purely) catalytic P systems generating the non-semilinear set of pairs of natural numbers $\{(n, m) \mid n \leq m \leq 2^n\}$. First we define the purely catalytic P system Π_9 generating $\{a_3{}^n a_4{}^m \mid n \leq m \leq 2^n\}$.

$$\Pi_9 = (O, C = \{c_1, c_2, c_3\}, \mu = [\ ]_1, w_1 = c_1 c_2 c_3 a_1 p_1 d_1 d_2, R_1, f = 1) \text{ where}$$
$$O = \{c_1, c_2, c_3\} \cup \{a_1, a_2, a_3, a_4, d_1, d_2, p_1, p_2, \#\},$$
$$R_1 = \{c_1 a_1 \rightarrow c_1, \ c_1 p_2 \rightarrow c_1 a_1 a_4 p_2, \ c_1 p_2 \rightarrow c_1 a_1 a_3 a_4 p_1, \ c_1 p_2 \rightarrow c_1 a_3 a_4,$$
$$c_2 a_2 \rightarrow c_2, \ c_2 p_1 \rightarrow c_2 a_2 a_2 p_1, \ c_2 p_1 \rightarrow c_2 a_2 a_2 p_2,$$
$$c_1 d_2 \rightarrow c_1, \ c_2 d_1 \rightarrow c_2, \ c_1 d_1 \rightarrow c_1 \#, \ c_2 d_2 \rightarrow c_2 \#,$$
$$c_3 p_1 \rightarrow c_3 \#, \ c_3 p_2 \rightarrow c_3 \#, \ c_3 \# \rightarrow c_3 \#\}.$$

This purely catalytic system has 14 rules, and with just omitting the third catalyst we obtain the corresponding catalytic P system having 14 rules, too. But with using toxic objects we can save some of (but again not all) the rules introducing the trap symbol $\#$, i.e., we obtain the purely catalytic P system with toxic objects Π_{10} with only 11 rules:

$$\Pi_{10} = (O, C = \{c_1, c_2\}, O_{tox}, \mu = [\ ]_1, w_1 = c_1 c_2 a_1 p_1 d_1 d_2, R_1, f = 1) \text{ where}$$
$$O = \{c_1, c_2\} \cup \{a_1, a_2, a_3, a_4, d_1, d_2, p_1, p_2, \#\},$$
$$O_{tox} = \{p_1, p_2, \#\},$$
$$R_1 = \{c_1 a_1 \rightarrow c_1, \ c_1 p_2 \rightarrow c_1 a_1 a_4 p_2, \ c_1 p_2 \rightarrow c_1 a_1 a_3 a_4 p_1, \ c_1 p_2 \rightarrow c_1 a_3 a_4,$$
$$c_2 a_2 \rightarrow c_2, \ c_2 p_1 \rightarrow c_2 a_2 a_2 p_1, \ c_2 p_1 \rightarrow c_2 a_2 a_2 p_2,$$
$$c_1 d_2 \rightarrow c_1, \ c_2 d_1 \rightarrow c_2, \ c_1 d_1 \rightarrow c_1 \#, \ c_2 d_2 \rightarrow c_2 \#\}.$$

In all cases, the derivations work as follows: the objects p_1, p_2 work as states, and the objects d_i, $i \in \{1,2\}$, are used to check that the corresponding catalyst c_i is busy at some stage, otherwise these objects d_i force the system to enter an infinite loop with the trap rules or to *kill* the derivation.

In state p_1, we decrement (the number of objects representing) register 1 by the rule $c_1 a_1 \to c_1$ and double their number by applying the rule $c_2 p_1 \to c_2 a_2 a_2 p_1$ in parallel. By using the rule $c_2 p_1 \to c_2 a_2 a_2 p_2$ instead, we change to state p_2, yet without checking whether register 1 is already empty. In case the latter rule is used too late, i.e., if no object a_1 is present any more, then we have to use the trap rule $c_1 d_1 \to c_1 \#$.

In state p_2, we decrement (the number of objects representing) register 2 by the rule $c_2 a_2 \to c_2$ and copy (the contents of) this register to register 1, at the same time adding this number to register 4 by using the rule $c_1 p_2 \to c_1 a_1 a_4 p_2$ in parallel. If this rule is used until no object a_2 is present any more, then we have to use the trap rule $c_2 d_2 \to c_2 \#$. If instead we use the rule $c_1 p_2 \to c_1 a_1 a_3 a_4 p_1$ in time, we switch back to state 1, at the same moment incrementing register 3, yet again without checking register a_2 for being zero. By using the rule $c_1 p_2 \to c_1 a_3 a_4$, we end this cycling between states p_1 and p_2, i.e., now both p_1 and p_2 are not present any more, and the two objects d_1 and d_2 have to be eliminated, which can be achieved by using the two rules $c_1 d_2 \to c_1$ and $c_2 d_1 \to c_2$ in parallel.

At the end of a computation, even if the two objects d_1 and d_2 have already been deleted, the catalysts c_1 and c_2 will still be active to delete all the remaining objects a_1 and a_2, hence, at the end only copies of objects a_3 and a_4 are present any more. In sum, we conclude that $Ps(\{a_3{}^n a_4{}^m \mid n \le m \le 2^n\})$ belongs to

$$Ps_{gen,maxpar} OP_1(pcat_3)_{14} \cap Ps_{gen,maxpar} O_{tox} P_1(pcat_2)_{11}. \quad \bullet$$

4.5   Purely Catalytic P systems with Label Selection

If we only allow purely catalytic rules with two catalysts, P systems with label selection can apply at most two rules in each derivation step and thus show a behavior rather similar to the way matrix grammars in binary normal form work, i.e., the set of labels defines the matrix of the two rules to be applied together.

We now construct a purely catalytic P system with label selection with two catalysts which generates the non-semilinear set of natural numbers $\{2^n \mid n \ge 1\}$.

$\Pi_{11} = (O, C = \{c_1, c_2\}, \mu = [\ ]_1, w_1 = c_1 c_2 p a_1, R_1, H, W, f = 1)$ where
$\quad O = \{c_1, c_2\} \cup \{a_1, a_2, a_3, p, q, r, \#\},$
$\quad H = \{i \mid 1 \le i \le 7\} \cup \{i' \mid i \in \{1,3,6\}\} \cup \{\#_{a_1}, \#_{a_2}, \#_p, \#_q, \#_r, \#_\#\},$
$\quad W = \{\{1, 1', \#_q, \#_r\}, \{2, \#_{a_1}, \#_q, \#_r\}, \{3, 3', \#_p, \#_r\}, \{4, \#_{a_2}, \#_p, \#_r\}$
$\qquad \{5, \#_{a_1}, \#_q, \#_r\}, \{6, 6', \#_p, \#_q\}, \{7, \#_{a_2}, \#_p, \#_q, \#_\#\}\},$
$\quad R_1 = \{1 : c_2 p \to c_2 p, \ 1' : c_1 a_1 \to c_1 a_2 a_2, \ 2 : c_2 p \to c_2 q,$
$\qquad 3 : c_2 q \to c_2 q, \ 3' : c_1 a_2 \to c_1 a_1, \ 4 : c_2 q \to c_2 p,$
$\qquad 5 : c_2 p \to c_2 r, \ 6 : c_2 r \to c_2 r, \ 6' : c_1 a_2 \to c_1 a_3,$
$\qquad 7 : c_2 r \to c_2, \ \#_{a_1} : c_1 a_1 \to c_1 \#, \ \#_{a_2} : c_1 a_2 \to c_1 \#, \ \#_\# : c_2 \# \to c_2 \#,$
$\qquad \#_p : c_2 p \to c_2 \#, \ \#_q : c_2 q \to c_2 \#, \ \#_r : c_2 r \to c_2 \#\}.$

In "state" p we double the number of symbols a_1, and in "state" q we rename them back from a_2 to a_1; in "state" r we rename every symbol a_2 to the output symbol a_3. The trap rules $\#_p, \#_q, \#_r$ guarantee that the second rule associated with the catalyst c_1 is only carried out with the right state symbol evolving with c_2. The system in total has 16 rules. We can avoid the trap rules $\#_p, \#_q, \#_r, \#_\#$ by using toxic objects, in fact exactly $p, q, r, \#$, thus obtaining a system with only 12 rules:

$$\Pi'_{11} = (O, C = \{c_1, c_2\}, \mu = [\ ]_1, w_1 = c_1 c_2 p a_1, R'_1, H', W', f = 1) \text{ where}$$
$$O = \{c_1, c_2\} \cup \{a_1, a_2, a_3, p, q, r\},$$
$$O_{tox} = \{p, q, r, \#\},$$
$$H' = \{i \mid 1 \leq i \leq 7\} \cup \{i' \mid i \in \{1, 3, 6\}\} \cup \{\#_{a_1}, \#_{a_2}\},$$
$$W' = \{\{1, 1'\}, \{2, \#_{a_1}\}, \{3, 3'\}, \{4, \#_{a_2}\}, \{5, \#_{a_1}\}, \{6, 6'\}, \{7, \#_{a_2}\}\},$$
$$R'_1 = \{1 : c_2 p \rightarrow c_2 p, \ 1' : c_1 a_1 \rightarrow c_1 a_2 a_2, \ 2 : c_2 p \rightarrow c_2 q,$$
$$3 : c_2 q \rightarrow c_2 q, \ 3' : c_1 a_2 \rightarrow c_1 a_1, \ 4 : c_2 q \rightarrow c_2 p,$$
$$5 : c_2 p \rightarrow c_2 r, \ 6 : c_2 r \rightarrow c_2 r, \ 6' : c_1 a_2 \rightarrow c_1 a_3,$$
$$7 : c_2 r \rightarrow c_2, \ \#_{a_1} : c_1 a_1 \rightarrow c_1 \#, \ \#_{a_2} : c_1 a_2 \rightarrow c_1 \#\}.$$

In sum, we have $mL_{gen,maxpar}(\Pi_{11}) = mL_{gen,maxpar}(\Pi'_{11}) = \{a_3^{2^n} \mid n \geq 1\}$, hence,

$$\{2^n \mid n \geq 1\} \in N_{gen,maxpar} OP_1(pcat_2, ls)_{16} \cap N_{gen,maxpar} O_{tox} P_1(pcat_2, ls)_{12}.$$

Computational completeness of purely catalytic P systems with label selection was shown in [12]. We here recall this proof for the generating case, but also show how toxic objects influence the descriptional complexity of the constructed P system:

Theorem 3. $PsRE = PsOP_1(pcat_2, ls) = PsO_{tox} P_1(pcat_2, ls)$.

Proof. We first prove the inclusion $PsRE \subseteq PsOP_1(pcat_2, ls)$. Let us consider a deterministic register machine $M = (2 + d, B, l_0, l_h, P)$ with the last d registers containing the output values, and let $A = \{a_1, \ldots, a_{d+2}\}$ be the set of objects for representing the contents of the registers 1 to $d + 2$ of M. We construct the following purely catalytic P system:

$$\Pi = (O, \{c_1, c_2\}, [\ ]_1, c_1 c_2 d l_0, R_1, H, W, 0),$$
$$O = A \cup B \cup \{c_1, c_2, d, \#\},$$
$$H = \{l, l', \#_l \mid l \in B\} \cup \{\#_\alpha \mid \alpha \in \{d, \#\}\} \cup \{l_r^-, \#_{a_r} \mid 1 \leq r \leq 2\};$$

the sets of labels in W and the rules for R_1 are defined as follows:

A. The trap rules are $\#_\# : c_2 \# \rightarrow c_2 \#$ and $\#_d : c_1 d \rightarrow c_1 \#$ as well as $\#_l : c_2 l \rightarrow c_2 \#$ for all $l \in B$ and $\#_{a_r} : c_1 a_r \rightarrow c_1 \#$ for all $a_r, 1 \leq r \leq 2$. Moreover, for every $j \in B$ we define

$$B_\#(j) = \{\#_l \mid l \in B \setminus \{j\}\}.$$

B. Let $l_i : (\text{ADD}\,(r), l_j, l_k)$ be an ADD-instruction in P. Then we introduce the two rules

$$l_i : c_2 l_i \to c_2 l_j a_r \text{ and } l'_i : c_2 l_i \to c_2 l_k a_r$$

and define $\{l_i, l'_i\}$ to be the corresponding set of labels in W. Observe that only one of these rules can be applied at the same computation step in Π. For the output registers r, $2 < r \le d+2$, we replace a_r by (a_r, out).

C. The simulation of a SUB-instruction $l_i : (\text{SUB}\,(r), l_j, l_k)$, for $1 \le r \le 2$, in P is carried out by the following rules and the corresponding sets of labels in W:

For the case that the register r is not empty we take $\{l_i, l_r^-, \#_d\} \cup B_\#\,(l_i)$ into W where

$$l_i : c_2 l_i \to c_2 l_j \text{ and } l_r^- : c_1 a_r \to c_1.$$

If no symbol a_r is present, i.e., if the register r is empty, then the trap symbol $\#$ is introduced by enforcing c_1 to be used with $\#_d : c_1 d \to c_1 \#$; moreover, this set of labels should only be used in the presence of l_i as otherwise c_2 is enforced to be used with $\#_l : c_2 l \to c_2 \#$ for the current label l just being present in the system.

For the case that the register r is empty, we take $\{l'_i, \#_{a_r}\} \cup B_\#\,(l_i)$ into W with the rule

$$l'_i : c_2 l_i \to c_2 l_k.$$

If at least one symbol a_r is present, i.e., if the register r is not empty, then the trap symbol $\#$ is introduced by the enforced application of the rule $\#_{a_r} : c_1 a_r \to c_1 \#$; again this set of labels should only be used in the presence of l_i as otherwise c_2 is enforced to be used with $\#_l : c_2 l \to c_2 \#$ for the current label l just being present in the system.

In both cases, the simulation of the SUB-instruction works correctly if we make the right choice with respect to the current label present in the system and the contents of register r.

D. At the end of a successful computation of the register machine M, all registers r, $1 \le r \le 2$, are empty, and M has reached label l_h. Hence, we finally add $\{l_h, l'_h\} \cup B_\#\,(l_h)$ to W where $l_h : c_2 l_h \to c_2$ and $l'_h : c_1 d \to c_1$. If during the simulation of the instructions of M by Π no trap symbol $\#$ has been generated, the P system Π halts with only the catalysts remaining in the skin region; otherwise, the system enters an infinite loop with the trap rule $\#_\# : c_2 \# \to c_2 \#$ and $\{\#_\#\}$ in W.

In sum, we have shown $L\,(M) = Ps_{gen,maxpar}\,(\Pi)$, which observation completes the first part of the proof.

We now prove the inclusion $PsRE \subseteq PsO_{tox}P_1\,(pcat_2, ls)$ and construct the following purely catalytic P system with toxic objects using the rules already explained above:

$$\Pi' = (O', \{c_1, c_2\}, [\ ]_1, c_1 c_2 d l_0, R'_1, H', W', 0),$$
$$O' = A \cup B \cup \{c_1, c_2, d, \#\},$$
$$O_{tox} = B \cup \{\#\},$$
$$H' = \{l, l' \mid l \in B\} \cup \{l_r^- \mid l_i : (\text{SUB}(r), l_j, l_k) \in P\} \cup \{\#_\alpha \mid \alpha \in \{d, a_1, a_2\}\},$$
$$W' = \{\{l_h, l'_h\}\} \cup \{\{l_i, l''_i\} \mid l_i : (\text{ADD}(r), l_j, l_k) \in P\}$$
$$\cup \{\{l_i, l_r^-, \#_d\}, \{l'_i, \#_{a_r}\} \mid l_i : (\text{SUB}(r), l_j, l_k) \in P\},$$
$$R'_1 = \{l_i : c_2 l_i \to c_2 l_j a_r, l'_i : c_2 l_i \to c_2 l_k a_r \mid l_i : (\text{ADD}(r), l_j, l_k) \in P, 1 \le r \le 2\}$$
$$\cup \{l_i : c_2 l_i \to c_2 l_j (a_r, out), l'_i : c_2 l_i \to c_2 l_k (a_r, out) \mid$$
$$\qquad l_i : (\text{ADD}(r), l_j, l_k) \in P, 2 < r \le d + 2\}$$
$$\cup \{l_i : c_2 l_i \to c_2 l_j, l_r^- : c_1 a_r \to c_1, l'_i : c_2 l_i \to c_2 l_k \mid l_i : (\text{SUB}(r), l_j, l_k) \in P\}$$
$$\cup \{\#_\alpha : c_1 \alpha \to c_1 \# \mid \alpha \in \{d, a_1, a_2\}\} \cup \{l_h : c_2 l_h \to c_2, l'_h : c_1 d \to c_1\}.$$

In this purely catalytic P system with toxic objects, besides the trap symbol itself, exactly the labels from B are toxic, i.e., they must evolve, which guarantees that a set from W' is used with the correct label. This observation concludes the proof showing $L(M) = Ps_{gen,maxpar}(\Pi')$.   □

4.6   Generating Number Sets with (Purely) Catalytic P Systems

We now are going to improve the result from [21], where a catalytic P system with 54 rules was elaborated, generating the non-semilinear set of natural numbers $\{2^n - 2n \mid n \ge 2\}$, and even the improved result from [22] where only 32 rules were needed.

In the following, we construct a (purely) catalytic P system with 29 rules, generating the (standard) non-semilinear set of natural numbers $\{2^n \mid n \ge 1\}$. Yet we will show even more, i.e., our construction works for any set of natural numbers representing a function $g : \mathbb{N} \to \mathbb{N}$ which is computed in r_3 by the following function program (starting with $r_1 = b_0$ and $r_2 = r_3 = 0$), with r_1, r_2, r_3 representing three registers of a register machine, and with the parameters b_0, b_1, b_2, b_3, b_4 being natural numbers, $b_0 \ge 1$:

```
function g(r₃):
1: if r₁ > 0
            then begin DEC(r₁); ADD(1,r₂); goto 1 end
            else goto 2
            orelse begin ADD(b₃,r₃); goto 3 end
2: if r₂ > 0
            then begin DEC(r₂); ADD(b₂,r₁); ADD(b₁,r₃); goto 2 end
            else begin ADD(b₄,r₁); goto 1 end;
3: HALT
endfunction
```

The idea of this program is that in label 1 we copy (register) r_1 to r_2; the notation $\text{DEC}(r)$ means decrementing (register) r by one, whereas $\text{ADD}(k,r)$

means adding k to (register) r. As soon as register r_1 is empty, we switch to label 2 or halt after having added b_3 to (the result register) r_3 before. In label 2, we copy back the value of register r_2 to r_1, but take it b_2 times, at the same time adding b_1 times the value of register r_2 to r_3, and at the end, when r_2 is empty, we add b_4 to r_1.

The structures

i: <u>if</u> $r_i > 0$

$\qquad$ <u>then</u> <u>begin</u> DEC(r_i); ADD$(1,r_{3-i})$; <u>goto</u> i <u>end</u>

$\qquad$ <u>else</u> <u>goto</u> j

in this function program correspond with the following instructions in a register machine program:

$i : (SUB(i), i', j)$
$i' : (ADD(3-i), i, i)$

We now describe the functions computed by specific values of the parameters b_0, b_1, b_2, b_3, b_4; thereby let $f_i(n)$, $i \in \{1, 2, 3\}$, denote the value of register i after n times, $n \geq 0$, having gone through the loops 1 and 2, and $g(n)$ the final value of the function when having gone through the loops 1 and 2 for n times and then having performed loop 1 once more, yet exiting at the end of loop 1 to halt.

In general, we get $f_2(0) = f_2(n) = 0$ for all $n \geq 0$ as well as the system of linear recursions

$$f_1(n+1) = b_2 f_1(n) + b_4,$$
$$f_3(n+1) = f_3(n) + b_1 f_1(n)$$

with $f_1(0) = b_0$ and $f_3(0) = 0$ as well as the final result $g(n) = f_3(n) + b_3$.

Case 1. $b_2 = 1$:

In this case, we get the system of linear recursions

$$f_1(n+1) = f_1(n) + b_4,$$
$$f_3(n+1) = f_3(n) + b_1 f_1(n).$$

Solving these recursions yields $f_1(n) = b_0 + b_4 n$ and, for $n \geq 0$,

$$f_3(n) = f_3(0) + \sum_{i=0}^{n-1} b_1 f_1(i) = b_1 \sum_{i=0}^{n-1} (b_0 + b_4 i)$$
$$= b_1 b_0 n + b_1 b_4 n(n-1)/2$$

hence, $g(0) = b_3$ and, for $n \geq 0$,

$$g(n) = f_3(n) + b_3 = (b_1 b_4/2)n^2 + (b_1 b_0 - b_1 b_4/2)n + b_3,$$

i.e., a quadratic function provided $b_1 \neq 0$ and $b_4 \neq 0$.

As a specific example, for $(b_0, b_1, b_2, b_3, b_4) = (1, 1, 1, 0, 2)$ we obtain $g(n) = n^2$.

Case 2. $b_2 > 1$, $b_1 = 1$, $b_4 = 0$:

In this case, we get the linear recursions

$$f_1(n+1) = b_2 f_1(n),$$
$$f_3(n+1) = f_3(n) + f_1(n)$$

with $f_1(0) = b_0$ and $f_2(0) = f_3(0) = 0$ as well as the final result $g(n) = f_3(n)+b_3$, i.e., for $n \geq 0$ we obtain $f_1(n) = b_0(b_2)^n$ and

$$f_3(n) = f_3(0) + \sum_{i=0}^{n-1} b_0(b_2)^i = b_0 \sum_{i=1}^{n-1}(b_2)^i = b_0(((b_2)^n - 1)/(b_2 - 1))$$

as well as

$$g(n) = f_3(n) + b_3 = b_0(((b_2)^n - 1)/(b_2 - 1)) + b_3.$$

As a specific example, for $(b_0, b_1, b_2, b_3, b_4) = (1, 1, 2, 1, 0)$ we therefore obtain $g(n) = 2^n$.

We now start from the constructions for simulating SUB-instructions as already exhibited in Subsection 4.3. In order to get even more efficient simulations, we save the first steps in a specific way; moreover, every ADD-instruction can be incorporated into the rules of the last steps of the simulations, in a similar way as this was already done in the construction elaborated in [21]. Thus, for the function g with the parameters b_0, b_1, b_2, b_3, b_4 we construct the catalytic P system

$$\Pi_{12}(b_0, b_1, b_2, b_3, b_4) = (O, C = \{c_1, c_2\}, \mu = [\ ]_1, w_1, R_1, f = 1) \text{ where}$$
$$O = \{a_1, a_2, a_3, a_1', a_2', d, \#\}$$
$$\cup \{p_j, p_j', p_j'', \bar{p}_j \mid j \in \{1, 2\}\},$$
$$w_1 = c_1 c_2 (a_1)^{b_0} p_1,$$
$$R_1 = R_{1,c} \cup R_{1,\#},$$

and $R_{1,c}$ consists of the catalytic rules contained in the following two tables:

Simulation of the instructions related with label 1 if

register 1 is not empty	register 1 is empty
$c_1 a_1 \rightarrow c_1 a_1'$	c_1 remains idle
$c_2 p_1 \rightarrow c_2 p_1'$	$c_2 \bar{p}_1 \rightarrow c_2 p_2$
$c_1 a_1' \rightarrow c_1 d$	
$c_2 p_1' \rightarrow c_2 p_1''$	
$c_1 p_1'' \rightarrow c_1 p_1 a_2$ or	
$c_1 p_1'' \rightarrow c_1 \bar{p}_1 a_2$	
$c_2 d \rightarrow c_2$	
halting:	$c_2 \bar{p}_1 \rightarrow c_2 (a_3)^{b_3}$

Simulation of the instructions related with label 2 if

register 2 is not empty	register 1 is empty
$c_2a_2 \rightarrow c_2a_2'$	c_2 remains idle
$c_1p_2 \rightarrow c_1p_2'$	$c_1\bar{p}_2 \rightarrow c_1p_1(a_1)^{b_4}$
$c_2a_2' \rightarrow c_2d$	
$c_1p_2' \rightarrow c_1p_2''$	
$c_2p_2'' \rightarrow c_2p_2(a_1)^{b_2}(a_3)^{b_1}$ or	
$c_2p_2'' \rightarrow c_2\bar{p}_2(a_1)^{b_2}(a_3)^{b_1}$	
$c_1d \rightarrow c_1$	

In addition, we have to add trap rules to guarantee that in case of wrong guesses, the derivation enters an infinite loop with the rule $\# \rightarrow \#$ in the catalytic case (or $c_3\# \rightarrow c_3\#$ in the purely catalytic case). The objects x for which we have such trap rules $x \rightarrow \#$ in the catalytic case (or $c_3x \rightarrow c_3\#$ in the purely catalytic case) are $\#$ and d as well as, for $j \in \{1,2\}$, the objects $a_j', p_j, p_j', p_j'', \bar{p}_j$, i.e.,

$$R_{1,\#} = \{x \rightarrow \# \mid x \in \{\#, d\} \cup \{a_j', p_j, p_j', p_j'', \bar{p}_j \mid j \in \{1,2\}\}\}.$$

In total this yields 17 catalytic rules in $R_{1,c}$ and 12 trap rules in $R_{1,\#}$, i.e., 29 rules in R_1. Obviously, the same number of rules is obtained for the corresponding purely catalytic P system $\Pi_{12}'(b_0, b_1, b_2, b_3, b_4)$ where we simply have to add the third catalyst c_3 and replace the non-cooperative trap rules $x \rightarrow \#$ by the corresponding catalytic trap rules $c_3x \rightarrow c_3\#$.

We can omit the trap rules when using toxic objects, i.e., if we take

$$\Pi_{12}''(b_0, b_1, b_2, b_3, b_4) = (O'', C = \{c_1, c_2\}, O_{tox}, \mu = [\ ]_1, w_1, R_{1,c}, f = 1) \text{ where}$$
$$O'' = \{a_1, a_2, a_3, a_1', a_2', d\}$$
$$\cup \{p_j, p_j', p_j'', \bar{p}_j \mid j \in \{1,2\}\},$$
$$O_{tox} = \{a_1', a_2', d\} \cup \{p_j, p_j', p_j'', \bar{p}_j \mid j \in \{1,2\}\},$$
$$w_1 = c_1c_2(a_1)^{b_0}p_1,$$

and $R_{1,c}$ contains the catalytic rules as listed above. This system now only contains 17 rules.

How to argue that the catalytic P system $\Pi_{12}(b_0, b_1, b_2, b_3, b_4)$ and the corresponding catalytic P systems $\Pi_{12}'(b_0, b_1, b_2, b_3, b_4)$ and $\Pi_{12}''(b_0, b_1, b_2, b_3, b_4)$ work correctly was exhibited in detail in [10] as well as in [21] and [22]. Yet as we have reduced the number of rules in a considerable way, we have to argue for any possible case of decrementing or zero-testing register r:

If decrementing of register r is possible, all steps have to be performed exactly as described in the table. If decrementing fails, then in the last (third) step c_{3-r} must be used with the rule $c_{3-r}a_{3-r} \rightarrow c_{3-r}a_{3-r}'$ as not both registers can be empty during a computation of the register machine. Yet in the next step the catalyst c_{3-r} is busy with the program symbol p_r or $\bar{p}_r$, hence, with a_{3-r}' and one of these program symbols competing for the same catalyst, one of these symbols will be trapped.

A successful simulation of testing register r for zero is performed in one step leaving catalyst c_r idle. In case the register is not empty, a'_r has to be generated, and this symbol in the next step will compete for the catalyst c_r with the program symbol p_{3-r} and thus one of these symbols will be trapped.

As already explained in [21], we here also mention that when using $c_2\bar{p}_2 \to c_2(a_3)^{b_3}$ instead of $c_2\bar{p}_1 \to c_2 p_2$ in order to reach a halting configuration, the system does not immediately halt, but instead, if having chosen the rule when register 1 is empty, uses the sequences of rules $c_2 a_2 \to c_2 a'_2$, $c_2 a'_2 \to c_2 d$, and $c_1 d \to c_1$ (or $c_2 d \to c_2$), to clear register 2, so that in the end only the objects a_3 remain besides the catalysts. If $c_2\bar{p}_2 \to c_2(a_3)^{b_3}$ is chosen too early, then both registers may be cleared by using the corresponding rules. The result expressed by the number of symbols a_3 is not affected, if we make such a wrong choice at the end only.

As specific examples, we therefore obtain

$$N_{gen,maxpar}(\Pi_{12}(1,1,1,0,2)) = \{n^2 \mid n \geq 0\}$$

and

$$N_{gen,maxpar}(\Pi_{12}(1,1,2,1,0)) = \{2^n \mid n \geq 0\}.$$

We observe that with respect to the complexity of the systems, especially concerning the number of rules, there is no difference at all between the sets of natural numbers growing in a quadratic and in an exponential way, respectively.

In sum, we conclude that all these non-linear sets of natural numbers as described above are contained in

$$N_{gen,maxpar}OP_1(cat_2)_{29} \cap N_{gen,maxpar}OP_1(pcat_3)_{29}$$

as well as in

$$N_{gen,maxpar}O_{tox}P_1(cat_2)_{17} \cap N_{gen,maxpar}O_{tox}P_1(pcat_2)_{17}.$$

If we do not limit ourselves with the number of catalysts, a better solution with respect to the number of rules is possible, i.e., for the function g with the parameters b_0, b_1, b_2, b_3, b_4 we construct the purely catalytic P system

$$\Pi_{13}(b_0, b_1, b_2, b_3, b_4) = (O, C, \mu = [\ ]_1, w_1, R_1, f = 1) \text{ where}$$
$$O = C \cup \{a_1, a_2, a_3, p_1, p_2, p_h, d_1, d_2, d'_1, d'_2, d, d', \#\},$$
$$C = \{c_{r,Decr}, c_{r,0Test} \mid r \in \{1,2\}\} \cup \{c_d, c_p, c_\#\},$$
$$w_1 = c_{1,Decr}c_{1,0Test}c_{2,Decr}c_{2,0Test}c_d c_p c_\# (a_1)^{b_0} p_1 d_2 d'_1 d'_2 dd',$$

and R_1 consists of the catalytic rules described in the following.

The main idea of this new construction is to use two catalysts for each register – one for the decrement ($c_{r,Decr}$) and one for the zero-test ($c_{r,0Test}$). Moreover, each SUB-instruction is simulated by two rules, one for the decrement and one for the zero-test, just allowing the corresponding catalyst to do its work, whereas all other catalysts are kept busy having introduced d_r for $c_{r,Decr}$ and d'_r

for $c_{r,0Test}$. The catalyst c_d for the special symbol d is kept busy by d'; the symbol d is used for trapping in case an intended decrement fails and can only be allowed to vanish in the last step. The catalyst c_p is used with the instruction labels p_1, p_2, and p_h. The catalyst $c_\#$ is only needed for handling the trap symbol $\#$.

For each of the two registers $r \in \{1, 2\}$, the following rules perform the decrement and the zero-test, respectively, in case this operation is initiated by omitting d_r or d'_r, respectively, in the step before.

decrement $c_{r,Decr}a_r \rightarrow c_{r,Decr}$: if register r is not empty, it is decremented;

$c_{r,Decr}d \rightarrow c_{r,Decr}\#$: if register r is empty, the catalyst $c_{r,Decr}$ has to be used with the symbol d thereby introducing the trap symbol $\#$;

$c_{r,Decr}d_r \rightarrow c_{r,Decr}$: d_r keeps $c_{r,Decr}$ busy if another instruction is to be simulated;

$c_\# d_r \rightarrow c_\#\#$: d_r is a "toxic" object which must not stay idle;

$c_d d' \rightarrow c_d$: d' keeps c_d busy until the end;

$c_\# d' \rightarrow c_\#\#$: d' is a "toxic" object which must not stay idle.

zero-test $c_{r,0Test}a_r \rightarrow c_{r,0Test}\#$: if register r is not empty, a trap symbol $\#$ is generated;

$c_{r,0Test}d'_r \rightarrow c_{r,0Test}$: d'_r keeps $c_{r,0Test}$ busy if another instruction is to be simulated; for the symbol d'_r we do not need an additional trap rule as the only alternative is already a trap rule.

The following rules initiate the decrement or the zero-test on register 1 or 2 and simulate the program for the function g:

1. $c_p p_1 \rightarrow c_p a_2 p_1 d_2 d'_1 d'_2 d'$: decrement register 1;
   $c_p p_1 \rightarrow c_p p_2 d_1 d_2 d'_2 d'$: zero-test register 1;
2. $c_p p_2 \rightarrow c_p (a_1)^{b_2} (a_3)^{b_1} p_2 d_1 d'_1 d'_2 d'$: decrement register 2;
   $c_p p_2 \rightarrow c_p (a_1)^{b_4} p_1 d_1 d_2 d'_1 d'$: zero-test register 2;
   $c_p p_1 \rightarrow c_p (a_3)^{b_3} p_h d_1 d_2 d'_2 d'$: zero-test register 1 and go to halting.
3. Whereas register 1 is already empty, now also register 2 has to be cleaned using the instruction label p_h:
   $c_p p_h \rightarrow c_p p_h d_1 d'_1 d'_2 d'$: decrement register 2;
   $c_p p_h \rightarrow c_p d_1 d_2 d'_1$: zero-test register 2 and eliminate p_h;
   $c_d d \rightarrow c_d$: finally c_d is allowed to eliminate d;
   $c_\# \# \rightarrow c_\#\#$: in case something goes wrong during a simulation of an instruction, this rule keeps the P system in an infinite loop.

In sum, this purely catalytic P system $\Pi_{13}(b_0, b_1, b_2, b_3, b_4)$ contains only 23 rules. We can save two catalysts by using non-cooperative rules instead of the catalytic rules assigned to the catalysts c_p and $c_\#$, thus obtaining the catalytic P system $\Pi'_{13}(b_0, b_1, b_2, b_3, b_4)$. Hence, all the non-linear sets of natural numbers described above are contained in

$$N_{gen,maxpar}OP_1(cat_5)_{23} \cap N_{gen,maxpar}OP_1(pcat_7)_{23}.$$

Besides the trap rule $c_\# \# \rightarrow c_\#\#$, only the rules $c_\# d_r \rightarrow c_\#\#$, $r \in \{1, 2\}$, and $c_\# d' \rightarrow c_\#\#$ can be omitted when considering a (purely) catalytic P system with "toxic" objects, yet this result with 19 rules is even weaker than the previous one where we also used less catalysts.

5   Conclusions

In this paper we have investigated and illustrated with several examples the effect of using toxic objects in various models of P systems. Moreover, we have given a lot of examples for small P systems accepting or generating specific non-semilinear sets of vectors of natural numbers or non-semilinear sets of natural numbers. As our main result, we have improved considerably the result established in [21] and even improved the newest result obtained in [22] by showing that 29 rules are enough for generating the non-semilinear set of numbers $\{2^n \mid n \geq 0\}$ with (purely) catalytic P systems and 2 (3) catalysts; using toxic objects, only 17 rules are needed. Allowing for a larger number of catalysts, with a new proof technique we could even reduce the number of rules to 23.

For the catalytic P systems/purely catalytic P systems it is still one of the most challenging questions in the area of P systems whether we really need two/three catalysts to get computational completeness or at least to accept or generate a non-semilinear set of (vectors of) natural numbers. Another direction for future research is to investigate the influence of toxic objects in further models of P systems.

Acknowledgements. The first author acknowledges project STCU-5384 *Models of high performance computations based on biological and quantum approaches* awarded by the Science and Technology Center in the Ukraine. Both authors are very grateful to Petr Sosík for pointing out the mistake in the proof of Corollary 8 in [10].

References

1. Alhazov, A., Freund, R.: Asynchronous and Maximally Parallel Deterministic Controlled Non-cooperative P Systems Characterize *NFIN* and *coNFIN*. In: Csuhaj-Varjú, E., Gheorghe, M., Rozenberg, G., Salomaa, A., Vaszil, Gy. (eds.) CMC 2012. LNCS, vol. 7762, pp. 101–111. Springer, Heidelberg (2013)
2. Alhazov, A., Freund, R.: Small P Systems Defining Non-semilinear Sets. Automata, Computation, Universality. Springer (to appear)
3. Alhazov, A.: P Systems without Multiplicities of Symbol-Objects. Information Processing Letters **100**(3), 124–129 (2006)
4. Alhazov, A., Freund, R., Păun, Gh.: Computational Completeness of P Systems with Active Membranes and Two Polarizations. In: Margenstern, M. (ed.) MCU 2004. LNCS, vol. 3354, pp. 82–92. Springer, Heidelberg (2005)
5. Alhazov, A., Freund, R., Riscos-Núñez, A.: One and Two Polarizations, Membrane Creation and Objects Complexity in P Systems. In: Seventh International Symposium on Symbolic and Numeric Algorithms for Scientific Computing, SYNASC 2005, 385–394. EEE Computer Society (2005)
6. Alhazov, A., Verlan, S.: Minimization Strategies for Maximally Parallel Multiset Rewriting Systems. Theoretical Computer Science **412**(17), 1581–1591 (2011)
7. Beyreder, M., Freund, R.: Membrane Systems Using Noncooperative Rules with Unconditional Halting. In: Corne, D.W., Frisco, P., Păun, Gh., Rozenberg, G., Salomaa, A. (eds.) WMC 2008. LNCS, vol. 5391, pp. 129–136. Springer, Heidelberg (2009)

8. Dassow, J., Păun, Gh.: Regulated Rewriting in Formal Language Theory. Springer (1989)

9. Freund, R.: Special Variants of P Systems Inducing an Infinite Hierarchy with Respect to the Number of Membranes. Bulletin of the EATCS **75**, 209–219 (2001)

10. Freund, R., Kari, L., Oswald, M., Sosík, P.: Computationally Universal P Systems without Priorities: Two Catalysts Are Sufficient. Theoretical Computer Science **330**(2), 251–266 (2005)

11. Freund, R., Leporati, A., Mauri, G., Porreca, A.E., Verlan, S., Zandron, C.: Flattening in (Tissue) P Systems. In: Alhazov, A., Cojocaru, S., Gheorghe, M., Rogozhin, Yu., Rozenberg, G., Salomaa, A. (eds.) CMC 2013. LNCS, vol. 8340, pp. 173–188. Springer, Heidelberg (2014)

12. Freund, R., Oswald, M., Păun, Gh.: Catalytic and Purely Catalytic P Systems and P Automata: Control Mechanisms for Obtaining Computational Completeness. Fundamenta Informaticae **136**, 59–84 (2015)

13. Ibarra, O.H., Woodworth, S.: On Symport/Antiport P Systems with a Small Number of Objects. International Journal of Computer Mathematics **83**(7), 613–629 (2006)

14. Minsky, M.L.: Computation: Finite and Infinite Machines. Prentice Hall, Englewood Cliffs (1967)

15. Păun, Gh.: Computing with Membranes. Journal of Computer and System Sciences **61**(1), 108–143 (2000) (and Turku Center for Computer Science-TUCS Report 208, November 1998, www.tucs.fi)

16. Păun, Gh.: Membrane Computing: An Introduction. Springer (2002)

17. Păun, Gh., Rozenberg, G., Salomaa, A.: The Oxford Handbook of Membrane Computing, pp. 118–143. Oxford University Press (2010)

18. Rozenberg, G., Salomaa, A.: The Mathematical Theory of L Systems. Academic Press, New York (1980)

19. Rozenberg, G., Salomaa, A. (eds.): Handbook of Formal Languages, 3 vol. Springer (1997)

20. Sburlan, D.: Further Results on P Systems with Promoters/Inhibitors. International Journal of Foundations of Computer Science **17**(1), 205–221 (2006)

21. Sosík, P.: A Catalytic P System with Two Catalysts Generating a Non-Semilinear Set. Romanian Journal of Information Science and Technology **16**(1), 3–9 (2013)

22. Sosík, P., Langer, M.: Improved Universality Proof for Catalytic P Systems and a Relation to Non-Semi-Linear Sets. In: Bensch, S., Freund, R., Otto, F. (eds.): Sixth Workshop on Non-Classical Models of Automata and Applications (NCMA 2014), books@ocg.at, Band 304, Wien, pp. 223–234 (2014)

23. The P systems webpage: http://ppage.psystems.eu

Promoters and Inhibitors
in Purely Catalytic P Systems

Artiom Alhazov[1], Rudolf Freund[2]([✉]), and Sergey Verlan[1,3]

[1] Institute of Mathematics and Computer Science,
Academy of Sciences of Moldova, Academiei 5, 2028 Chişinău, Moldova
artiom@math.md
[2] Faculty of Informatics, Vienna University of Technology,
Favoritenstr. 9, 1040 Vienna, Austria
rudi@emcc.at
[3] LACL, Département Informatique, Université Paris Est,
61, av. Général de Gaulle, 94010 Créteil, France
verlan@u-pec.fr

Abstract. We consider purely catalytic P systems with two catalysts together with promoters and inhibitors on the rules. We show that computational completeness can be achieved in a deterministic way by using atomic promoters or sets of atomic inhibitors. By using atomic inhibitors computational completeness is achieved only with a non-deterministic construction.

1 Introduction

Catalytic P systems are one of the first models in the area of P systems. This model allows for context-free (non-cooperative) rewriting rules like $a \to u$, where a is a single symbol, as well as contextual (cooperative) catalytic rules of the form $ca \to cu$, where c is a special object – the catalyst – present in one copy. The number of catalysts is a natural descriptional complexity parameter for such systems. It is known that systems with two catalysts are computationally complete, see [5,14], while systems with no catalysts generate *PsREG*. The computational power of systems with one catalyst is still an open question. When additional ingredients are used, then such systems become computationally complete, e.g. when using promoters/inhibitors [11,16] or different rule control mechanisms [8].

In purely catalytic P systems only catalytic rules are allowed, which limits the degree of the parallelism to the number of catalysts in the system. Such systems are very similar to catalytic P systems, however, not always the proofs can be translated from one model to the other one because they have to take into account the limitation of the parallelism. In many cases, the same results hold for purely catalytic P systems with n catalysts and catalytic P systems with $n-1$ catalysts. For example, three catalysts are sufficient for the computational completeness of purely catalytic P systems. With one catalyst such systems are identical to sequential context-free multiset rewriting grammars, so they can

© Springer International Publishing Switzerland 2014
M. Gheorghe et al. (Eds.): CMC 2014, LNCS 8961, pp. 126–138, 2014.
DOI: 10.1007/978-3-319-14370-5_8

generate exactly *PsREG*. As in the previous case, the computational power of purely catalytic P systems with two catalysts is not yet known and different extensions have been studied in order to increase the computational power.

Promoters/inhibitors are special variants of permitting/forbidding contexts, which correspond to a single permitting/forbidding set and an empty forbidding/permitting set. It is known that non-cooperative P systems with either promoters or inhibitors of weight 2 are computationally complete, see [3]. Recently, in [1] it was shown that computational completeness cannot be achieved by deterministic non-cooperative systems with promoters, inhibitors and priorities (in the maximally parallel or the asynchronous mode, unlike the sequential mode). In [2] some interesting questions on the power of P systems in the maximally parallel mode using only priorities or restricting the weight of the promoting/inhibiting multisets were addressed.

In this paper we consider purely catalytic P systems having two catalysts and rules with promoters and inhibitors of weight 1 (consisting of a single object, and we call them atomic). We show that using atomic promoters or sets of atomic inhibitors it is possible to achieve computational completeness even with a deterministic construction. In the case of atomic inhibitors, our construction for computational completeness is non-deterministic. Moreover, our results can easily be adapted to the case of catalytic P systems yielding simpler proofs for the results established in [11]. We remark that the converse is not true, as the proofs from the cited article make use of a massive unbounded parallelism, so they cannot be adapted to the purely catalytic case.

2   Definitions

An *alphabet* is a finite non-empty set V of abstract *symbols*. The free monoid generated by V under the operation of concatenation is denoted by V^*; the *empty string* is denoted by λ, and $V^* \setminus \{\lambda\}$ is denoted by V^+. The families of all finite, regular, and recursively enumerable sets of strings are demoted by *FIN*, *REG*, and *RE*, respectively. The set of non-negative integers is denoted by $\mathbb{N}$. The families of all finite, linear (or regular), and recursively enumerable sets of non-negative integers are denoted by *NFIN*, *NREG*, and *NRE*, respectively. If we consider vectors of non-negative integers, N is replaced by *Ps* in these notations. In the following, we will use $\subseteq$ both for the subset as well as the submultiset relation and we will represent multisets by a string notation. The corresponding functions and relations on all these sets are indicated by the prefix *Fun* and *Rel*, respectively.

2.1   Register Machines

A *register machine* is a tuple $M = (m, B, l_0, l_h, P)$, where m is the number of registers, B is a set of labels, $l_0 \in B$ is the initial label, $l_h \in B$ is the final label, and P is the set of instructions bijectively labeled by elements of B. The instructions of M can be of the following forms:

- $l_1 : (ADD(j), l_2, l_3)$, with $l_1 \in B \setminus \{l_h\}$, $l_2, l_3 \in B$, $1 \le j \le m$.
  Increases the value of register j by one, followed by a non-deterministic jump to instruction l_2 or l_3. This instruction is usually called *increment*.
- $l_1 : (SUB(j), l_2, l_3)$, with $l_1 \in B \setminus \{l_h\}$, $l_2, l_3 \in B$, $1 \le j \le m$.
  If the value of register j is zero then jump to instruction l_3; otherwise, the value of register j is decreased by one, followed by a jump to instruction l_2. The two cases of this instruction are usually called *zero-test* and *decrement*, respectively.
- $l_h : HALT$. Stops the execution of the register machine.

A *configuration* of a register machine $(l; v_1, \ldots, v_m)$ is described by the value of the current label l indicating the next instruction to be executed and the contents of each register. Computations start by executing the instruction l_0 of P, and terminate with reaching the HALT-instruction l_h.

In order to deal with strings, this basic model of register machines can be extended by instructions for reading from an input tape and writing to an output tape containing strings over an input alphabet T_{in} and an output alphabet T_{out}, respectively:

- $l_1 : (read(a), l_2)$, with $l_1 \in B \setminus \{l_h\}$, $l_2 \in B$, $a \in T_{in}$.
  Reads the symbol a from the input tape and jumps to instruction l_2.
- $l_1 : (write(a), l_2)$, with $l_1 \in B \setminus \{l_h\}$, $l_2 \in B$, $a \in T_{out}$.
  Writes the symbol a on the output tape and jumps to instruction l_2.

2.2   (Purely) Catalytic P Systems

Since flattening [7] the membrane structure of a membrane system preserves both determinism and the model, in the following we restrict ourselves to consider membrane systems with only one membrane, eventually communicating with the environment, hence, in the description we omit the trivial membrane structure only consisting of the skin membrane.

Definition 1. *A catalytic P system is a tuple*

$$\Pi = (O, C, \Sigma, T, w, R', m_{in}, m_{out})$$

where O is a finite alphabet, $C \subset O$ is the set of catalysts, $\Sigma \subseteq O$ is the input sub-alphabet, $T \subseteq O$ is the output sub-alphabet, $w \in O^*$ is a string representing the initial multiset in the skin membrane, m_{in} and m_{out} are the input and output membranes with 1 indicating the skin membrane and 0 indicating the environment, and R' is a set of rules of one of the following forms:

- $r : a \to v$, $a \in O$, $v \in O^*$ *(non-cooperative rule);*
- $r : ca \to cv$, $a \in O$, $c \in C$, $v \in O^*$ *(catalytic rule);*

for communication with the environment, in both non-cooperative and catalytic rules, an object b in v may be replaced by $(b, come)$ meaning that the symbol b is taken from the environment, or by (b, out) meaning that the symbol b is sent out to the environment.

If only catalytic rules occur in R', then the system is called purely catalytic.

Below, we briefly describe the semantics of catalytic P systems; more formal details can be found in [9, 14].

A configuration of the system Π is represented by a multiset of objects from O contained in the skin membrane region, the set of all configurations over O is denoted by $\mathbb{C}(O)$. A rule $r : u \to v$ is applicable if the current configuration contains the multiset specified by u.

Furthermore, applicability may be controlled by *context conditions*, specified by two sets of multisets.

Definition 2. *Let P and Q be (finite) sets of multisets over O. A (simple) rule with context conditions $(r; P, Q)$ is applicable to a configuration C if r is applicable, and moreover,*

- *for all $p \in P$, $p \subseteq C$, and*
- *for all $q \in Q$, $q \not\subseteq C$.*

The more general variant of a rule with context conditions is of the form $(r; (P_1, Q_1), \ldots, (P_m, Q_m))$ where any of the corresponding triples $(r; (P_i, Q_i))$, $1 \leq i \leq m$, is a simple rule with context conditions, and its applicability is defined as the applicability of any of these simple rules with context conditions.

In the definition of a (simple) rule with context conditions $(r; P, Q)$ as given above the set P is called the *permitting set*, while the set Q is called the *forbidding set* (for r). In words, context conditions are satisfied if all multisets in the permitting set are submultisets of the current configuration, and no multiset in the forbidding set is a submultiset of the current configuration.

By a promoter/inhibitor we understand an element of a permitting/forbidding set. Traditionally, P systems with promoters use the notation $r|_{p_1, \cdots, p_n}$, which is equivalent to $(r; \{p_1, \ldots, p_n\}; \emptyset)$. In the case of P systems with inhibitors the notation $r|_{\neg q_1, \cdots, \neg q_n}$ is used, which is equivalent to $(r; \emptyset, \{q_1, \ldots, q_n\})$. Finally, promoters and inhibitors consisting of one symbol are called *atomic*.

Definition 3. *A P system with context conditions and priorities on the rules is a construct*

$$\Pi = (O, C, \Sigma, T, w, R', R, l_{in}, l_{out}, >)$$

where $(O, C, \Sigma, T, w, R', m_{in}, m_{out})$ is a catalytic P system as defined above, R is a set of rules with context conditions and $>$ is a priority relation on the rules in R.

During a computational step the applicability of a rule can additionally be restricted by a priority relation $>$: if rule r' has priority over rule r, denoted by $r' > r$, then r cannot be applied if r' is applicable.

The computation of the system follows the usual maximally parallel derivation mode, meaning that a maximal applicable multiset of rules is chosen to be applied in each step. Also other strategies for a computational step exist, e.g., the sequential or the asynchronous derivation mode; we refer to [9,14] for a detailed discussion on this topic. The computation step between two configurations C and C' is denoted by $C \Longrightarrow C'$, thus yielding the binary relation $\Rightarrow$: $\mathbb{C}(O) \times \mathbb{C}(O)$. A computation halts when there are no rules applicable to the current configuration in the corresponding mode; such a configuration is called a *halting configuration*.

In the *generative case*, a halting computation has associated a result, in the form of the number of objects present in membrane m_{out} in a halting configuration (m_{in} can be omitted). The set of non-negative integers and the set of (Parikh) vectors of non-negative integers obtained as results of halting computations in Π are denoted by $N_{gen}(\Pi)$ and $Ps_{gen}(\Pi)$, respectively.

In the *accepting case*, for $m_{in} \neq 0$, we accept all (vectors of) non-negative integers whose input, given as the corresponding numbers of objects in membrane m_{in}, leads to a halting computation (m_{out} can be omitted); the set of non-negative integers and the set of (Parikh) vectors of non-negative integers accepted in that way by halting computations in Π are denoted by $N_{acc}(\Pi)$ and $Ps_{acc}(\Pi)$, respectively.

For the input being taken from the environment, i.e., for $m_{in} = 0$, we need the additional target indication *come*; $(a, come)$ means that the object a is taken into the skin from the environment (all objects there are assumed to be available in an unbounded number). The multiset of all objects taken from the environment during a halting computation then is the multiset accepted by this accepting P system, which in this case we shall call a *P automaton*, e.g., see [4]; the set of non-negative integers and the set of (Parikh) vectors of non-negative integers accepted by halting computations in Π are denoted by $N_{aut}(\Pi)$ and $Ps_{aut}(\Pi)$, respectively.

A P system Π can also be considered as a system computing a partial recursive function (in the deterministic case) or even a partial recursive relation (in the non-deterministic case), with the input being given in a membrane region $m_{in} \neq 0$ as in the accepting case or being taken from the environment as in the automaton case. The corresponding functions/relations computed by halting computations in Π are denoted by $ZY_\alpha(\Pi)$, $Z \in \{Fun, Rel\}$, $Y \in \{N, Ps\}$, $\alpha \in \{acc, aut\}$.

Moreover, P systems can also be considered as devices computing with languages: the objects sent out can be concatenated to strings over a given alphabet, and the objects taken in during a halting computation can be assumed to form a string. For sake of simplicity, we assume that in each computation step at most one symbol is sent out or taken in; otherwise, as usual, e.g., see [4], we may take any permutation of the symbols sent out or taken in to be part of a string to be considered as output or input, respectively. Obviously, according to this method of getting an input string, for the accepting case only the automaton variant is to be considered now, as otherwise we would have to take an encoding of the input string by a multiset. The set of strings generated or accepted (in the sense of automata) by a P system Π is denoted by $L_\gamma(\Pi)$, $\gamma \in \{gen, aut\}$, the function/relation computed by Π is denoted by $ZL_{aut}(\Pi)$, $Z \in \{Fun, Rel\}$.

The families of sets $Y_\delta(\Pi)$, $Y \in \{N, Ps\}$, $\delta \in \{gen, acc, aut\}$, and of sets $L_\gamma(\Pi)$, $\gamma \in \{gen, aut\}$, computed by purely catalytic P systems with context conditions and priorities on the rules having at most m catalysts are denoted by $Y_\delta OP(pcat_m, (pro_{k,l}, inh_{k',l'})_d, pri)$ and $L_\gamma OP(pcat_m.(pro_{k,l}, inh_{k',l'})_d, pri)$, respectively; d denotes the maximal number m in the rules with context conditions $(r, (P_1, Q_1), \cdots, (P_m, Q_m))$; k and k' denote the maximum number of promoters and inhibitors in the P_i and Q_i, respectively; l and l' indicate the maximum of weights of promoters and inhibitors, respectively.

For $Z \in \{Fun, Rel\}$, the corresponding families of functions and relations are denoted by $FY_\delta OP(pcat_m, (pro_{k,l}, inh_{k',l'})_d, pri)$ for $Y \in \{N, Ps\}$ and $\delta \in \{acc, aut\}$, and by $FL_{aut}OP(pcat_m, (pro_{k,l}, inh_{k',l'})_d, pri)$.

In the case of catalytic P systems, we replace $pcat$ by cat. If any of the numbers k, k', l, l' is not bounded, we replace it by $*$.

In the case of accepting systems and of systems computing functions, we also consider the idea of determinism, which means that in each step of any computation at most one (multiset of) rule(s) is applicable; in this case, we write $detacc$.

In the literature, we find a lot of restricted variants of P systems with context conditions and priorities on the rules, e.g., we may omit the priorities or the context conditions completely.

Remark 1. As in a P system $(O, C, \Sigma, T, w, R', R, m_{in}, m_{out}, >)$ the set of rules R' can easily be deduced from the set of rules with context conditions R, we omit R' in the description of the P system. Moreover, for systems having only rules with a simple context condition, we omit d in the description of the families, and each control mechanism not used can be omitted, too.

Remark 2. It is worth to note, see also [6], that if no other control is used, the priorities can be mapped to sets of atomic inhibitors. Indeed, a rule is inhibited precisely by the left side of each rule with higher priority. This is straightforward in the case when the priority relation is assumed to be a partial order. Therefore, we will restrict ourselves to consider systems without priorities in the following.

3   Results

In this section we present the main results of the paper. First we show that purely catalytic P systems with atomic promoters are computationally complete.

Theorem 1. *The computations of a register machine can be simulated by a purely catalytic P system with only two catalysts and atomic promoters. Moreover, the simulation preserves determinism.*

Proof. Let $M = (m, B, l_0, l_h, P)$ be a register machine. We construct a purely catalytic P system with promoters

$$\Pi = (O, C, \Sigma, T, w, R, m_{in}, m_{out}) \text{ where}$$
$$O = C \cup \{a_r \mid 1 \leq r \leq m\} \cup \{X, Y\} \cup \{l \mid l \in B\} \cup$$
$$\{i', i'', i''', b_i \mid i : (SUB(r), j, k) \in P\},$$
$$C = \{c_1, c_2\},$$
$$\Sigma, T \subseteq \{a_r \mid 1 \leq r \leq m\},$$
$$w = l_0, \ m_{in} = m_{out} = 1,$$
$$R = \{c_1 i \to c_1 j a_r, \ c_1 i \to c_1 k a_r \mid i : (ADD(r), j, k) \in P\}$$
$$\cup \bigcup_{i:(SUB(r),j,k) \in P} R_i,$$

where R_i is the set of rules corresponding to the conditional decrement instruction labeled by i, consisting of the rules below.

$i.1.1 : c_1 i \to c_1 i' X$	$i.2.1 : c_2 a_r \to c_2 b_i \mid_i$
$i.1.2 : c_1 i' \to c_1 i'' \mid_{b_i}$	$i.2.2 : c_2 X \to c_2 Y$
$i.1.3 : c_1 i'' \to c_1 i'''$	$i.2.3 : c_2 Y \to c_2$
$i.1.4 : c_1 i''' \to c_1 j$	$i.2.4 : c_2 b_i \to c_2 \mid_{i'''}$
$i.1.5 : c_1 i' \to c_1 k \mid_Y$	

The simulation of the instructions of the register machine M is performed as described in the following; each configuration $(i ; v_1, \ldots, v_m)$ of M is encoded as $i \, a_1^{v_1} \ldots a_m^{v_m}$ in Π.

The simulation of the increment instruction is done directly by changing the label i and incrementing the corresponding register. The catalyst c_1 is used for this operation.

The conditional decrement instruction $i : (SUB(r), j, k)$ is simulated as follows: In the first step, the rule $i.1.1$ is applicable, and if register r is not empty, then the rule $i.2.1$ is applicable, too, yielding the configuration $i' X a_1^{v_1} \ldots a_r^{v_r - 1} b_i \ldots a_m^{v_m}$. Then only the rules $i.1.2$ and $i.2.2$ are applicable, yielding the configuration $i'' Y a_1^{v_1} \ldots a_r^{v_r - 1} b_i \ldots a_m^{v_m}$. After that only the sequences of rules $i.1.3$, $i.1.4$ and $i.2.3$, $i.2.4$ can be applied, finally yielding the configuration $j \, a_1^{v_1} \ldots a_r^{v_r - 1} \ldots a_m^{v_m}$ corresponding to the configuration $(j ; v_1, \ldots, v_r - 1, \ldots, v_m)$ of M. If the register r is empty, then in the second step only rule $i.2.2$ is applicable. In the next step, only the rules $i.1.5$ and $i.2.3$ can be applied yielding the configuration $k \, a_1^{v_1} \ldots a_r^{0} \ldots a_m^{v_m}$, which correctly encodes the corresponding configuration $(k ; v_1, \ldots, 0, \ldots, v_m)$ of M. $\square$

Remark 3. We remark that only the rule with a_r on the left side actually requires the catalyst; removing the catalysts from all other rules would still yield an equivalent system, except that this system would not be purely catalytic. Hence, the catalysts could be assigned in an arbitrary way, provided no catalyst is assigned to both rules in any line.

Remark 4. We observe that Π is deterministic if M is deterministic, but also that the construction was made in such a way that the rules with the same left side and the same right side never have different promoters (without fulfilling this condition, a simpler deterministic construction could be obtained).

The next theorem shows a similar result with inhibitors. However, this proof does not preserve the determinism.

Theorem 2. *The computations of a register machine can be simulated by a purely catalytic P system with only two catalysts and atomic inhibitors.*

Proof. Let $M = (m, B, l_0, l_h, P)$ be a register machine. We construct a purely catalytic P system with inhibitors

$$\Pi = (O, C, \Sigma, T, w, R, m_{in}, m_{out}) \text{ where}$$

$$O = C \cup \{l \mid l \in B\} \cup \{a_r \mid 1 \le r \le m\} \cup \{f, S_1, S_2, Z, \#\}$$
$$\cup \{i', i_-, Z_i, \bar{Z}_i, \bar{Z}_i', b_i, \bar{b}_i \mid i : (SUB(r), j, k) \in P\},$$
$$C = \{c_1, c_2\},$$
$$\Sigma, T \subseteq \{a_r \mid 1 \le r \le m\},$$
$$w = l_0 Z, \ m_{in} = m_{out} = 1,$$
$$R = \{c_2 i \to c_2 j a_r, \ c_2 i \to c_2 k a_r, c_1 i \to c_1 \# \mid i : (ADD(r), j, k) \in P\}$$
$$\cup \{c_1 \# \to c_1 \#, c_2 \# \to c_2 \#, c_2 l_h \to c_2 f S_1 S_2, c_1 l_h \to c_1 \#\}$$
$$\cup \bigcup\nolimits_{i:(SUB(r),j,k) \in P} R_i,$$

where R_i is the set of rules corresponding to the conditional decrement instruction labeled by i, consisting of the rules below.

$i.1.1 : c_1 i \to c_1 i_- S_1 S_1 S_2 \mid_{\neg S_1}$	$i.2.1 : c_2 a_r \to c_2 b_i \mid_{\neg S_1}$	$i.3.1 : c_2 Z \to c_2 Z_i \mid_{\neg S_1}$
$i.1.2 : c_1 i \to c_1 i' S_1 S_1 S_1 S_2 \mid_{\neg S_1}$	$i.2.2 : c_2 b_i \to c_2 \# \mid_{\neg i_-}$	$i.3.2 : c_2 Z_i \to c_2 \# \mid_{\neg i'}$
$i.1.3 : c_1 S_1 \to c_1 \mid_{\neg S_2}$	$i.2.3 : c_2 b_i \to c_2 \bar{b}_i \mid_{\neg S_2}$	$i.3.3 : c_2 Z_i \to c_2 \bar{Z}_i \mid_{\neg S_2}$
$i.1.4 : c_1 S_2 \to c_1 \mid_{\neg f}$	$i.2.4 : c_2 \bar{b}_i \to c_2$	$i.3.4 : c_2 \bar{Z}_i \to c_2 \#$
$i.1.5 : c_1 i_- \to c_1 j \mid_{\neg S_1}$		$i.3.5 : c_2 \bar{Z}_i \to c_2 \bar{Z}_i' \mid_{\neg a_r}$
$i.1.6 : c_1 i' \to c_1 k \mid_{\neg S_1}$		$i.3.6 : c_2 \bar{Z}_i' \to c_2 Z$

The simulation of the instructions of the register machine M is performed as described in the following; each configuration $(i; v_1, \ldots, v_m)$ of M is encoded as $i Z a_1^{v_1} \ldots a_m^{v_m}$ in Π.

The simulation of the increment instruction $i : (ADD(r), j, k) \in P$ is done directly by changing the label i and incrementing the corresponding register. The catalyst c_2 has to be used for this operation and thus to evolve label i, as otherwise catalyst c_1 would enforce the generation of the trap symbol $\#$.

The conditional decrement instruction $i : (SUB(r), j, k)$ is simulated as follows: As can easily be seen, the rules from R_i have the property that if $c_1 x \to c_1 y \in R_i$ and $c_2 z \to c_2 u \in R_i$, then $x \ne z$. Hence, the contents of a configuration can be split into two parts C_1 and C_2 with respect to this property (objects that involve catalyst c_1 will be part of C_1, those that involve c_2 will be part of C_2). For the case of the configuration $i\,Za_1^{v_1}\ldots a_m^{v_m}$ in Π, $C_1 = \{i\}$ and $C_2 = \{Za_1^{v_1}\ldots a_m^{v_m}\}$. Moreover, since the forbidding contexts of the rules $i.1.*$ do not involve objects from C_2, their application is independent from rules involving catalyst c_2.

First we examine the evolution of objects from C_1, i.e., of symbol i. Using catalyst c_1, a non-deterministic guess is made about the contents of register r. If rule $i.1.1$ is used, then it is guessed that register r is not zero, yielding $i_- S_1 S_1 S_2$, while if rule $i.1.2$ is used, then it is guessed that register r is empty, yielding $i' S_1 S_1 S_1 S_2$. In the first case only rule $i.1.4$ is applicable in the next step, leading to the removal of S_2. During the next two steps only $i.1.3$ is applicable, removing the two occurrences of S_1. Finally, symbol j replaces i_-.

When using the second group of rules, the computation is one step longer (because of the presence of three copies of S_1) and yields k.

Now we consider the evolution of objects from C_2, i.e., of $Za_1^{v_1}\ldots a_m^{v_m}$. Initially a guess is made about which is the current decrement instruction and whether using c_1 it was guessed that the corresponding register is empty or not. In some sense this permits to synchronize with the guess done in parallel using catalyst c_1. This materializes in two groups of rules $i.2.*$ and $i.3.*$; the first one corresponds to the case when the parallel guess is that register r is not empty, while the second case corresponds to the guess that register r is empty.

Let us consider the evolution of the system in the first case. Rule $i.2.1$ takes symbol a_r corresponding to a non-empty register r and transforms it to b_i. In the next step, rule $i.2.3$ is not applicable because symbol S_2 is still present in the configuration (it disappears on the next step as shown above). Now, if symbol i_- is present in the configuration (this means that the parallel guess was to decrement register r being in state i), then no rule using catalyst c_2 is applicable. Otherwise, rule $i.2.2$ is applied introducing the trap symbol $\#$ into the system. So, if at the beginning of the third step no symbol $\#$ has been introduced, then the labels i of i_- and b_i must coincide. After that, symbol b_i is transformed to $\bar{b}_i$, which is erased in the next step. We note that at the same moment rule $i.1.5$ is applied, hence, the resulting configuration is $j\,Za_1^{v_1}\ldots a_r^{v_r-1}\ldots a_m^{v_m}$, corresponding to the configuration $(j; v_1, \ldots, v_r - 1, \ldots, v_m)$ of M.

In the case of the application of rule $i.3.1$, a similar mechanism involving rules $i.3.2$ and $i.3.3$ permits to check if the parallel guess was that register r is empty. In this case, the rules $i.3.4$ and $i.3.5$ verify that this register is indeed empty by introducing a trap symbol if this is not the case. Finally, rule $i.3.6$ introduces back the additional symbol Z used for the zero check.

When the final label l_h is reached, rule $c_1 l_h \rightarrow f S_1 S_2$ is applied and after that the system halts as S_1 and S_2 cannot be removed, so no rule involving the first or the second catalyst can be applied. $\square$

We remark that the proof given above is highly non-deterministic. We conjecture that in the deterministic case atomic inhibitors should not suffice to obtain computational completeness.

The next theorem shows that forbidding conditions using sets of atomic inhibitors allow a computational completeness proof preserving the determinism.

Theorem 3. *The computations of a register machine can be simulated by a purely catalytic P system with only two catalysts and sets of atomic inhibitors. Moreover, the simulation preserves determinism.*

Proof. Let $M = (m, B, l_0, l_h, P)$ be a register machine. Let B_{sub} be the subset of B corresponding to the labels of SUB-instructions of M. We construct a purely catalytic P system with inhibitors

$$\Pi = (O, C, \Sigma, T, w, R, m_{in}, m_{out}) \text{ where}$$
$$O = C \cup \{l \mid l \in B\} \cup \{a_r \mid 1 \le r \le m\} \cup \{X\} \cup B'_{sub},$$
$$B'_{sub} = \{i' \mid i : (SUB(r), j, k) \in P\},$$
$$C = \{c_1, c_2\},$$
$$\Sigma, T \subseteq \{a_r \mid 1 \le r \le m\},$$
$$w = l_0, \ m_{in} = m_{out} = 1,$$
$$R = \{c_1 i \to c_1 j a_r, \ c_1 i \to c_1 k a_r \mid i : (ADD(r), j, k) \in P\}$$
$$\cup \bigcup_{i:(SUB(r),j,k)\in P} R_i,$$

where R_i is the set of rules corresponding to the conditional decrement instruction labeled by i, consisting of the rules below.

$i.1.1 : c_1 i \to c_1 i' X$

$i.1.2 : (c_1 i' \to c_1 k; \emptyset, \{a_r\})$ $i.2.1 : c_2 X \to c_2$

$i.1.3 : (c_1 i' \to c_1 j; \emptyset, \{X\})$ $i.2.2 : (c_2 a_r \to c_2; \emptyset, \{X\} \cup B \cup (B'_{sub} \setminus \{i'\}))$

The simulation of the instructions of the register machine M is performed as described in the following; each configuration $(i; v_1, \ldots, v_m)$ of M is encoded as $i(a_1)^{v_1} \ldots a_m{}^{v_m}$ in Π.

As in the previous proofs, the simulation of the increment instruction $i : (ADD(r), j, k) \in P$ is done directly by changing the label i and incrementing the corresponding register. The catalyst c_1 is used for this operation.

The conditional decrement instruction $i : (SUB(r), j, k)$ is simulated as follows: In the first step the only applicable rule is $i.1.1$, which rewrites symbol i to $i'X$. In the next step rule $i.2.1$ is applicable, and only if register r is empty, then rule $i.1.2$ is applicable as well. In this way, the zero check is simulated. If register r is not empty, then in the next step rules $i.1.3$ and $i.2.2$ have to be applied performing the decrement operation.

We finally remark that the conditions from rule $i.2.2$ allow its application only in the case when i' is present and X is absent.   □

Summing up the results from the preceding three theorems we obtain the following results for computations on (vectors of) non-negative integers as well as on strings:

Theorem 4. *For any $Z \in \{Fun, Rel\}$ and any $Y \in \{N, Ps\}$ as well as any $\gamma \in \{acc, aut\}$, any $\delta \in \{gen, acc, aut\}$, and any $\beta \in \{gen, aut\}$,*

- $ZY_\gamma OP_1 (pcat_2, pro_{1,1}) = ZYRE.$
- $ZY_\gamma OP_1 (pcat_2, inh_{1,1}) = ZYRE.$

- $FunY_{detacc} OP_1 (pcat_2, pro_{1,1}) = FunYRE.$
- $FunY_{detacc} OP_1 (pcat_2, inh_{*,1}) = FunYRE.$

- $Y_\delta OP_1 (pcat_2, pro_{1,1}) = YRE.$
- $Y_\delta OP_1 (pcat_2, inh_{1,1}) = YRE.$

- $Y_{detacc} OP_1 (pcat_2, pro_{1,1}) = YRE.$
- $Y_{detacc} OP_1 (pcat_2, inh_{*,1}) = YRE.$

- $ZL_{aut} OP_1 (pcat_2, pro_{1,1}) = ZRE.$
- $ZL_{aut} OP_1 (pcat_2, inh_{1,1}) = ZRE.$

- $L_\beta OP_1 (pcat_2, pro_{1,1}) = RE.$
- $L_\beta OP_1 (pcat_2, inh_{1,1}) = RE.$

Proof. Generation and acceptance of a set of (vectors of) natural numbers L can be interpreted as a specific relation $\{0\} \times L$ and a function $L \times \{0\}$, respectively.

By well-known techniques, input symbols composing an input string can be encoded as numbers in an input register and thus as a multiset in a simulating P system. In the same way, the results of a computation in the P system can be decoded from the multiset representing the output register of the underlying register machine. An input symbol $a \in T_{in}$ read by a register machine using the instruction $l_1 : (read(a), l_2)$ is taken in by the corresponding catalytic rule $c_1 l_1 \rightarrow c_1 l_2 (a, come)$, and an output symbol $a \in T_{out}$ written by a register machine using the instruction $l_1 : (write(a), l_2)$ is sent out by the corresponding rule $c_1 l_1 \rightarrow c_1 l_2 (a, out)$. Hence, it is easy to see that in this way all the computational completeness results established above for non-negative integers carry over to string languages, too.   □

4   Conclusion

We have shown computational completeness for purely catalytic P systems with only two catalysts and either atomic promoters or sets of atomic inhibitors in such a way that for accepting P systems and for systems computing functions, we even get deterministic systems. The main open question is whether computational completeness can even be achieved with atomic inhibitors instead of sets of atomic inhibitors.

Acknowledgements. Artiom Alhazov acknowledges project STCU-5384 *Models of high performance computations based on biological and quantum approaches* awarded by the Science and Technology Center in the Ukraine.

References

1. Alhazov, A., Freund, R.: Asynchronous and Maximally Parallel Deterministic Controlled Non-cooperative P Systems Characterize *NFIN* and *coNFIN*. In: Martínez-del-Amor, M.Á., Păun, Gh., Pérez-Hurtado, I., Romero-Campero, F.J. (eds.): The Tenth Brainstorming Week in Membrane Computing, vol. 1, pp. 25–34. Fénix Editora, Sevilla (2012), and in: Csuhaj-Varjú, E., Gheorghe, M., Rozenberg, G., Salomaa, A., Vaszil, Gy. (eds.) CMC 2012. LNCS, vol. 7762, pp. 101–111. Springer, Heidelberg (2013)
2. Alhazov, A., Freund, R.: Priorities, Promoters and Inhibitors in Deterministic Non-Cooperative P Systems. In: Macías-Ramos, L.F., Martínez-del-Amor, M.Á., Păun, Gh., Riscos-Núñez, A., Valencia-Cabrera, L. (eds.) Proceedings of the Twelfth Brainstorming Week on Membrane Computing, pp. 27–36. Fénix Editora, Sevilla (2014)
3. Alhazov, A., Sburlan, D.: Ultimately Confluent Rewriting Systems. Parallel Multiset–Rewriting with Permitting or Forbidding Contexts. In: Mauri, G., Păun, Gh., Pérez-Jímenez, M.J., Rozenberg, G., Salomaa, A. (eds.) WMC 2004. LNCS, vol. 3365, pp. 178–189. Springer, Heidelberg (2005)
4. Csuhaj-Varjú, E., Vaszil, Gy.: P Automata or Purely Communicating Accepting P Systems. In: Păun, Gh., Rozenberg, G., Salomaa, A., Zandron, C. (eds.) WMC-CdeA 2002. LNCS, vol. 2597, pp. 219–233. Springer, Heidelberg (2003)
5. Freund, R., Kari, L., Oswald, M., Sosík, P.: Computationally Universal P Systems without Priorities: Two Catalysts are Sufficient. Theoretical Computer Science **330**(2), 251–266 (2005)
6. Freund, R., Kogler, M., Oswald, M.: A General Framework for Regulated Rewriting Based on the Applicability of Rules. In: Kelemen, J., Kelemenová, A. (eds.) Computation, Cooperation, and Life. LNCS, vol. 6610, pp. 35–53. Springer, Heidelberg (2011)
7. Freund, R., Leporati, A., Mauri, G., Porreca, A.E., Verlan, S., Zandron, C.: Flattening in (Tissue) P Systems. In: Alhazov, A., Cojocaru, S., Gheorghe, M., Rogozhin, Yu., Rozenberg, G., Salomaa, A. (eds.) CMC 2013. LNCS, vol. 8340, pp. 173–188. Springer, Heidelberg (2014)
8. Freund, R., Păun, Gh.: How to Obtain Computational Completeness in P Systems with One Catalyst. In: Neary, T., Cook, M. (eds.): Proceedings Machines, Computations and Universality 2013, MCU 2013, Zürich, Switzerland, September 9–11. EPTCS, vol. 128, pp. 47–61 (2013)
9. Freund, R., Verlan, S.: A Formal Framework for Static (Tissue) P Systems. In: Eleftherakis, G., Kefalas, P., Păun, Gh., Rozenberg, G., Salomaa, A. (eds.) WMC 2007. LNCS, vol. 4860, pp. 271–284. Springer, Heidelberg (2007)
10. Ibarra, O.H., Yen, H.-C.: Deterministic Catalytic Systems are Not Universal. Theoretical Computer Science **363**, 149–161 (2006)
11. Ionescu, M., Sburlan, D.: On P Systems with Promoters/Inhibitors. JUCS **10**(5), 581–599 (2004)

12. Minsky, M.L.: Finite and Infinite Machines. Prentice Hall, Englewood Cliffs (1967)
13. Păun, Gh.: Membrane Computing. An Introduction. Springer (2002)
14. Păun, Gh., Rozenberg, G., Salomaa, A.: The Oxford Handbook of Membrane Computing. Oxford University Press (2010)
15. Rozenberg, G., Salomaa, A.: Handbook of Formal Languages, 3 vol. Springer (1997)
16. Sburlan, D.: Further Results on P Systems with Promoters/Pnhibitors. Int. J. Found. Comput. Sci. **17**(1), 205–221 (2006)
17. P systems webpage: http://ppage.psystems.eu

Red–Green P Automata

Bogdan Aman[1], Erzsébet Csuhaj-Varjú[2], and Rudolf Freund[3(✉)]

[1] Institute of Computer Science, Romanian Academy,
Iaşi, Romania
bogdan.aman@gmail.com
[2] Faculty of Informatics, Eötvös Loránd University,
Budapest, Hungary
csuhaj@inf.elte.hu
[3] Faculty of Informatics, Vienna University of Technology,
Vienna, Austria
rudi@emcc.at

Abstract. Acceptance and recognizability of finite strings by red–green Turing machines are defined via infinite runs on the input string and the way how to distinguish between red and green states. We extend the notion of red–green Turing machines to register machines with an input tape and then to several variants of P automata. In order to allow for correct simulations of infinite computations of register machines, the models of P automata have to avoid trapping leading to unwanted infinite computations. Therefore, besides the original model of P automata using antiport rules we here consider two models introduced just recently and also allowing for deterministic simulations of register machine instructions, i.e., we consider the models of P systems with anti-matter as well as catalytic P systems with toxic objects. For all these models of P automata we define their red–green variants and show that they can simulate red–green register machines and therefore red–green Turing machines.

1 Introduction

In this paper we introduce the notion of red–green automata for register machines with input strings given on an input tape (often also called *counter automata*) as well as *red–green P automata* for several specific models of membrane systems. Acceptance and recognizability of finite strings by a red–green Turing machine are defined via infinite runs of the automaton on the input string and the way how to distinguish between red and green states; via infinite runs which are allowed to change between red and green states more than once, more than the recursively enumerable sets of strings can be obtained, i.e., in that way we can "go beyond Turing". Various possibilities how to "go beyond Turing" to be already found in the literature are discussed in [9]; most of the definitions and results for red–green Turing machines are taken from this paper. In the area of P systems, first attempts to do that can be found in [5] and [15]. Computations with infinite words by P automata have been investigated in [8].

© Springer International Publishing Switzerland 2014
M. Gheorghe et al. (Eds.): CMC 2014, LNCS 8961, pp. 139–157, 2014.
DOI: 10.1007/978-3-319-14370-5_9

Here we focus on the idea of being able to switch between red and green states in P automata, where states are specific properties of a configuration, for example, the occurrence or the non-occurrence of a specific symbol. As for Turing machines, with one change from red to green states, we can accept all recursively enumerable languages. Such a result can easily be obtained especially for the basic model of P automata using antiport rules assigned to the skin membrane, yet also for several other models of P automata which can simulate the instructions of a register machine without needing trapping rules to force incorrect guesses into infinite computations; instead, wrong guesses should lead to computations halting without yielding a result, whereas the infinite computations are those defining acceptance or recognizability of the finite strings defined by the input symbols taken in during the computation. Therefore, as further models of red–green P automata we consider catalytic P systems with toxic objects as well as P systems with anti-matter with the matter/anti-matter annihilation rules having weak priority over all other rules. Both these models have been introduced just recently; the main results for these new models are described in [3] as well as in [1] and [2].

Before we extend the concept of red–green Turing machines to red–green P automata, we discuss the concept of red–green register machines; based on the corresponding simulations of the infinite runs of red–green Turing machines by the corresponding infinite computations of red–green register machines, for all the models of P systems mentioned above we describe their red–green automata variants and how they can simulate the instructions of a register machine on its registers in a deterministic way or at least quasi-deterministic way. We emphasize that P automata, when dealing with strings, in some sense themselves during a computation define the input string to be analyzed, as this string is defined as the sequence of terminal symbols taken in from the environment. This causes an inherent non-determinism with respect to these input rules; only when using an encoding by numbers for the input string, we can avoid this kind of non-determinism. Throughout the paper, with a (quasi-)deterministic simulation of a register machine with string input by a P automaton we will understand the (quasi-)deterministic simulation of the instructions on the registers, excluding the read-operations: in that sense, the classic definition of determinism can be applied for P automata with antiport rules as well as for P automata with anti-matter with the matter/anti-matter annihilation rules having weak priority over all other rules, i.e., at most one multiset of rules is applicable to a configuration; for catalytic P systems with toxic objects, we will use the notion "quasi-determinism" – at most one multiset of rules exists such that the resulting configuration can evolve further one step without leaving any toxic object idle; in some sense this corresponds with a look-ahead of one step, also see [16].

The paper is organized as follows: After recalling some basic definitions from formal language theory, we give a short description of the arithmetical hierarchy, e.g., see [4]. Then we restate some results from [9] for red–green Turing machines and extend the notion and the results of red–green Turing machines to register machines. In the fourth section we define the basic model of P automata using antiport rules as well as the newly introduced models of catalytic P systems with toxic objects and P systems with anti-matter with the matter/anti-matter annihilation rules having weak priority over all other rules; we show how the results for red–green Turing machines and red–green register machines can easily be carried over to red–green P automata based on these three models of P systems with antiport rules, with toxic objects, and with anti-matter. We conclude the paper with an overview of the most important results established in this paper and an outlook to future research.

2   Definitions

In this section, we first recall some of the definitions from formal language theory. Then we give a short description of the arithmetical hierarchy.

We assume the reader to be familiar with the underlying notions and concepts from formal language theory, e.g., see [14], as well as from the area of P systems, e.g., see [13].

2.1   Prerequisites

The set of integers is denoted by $\mathbb{Z}$, and the set of non-negative integers by $\mathbb{N}$. Given an alphabet V, a finite non-empty set of abstract symbols, the free monoid generated by V under the operation of concatenation is denoted by V^*. The elements of V^* are called strings, the empty string is denoted by λ, and $V^* \backslash \{\lambda\}$ is denoted by V^+. For an arbitrary alphabet $V = \{a_1, \ldots, a_n\}$, the number of occurrences of a symbol a_i in a string x is denoted by $|x|_{a_i}$, while the length of a string x is denoted by $|x| = \sum_{a_i \in V} |x|_{a_i}$. A (finite) multiset over a (finite) alphabet $V = \{a_1, \ldots, a_n\}$ is a mapping $f : V \to \mathbb{N}$ and can be represented by $\left\langle a_1^{f(a_1)}, \ldots, a_n^{f(a_n)} \right\rangle$ or by any string x for which $(|x|_{a_1}, \ldots, |x|_{a_n}) = (f(a_1), \ldots, f(a_n))$. The families of regular and recursively enumerable string languages are denoted by REG and RE, respectively.

2.2   Register Machines

A *register machine* is a tuple $M = (m, B, l_0, l_h, P)$, where m is the number of registers, B is a set of labels, $l_0 \in B$ is the initial label, $l_h \in B$ is the final label, and P is the set of instructions bijectively labeled by elements of B. The instructions of M can be of the following forms:

- $l_1 : (ADD\,(r), l_2, l_3)$, with $l_1 \in B \backslash \{l_h\}$, $l_2, l_3 \in B$, $1 \leq j \leq m$.
  Increases the value of register r by one, followed by a non-deterministic jump to instruction l_2 or l_3. This instruction is usually called *increment*.
- $l_1 : (SUB\,(r), l_2, l_3)$, with $l_1 \in B \backslash \{l_h\}$, $l_2, l_3 \in B$, $1 \leq j \leq m$.
  If the value of register r is zero then jump to instruction l_3; otherwise, the value of register r is decreased by one, followed by a jump to instruction l_2. The two cases of this instruction are usually called *zero-test* and *decrement*, respectively.

- $l_h : HALT$. Stops the execution of the register machine.

A *configuration* of a register machine is described by the contents (i.e., by the number stored in the register) of each register and by the current label, which indicates the next instruction to be executed. Computations start by executing the instruction l_0 of P, and terminate with reaching the HALT-instruction l_h.

In order to deal with strings, this basic model of register machines can be extended by instructions for reading from an input tape and writing to an output tape containing strings over an input alphabet T_{in} and an output alphabet T_{out}, respectively:

- $l_1 : (read\,(a)\,,l_2)$, with $l_1 \in B \setminus \{l_h\}$, $l_2 \in B$, $a \in T_{in}$.
  Reads the symbol a from the input tape and jumps to instruction l_2.
- $l_1 : (write\,(a)\,,l_2)$, with $l_1 \in B \setminus \{l_h\}$, $l_2 \in B$, $a \in T_{out}$.
  Writes the symbol a on the output tape and jumps to instruction l_2.

Such a register machine working on strings often is also called a *counter automaton*, and we write $M = (m, B, l_0, l_h, P, T_{in}, T_{out})$. If no output is written, we omit T_{out}.

As is well known (e.g., see [10]), for any recursively enumerable set of natural numbers there exists a register machine with (at most) three registers accepting the numbers in this set. Counter automata, i.e., register machines with an input tape, with two registers can simulate the computations of Turing machines and thus characterize RE. All these results are obtained with deterministic register machines, where the ADD-instructions are of the form $l_1 : (ADD\,(r)\,,l_2)$, with $l_1 \in B \setminus \{l_h\}$, $l_2 \in B$, $1 \leq j \leq m$.

2.3   The Arithmetical Hierarchy

We now describe the *Arithmetical Hierarchy* (for example, see [4]). The Arithmetical Hierarchy is usually developed with the universal ($\forall$) and existential ($\exists$) quantifiers restricted to the integers. Levels in the Arithmetical Hierarchy are labeled as Σ_n if they can be defined by expressions beginning with a sequence of n alternating quantifiers starting with $\exists$; levels are labeled as Π_n if they can be defined by such expressions of n alternating quantifiers that start with $\forall$. Σ_0 and Π_0 are defined as having no quantifiers and are equivalent. Σ_1 and Π_1 only have the single quantifier $\exists$ and $\forall$, respectively. We only need to consider alternating pairs of the quantifiers $\forall$ and $\exists$ because two quantifiers of the same type occurring together are equivalent to a single quantifier.

Another way of looking at the Arithmetical Hierarchy is to consider the Halting Problem for Turing machines and machines equipped with an oracle solving this problem. Then one can apply the original proof for the undecidability of the Halting Problem to such a machine to prove it cannot solve its own Halting Problem. Then one can give an oracle for this higher level Halting Problem and generate an even higher level problem. Thus the Arithmetical Hierarchy reflects degrees of unsolvability.

A related way to extend the hierarchy of unsolvable problems is to ask if a computer program will generate an infinite number of outputs. This property can be generalized by interpreting the output of a computer as the Gödel number of another computer. Then one can ask the question "Does a program have an infinite number of outputs an infinite subset of which, when interpreted as computer programs, have an infinite number of outputs?" This can be iterated any finite number of times to create the Arithmetical Hierarchy. In that sense, the Arithmetical Hierarchy can be described as in the following table taken from [4]:

Table 1. Arithmetical Hierarchy

Level	Question: will the computer program
$\Sigma_0 = \Pi_0$	halt in fixed time
Σ_1	ever halt
Π_1	never halt
Σ_2	have at most a finite number of outputs
Π_2	have an infinite number of outputs
Σ_3	have at most a finite number of Π_2 outputs
Π_3	have an infinite number of Π_2 outputs
Σ_n	have at most a finite number of Π_{n-1} outputs
Π_n	have an infinite number of Π_{n-1} outputs

3 Red–Green Turing Machines

A Turing machine M is called a *red–green Turing machine* if its set of internal states Q is partitioned into two subsets, Q_{red} and Q_{green}, and M operates without halting. Q_{red} is called the set of "red states", Q_{green} the set of "green states". Moreover, we shall assume M to be deterministic, i.e., for each configuration there exists exactly one transition to the next one.

Red–green Turing machines can be seen as a type of ω-Turing machines on finite inputs with a recognition criterion based on some property of the set(s) of states visited (in)finitely often, in the tradition of ω-automata (see [8]), i.e., we call an infinite run of the Turing machine on input w *recognizing* if and only if

- no red state is visited infinitely often and
- some green states (one or more) are visited infinitely often.

Remark 1. In the following, we use the phrase "mind change" in the sense of changing the color, i.e., changing from red to green or vice versa.

To get the reader familiar with the basic idea of red–green automata, we give a short sketch of the proofs for some well-known results (see [9]):

Theorem 1. *A set of strings L is recognized by a red–green Turing machine with one mind change if and only if $L \in \Sigma_1$, i.e., if L is recursively enumerable.*

Proof. Let L be the set of strings recognized by a red–green Turing machine M with one mind change. Then design a Turing machine that enumerates all possible inputs, simulates and dovetails the computations of M on these inputs, and outputs string w whenever M makes its first mind change (if any) during the computation on w.

Conversely, if $L \in \Sigma_1$ and M is the Turing machine that enumerates L, then design a red–green Turing machine that on input w simulates the computation of M in red but switches to green when w appears in the enumeration. This red–green Turing machine precisely recognizes L.   □

3.1   Red–Green Turing Machines – Going Beyond Turing

If more mind changes are allowed, the full power of red–green Turing machines is revealed. For example, the complement of a recursively enumerable set L need not be recursively enumerable, too, but it is always red–green recognizable:

Let M' be the Turing machine recognizing L. Then construct a red–green Turing machine M that operates on inputs w as follows: starting in red, the machine immediately switches to green and starts simulating M' on w. If M' halts (thus recognizing w), the machine switches to red and stays in red from then onward. It follows that M precisely recognizes, in fact *accepts*, the set L. *Acceptance* means that for every word not recognized by the Turing machine it will never make an infinite number of mind changes, i.e., it finally will end up in red.

The following result characterizes the computational power of red–green Turing machines (see [9]):

Theorem 2. *(Computational power of red–green Turing machines)*

(a) *Red–green Turing machines recognize exactly the Σ_2-sets of the Arithmetical Hierarchy.*

(b) *Red–green Turing machines accept exactly the Π_2-sets of the Arithmetical Hierarchy.*

3.2   Red–Green Register Machines

As is well-known folklore, e.g., see [10], the computations of a Turing machine can be simulated by a counter automaton with (only two) counters; in this paper, we will rather speak of a register machine with (two) registers and with string input. As for red–green Turing machines, we can also color the "states", i.e., the labels, of a register machine $M = (m, B, l_0, l_h, P, T_{in})$ by the two colors red and green, i.e., partition its set of labels B into two disjoint sets B_{red} (red "states") and B_{green} (green "states"), and we then write $RM = (m, B, B_{red}, B_{green}, l_0, P, T_{in})$, as we can omit the halting label l_h.

Theorem 3. *The computations of a red–green Turing machine TM can be simulated by a red–green register machine RM with two registers and with string* *input in such a way that during the simulation of a transition of TM leading from a state p with color c to a state p' with color c' the simulating register machine uses instructions with labels ("states") of color c and only in the last step of the simulation changes to a label ("state") of color c'.*

Proof. (Sketch) As the underlying model of Turing machines we consider the variant having a separate input tape from which the input string is read from left to right as well as a working tape for carrying out the computations. Let TM be such a Turing machine having its set of internal states Q partitioned into two subsets, Q_{red} (the set of red states) and Q_{green} (the set of green states); TM operates without halting, i.e., with an infinite run on each input string. The register machine RM with string input simulating TM also has to color its labels into red and green "states", i.e., to partition its set of labels B into two disjoint sets B_{red} (red "states") and B_{green} (green "states") according to the strategy described in the following. The register machine $RM = (m, B, B_{red}, B_{green}, l_0, P, T_{in})$ can directly simulate a read-operation of the Turing machine TM by the corresponding read-operation on its input tape, i.e., one step of TM corresponds with one step of RM and the corresponding states in TM and RM have to get the same colors. When simulating one computation step of TM leading from a state p with color $c \in \{red, green\}$ to a state p' with color $c' \in \{red, green\}$ on its working tape, RM has to use only "states", i.e., labels, with color c until the simulation is completed with entering a "state" of color c'.   □

It is rather obvious that also the other direction of the preceding lemma works, i.e., red–green register machines, even with an arbitrary number of registers, with string input can be simulated by red–green Turing machines observing the corresponding colors of states:

Lemma 1. *The computations of a red–green register machine RM with an arbitrary number of registers and with string input can be simulated by a red–green Turing machine TM in such a way that during the simulation of a computation step of RM leading from an instruction with label ("state") p with color c to an instruction with label ("state") p' with color c' the simulating Turing machine stays in states of color c and only in the last step of the simulation changes to a state of color c'.*

Proof. (Sketch) Let $RM = (m, B, B_{red}, B_{green}, l_0, P, T_{in})$ be a red–green register machine, i.e., its set of labels B is partitioned into two disjoint sets B_{red} (red "states") and B_{green} (green "states"); for every input string, the computation of RM never stops. Then one can easily construct a red–green Turing machine having its set of internal states Q partitioned into two subsets, Q_{red} (the set of red states) and Q_{green} (the set of green states); TM operates without halting, i.e., with an infinite run on each input string. The simulating red–green Turing machine TM has to color its states in red and green states according to the strategy described in the following. The Turing machine TM can directly simulate a read-operation of the register machine RM by the corresponding read-operation on its input tape, i.e., one step by RM corresponds to one step of TM and the corresponding states in RM and TM have to get the same colors. When simulating one computation step of RM leading from a label ("state") p with color c to a label ("state") p' with color c', TM has to use only states with color c until the simulation is completed with entering a state of color c'.   □

As an immediate consequence, the preceding two lemmas yield the characterization of Σ_2 and Π_2 by red–green register machines as Theorem 2 does for red–green Turing machines:

Theorem 4. *(Computational power of red–green register machines)*

(i) *A set of strings L is recognized by a red–green register machine with one mind change if and only if $L \in \Sigma_1$, i.e., if L is recursively enumerable.*

(ii) *Red–green register machines recognize exactly the Σ_2-sets of the Arithmetical Hierarchy.*

(iii) *Red–green register machines accept exactly the Π_2-sets of the Arithmetical Hierarchy.*

The step from red–green Turing machines to red–green register machines is important for the succeeding section, as usually register machines are simulated when proving a model of P systems to be computationally complete. Hence, when showing models of red–green P automata to characterize Σ_2 and Π_2, we only have to show how red–green register machines can be simulated.

Let us finally cite from [15]:

"... a super-Turing potential is naturally and inherently present in evolution of living organisms."

In that sense, we now seek for this potential in specific models of P automata by defining their red–green variants.

4   Variants of Red–Green P Automata

In this section, we consider several models of P systems which allow for defining the corresponding variant of red–green P automata in a straightforward manner. Besides the original model of *P automata with antiport rules*, we also take into account two other models of P systems introduced just recently, i.e., *P automata with toxic objects* as well as *P automata with anti-matter*, see [3] as well as [1] and [2] in this volume.

The main challenge is how to define the "red" and "green" states in P automata. In fact, states sometimes are considered to simply be the configurations a P automaton may reach during a computation, or some specific elements occurring in a configuration define its state. Another variant is to consider the multiset of rules applicable to a configuration as its state, which especially may make sense in the case of deterministic systems. Obviously, in any case we have to restrict ourselves to recursive, i.e., computable, features to distinguish between "red" and "green" states. Although in principle this definition would allow us to deal with an infinite number of "states", for all the variants considered in the following, we will be able to restrict ourselves to a finite number of "states", i.e., a finite number of different multisets of objects occurring in the configurations reachable from the initial configuration will define the set of "states" which then can be partitioned into two disjoint sets of "red states" and "green states".

4.1   The Basic Model of P Automata with Antiport Rules

The basic model of P automata as introduced in [6] and in a similar way in [7] is based on antiport rules, i.e., on rules of the form u/v, which means that the multiset u goes out through the membrane and v comes in instead. As it is already folklore, only one membrane is needed for obtaining computational completeness with antiport rules in the maximally parallel derivation mode; the input string is defined as the sequence of terminal symbols taken in during a halting computation (without loss of generality we may assume that at most one terminal symbol is taken in from the environment in each computation step). Restricting ourselves to P automata with only one membrane as the basic model, we define a P automaton (with antiport rules) as follows:

A *P automaton (with antiport rules)* is a construct

$$\Pi = (O, T, w, R)$$

where

- O is the alphabet of *objects*,
- $T \subset O$ is the alphabet of *terminal objects*,
- $w \in (O \setminus T)^*$ is the *initial multiset*, i.e., the multiset of objects present in the skin membrane at the beginning of a computation, and
- R is a finite set of *antiport rules*.

The strings accepted by Π consist of the sequences of terminal symbols taken in during a halting computation.

In order to define a *red–green P automaton (with antiport rules)*, we first mention that in this case we only look at infinite computations and that we *accept or recognize finite strings consisting of the finite sequences of terminal symbols taken in during an infinite computation.* In its most general form, we can use a recursive function on the set of all configurations $f_{red/green}$ yielding as a result the color, i.e., red or green, of the given configuration, and we write

$$\Pi = \left(O, T, w, R, f_{red/green} \right).$$

As we shall see later, for P automata with antiport rules instead of such a general function we may simply define disjoint subsets of singleton objects to determine the color of the underlying configuration, i.e., we take O_{red} and O_{green} with $O_{red} \cup O_{green} \subseteq O$ and require that every configuration over Π reachable from the initial configuration has to contain exactly one element from $O_{red} \cup O_{green}$; in this case, we simply write

$$\Pi = (O, T, w, R, O_{red}, O_{green}) \,.$$

We now show how the instructions of a (red–green) register machine with string input on its registers can be simulated by a (red–green) P automaton even in a deterministic way and preserving the coloring of the states. We recall our convention that determinism here does not apply to the read-instructions defining the input string.

Lemma 2. *For every red–green register machine*

$$RM = (m, B, B_{red}, B_{green}, l_0, P, T_{in})$$

we can construct a red–green P automaton with antiport rules

$$\Pi = (O, T, w, R, O_{red}, O_{green})$$

simulating the computations of RM in such a way that during the simulation of an instruction of RM leading from a label ("state") p with color c to a label ("state") p' with color c' the simulating P automaton Π only goes through configurations ("states") of color c and only in the last step of the simulation changes to a configuration ("state") of color c'.

Proof. Let $RM = (m, B, B_{red}, B_{green}, l_0, P, T_{in})$ be a red–green register machine. Following the deterministic proof given in [13], Chapter 5, Theorem 5.1, we now construct a red–green P automaton with antiport rules simulating the instructions of RM on its registers in a deterministic way as follows:

The number n_r contained in register r of the register machine is represented by the multiset $a_r{}^{n_r}$.

$$
\begin{aligned}
\Pi &= (O, T, w, R, O_{red}, O_{green})\,, \\
O &= T_{in} \cup \{a_r \mid 1 \leq r \leq m\} \cup \{l_1 \mid l_1 : (read\,(a)\,, l_2) \in P\} \\
&\quad \cup \{l_1 \mid l_1 : (ADD\,(r)\,, l_2) \in P\} \\
&\quad \cup \left\{ l_1, l_1', l_1'', \tilde{l}_1, \bar{l}_1 \mid l_1 : (SUB\,(r)\,, l_2, l_3) \in P \right\}, \\
O_{red} &= \{l_1 \mid l_1 : (read\,(a)\,, l_2) \in P, l_1 \in B_{red}\} \\
&\quad \cup \{l_1 \mid l_1 : (ADD\,(r)\,, l_2) \in P, l_1 \in B_{red}\} \\
&\quad \cup \{l_1, l_1', l_1'' \mid l_1 : (SUB\,(r)\,, l_2, l_3) \in P, l_1 \in B_{red}\}, \\
O_{green} &= \{l_1 \mid l_1 : (read\,(a)\,, l_2) \in P, l_1 \in B_{green}\} \\
&\quad \cup \{l_1 \mid l_1 : (ADD\,(r)\,, l_2) \in P, l_1 \in B_{green}\} \\
&\quad \cup \{l_1, l_1', l_1'' \mid l_1 : (SUB\,(r)\,, l_2, l_3) \in P, l_1 \in B_{green}\}, \\
T &= T_{in}, \\
w &= l_0,
\end{aligned}
$$

and R contains the following antiport rules:

- $l_1 : (read(a), l_2)$, with $l_1, l_2 \in B$, $a \in T$, is simulated by the corresponding antiport rule l_1/al_2.
- $l_1 : (ADD(r), l_2)$, with $l_1, l_2 \in B$, $1 \leq j \leq m$, is simulated by the corresponding antiport rule $l_1/a_r l_2$.
- $l_1 : (SUB(r), l_2, l_3)$, with $l_1, l_2, l_3 \in B$, $1 \leq j \leq m$, is simulated by the following rules:

$l_1/l_1'\tilde{l}_1,\ \tilde{l}_1 a_r/\bar{l}_1,\ l_1'/l_1'',\ l_1''\bar{l}_1/l_2,\ l_1''\tilde{l}_1/l_3.$

Depending on the contents of register r, we either can apply $\tilde{l}_1 a_r/\bar{l}_1$ if it is non-empty or else the object $\tilde{l}_1$ has to stay idle for one computation step in Π. The two possible situations are illustrated in the following table:

register r is non-empty	register r is empty
$l_1 a_r$	l_1
$l_1' \tilde{l}_1 a_r$	$l_1' \tilde{l}_1$
$l_1'' \bar{l}_1$	$l_1'' \tilde{l}_1$
l_2	l_3

As it is easy to see, l_1' and l_1'' have to keep the same color as l_1 and can be interpreted as the "states" of the P system Π during the intermediate simulation steps, hence, the coloring of the objects from O into state objects in O_{red} and O_{green} exactly follows the colorings of the red–green register machine M in B_{red} and B_{green}.

In sum, we conclude that for any infinite computation in RM we get a correct simulation in Π with respecting the coloring of states, and even in a deterministic way as far as only the simulation of instructions on the registers are taken into account. $\square$

4.2   Catalytic P Automata with Toxic Objects

In *catalytic P automata with toxic objects* we use non-cooperative and catalytic rules, yet with the additional condition that a computation branch is halting without yielding any result if we cannot find an applicable multiset of rules not covering all toxic objects, where the *toxic objects* are a specified subset of all objects used in the P system. In that way, the usual trapping with a trap symbol # yielding infinite computations by the trap rule # $\rightarrow$ # can be avoided. Again we restrict ourselves to P automata with only one membrane, the skin membrane.

A *catalytic P automaton with toxic objects* is a construct

$$\Pi = (O, O_{tox}, C, T, w, R)$$

where

- O is the alphabet of *objects*,
- $O_{tox} \subseteq O \setminus T$ is the set of *toxic objects* in O,

- $C \subset O \setminus T$ is the set of *catalysts* in O,
- $T \subset O \setminus C$ is the alphabet of *terminal objects*,
- $w \in (O \setminus T)^*$ is the *initial multiset*, i.e., the multiset of objects present in the skin membrane at the beginning of a computation, and
- R is a finite set of rules of the following forms:

> **non-cooperative rules:** are rules of the form $u \to v$ where $u \in O \setminus (T \cup C)$ and $v \in (O \setminus (T \cup C))^*$;
>
> **catalytic rules:** are rules of the form $cu \to cv$ where $c \in C$, $u \in O \setminus (T \cup C)$ and $v \in (O \setminus (T \cup C))^*$;
>
> **input rules:** are special non-cooperative rules of the form $p \to q\,(a, come)$ or catalytic rules of the form $cp \to cq\,(a, come)$ where $c \in C$, $p, q \in O \setminus (T \cup C)$ and $a \in T$; whereas p changes to q in the skin membrane, at the same moment the terminal symbol a is taken in from the environment; without loss of generality, we will also assume that there are no rules for the terminal symbols $a \in T$ in R except for these input rules. The sequence of terminal symbols taken in by these input rules forms the string to be accepted by the P automaton.

Again, *catalytic red–green P automata with toxic objects* are catalytic P automata with toxic objects where we are only interested in their infinite computations *accepting or recognizing finite strings consisting of the finite sequences of terminal symbols taken in during an infinite computation*. In its most general form, as for red–green P automata with antiport rules we could use a recursive function on the set of all configurations $f_{red/green}$ yielding as a result the color, i.e., red or green, of the given configuration, and write

$$\Pi = \left(O, O_{tox}, C, T, w, R, f_{red/green}\right).$$

As for P automata with antiport rules, instead of such a general function we may simply define disjoint subsets of the objects to determine the color of the underlying configuration, i.e., we take O_{red} and O_{green} with $O_{red} \cup O_{green} \subseteq O \setminus (T \cup C)$ and require that every configuration over Π reachable from the initial configuration has to contain exactly one element from $O_{red} \cup O_{green}$; in this case, we simply write

$$\Pi = (O, O_{tox}, C, T, w, R, O_{red}, O_{green}).$$

Catalytic (red–green) P automata with toxic objects are called *purely catalytic* if all rules involve a catalyst.

Lemma 3. *For every red–green register machine*

$$RM = (m, B, B_{red}, B_{green}, l_0, P, T_{in})$$

we can construct a purely catalytic red–green P automaton with toxic objects

$$\Pi = (O, O_{tox}, C, T, w, R, O_{red}, O_{green})$$

simulating the computations of RM in such a way that during the simulation of an instruction of RM leading from a label ("state") p with color c to a label ("state") p′ with color c′ the simulating P automaton Π only goes through configurations ("states") of color c and only in the last step of the simulation changes to a configuration ("state") of color c′.

Proof. Let $RM = (m, B, B_{red}, B_{green}, l_0, P, T_{in})$ be a red–green register machine. Our goal is to obtain a quasi-deterministic construction, i.e., a proof where for every input string defined by the terminal symbols taken in by the input rules $p \rightarrow q(a, come)$ there exists only one prolongation to an infinite computation. The purely catalytic red–green P automaton with toxic objects we are going to describe below is constructed in such a way that it simulates the instructions of M in a quasi-deterministic way – as already mentioned earlier, this means that if the wrong multiset of rules is applied, in the next step we cannot find an applicable multiset of rules covering all toxic objects, hence, this computation branch is abandoned. The only non-determinism will remain with the choice of the input rules $p \rightarrow q(a, come)$, i.e., for p there can be several rules with different input symbols a from T (and, of course, eventually different states q) on their right sides, yet this only means that we are simulating RM on a different input. Finally, as we want to simulate register machines with an arbitrary number of registers, we adapt a new proof technique for the simulation of register machine instructions as exhibited in [3], see this volume. This new proof technique allows for a very simple simulation of the register machine instructions in real-time, i.e., each computation step in RM has exactly one correct simulation step in Π.

The main idea of this new construction is to use two catalysts for each register – one for the decrement ($c_{r,Decr}$) and one for the zero-test ($c_{r,0Test}$). Moreover, each SUB-instruction is simulated by two rules, one for the decrement and one for the zero-test, just allowing the corresponding catalyst to do its work, whereas all the other catalysts are kept busy by the symbols d_r for $c_{r,Decr}$ and e_r for $c_{r,0Test}$, respectively, with these symbols d_r and e_r having been introduced one step before. The symbol d is used to introduce the toxic object $\#$ which usually would be used as a trap symbol for causing an infinite computation for wrong choices of multisets of rules. The catalyst c_B is used with the instruction labels in B. As usual, the number n_r contained in register r of the register machine is represented by the multiset $a_r{}^{n_r}$. For each of the registers r, the following rules perform the decrement and the zero-test, respectively, in case this operation is initiated by omitting d_r or e_r, respectively, in the step before.

decrement

$c_{r,Decr}a_r \rightarrow c_{r,Decr}$: if register r is not empty, it is decremented;

$c_{r,Decr}d \rightarrow c_{r,Decr}\#$: if register r is empty, the catalyst $c_{r,Decr}$ has to be used with the symbol d thereby introducing the toxic symbol $\#$, for which no rule exists, hence, with the application of this rule the whole computation branch is abandoned.

$c_{r,Decr}d_r \rightarrow c_{r,Decr}$: d_r keeps $c_{r,Decr}$ busy if another instruction is to be simulated; d_r is a toxic object which must not stay idle;

zero-test

$c_{r,0Test}a_r \rightarrow c_{r,0Test}\#$: if register r is not empty, the toxic symbol $\#$ is generated in case it cannot be used with the symbol e_r being present if another instruction is to be simulated;

$c_{r,0Test}e_r \rightarrow c_{r,0Test}$: the toxic object e_r keeps $c_{r,0Test}$ busy if another instruction is to be simulated.

As for each computation step in RM there exists exactly one correct simulation step in Π with exactly the same symbols representing the corresponding states, the coloring is trivial.

$$\Pi = (O, O_{tox}, C, T, w, R, O_{red}, O_{green}),$$
$$O = T_{in} \cup \{a_r, d_r, e_r, c_{r,Decr}, c_{r,0Test} \mid 1 \leq r \leq m\} \cup B \cup \{c_B, d, \#\},$$
$$O_{tox} = \{d_r, e_r \mid 1 \leq r \leq m\} \cup \{\#\},$$
$$C = \{c_{r,Decr}, c_{r,0Test} \mid 1 \leq r \leq m\} \cup \{c_B\},$$
$$T = T_{in},$$
$$w = l_0 d \prod_{1 \leq i \leq m} d_i \prod_{1 \leq i \leq m} e_i,$$
$$R = \left\{ c_B l_1 \rightarrow c_B l_2 \, (a, come) \prod_{1 \leq i \leq m} d_i \prod_{1 \leq i \leq m} e_i \mid l_1 : (read\,(a)\,, l_2) \in P \right\}$$
$$\cup \left\{ c_B l_1 \rightarrow c_B l_2 a_r \prod_{1 \leq i \leq m} d_i \prod_{1 \leq i \leq m} e_i \mid l_1 : (ADD\,(r)\,, l_2) \in P \right\}$$
$$\cup \left\{ c_B l_1 \rightarrow c_B l_2 \prod_{1 \leq i \leq m, i \neq r} d_i \prod_{1 \leq i \leq m} e_i \mid l_1 : (SUB\,(r)\,, l_2, l_3) \in P \right\}$$
$$\cup \left\{ c_B l_1 \rightarrow c_B l_3 \prod_{1 \leq i \leq m} d_i \prod_{1 \leq i \leq m, i \neq r} e_i \mid l_1 : (SUB\,(r)\,, l_2, l_3) \in P \right\}$$
$$\cup \{ c_{r,Decr}a_r \rightarrow c_{r,Decr}, c_{r,Decr}d \rightarrow c_{r,Decr}\#, c_{r,Decr}d_r \rightarrow c_{r,Decr},$$
$$\cup \; c_{r,0Test}a_r \rightarrow c_{r,0Test}\#, c_{r,0Test}e_r \rightarrow c_{r,0Test} \mid 1 \leq i \leq m\},$$
$$O_{red} = B_{red},$$
$$O_{green} = B_{green}.$$

The rule $c_B l_1 \rightarrow c_B l_2 \prod_{1 \leq i \leq m, i \neq r} d_i \prod_{1 \leq i \leq m} e_i$ leaves free the catalyst $c_{r,Decr}$ for using the rule $c_{r,Decr}a_r \rightarrow c_{r,Decr}$, i.e., for simulating the decrement case, whereas the rule $c_B l_1 \rightarrow c_B l_3 \prod_{1 \leq i \leq m} d_i \prod_{1 \leq i \leq m, i \neq r} e_i$ leaves free the catalyst $c_{r,0Test}$ for the zero-test, as with the occurrence of a symbol a_r the rule $c_{r,0Test}a_r \rightarrow c_{r,0Test}\#$ is enforced, which introduces the toxic symbol $\#$, for which no rule exists, hence it enforces the computation to be abandoned. By construction, the states of RM directly correspond with the "states" of Π, hence, we can directly take over the coloring from the states in B into the two disjoint sets B_{red} and B_{green} to the coloring of "states" of Π into O_{red} and O_{green}.

In sum, we conclude that each step of any infinite computation in RM is correctly simulated by one step of Π – even in a quasi-deterministic way as far as only the simulations of instructions on the registers are taken into account – with respecting the coloring of states.   □

4.3   P Automata with Anti-Matter

In *P automata with anti-matter*, for each object a we may have its anti-matter object a^-. If an object a meets its anti-matter object a^-, then these two objects annihilate each other, which corresponds to the application of the non-cooperative erasing rule $aa^- \to \lambda$. In the following, we shall only consider the variant where these annihilation rules have priority over all other rules, which allows for a deterministic simulation of deterministic register machines or counter automata, see [2].

Whereas in [2] non-cooperative and catalytic rules are allowed in P systems with anti-matter, we here only use non-cooperative rules, and again we restrict ourselves to P automata with only one membrane, the skin membrane. Yet this basic variant of catalytic P systems is now extended by also allowing for annihilation rules $aa^- \to \lambda$, with these rules having weak priority over all other rules, i.e., other rules can only be applied if no annihilation rule could still bind the corresponding objects.

A *P automaton with anti-matter* is a construct

$$\Pi = (O, T, w, R)$$

where

- O is the alphabet of *objects*,
- $T \subset O$ is the alphabet of *terminal objects*,
- $w \in (O \setminus T)^*$ is the *initial multiset*, i.e., the multiset of objects present in the skin membrane at the beginning of a computation, and
- R is a finite set of rules of the following forms:

  non-cooperative rules: are rules of the form $u \to v$ where $u \in O \setminus T$ and $v \in (O \setminus T)^*$;

  input rules: are special non-cooperative rules of the form $p \to q\,(a, come)$ where $p, q \in O \setminus T$ and $a \in T$; whereas p changes to q in the skin membrane, at the same moment the terminal symbol a is taken in from the environment; without loss of generality, we will also assume that there are no rules for the terminal symbols $a \in T$ in R except for these input rules. The sequence of terminal symbols taken in by these input rules forms the string to be accepted by the P automaton;

  matter/anti-matter annihilation rules: are cooperative rules of the form $aa^- \to \lambda$, i.e., the matter object a and its anti-matter object a^- annihilate each other, and these annihilation rules have weak priority over all other rules.

Again, *red–green P automata with anti-matter* are P automata with anti-matter where we are only interested in its infinite computations *accepting or recognizing finite strings consisting of the finite sequences of terminal symbols taken in during an infinite computation.* In its most general form, as for red–green P automata with antiport rules we could use a recursive function on the set of all configurations $f_{red/green}$ yielding as a result the color, i.e., red or green, of the given configuration, and write

$$\Pi = \left(O, T, w, R, f_{red/green}\right).$$

As for red–green P automata with antiport rules, we cannot avoid the inherent non-determinism coming along with the input rules. Yet following the poof given in [2], the simulation of all the other instructions working on the registers of the underlying red–green register machine can be carried out in a deterministic way. In contrast to red–green P automata with antiport rules, this general function cannot simply be replaced by disjoint subsets of singleton objects to determine the color of the underlying configuration, instead we have to specify finite sets S_{red} and S_{green} of finite multisets over $O \setminus T$ and require that every configuration over Π reachable from the initial configuration has to contain exactly one multiset from $S_{red} \cup S_{green}$; in this case, we then write

$$\Pi = (O, T, w, R, S_{red}, S_{green}).$$

Lemma 4. *For every red–green register machine*

$$RM = (m, B, B_{red}, B_{green}, l_0, P, T_{in})$$

we can construct a red–green P automaton with anti-matter

$$\Pi = (O, T, w, R, S_{red}, S_{green})$$

simulating the computations of RM in such a way that during the simulation of an instruction of RM leading from a label ("state") p with color c to a label ("state") p' with color c' the simulating P automaton Π only goes through configurations ("states") of color c and only in the last step of the simulation changes to a configuration ("state") of color c'.

Proof. Let $RM = (m, B, B_{red}, B_{green}, l_0, P, T_{in})$ be a red–green register machine. Following the deterministic proof given in [2], we now construct a red–green P automaton with anti-matter simulating the instructions of RM on its registers in a deterministic way as follows:

As usual, the number n_r contained in register r of the register machine is represented by the multiset $a_r^{n_r}$. Moreover, for every register r, $1 \leq r \leq m$, we use the notation $B_-(r) = \{l \mid l : (SUB(r), l', l'') \in P\}$, and the rule $a_r^- \rightarrow \prod_{l \in B_-(r)} \tilde{l}^- \prod_{l \in B_-(r)} \hat{l}$ as well as the annihilation rules $a_r a_r^- \rightarrow \lambda$ and $\hat{l}\hat{l}^- \rightarrow \lambda, \tilde{l}\tilde{l}^- \rightarrow \lambda$ for $l \in B_-(r)$.

$$\Pi = (O, T, w, R, S_{red}, S_{green}),$$
$$O = T_{in} \cup \{a_r, a_r^- \mid 1 \leq r \leq m\} \cup B$$
$$\cup \left\{\bar{l}, \hat{l}, \tilde{l}, l^{(d)}, l^{(0)}, \hat{l}^-, \tilde{l}^- \mid l \in B_-(r), 1 \leq r \leq m\right\},$$
$$T = T_{in},$$
$$w = l_0,$$
$$S_{red} = B_{red} \cup \{\bar{l}, l^{(d)}, l^{(0)} \mid l \in B_-(r) \cap B_{red}, 1 \leq r \leq m\}$$
$$\cup \left\{\hat{l_1}^- \prod_{l \in B_-(r)\setminus\{l_1\}} \tilde{l}, \hat{l_1}^- \prod_{l \in B_-(r)\setminus\{l_1\}} \tilde{l} \prod_{l \in B_-(r)} \tilde{l}^- \prod_{l \in B_-(r)} \hat{l} \mid \right.$$
$$\left. l_1 \in B_-(r) \cap B_{red}, 1 \leq r \leq m\right\},$$
$$S_{green} = B_{green} \cup \{\bar{l}, l^{(d)}, l^{(0)} \mid l \in B_-(r) \cap B_{green}, 1 \leq r \leq m\}$$
$$\cup \left\{\hat{l_1}^- \prod_{l \in B_-(r)\setminus\{l_1\}} \tilde{l}, \hat{l_1}^- \prod_{l \in B_-(r)\setminus\{l_1\}} \tilde{l} \prod_{l \in B_-(r)} \tilde{l}^- \prod_{l \in B_-(r)} \hat{l} \mid \right.$$
$$\left. l_1 \in B_-(r) \cap B_{green}, 1 \leq r \leq m\right\},$$

and the set of rules R is defined as follows:

$$R = \{a_r a_r^- \to \lambda \mid 1 \le r \le m\}$$
$$\cup \left\{ a_r^- \to \prod_{l \in B_-(r)} \tilde{l}^- \prod_{l \in B_-(r)} \hat{l} \mid 1 \le r \le m \right\}$$
$$\cup \left\{ \hat{l}\hat{l}^- \to \lambda, \tilde{l}\tilde{l}^- \to \lambda \mid l \in B_-(r), 1 \le r \le m \right\}$$
$$\cup \{l_1 \to l_2 (a, come) \mid l_1 : (read(a), l_2) \in P\}$$
$$\cup \{l_1 \to l_2 a_r \mid l_1 : (ADD(r), l_2) \in P\}$$
$$\cup \left\{ l_1 \to \bar{l}_1 a_r^-, \bar{l}_1 \to \hat{l}_1^- \prod_{l \in B_-(r)\setminus\{l_1\}} \tilde{l}, \hat{l}_1^- \to l_1^{(d)} \prod_{l \in B_-(r)\setminus\{l_1\}} \tilde{l}^-, \right.$$
$$\left. \tilde{l}_1^- \to l_1^{(0)} \prod_{l \in B_-(r)\setminus\{l_1\}} \hat{l}^-, l_1^{(d)} \to l_2, l_1^{(0)} \to l_3 \mid \right.$$
$$\left. l_1 : (SUB(r), l_2, l_3) \in P \right\}.$$

Depending on the contents of register r, we have two possible situations for the simulation of a SUB-instruction $l_1 : (SUB(r), l_2, l_3) \in P$ which are illustrated in the following table; the main idea is that the symbol $\hat{l}_1^-$ generated by the rule $\bar{l}_1 \to \hat{l}_1^- \prod_{l \in B_-(r)\setminus\{l_1\}} \tilde{l}$, is eliminated again and replaced by $\tilde{l}_1^-$ if a_r^- is not annihilated (which indicates that the register is empty):

register r is non-empty	register r is empty
$l_1 a_r$	l_1
$\bar{l}_1 a_r^- a_r$	$\bar{l}_1 a_r^-$
$\hat{l}_1^- \prod_{l \in B_-(r)\setminus\{l_1\}} \tilde{l}$	$\hat{l}_1^- \prod_{l \in B_-(r)\setminus\{l_1\}} \tilde{l} \prod_{l \in B_-(r)} \tilde{l}^- \prod_{l \in B_-(r)} \hat{l}$
$l_1^{(d)} \prod_{l \in B_-(r)\setminus\{l_1\}} \tilde{l}^- \prod_{l \in B_-(r)\setminus\{l_1\}} \tilde{l}$	$l_1^{(0)} \prod_{l \in B_-(r)\setminus\{l_1\}} \tilde{l}^- \prod_{l \in B_-(r)\setminus\{l_1\}} \hat{l}$
l_2	l_3

Whereas anywhere else only singletons can be used as "states", i.e., $l_1, \bar{l}_1, l_1^{(d)}$, and $l_1^{(0)}$, respectively, only for the configuration in the third line of this table, the whole multisets

$$\hat{l}_1^- \prod_{l \in B_-(r)\setminus\{l_1\}} \tilde{l}$$

and

$$\hat{l}_1^- \prod_{l \in B_-(r)\setminus\{l_1\}} \tilde{l} \prod_{l \in B_-(r)} \tilde{l}^- \prod_{l \in B_-(r)} \hat{l}$$

have to be used as "states", but even here the singletons $\hat{l}_1^-$ and $\tilde{l}_1^-$ characterize these "states", as they are the only ones in the current configuration with the marking by $\hat{\ }$ and $\tilde{\ }$, respectively. □

4.4   The Computational Power of Red–Green P Automata

In this subsection we summarize the results of the three preceding subsections for the three models of P automata – with antiport rules, purely catalytic with toxic objects, with anti-matter:

Theorem 5. *(Computational power of red–green P automata)*

(i) *A set of strings L is recognized by a red–green P automaton (with antiport rules, purely catalytic with toxic objects, with anti-matter) with one mind change if and only if $L \in \Sigma_1$, i.e., if L is recursively enumerable.*
(ii) *Red–green P automata (with antiport rules, purely catalytic with toxic objects, with anti-matter) recognize exactly the Σ_2-sets of the Arithmetical Hierarchy.*
(iii) *Red–green P automata (with antiport rules, purely catalytic with toxic objects, with anti-matter) accept exactly the Π_2-sets of the Arithmetical Hierarchy.*

Proof. (Sketch) As we have shown in Lemma 2, Lemma 3, and Lemma 4, all these variants of red–green P automata (with antiport rules, purely catalytic with toxic objects, with anti-matter) can simulate the infinite computations of any red–green register machine, even with a clearly specified finite set of "states" having the same color as the corresponding labels ("states") of the instructions of the red–green register machine with string input.

Therefore, according to Theorem 4, these variants of red–green P automata have at least the same computational power as red–green Turing machines.

But also the converse can be shown in a similar way as outlined for register machines in Lemma 1 now for all these variants of red–green P automata, yet we omit the tedious details how Turing machines can simulate these variants of red–green P automata even in their most general form $\Pi = (O, T, w, R, f_{red/green})$ equipped with a computable function $f_{red/green}$. □

One of the main reasons that the proofs of the lemmas in the preceding subsections are possible is that they are based on the fact that the simulation does not need the trick to trap non-wanted evolutions of the system, which is a trick used very often in the area of P systems. Yet this exactly would contradict the basic feature of the red–green automata way of acceptance by looking at *infinite* computations. Fortunately, the basic model of P automata, i.e., P automata with antiport rules, comes along with this nice feature of not needing trap rules for being able to simulate the instructions of a register machines on its registers, and the models of P systems with toxic objects and P systems with anti-matter have this nice feature, too.

5   Summary and Future Research

A lot of research topics wait for being investigated for P automata "going beyond Turing", not only the different variants of defining red–green P automata as already discussed in this paper. For instance, the idea of having red and green configurations should also be investigated together with models of P automata which are not computationally complete, as for example dP automata.

There are already a lot of strategies and models to be found in the literature how to "go beyond Turing"; some of them should also be of interest to be considered in the P systems area. Thus, a wide range of possible variants to be investigated remains for future research.

References

1. Alhazov, A., Aman, B., Freund, R., Păun, Gh.: Matter and Anti-Matter in Membrane Systems. In: Macías-Ramos, L.F., Martínez-del-Amor, M.Á., Păun, Gh., Riscos-Núñez, A., Valencia-Cabrera, L. (eds.) Proceedings of the Twelfth Brainstorming Week on Membrane Computing, pp. 1–26 (2014)
2. Alhazov, A., Aman, B., Freund, R.: P Systems with Anti-Matter. In: Gheorghe, M., Rozenberg, G., Salomaa, A., Sosík, P., Zandron, C. (eds.) CMC 2014. LNCS, vol. 8961, pp. 66–85. Springer, Heidelberg (2014)
3. Alhazov, A., Freund, R.: P Systems with Toxic Objects. In: Gheorghe, M., Rozenberg, G., Salomaa, A., Sosík, P., Zandron, C. (eds.) CMC 2014. LNCS, vol. 8961, pp. 99–125. Springer, Heidelberg (2014)
4. Budnik, P.: What Is and What Will Be. Mountain Math Software (2006)
5. Calude, C.S., Păun, Gh.: Bio-steps Beyond Turing. Biosystems **77**, 175–194 (2004)
6. Csuhaj-Varjú, E., Vaszil, Gy.: P Automata or Purely Communicating Accepting P Systems. In: Păun, Gh., Rozenberg, G., Salomaa, A., Zandron, C. (eds.) WMC-CdeA 2002. LNCS, vol. 2597, pp. 219–233. Springer, Heidelberg (2003)
7. Freund, R., Oswald, M.: A Short Note on Analysing P Systems. Bulletin of the EATCS **78**, 231–236 (2002)
8. Freund, R., Oswald, M., Staiger, L.: ω-P Automata with Communication Rules. In: Martín-Vide, C., Mauri, G., Păun, Gh., Rozenberg, G., Salomaa, A. (eds.) WMC 2003. LNCS, vol. 2933, pp. 203–217. Springer, Heidelberg (2004)
9. van Leeuwen, J., Wiedermann, J.: Computation as an Unbounded Process. Theoretical Computer Science **429**, 202–212 (2012)
10. Minsky, M.L.: Computation: Finite and Infinite Machines. Prentice Hall, Englewood Cliffs (1967)
11. Păun, Gh.: Computing with Membranes. Journal of Computer and System Sciences **61**(1), 108–143 (2000) (and Turku Center for Computer Science-TUCS Report 208, November 1998, www.tucs.fi)
12. Păun, Gh.: Membrane Computing. An Introduction. Springer (2002)
13. Păun, Gh., Rozenberg, G., Salomaa, A. (eds.): The Oxford Handbook of Membrane Computing. Oxford University Press (2010)
14. Rozenberg, G., Salomaa, A. (eds.): Handbook of Formal Languages, 3 vol. Springer (1997)
15. Sosík, P., Valík, O.: On Evolutionary Lineages of Membrane Systems. In: Freund, R., Păun, Gh., Rozenberg, G., Salomaa, A. (eds.) WMC 2005. LNCS, vol. 3850, pp. 67–78. Springer, Heidelberg (2006)
16. Verlan, S.: Look-Ahead Evolution for P Systems. In: Păun, Gh., Pérez-Jiménez, M.J., Riscos-Núñez, A., Rozenberg, G., Salomaa, A. (eds.) WMC 2009. LNCS, vol. 5957, pp. 479–485. Springer, Heidelberg (2010)
17. The P Systems Website: www.ppage.psystems.eu

Extended Simulation and Verification Platform for Kernel P Systems

Mehmet E. Bakir[1], Florentin Ipate[2], Savas Konur[1(✉)],
Laurentiu Mierla[2], and Ionut Niculescu[3]

[1] Department of Computer Science, University of Sheffield, Regent Court,
Portobello Street, Sheffield S1 4DP, UK
{mebakir1,s.konur}@sheffield.ac.uk

[2] Department of Computer Science, University of Bucharest, Str. Academiei nr. 14,
010014 Bucharest, Romania
florentin.ipate@ifsoft.ro, laurentiu.mierla@gmail.com

[3] Department of Computer Science, University of Pitesti, Str. Targul din Vale, nr.1,
110040 Pitesti, Arges, Romania
ionutmihainiculescu@gmail.com

Abstract. *Kernel P systems* integrate in a coherent and elegant manner many of the features of different P system variants, successfully used for modelling various applications. In this paper, we present our initial attempt to extend the software framework developed to support kernel P systems: a formal verification tool based on the NuSMV model checker and a large scale simulation environment based on FLAME. The use of these two tools for modelling and analysis of biological systems is illustrated with a synthetic biology example.

1 Introduction

Membrane computing [16] is a branch of natural computing inspired by the hierarchical structure of living cells. The central model, called *P systems*, consists of a membrane structure, the regions of which contain rewriting rules operating on multisets of objects [16]. P systems *evolve* by repeatedly applying rules, mimicking chemical reactions and transportation across membranes or cellular division or death processes, and halt when no more rules can be applied. The most recent developments in this field are reported in [17].

The origins of P systems make it highly suited as a formalism for representing biological systems, especially (multi-)cellular systems and molecular interactions taking place in different locations of living cells [7]. Different simple molecular interactions or more complex gene expressions, compartment translocation, as well as cell division and death are specified using multiset rewriting or communication rules, and compartment division or dissolution rules. In the case of *stochastic P systems*, constants are associated with rules in order to compute their probabilities and time needed to be applied, respectively, according to the Gillespie algorithm [18]. This approach is based on a Monte Carlo algorithm for the stochastic simulation of molecular interactions taking place inside a single volume or across multiple compartments.

© Springer International Publishing Switzerland 2014
M. Gheorghe et al. (Eds.): CMC 2014, LNCS 8961, pp. 158–178, 2014.
DOI: 10.1007/978-3- 319-14370-5_10

The recently introduced class of *kernel P (kP) systems* [8] integrates in a coherent and elegant manner many of the features of different P system variants, successfully used for modelling various applications. The kP model is supported by a modelling language, called *kP-Lingua*, capable of mapping a kernel P system specification into a machine readable representation. Furthermore, the KPWORK-BENCH framework that allows simulation and formal verification of the obtained models using the model checker SPIN was presented in a recent paper [5].

In this paper, we present two new extensions to KPWORKBENCH: a formal verification tool based on the NuSMV model checker [4] and a large scale simulation environment using FLAME (Flexible Large-Scale Agent Modelling Environment) [6], a platform for agent-based modelling on parallel architectures, successfully used in various applications ranging from biology to macroeconomics. The use of these two tools for modelling and analysis of biological systems is illustrated with a synthetic biology case study, the pulse generator.

The paper is structured as follows. Section 2 defines the formalisms used in the paper, stochastic and kernel P systems as well as stream X-machines and communicating stream X-machine systems, which are the basis of the FLAME platform. Section 3 presents an overview on the kP-lingua language and the simulation and model checking tools. The case study and the corresponding experiments are presented in Section 4 and 5, respectively, while conclusions are drawn in Section 6.

2 Basic Definitions

2.1 Stochastic and Kernel P Systems

Two classes of P systems, used in this paper, will be now introduced. The first model is a **stochastic P system** with its components distributed across a lattice, called *lattice population P systems* [3,18], which have been applied to some unconventional models e.g. the genetic Boolean gates [12,13,19]. For the purpose of this paper we will consider stochastic P systems with only one compartment and the lattice will be regarded as a tissue with some communication rules defined in accordance to its structure.

Definition 1. *A stochastic P system (SP system) with one compartment is a tuple:*

$$SP = (O, M, R) \tag{1}$$

where O is a finite set of objects, called alphabet; M *is the finite* initial multiset of objects *of the compartment, an element of O^*; R is a set of* multiset rewriting rules, *of the form $r_k : x \xrightarrow{c_k} y$, where x, y are multisets of objects over O (y might be empty), representing the molecular species consumed (x) and produced (y).*

We consider a finite set of labels, L, and a population of SP systems indexed by this family, SP_h, $h \in L$. A lattice, denoted by Lat, is a bi-dimensional finite array of coordinates, (a, b), with a and b positive integer numbers. Now we can define a lattice population P system, by slightly changing the definition provided in [3].

Definition 2. *A lattice population P system (LPP system) is a tuple*

$$LPP = (Lat, (SP_h)_{h \in L}, Pos, Tr) \qquad (2)$$

where Lat, SP_h and L are as above and $Pos : Lat \rightarrow \{SP_h | h \in L\}$ is a function associating to each coordinate of Lat a certain SP system from the given population of SP systems. Tr is a set of translocation rules of the form $r_k : [x]_{h_1} \overset{c_k}{\rightarrow} [x]_{h_2}$, where $h_1, h_2 \in L$; this means that the multiset x from the SP system SP_{h1}, at a certain position in Lat, will move to any of the neighbours (east, west, south, north) in Lat that contains an SP system SP_{h_2}.

The stochastic constant c_k, that appears in both definitions above, is used by Gillespie algorithm [9] to compute the next rule to be applied in the system.

One can see the lattice as a tissue system and the SP systems as nodes of it with some communication rules defined according to the neighbours and also to what they consist of.

Another class of P systems, called **kernel P systems**, has been introduced as a unifying framework allowing to express within the same formalism many classes of P systems [5,8].

Definition 3. *A kernel P system (kP system) of degree n is a tuple*

$$k\Pi = (O, \mu, C_1, \ldots, C_n, i_0) \qquad (3)$$

where O is a finite set of objects, called alphabet; *μ defines the* membrane struc- *ture, which is a graph, (V, E), where V are vertices indicating compartments, and E edges; $C_i = (t_i, w_i)$, $1 \le i \le n$, is a compartment of the system consisting of a compartment type from T and an initial multiset, w_i over O; i_0 is the output compartment where the result is obtained (this will not be used in the paper).*

Definition 4. *T is a set of compartment types, $T = \{t_1, \ldots, t_s\}$, where $t_i = (R_i, \sigma_i)$, $1 \le i \le s$, consists of a set of rules, R_i, and an execution strategy, σ_i, defined over $Lab(R_i)$, the labels of the rules of R_i.*

In this paper we will use only one execution strategy, corresponding to the execution of a rule in each compartment, if possible. For this reason the execution strategy will be no longer mentioned in the further definition of the systems. The rules utilised in the paper are defined below.

Definition 5. *A rewriting and communication rule, from a set of rules, R_i, $1 \le i \le s$, used in a compartment $C_{l_i} = (t_{l_i}, w_{l_i})$, $1 \le i \le n$, has the form $x \rightarrow y \{g\}$, where $x \in O^+$ and y has the form $y = (a_1, t_1) \ldots (a_h, t_h)$, $h \ge 0$, $a_j \in O$ and t_j indicates a compartment type from T – see Definition 3 – with instance compartments linked to the current compartment, C_{l_i}; t_j might indicate the type of the current compartment, i.e., t_{l_i} – in this case it is ignored; if a link does not exist (the two compartments are not in E) then the rule is not applied; if a target, t_j, refers to a compartment type that has more than one instance connected to C_{l_i}, then one of them will be non-deterministically chosen.*

The definition of a rule from R_i, $1 \le i \le s$, is more general than the form provided above, see [5,8], but in this paper we only use the current form. The guards, denoted by g, are Boolean conditions and their format will be discussed latter on. The guard must be true when a rule is applied.

2.2   X-Machines and Communicating Stream X-Machine Systems

We now introduce the concepts of stream X-machine and communicating stream X-machine and also discuss how these are implemented in FLAME [6]. The definitions are largely from [11].

A stream X-machine is like a finite automaton in which the transitions are labelled by (partial) functions (called processing functions) instead of mere symbols. The machine has a memory (that represents the domain of the variables of the system to be modelled) and each processing function will read an input symbol, discard it and produce an output symbol while (possibly) changing the value of the memory.

Definition 6. *A Stream X-Machine (SXM for short) is a tuple*
$Z = (\Sigma, \Gamma, Q, M, \Phi, F, I, T, m_0)$, *where:*

- *Σ and Γ are finite sets called the* input alphabet *and* output alphabet *respectively;*
- *Q is the finite set of* states;
- *M is a (possibly) infinite set called* memory;
- *Φ is the* type *of Z, a finite set of* function symbols. *A basic processing function $\phi : M \times \Sigma \longrightarrow \Gamma \times M$ is associated with each function symbol ϕ.*
- *F is the (partial)* next state function, *$F : Q \times \Phi \nrightarrow 2^Q$. As for finite automata, F is usually described by a* state-transition diagram.
- *I and T are the sets of* initial *and* terminal *states respectively, $I \subseteq Q, T \subseteq Q$;*
- *m_0 is the* initial memory *value, where $m_0 \in M$;*
- *all the above sets, i.e., Σ, Γ, Q, M, Φ, F, I, T, are non-empty.*

A configuration of a SXM is a tuple (m, q, s, g), where $m \in M, q \in Q, s \in \Sigma^*, g \in \Gamma^*$. An initial configuration will have the form (m_0, q_0, s, ϵ), where m_0 is as in Definition 6, $q_0 \in I$ is an initial state, and ϵ is the empty word. A final configuration will have the form (m, q_f, ϵ, g), where $q_f \in T$ is a terminal state. A change of *configuration*, denoted by $\vdash$, $(m, q, s, g) \vdash (m', q', s', g')$, is possible if $s = \sigma s'$ with $\sigma \in \Sigma$, $g' = g\gamma$ with $\gamma \in \Gamma$ and there exists $\phi \in \Phi$ such that $q' \in F(q, \phi)$ and $\phi(m, \sigma) = (\gamma, m')$. A change of configuration is called a *transition* of a SXM. We denote by $\vdash^*$ the reflexive and transitive closure of $\vdash$.

A number of communicating SXMs variants have been defined in the literature. In what follows we will be presenting the communicating SXM model as defined in [11] since this is the closest to the model used in the implementation of FLAME [6] (there are however, a few differences that will be discussed later). The model defined in [11] appears to be also the most natural of the existing models of communicating SXMs since each communicating SXM is a standard SXM as defined by Definition 6. In this model, each communicating SXM has only one (global) input stream of inputs and one (global) stream of outputs. Depending on the value of the output produced by a communicating SXM, this is placed in the global output stream or is processed by a SXM component. For a more detailed discussion about the differences between various models of communicating SXMs see [15].

The following definitions are largely from [11].

Definition 7. *A Communicating Stream X-Machine System (CSXMS for short) with n components is a tuple $S_n = ((Z_i)_{1 \leq i \leq n}, E)$, where:*

- $Z_i = (\Sigma_i, \Gamma_i, Q_i, M_i, \Phi_i, F_i, I_i, T_i, m_{i,0})$ *is the SXM with number $i, 1 \leq i \leq n$.*
- $E = (e_{ij})_{1 \leq i,j \leq n}$ *is a matrix of order $n \times n$ with $e_{ij} \in \{0,1\}$ for $1 \leq i,j \leq n$, $i \neq j$ and $e_{ii} = 0$ for $1 \leq i \leq n$.*

A CSXMS works as follows:

- Each individual *Communicating SXM (CSXM for short)* is a SXM plus an implicit input queue (i.e., of FIFO (first-in and first-out) structure) of infinite length; the CSXM only consumes the inputs from the queue.
- An input symbol σ received from the external environment (of FIFO structure) will go to the input queue of a CSXM, say Z_j, provided that it is contained in the input alphabet of Z_j. If more than one such Z_j exist, then σ will enter the input queue of one of these in a non-deterministic fashion.
- Each pair of CSXMs, say Z_i and Z_j, have two FIFO channels for communication; each channel is designed for one direction of communication. The communication channel from Z_i to Z_j is enabled if $e_{ij} = 1$ and disabled otherwise.
- An output symbol γ produced by a CSXM, say Z_i, will pass to the input queue of another CSXM, say Z_j, providing that the communication channel from Z_i to Z_j is enabled, i.e. $e_{ij} = 1$, and it is included in the input alphabet of Z_j, i.e. $\gamma \in \Sigma_j$. If these conditions are met by more than one such Z_j, then γ will enter the input queue of one of these in a non-deterministic fashion. If no such Z_j exists, then γ will go to the output environment (of FIFO structure).
- A CSXMS will receive from the external environment a sequence of inputs $s \in \Sigma^*$ and will send to the output environment a sequence of outputs $g \in \Gamma^*$, where $\Sigma = \Sigma_1 \cup \cdots \cup \Sigma_n$, $\Gamma = (\Gamma_1 \setminus In_1) \cup \cdots \cup (\Gamma_n \setminus In_n)$, with $In_i = \cup_{k \in K_i} \Sigma_k$, and $K_i = \{k \mid 1 \leq k \leq n, e_{ik} = 1\}$, for $1 \leq i \leq n$.

A *configuration* of a CSXMS S_n has the form $z = (z_1, \ldots, z_n, s, g)$, where:

- $z_i = (m_i, q_i, \alpha_i, \gamma_i), 1 \leq i \leq n$, where $m_i \in M_i$ is the current value of the memory of Z_i, $q_i \in Q_i$ is the current state of Z_i, $\alpha_i \in \Sigma_i^*$ is the current contents of the input queue and $\gamma_i \in \Gamma_i^*$ is the current contents of the output of Z_i;
- s is the current value of the input sequence;
- g is the current value of the output sequence.

An *initial configuration* has the form $z_0 = (z_{1,0}, \ldots, z_{n,0}, s, \epsilon)$, where $z_{i,0} = (m_{i,0}, q_{i,0}, \epsilon, \epsilon)$, with $q_{i,0} \in I_i$. A *final configuration* has the form $z_f = (z_{1,f}, \ldots, z_{n,f}, \epsilon, g)$, where $z_{i,f} = (m_i, q_{i,f}, \alpha_i, \gamma_i)$, with $q_{i,f} \in T_i$.

A change of configuration happens when at least one of the X-machines changes its configuration, i.e., a processing function is applied. More formally, a change of configuration of a CSXMS S_n, denoted by $\models$,

$$z = (z_1, \ldots, z_n, s, g) \models z' = (z'_1, \ldots, z'_n, s', g'),$$

with $z_i = (m_i, q_i, \alpha_i, \gamma_i)$ and $z'_i = (m'_i, q'_i, \alpha'_i, \gamma'_i)$, is possible if one of the following is true for some $i, 1 \leq i \leq n$:

1. $(m'_i, q'_i, \alpha'_i, \gamma'_i) = (m_i, q_i, \alpha_i \sigma, \epsilon)$, with $\sigma \in \Sigma_i$; $z'_k = z_k$ for $k \neq i$; $s = \sigma s'$, $g' = g$;
2. $(m_i, q_i, \sigma \alpha_i, \gamma_i) \vdash (m'_i, q'_i, \alpha'_i, \gamma)$ with $\sigma \in \Sigma_i$, $\gamma \in (\Gamma_i \setminus In_i)$; $z'_k = z_k$ for $k \neq i$; $s' = s$, $g' = g\gamma$;
3. $(m_i, q_i, \sigma \alpha_i, \gamma_i) \vdash (m'_i, q'_i, \alpha'_i, \gamma)$ with $\sigma \in \Sigma_i \cup \{\epsilon\}$, $\gamma \in (\Gamma_i \cap \Sigma_j) \cup \{\epsilon\}$ for some $j \neq i$ such that $e_{ij} = 1$; $(m'_j, q'_j, \alpha'_j, \gamma'_j) = (m_j, q_j, \alpha_j \gamma, \epsilon)$; $z'_k = z_k$ for $k \neq i$ and $k \neq j$; $s' = s$, $g' = g$;

A change of configuration is called a *transition* of a CSXMS. We denote by $\models^*$ the reflexive and transitive closure of $\models$.

The correspondence between the input sequence applied to the system and the output sequence produced gives rise to the *relation computed by the system*, f_{S_n}. More formally, $f_{S_n} : \Sigma \longleftrightarrow \Gamma$ is defined by: $s\, f_{S_n}\, g$ if there exists $z_0 = (z_{1,0}, \ldots, z_{n,0}, s, \epsilon)$ and $z_f = (z_{1,f}, \ldots, z_{n,f}, \epsilon, g)$ an initial and final configuration, respectively, such that $z_0 \models^* z_f$ and there is no other configuration z such that $z_f \models z$.

In [15] it is shown that for any kP system, $k\Pi$, of degree n, $k\Pi = (O, \mu, C_1, \ldots, C_n, i_0)$, using only rewriting and communication rules, there is a communicating stream X-machine system, $S_{n+1} = ((Z_{i,t_i})_{1 \leq i \leq n}, Z_{n+1}, E')$ with $n + 1$ components such that, for any multiset w computed by $k\Pi$, there is a complete sequence of transitions in S_{n+1} leading to $s(w)$, the sequence corresponding to w. The first n CSXM components simulate the behaviour of the compartment C_i and the $(n + 1)th$ component Z_{n+1} helps synchronising the other n CSXMs. The matrix $E' = (e'_{i,j})_{1 \leq i,j \leq n+1}$ is defined by: $e'_{i,j} = 1, 1 \leq i, j \leq n$, iff there is an edge between i and j in the membrane structure of $k\Pi$ and $e'_{i,n+1} = e'_{n+1,i} = 1, 1 \leq i \leq n$ (i.e., there are connections between any of the first n CSXMs and Z_{n+1}, and vice-versa). Only one input symbol σ_0 is used; this goes into the input queue of Z_{n+1}, which, in turn, sends $[\sigma_0, i]$ to each CSXM Z_i and so initializes their computation, by processing the strings corresponding to their initial multisets. Each computation step in $k\Pi$ is reproduced by a number of transitions in S_{n+1}. Finally, when the kP system stops the computation, and the multiset w is obtained in C_{i_0}, then S_{n+1} moves to a final state and the result is sent out as an output sequence, $s(w)$.

We now briefly discuss the implementation of CSXMSs in FLAME. Basically, there are two restrictions that the FLAME implementation places on CSXMSs: (i) the associated FA of each CSXM has no loops; and (ii) the CSXMSs receive no inputs from the environment, i.e., the inputs received are either empty inputs or outputs produced (in the previous computation step) by CSXM components of the system. As explained above, a kP system is transformed into a communicating X-machine system by constructing, for each membrane, a communicating X-machine that simulates its behaviour; an additional X-machine, used for the synchronization of the others, is also used. In FLAME, however, the additional X-machine is no longer needed since the synchronization is achieved through message passing - for more details see Section 3.1 and Appendix.

3   Tools Used for kP System Models

The kP system models are specified using a machine readable representation, called *kP–Lingua* [5]. A slightly modified version of an example from [5] is presented below, showing how various kP systems concepts are represented in kP–Lingua.

Example 1. A type definition in kP–Lingua.

```
type C1 {
    choice {
        > 2b : 2b -> b, a(C2) .
         b ->  2b .
    }
}
  type C2 {
    choice {
        a -> a, {b, 2c}(C1) .
    }
 }
m1 {2x, b} (C1) - m2 {x} (C2) .
```

Example 1 shows two compartment types, C1, C2, with corresponding instances m1, m2, respectively. The instance m1 starts with the initial multiset 2x, b and m2 with an x. The rules of C1 are selected non-deterministically, only one at a time. The first rule is executed only when its guard is true, i.e., only when the current multiset has at least three b's. This rule also sends an a to the instance of the type C2 linked to it. In C2, there is only a rule which is executed only when there is an a in the compartment.

The specifications written in kP–Lingua can be simulated and formally verified using a model checker called SPIN. In this paper, we show two further extensions, another verification mechanism based on the NuSMV model checker [4] and a large scale simulation environment using FLAME [6]. These two tools are are integrated into KPWORKBENCH, which can be downloaded from the KPWORKBENCH web page [14].

3.1   Simulation

The ability of simulating kernel P systems is one important aspect provided by a set of tools supporting this formalism. Currently, there are two different simulation approaches (a performance comparison can be found in [1]). Both receive as input a kP–Lingua model and outputs a trace of the execution, which is mainly used for checking the evolution of a system and for extracting various results out of the simulation.

KPWorkbench Simulator. KPWORKBENCH contains a simulator for kP system models and is written in the C# language. The simulator is a command line tool, providing a means for configuring the traces of execution for the given model, allowing the user to explicitly define the granularity of the output information by setting the values for a concrete set of parameters:

- *Steps* - a positive integer value for specifying the maximum number of steps the simulation will run for. If omitted, it defaults to 10.
- *SkipSteps* - a positive integer value representing the number of steps to skip the output generation. By using this parameter, the simulation trace will be generated from the step next to the currently specified one, onward. If not set, the default value is 0.
- *RecordRuleSelection* - defaulting to *true*, takes a boolean value on which to decide if the rule selection mechanism defined by the execution strategy will be generated into the output trace.
- *RecordTargetSelection* - if *true* (which is also the default value), traces the resolution of the communicating rules, outputting the non-deterministically selected membrane of a specified type to send the objects to.
- *RecordInstanceCreation* - defaulting to *true*, specifies if the membrane creation processes should be recorded into the output simulation trace.
- *RecordConfigurations* - if *true* (being also the default setting), generates as output, at the end of a step, the multiset of objects corresponding to each existing membrane.
- *ConfigurationsOnly* - having precedence over the other boolean parameters, sets the value of the above flags to *false*, except the one of the *RecordConfigurations*, causing the multiset configuration for each of the existing membranes to be the only output into the simulation trance. The default value is *false*.

FLAME-Based Simulator. The agent-based modeling framework FLAME can be used to simulate kP–Lingua specifications. One of the main advantages of this approach is the high scalability degree and efficiency for simulating large scale models.

A general FLAME simulation requires the provision of a model for specifying the agents representing the definitions of communicating X-machines, whose behaviour is to be simulated, together with the input data representing the initial values of the memory for the generated X-machines. The model specification is composed of an xml file defining the structure of the agents, while their behaviour is provided as a set of functions in the C programming language.

In order to be able to simulate kernel P system models using the FLAME framework, an automated model translation has been implemented for converting the kP–Lingua specification into the above mentioned formats. Thus, the various compartments defined into the kP-Lingua model are translated into agent definitions, while the rule execution strategies corresponds to the transitions describing the behaviour of the agents. More specifically, each membrane of the kP system is represented by an agent. The rules are stored together with the membrane multiset as agent data. For each type of membrane from the kP system, a type of agent is defined, and for each execution strategy of the membrane, states are created in the X-machine. Transitions between the two states are represented by C functions that are executed in FLAME when passing from one state to another. Each type of strategy defines a specific function that applies the rules according to the execution strategy. A detailed description of the algorithm for translating a kP system into FLAME is given in the Appendix.

Each step of the simulation process modifies the memory of the agents, generating at the same time output xml files representing the configuration of the corresponding membranes at the end of the steps. The granularity level of the information defining the simulation traces is adjustable by providing a set of concrete parameters for the input data set.

3.2   Model Checking

KPWORKBENCH already integrates the SPIN model checker [10]. A more detailed account can be found in [5]. In this paper, we also integrate the NuSMV model checker [4] to the KPWORKBENCH platform to be able to verify branching-time semantics. NuSMV is designed to verify synchronous and asynchronous systems. Its high-level modelling language is based on *Finite State Machines* (FSM) and allows the description of systems in a modular and hierarchical manner. NuSMV supports the analysis of specification expressed in *Linear-time Temporal Logic* (LTL) and *Computation Tree Logic* (CTL). NuSMV employs *symbolic* methods, allowing a compact representation of the state space to increase the efficiency and performance. The tool also permits conducting simulation experiments over the provided FSM model by generating traces either interactively or randomly.

We note that the NuSMV tool is currently considered for a restricted subset of the kP-Lingua language, and we only consider one execution strategy, *nondeterministic choice*.

4   Case Study: Pulse Generator

The *pulse generator* [2] is a synthetic biology system, which was analysed stochastically in [3,13]. It is composed of two types of bacterial strains: *sender* and *pulsing* cells (see Figure 1). The sender cells produce a signal (30C6-HSL) and propagates it through the pulsing cells, which express the green fluorescent protein (GFP) upon sensing the signal. The excess of the signalling molecules are propagated to the neighbouring cells.

Sender cells synthesize the signalling molecule 30C6-HSL (AHL) through the enzyme LuxI, expressed under the constitutive expression of the promoter PLtet01. Pulsing cells express GFP under the regulation of the PluxPR promoter, activated by the LuxR_30C6_2 complex. The LuxR protein is expressed under the control of the PluxL promoter. The GFP production is repressed by the transcription factor CI, codified under the regulation of the promoter PluxR that is activated upon binding of the transcription factor LuxR_30C6_2.

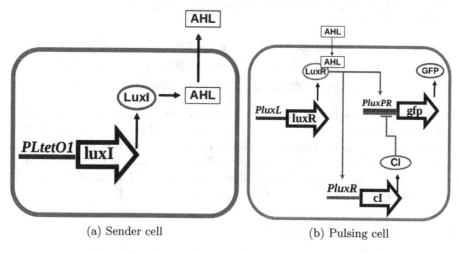

(a) Sender cell   (b) Pulsing cell

Fig. 1. Two cell types of the pulse generator system (taken from [3])

4.1 Stochastic Model

The formal model consists of two bacterial strains, each one is represented by an SP system model. So, $L = \{sender, pulsing\}$, describes these two labels and accordingly:

$$SP_h = (O_h, M_h, R_h), h \in L \tag{4}$$

where

$O_{sender} = \{\texttt{PLtet01\_geneLuxI}, \texttt{proteinLuxI}, \texttt{proteinLuxI\_Rib}, \texttt{rnaLuxI},$
$\qquad\quad \texttt{rnaLuxI\_RNAP}, \texttt{signal30C6}\}$

$M_{sender} = \texttt{PLtet01\_geneLuxI}$

$R_{sender} = \{r_1 : \texttt{PLtet01\_geneLuxI} \xrightarrow{k_1} \texttt{PLtet01\_geneLuxI} + \texttt{rnaLuxI\_RNAP} \ k_1 = 0.1,$
$\qquad\quad r_2 : \texttt{rnaLuxI\_RNAP} \xrightarrow{k_2} \texttt{rnaLuxI} \ k_2 = 3.36,$
$\qquad\quad r_3 : \texttt{rnaLuxI} \xrightarrow{k_3} \texttt{rnaLuxI} + \texttt{proteinLuxI\_Rib} \ k_3 = 0.0667,$
$\qquad\quad r_4 : \texttt{rnaLuxI} \xrightarrow{k_4} \ k_4 = 0.004,$
$\qquad\quad r_5 : \texttt{proteinLuxI\_Rib} \xrightarrow{k_5} \texttt{proteinLuxI} \ k_5 = 3.78,$
$\qquad\quad r_6 : \texttt{proteinLuxI} \xrightarrow{k_6} \ k_6 = 0.067,$
$\qquad\quad r_7 : \texttt{proteinLuxI} \xrightarrow{k_7} \texttt{proteinLuxI} + \texttt{signal30C6} \ k_7 = 5\}$

and

$O_{pulsing} = \{\texttt{CI2}, \texttt{LuxR2}, \texttt{PluxL\_geneLuxR}, \texttt{PluxPR\_CI2\_geneGFP},$
$\qquad\quad \texttt{PluxPR\_LuxR2\_CI2\_geneGFP}, \texttt{PluxPR\_LuxR2\_geneGFP}, \texttt{PluxPR\_geneGFP},$
$\qquad\quad \texttt{PluxR\_LuxR2\_geneCI}, \texttt{PluxR\_geneCI}, \texttt{proteinCI}, \texttt{proteinCI\_Rib}, \texttt{proteinGFP},$
$\qquad\quad \texttt{proteinGFP\_Rib}, \texttt{proteinLuxR}, \texttt{proteinLuxR\_30C6}, \texttt{proteinLuxR\_Rib}, \texttt{rnaCI},$
$\qquad\quad \texttt{rnaCI\_RNAP}, \texttt{rnaGFP}, \texttt{rnaGFP\_RNAP}, \texttt{rnaLuxR}, \texttt{rnaLuxR\_RNAP}, \texttt{signal30C6}\}$

$M_{pulsing} = \texttt{PluxL\_geneLuxR}, \texttt{PluxR\_geneCI}, \texttt{PluxPR\_geneGFP}.$

The set of rules ($R_{pulsing}$) is presented in Table 6 (Appendix).

The translocation rules are:

$$Tr = \{r_1 : [\texttt{signal30C6}]_{sender} \overset{k_1}{\rightarrow} [\texttt{signal30C6}]_{pulsing} \quad k_1 = 1.0,$$
$$r_2 : [\texttt{signal30C6}]_{sender} \overset{k_2}{\rightarrow} [\texttt{signal30C6}]_{sender} \quad k_2 = 1.0,$$
$$r_3 : [\texttt{signal30C6}]_{pulsing} \overset{k_3}{\rightarrow} [\texttt{signal30C6}]_{pulsing} \quad k_3 = 1.0\}.$$

The lattice, given by Lat, is an array with n rows and m columns of coordinates (a,b), where $0 \le a \le n-1$ and $0 \le b \le m-1$. The values n and m will be specified for various experiments conducted in this paper. If we assume that the first column is associated with *sender* SP systems and the rest with *pulsing* systems, we formally express this as follows: $Pos(a,0) = SP_{sender}, 0 \le a \le n-1$, and $Pos(a,b) = SP_{pulsing}, 0 \le a \le n-1$ and $1 \le b \le m-1$.

4.2   Nondeterministic Model

Non-deterministic models are used for qualitative analysis. They are useful for detecting the existence of molecular species rather than for measuring their concentration. A typical non-deterministic model can be obtained from a stochastic model by removing the kinetics constants.

More precisely, one can define two types corresponding to the two bacterial strains in accordance with Definition 4, namely $T = \{sender, pulsing\}$, and the corresponding rule sets, R'_{sender} and $R'_{pulsing}$. The rules from R'_{sender} are obtained from R_{sender} and $r_1, r_2 \in Tr$, and those from $R'_{pulsing}$ are obtained from $R_{pulsing}$ and $r_3 \in Tr$, by removing the kinetic rates. For each rule from the set Tr, namely $r_k : [x]_{h_1} \overset{c_k}{\rightarrow} [x]_{h_2}$, the corresponding rule of the kP system will be $r_k : x \rightarrow x(t)$, where $t \in T$. The execution strategies are those described in the associated definitions of the kP systems.

The kP system with $n \times m$ components is given, in accordance with Definition 3, by the graph with vertices $C_{a,b} = (t_{a,b}, w_{a,b})$, where $t_{a,b} \in T$ and $w_{a,b}$ is the initial multiset, $0 \le a \le n-1, 0 \le b \le m-1$; and edges where each component $C_{a,b}$, with $0 \le a \le n-1, 0 \le b \le m-2$, is connected to its east neighbor, $C_{a,b+1}$, and each component $C_{a,b}$, with $0 \le a \le n-2, 0 \le b \le m-1$ is connected to the south neighbor, $C_{a+1,b}$. The types of these components are $t_{a,0} = sender$, $0 \le a \le n-1$, and $t_{a,b} = pulsing, 0 \le a \le n-1$ and $1 \le b \le m-1$. The initial multisets are $w_{a,0} = M_{sender}, 0 \le a \le n-1$, and $w_{a,b} = M_{pulsing}, 0 \le a \le n-1$ and $1 \le b \le m-1$.

So, one can observe the similitude between the lattice and function Pos underlying the definition of the LPP system and the graph and the types associated with the kP system.

4.3   Nondeterministic Simplified Model

In order to relieve the state explosion problem, models can also be simplified by replacing a long chain of reactions by a simpler rule set which will capture the starting and ending parts of this chain, and hence eliminating species that do not appear in the new rule set. With this transformation we achieve a simplification of the state space, but also of the number of transitions associated with the model.

The non-deterministic system with a set of compacted rules for the sender cell is obtained from the kP system introduced above and consists of the same graph with the same types, T, and initial multisets, $w_{a,b}$, $0 \leq a \leq n-1$, $0 \leq b \leq m-1$, but with simplified rule sets obtained from R'_{sender} and $R'_{pulsing}$, denoted R''_{sender} and $R''_{pulsing}$, respectively, where R''_{sender} is defined as follows:

$$R''_{sender} = \{r_1 : \texttt{PLtet01\_geneLuxI} \rightarrow \texttt{PLtet01\_geneLuxI} + \texttt{rnaLuxI\_RNAP},$$
$$r_2 : \texttt{proteinLuxI} \rightarrow,$$
$$r_3 : \texttt{proteinLuxI} \rightarrow \texttt{proteinLuxI} + \texttt{signal30C6},$$
$$r_4 : \texttt{signal30C6} \rightarrow \texttt{signal30C6} \text{ (pulsing)},$$
$$r_5 : \texttt{signal30C6} \rightarrow \texttt{signal30C6} \text{ (sender)}\}$$

and $R''_{pulsing}$ is defined in Table 7 (Appendix).

5   Experiments

5.1   Simulation

The simulation tools have been used to check the temporal evolution of the system and to infer various information from the simulation results. For a kP system of 5×10 components, which comprises 25 sender cells and 25 pulsing cells, we have observed the production and transmission of the signalling molecules from the sender cells to the furthest pulsing cell and the production of the green fluorescent protein.

FLAME Results. As explained before, in FLAME each agent is represented by an X-machine. When an X-machine reaches its final state, the data is written to the hard disk and then used as input for the next iteration. Since the volume of data increases with the number of membranes, the more membranes we have, the more time for reading and writing the data (from or to the hard disk) is required. Consequently, when the number of membranes is large, the time required by the read and write operations increases substantially, so the simulation may become infeasible[1]. For example, for the pulsing generator system it was difficult to obtain simulation results after 100,000 steps; the execution time for 100,000 steps was approximately one hour.

The signalling molecule $\texttt{signal30C6}$ appeared for the first time in the sending cell $\texttt{sender}_{1,1}$ at the 27th step; after that, it appeared and disappeared many times. In the pulsing cell $\texttt{pulse}_{5,9}$, the signalling molecule appeared for the first time at 4963 steps, while $\texttt{proteinGFP}$ was produced for the first time after 99,667 steps.

---

[1] On the other hand, the distributed architecture of FLAME allows the simulation to be run on parallel supercomputers with great performance improvements, but this is beyond the scope of this paper.

Table 1. FLAME results

Step Interval	$\text{sender}_{1,1}$ signal30C6	$\text{pulse}_{5,9}$ signal30C6	proteinGFP
0 – 10,000	Exist	Exist	None
10,001 – 20,000	Exist	Exist	None
20,001 – 30,000	Exist	Exist	None
30,001 – 40,000	Exist	Exist	None
40,001 – 50,000	Exist	Exist	None
50,001 – 60,000	Exist	Exist	None
60,001 – 70,000	Exist	Exist	None
70,001 – 80,000	Exist	Exist	None
80,001 – 90,000	Exist	Exist	None
90,001 – 99,666	Exist	Exist	None
99,667 – 100,000	Exist	Exist	Exist

The results of the FLAME simulation show that the signaling molecules produced in the sending cells are propagated to the pulsating cells which, in turn, produce `proteinGFP`. The results of the simulation are given in Table 1. In 100,000 steps (the maximum number of steps considered for the FLAME simulation), the farthest cell in which `proteinGFP` was produced was $\text{pulse}_{5,9}$ - this was produced after 99,667 steps.

KPWorkbench Simulator Results. KPWORKBENCH SIMULATOR is a specialised simulation tool and provides better results, in terms of execution time, then a general purpose simulation environment like FLAME. This is mainly due to the fact that this approach makes the simulation to be performed in a single memory space, that scales according to the number of membranes used in the model and the number of objects resulting from applying the rules in each simulation step.

Table 2 presents the production and availability of the signaling molecule at the first sender cell (i.e. $\text{sender}_{1,1}$) and the transmission of the signaling molecule and the production of the green fluorescent protein at the furthest pulsing cell (i.e. $\text{pulse}_{5,10}$).

We have run the simulator for 3,000,000 time steps. The $\text{sender}_{1,1}$ cell was able to produce the signaling molecule at 22 steps, and later produced more signaling molecules. The $\text{pulse}_{5,10}$ cell, as the furthest pulse generator cell, was able to receive the signaling molecule at the 5474 step. But, the production of `proteinGFP` was possible at the 2,476,813 step, and it remained inside the cell until the 2,476,951 step, then it was consumed.

The simulation results show that the signaling molecule can be produced and transmitted by a sender cell. In addition, a pulse generator cell can have a signaling molecule only after a sender cell sends it, and can use the signal for the production of `proteinGFP` in later steps.

Table 2. KPWORKBENCH SIMULATOR results

	$sender_{1,1}$	$pulse_{5,10}$	
Step Interval	signal30C6	signal30C6	proteinGFP
0 – 300,000	Exist	Exist	None
300,001 – 600,000	Exist	Exist	None
600,001 – 900,000	Exist	Exist	None
900,001 – 1,200,000	Exist	Exist	None
1,200,001 – 1,500,000	Exist	Exist	None
1,500,001 – 1,800,000	Exist	Exist	None
1,800,001 – 2,100,000	Exist	Exist	None
2,100,001 – 2,400,000	Exist	Exist	None
2,400,001 – 2,700,000	Exist	Exist	Exist
2,700,001 – 3,000,000	Exist	Exist	None

Table 3. Property patterns used in the verification experiments

Prop.	Informal specification and the corresponding CTL translations
1	X *will eventually be produced.* EF X>0
2	*The availability/production of* X *will eventually lead to the production of* Y. AG (X ⇒ EF Y)
3	Y *cannot be produced before* X *is produced.* ¬ E (X=0 U Y>0)

5.2   Verification

The properties of the system are verified using the NuSMV model checker, fully integrated into the KPWORKBENCH platform. In this section, we first verify individual cell properties, and then verify the properties of the whole kP system, involving multiple cells that are distributed within the lattice and interact with each other via the translocation rules.

Our verification results show that when the cell population is small, the properties can be verified using reasonable computational resources. However, given that the complete rule set is used, when the number of cell increases, verification becomes no longer feasible due to the state explosion problem. To mitigate this problem, we have used a simplified rule set to verify the cell interaction properties when the cell population is large.

Complete Rule Sets. Experiments under this section are conducted on a small population of multi-cellular systems including the complete set of rules. We have analysed two pulse-generator systems that differ only in the number of pulse generator cells. The first group consists of one sender cell and one pulse generator cell, i.e. 1 × 2 components, whereas the second group has one more pulse generator cell, i.e. 1 × 3 components.

Table 4. Verification experiments for the complete rule sets

Lattice	Property	X, Y
1×2	Prop. 1	X = $sender_1$.signal30C6 X = $pulsing_1$.signal30C6
	Prop. 2	X = $pulsing_1$.signal30C6, Y = $pulsing_1$.proteinGFP X = $sender_1$.signal30C6, Y = $pulsing_1$.proteinGFP
	Prop. 3	X = $pulsing_1$.signal30C6, Y = $pulsing_1$.proteinGFP X = $sender_1$.signal30C6, Y = $pulsing_1$.proteinGFP
1×3	Prop. 1	X = $pulsing_2$.signal30C6 X = $pulsing_2$.proteinGFP
	Prop. 2	X = $pulsing_1$.signal30C6, Y = $pulsing_2$.proteinGFP X = $sender_1$.signal30C6, Y = $pulsing_2$.proteinGFP
	Prop. 3	X = $pulsing_1$.signal30C6, Y = $pulsing_2$.signal30C6 X = $sender_1$.signal30C6, Y = $pulsing_2$.signal30C6

For our experiments, we use the property patterns provided in Table 3. Table 4 shows the verification results for the properties given in Table 3 using two different groups. NuSMV has returned TRUE for all the properties. In the group with 1×2 components, we have verified that the sender cell ($sender_1$) can produce a signalling molecule and transmit it to the pulsing cell ($pulsing_1$). In addition, the pulse generator cell can use that signal to produce the green fluorescent protein (proteinGFP). In the group with 1×3 components, we have verified similar properties. In addition, we have verified that the first pulsing cell ($pulsing_1$) can transmit the signalling molecule to the second pulsing cell ($pulsing_2$).

Reduced Rule Sets. Using a larger sets of components, we want to prove that the signalling molecules can be transmitted to the furthest pulsing cells. However, when we increase the number of cells, verification becomes no longer feasible due to the state explosion problem. In order to achieve the verification results within a reasonable time, we have compacted the rules sets such that an entire chain of reactions is replaced by a fewer simple rules. Consequently, the overall number of interactions is reduced and all the species which do not appear in the new set of rules are removed from the model. These changes are made in the non-deterministic models as these are used for qualitative analyses where the concentration of certain molecules is not significant or chain of reaction already analysed can be replaced by some abstractions mimicking their behaviour through simpler rewriting mechanisms.

Here, we define a group of cells with 1×5 components, where 1 sender and 4 pulsing cells are placed in row. For this scenario, we could verify the same properties in Table 4 using the reduced rule sets (as defined in Section 4.3). In addition, we have verified additional properties to analyse the other pulsing

Table 5. Verification experiments for the reduced rule sets

Lattice	Property	X, Y
1×5	Prop. 1	X = pulsing$_4$.signal30C6
		X = pulsing$_4$.proteinGFP
	Prop. 2	X = pulsing$_1$.signal30C6, Y = pulsing$_4$.proteinGFP
		X = sender$_1$.signal30C6, Y = pulsing$_4$.proteinGFP
	Prop. 3	X = pulsing$_3$.signal30C6, Y = pulsing$_4$.signal30C6
		X = pulsing$_3$.signal30C6, Y = pulsing$_4$.proteinGFP

cells. Table 5 shows these properties, for which NuSMV has returned TRUE. The verification results show that the sender cell can produce the signalling molecule and transmit it to the adjacent pulsing cell, and the pulsing cells can use the signalling molecule to produce proteinGFP and transmit it to the its neighbour pulsing cells.

6   Conclusions

In this paper, we have presented two extensions to KPWORKBENCH: a formal verification tool based on the NuSMV model checker and a large scale simulation environment using FLAME, a platform for agent-based modelling on parallel architectures. The use of these two tools for modelling and analysis of biological systems is illustrated with a pulse generator, a synthetic biology system. We have provided both the stochastic model as stochastic P systems and the non-deterministic model as kernel P systems as well as a reduced model. We have also provided both simulation and verification results, confirming the desired behaviour of the pulse generator system.

The NuSMV tool currently works for a restricted subset of the kP-Lingua language, and we only consider one execution strategy, the nondeterministic choice. As a future work, we will extend the compatibility of the tool to cover the full language and the other execution strategies, e.g. sequence and maximal parallelism. The future work will also involve modeling, simulation and verification of even more complex biological systems as well as performance comparisons of simulators and model checking tools integrated within KPWORKBENCH.

Acknowledgments. The work of FI, LM and IN was supported by a grant of the Romanian National Authority for Scientific Research, CNCS-UEFISCDI (project number: PN-II-ID-PCE-2011-3-0688). SK acknowledges the support provided for synthetic biology research by EPSRC ROADBLOCK (project number: EP/I031812/1). MB is supported by a PhD studentship provided by the Turkey Ministry of Education.

The authors would like to thank Marian Gheorghe for his valuable comments to this paper.

Appendix

Algorithm 1. Transforming a kP Systems into Flame algorithm

1: **procedure** ADDTTRANSITION(startState, stopState, strategy, guard)
   ▷ *procedure adding the appropriate transition strategy to the current agent stack given as parameter and FLAME function applying rules conforming to execution strategy*
   ▷ *guard is an optional parameter that represents the transition guard*
2:    **if** strategy is Sequence **then**
3:        agentTtransitions.Push(startState, stopState, SequenceFunction, guard)
          ▷ *FLAME function SequenceFunction applies rules in sequentially mode*
4:    **else if** strategy is Choice **then**
5:        agentTtransitions.Push(startState, stopState, ChoiceFunction, guard)
          ▷ *FLAME function ChoiceFunction applies rules in choice mode*
6:    **else if** strategy is ArbitraryParallel **then**
7:        agentTtransitions.Push(startState, stopState, ArbitraryParallelFunction, guard)
          ▷ *FLAME function ArbitraryParallelFunction applies rules in arbitrary parallel mode*
8:    **else if** strategy is MaximalParallel **then**
9:        agentTtransitions.Push(startState, stopState, MaximalParallelFunction, guard)
          ▷ *FLAME function MaximalParallelFunction applies rules in maximal parallel mode*
10:   **end if**
11: **end procedure**
12:
      ▷ *main algorithm for traforming a kP system into Flame*
13:
14: agentsStates.Clear()
15: agentsTtransitions.Clear()
      ▷ *empty state and transition stacks of agents*
16: **foreach** membrane in kPSystem **do**
      ▷ *for each membrane of kP system build corresponding agent, consisting of states and transitions*
17:   agentStates.Clear()
18:   agentTtransitions.Clear()
      ▷ *empty state and transition stacks of agent that is built for the current membrane*
19:   agentStates.Push(startState)
      ▷ *adding the initial state of the X machine*
20:   agentStates.Push(initializationState)
      ▷ *adding initialization state*
21:   agentTtransitions.Push(startState, initializationState)
      ▷ *adding transition between the initial and initialization states; this transition performs objects allocation on rules and other initializations*
22:   **foreach** strategy in membrane **do**
      ▷ *for each strategy of the current membrane the corresponding states and transitions are built*
23:      previousState = agentStates.Top()
          ▷ *the last state is stored in a temporary variable*
24:      **if** is first strategy and strategy.hasNext() **then**
          ▷ *when the strategy is the first of several, state and transition corresponding to the execution strategy are added*
25:         agentStates.Push(strategy.Name)
26:         AddTtransition(previousState, strategy.Name, strategy)
27:      **else**
28:         **if** not strategy.hasNext() **then**
             ▷ *if it is the last strategy, the transition corresponding to the execution strategy is added*
29:            AddTtransition(previousState, applyChangesState, strategy)
30:         **else**

Algorithm 1. Transforming a kP Systems into Flame algorithm (continued)

31:           agentStates.Push(strategy.Name)
              ▷ add corresponding state of the current strategy
32:           if strategy.Previous() is Sequence then
              ▷ verify that previous strategy is of sequence type
33:               AddTtransition(previousState,strategy.Name,strategy, IsApplyAllRules)
                  ▷ add transition from preceding strategy state to the current strategy state. The guard is
                  active if all the rules have been applied in the previous strategy transition.
34:               agentTtransitions.Push(previousState, applyChangesState, IsNotApplyAllRules)
                  ▷ add transition from preceding strategy state to state where changes produced by rules are
                  applied. The guard is active if not all rules have been applied in the previous strategy
                  transition
35:           else
36:               AddTtransition(previousState, strategy.Name, strategy)
                  ▷ add transition from preceding strategy state to the current strategy state
37:               agentTtransitions.Push(previousState, applyChangesState, IsApplyStructureRule)
                  ▷ add transition from preceding state strategy to state in which changes produced by the
                  applied rules are committed. The guard is active when the structural rule has been applied
                  on the previous strategy transition
38:           end if
39:        end if
40:      end if
41:    end for
42:    agentStates.Push(applyChangesState)
       ▷ adding state in which changes produced by the applied rules are committed
43:    agentTtransitions.Push(applyChangesState, receiveState)
       ▷ adding transition on which changes produced by the applied rules are committed
44:    agentStates.Push(receiveState)
       ▷ add state that receives objects sent by applying the communication rules in other membranes
45:    agentTtransitions.Push(receiveState, s0State)
       ▷ add transition that receives objects sent by applying the communication rules in other membranes
46:    agentStates.Push(s0State)
       ▷ add an intermediary state
47:    agentTtransitions.Push(s0State, endState, IsNotApplyStructureRule)
       ▷ add transition to the final state in which nothing happens unless a structural rule was applied
48:    agentTtransitions.Push(s0State, endState, IsApplyStructureRule)
       ▷ add the transition to the final state on which structural changes are made if the structure rule has been
       applied
49:    agentStates.Push(endState)
       ▷ add the final state
50:    agentsStates.PushAll(agentStates.Content())
       ▷ add the contents of the stack that holds the current agent states to the stack that holds the states of all
       agents
51:    agentsTtransitions.PushAll(agentStates.Content())
       ▷ add the contents of the stack that holds the current agent transitions to the stack that holds the transitions
       of all agents
52: end for

Table 6. Multiset rules ($R_{pulsing}$) of the SP systems model of the pulsing cell

Rule	Kinetic constant
r_1 : PluxL_geneLuxR $\xrightarrow{k_1}$ PluxL_geneLuxR + rnaLuxR_RNAP	$k_1 = 0.1$
r_2 : rnaLuxR_RNAP $\xrightarrow{k_2}$ rnaLuxR	$k_2 = 3.2$
r_3 : rnaLuxR $\xrightarrow{k_3}$ rnaLuxR + proteinLuxR_Rib	$k_3 = 0.3$
r_4 : rnaLuxR $\xrightarrow{k_4}$	$k_4 = 0.04$
r_5 : proteinLuxR_Rib $\xrightarrow{k_5}$ proteinLuxR	$k_5 = 3.6$
r_6 : proteinLuxR $\xrightarrow{k_6}$	$k_6 = 0.075$
r_7 : proteinLuxR + signal3OC6 $\xrightarrow{k_7}$ proteinLuxR_3OC6	$k_7 = 1.0$
r_8 : proteinLuxR_3OC6 $\xrightarrow{k_8}$	$k_8 = 0.0154$
r_9 : proteinLuxR_3OC6 + proteinLuxR_3OC6 $\xrightarrow{k_9}$ LuxR2	$k_9 = 1.0$
r_{10} : LuxR2 $\xrightarrow{k_{10}}$	$k_{10} = 0.0154$
r_{11} : LuxR2 + PluxR_geneCI $\xrightarrow{k_{11}}$ PluxR_LuxR2_geneCI	$k_{11} = 1.0$
r_{12} : PluxR_LuxR2_geneCI $\xrightarrow{k_{12}}$ LuxR2 + PluxR_geneCI	$k_{12} = 1.0$
r_{13} : PluxR_LuxR2_geneCI $\xrightarrow{k_{13}}$ PluxR_LuxR2_geneCI + rnaCI_RNAP	$k_{13} = 1.4$
r_{14} : rnaCI_RNAP $\xrightarrow{k_{14}}$ rnaCI	$k_{14} = 3.2$
r_{15} : rnaCI $\xrightarrow{k_{15}}$ rnaCI + proteinCI_Rib	$k_{15} = 0.3$
r_{16} : rnaCI $\xrightarrow{k_{16}}$	$k_{16} = 0.04$
r_{17} : proteinCI_Rib $\xrightarrow{k_{17}}$ proteinCI	$k_{17} = 3.6$
r_{18} : proteinCI $\xrightarrow{k_{18}}$	$k_{18} = 0.075$
r_{19} : proteinCI + proteinCI $\xrightarrow{k_{19}}$ CI2	$k_{19} = 1.0$
r_{20} : CI2 $\xrightarrow{k_{20}}$	$k_{20} = 0.00554$
r_{21} : LuxR2 + PluxPR_geneGFP $\xrightarrow{k_{21}}$ PluxPR_LuxR2_geneGFP	$k_{21} = 1.0$
r_{22} : PluxPR_LuxR2_geneGFP $\xrightarrow{k_{22}}$ LuxR2 + PluxPR_geneGFP	$k_{22} = 1.0$
r_{23} : LuxR2 + PluxPR_CI2_geneGFP $\xrightarrow{k_{23}}$ PluxPR_LuxR2_CI2_geneGFP	$k_{23} = 1.0$
r_{24} : PluxPR_LuxR2_CI2_geneGFP $\xrightarrow{k_{24}}$ LuxR2 + PluxPR_CI2_geneGFP	$k_{24} = 1.0$
r_{25} : CI2 + PluxPR_geneGFP $\xrightarrow{k_{25}}$ PluxPR_CI2_geneGFP	$k_{25} = 5.0$
r_{26} : PluxPR_CI2_geneGFP $\xrightarrow{k_{26}}$ CI2 + PluxPR_geneGFP	$k_{26} = 0.0000001$
r_{27} : CI2 + PluxPR_LuxR2_geneGFP $\xrightarrow{k_{27}}$ PluxPR_LuxR2_CI2_geneGFP	$k_{27} = 5.0$
r_{28} : PluxPR_LuxR2_CI2_geneGFP $\xrightarrow{k_{28}}$ CI2 + PluxPR_LuxR2_geneGFP	$k_{28} = 0.0000001$
r_{29} : PluxPR_LuxR2_geneGFP $\xrightarrow{k_{29}}$ PluxPR_LuxR2_geneGFP + rnaGFP_RNAP	$k_{29} = 4.0$
r_{30} : rnaGFP_RNAP $\xrightarrow{k_{30}}$ rnaGFP	$k_{30} = 3.36$
r_{31} : rnaGFP $\xrightarrow{k_{31}}$ rnaX + proteinGFP_Rib	$k_{31} = 0.667$
r_{32} : rnaGFP $\xrightarrow{k_{32}}$	$k_{32} = 0.04$
r_{33} : proteinGFP_Rib $\xrightarrow{k_{33}}$ proteinGFP	$k_{33} = 3.78$
r_{34} : proteinGFP $\xrightarrow{k_{34}}$	$k_{34} = 0.0667$

Table 7. Multiset rules ($R''_{pulsing}$) of the kP systems model of the pulsing cell

Rule

r_1 :	PluxL_geneLuxR $\rightarrow$ PluxL_geneLuxR + rnaLuxR_RNAP
r_2 :	proteinLuxR $\rightarrow$
r_3 :	proteinLuxR + signal30C6 $\rightarrow$ proteinLuxR_30C6
r_4 :	proteinLuxR_30C6 $\rightarrow$
r_5 :	proteinLuxR_30C6 + PluxPR_geneGFP $\rightarrow$ PluxPR_LuxR2_geneGFP
r_6 :	PluxPR_LuxR2_geneGFP $\rightarrow$ PluxPR_LuxR2_geneGFP + proteinGFP
r_7 :	proteinGFP $\rightarrow$
r_8 :	signal30C6 $\rightarrow$ signal30C6 (pulsing)

References

1. Bakir, M.E., Konur, S., Gheorghe, M., Niculescu, I., Ipate, F.: High performance simulations of kernel P systems. In: The 16th IEEE International Conference on High Performance Computing and Communications (2014)
2. Basu, S., Mehreja, R., Thiberge, S., Chen, M.T., Weiss, R.: Spatio-temporal control of gene expression with pulse-generating networks. PNAS **101**(17), 6355–6360 (2004)
3. Blakes, J., Twycross, J., Konur, S., Romero-Campero, F.J., Krasnogor, N., Gheorghe, M.: Infobiotics Workbench: A P systems based tool for systems and synthetic biology. In: [7], pp. 1–41. Springer (2014)
4. Cimatti, A., Clarke, E., Giunchiglia, E., Giunchiglia, F., Pistore, M., Roveri, M., Sebastiani, R., Tacchella, A.: NuSMV 2: An opensource tool for symbolic model checking. In: Brinksma, E., Larsen, K.G. (eds.) CAV 2002. LNCS, vol. 2404, p. 359. Springer, Heidelberg (2002)
5. Dragomir, C., Ipate, F., Konur, S., Lefticaru, R., Mierla, L.: Model checking kernel P systems. In: Alhazov, A., Cojocaru, S., Gheorghe, M., Rogozhin, Yu., Rozenberg, G., Salomaa, A. (eds.) CMC 2013. LNCS, vol. 8340, pp. 151–172. Springer, Heidelberg (2014)
6. FLAME: Flexible large-scale agent modeling environment. http://www.flame.ac.uk/
7. Frisco, P., Gheorghe, M., Pérez-Jiménez, M.J. (eds.): Applications of Membrane Computing in Systems and Synthetic Biology. Springer (2014)
8. Gheorghe, M., Ipate, F., Dragomir, C., Mierlă, L., Valencia-Cabrera, L., García-Quismondo, M., Pérez-Jiménez, M.J.: Kernel P systems - Version 1. 12th BWMC, pp. 97–124 (2013)
9. Gillespie, D.: A general method for numerically simulating the stochastic time evolution of coupled chemical reactions. Journal of Computational Physics **22**(4), 403–434 (1976)
10. Holzmann, G.J.: The model checker SPIN. IEEE Transactions on Software Engineering **23**(5), 275–295 (1997)
11. Ipate, F., Bălănescu, T., Kefalas, P., Holcombe, M., Eleftherakis, G.: A new model of communicating stream X-machine systems. Romanian Journal of Information Science and Technology **6**, 165–184 (2003)

12. Konur, S., Gheorghe, M., Dragomir, C., Ipate, F., Krasnogor, N.: Conventional verification for unconventional computing: a genetic XOR gate example. Fundamenta Informaticae (2014)
13. Konur, S., Gheorghe, M., Dragomir, C., Mierla, L., Ipate, F., Krasnogor, N.: Qualitative and quantitative analysis of systems and synthetic biology constructs using P systems. ACS Synthetic Biology (2014)
14. KPWorkbench. http://kpworkbench.org
15. Niculescu, I.M., Gheorghe, M., Ipate, F., Stefanescu., A.: From kernel P systems to X-machines and FLAME. Journal of Automata, Languages and Combinatorics (to appear, 2014)
16. Păun, Gh.: Computing with membranes. Journal of Computer and System Sciences **61**(1), 108–143 (2000)
17. Păun, Gh., Rozenberg, G., Salomaa, A. (eds.): The Oxford Handbook of Membrane Computing. Oxford University Press (2010)
18. Romero-Campero, F.J., Twycross, J., Cao, H., Blakes, J., Krasnogor, N.: A multiscale modeling framework based on P systems. In: Corne, D.W., Frisco, P., Păun, Gh., Rozenberg, G., Salomaa, A. (eds.) WMC 2008. LNCS, vol. 5391, pp. 63–77. Springer, Heidelberg (2009)
19. Sanassy, D., Fellermann, H., Krasnogor, N., Konur, S., Mierlă, L., Gheorghe, M., Ladroue, C., Kalvala, S.: Modelling and stochastic simulation of synthetic biological boolean gates. In: The 16th IEEE International Conference on High Performance Computing and Communications (2014)

The Abilities of P Colony Based
Models in Robot Control

Luděk Cienciala, Lucie Ciencialová[(✉)], Miroslav Langer, and Michal Perdek

Institute of Computer Science and Research Institute of the IT4Innovations
Centre of Excellence, Silesian University in Opava, Opava, Czech Republic
{ludek.cienciala,lucie.ciencialova,miroslav.langer,
michal.perdek}@fpf.slu.cz

Abstract. P colonies were introduced in 2004 (see [10]) as an abstract
computing device composed of independent single membrane agents,
reactively acting and evolving in a shared environment. Each agent is
equipped with a set of rules which are structured into simple programs.
There are some models based on from original P colony. In most cases,
models are equipped with such components which are associated with the
environment. This is the case of Pcol automaton too. The agents work
not only with environment but also with an input tape. We use this two
theoretical computational devices to build complex robot controllers. In
this paper we introduce simple controllers; the first one is used for fulfilling instructions and the other one for passing the maze using right-hand
rule. We followed two different approaches and ideas and we present the
obtained results in this paper.

1 Introduction

Recently, the robotics has been more and more expanding and intervening in
various branches of science like biology, psychology, genetics, engineering, cognitive science, neurology etc. Hardware and software equipment limits the efforts
to create robots with artificial intelligence, which are able to act autonomously
and solve various types of problems. Many of these limits are managed to be
eliminated by the interdisciplinary approach which allows creating new concepts
and technics suitable for the robot control and facture of the new hardware.

The robot control is often realized by the classical procedures known from
the control theory (see [17]), concepts inspired by the biology, evolution concepts
(see [7]) or with use of the decentralized approaches (see [16]).

Another proposal to use the P systems as an instrument for the realization of the robot control can be found in [1], [2]. The controller based on the
numerical P systems allows the parallelization of the computation of the function which the controller has to perform. In [18] the authors showed the use
of P systems for modelling mobile robot path planning. The authors proposed
a modified membrane-inspired algorithm based on particle swarm optimization,
which combines membrane systems with particle swarm optimization.

© Springer International Publishing Switzerland 2014
M. Gheorghe et al. (Eds.): CMC 2014, LNCS 8961, pp. 179–193, 2014.
DOI: 10.1007/978-3-319-14370-5_11

The robot's control is realized by the control unit. Robots are equipped with the various types of sensors, cameras, gyroscopes and further hardware which all together represent the robots perception. These hardware components provide to the control unit the information about the actual state of the environment in which the robot is present and also the information about the internal state of the robot. After the transformation of these inputs, new data, which is then forwarded to the actuators like the wheels or the robotic arm, is generated. Thus the robot can pass the obstacle by using the sensors and adjusting the speed of the particular wheels. So the objective of the control unit is to transform input signals to the output signals which consequently affect the behaviour of the robot. Transformation of these signals can be done computationally in various ways with use of the knowledge or fuzzy knowledge systems, artificial neural networks, or just with use of the membrane systems, namely P colonies as it will be shown in this paper.

P colonies were introduced in 2004 as an abstract computing devices composed from independent single membrane agents, reactively acting and evolving in a shared environment ([9]). P colonies reflect motivation from colonies of grammar systems, i.e. the idea of the devices composed from as simple as possible agents placed in a common environment; the system which produces nontrivial emergent behaviour, using the environment only as the communication medium with no internal rules. P colonies consist of single membrane agents, cells "floating" in a common environment. Sets of rules of cells are structured to simple programs in P colonies. Rules in a program have to act in parallel in order to change all objects placed into the cell, in one derivation step. Objects are grouped into cells or they can appear in their completely passive environment in which these cells act. In [9] the set of programs was extended by the checking rules. These rules give an opportunity to the agents to opt between two possibilities. They have form r_1/r_2. If the checking rule is performed, the rule r_1 has higher priority to be executed than the rule r_2 has. It means that the agent checks the possibility to use rule r_1. If it can be executed, the agent has to use it. If the first rule cannot be applied, the agent uses the second one.

Pcol automaton was introduced in order to describe the situation when P colonies behave according to the direct signals from the environment (see [3]). This modification of the P colony is constructed in order to recognize input strings. In addition to the writing and communication rules usual for P colony cells Pcol automata have also tape rules. Tape rules are used for reading next symbol from the input tape and changing an object in cell(s) to the read symbol. Depending on the way tape rules and other rules can take a part in derivation process several computation modes are treated. After reading the whole input word, computation ends with success if the Pcol automaton reaches one of its accepting configurations. So, in accordance with finite automata, Pcol automata are string accepting devices based on the P colony computing mechanisms. Controller based on P colonies described in this paper is drawn up as a group of cooperating agents which live in a shared environment, through which the agents can communicate. Such controller can be used for wide range of tasks associated with control issues.

In this paper we follow two ideas of controlling a robot with use of P colonies. The first controller model uses the Pcol automaton for which we put the instructions for the robot on the input tape. The agents have to read the current information from the tape and together with objects in the environment coming from the receptors, they generate objects - commands for actuators. The second idea is to use original model of P colony and put all information to the environment. We divide the agents into modules that will perform the individual functions in the control of the robot.

The paper is structured as follows: After the brief introduction, we present a formal model of the P colony and of the Pcol automata in section 2.

In section 3 the Pcol automaton is used for robot control. Our device consists of 7 agents structured into four natural modules; namely control unit, left actuator controller, right actuator controller and infra-red receptor. The Pcol automaton uses checking rules but it can be redesigned to the Pcol automaton without using checking rules with the number of agents higher than 7. In section 4 we describe P colony controller which can go through the maze using the right-hand rule. The P colony has 5 agents with capacity 3. In conclusion we compare both models and we outline one of possible directions for further research.

Throughout the paper we assume that the reader is familiar with the basics of the formal language theory.

2 Preliminaries on the P Colonies and Pcol Automata

P colonies were introduced in 2004 (see [10]) as an abstract computing device composed of independent single membrane agents, reactively acting and evolving in a shared environment. This model is inspired by structure and function of a community of living organisms in a shared environment.

Each agent is represented by a collection of objects embedded in a membrane. The number of objects inside each agent is constant during the computation. With each agent is associated a set of simple programs. Each program is composed of the rules which can be of two types. The first type of rules, called the evolution rules, are of the form $a \rightarrow b$. It means that the object a inside the agent is rewritten (evolved) to the object b. The second type of rules, called the communication rules, are of the form $c \leftrightarrow d$. If the communication rule is performed, the object c inside the agent and the object d outside the agent swap their places. Thus after executing the rule, the object d appears inside the agent and the object c is placed outside the agent.

If the checking rule r_1/r_2 is performed, then the rule r_1 has higher priority to be executed over the rule r_2. It means that the agent checks whether the rule r_1 is applicable. If the rule can be executed, then it is compulsory for the agent to use it. If the rule r_1 cannot be applied, then the agent uses the rule r_2. The program determines the activity of the agent. The agent can change the content of itself or of the environment.

The environment contains several copies of the basic environmental object denoted by e. The environmental object e appears in arbitrary large number of copies in the environment.

This interaction between agents is the key factor of the P colony function. In each moment each object inside the agent is affected by execution of the program.

For more information about P systems see [14] or [15].

Definition 1. *The P colony of the capacity k is a construct*
$$\Pi = (A, e, f, V_E, B_1, \ldots, B_n), \text{ where}$$

- *A is an alphabet of the colony, its elements are called objects;*
- *$e \in A$ is the basic object of the colony;*
- *$f \in A$ is the final object of the colony;*
- *V_E is a multiset over $A - \{e\}$, it determines the initial state (content) of the environment;*
- *B_i, $1 \le i \le n$, are agents, each agent is a construct $B_i = (O_i, P_i)$, where*
  - *O_i is a multiset over A, it determines the initial state (content) of the agent, $|O_i| = k$;*
  - *$P_i = \{p_{i,1}, \ldots, p_{i,k_i}\}$ is a finite multiset of programs, where each program contains exactly k rules, which are in one of the following forms each:*
    - *$a \to b$, called the evolution rule;*
    - *$c \leftrightarrow d$, called the communication rule;*
    - *r_1/r_2, called the checking rule; r_1, r_2 are the evolution rules or the communication rules.*

The initial configuration of a P colony is an $(n+1)$-tuple of strings of objects present in the P colony at the beginning of the computation. It is given by the multiset O_i for $1 \le i \le n$ and by the set V_E. Formally, the configuration of the P colony Π is given by $(w_1, \ldots, w_n, w_E)$, where $|w_i| = k$, $1 \le i \le n$, w_i represents all the objects placed inside the i-th agent, and $w_E \in (A - \{e\})^*$ represents all the objects in the environment different from the object e.

We will use the parallel model of P colonies for the robot controller. It means that each agent tries to find one usable program in current configuration at each step of the parallel computation. If the number of applicable programs is higher than one, then the agent nondeterministically chooses one of the programs. The maximal possible number of agents is active at each step of the computation. Using the chosen programs, the P colony goes from one configuration to another one.

The configuration is called halting if any of the agents has no applicable program. The result of computation is associated with the halting configuration. It is the number of final objects placed in the environment at the end of computation.

By extending the P colony with the input tape, we obtain a string accepting/recognizing device; the PCol automaton (see [3]). The input tape contains an input string which can be read by the agents. The input string is a sequence of the symbols. To access the tape, the agents use special tape rules (T-rules).

The rules which are not accessing the tape are called the non-tape rules (N-rules). The computation and use of the T-rules is very similar to the use of the rules in the P colonies. Once any of the agents uses its T-rule, the current symbol on the tape is considered as read.

Definition 2. *A PCol automaton of the capacity k and with n agents, $k, n \geq 1$, is a construct*

$$\Pi = (A, e, w_E, (O_1, P_1), \ldots (O_n, P_n)), \text{ where}$$

- *A is a finite set, an alphabet of the PCol automaton, its elements are called objects;*
- *e is an environmental object, $e \in A$;*
- *w_E is a multiset over $A - \{e\}$ defining the initial content of the environment;*
- *$(O_i, P_i), 1 \leq i \leq n$ is an i-th agent, where*
  - *O_i is a multiset over A defining the initial content of the agent, $|O_i| = k$;*
  - *P_i is a finite set of the programs, $P_i = T_i \cup N_i$, $T_i \cap N_i = \emptyset$; where each program is formed from k rules of the following types:*
    - *the tape rules (T-rules for short)*
      - *$a \xrightarrow{T} b$ are called the rewriting T-rules, $a, b \in A$;*
      - *$a \xleftrightarrow{T} b$ are called the communication T-rules, $a, b \in A$;*
    - *the non-tape rules (N-rules for short)*
      - *$a \rightarrow b$ are called the rewriting N-rules, $a, b \in A$;*
      - *$a \leftrightarrow b$ are called the communication N-rules, $a, b \in A$;*
      - *r_1/r_2 are called the checking N-rules, r_1, r_2 are rewriting or communication rules;*
    - *T_i is a finite set of tape programs (T-programs for short) consisting from one T-rule and $k - 1$ N-rules;*
    - *N_i is a finite set of non-tape programs (N-programs for short) consisting from k N-rules.*

The configuration of the PCol automaton is the $(n+2)$-tuple $(v_T; v_E; v_1, \ldots, v_n)$, where $v_T \in A^*$ the unprocessed (unread) part of the input string, $v_E \in (A - \{e\})^*$ is a multiset of the objects different from the object e placed in the environment of the PCol automaton and v_i, $1 \leq i \leq n$ is a content of the i-th agent.

The computation starts in the initial configuration defined by the input string ω on the tape, the initial content of the environment w_E and the initial content of the agents $O_i, 1 \leq i \leq n$. The computation is performed similarly as in the case of P colonies. When an agent looks for applicable program, it scans the set of T-programs at first. If there is at least one applicable program, the agent uses one of applicable programs. If there is no suitable T-program, the agent proceeds with the set of N-programs. The current symbol on the input tape is considered as read iff at least one agent uses its T-program in the particular derivation step.

The computation halts if no agent has an applicable program. The halting configuration is accepting iff all symbols on the input tape are already read. In the case Pcol automaton accepts the input word ω if there exists at least one accepting halting computation starting in the initial configuration with ω on the input tape.

3   Pcol Automaton Controller with Commands on the Input Tape

The main advantage of using a PCol automaton in the controlling robot behaviour is the parallel processing of the data done by very primitive computational units using very simple rules.

Combining the modularity and the PCol automaton results in obtaining a powerful tool for controlling the robot behaviour. A PCol automaton is a parallel computation device. Collaterally working autonomous units sharing common environment provide a fast computation device. Dividing agents into the modules allows us to compound agents controlling single robot sensors and actuators. All the modules are controlled by the main control unit. The input tape gives us an opportunity to plan robot actions. Each input symbol represents a single instruction which has to be done by the robot, so the input string is the sequence of the actions which guides the robot in reaching its goal; performing all the actions. In this meaning the computation ends by halting, and it is successful if the whole input tape is read. For this purpose we use a special symbol which marks the end of the action. When the last tape symbol is read, the control unit sends halting symbol to the receptor modules, which stops their action. All the other modules will stop their actions independently on the halting symbols, because they will not obtain any other instruction from the control unit.

We construct a PCol automaton with capacity of two and seven agents. The agents are divided into four modules: *The control unit* consists of two agents, *the left actuator controller* and *the right actuator controller*, one agent each and *the infra-red receptor* consists of three agents. The entire automaton is completed with the *input* and *output filters*. The input filter codes signals from the robots receptors and spreads the coded signal into the environment. In the environment, the coded signal is used by the agents. The output filter decodes the signal from the environment which the actuator controllers have sent into. Decoded signal is forwarded to the robots actuators.

If the program is formed from rules of the same kind we can write $\langle ab \rightarrow cd \rangle$ or $\langle ab \leftrightarrow cd \rangle$ instead of $\langle a \rightarrow c; b \rightarrow d \rangle$ or $\langle a \leftrightarrow c; b \leftrightarrow d \rangle$. Let us introduce the formal specification of the mentioned PCol automaton. We will not present all the programs entirely, but we will focus on the individual sets of programs and their functions.

We define Pcol automaton as follows:

$\Pi = (A, e, w_E, (O_1, P_1), \ldots (O_7, P_7))$, where

$A = \{0_L, 0_R, 1_L, 1_R, e, F_F, \overline{F_F}, F_L, \overline{F_L}, F_R, \overline{F_R}, G_F, G_L, G_R, I_F, I_L, I_R, M_F,$
$\quad M_L, M_R, N_F, \overline{N_F}, N_L, \overline{N_L}, N_R, \overline{N_R}, R_T, W_F, W_L, W_R, W_T, H\},$

$w_E = \{\varepsilon\}.$

Let us describe the meaning of the particular objects:

$0_L, 0_R$	Signal for the output filter - do not move the left/right wheel.
$1_L, 1_R$	Signal for the output filter - move the left/right wheel.
$\overline{F_F}, \overline{F_L}, \overline{F_R}$	Signal from the input filter - no obstacle in front/on the left/right.
$\overline{N_F}, \overline{N_L}, \overline{N_R}$	Signal from the input filter - obstacle in front/on the left/right.
F_F, F_L, F_R	Signal from the IR module to the control unit- no obstacle in front/on the left/right.
N_F, N_L, N_R	Signal from the IR module to the control unit- obstacle in front/on the left/right.
I_F, I_L, I_R	Signal from the control unit to the IR module - is there an obstacle in front/on the left/right?
M_F, M_L, M_R	Signal from the control unit to the actuator controllers - move front, turn left/right.
R_T	Signal from the actuator controllers to the control unit - read next tape symbol.
H	Halting symbol - the last symbol on the tape.

Remaining objects (W_F, W_L, W_R, G) are used for inner representation of the actions and as the complementary objects.

Particular modules and agents which the modules contain are defined as follows:

Control unit: The control unit has two agents $B1$ and B_2 with the initial contents $O_1 = eR_T$ and $O_2 = eR_T$. They process the input string in parallel. The first programs are designed for reading instruction from the input tape.

$P_1 : \ < R_T \xrightarrow{T} M_F; e \rightarrow e >$ - instruction "move front";

$\qquad < R_T \xrightarrow{T} M_L; e \rightarrow e >$ - instruction "move left";

$\qquad < R_T \xrightarrow{T} M_R; e \rightarrow e >$ - instruction "move right";

$\qquad < R_T \xrightarrow{T} H; e \rightarrow H >$ - instruction "halt";

$P_2 : \ < R_T \xrightarrow{T} M_F; e \rightarrow I_F >;$

$\qquad < R_T \xrightarrow{T} M_L; e \rightarrow I_L >;$

$\qquad < R_T \xrightarrow{T} M_R; e \rightarrow I_R >;$

$\qquad < R_T \xrightarrow{T} H; e \rightarrow H >;$

The second agent generates the object for sending to infra-red modules. This object carries information about the next move which the robot is obliged to do. The following programs are to send this object of type I_x to the environment; $x \in \{F, L, R\}$.

$P_2 : \ < I_x \leftrightarrow e; M_x \rightarrow W_x >$

There are two different types of symbols which can appear in the environment after some steps - F_x the space in requested direction is free or N_x there is obstacle in requested direction. The agent B_2 consumes the object and if the object is of the type F_x it generates the instruction for agent B_1 to generate command for actuators.

P_2 : $< W_x \to e; e \leftrightarrow F_x/e \leftrightarrow N_x >$;
    $< F_x \to G_x; e \to e >$;
    $< G_x \leftrightarrow e; e \to W_T >$

The object of type G_x is processed by the agent B_1. After consuming G_x it generates two objects M_x, the information for actuator module to generate commands for wheels.

P_1 : $< e \leftrightarrow G_x; M_x \to M_x >$;
    $< G_x M_x \to M_x M_x >$;
    $< M_x M_x \leftrightarrow ee >$;
    $< ee \to eW_T >$

When inside both agents there are objects W_T it means that agents have to wait for execution of their command. It is performed before object R_T appears in the environment. They are generated by actuator module after sending the command for the wheels to the environment.

P_1 : $< W_T \to e; e \leftrightarrow R_T >$
P_2 : $< W_T \to e; e \leftrightarrow R_T >$

Now the control unit is prepared to read a new symbol from the input tape. If the symbol read from the input tape is H, both agents generate a pair of Hs. These objects are needed for halting three agents in infra-red module.

P_1 : $< H \to H; H \leftrightarrow e >$
P_2 : $< HH \leftrightarrow ee >$

Infra-red unit: The infra-red module is composed of three agents with similar programs. Each agent is to utilize object coming from the infra-red sensors $\overline{F_x}; x \in \{F, L, R\}$. Each one for one direction (F - front, L - left, R - right). The initial content of all agents in infra-red module is ee - $O_i = ee; i = \{3, 4, 5\}$. If there is object $\overline{F_x}$ or $\overline{N_x}$ in the environment - comes from infra-red sensors, the corresponding agent consumes it. It remakes the object F_x or N_x. If the control unit needs information about situation in the direction x which object I_x is present in the environment. The infra-red unit replaces the object F_x or N_x for I_x. If there is no request from control unit, the agents shred the information (they rewrite object F_x or N_x to e). If the object H appears in the environment, each agent consumes it preferably and the agent halts.

$P_i = \{ < e \leftrightarrow H/e \leftrightarrow \overline{F_x}; e \to F_x >$;
    $< F_x \leftrightarrow I_x/F_x \to e; \overline{F_x} \to e >$;
    $< e \leftrightarrow H/e \leftrightarrow \overline{N_x}; e \to N_x >$;
    $< N_x \leftrightarrow I_x/N_x \to e; \overline{N_x} \to e >$;
    $< I_x e \to ee; >\}$; $i = \{3, 4, 5\}$

The left and right actuator controllers wait for the activating signal (M_x) from the control unit. After obtaining the activating signal, the controllers try to provide demanded action by sending special objects - coded signal for the output filter into the environment. If the action is performed successfully, the actuators send an announcement of the successful end of the action to the control unit.

The left actuator controller:
$O_6 = \{ e, e \}$,
$P_6 = \{ < e \leftrightarrow M_F; e \rightarrow 1_L >; < M_F \rightarrow R_T; 1_L \leftrightarrow e >;$
$\qquad < e \leftrightarrow M_R; e \rightarrow 1_L >; < M_R \rightarrow R_T; 1_L \leftrightarrow e >;$
$\qquad < e \leftrightarrow M_L; e \rightarrow 0_L >; < M_L \rightarrow R_T; 0_L \leftrightarrow e >;$
$\qquad < R_T \leftrightarrow e; e \rightarrow e >\}$.

The right actuator controller:
$O_7 = \{ e, e \}$,
$P_7 = \{ < e \leftrightarrow M_F; e \rightarrow 1_R >; < M_F \rightarrow R_T; 1_R \leftrightarrow e >;$
$\qquad < e \leftrightarrow M_R; e \rightarrow 0_R >; < M_R \rightarrow R_T; 0_R \leftrightarrow e >;$
$\qquad < e \leftrightarrow M_L; e \rightarrow 1_R >; < M_L \rightarrow R_T; 1_R \leftrightarrow e >;$
$\qquad < R_T \leftrightarrow e; e \rightarrow e >\}$.

The robot driven by this very simple PCol automaton is able to follow the instruction on the tape safely without crashing into any obstacle. If the instruction cannot be proceeded, the robot stops. This solution is suitable for known robots environment. If the environment is changed before or during the journey and the robot cannot reach the final place it will not crash, either. We consider the computation as successful if the input string is processed and the robot fulfills the last action. The computation is unsuccessful otherwise.

4   P Colony Robot Controller

We construct a P colony with four modules: *The control unit, the left actuator controller, the right actuator controller* and *the infra-red receptors*. Entire colony is completed by the *input* and *output filter*. The input filter codes signals from the robots receptors and spread the coded signal into the environment. In the environment there is the coded signal used by the agents. The output filter decodes the signal from the environment which the actuator controllers sent into it. Decoded signal is forwarded to the robots actuators.

Let us introduce the formal definition of the mentioned P colony:
$$\Pi = (A, e, V_E, (O_1, P_1), \dots (O_5, P_5), \emptyset), \text{ where}$$
$$A = \{1_L, 1_R, -1_L, -1_R, A_L, A_R, F, F_F, F_O, F_F^F, F_O^F, G, I_F, I_R, H, H_1, L, M_F,$$
$$R, R_F, R_O, R_F^F, R_O^F, W_i\}$$
$$V_E = \{e\},$$

Let us describe the meaning of the particular objects:

$1_L, -1_L$ Signal for the output filter - move the left wheel forward/backward.

$1_R, -1_R$ Signal for the output filter - move the right wheel forward/backward.

F, L, R Signal from the control unit to the actuator controllers - move forward, turn left/right.

F_F^F, R_F^F Signal from the input filter - no obstacle in front/on the right.

F_O^F, R_O^F Signal from the input filter - obstacle in front/on the right.

F_F, R_F Signal from the IR module to the control unit - no obstacle in front/on the right.

F_O, R_O Signal from the IR module to the control unit - obstacle in front/on the right.

I_F, I_R Signal from the control unit to the IR module - is there an obstacle
in front/on the right?

G Maze exit.

H Halting symbol.

Remaining objects (A_L, A_R, H_1,...) are used for inner representation of the actions and as complementary objects.

Particular modules and agents which they contain are defined as follows:

Control unit: The control unit ensures the computation. It controls the behaviour of the robot, asks the data from the sensors and sends instructions to the actuators by sending particular symbols to the environment. The controlling unit contains a set of programs which ensures fulfillment of given goal, in this case passing through the maze using the right-hand rule. If the exit from the maze is found, symbol G appears in the environment, the control unit releases into the environment special symbol H, which stops the infra-red receptors and the P colony stops and so the robot.

The control unit is realized by one agent B_1. Initial content of the agent is $O_1 = I_F I_R W_i$. At first the agent sends the request for information about obstacles to the environment.

$P_1 : < I_F I_R \leftrightarrow ee; W_i \rightarrow W_i >$

Then the agent waits until it receives the answer form infra-red modules.

$P_1 : < W_i \rightarrow W_i; ee \leftrightarrow R_F F_F >; \quad < W_i \rightarrow W_i; ee \leftrightarrow R_O F_F >;$
$\quad\quad < W_i \rightarrow W_i; ee \leftrightarrow R_O F_O >; \quad < W_i \rightarrow W_i; ee \leftrightarrow R_F F_O >;$

Based on the information about obstacles the agent generates commands to actuator units and sends objects to the environment.

$P_1 : < R_O F_O e \rightarrow LLe >; \quad < R_F F_F e \rightarrow RRM_F >;$
$\quad\quad < R_O F_F e \rightarrow FFe >; \quad < R_F F_O e \rightarrow RRM_F >;$
$\quad\quad < LL \leftrightarrow ee; e \rightarrow e >; \quad < RR \leftrightarrow ee; M_F \rightarrow M_F >;$
$\quad\quad < FF \leftrightarrow ee; e \rightarrow e >; \quad < M_F ee \rightarrow FFe >$

After emitting object F, L or R to the environment the content of the agent is eee and agent B_1 has to prepare for the next step. It consumes objects A_L and A_R - the information about successfully performed motion and consumes G or e from the environment. If there is G on the environment, it means that the robot finds the exit from the maze and computation can halt. If there is no G in the environment, the control unit must generate a new request.

$P_1: < ee \leftrightarrow A_L A_R; e \leftrightarrow G/e \rightarrow e >;$
$\quad\quad < A_L A_R e \rightarrow I_F I_R W_i >;$
$\quad\quad < A_L A_R G \rightarrow HHH >;$
$\quad\quad < HH \leftrightarrow ee; H \rightarrow H_1 >$

Control unit contains a program which controls robots' behaviour. According to the data obtained from the infra-red module it sends instructions to the actuator controllers. It passes the maze using the right-hand rule until it finds a symbol G which represents the exit from the maze. While it founds the exit the control unit releases a symbol H into the environment which stops the computation.

The actuator controllers wait for the activating signal from the control unit. After obtaining the activating signal the controllers try to provide demanded action by sending special objects - coded signal for the output filter into the environment. When the action is performed successfully, the actuators send an announcement of the successful end of the action to the control unit, an announcement of the unsuccessful end of the action otherwise.

Left Actuator controller:

$$O_2 = \{\ e,e,e\ \},$$
$$P_2 = \{\ < e{\leftrightarrow}F; e \rightarrow 1_L; e \rightarrow A_L >;$$
$$< F{\rightarrow}e; 1_L \leftrightarrow e; A_L \leftrightarrow e >;$$
$$< e{\leftrightarrow}R; e \rightarrow 1_L; e \rightarrow A_L >;$$
$$< R{\rightarrow}e; 1_L \leftrightarrow e; A_L \leftrightarrow e >;$$
$$< e{\leftrightarrow}L; e \rightarrow -1_L; e \rightarrow A_L >;$$
$$< L{\rightarrow}e; -1_L \leftrightarrow e; A_L \leftrightarrow e > \quad\}.$$

Right Actuator controller:

$$O_3 = \{\ e,e,e\ \},$$
$$P_3 = \{\ < e{\leftrightarrow}F; e \rightarrow 1_R; e \rightarrow A_R >;$$
$$< F{\rightarrow}e; 1_R \leftrightarrow e; A_R \leftrightarrow e >;$$
$$< e{\leftrightarrow}R; e \rightarrow -1_R; e \rightarrow A_R >;$$
$$< R{\rightarrow}e; -1_R \leftrightarrow e; A_R \leftrightarrow e >;$$
$$< e{\leftrightarrow}L; e \rightarrow 1_R; e \rightarrow A_R >;$$
$$< L{\rightarrow}e; 1_R \leftrightarrow e; A_R \leftrightarrow e >\}.$$

Right and left actuator controllers wait for the activating signal from the control unit. According to the signal they move the robot in required direction by sending an appropriate signal to the output filter.

The infra-red receptors consume all the symbols released into the environment by the input filter. They release actual information from the sensors on demand of the control unit. The infra-red receptors remove unused data from the environment.

Front Infra-red module:

$$O_4 = \{\ e,e,e\ \},$$
$$P_4 = \{\ < e \leftrightarrow H/e \leftrightarrow F_F^F; ee \rightarrow eF_F >;$$
$$< e \leftrightarrow H/e \leftrightarrow F_O^F; ee \rightarrow eF_O >;$$
$$< F_F \leftrightarrow I_F/F_F \leftrightarrow e; F_F^F e \rightarrow ee >;$$
$$< F_O \leftrightarrow I_F/F_O \leftrightarrow e; F_O^F e \rightarrow ee >;$$
$$< I_F ee \rightarrow eee; >\}.$$

Right Infra-red module:

$$O_5 = \{\ e,e,e\ \},$$
$$P_5 = \{\ < e \leftrightarrow H/e \leftrightarrow R_F^F; ee \rightarrow eR_F >;$$
$$< e \leftrightarrow H/e \leftrightarrow R_O^F; ee \rightarrow eR_O >;$$
$$< R_F \leftrightarrow I_R/R_F \leftrightarrow e; R_F^F e \rightarrow ee >;$$
$$< R_O \leftrightarrow I_R/R_O \leftrightarrow e; R_O^F e \rightarrow ee >;$$
$$< I_R ee \rightarrow eee; >\}.$$

Infra-red modules consume all the symbols sent by the input filter into the environment. They send actual data to the control unit on demand.

Robot driven by this P colony is able to pass through simple mazes that are possible to pass using the right-hand rule.

5   Experimental Results

We have used the mobile robotics simulation software Webots for the implementation of our controller. Webots is a visualizing tool which allows us to work with the model of a robot and verify the functionality of our controller. The simulators of the P colony and PCol automaton are written in the Java and they process text files with the specification of the P colony systems. The file contains initial content of the environment, the definition of the agents, including their rules and the initial content, and the initial content of the input tape, eventually. Both of these simulation tools are interconnected. That allows us to perform our experiments.

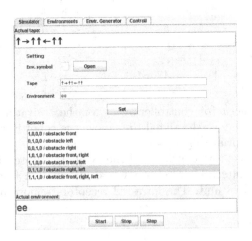

Fig. 1. Simulator environment

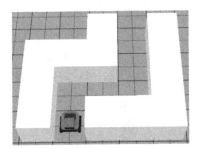

Fig. 2. Starting position

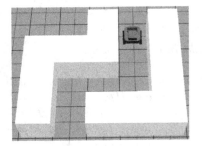

Fig. 3. Ending position

To verify our concept we have performed following simulation. The robot, namely the koala, was placed into the simulation environment in the grid shape with obstacles. According to the instructions on the input tape (see figure 1) the robot went through prepared maze (see figures 2, 3). All the instructions on the tape were interpreted as performable so the robot went through the maze with use of our controller.

In the second experiment, the P colony controller was used. A robot passed the maze from the starting position to the final position using the right-hand rule.

Both of the experiments suggest that using these types of controllers on real robots is feasible. Parallel processing of the instructions and the cooperation between the agents appear to be convenient with respect to the possible extension of the controllers by new functions, i.e. by adding new modules.

6   Other P System Based Controllers

Other approach to use the P systems as an instrument for realization of the robot control can be found in [1], [2]. Controller based on the numerical P systems (NPS for short) allows to parallelize the computation of the function which the controller has to perform. In the particular membranes there are placed particular parts of the function which are computed in the particular iterations of the computation and the partial results are forwarded through the membranes and they are composed into the resulting variables. NSP returns values for particular actuators of the robots and is using advantages of the P systems such the parallelization and distribution of the controller.

7   Conclusion and Future Research

In this paper we have introduced two variants of the robot controller based on the P systems, the P colony and the Pcol automaton.

We constructed the Pcol automaton with seven agents with capacity of two which can follow the instructions written on the input tape. The Pcol automaton controller is suitable for use in a well-known environment, where the actions can be planned accurately. Unexpected obstacle causes halt of the computation, the goal will not be fulfilled, but the robot will not crash.

We also constructed the P colony with five agents with capacity three for passing the maze using right-hand rule. The P colony controller is suitable for the autonomous systems. The behaviour of the robot is given by the rules of the control unit.

Further research can follow the idea of combining the advantages of both constructed models. Our idea is to construct a Pcol automaton with a dynamically changing input tape because the receptors will write the information in here. One input symbol can be a vector of inputs or we can precompute or filter and scale the values. The active agents will be formed to layers, the first layer is formed from agents that can read the current input symbol, the agents "controlling" behaviour of robot belong to the second layer. The last layer is composed of agents generating output for actuators. The layers are formed from active agents only. So the controlling layer can activate different agents in different situations (guiding closer to the obstacle, avoiding the obstacle or touching and pushing obstacle).

Remark 1. Article has been made in connection with project IT4Innovations Centre of Excellence, reg. no. CZ.1.05/1.1.00/02.0070.

Research was also supported by project OPVK no. CZ.1.07/2.2.00/28.0014 and by projects SGS/24/2013 and SGS/6/2014 .

References

1. Arsene, O., Buiu, C., Popescu, N.: SNUPS - A simulator for numerical membrane computing. International Journal of Innovative Computing, Information and Control **7**(6), 3509–3522 (2011)
2. Buiu, C., Vasile, C., Arsene, O.: Development of membrane controllers for mobile robots. Information Sciences **187**, 33–51 (2012)
3. Cienciala, L., Ciencialová, L., Csuhaj-Varjú, E., Vazsil, G.: PCol Automata: Recognizing Strings with P colonies. In: Martínez del Amor, M.A., Păun, Gh., Hurtado de Mendoza, I.P., Riscon-Núnez, A. (eds.) Eight Brainstormung Week on Membrane Computing, Sevilla, pp. 65–76 (2010)
4. Cienciala, L., Ciencialová, L., Langer, M.: Modularity in P colonies with Checking Rules. In: Gheorghe, M., Păun, Gh., Rozenberg, G., Salomaa, A., Verlan, S. (eds.) CMC 2011. LNCS, vol. 7184, pp. 104–119. Springer, Heidelberg (2012)
5. Csuhaj-Varjú, E., Kelemen, J., Kelemenová, A., Păun, Gh., Vaszil, Gy.: Cells in environment: P colonies. Multiple-valued Logic and Soft Computing **12**(3–4), 201–215 (2006)
6. Csuhaj-Varjú, E., Margenstern, M., Vaszil, Gy.: P colonies with a bounded number of cells and programs. In: Hoogeboom, H.J., Păun, Gh., Rozenberg, G., Salomaa, A. (eds.) WMC 7. LNCS, vol. 4361, pp. 352–366. Springer, Heidelberg (2006)
7. Floreano, D., Mattiussi, C.: Bio-inspired Artificial Inteligence: Theories, Methods, and Technologies. MIT Press (2008)
8. Freund, R., Oswald, M.: P colonies working in the maximally parallel and in the sequential mode. In: Ciobanu, G., Păun, Gh. (eds.) Pre-Proceedings of the 1st International Workshop on Theory and Application of P Systems, Timisoara, Romania, pp. 49–56 (2005)
9. Kelemen, J., Kelemenová, A.: On P colonies, a biochemically inspired model of computation. In: Proc. of the 6th International Symposium of Hungarian Researchers on Computational Intelligence, Budapest TECH, Hungary, pp. 40–56 (2005)
10. Kelemen, J., Kelemenová, A., Păun, Gh.: Preview of P colonies: A biochemically inspired computing model. In: Bedau, M., et al. (eds.) Workshop and Tutorial Proceedings, Ninth International Conference on the Simulation and Synthesis of Living Systems, ALIFE IX, Boston, Mass., pp. 82–86 (2004)
11. Minsky, M.L.: Computation: Finite and Infinite Machines. Prentice Hall, Engle-wood Cliffs (1967)
12. Păun, Gh.: Computing with membranes. Journal of Computer and System Sciences **61**, 108–143 (2000)
13. Păun, Gh.: Membrane Computing: An Introduction. Springer, Berlin (2002)

14. Păun, Gh., Rozenberg, G., Salomaa, A.: The Oxford Handbook of Membrane Computing. Oxford University Press (2009)
15. P systems web page. http://ppage.psystems.eu. Web. 29 September 2014
16. Weiss, G.: Multiagent systems. A Modern Approach to Distributed Artificial Intelligence. MIT Press, Cambridge (1999)
17. Wit, C.C., Bastin, G., Siciliano, B.: Theory of Robot Control. Springer, New York (1996)
18. Wang, X.Y., Zhang, G.X., Zhao, J.B., Rong, H.N., Ipate, F., Lefticaru, R.: A Modified Membrane-Inspired Algorithm Based on Particle Swarm Optimization for Mobile Robot Path Planning. International Journal of Computers, Communications & Control (accepted, 2014)

Probabilistic Guarded P Systems, A New Formal Modelling Framework

Manuel García-Quismondo, Miguel A. Martínez-del-Amor[✉],
and Mario J. Pérez-Jiménez

Research Group on Natural Computing,
Department of Computer Science and Artificial Intelligence,
University of Seville, Avda. Reina Mercedes s/n, 41012 Sevilla, Spain
{mgarciaquismondo,mdelamor,marper}@us.es

Abstract. Multienvironment P systems constitute a general, formal framework for modelling the dynamics of population biology, which consists of two main approaches: stochastic and probabilistic. The framework has been successfully used to model biologic systems at both micro (e.g. bacteria colony) and macro (e.g. real ecosystems) levels, respectively.

In this paper, we extend the general framework in order to include a new case study related to *P. Oleracea* species. The extension is made by a new variant within the probabilistic approach, called Probabilistic Guarded P systems (in short, PGP systems). We provide a formal definition, a simulation algorithm to capture the dynamics, and a survey of the associated software.

Keywords: Modelling Framework · Multienvironment P systems · Probabilistic Guarded P systems

1 Introduction

Since P systems were introduced in 1998 [19], they have been utilised as a high level computational modelling framework [10,20]. Their main advantage is the integration of the structural and dynamical aspects of complex systems in a comprehensive and relevant way, while providing the required formalisation to perform mathematical and computational analysis [2].

In this respect, multienvironment P systems are a general formal framework for population dynamics modelling in biology [7]. This framework has two approaches: stochastic and probabilistic. Stochastic approach is usually applied to model *micro*-level systems (such as bacteria colonies), whereas the probabilistic approach is normally used for *macro*-level modelling (real ecosystems, for example). Population Dynamics P systems [2,3,16,17] (PDP systems, in short) are a variant of multienvironment P systems, in the probabilistic approach. PDP systems have been successfully applied to ecological modelling, specially with real ecosystems of some endanger [3,6] and exotic species [3].

© Springer International Publishing Switzerland 2014
M. Gheorghe et al. (Eds.): CMC 2014, LNCS 8961, pp. 194–214, 2014.
DOI: 10.1007/978-3-319-14370-5_12

In this paper, we introduce a brand new variant inside the probabilistic approach of multienvironment P systems: Probabilistic Guarded P systems (*PGP systems*, for short). They are specifically oriented for ecological processes. PGP systems are a computational probabilistic framework which takes inspiration from different Membrane Computing paradigms, mainly from tissue–like P systems [23], PDP systems [2] and Kernel P systems [12]. This framework aims for simplicity, considering these aspects:

Model designers: In PGP systems, model designers do not need to worry about context consistency. That is to say, they do not need to take into account that all rules simultaneously applied in a elementary processor of the system (referred as a cell) must define the same polarization in the right–hand side [16]. This is because the framework centralizes all context changes in a single rule per cycle, rather than distributing them across all rules. Therefore, there exist two types of rules: *context–changing* rules and *non context–changing* rules. Due to the nature of the model, only one of such rules can be applied at the same time on each cell, so context inconsistency is not possible. Moreover, the fact that the context is explicitly expressed in each cell and that cells do not contain internal cell structures simplifies transitions between contexts without loss of computational or modelling power.

Simulator developers: The fact that the framework implicitly takes care of context consistency simplifies the development of simulators for these models, as it is a non–functional requirement which does not need to be supported by simulators. In addition, the lack of internal structure in cells simplifies the simulation of object transmission; the model can be regarded as a set of memory regions with no hierarchical arrangement, thus enabling direct region fetching.

Probabilistic Guarded P Systems can be seen as an extension of Population Dynamic P systems. In this context, PGP systems propose a modelling framework for ecology in which inconsistency (that is to say, undefined context of membranes) is handled by the framework itself, rather than delegating to simulation algorithms. In addition, by replacing alien concepts to biology (such as electrical polarizations and internal compartment hierarchies) by state variables known as *flags* and defined by designers models seem more natural to experts, thus simplifying communication between expert and designer.

This paper is structured as follows. Section 2 introduces some preliminaries. The formal framework of multienvironment P systems, and the two main approaches, are shown in Section 3. Section 4 describes the framework of PGP systems, providing a formal definition, some remarks about the semantics of the model, and a comparison with other similar frameworks of Membrane Computing. Section 5 provides a simulation algorithm, and a software environment based on P–Lingua and a C++ simulator. Section 6 summarizes an ecosystem under study with PGP systems. Finally, Section 7 ends the paper with conclusions and future work.

2   Preliminaries

An *alphabet* Γ is a non–empty set whose elements are called *symbols*. An ordered finite sequence of symbols of Γ is a *string* or *word* over Γ. As usual, the empty string (with length 0) will be denoted by λ. The set of all strings over an alphabet Γ is denoted by Γ^*. A *language* over Γ is a subset of Γ^*.

A *multiset* m over an alphabet Γ is a pair $m = (\Gamma, f)$ where $f : \Gamma \to \mathbb{N}$ is a mapping. For each $x \in \Gamma$ we say that $f(x)$ is the *multiplicity* of the symbol x in m. If $m = (\Gamma, f)$ is a multiset, then its *support* is defined as $supp(m) = \{x \in \Gamma \mid f(x) > 0\}$. A multiset is finite if its support is a finite set. A *set* is a multiset such that the multiplicity of each element of its support, is equal to 1.

If $m = (\Gamma, f)$ is a finite multiset over Γ, and $supp(m) = \{a_1, \ldots, a_k\}$ then it will be denoted as $m = a_1^{f(a_1)} \ldots a_k^{f(a_k)}$ (here the order is irrelevant), and we say that $f(a_1) + \cdots + f(a_k)$ is the cardinal of m, denoted by $|m|$. The empty multiset is denoted by $\emptyset$. We also denote by $M_f(\Gamma)$ the set of all finite multisets over Γ.

Let $m_1 = (\Gamma, f_1)$ and $m_2 = (\Gamma, f_2)$ multisets over Γ. We define the following concepts:

- The union of m_1 and m_2, denoted by $m_1 + m_2$ is the multiset (Γ, g), where $g = f_1 + f_2$, that is, $g(x) = f_1(x) + f_2(x)$ for each $x \in \Gamma$.
- The relative complement of m_2 in m_1, denoted by $m_1 \setminus m_2$ is the multiset (Γ, g), where $g = f_1(x) - f_2(x)$ if $f_1(x) \geq f_2(x)$ and $g(x) = 0$ otherwise.

We also say that m_1 is a submultiset of m_2, denoted by $m_1 \subseteq m_2$, if $f_1(x) \leq f_2(x)$ for each $x \in \Gamma$.

Let $m = (\Gamma, f)$ a multiset over Γ and A a set. We define the intersection $m \cap A$ as the multiset (Γ, g), where $g(x) = f(x)$ for each $x \in \Gamma \cap A$, and $g(x) = 0$ otherwise.

3   (Extended) Multienvironment P Systems

Definition 1. *A (extended) multienvironment P system of degree (m, n, q) with $q \geq 1$, $m \geq 1$, $n \geq 0$, taking T time units, $T \geq 1$, is a tuple*

$$\Pi = (G, \Gamma, \Sigma, \Phi, \mu, T, n = \sum_{j=1}^{m} n_j, \{\Pi_{k,j} \mid 1 \leq k \leq n_j, 1 \leq j \leq m\}, \{A_j \mid 1 \leq j \leq m\}, \mathcal{R}_E)$$

where:

- *$G = (V, S)$ is a directed graph. Let $V = \{e_1, \ldots, e_m\}$ whose elements are called environments;*
- *Γ, Σ and Φ are finite alphabets such that $\Sigma \subsetneq \Gamma$ and $\Gamma \cap \Phi = \emptyset$.*
- *μ is a rooted tree with $q \geq 1$ nodes labelled by elements from $\{1, \ldots, q\} \times \{0, +, -\}$.*
- *$n = \sum_{j=1}^{m} n_j$, with $n_j \geq 0$*

- For each k $(1 \le k \le n_j, 1 \le j \le m)$, $\Pi_{k,j}$ is a tuple $(\Gamma, \mu, \mathcal{M}_{1,j}^k, \ldots, \mathcal{M}_{q,j}^k, \mathcal{R}_j^k, i_{in})$, where:
  - For each i, $1 \le i \le q$, $\mathcal{M}_{i,j}^k \in M_f(\Gamma)$.
  - $\mathcal{R}_j^k$ is a finite set of rules of the type: $u[v]_i^\alpha \xrightarrow{p} u'[v']_i^{\alpha'}$, being $u, v, u', v' \in M_f(\Gamma)$, $1 \le i \le q$, $\alpha, \alpha' \in \{0, +, -\}$ and p is a real computable function whose domain is $\{0, \ldots, T\}$.
  - i_{in} is a node from μ.

  Let us note that n_j can be eventually 0, so that there would not exist any $\Pi_{k,j}$ for such an environment j.
- For each j, $1 \le j \le m$, $f_j \in \Phi$ and $E_j \in M_f(\Sigma)$.
- $\mathcal{R}_E$ is a finite set of rules among environments of the types:

$$(x)_{e_j} \xrightarrow{p_1} (y_1)_{e_{j_1}} \cdots (y_h)_{e_{j_h}} \qquad (\Pi_{k,j})_{e_j} \xrightarrow{p_2} (\Pi_{k,j})_{e_{j_1}}$$
$$\{f\}\,(u)_{e_j} \xrightarrow{p_3} (v)_{e_{j_1}} \qquad \{f\}\,(u, f)_{e_j} \xrightarrow{p_4} (v, g)_{e_j}$$

being $x, y_1, \ldots y_h \in \Sigma$, $(e_j, e_{j_i}) \in S$, $1 \le j \le m, 1 \le i \le h$, $1 \le k \le n, f, g \in \Phi, u, v \in M_f(\Gamma)$ and p_1, p_2, p_3, p_4 are computable functions whose domain is $\{0, \ldots, T\}$.
- For each j, $1 \le j \le m$, $A_j \in M_f(\Sigma \cup \Phi)$.

A (extended) multienvironment P system of degree (m, n, q) can be viewed as a set of m environments $e_1, \ldots, e_m$, n systems $\Pi_{k,j}$ of order q, and a set Φ of flags, in such a way that: (a) the links between the m environments are given by the arcs from the directed graph G; (b) each environment has a flag from Φ at any instant; (c) all P systems have the same working alphabet, the same membrane structure and the same evolution rules; (d) each environment e_j contains several P systems, $\Pi_{1,j}, \ldots, \Pi_{n_j,j}$, where each evolution rule has associated a computable function p_j, and each one of them has an initial multiset which depends on j. Furthermore, inside the environments, only objects from the alphabet Σ can exist; that is, there are symbols from the working alphabet that cannot circulate through the environments.

A *configuration* of the system at any instant t is a tuple whose components are the following: (a) the flags associated with each environment at instant t (initially $f_1, \ldots, f_m$); (b) the multisets of objects present in the m environments at instant t (initially $E_1, \ldots, E_m$); and (c) the multisets of objects associated with each of the regions of each P system $\Pi_{k,j}$ (initially $\mathcal{M}_{1,j}^k, \ldots, \mathcal{M}_{q,j}^k$), together with the polarizations of their membranes (initially all membranes have a neutral polarization).

We assume that a global clock exists, marking the time for the whole system, that is, all membranes and the application of all rules (both from $\mathcal{R}_E$ and $\mathcal{R}_j^k, 1 \le k \le n_j, n_j \ge 0$) are synchronized in all environments. We will denote the set of all defined rules in the system as $\mathcal{R}$.

The P system can pass from one configuration to another by using the rules from $\mathcal{R}$ as follows: at each transition step, the rules to be applied are selected according to the probabilities assigned to them, and all applicable rules are simultaneously applied.

A rule of the type $u[v]_i^\alpha \xrightarrow{p} u'[v']_i^{\alpha'}$ is applicable to a configuration at any instant t if the following is satisfied: in that configuration membrane i has polarization α, contains multiset v and its parent (the environment if the membrane is the skin membrane) contains multiset u. When that rule is applied, multisets u, v produce u', v', respectively, and the new polarization is α' (the value of function p in that moment provide the affinity of the application of that rule). For each j $(1 \le j \le m)$ there is just one further restriction, concerning the consistency of charges: in order to apply several rules of $\mathcal{R}_j^k$ simultaneously to the same membrane, all the rules must have the same electrical charge on their right-hand side.

A rule of the environment of the type $(x)_{e_j} \xrightarrow{p_1} (y_1)_{e_{j_1}} \cdots (y_h)_{e_{j_h}}$ is applicable to a configuration at any instant t if the following is satisfied: in that configuration environment e_j contains object x. When that rule is applied, object x passes from e_j to $e_{j_1}, \ldots, e_{j_h}$ possibly transformed into objects $y_1, \ldots, y_h$, respectively (the value of function p_1 in that moment provide the affinity of the application of that rule).

A rule of the environment of the type $(\Pi_{k,j})_{e_j} \xrightarrow{p_2} (\Pi_{k,j})_{e_{j'}}$: is applicable to a configuration at any instant t if the following is satisfied: in that configuration environment e_j contains the P system $\Pi_{k,j}$. When that rule is applied, the system $\Pi_{k,j}$ passes from environment e_j to environment $e_{j'}$ (the value of function p_2 in that moment provide the affinity of the application of that rule).

A rule of the environment of the type $\{f\}(u)_{e_j} \xrightarrow{p_3} (v)_{e_{j_1}}$, where e_{j_1} can be equal to e_j or not, is applicable to a configuration at any instant t if the following is satisfied: in that configuration environment e_j has flag f and contains the multiset u. When that rule is applied multiset u produces multiset v and environment e_j keep the same flag. This kind of rule can be applied many times in a computation step. The value of function p_3 in that moment provide the affinity of the application of that rule.

A rule of the environment of the type $\{f\}(u, f)_{e_j} \xrightarrow{p_4} (v, g)_{e_j}$ is applicable to a configuration at any instant t if the following is satisfied: in that configuration environment e_j has flag f and contains the multiset u. When that rule is applied multiset u produces multiset v and flag f of environment e_j is replaced by flag g. Bearing in mind that each environment only has a flag in any instant, this kind of rules can only be applied once in any moment.

Next, we depict the two approaches (stochastic and probabilistic) for multienvironment P systems.

3.1   Stochastic Approach

We say that a multienvironment P system has a stochastic approach if the following holds:

(a) The alphabet of flags, Φ, is an empty set.
(b) The computable functions associated with the rules of the P systems are **propensities** (obtained from the kinetic constants) [22]: These rules is function of the time but they do not depend on the environment.

(c) Initially, the P systems $\Pi_{k,j}$ are randomly distributed among the m environments of the system.

Multicompartmental P Systems. Multicompartmental P systems are multienvironment P systems with a stochastic approach which can be formally expressed as follows:

$$\Pi = (G, \Gamma, \Sigma, T, n = \sum_{j=1}^{m} n_j, \{\Pi_{k,j} \mid 1 \leq k \leq n_j, 1 \leq j \leq m\}, \{E_j \mid 1 \leq j \leq m\}, \mathcal{R}_E)$$

These systems can be viewed as a set of m environment connected by the arcs of a directed graph G. Each environment e_j only can contains P systems of the type $\Pi_{k,j}$. The total number of P systems is n, all of them with the same skeleton. The functions associated with the rules of the system are propensities which are computed as follows: stochastic constants are computed from kinetic constants by applying the mass action law, and the propensities are obtained from the stochastic constants by using the concentration of the objects in the LHS at any instant. In these systems there are rules of the following types:

1. $u[v]_i^\alpha \xrightarrow{p} u'[v']_i^{\alpha'}$
2. $(x)_{e_j} \xrightarrow{p_1} (y_1)_{e_{j_1}} \cdots (y_h)_{e_{j_h}}$
3. $(\Pi_{k,j})_{e_j} \xrightarrow{p_2} (\Pi_{k,j})_{e_{j'}}$

The dynamics of these systems is captured by the multicompartmental Gillespie's algorithm [22] or the deterministic waiting time [4]. Next, some practical examples of multicompartmental P systems applications are highlighted: Quorum sensing in Vibrio Fischeri [24], gene expression control in Lac Operon [25], and FAS-induced apoptosis [4]. A software environment supporting this model is Infobiotics Workbench [1], which provides (in version 0.0.1): a modelling language, a multi-compartmental stochastic simulator based on Gillespie's Stochastic Simulation Algorithm, a formal model analysis, and a structural and parameter model optimisation.

3.2   Probabilistic Approach

We say that a multienvironment P system has a probabilistic approach if the following holds:

(a) The total number of P systems $\Pi_{k,j}$ is, at most, the number m of environment, that is, $n \leq m$.
(b) Functions p_r associated with rule $r \equiv u[v]_i^\alpha \xrightarrow{p_r} u'[v']_i^{\alpha'}$ from $\Pi_{k,j}$ are **probability functions** such that for each $u, v \in M_f(\Gamma)$, $i \in \{1, \ldots, q\}$, $\alpha \in \{0, +, -\}$, if $r_1, \ldots, r_z$ are the rules in R_j^k whose LHS is $u \, [\, v \,]_i^\alpha$, then

$$\sum_{j=1}^{z} p_{r_j}(t) = 1, \text{ for each } t \ (1 \leq t \leq T).$$

(c) Functions p_1 associated with the rules of the environment $(x)_{e_j} \xrightarrow{p_1} (y_1)_{e_{j_1}} \cdots (y_h)_{e_{j_h}}$ are **probability functions** such that for each $x \in \Sigma$ and each environment e_j, the sum of all functions associated with the rules whose LHS is $(x)_{e_j}$, is equal to 1.

(d) Functions p_2 associated with the rules of the environment $(\Pi_{k,j})_{e_j} \xrightarrow{p_2} (\Pi_{k,j})_{e_{j'}}$ are constant functions equal to 0; that is, these rules will never be applied.

(e) Functions p_3 associated with the rules of the environment $\{f\}(u)_{e_j} \xrightarrow{p_3} (v)_{e_{j_1}}$ are **probability functions**.

(f) Functions p_4 associated with the rules of the environment $\{f\}(u,f)_{e_j} \xrightarrow{p_4} (v,g)_{e_j}$ are constant functions equal to 1.

(g) There exist no rules $u[v]_i^\alpha \xrightarrow{p} u'[v']_i^{\alpha'}$ in the skin membrane of $\Pi_{k,j}$ and rules of the environment $(x)_{e_j} \xrightarrow{p_1} (y_1)_{e_{j_1}} \cdots (y_h)_{e_{j_h}}$ such that $x \in u$.

(h) Initially, each environment e_j contains at most one P system $\Pi_{k,j}$.

Population Dynamics P Systems (PDP). Population Dynamics P systems are multienvironment P systems with a probabilistic approach such that the alphabet Φ of the flags is an empty set and $n = m$, that is, the environment has not any flag and the total number n of P systems are equal to the number m of environments. Then in a PDP system Π each environment e_j contains exactly one P system $\Pi_{k,j}$, which will be denoted henceforth by Π_j; that is, $\forall j, 1 \le j \le m, n_j = 1$.

$$\Pi = (G, \Gamma, \Sigma, T, n = m, \{\Pi_j \mid 1 \le j \le m\}, \{E_j \mid 1 \le j \le m\}, \mathcal{R}_E)$$

In these systems there are rules of the following types:

1. $u[v]_i^\alpha \xrightarrow{p} u'[v']_i^{\alpha'}$
2. $(x)_{e_j} \xrightarrow{p_1} (y_1)_{e_{j_1}} \cdots (y_h)_{e_{j_h}}$

Let us recall that in this kind of systems each rule has an associated probability function that depends on the time and on the environment where the rule is applied.

Finally, in order to ease the understandability of the whole framework, Figure 1 shows a graphical summary of multienvironment P systems and the two approaches (stochastic and probabilistic).

Some practical examples of using PDP systems on the modelling of real ecosystems are: the Bearded Vulture at the Pyrenees (Spain) [3,6], the Zebra mussel at the Ribarroja reservoir (Spain) [3], and the Pyrenean Chamois [5]. A simple example of modelling pandemics dynamics can be seen in [2].

The dynamics of these systems is captured by the Direct Non-deterministic Distribution algorithm with Probabilities (DNDP) algorithm [17], or the Direct distribution based on Consistent Blocks Algorithm (DCBA) [16]. DNDP aims to perform a random distribution of rule applications without using the concept

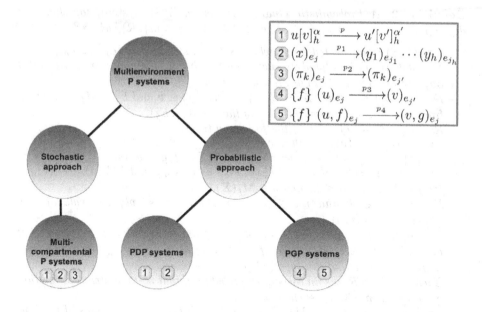

Fig. 1. The formal framework of Multienvironment P systems

of rule block, but this selection process is biased towards those rules with the highest probabilities. DCBA was first conceived to overcome the accuracy problem of DNDP, by performing an object distribution along the rule blocks, before applying the random distribution process. Although the accuracy achieved by the DCBA is better than the DNDP algorithm, the latter is much faster. In order to improve the performance of simulators implementing DCBA, parallel architectures has been used [15]. For example, a GPU-based simulator, using CUDA, reaches the acceleration of up to 7x, running on a NVIDIA Tesla C1060 GPU (240 processing cores). However, these accelerated simulators are still to be connected to those general environments to run virtual experiments. Therefore, P–Lingua and pLinguaCore are being utilised to simulate PDP systems [2,11]. The provided virtual experimentation environment is called MeCoSim [21], and it is based on P–Lingua.

4   Probabilistic Guarded P Systems (PGP)

Probabilistic Guarded P systems are multienvironment P systems with a probabilistic approach such that $n = 0$, that is, there is no P systems $\Pi_{k,j}$ (so the alphabet Γ can be considered as an emptyset), and the alphabet of the flags, Φ, is a nonempty set such that every environment has a unique flag in the initial configuration.

Definition 2. *A Probabilistic Guarded P system* (PGP system, *for short*) *of degree* $m \geq 1$ *is a tuple* $\Pi = (G, \Sigma, \Phi, T, \{A_j \mid 1 \leq j \leq m\}, \mathcal{R})$, *where:*

- $G = (V, S)$ *is a directed graph whose set of nodes is* $V = \{e_1, \ldots, e_m\}$.
- Σ *and* Φ *are finite alphabets such that* $\Sigma \cap \Phi = \emptyset$. *Elements in* Σ *are called* **objects** *and elements in* Φ *are called* **flags**.
- *For each* j, $1 \leq j \leq m$, $A_j = E_j \cup \{f_j\}$, *with* $f_j \in \Phi$ *and* $E_j \in M_f(\Sigma)$. *Thus, from now on, we "represent"* A_j *by the pair* (f_j, E_j).
- $\mathcal{R}$ *is a finite set of rules of the following types:*
  - $\{f\}(u)_{e_j} \rightarrow (v)_{e_{j_1}}$ *with* $u, v \in M_f(\Sigma)$, $f \in \Phi$ *and* $1 \leq j, j_1 \leq m$.
  - $\{f\}(u, f)_{e_j} \rightarrow (v, g)_{e_j}$ *with* $u, v \in M_f(\Sigma)$, $f, g \in \Phi$ *and* $1 \leq j \leq m$.

  There are no rules of types $\{f\}(u, f)_{e_j} \rightarrow (v, g)_{e_j}$ *and* $\{f\}(u)_{e_j} \longrightarrow (v)_{e_{j_1}}$, *for* $f \in \Phi$, $1 \leq j, j_1 \leq m$ *and* $u \in M_f(\Sigma)$).
  For each $f \in \Phi$ *and* $j, 1 \leq j \leq m$, *there exists only one rule of type* $\{f\}(u, f)_{e_j} \rightarrow (v, g)_{e_j}$.
- *The arcs of graph* $G = (V, S)$ *are defined from* $\mathcal{R}$ *as follows:* $(e_j, e_{j_1}) \in S$ *if and only if there exists a rule of the type* $\{f\}(u)_{e_j} \rightarrow (v)_{e_{j_1}}$, *or* $j = j_1$ *and there exists a rule of the type* $\{f\}(u, f)_{e_j} \rightarrow (v, g)_{e_j}$.
- *Each rule from* $\mathcal{R}$ *has an associated probability, that is, there exists a function* $p_{\mathcal{R}}$ *from* $\mathcal{R}$ *into* $[0, 1]$, *such that:*
  - *For each* $f \in \Phi, u \in M_f(\Sigma), 1 \leq j \leq m$, *if* $r_1, \ldots, r_t$ *are rules of the type* $\{f\}(u)_{e_j} \rightarrow (v)_{e_{j_1}}$, *then* $\sum_{s=1}^{t} p_{\mathcal{R}}(r_s) = 1$.
  - *If* $r \equiv \{f\}(u, f)_{e_j} \rightarrow (u, g)_{e_j}$, *then* $p_{\mathcal{R}}(r) = 1$.

A Probabilistic Guarded P system can be viewed as a set of m environments, called *cells*, labelled by $1, \ldots, m$ such that: (a) $E_1, \ldots, E_m$ are finite multisets over Σ representing the objects initially placed in the cells of the system; (b) $f_1, \ldots, f_m$ are flags that initially mark the cells; (c) G is a directed graph whose arcs specify connections among cells; (d) $\mathcal{R}$ is the set of rules that allow the evolution of the system and each rule r is associated with a real number $p_{\mathcal{R}}(r)$ in $[0, 1]$ describing the probability of that rule to be applied in the case that it is applicable. That is to say, each rule r has a probability $p_{\mathcal{R}}(r)$ to be applied at an instant t for each possible application of r at such an instant. Γ and n are omitted, as they are $\Gamma =$ and $n = 0$, respectively. Let us point out that the set of rules $\mathcal{R}$ is exactly the set $\mathcal{R}_E$ in Definition 1, since $n_j = 0, 1 \leq j \leq m$.

In PGP systems, two types of symbols are used: *objects* (elements in Σ) and *flags* (elements in Φ). It can be considered that objects are **in** cells and flags are **on** (the borderline of) cells.

4.1   Semantics of PGP Systems

Definition 3. *A configuration at any instant* $t \geq 0$ *of a PGP system* Π *is a tuple* $\mathcal{C}_t = (x_1, u_1, \ldots, x_m, u_m)$ *where, for each* i, $1 \leq i \leq m$, $x_i \in \Phi$ *and* $u_i \in M_f(\Sigma)$. *That is to say, such a configuration is described by all multisets of objects over* Σ *associated with all the cells present in the system and the flags marking these cells.* $(f_1, E_1, \ldots, f_m, E_m)$ *is said to be the* initial configuration *of* Π. *At any instant, each cell has exactly one flag, in a similar manner to polarizations in cell–like P systems.*

Definition 4. *A rule r of the type $\{f\}(u)_i \to (v)_j$ is applicable to a configuration $C_t = (x_1, u_1, \ldots x_m, u_m)$ if and only if $x_i = f$ and $u \subseteq u_i$, for all i $(1 \leq i \leq m)$.*

When applying r to C_t, objects in u are removed from cell i and objects in v are produced in cell j. Flag f is not changed; it plays the role of a catalyst assisting the evolution of objects in u.

Definition 5. *A rule r of the type $\{f\}(u, f)_i \to (v, g)_i$, where $1 \leq i \leq m$, is applicable to a configuration $C_t = (x_1, u_1, \ldots x_m, u_m)$ if and only if $x_i = f$ and $u \subseteq u_i$.*

When applying r to C_t, in cell i objects in u are replaced by those in v and f is replaced by g. In this case, flag f is consumed, so r can be applied only once in instant t in cell i.

Remark 1. After applying a rule r of the type $\{f\}(u, f)_i \to (v, g)_i$, other rules r' of the type $\{f\}(u)_i \to (v)_j$ can still be applied (the flag remains in vigor). However, f has been consumed (in the same sense that an object $x \in \Sigma$ is consumed), so no more rules of the type $\{f\}(u, f)_i \to (v, g)_i$ can be applied.

Definition 6. *A configuration is a halting configuration if no rule is applicable to it.*

Definition 7. *We say that configuration C_1 yields configuration C_2 in a transition step if we can pass from C_1 to C_2 by applying rules from $\mathcal{R}_\mathcal{E}$ in a non-deterministic, maximally parallel manner, according to their associated probabilities denoted by map $p_{\mathcal{R}_\mathcal{E}}$. That is to say, a maximal multiset of rules from $\mathcal{R}_\mathcal{E}$ is applied, no further rule can be added.*

Definition 8. *A computation of a PGP system Π is a sequence of configurations such that: (a) the first term of the sequence is the initial configuration of Π, (b) each remaining term in the sequence is obtained from the previous one by applying the rules of the system following Definition 7, (c) the sequence will have, at most, $T + 1$ terms. That is, we consider that the execution of a PGP system will perform, at most, T steps.*

4.2 Comparison Between PGP Systems and Other Frameworks in Membrane Computing

Probabilistic Guarded P systems display similarities with other frameworks in Membrane Computing. For example, *P systems with proteins on membranes* [18] are a type of cell-like systems in which membranes might have attached a set of proteins which regulate the application of rules, whilst in PGP systems each cell has only one flag. Therefore, some rules are applicable if and only if the corresponding protein is present.

When comparing PGP systems and *Population Dynamics P systems* [2], it is important to remark the semantic similarity between flags and polarizations, as they both define at some point the context of each compartment. Nevertheless, as described at the beginning of this paper, upon the application of a rule

$r \equiv \{f\} (u, f)_i \rightarrow (v, g)_i$ flag f is consumed, thus ensuring that r can be applied at most once to any configuration. This property keeps PGP transitions from yielding inconsistent flags; at any instant, only one rule at most can change the flag in each membrane, so scenarios in which inconsistent flags produced by multiple rules are impossible. Moreover, in PDP systems the number of polarizations is limited to three ($+$, $-$ and 0), whereas in their PGP counterpart depends on the system itself. Finally, each compartment in PDP systems contains a hierarchical structure of membranes, which is absent in PGP systems.

5 Simulation of PGP Systems

When simulating PGP systems, there exist two cases, according to if there exists object competition or not. In this work, only algorithms for the second case are introduced, but some ideas are given to handle object competition among rules in the model, and kept for future developments.

5.1 Some Definitions on the Model

The following concepts defined for PGP systems are analogous to those described in [16], but adapted to the syntax of PGP systems.

Remark 2. For the sake of simplicity, henceforth the following notation will be used. For every cell i, $1 \leq i \leq m$, and time t, $0 \leq t \leq T$, the flag and multiset of cell i in step t are denoted as $x_{i,t} \in \Phi$ and $u_{i,t} \in M_f(\Sigma)$, respectively. Similarly, $|u|_y$, where $u \in M_f(\Sigma)$, $y \in \Sigma$ denotes the number of objects y in multiset u.

Definition 9 shows the notation regarding the left-hand and right-hand sides of rules.

Definition 9. *For each rule $r \in \mathcal{R_E}$:*

Type 1: *If r is of the form $r \equiv \{f\} (u)_i \rightarrow (v)_j$, we denote the left–hand side of r ($LHS(r)$) as $LHS(r) = (i, f, u)$ and the right–hand side of r ($RHS(r)$) as $RHS(r) = (j, f, v)$.*
Type 2: *If r is of the form $r \equiv \{f\} (u, f)_i \rightarrow (v, g)_i$, we denote the left–hand side as $LHS(r) = (i, f, u, f)$ and the right–hand side as $RHS(r) = (i, g, v)$.*

Let us recall that for each i, $1 \leq i \leq m$, and $f \in \Phi$, there exists a *unique* rule of type 2: $r \equiv \{f\} (u, f)_i \rightarrow (v, g)_i$.

Next, Definition 10 introduces the concept of rule blocks in PGP systems, which is inspired by the one used in PDP systems [16].

Definition 10. *For each $1 \leq i \leq q$, $f \in \Phi$, and $u \in M_f(\Sigma)$, we will denote:*

- *The block of communication rules $B^1_{i,f,u} = \{r \in \mathcal{R} : LHS(r) = (i, f, u)\}$.*
- *The block of context–changing rules $B^2_{i,f,u} = \{r \in \mathcal{R} : LHS(r) = (i, f, u, f)\}$.*

Obviously, $B_{i,f,u}^1 \cap B_{i,f,u}^2 = \emptyset$. It is important to recall that, as it is the case in PDP systems, the sum of probabilities of all the rules belonging to the same block is always equal to 1 – in particular, rules with probability equal to 1 form individual blocks. Consequently, non–empty blocks of context–changing rules (type 2) are composed of single rules. In addition, rules with overlapping (but different) left–hand sides are classified into different blocks.

Definition 11. *For each $i, 1 \leq i \leq m$, we will consider the set of all rule blocks associated with cell i as $B_i = \{B_{i,f,u}^1, B_{i,f,u}^2 : f \in \Phi \wedge u \in M_f(\Sigma)\}$.*

We will also consider a total order in B_i, for $1 \leq i \leq m$, $B_i = \{B_{i,1}, B_{i,2}, \ldots, B_{i,\alpha_i}\}$. Therefore, there are α_i blocks associated to cell i.

Furthermore, let $B_{i,j}, 1 \leq i \leq m, 1 \leq j \leq \alpha_i$ be a block associated to cell i. We define the following notations:

- $Type(B_{i,j})$ is equal to:
  - 1, if $\exists f \in \Phi, u \in M_f(\Sigma)$ such that $B_{i,j} = B_{i,f,u}^1$
  - 2, if $\exists f \in \Phi, u \in M_f(\Sigma)$ such that $B_{i,j} = B_{i,f,u}^2$
- $Flag(B_{i,j}) = f$, if $\exists k(1 \leq k \leq 2) \wedge \exists u \in M_f(\Sigma)$ such that $B_{i,j} = B_{i,f,u}^k$
- $Mult(B_{i,j}) = u$, if $\exists k(1 \leq k \leq 2) \wedge \exists f \in \Phi$ such that $B_{i,j} = B_{i,f,u}^k$

In addition, for each block $B_{i,j}, 1 \leq i \leq m$ and $1 \leq j \leq \alpha_i$, associated to cell i, we consider a total order in its set of rules: $B_{i,j} = \{r_{i,j,1}, \ldots, r_{i,j,h_{i,j}}\}$, where $h_{i,j}(1 \leq i \leq m, 1 \leq j \leq \alpha_i)$ denotes the number of rules in block $B_{i,j}$. Obviously, all the rules of a block are of the same type.

Definition 12. *A PGP system is said to feature object competition, if there exists at least two different blocks $B_{i,j}$ and $B_{i,j'}$ (possibly of different type), such that $Flag(B_{i,j}) = Flag(B_{i,j'})$, and $Mult(B_{i,j}) \cap Mult(B_{i,j'}) \neq \emptyset$. That is, their rules have overlapping (but not equal) left–hand sides.*

Remark 3. It is worth noting that all rules in the model can be consistently applied. This is because there can only exists one flag $f \in \Phi$ at every membrane at the same time, and, consequently, at most one context–changing rule $r \equiv \{f\}(u, f)_i \rightarrow (v, g)_i$ can consume f and replace it (where possibly $f = g$).

Definition 13. *Given a block $B_{i,f,u}^1$ or $B_{i,f,u}^2$, where $u \in M_f(\Sigma), f \in \Phi, 1 \leq i \leq m$ and a configuration $C_t = \{x_1, u_1, \ldots, x_m, u_m\}, 0 \leq t \leq T$, the maximum number of applications of such a block in C_t is the maximum times that each one of its rules can be applied in C_t.*

5.2 Simulation Algorithm

Next, we define some auxiliary data structures to be used in the simulation algorithms.

NBA **(Number of Block Applications):** a matrix of integer numbers of dimension $m \times N_{BM}$, where $N_{BM} = \max(\alpha_i \mid 1 \leq i \leq m)$ (maximum number of blocks for all cells). Each element $NBA_{i,j}$, $1 \leq i \leq m$, $1 \leq j \leq N_{BM}$ stores the number of applications of block $B_{i,j}$.

NRA **(Number of Rule Applications):** a matrix of integer numbers of dimension $m \times N_{BM} \times N_{RM}$, where $N_{RM} = max(h_{i,j})$, $1 \leq i \leq m$, $1 \leq j \leq \alpha_i$ (maximum number of rules for all blocks in all membranes). Each element $NRA_{i,j,k}$, $1 \leq i \leq m$, $1 \leq j \leq \alpha_i$, $1 \leq k \leq h_{i,j}$, stores the number of applications of rule $r_{i,j,k}$, identified by its cell, block and local identifier inside its block, according to the established total order.

The algorithm for simulation of PGP systems receives three parameters:

- The PGP system Π of degree m.
- The integer number $T > 0$ (number of time steps).
- An integer number $K > 0$ (random accuracy). It indicates for how many cycles block applications are assigned among their rules in random fashion. That is, the algorithm distributes the applications of each block among its rules for K cycles, and after that, block applications are maximally assigned among rules in a single cycle. Therefore, the greater K is, the more accurate the distribution of rule applications for each block becomes, but at the expense of a greater computational cost. It is used as an accuracy parameter for the probabilistic method. Algorithm 5.4 performs this function.

When simulating PGP systems without object competition, it is not necessary to randomly assign objects among blocks; as they do not compete for objects, then the number of times that each block is applied is always equal to its maximum number of applications. As it is the case of DCBA for PDP systems [16], the simulation algorithm heavily relies on the concept of block, being rule applications secondary. However, DCBA handles object competition among blocks, penalizing more those blocks which require a larger number of copies of the same object which is inspired by the amount of energy required to join individuals from the same species. On the other hand, object competition is not supported on the proposed algorithm. Algorithm 5.1 describes a simulation algorithm for PGP systems without object competition.

On each simulation step t, $1 \leq t \leq T$ and cell i, $1 \leq i \leq m$, the following stages are applied: *Object distribution* (selection), *Rule application distribution* (selection) and *Object generation* (execution).

However, before starting the simulation process, we must initialize some data structures. In *Initialization* (Algorithm 5.2), the initial configuration C_0 is constructed with the input PGP system Π. Moreover, the information about blocks are created; that is, the blocks of rules are computed, and ordered for each cell. Moreover, the rules inside each block are also ordered. Finally, the data structures NBA and NRA are initialized with zeros.

In the *Object distribution* stage (Algorithm 5.3), objects are distributed among blocks. As the system to simulate does not feature object competition, the number

---

Algorithm 5.1. Algorithm for simulation of PGP systems

Input:

- T: an integer number $T \geq 1$ representing the iterations of the simulation.
- K: an integer number $K \geq 1$ representing non–maximal rule iterations (i.e., iterations in which the applications selected for each rule do not necessarily need to be maximal).
- $\Pi = (G, \Sigma, \Phi, T, \{(f_j, E_j) \mid 1 \leq j \leq m\}, \mathcal{R})$: a PGP system of degree $m \geq 1$.

1: Initialization (Π)
2: **for** $t \leftarrow 1$ **to** T **do** $\triangleright$ See Algorithm 5.2
3:     $C'_t \leftarrow C_{t-1}$
4:     SELECTION of rules:
5:         PHASE 1: Objects distribution (C'_t) $\triangleright$ See Algorithm 5.3
6:         PHASE 2: Rule application distribution (C'_t) $\triangleright$ See Algorithm 5.4
7:     EXECUTION of rules:
8:         PHASE 3: Object production (C'_t) $\triangleright$ See Algorithm 5.5
9:     $C_t \leftarrow C'_t$
10: **end for**

Algorithm 5.2. Initialization

Input: $\Pi = (G, \Sigma, \Phi, T, \{(f_j, E_j) \mid 1 \leq j \leq m\}, \mathcal{R})$
1: $C_0 \leftarrow \{f_1, E_1, \ldots, f_m, E_m\}$ $\triangleright$ Initial configuration
2: **for** $i \leftarrow 1$ **to** m **do** $\triangleright$ For each cell
3:     $B_i \leftarrow$ ordered set of blocks formed by rules of $\mathcal{R}$ associated with cell i
4:     $\alpha_i \leftarrow |B_i|$ $\triangleright$ Number of rule blocks
5:     **for** $j \leftarrow 1$ **to** α_i **do** $\triangleright$ For each block associated with the cell
6:         $B_{i,j} \leftarrow$ ordered set of rules from j^{th} block in B_i.
7:         $h_{i,j} \leftarrow |B_{i,j}|$ $\triangleright$ Number of rules within the block
8:         $NBA_{i,j} \leftarrow 0$ $\triangleright$ Initially, all blocks applications are 0
9:         **for** $k \leftarrow 1$ **to** $h_{i,j}$ **do** $\triangleright$ Initially, all rule applications are 0
10:             $NRA_{i,j,k} \leftarrow 0$
11:         **end for**
12:     **end for**
13: **end for**

---

of applications of each block is its maximum. Then, objects are consumed accordingly. It is in this stage that the flag checking for each block is performed. Moreover, blocks of type 2 (context–changing rules) consume and generate the new flag.

Next, objects are distributed among rules according to a binomial distribution with rule probabilities and maximum number of block applications as parameters. This algorithm is composed of two stages *non–maximal* and *maximal* repartition. In the non–maximal repartition stage, a rule in the block is randomly selected according to a uniform distribution, so each rule has the same probability to be chosen. Then, its number of applications is calculated according to an *ad–hoc* procedure based on a binomially distributed variable $Binomial(n, p)$, where n is the remaining number of block applications to be assigned among

---

Algorithm 5.3. Phase 1: Object distribution among blocks

Input: $C'_t = \{x_{1,t}, u_{1,t}, \ldots, x_{m,t}, u_{m,t}\}$

1: **for** $i \leftarrow 1$ **to** m **do**   ▷ For each cell
2:     **for** $j \leftarrow 1$ **to** α_i **do**   ▷ For each block associated with the cell
3:        **if** $Flag(B_{i,j}) = x_{i,t}$ **then**
4:           **if** $Type(B_{i,j}) = 1 \wedge Mult(B_{i,j}) \subseteq u_{i,t}$ **then**
5:             $NBA_{i,j} \leftarrow \min(\lfloor \frac{|u_{i,t}|_z}{|Mult(B_{i,j})|_z} \rfloor : z \in \Sigma)$ ▷ Maximal application
6:             $u_{i,t} \leftarrow u_{i,t} - NBA_{i,j} \cdot Mult(B_{i,j})$ ▷ Update the configuration
7:           **end if**
8:           **if** $Type(B_{i,j}) = 2 \wedge Mult(B_{i,j}) \subseteq u_{i,t}$ **then**
9:             $NBA_{i,j} \leftarrow 1$ ▷ Just one application
10:            $x_{i,t} \leftarrow g$, being $RHS(r_{i,j,1}) = (i, g, v)$ with $B_{i,j} = \{r_{i,j,1}\}$ ▷ Update
                 cell flag
11:            $u_{i,t} \leftarrow u_{i,t} - NBA_{i,j} \cdot Mult(B_{i,j})$ ▷ Update the configuration
12:           **end if**
13:        **end if**
14:     **end for**
15: **end for**

Algorithm 5.4. Phase 2: Rule application distribution

Input: $C'_t = \{x_{1,t}, u_{1,t}, \ldots, x_{m,t}, u_{m,t}\}$

    for $k \leftarrow 1$ **to** K **do**   ▷ Non-maximal repartition stage
       for $i \leftarrow 1$ **to** m **do**
          for $j \leftarrow 1$ **to** α_i **do**
            $l \leftarrow Uniform\{1, \ldots, h_{i,j}\}$ ▷ Select a random rule $r_{i,j,l}$ in Block $B_{i,j}$
            $lnrap \leftarrow Binomial(NBA_{i,j}, p_{\mathcal{R}}(r_{i,j,l}))$
            $NRA_{i,j,l} \leftarrow NRA_{i,j,l} + lnrap$ ▷ Update rule applications
            $NBA_{i,j} \leftarrow NBA_{i,j} - lnrap$
          end for
       end for
    end for
    for $i \leftarrow 1$ **to** m **do**   ▷ Maximal repartition stage
       for $j \leftarrow 1$ **to** α_i **do**
          $l \leftarrow Uniform\{1, \ldots, h_{i,j}\}$
          $NRA_{i,j,l} \leftarrow NRA_{i,j,l} + NBA_{i,j}$
          $NBA_{i,j} \leftarrow 0$
       end for
    end for

---

its rules and p is the corresponding rule probability. This process is repeated a number K of iterations for each block $B_{i,j}, 1 \leq i \leq m, 1 \leq j \leq \alpha_i$. We propose this procedure to simulate a multinomial distribution, but it could be easily interchangeable by another one. Algorithm 5.4 describes this procedure. If, after this process, there are still applications to assign among rules, a rule per applicable block is chosen at random and as many applications as possible are assigned to it in the maximal repartition stage. An alternative approach would be to

Algorithm 5.5. Phase 3: Object production

---

for $i \leftarrow 1$ to m do   ▷ For each cell
   for $j \leftarrow 1$ to α_i do   ▷ For each block associated with the cell
      for $k \leftarrow 1$ to $h_{i,j}$ do   ▷ For each rule belonging to the block
         $u_{i,t} \leftarrow u_{i,t} + NRA_{i,j,k} \cdot v$, where $RHS(r_{i,j,k}) = (i', f', v)$
         $NRA_{i,j,k} \leftarrow 0$
      end for
   end for
end for

---

implement a multinomial distribution of applications for the rules inside each block, such as the way that it is implemented on the DCBA algorithm [16]. A method to implement a multinomial distribution would be the conditional distribution method, which emulates a multinomial distribution based on a sequence of binomial distributions [9]. This would require to normalize rule probabilities for each rule application distribution iteration. This approach has also been tested on the simulation algorithm, but was discarded because it tends to distribute too few applications in the non–maximal repartition stage, thus leaving too many applications for the rule selected in the maximal repartition one.

Lastly, rules produce objects as indicated by their right–hand side. Each rule produces objects according to its previously assigned number of applications. Algorithm 5.5 describes this procedure.

The algorithm proposed in this paper works only for models without object competition. This is because the models studied so far (such as the *Pieris oleracea* model to be mentioned on Section 6) did not have object competition, so this feature was not required. However, it might be interesting to develop new algorithms supporting it. They would be identical to their counterpart without object competition, solely differing in the protocol by which objects are distributed among blocks. As an example, it would be possible to adapt the way in which objects are distributed in the DCBA algorithm [16].

5.3   Software Environment

This section provides an overview of the developed simulators, the P–Lingua extension, and the GUI for PGP systems.

Software Enviornment. A simulator for PGP systems without object competition has been incorporated on P–Lingua [11]. In addition, a C++ simulator for PGP systems (namely PGPC++) has also been implemented. The libraries used for random number generation are COLT [26] in the P–Lingua simulator, and standard std::rand [27] for PGPC++. In the latter, the facilities provided by std::rand are directly used. These libraries provide a wide range of functionality to generate and handle random numbers, and are publicly available under open source licenses.

P–Lingua Extension. In order to define PGP systems, P–Lingua has been extended to support PGP rules. Specifically, given $f, g \in \Phi$, $u, v \in M_f(\Sigma)$, $1 \leq i, j \leq m$, $p = p_{\mathcal{R}}(r)$, rules are represented as follows:

$$\{f\}\,(u)_i \xrightarrow{p} (v)_j, \equiv \texttt{@guard } f \texttt{ ?[}u\texttt{]'}i \texttt{ --> [}v\texttt{]'}j \texttt{ :: } p\texttt{;}$$

$$\{f\}\,(u, f)_i \to (v, g)_i \equiv \texttt{@guard } f \texttt{ ?[}u,f\texttt{]'}i \texttt{ --> [}v,g\texttt{]'}i \texttt{ :: } 1.0\texttt{;}$$

In both cases, if $p = 1.0$, then $\texttt{:: } p$ can be omitted. If $i = j$, then $\{f\}\,(u)_i \xrightarrow{p} (v)_j$ can be written as $\texttt{@guard } f \texttt{ ?[}u \texttt{ --> } v\texttt{]'}i \texttt{ :: } p\texttt{;}$. Likewise, $\{f\}\,(u, f)_i \to (v, g)_i$ can always be written as $\texttt{@guard } f \texttt{ ?[}u,f \texttt{ --> } v,g\texttt{]'}i\texttt{;}$.

Further additional constructs have been included to ease parametrization of P systems. The idea is to enable completely parametric designs, so as experiments can be tuned by simply adjusting parameters leaving modifications of P–Lingua files for cases in which changes in semantics are in order. This extension is going to be released on the next version of P–Lingua.

In addition, two new formats have been integrated into P-Lingua. These formats (XML–based and binary) encode P systems representing labels and objects as numbers instead of strings, so they are easily parsed and simulated by third–part simulators such as PGPC++.

A Graphical Environment for PGP Systems. *MeCoGUI* is a new Graphical User Interface (GUI) developed for the simulation of PGP systems. MeCoSim [21] could have been used instead. However, in the environment in which the simulators were developed there exist some pros and cons on this approach versus and ad–hoc simulator.

MeCoSim is an integrated development environment (IDE). That is to say, it provides all functionality required for the simulation and computational analysis of P systems. To define the desired input and output displays, it is necessary to configure a spreadsheet by using an *ad–hoc* programming language. However, it would entail teaching this language to prospective users, who can be proficient in any other statistic programming language instead, such as R. In this sense, a more natural approach for them is to develop a GUI in which users can define input parameters and results analysis on R.

To do so, the developed GUI takes as input a P system file on P–Lingua format and a CSV file encoding its parameters, and outputs a CSV file which contains simulation results. This way, users can define inputs and analyse outputs on their programming language of choice. CSV is a widespread, simple and free format with plenty of libraries for different languages. This flexibility comes at the cost concerning that the developed GUI is not an IDE, as input parameters and simulation analysis cannot be directly input and viewed on the GUI. Rather, it is necessary to develop applications to generate and process these CSV files which depend on the domain of use. In some simulators (such as PGPC++), the output CSV files represent labels and objects as integers, but this application includes a button to translate output files from PGPC++ into string–representative file formats. Figure 2 displays the main screen of this application.

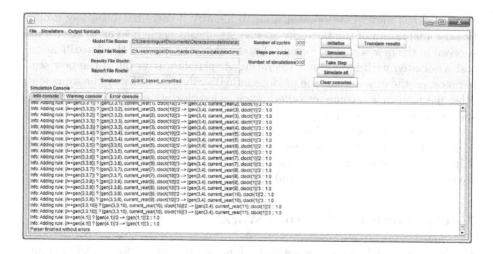

Fig. 2. Main screen of MeCoGUI

MeCoGUI can also translate P systems into machine–readable formats, such as those read by PGPC++. Finally, it is important to remark that these applications play the role of domain–specific spreadsheets on MeCoSim, so MeCoGUI can simulate any type of P system supported by P–Lingua. This is because only external applications for input data and simulation processing depend on the domain, not MeCoGUI itself, which is general for any type of P system.

6   Applications of PGP Systems

A model of the ecosystem of the white cabbage butterfly (*Pieris oleracea*) [8], based on PGP systems, is a currently ongoing project. Such a species is suffering the invasion of the garlic mustard (*Alliaria petiolata*), which is replacing native host broadleaf toothwort (*Cardamine diphylla*) and ravaging the butterfly's natural habitat. Specifically, *A. petiolata* contains a deterrent agent for larvae of *P. oleracea*. Moreover, such a plant is toxic for these larvae, although it contains a chemical compound which lures mature butterflies and frames them into laying eggs. Nevertheless, a minority of individuals tolerates such a deterrent, metabolize the toxin and reach the pupa stage [13,14].

The distribution of phylogenetic profiles across the species consists of a majority of homozygous individuals unable to thrive on *A. petiolata* patches, a minority of homozygous individuals which do well on *A. petolata* rosettes and, in the midterm, an slightly larger population of heterozygous individuals with both alleles. The allele which enables butterflies to overcome the dietary restrictions imposed by *A. petiolata* is dominant, but individuals carrying this allele undergo a detoxification mechanism which entails an energetic cost and hampers their arrival at adulthood [13].

The model under development aims to identify if there has been any evolutionary adaptation of the butterfly species significant enough so as to ensure its survival in the new scenario. Specifically, the idea is to assess if the detoxification cost associated with individuals tolerating *A. petiolata* pays off in the new scenario or, on the other hand, the phylogenetic distribution will stay the same and other mechanism will come into effect, such as hybridization with other butterfly species such as *Pieris rapae* [8].

The approach taken in this project aims to validate the model *qualitatively*. A *qualitative validation* is defined as follows: a model is qualitatively validated if it can reproduce some properties verified by the ecosystem under different scenarios (according to the experts).

7   Conclusions and Future Work

Multienvironment P systems are a general, formal framework for modelling population dynamics in biology. The framework has two main approaches: stochastic (micro–level oriented) and probabilistic (macro–level oriented). The framework has been extended in the probabilistic approach, with the inclusion of a new modelling framework called Probabilistic Guarded P (PGP) systems. PGP systems are inspired by Population Dynamics P systems, and aim to simplify the design and simulation of models of ecological phenomena. The model has been formalized in this paper, and a simulation algorithm is introduced. This algorithm is restricted for models which do not feature object competition. Moreover, an extension of the P–Lingua language is provided to enable PGP systems in P–Lingua, as well as a Graphical User Interface (GUI) to simulate PGP systems (MeCoGUI).

The framework of PGP systems is being utilized for modelling the ecosystem of *Pieris napi oleracea*, a butterfly native to Northeastern America. The aim is to validate the model qualitatively; that is, checking that if the ecosystem verifies some properties under different scenarios (experts), our model reproduces those properties as well.

Although PGP systems provide a simplified alternative to PDP systems, some constraints to the supported models are imposed: only models without object competition are allowed. Therefore, future research lines will be focused on overcoming this constraint, providing new simulation algorithms permitting object competition. Moreover, new case studies will be considered, which can help to extend the framework. Finally, PGP simulation will be accelerated by using parallel architectures, such as GPU computing with CUDA.

Acknowledgements. The authors acknowledge the support of the project TIN2012-37434 of the "Ministerio de Economía y Competitividad" of Spain, co-financed by FEDER funds. Manuel García–Quismondo also acknowledges the support from the National FPU Grant Programme from the Spanish Ministry of Education. Miguel A. Martínez-del-Amor also acknowledges the support of the 3rd Postdoctoral phase of the PIF program associated with "Proyecto de Excelencia con Investigador de Reconocida

Valía" of the "Junta de Andalucía" under grant P08-TIC04200. The authors also recognize the assistance provided by Profs. Michael Reed and Frances Chew from TUFTS University on the development of the proposed framework.

References

1. Blakes, J., Twycross, J., Romero-Campero, F.J., Krasnogor, N.: The Infobiotics Workbench: an integrated in silico modelling platform for Systems and Synthetic Biology. Bioinformatics **27**(23), 3323–3324 (2011)
2. Colomer, M.A., García-Quismondo, M., Macías-Ramos, L.F., Martínez-del-Amor, M.A., Pérez-Hurtado, I., Pérez-Jiménez, M.J., Riscos-Núñez, A., Valencia-Cabrera, L.: Membrane system-based models for specifying Dynamical Population systems. In: Applications of Membrane Computing in Systems and Synthetic Biology. Emergence, Complexity and Computation series, Chap. 4, vol. 7, pp. 97–132. Springer (2014)
3. Cardona, M., Colomer, M.A., Margalida, A., Palau, A., Pérez-Hurtado, I., Pérez-Jiménez, M.J., Sanuy, D.: A computational modeling for real ecosystems based on P systems. Natural Computing **10**(1), 39–53 (2011)
4. Cheruku, S., Păun, A., Romero-Campero, F.J., Pérez-Jiménez, M.J., Ibarra, O.H.: Simulating FAS-induced apoptosis by using P systems. Progress in Natural Science **17**(4), 424–431 (2007)
5. Colomer, M.A., et al.: Modeling population growth of Pyrenean Chamois (Rupicapra p. pyrenaica) by using P-systems. In: Gheorghe, M., Hinze, T., Păun, Gh., Rozenberg, G., Salomaa, A. (eds.) CMC 2010. LNCS, vol. 6501, pp. 144–159. Springer, Heidelberg (2010)
6. Colomer, M.A., Margalida, A., Sanuy, D., Pérez-Jiménez, M.J.: A bio-inspired computing model as a new tool for modeling ecosystems: The avian scavengers as a case study. Ecological Modelling **222**(1), 33–47 (2011)
7. Colomer, M.A., Martínez-del-Amor, M.A., Pérez-Hurtado, I., Pérez-Jiménez, M.J., Riscos-Núñez, A.: A uniform framework for modeling based on P Systems. In: Proceedings IEEE Fifth International Conference on Bio-inpired Computing: Theories and Applications (BIC-TA 2010), vol. 1, pp. 616–621 (2010)
8. Chew, F.S.: Coexistence and local extinction in two pierid butterflies. The American Naturalist **118**(5), 655–672 (1981)
9. Davis, C.S.: The computer generation of multinomial random variates. Computational Statistics and Data Analysis **16**(2), 205–217 (1993)
10. Frisco, P., Gheorghe, M., Pérez-Jiménez, M.J. (eds.): Applications of Membrane Computing in Systems and Synthetic Biology. Springer (2014)
11. García-Quismondo, M., Gutiérrez-Escudero, R., Pérez-Hurtado, I., Pérez-Jiménez, M.J., Riscos-Núñez, A.: An overview of P-Lingua 2.0. In: Păun, Gh., Pérez-Jiménez, M.J., Riscos-Núñez, A., Rozenberg, G., Salomaa, A. (eds.) WMC 2009. LNCS, vol. 5957, pp. 264–288. Springer, Heidelberg (2010)
12. Gheorghe, M., Ipate, F., Dragomir, C., Mierla, L., Valencia-Cabrera, L., García-Quismondo, M., Pérez-Jiménez, M.J.: Kernel P systems - Version I. In: Proceedings of the Eleventh Brainstorming Week on Membrane Computing (BWMC 2013), pp. 97–124 (2013)
13. Keeler, M.S., Chew, F.S.: Escaping an evolutionary trap: preference and performance of a native insect on an exotic invasive host. Oecologia **156**(3), 559–568 (2008)

14. Keeler, M.S., Chew, F.S., Goodale, B.C., Reed, J.M.: Modelling the impacts of two exotic invasive species on a native butterfly: top-down vs. bottom-up effects. Journal of Animal Ecology **75**(3), 777–788 (2006)
15. Martínez-del-Amor, M.A., Pérez-Hurtado, I., Gastalver-Rubio, A., Elster, A.C., Pérez-Jiménez, M.J.: Population Dynamics P systems on CUDA. In: Gilbert, D., Heiner, M. (eds.) CMSB 2012. LNCS (LNBI), vol. 7605, pp. 247–266. Springer, Heidelberg (2012)
16. Martínez-del-Amor, M.A., et al.: DCBA: Simulating Population Dynamics P Systems with Proportional Object Distribution. In: Csuhaj-Varjú, E., Gheorghe, M., Rozenberg, G., Salomaa, A., Vaszil, Gy. (eds.) CMC 2012. LNCS, vol. 7762, pp. 257–276. Springer, Heidelberg (2013)
17. Martínez-del-Amor, M.A., Pérez-Hurtado, I., Pérez-Jiménez, M.J., Riscos-Núñez, A., Sancho-Caparrini, F.: A simulation algorithm for multienvironment probabilistic P systems: A formal verification. International Journal of Foundations of Computer Science **22**(1), 107–118 (2011)
18. Păun, A., Popa, B.: P systems with proteins on membranes. Fundamenta Informaticae **72**(4), 467–483 (2006)
19. Păun, Gh.: Computing with membranes. Journal of Computer and System Sciences **61**(1), 108–143 (2000). and TUCS Report No. 208 (2000)
20. Păun, Gh., Rozenberg, G., Salomaa, A. (eds.): The Oxford Handbook of Membrane Computing. Oxford University Press (2010)
21. Pérez-Hurtado, I., Valencia-Cabrera, L., Pérez-Jiménez, M.J., Colomer, M.A., Riscos-Núñez, A.: MeCoSim: A general purpose software tool for simulating biological phenomena by means of P Systems. In: Proceedings IEEE Fifth International Conference on Bio-inpired Computing: Theories and Applications (BIC-TA 2010), vol. I, pp. 637–643 (2010)
22. Pérez-Jímenez, M.J., Romero-Campero, F.J.: P systems, A new computational modelling tool for Systems Biology. In: Priami, C., Plotkin, G. (eds.) Trans. on Comput. Syst. Biol. VI. LNCS (LNBI), vol. 4220, pp. 176–197. Springer, Heidelberg (2006)
23. Pan, L., Pérez-Jiménez, M.J.: Computational complexity of tissue-like P systems. Journal of Complexity **26**(3), 296–315 (2010)
24. Romero-Campero, F.J., Pérez-Jiménez, M.J.: A model of the Quorum Sensing system in Vibrio fischeri using P systems. Artificial Life **14**(1), 95–109 (2008)
25. Romero-Campero, F.J., Pérez-Jiménez, M.J.: Modelling gene expression control using P systems: The Lac Operon, a case study. BioSystems **91**(3), 438–457 (2008)
26. COLT library. http://acs.lbl.gov/software/colt/index.html
27. RAND function in C++/C Standard General Utilities Library (cstdlib). http://www.cplusplus.com/reference/cstdlib/rand

Solving the ST-Connectivity Problem
with Pure Membrane Computing Techniques

Zsolt Gazdag[1]([✉]) and Miguel A. Gutiérrez-Naranjo[2]

[1] Department of Algorithms and Their Applications, Faculty of Informatics,
Eötvös Loránd University, Budapest, Hungary
gazdagzs@inf.elte.hu
[2] Research Group on Natural Computing,
Department of Computer Science and Artificial Intelligence,
University of Sevilla, 41012 Sevilla, Spain
magutier@us.es

Abstract. In Membrane Computing, the solution of a decision problem X belonging to the complexity class **P** via a polynomially uniform family of recognizer P systems is trivial, since the polynomial encoding of the input can involve the solution of the problem. The design of such solution has one membrane, two objects, two rules and one computation step. *Stricto sensu*, it is a solution in the framework of Membrane Computing, but it does not use Membrane Computing strategies. In this paper, we present three designs of uniform families of P systems that solve the decision problem STCON by using Membrane Computing strategies (*pure* Membrane Computing techniques): P systems with membrane creation, P systems with active membranes with dissolution and without polarizations and P systems with active membranes without dissolution and with polarizations. Since STCON is **NL**-complete, such designs are *constructive* proofs of the inclusion of **NL** in $\mathbf{PMC}_{\mathcal{MC}}$, $\mathbf{PMC}_{\mathcal{AM}^0_{+d}}$ and $\mathbf{PMC}_{\mathcal{AM}^+_{-d}}$.

1 Introduction

Membrane Computing [14] is a well-established model of computation inspired by the structure and functioning of cells as living organisms able to process and generate information. It starts from the assumption that the processes taking place in the compartmental structures as living cells can be interpreted as computations. The devices of this model are called *P systems*.

Among the different research lines in Membrane Computing, one of the most vivid is the search of frontiers between complexity classes of decision problems, i.e., to identify collections of problems that can be solved (or languages that can be decided) by families of P systems with *similar* computational resources. In order to settle the correspondence between complexity classes and P system families, recognizer P systems were introduced in [10,11]. Since then, recognizer P systems are the natural framework to study and solve decision problems within Membrane Computing.

© Springer International Publishing Switzerland 2014
M. Gheorghe et al. (Eds.): CMC 2014, LNCS 8961, pp. 215–228, 2014.
DOI: 10.1007/978-3-319-14370-5_13

In the last years, many papers have been published about the problem of deciding if a uniform family of recognizer P systems of type $\mathcal{F}$ built in polynomial time is able to solve a given decision problem X . This is usually written as the problem of deciding if X belongs to $\mathbf{PMC}_{\mathcal{F}}$ or not. It has been studied for many P system models $\mathcal{F}$ and for many decision problems X (see, e.g., [3–6] and references therein).

The solution of a decision problem X belonging to the complexity class $\mathbf{P}$ via a polynomially uniform family of recognizer P systems is trivial (see [9,12]), since the polynomial encoding of the input can involve the solution of the problem. On the one hand, by definition, $X \in \mathbf{P}$ if there exists a deterministic algorithm A working in polynomial time that *solves* X. On the other hand, the belonging of X to $\mathbf{PMC}_{\mathcal{F}}$ requires a polynomial time mapping *cod* that encodes the instances u of the problem X as multisets which will be provided as inputs. Formally, given a decision problem X and an algorithm A as described above, two different functions s *(size)* and *cod (encoding)* can be defined for each instance u of the decision problem:

- $s(u) = 1$, for all u
- $cod(u) = \begin{cases} yes & \text{if } A(u) = yes \\ no & \text{if } A(u) = no. \end{cases}$

The family of P systems which solves X is $\boldsymbol{\Pi} = \{\Pi(n)\}_{n \in \mathbb{N}}$ with

$$\Pi(n) = \langle \Gamma, \Sigma, H, \mu, w, \mathcal{R}, i \rangle, \text{ where}$$

- *Alphabet:* $\Gamma = \{yes, no\}$
- *Input alphabet:* $\Sigma = \Gamma$
- *Set of labels:* $H = \{skin\}$
- *Membrane structure:* $[\,]_{skin}$
- *Initial multisets:* $w = \emptyset$
- *Input label:* $i = skin$
- *Set of rules:* $[\,yes\,]_{skin} \rightarrow yes\,[\,]_{skin}$ and $[\,no\,]_{skin} \rightarrow no\,[\,]_{skin}$. Both are send-out rules.

Let us notice that $\boldsymbol{\Pi}$ is formally a family, but all the members of the family are the same. It is trivial to check that, for all instance u of the problem, $\Pi(s(u)) + cod(u)$ provides the right solution in one computation step, i.e., it suffices to provide $cod(u)$ as input to the unique member of the family in order to obtain the right answer. *Stricto sensu*, it is a solution in the framework of Membrane Computing, but it does not use Membrane Computing strategies. All the work is done in the algorithm A and one can wonder if the computation itself can be performed by using *pure* Membrane Computing techniques.

We focus now on the well-known ST-CONNECTIVITY problem (also known as STCON). It can be settled as follows: *Given a directed graph $\langle V, E \rangle$ and two vertices s and t in V, the STCON problem consists of deciding if t is reachable from s, i.e., if there exists a sequence of adjacent vertices (i.e., a path) starting with s and ending with t.* It is known that it is an $\mathbf{NL}$-complete problem, i.e., it can be solved by a nondeterministic Turing machine using a logarithmic amount of memory space and every problem in the class **NL** is reducible to STCON under a log-space reduction.

In this paper, we study the STCON in the framework of P systems. As shown above, since STCON $\in$ **NL** $\subseteq$ **P**, there exist a trivial family of P systems in **PMC**$_\mathcal{F}$ which solves it, regardless of the model $\mathcal{F}$. It suffices that $\mathcal{F}$ deals with *send-out* rules. In this paper, we present three designs of uniform families of P systems that solve the decision problem STCON by *pure* Membrane Computing techniques, i.e., techniques where the features of the model $\mathcal{F}$ are exploited in the computation: P systems with membrane creation, P systems with active membranes with dissolution and without polarizations and P systems with active membranes without dissolution and with polarizations. Recently, in some papers (see e.g. [1,8,13]), the fact that a language L is decided using pure Membrane Computing techniques is proved by showing that L can be decided by an $(\mathbf{E}, \mathbf{F})$-uniform family of P systems, for some appropriately small complexity classes **E** and **F**. This means that L can be decided by such a uniform family Π, where the encoding of words in L and the construction of members of Π can be carried out by Turing machines which compute functions belonging to **E** and **F**, respectively. We will see that in our solutions **E** and **F** can be the complexity class **L**, the family of all functions computable by deterministic Turing machines using logarithmic space.

Since STCON is **NL**-complete, our solutions are *constructive* proofs of that **NL** belongs to the $(\mathbf{L}, \mathbf{L})$-uniform sub-classes of the well known complexity classes **PMC**$_{\mathcal{MC}}$, **PMC**$_{\mathcal{AM}^0_{+d}}$ and **PMC**$_{\mathcal{AM}^+_{-d}}$. Moreover, as **L** is widely believed to be strictly contained in **NL**, our solutions can be considered as solutions using pure Membrane Computing techniques.

The paper is structured as follows: First of all, we recall some basic definitions used along the paper. In Section 3, some previous works on STCON in Membrane Computing are revisited. Next, our designs of solutions are provided and the paper finishes with some conclusions and presenting research lines for a future work.

2 Preliminaries

Next, some basic concepts used along the paper are recalled. We assume that the reader is familiar with Membrane Computing techniques (for a detailed description, see [14]).

A decision problem X is a pair (I_X, θ_X) such that I_X is a language over a finite alphabet (whose elements are called *instances*) and θ_X is a total Boolean function over I_X. A *P system with input* is a tuple (Π, Σ, i_Π), where Π is a P system, with working alphabet Γ, with p membranes labelled by $1, \ldots, p$, and initial multisets $\mathcal{M}_1, \ldots, \mathcal{M}_p$ associated with them; Σ is an (input) alphabet strictly contained in Γ; the initial multisets are over $\Gamma - \Sigma$; and i_Π is the label of a distinguished (input) membrane. Let (Π, Σ, i_Π) be a P system with input, Γ be the working alphabet of Π, μ its membrane structure, and $\mathcal{M}_1, \ldots, \mathcal{M}_p$

the initial multisets of Π. Let m be a multiset over Σ. The *initial configuration of* (Π, Σ, i_Π) *with input* m is $(\mu, \mathcal{M}_1, \ldots, \mathcal{M}_{i_\Pi} \cup m, \ldots, \mathcal{M}_p)$. We denote by I_Π the set of all inputs of the P system Π (i.e. I_Π is a collection of multisets over Σ). In the case of P systems with input and *with external output*, the above concepts are introduced in a similar way.

Definition 1. *A* recognizer P system *is a P system with input and with external output such that:*

1. *The working alphabet contains two distinguished elements yes, no.*
2. *All its computations halt.*
3. *If C is a computation of Π, then either the object yes or the object no (but not both) must have been released into the environment, and only in the last step of the computation. We say that C is an accepting computation (respectively, rejecting computation) if the object yes (respectively, no) appears in the external environment associated to the corresponding halting configuration of C.*

In this paper, we will use uniform families of recognizer P system to decide a language $L \subseteq \Sigma^*$. We follow the notion of uniformity used in [13]. Let **E** and **F** be classes of computable functions. A family $\mathbf{\Pi} = \{\Pi(n)\}_{n \in \mathbb{N}}$ of recognizing P systems is called $(\mathbf{E}, \mathbf{F})$-*uniform* if and only if (i) there is a function $f \in \mathbf{F}$ such that, for every $n \in \mathbb{N}$, $\Pi(n) = f(1^n)$ (i.e., f maps the unary representation of each natural number to an encoding of the P system processing all the inputs of length n); (ii) there is a function $e \in \mathbf{E}$ that maps every word $x \in \Sigma^*$ with length n to a multiset $e(x) = w_x$ over the input alphabet of $\Pi(n)$. We denote by $(\mathbf{E}, \mathbf{F}) - \mathbf{PMC}_{\mathcal{F}}$ the set of problems decidable in polynomial time using an $(\mathbf{E}, \mathbf{F})$-uniform family of P systems of type $\mathcal{F}$. As usual, $\mathbf{PMC}_{\mathcal{F}}$ denotes the class $(\mathbf{P}, \mathbf{P}) - \mathbf{PMC}_{\mathcal{F}}$.

3   Previous Works

The relation between the complexity class **NL** and Membrane Computing models has already been explored in the literature. In [8], Murphy and Woods claim that $\mathbf{NL} \subseteq \mathbf{PMC}_{\mathcal{AM}^0_{-d,-u}}$, i.e., every problem in the complexity class **NL** can be solved by a semi-uniform family of recognizer P systems with active membranes without polarization and without dissolution.

The proof shows the design of a family of P systems with active membranes without polarization and without dissolution which solves STCON and considers the **NL**-completeness of STCON. Nonetheless, the authors use a non standard definition of recognizer P systems. According to the usual definition of *recognizer P system* (see, e.g., [5]), *either one object yes or one object no (but no both) must have been released into the environment, and only in the last step of the computation*. In the proposed family by Murphy and Woods, it is easy to find a P system which sends *yes* to the environment in an intermediate step of the computation and sends *no* to the environment in the last step of the computation, so their proof of $\mathbf{NL} \subseteq \mathbf{PMC}_{\mathcal{AM}^0_{-d,-u}}$ cannot be considered valid with respect to the standard definition of recognizer P systems.

Counterexample: Let us consider the instance (s, t, G) of STCON where G has only two vertices s and t and only one edge (s, t). According to [8], the P system of the cited model that solves this instance has $\Gamma = \{s, t, yes, no, c_0, \ldots, c_3\}$ as alphabet, skn as unique label and $[\,]_{skn}$ as membrane structure. The initial configuration is $[s\, c_3]_{skn}$ and the set of rules consists of the following six rules:

$$[s \rightarrow t]_{skn} \qquad [t \rightarrow yes]_{skn}$$
$$[c_0 \rightarrow no]_{skn} \quad [c_i \rightarrow c_{i-1}]_{skn}, \text{ for } i \in \{1, 2, 3\}.$$

According to [8], in this example the answer of the system appears in the membrane with label skn rather then in the environment. It easy to check that this P system introduces yes in membrane skn in the second step of computation and introduces no in the fourth (and last) step. Thus, according to the standard definition, this system is not a recognizer P system. In [7] Murphy and Woods revisited the solution of STCON by semi-uniform families of recognizer P systems and considered three different ways of the acceptance in recognizer P systems, one of them was the standard one (Def. 1).

4 Three Designs for the STCON Problem

In this section, we provide three uniform families of P systems that solve the STCON problem in three different P system models. All these models use the same encoding of an instance of the problem. We do not loss generality if we consider the n vertices of the graph as $\{1, \ldots, n\}$. In this case, a concrete instance $I = (s, t, \langle V, E \rangle)$ of the STCON on a graph $\langle V, E \rangle$ with vertices $\{1, \ldots, n\}$, can be encoded as

$$cod(I) = \{x_s, y_t\} \cup \{a_{ij} : (i, j) \in E\},$$

i.e., x_s stands for the starting vertex, y_t for the ending vertex and a_{ij} for each edge (i, j) in the graph. By using this coding, all the instances of the STCON problem with n vertices, can be encoded with the alphabet

$$\Sigma = \{x_i : i \in \{1, \ldots, n\}\} \cup$$
$$\{y_j : j \in \{1, \ldots, n\}\} \cup$$
$$\{a_{ij} : i, j \in \{1, \ldots, n\}\}$$

whose cardinality is $2n + n^2$.

Next we present three solutions of the STCON problem by P systems. The first two of them are based on P systems with active membranes, while the last one uses P systems with membrane creation. The first solution does not use membrane dissolution rules but uses the polarizations of the membranes. The second solution does not use polarizations but uses membrane dissolution instead. Moreover, none of these solutions use membrane division rules.

All the three solutions, roughly speaking, work in the following way. For a given directed graph $G = \langle V, E \rangle$ and vertices s and t, the system creates/activates certain membranes in the initial configuration corresponding to the edges in E. Then, these membranes will be used to create those objects that represent the vertices reachable from s. Meanwhile, it is tested whether or not the vertex t is created or not. If yes, the system initiates a process which will send *yes* out to the environment. If the vertex t is not produced by the system, i.e., t is not reachable from s in G, then a counter will create the symbol *no* which is then sent out to the environment.

Although these solutions are similar, they use different techniques according to the class of P systems that we employ. We believe that some of the constructions used in the following designs might be useful also in solutions of other problems by these classes of P systems.

4.1 P Systems with Active Membranes with Polarization and Without Dissolution

As a first approach, we provide a design of a uniform family $\mathbf{\Pi} = \{\Pi_n\}_{n \in \mathbb{N}}$ of P systems with active membranes which solves STCON without using dissolution rules. Each P system Π_n of the family decides on *all the possible* instances of the STCON problem on a graph with n nodes. Such P systems use two polarizations, but they do not use division or dissolution rules, so *not all the types of rules* of P systems with active membranes are necessary to solve STCON. Each Π_n will receive as input an instance of the STCON as described above and will release *yes* or *no* into the environment in the last step of the computation as the answer of the decision problem. The family presented here consists of P systems of the form

$$\Pi_n = \langle \Gamma_n, \Sigma_n, H_n, EC_n, \mu_n, w_n^a, w_n^1, \ldots, w_n^n, w_n^{11}, \ldots, w_n^{nn}, w_n^{skin}, \mathcal{R}_n, i_n \rangle.$$

For the sake of simplicity, thereafter we will omit the sub-index n. The components of Π_n are as follows.

- **Alphabet:**
$$\begin{aligned} \Gamma = \{x_i, y_i, t_i \; : \; i \in \{1, \ldots, n\}\} \cup \\ \{a_{ij}, z_{ij} \; : \; i, j \in \{1, \ldots, n\}\} \cup \\ \{c_i \; : \; i \in \{0, \ldots, 3n+1\}\} \cup \\ \{k, yes, no\}. \end{aligned}$$

- **Input alphabet:** Σ, as described at the beginning of the section. Let us remark that $\Sigma \subset \Gamma$.
- **Set of labels:** $H = \{\langle i, j \rangle \; : \; i, j \in \{1, \ldots, n\}\} \cup \{1, \ldots, n\} \cup \{a, skin\}$.
- **Electrical charges:** $EC = \{0, +\}$.
- **Membrane structure:** $[\, [\,]_1^0 \cdots [\,]_n^0 \, [\,]_{\langle 1,1 \rangle}^0 \cdots [\,]_{\langle n,n \rangle}^0 \, [\,]_a^0 \,]_{skin}^0$.
- **Initial multisets:** $w^a = c_0$, $w^{skin} = w^{ij} = w^k = \lambda$ for $i, j, k \in \{1, \ldots, n\}$.
- **Input label:** $i = skin$.

The set of rules $\mathcal{R}$:

R1. $a_{ij} [\,]_{\langle i,j \rangle}^0 \to [a_{ij}]_{\langle i,j \rangle}^+$ for $i, j \in \{1, \ldots, n\}$.

Each input object a_{ij} activates the corresponding membrane by changing its polarization. Notice that such a symbol a_{ij} represents an edge in the input graph.

R2. $y_j \, []^0_j \rightarrow [y_j]^+_j$ for $j \in \{1, \ldots, n\}$.

The object y_j activates the membrane j by changing its polarization. As the input multiset always has exactly one object of the form y_j, Π_n will have a unique membrane with label in $\{1, \ldots, n\}$ and polarization $+$.

R3. $[x_i \rightarrow z_{i1} \ldots z_{in} t_i]^0_{skin}$ for $i \in \{1, \ldots, n\}$.

The goal of these rules is to create $n + 1$ copies of an object x_i. A copy z_{ij} will be able to produce an object x_j if the edge (i, j) belongs to E. The object t_i will be used to witness that vertex i is reachable.

R4. $\left. \begin{array}{l} z_{ij} \, []^+_{\langle i,j \rangle} \rightarrow [x_j]^0_{\langle i,j \rangle} \\ t_j \, []^+_j \rightarrow [k]^0_j \end{array} \right\}$ for $i, j \in \{1, \ldots, n\}$.

If the membrane with label $\langle i, j \rangle$ has polarization $+$, then the symbol z_{ij} produces a symbol x_j inside this membrane. Meanwhile, the polarization of this membrane changes from $+$ to 0, i.e., the membrane is deactivated. Moreover, if the symbol t_j appears in the skin and the membrane with label j has positive polarization, then an object k is produced inside this membrane. Such object k will start the process to send out *yes* to the environment.

R5. $[k]^0_j \rightarrow k \, []^0_j$ $k \, []^0_a \rightarrow [k]^+_a$.

The object k is a witness of the success of the STCON problem. If it is produced, it goes into the membrane with label a and changes its polarization to $+$.

R6. $[x_j]^0_{\langle i,j \rangle} \rightarrow x_j \, []^0_{\langle i,j \rangle}$ for $i, j \in \{1, \ldots, n\}$.

The produced object x_j is sent to the membrane *skin* in order to continue the computation by rules form **R3**.

R7. $\left. \begin{array}{l} [c_i \rightarrow c_{i+1}]^0_a, \; [c_{3n+1}]^0_a \rightarrow no \, []^0_a \\ [c_i \rightarrow c_{i+1}]^+_a, \; [c_{3n+1}]^+_a \rightarrow yes \, []^0_a \end{array} \right\}$ for $i \in \{0, \ldots, 3n\}$.

Object c_i evolves to c_{i+1} regardless of the polarization of the membrane with label a. If during the evolution the object k enters the membrane with label a, then the polarization of this membrane changes to $+$ and the object c_{3n+1} will produce *yes* in the skin membrane. Otherwise, if the object k is not produced, the polarization is not changed and the object c_{3n+1} will produce *no*.

R8. $[no]_{skin} \rightarrow no \, []_{skin}, \quad [yes]_{skin} \rightarrow yes \, []_{skin}$.

Finally, *yes* or *no* is sent out the P system in the last step of computation.

To see in more details how a computation of the presented P system goes, let us consider an instance $I = (s, t, G)$ of STCON where G is a graph $\langle \{1, \ldots, n\}, E \rangle$. The computation of Π_n on $cod(I)$ can be described as follows. During the first step, using rules in **R1**, every a_{ij} enters the membrane with label $\langle i, j \rangle$ and changes its polarization to $+$. Thus, after the first step the edges in E are encoded by the positive polarizations of the membranes with labels of the form $\langle i, j \rangle$. During the same step, using the corresponding rule in **R2**, y_t enters the membrane with label t and changes its polarization to $+$. This membrane will be used to recognize if an object representing that t is reachable from s is introduced by the system.

Now let $l \in \{1, 4, \ldots, 3(n-1) + 1\}$ and consider an object x_i in the skin membrane. During the lth step, using rules in **R3**, x_i creates $n + 1$ copies of itself. The system will try to use a copy z_{ij} ($j \in \{1, \ldots, n\}$) in the next step to create a new object x_j. The copy t_i will be used to decide if $i = t$.

During the $(l+1)$th step, using rules in **R4**, the systems sends z_{ij} into the membrane with label $\langle i, j \rangle$ if that membrane has a positive polarization. Meanwhile, z_{ij} evolves to x_j and the polarization of the membrane changes to neutral. During the same step, if $i = t$ and the membrane with label t has positive polarization, then the system sends t_i into this membrane. Meanwhile, t_i evolves to k and the polarization of the membrane changes to neutral.

During the $(l+2)$th step, using rules in **R6**, the object x_j is sent out of the membrane with label $\langle i, j \rangle$. Moreover, if the membrane with label t contains k, then this k is sent out of this membrane.

One can see that during the above three steps the system introduces an object x_j if and only if (i, j) is an edge in E. Using this observation we can derive that during the computation of the system, an object x_j appears in the skin if and only if there is a path in G from s to j. Thus, t is reachable from s in G if and only if there is a configuration of Π_n where the skin contains x_t. However, in this case an object k is introduced in the membrane with label t. It can also be seen that Π_n sends out to the environment *yes* if and only if k appears in membrane t. Moreover, if k does not appear in membrane t, then the systems sends out to the environment *no*. Thus, Π_n sends out to the environment *yes* or *no* according to that t is reachable from s or not. As Π_n stops in at most $3n + 2$ steps, we can conclude that the family **Π** decides STCON in linear time in the number of vertices of the input graph.

4.2   P Systems with Active Membranes with Dissolution and Without Polarization

Based on the solution presented in the previous sub-section, we give here a uniform family **$\Pi = \{\Pi_n\}_{n \in \mathbb{N}}$** of P systems with active membranes which solves STCON without using the polarizations of the membranes. Since here we cannot use polarizations, we use membrane dissolution to select those membranes of the initial configuration that correspond to the edges of the input graph. The members of the family **Π** are P systems of the form

$$\Pi_n = \langle \Gamma, \Sigma, H, EC, \mu, W, \mathcal{R}, i \rangle.$$

The components of Π_n are as follows (notice that since Π_n does not use polarizations, we do not indicate them at the upper-right corner of the membranes).

- **Alphabet:**

$$\Gamma = \{x_i, v_{1i}, v_{2i}, v_{3i}, v_i, y_i, t_i \; : \; i \in \{1, \ldots, n\}\} \cup$$
$$\{a_{ij}, z_{ij} \; : \; i, j \in \{1, \ldots, n\}\} \cup$$
$$\{c_i \; : \; i \in \{0, \ldots, 3n + 4\}\} \cup$$
$$\{k, yes, no\}.$$

- **Input alphabet:** Σ, as described at the beginning of the section.

- **Set of labels:** $H = \{\langle i,j,in\rangle, \langle i,j,out\rangle : i,j \in \{1,\ldots,n\}\} \cup \{\langle i,in\rangle,$
  $\langle i,out\rangle : i \in \{1,\ldots,n\} \cup \{a,skin\}.$
- **Electrical charges:** $EC = \varnothing.$
- **Membrane structure:** $[[[\,]\langle 1,in\rangle]\langle 1,out\rangle \cdots [[\,]\langle n,in\rangle]\langle n,out\rangle [[\,]\langle 1,1,in\rangle]\langle 1,1,out\rangle \cdots$
  $\cdots [[\,]\langle n,n,in\rangle]\langle n,n,out\rangle [\,]a]skin.$
- **Initial multisets:** $W = \{w^a, w^{\langle 1,in\rangle}, \ldots, w^{\langle n,in\rangle}, w^{\langle 1,out\rangle}, \ldots, w^{\langle n,out\rangle},$
  $w^{\langle 1,1,in\rangle}, \ldots, w^{\langle n,n,in\rangle}, w^{\langle 1,1,out\rangle}, \ldots, w^{\langle n,n,out\rangle}, w^{skin}\}$, where
  $w^a = c_0,\ w^{skin} = w^{\langle i,j,out\rangle} = w^{\langle k,out\rangle} = \lambda,\ w^{\langle i,j,in\rangle} = w^{\langle k,in\rangle} = f_0,$ for
  $i,j,k \in \{1,\ldots,n\}.$
- **Input label:** $i = skin.$

The set of rules $\mathcal{R}$:

R0. $[x_i \rightarrow v_{1i}]skin,\ [v_{ji} \rightarrow v_{j+1,i}]skin,\ [v_{3i} \rightarrow v_i]skin$ for $i \in \{1,\ldots,n\}$ and $j \in \{1,2\}$.

In this solution we cannot use an object x_i in the same role as we did in the previous sub-section because of the following reason. The system needs four steps to select those membranes in the initial membrane configuration that correspond to the edges in E. Thus, the system introduces in four steps the object v_i which will act in this solution as x_i did in the previous one.

R1. $\left.\begin{array}{l}[f_m \rightarrow f_{m+1}]\langle i,j,in\rangle \\ [f_3]\langle i,j,in\rangle \rightarrow f_4 \\ [f_4]\langle i,j,out\rangle \rightarrow f_4\end{array}\right\}$ for $i,j \in \{1,\ldots,n\},\ m \in \{0,1,2\}$.

These rules can dissolve the membranes with label $\langle i,j,in\rangle$ or $\langle i,j,out\rangle$. However, if a_{ij} is in the input multiset, then it prevents the dissolution of the membrane with label $\langle i,j,out\rangle$ using the following rules.

R2. $\left.\begin{array}{l}a_{ij}[\,]\langle i,j,m\rangle \rightarrow [a_{ij}]\langle i,j,m\rangle \\ [a_{ij}]\langle i,j,in\rangle \rightarrow a_{ij}\end{array}\right\}$ for $i,j \in \{1,\ldots,n\},\ m \in \{in,out\}$.

By these rules the input symbol a_{ij} goes into the membrane with label $\langle i,j,in\rangle$ and dissolves that. This way the second rule in **R1** cannot be applied, thus the membrane with label $\langle i,j,out\rangle$ cannot be dissolved by the third rule.

R3. $\left.\begin{array}{l}[f_m \rightarrow f_{m+1}]\langle j,in\rangle \\ [f_3]\langle j,in\rangle \rightarrow f_4 \\ [f_4]\langle j,out\rangle \rightarrow f_4\end{array}\right\}$ for $j \in \{1,\ldots,n\},\ m \in \{0,1,2\}$.

These rules can dissolve the membranes with label $\langle j,in\rangle$ or $\langle j,out\rangle$. However, if y_j is in the input multiset, then it prevents the dissolution of the membrane with label $\langle j,out\rangle$ using the following rules.

R4. $\left.\begin{array}{l}y_j[\,]\langle j,m\rangle \rightarrow [y_j]\langle j,m\rangle \\ [y_j]\langle j,in\rangle \rightarrow y_j\end{array}\right\}$ for $j \in \{1,\ldots,n\}$ and $m \in \{in,out\}$.

By these rules the input symbol y_j goes into the membrane with label $\langle j,in\rangle$ and dissolves that. With this it is achieved that the membrane with label $\langle j,out\rangle$ is not dissolved by the rules in **R3**.

R5. $[v_i \rightarrow z_{i1}\ldots z_{in}t_i]skin$ for $i \in \{1,\ldots,n\}$.

The role of these rules is the same as that of the rules in **R3** in Section 4.1.

R6. $\left.\begin{array}{l}z_{ij}[\,]\langle i,j,out\rangle \rightarrow [v_j]\langle i,j,out\rangle \\ t_j[\,]\langle j,out\rangle \rightarrow [k]\langle j,out\rangle\end{array}\right\}$ for $i,j \in \{1,\ldots,n\}$.

The role of these rules is similar to that of the rules in **R4** in Section 4.1: If the membrane with label $\langle i, j, out \rangle$ has not been dissolved, then the object z_{ij} produces a symbol v_j inside this membrane. Analogously, if the symbol t_j appears in the skin and the membrane with label $\langle j, out \rangle$ is not dissolved, then an object k is produced inside this membrane. Such object k will start the process to send *yes* out to the environment.

R7. $[k]_{\langle j, out \rangle} \rightarrow k\,[\,]_{\langle j, out \rangle}, \quad k\,[\,]_a \rightarrow [k]_a, \quad [k]_a \rightarrow k.$

The object k is a witness of the success of the STCON problem. If it is produced, it goes into the membrane with label a and dissolves it.

R8. $[v_j]_{\langle i,j \rangle} \rightarrow v_j$ for $i, j \in \{1, \ldots, n\}.$

The produced object v_j dissolves the membrane with label $\langle i, j \rangle$ as the computation does not need this membrane any more. This way the object v_j appears in the skin and the computation can continue using the rules in **R5**.

R9. $\left. \begin{array}{l} [c_i \rightarrow c_{i+1}]_a, \ [c_{3n+4}]_a \rightarrow no\,[\,]_a \\ \quad [c_{i+1}]_{skin} \rightarrow [yes]_{skin} \end{array} \right\}$ for $i \in \{0, \ldots, 3n+3\}.$

Object c_i evolves to c_{i+1} in membrane with label a. If during this evolution the object k appears in this membrane, then it dissolves it and the object c_{i+1} gets into the skin membrane where it produces *yes*. Otherwise, if the object k is not produced, c_{3n+4} remains in membrane with label a and produces *no*.

R10. $[no]_{skin} \rightarrow no\,[\,]_{skin}, \quad [yes]_{skin} \rightarrow yes\,[\,]_{skin}.$

Finally, *yes* or *no* is sent out the P system in the last step of computation.

One can observe that during the first four steps of Π_n a membrane with label $\langle i, j, out \rangle$ is not dissolved if and only if a_{ij} is in the input. Thus, Π_n has a membrane with label $\langle i, j, out \rangle$ after the first four steps if and only if Π_n defined in Section 4.1 has a membrane $\langle i, j \rangle$ with positive polarization after the first step. Similar observations apply in the case of membranes with label $\langle j, out \rangle$. Thus, the correctness of Π_n defined in this section follows from the correctness of Π_n defined in Section 4.1. One can also observe that Π_n stops after at most $3n + 5$ steps, which means that the family Π defined in this section decides STCON in linear time.

4.3 P Systems with Membrane Creation

Here we provide a solution of the problem STCON by a uniform family of P systems in the framework of *P systems with Membrane Creation*. Since STCON is **NL**-complete, we have a direct proof of **NL** $\subseteq$ **PMC**$_{MC}$. This result is well-know, since **NL** $\subseteq$ **NP** and **NP** $\subseteq$ **PMC**$_{MC}$ (see [5]). Nonetheless, to the best of our knowledge, this is the first design of a P system family which solves STCON in **PMC**$_{MC}$.

Next we describe a family $\Pi = \{\Pi_n\}_{n \in \mathbb{N}}$ of P systems in **PMC**$_{MC}$ which solves STCON. Π consists of P systems of the form

$$\Pi_n = \langle \Gamma, \Sigma, H, \mu, w^a, w^b, w^c, \mathcal{R}, i \rangle.$$

The components of Π_n are as follows.

- **Alphabet:**

$$\begin{aligned}
\Gamma = \ &\{x_i, y_i, t_i \ : \ i \in \{1, \ldots, n\}\} \cup \\
&\{a_{ij}, z_{ij} \ : \ i, j \in \{1, \ldots, n\}\} \cup \\
&\{no_i \ : \ i \in \{0, \ldots, 3n+3\}\} \cup \\
&\{yes_i \ : \ i \in \{1, \ldots, 4\}\} \cup \\
&\{yes, no\}.
\end{aligned}$$

- **Input alphabet:** Σ, as it is described at beginning of the section.
- **Set of labels:** $H = \{\langle i, j \rangle \ : \ i, j \in \{1, \ldots, n\}\} \cup \{1, \ldots, n\} \cup \{a, b, c\}$.
- **Membrane structure:** $[\,[\,]_a\,[\,]_b\,]_c$.
- **Initial multisets:** $w^a = no_0$, $w^b = w^c = \lambda$.
- **Input label:** $i = b$.

The set of rules $\mathcal{R}$:

R1. $[[a_{ij} \rightarrow [\lambda]_{\langle i,j \rangle}]_b$ for $i, j \in \{1, \ldots, n\}$.
Each input symbol a_{ij} creates a new membrane with label $\langle i, j \rangle$. Recall that such a symbol a_{ij} represents an edge in the directed graph.
R2. $[y_j \rightarrow [\lambda]_j]_b$ for $j \in \{1, \ldots, n\}$.
By these rules an input symbol y_j creates a new membrane with label j.
R3. $[x_i \rightarrow z_{i1} \ldots z_{in} t_i]_b$ for $i \in \{1, \ldots, n\}$.
The role of these rules is the same as that of the rules in **R3** in Section 4.1.
R4. $\left.\begin{aligned} z_{ij}\,[\,]_{\langle i,j \rangle} &\rightarrow [x_j]_{\langle i,j \rangle} \\ t_j\,[\,]_j &\rightarrow [yes_0]_j \end{aligned}\right\}$ for $i, j \in \{1, \ldots, n\}$.
The role of these rules is similar to that of the rules in **R4** in Section 4.1 except that here an object t_j introduces an object yes_0 in the membrane with label j. This new object yes_0 will evolve with the rules in **R6** and **R7** until the final object yes is produced in the environment.
R5. $[x_j]_{\langle i,j \rangle} \rightarrow x_j$ for $i, j \in \{1, \ldots, n\}$.
The object x_j dissolves the membrane with label $\langle i, j \rangle$. The useful information is that x_j is reachable. We keep this information, but the membrane can be dissolved. This way x_j gets to the membrane b and the computation can go on using the rules in $\mathbf{R_3}$.
R6. $[yes_0]_j \rightarrow yes_1$ for $j \in \{1, \ldots, n\}$.
For each possible value of j, if yes_0 is produced, the corresponding membrane is dissolved and yes_1 appears in the membrane with label b.
R7. $[yes_1]_b \rightarrow yes_2$, $yes_2\,[\,]_a \rightarrow [yes_3]_a$,
$\quad\ [yes_3]_a \rightarrow yes_4$, $[yes_4]_c \rightarrow yes\,[\,]_c$.
The evolution of the object yes_i firstly dissolves the membrane with label b. If this membrane is dissolved, the rules from **R3** will be no longer applied. In a similar way, object yes_3 dissolves the membrane with label a and this stops the evolution of the objects inside this membrane.
R8. $[no_i \rightarrow no_{i+1}]_a$ for $i \in \{1, \ldots, 3n+2\}$.
The object no_i evolves inside the membrane with label a. If this evolution is not halted by the dissolution of this membrane, these objects will produce an object no in the environment.
R9. $[no_{3n+3}]_a \rightarrow no$, $\quad [no]_c \rightarrow no\,[\,]_c$.

If the evolution of no_i is not stopped, the object no_{3n+3} dissolves the membrane with label a and creates a new object no. This object will be sent to the environment in the next step of the computation.

It is not difficult to see using the comments given after the rules that this solution works essentially in the same way as our first solution. The main difference is that while in Section 4.1 an input symbol a_{ij} is used to change the polarization of a membrane $\langle i, j \rangle$, here this symbol is used to create such a membrane. Thus, the correctness of the solution presented here can be seen using the correctness of the solution given in Section 4.1. It is also clear that the P systems presented here work in linear time in the number of vertices of the input graph.

($\mathbf{L}, \mathbf{L}$)-uniformity. As it is discussed earlier, in solutions of problems in $\mathbf{P}$ via uniform families of P systems it is important to use such input encoding and P system constructing devices that are not capable to compute the correct answer. In our solutions these devices can be realized by deterministic logarithmic-space Turing machines. Indeed, for an instance I of STCON, the multiset $cod(I)$ can be easily computed by such a Turing machine. Moreover, as in our P systems the working alphabet Γ, the set of labels H, and the rule set $\mathcal{R}$ have size $O(n^2)$ and every rule in $\mathcal{R}$ has size $O(n)$, there is a deterministic Turing machine that can enumerate the elements of Γ, H, and $\mathcal{R}$ using $O(\log n)$ space. This, together with the discussion about the correctness and running time of the P systems described in our solutions, implies the following theorem.

Theorem 1. STCON $\in$ ($\mathbf{L}, \mathbf{L}$)$-\mathbf{PMC}_{\mathcal{AM}^+_{-d}}$, STCON $\in$ ($\mathbf{L}, \mathbf{L}$)$-\mathbf{PMC}_{\mathcal{AM}^0_{+d}}$, and STCON $\in$ ($\mathbf{L}, \mathbf{L}$)$-\mathbf{PMC}_{\mathcal{MC}}$.

5   Conclusions

The design of a uniform family of recognizer P systems working in polynomial time which solves a decision problem with *pure* Membrane Computing techniques is a hard task, regardless of the complexity class of the problem. The difficulty comes from the hard restrictions imposed on such family. Firstly, the use of *input* P systems implies that each instance of the problem must be encoded as a multiset and such multiset must be introduced at the starting configuration in *one* input membrane. The multiset encoding the instance cannot be distributed in several membranes in the starting configuration. Secondly, in *uniform* families, each P system must solve *all* the instances of the problem of the same *size* (regardless of whether the answer is positive or not). This means that the set of rules which leads to send *yes* to the environment and the set of rules which leads to send *no* must be present in the design of the P system; and thirdly, the standard definition of recognizer P systems claims that an object *yes* or *no* (but no both) is sent to the environment in the *last* step of computation.

A deep study of these constraints shows that it is not sufficient to implement a design of P system with the control scheme "*if* the restrictions of the decision problem are satisfied, *then* an object *yes* must be sent to the environment".

Instead of such scheme, the design must consider the following structure: "*if* the restrictions are satisfied, *then* an object *yes* must be sent to the environment, *else* an object *no* must be sent". This scheme *if-then-else* must be controlled with the ingredients of the P system model. In the three presented designs, this *if-then-else* scheme is implemented via dissolution, polarization, or membrane creation.

These ideas lead us to consider the necessity of revisiting the complexity classes under **P** and adapt the definition of recognizer P systems for these classes. Some papers in this new research line can be found in the literature (see, e.g., [13]), but further research is needed.

Acknowledgements. This work was partially done during Zsolt Gazdag's visit at the Research Institute of Mathematics of the University of Sevilla (IMUS) partially supported by IMUS. Miguel A. Gutiérrez–Naranjo acknowledges the support of the project TIN2012-37434 of the Ministerio de Economía y Competitividad of Spain.

References

1. Alhazov, A., Leporati, A., Mauri, G., Porreca, A.E., Zandron, C.: Space complexity equivalence of P systems with active membranes and Turing machines. Theoretical Computer Science **529**, 69–81 (2014)
2. Csuhaj-Varjú, E., Gheorghe, M., Rozenberg, G., Salomaa, A., Vaszil, Gy. (eds.): CMC 2012. LNCS, vol. 7762. Springer, Heidelberg (2013)
3. Díaz-Pernil, D., Gutiérrez-Naranjo, M.A., Pérez-Jiménez, M.J., Riscos-Núñez, A.: A Linear Time Solution to the Partition Problem in a Cellular Tissue-Like Model. Journal of Computational and Theoretical Nanoscience **7**(5), 884–889 (2010)
4. Gazdag, Z., Kolonits, G.: A new approach for solving SAT by P systems with active membranes. In: Csuhaj-Varjú et al. [2], pp. 195–207
5. Gutiérrez-Naranjo, M.A., Pérez-Jiménez, M.J., Romero-Campero, F.J.: A uniform solution to SAT using membrane creation. Theoretical Computer Science **371** (1–2), 54–61 (2007)
6. Leporati, A., Zandron, C., Ferretti, C., Mauri, G.: Solving numerical NP-complete problems with spiking neural P systems. In: Eleftherakis, G., Kefalas, P., Păun, Gh., Rozenberg, G., Salomaa, A. (eds.) WMC 2007. LNCS, vol. 4860, pp. 336–352. Springer, Heidelberg (2007)
7. Murphy, N., Woods, D.: On acceptance conditions for membrane systems: characterisations of L and NL. In: Proceedings International Workshop on The Complexity of Simple Programs. Electronic Proceedings in Theoretical Computer Science, Cork, Ireland, December 6–7 2008, vol. 1, pp. 172–184 (2009)
8. Murphy, N., Woods, D.: The computational power of membrane systems under tight uniformity conditions. Natural Computing **10**(1), 613–632 (2011)
9. Pérez-Jiménez, M.J., Riscos-Núñez, A., Romero-Jiménez, A., Woods, D.: Complexity - membrane division, membrane creation. In: Păun et al. [14], pp. 302–336
10. Pérez-Jiménez, M.J., Romero-Jiménez, A., Sancho-Caparrini, F.: A polynomial complexity class in P systems using membrane division. In: Csuhaj-Varjú, E., Kintala, C., Wotschke, D., Vaszil, Gy. (eds.) Proceeding of the 5th Workshop on Descriptional Complexity of Formal Systems, DCFS 2003, pp. 284–294 (2003)

11. Pérez-Jiménez, M.J., Romero-Jiménez, Á., Sancho-Caparrini, F.: A polynomial complexity class in P systems using membrane division. Journal of Automata, Languages and Combinatorics **11**(4), 423–434 (2006)
12. Porreca, A.E.: Computational Complexity Classes for Membrane System. Master's thesis, Univertità di Milano-Bicocca, Italy (2008)
13. Porreca, A.E., Leporati, A., Mauri, G., Zandron, C.: Sublinear-space P systems with active membranes. In: Csuhaj-Varjú et al. [2], pp. 342–357
14. Păun, Gh., Rozenberg, G., Salomaa, A. (eds.): The Oxford Handbook of Membrane Computing. Oxford University Press, Oxford (2010)

Simulating Turing Machines with Polarizationless P Systems with Active Membranes

Zsolt Gazdag[1]([⊠]), Gábor Kolonits[1], and Miguel A. Gutiérrez-Naranjo[2]

[1] Department of Algorithms and Their Applications, Faculty of Informatics,
Eötvös Loránd University, Budapest, Hungary
{gazdagzs,kolomax}@inf.elte.hu
[2] Research Group on Natural Computing,
Department of Computer Science and Artificial Intelligence,
University of Sevilla, 41012 Sevilla, Spain
magutier@us.es

Abstract. We prove that every single-tape deterministic Turing machine working in $t(n)$ time, for some function $t : \mathbb{N} \to \mathbb{N}$, can be simulated by a uniform family of polarizationless P systems with active membranes. Moreover, this is done without significant slowdown in the working time. Furthermore, if $\log t(n)$ is space constructible, then the members of the uniform family can be constructed by a family machine that uses $O(\log t(n))$ space.

1 Introduction

The simulation of the behaviour of Turing machines by families of P systems has a long tradition in Membrane Computing (see, e.g., [1,8,11,13]). The purpose of such simulations is twofold. On the one hand, they allow to prove new properties on complexity classes and, on the other hand, they provide constructive proofs of results which have been proved via indirect methods[1].

In this paper, we give a new step on the second research line, by showing that Turing machines can be simulated efficiently by families of polarizationless P systems with active membranes. By efficiency we mean that these P systems can simulate Turing machines without significant slowdown in the working time. Moreover, the space complexity of the presented P systems is quadratic in the time complexity of the Turing machine.

The conclusions obtained from such simulations are well-known: the decision problems solved by Turing machines can also be solved by families of devices in the corresponding P system models. However, one has to be careful when giving such simulations. It is well known, for example, that the solution of a decision problem X belonging to the complexity class **P** via a polynomially uniform

---

[1] The reader is supposed to be familiar with standard techniques and notations used in Membrane Computing. For a detailed description see [10].

© Springer International Publishing Switzerland 2014
M. Gheorghe et al. (Eds.): CMC 2014, LNCS 8961, pp. 229–240, 2014.
DOI: 10.1007/978-3-319-14370-5_14

family of recognizer P systems is trivial, since the polynomial encoding of the input can involve the solution of the problem (see [3,7]).

This fact can be generalized to wider situations: the solution of a decision problem X by a uniform family of P systems Π may be trivial in the following sense. Let us consider a Turing machine that computes the encoding of the instances of X (also called the *encoding machine*). If this machine is powerful enough to decide if an instance is a positive instance of X or not, then a trivial P system can be used to send out to the environment the correct answer.

In order to avoid such trivial solutions, the encoding machine and the Turing machine that computes the members of Π (often called the *family machine*) should be reasonably weak. More precisely, if the problem X belongs to a complexity class $\mathcal{C}$, then the family machine and the encoding machine should belong to a class of Turing machines that can compute only a strict subclass of $\mathcal{C}$ (see [8]).

According to this, to simulate a Turing machine M working in $t(n)$ time, for some function $f : \mathbb{N} \to \mathbb{N}$ such that $\log t(n)$ is space constructible, we will use a family of P systems whose members can be constructed by a family machine using $O(\log t(n))$ space. In particular, if t is a polynomial, then the family machine uses logarithmic space. Moreover, we will use the following function *pos* to encode the input words of M: For a given input word w, $pos(w)$ is a multiset where every letter of w is coupled with its position in w. Furthermore, the positions of the letters are encoded in binary words. It was discussed in [8] that *pos* is computable by deterministic random-access Turing machines using logarithmic time (in other words, *pos* is **DLOGTIME** computable). In this way, there is no risk that *pos* can compute a solution of a problem outside of **DLOGTIME**. Since **DLOGTIME** is a rather small complexity class, it follows that we can use *pos* safely as the input encoding function during the simulation of M.

The result presented in this paper resembles the one appearing in [1] stating that every single-tape deterministic Turing machine can be simulated by uniform families of P systems with active membranes with a cubic slowdown and quadratic space overhead. However, this result and ours are not directly comparable, as the constructions in [1] use the polarizations of the membranes, while our solution does not.

The paper is organized as follows. First of all, we recall some basic definitions used along the paper. Then, in Section 3, we present the main result. Finally, we give some concluding remarks in Section 4.

2 Preliminaries

First, we recall some basic concepts used later.

Alphabets, Words, Multisets. An *alphabet* Σ is a non-empty and finite set of symbols. The elements of Σ are called *letters* and Σ^* denotes the set of all finite *words* (or *strings*) over Σ, including the *empty word* ε. The length of a word $w \in \Sigma^*$ is denoted by $l(w)$. We will use *multisets* of objects in the membranes of a P system. As usual, these multisets will be represented by strings over the object alphabet of the P system.

The set of natural numbers is denoted by $\mathbb{N}$. For $i, j \in \mathbb{N}$, $[i, j]$ denotes the set $\{i, i+1, \ldots, j\}$ (notice that if $j < i$, then $[i, j] = \varnothing$). For the sake of simplicity, we will write $[n]$ instead of $[1, n]$. For a number $i \in \mathbb{N}$, $b(i)$ denotes its binary form and $b(\mathbb{N}) = \{b(i) \mid i \in \mathbb{N}\}$. Given an alphabet Σ, the function $pos : \Sigma^* \rightarrow (\Sigma \times b(\mathbb{N}))^*$ is defined in the following way. For a word $w = a_1 \ldots a_n \in \Sigma^*$, where $a_i \in \Sigma$, $i \in [n]$, $pos(w) := (a_1, b(1)) \ldots (a_n, b(n))$. If a is the ith letter of w, then we will also write the ith letter of $pos(w)$ in the form $a_{b(i)}$.

Turing Machines. Turing machines are well known computational devices. In the following we describe the variant appearing, e.g., in [12]. A *(deterministic) Turing machine* is a 7-tuple $M = (Q, \Sigma, \Gamma, \delta, q_0, q_a, q_r)$ where

- Q is the finite set of *states*,
- Σ is the *input alphabet*,
- Γ is the *tape alphabet* including Σ and a distinguished symbol $\sqcup \notin \Sigma$, called the *blank symbol*,
- $\delta : (Q - \{q_a, q_r\}) \times \Gamma \rightarrow Q \times \Gamma \times \{L, R\}$ is the *transition function*,
- $q_0 \in Q$ is the *initial state*,
- $q_a \in Q$ is the *accepting state*,
- $q_r \in Q$ is the *rejecting state*.

M works on a single infinite tape that is closed on the left-hand side. During the computation of M, the tape contains only finitely many non-blank symbols, and it is blank everywhere else. Let us consider a word $w \in \Sigma^*$. The initial configuration of M on w is the configuration where w is placed at the beginning of the tape, the head points to the first letter of w, and the current state of M is q_0. A configuration step performed by M can be described as follows. If M is in state p and the head of M reads the symbol X, then M can change its state to q and write X' onto X if and only if $\delta(p, X) = (q, X', d)$, for some $d \in \{L, R\}$. Moreover, if $d = R$ (resp. $d = L$), then M moves its head one cell to the right (resp. to the left) (as usual, M can never move the head off the left-hand end of the tape even if the head points to the first cell and $d = L$). We say that M accepts (resp. rejects) w, if M can reach from the initial configuration on w the accepting state q_a (resp. the rejecting state q_r). Notice that M can stop only in these states. The language accepted by M is the set $L(M)$ consisting of those words in Σ^* that are accepted by M. It is said that M works in $t(n)$ time ($t : \mathbb{N} \rightarrow \mathbb{N}$) if, for every word $w \in \Sigma^*$, w stops on w after at most $t(l(w))$ steps; M works using $s(n)$ space ($s : \mathbb{N} \rightarrow \mathbb{N}$) if it uses at most $s(n)$ cells when it is started on an input word with length n. As usual, if M is a multi-tape Turing machine and it does not write any symbol on its input tape, then those cells that are used to hold the input word are not counted when the space complexity of M is measured[2]. Let us consider a function $f : \mathbb{N} \rightarrow \mathbb{N}$ such that $f(n)$ is at least

---

[2] For the formal definitions of the well known complexity classes concerning Turing machines (such as **L**, **P**, **TIME**$(t(n))$ and **SPACE**$(s(n))$), the interested reader is referred to [12].

$O(\log n)$. We say that f is *space constructible* if there is a Turing machine M that works using $O(f(n))$ space and M always halts with the unary representation of $f(n)$ on its tape when started on input 1^n.

Recognizer P Systems. A *P system* is a construct of the form $\Pi = (\Gamma, H, \mu, w_1, \ldots, w_m, R)$, where $m \geq 1$ (the *initial degree* of the system); Γ is the *working alphabet of objects*; H is a finite set of *labels* for membranes; μ is a *membrane structure* (a rooted tree), consisting of m membranes, labelled with elements of H; $w_1, \ldots, w_m$ are strings over Γ, describing the *initial multisets of objects* placed in the m regions of μ; and R is a finite set of *developmental rules*.

A *P system with input* is a tuple (Π, Σ, i_0), where Π is a P system with working alphabet Γ, with m membranes, and initial multisets $w_1, \ldots, w_m$ associated with them; Σ is an (input) alphabet strictly contained in Γ; the initial multisets are over $\Gamma - \Sigma$; and i_0 is the label of a distinguished (input) membrane.

We say that Π is a *recognizer P system* [4,5] if Π is a P system with input alphabet Σ and working alphabet Γ; Γ has two designated objects *yes* and *no*; every computation of Π halts and sends out to the environment either *yes* or *no*, but not both, and this is done exactly in the last step of the computation; and, for a word $w \in \Sigma^*$, called the *input of Π*, w can be added to the system by placing it into the input membrane i_0 in the initial configuration.

A P system Π is *deterministic* if it has only a single computation from its initial configuration to its unique halting configuration. Π is *confluent* if every computation of Π halts and sends out to the environment the same object. Notice that, by definition, recognizing P systems are confluent.

P Systems with Active Membranes. In this paper, we investigate recognizer P systems with active membranes [9]. These systems have the following types of rules. As we are dealing with P systems that do not use the polarizations of the membranes, we leave out this feature from the definition.

(a) $[a \rightarrow v]_h$, for $h \in H, a \in \Gamma, v \in \Gamma^*$
    (object evolution rules, associated with membranes and depending on the label of the membranes, but not directly involving the membranes, in the sense that the membranes are neither taking part in the application of these rules nor are they modified by them);

(b) $a[\ ]_h \rightarrow [b]_h$, for $h \in H, a, b \in \Gamma$
    (*send-in* communication rules, sending an object into a membrane, maybe modified during this process);

(c) $[a]_h \rightarrow [\ ]_h u$, for $h \in H, a \in \Gamma, u \in \Gamma^*$
    (*send-out* communication rules; an object is sent out of the membrane, maybe modified during this process);

(d) $[a]_h \rightarrow u$, for $h \in H, a \in \Gamma, u \in \Gamma^*$
    (membrane dissolving rules; in reaction with an object, a membrane can be dissolved, while the object specified in the rule can be modified);

(e) $[a]_h \rightarrow [b]_h[c]_h$, for $h \in H, a, b, c \in \Gamma$
    (division rules for elementary membranes; in reaction with an object, the

membrane is divided into two membranes; the object a specified in the rule is replaced in the two new membranes by (possibly new) objects b and c respectively, and the remaining objects are duplicated; the new membranes have the same labels as the divided one).

We note that we use the rules of type (c) and (d) in a slightly generalized way as we allow here an object a to evolve into an arbitrary string u over Γ. It is clear, however, that an application of a rule $[a]_h \rightarrow [\ ]_h u$ (resp. a rule $[a]_h \rightarrow u$) can be simulated by applying a rule of the form $[a]_h \rightarrow [\ ]_h b$ (resp. $[a]_h \rightarrow b$), where $b \in \Gamma$, and an object evolution rule. Thus, the use of these generalized rules will not speed up the running time of our P systems significantly.

As usual, a P system with active membranes works in a *maximally parallel* manner:

- In one step, any object of a membrane that can evolve must evolve, but one object can be used by only one rule in (a)-(e);
- when some rules in (b)-(e) can be applied to a certain membrane, then one of them must be applied, but a membrane can be the subject of only one of these rules during each step.

We will use uniform families of P system to decide a language $L \subseteq \Sigma^*$. In this paper, we follow the notion of uniformity used in [8]. Let E and F be classes of computable functions. A family $\mathbf{\Pi} = (\Pi(i))_{i \in \mathbb{N}}$ of recognizing P systems is called (E, F)-*uniform* if and only if (i) there is a function $f \in F$ such that, for every $n \in \mathbb{N}$, $\Pi(n) = f(1^n)$ (i.e., f maps the unary representation of each natural number to an encoding of the P system processing all the inputs of length n); (ii) there is a function $e \in E$ that maps every word $x \in \Sigma^*$ to a multiset $e(x) = w_x$ over the input alphabet of $\Pi(l(x))$.

An (E, F)-*uniform* family of P systems $\mathbf{\Pi} = (\Pi(i))_{i \in \mathbb{N}}$ *decides a language* $L \subseteq \Sigma^*$ if, for every word $x \in \Sigma^*$, starting $\Pi(l(x))$ with w_x in its input membrane, $\Pi(l(x))$ sends out to the environment *yes* if and only if $x \in L$. In general, E and F are well known complexity classes such as $\mathbf{P}$ or $\mathbf{L}$.

We say that $\Pi(n)$ *works in* $t(n)$ *time* ($t : \mathbb{N} \rightarrow \mathbb{N}$) if $\Pi(n)$ halts in at most $t(n)$ steps, for every input multiset in its input membrane. Next, we adopt the notion of space complexity for families of recognizer P systems similarly to the definition appearing in [8] (see also [6]). Let $\mathcal{C}$ be a configuration of a P system Π. The *size of* $\mathcal{C}$ (denoted by $|\mathcal{C}|$) is the sum of the number of membranes and the total number of objects in $\mathcal{C}$. If $\mathcal{C} = (\mathcal{C}_0, \dots, \mathcal{C}_k)$ is a halting computation of Π, then the space required by $\mathcal{C}$ is defined as $|\mathcal{C}| = max\{|\mathcal{C}_0|, \dots, |\mathcal{C}_k|\}$. The space required by Π is $|\Pi| = sup\{|\mathcal{C}| \mid \mathcal{C} \text{ is a halting computation of } \Pi\}$. Let us note that in this paper the presented P systems will have finitely many different halting computations. This clearly implies that $|\Pi| \in \mathbb{N}$. Finally, $\Pi(n)$ *works using* $s(n)$ *space* ($s : \mathbb{N} \rightarrow \mathbb{N}$), if $|\Pi(n)| \leq s(n)$, for every input multiset in its input membrane.

3   The Main Result

In this section we prove the following result:

Theorem 1. *Let* $t : \mathbb{N} \to \mathbb{N}$ *be a function such that* $\log t(n)$ *is space constructible and consider a Turing machine* M *working in* $t(n)$ *time. Then* M *can be simulated by a* (**DLOGTIME, SPACE**$(\log t(n))$)-*uniform family* $\mathbf{\Pi}_M = (\Pi_M(i))_{i \in \mathbb{N}}$ *of recognizer* P *systems with the following properties:*

- *the members of* $\mathbf{\Pi}_M$ *are polarizationless P systems with active membranes, without using membrane division rules, and*
- *for every* $n \in \mathbb{N}$, $\Pi_M(n)$ *works in* $O(t(n))$ *time and in* $O(t^2(n))$ *space.*

The rest of this section is devoted to the proof of this theorem. Let us consider a Turing machine $M = (Q, \Sigma, \Gamma, \delta, q_0, q_a, q_r)$ working in $t(n)$ time. We construct a uniform family of recognizer P systems $\mathbf{\Pi}_M = (\Pi_M(i))_{i \in \mathbb{N}}$ that decides the language $M(L)$. Assume that $Q = \{s_1, \ldots, s_m\}$, for some $m \geq 3$, where $s_1 = q_0$, $s_{m-1} = q_a$ and $s_m = q_r$. Moreover, $\Gamma = \{X_1, \ldots, X_k\}$ for some $k > |\Sigma|$, where $X_k = \sqcup$ is the blank symbol of the working tape.

Before giving the precise construction of $\Pi_M(n)$, we describe informally some of its components. As the number of certain components of $\Pi_M(n)$ will depend on n, when the family machine that constructs $\Pi_M(n)$ enumerates these components, an efficient representation of numbers depending on n should be used. Thus, instead of using a number to denote a component of $\Pi_M(n)$, we will use the binary form of this number.

As M stops in at most $t(n)$ steps, the segment of the tape of M that is used during its work consists of at most $t(n)$ cells. This segment of the tape will be represented by the nested membrane structure appearing on Fig. 1. Here the first membrane in the skin represents the first cell of the tape, while the innermost membrane represents the $t(n)$th one. We will call these membranes of $\Pi_M(n)$ *tape-membranes*. Let us consider a tape-membrane representing the lth cell of the tape. We call this membrane the lth *tape-membrane*. Notice that the lth tape-membrane has label $b(l)$, if $l \leq n$, and it has label $b(n+1)$ otherwise (we distinguish the indexes of the first $n+1$ tape-membranes in order to ensure that the objects in the input multiset are able to find their corresponding tape-membranes).

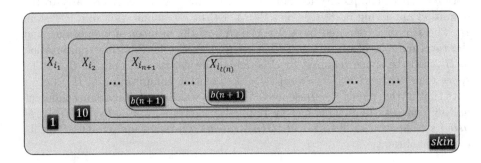

Fig. 1. The membrane structure corresponding to the simulated tape

For every $l \in [t(n)]$, the lth tape-membrane contains further membranes: for every state s_i ($i \in [m-2]$), it contains $t(n)$ copies of a membrane with label s_i. Such a membrane contains a further elementary membrane with label s_i'. Moreover, the lth tape-membrane contains a symbol $X_j \in \Gamma$ if and only if the lth cell of M contains the symbol X_j. Furthermore, if M is in state s_i and the head of M points to the lth cell, then an object $\uparrow_i$ is placed into the lth tape-membrane to represent this information (see Fig. 2 where we assumed that the head of M points to the third cell).

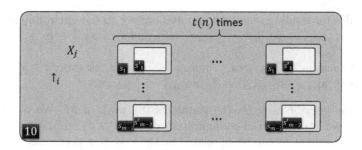

Fig. 2. The membrane structure of the third tape-membrane

We will see that when $\uparrow_i$ and X_j appear in the lth tape-membrane, then these objects will dissolve a membrane pair $[[\ ]_{s_i'}]_{s_i}$ and introduce new objects corresponding to the value $\delta(s_j, X_i)$. With these new objects $\Pi_M(n)$ will be able to maintain its configurations so that finally its current configuration corresponds to the new configuration of M.

The formal definition of $\Pi_M(n)$ is as follows. For every $n \in \mathbb{N}$, let $\Pi_M(n) := (\Sigma', \Gamma', H, \mu, W, R)$, where:

- $\Sigma' := \{a_{b(i)} \mid a \in \Sigma, 1 \le i \le n\}$
- $\Gamma' := \Sigma' \cup \Gamma \cup \{\uparrow_i, \downarrow_{i,d}\mid 1 \le i \le m, d \in \{L, R\}\} \cup \{d_{b(0)}, \ldots, d_{b(2n)}\} \cup \{yes, no\}$
- $H := \{skin, b(1), \ldots, b(n+1)\} \cup \{s_1, \ldots, s_m, s_1', \ldots, s_m'\}$;
- μ is a nested membrane structure $[[[\ldots[\ldots[\ ]_{b(n+1)} \cdots]_{b(n+1)} \cdots]_{b(2)}]_{b(1)}]_{skin}$ (containing $t(n)-n$ membranes with label $b(n+1)$), such that each membrane in this structure contains a further membrane structure ν, where ν consists of $t(n)$ copies of the membrane structure $[[\ ]_{s_i'}]_{s_i}$, for every $i \in [m-2]$. The input membrane is $[\ ]_{skin}$;
- $W := w_{skin}, w_{b(1)}, \ldots, w_{b(n+1)}, w_{s_1}, \ldots, w_{s_m}, w_{s_1'}, \ldots, w_{s_m'}$, where
  - $w_{skin} := \varepsilon$;
  - $w_{b(1)} := d_0$, $w_{b(l)} := \varepsilon$, for every $l \in [2, n]$, and $w_{b(n+1)} := X_k$ (i.e., $w_{b(n+1)}$ is the blank symbol);
  - $w_{s_i} = w_{s_i'} := \varepsilon$, for every $i \in [m-2]$;
- R is the set of the following rules:
  - Rules to set up the initial configuration of M:

(a) $a_{b(i)}[\ ]_{b(l)} \rightarrow [a_{b(i)}]_{b(l)}, \quad a_{b(i)}[\ ]_{b(i)} \rightarrow [a]_{b(i)}$, for every $i \in [n]$ and $l < i$;

(b) $[d_{b(i)} \rightarrow d_{b(i+1)}]_1, \quad [d_{b(2n)} \rightarrow \uparrow_1]_1$, for every $i \in [2n-1]$;

- Rules for simulating a configuration step of M:

(c) $\uparrow_i [\ ]_{s_i} \rightarrow [\uparrow_i]_{s_i}, \quad [\uparrow_i]_{s_i} \rightarrow \varepsilon$, for every $i \in [m-2]$;

(d) $X_j[\ ]_{s'_i} \rightarrow [X_j]_{s'_i}, \quad [X_j]_{s'_i} \rightarrow X_r \downarrow_{t,d}$, for every $i \in [m-2], j \in [k]$ and $(X_r, s_t, d) = \delta(s_i, X_j)$;

(e) $\downarrow_{i,R} [\ ]_{b(l)} \rightarrow [\uparrow_i]_{b(l)}$, for every $i \in [m-2], l \in [n+1]$;

(f) $[\downarrow_{i,L}]_{b(l)} \rightarrow [\ ]_{b(l)} \uparrow_i, \quad [\downarrow_{i,L}]_1 \rightarrow [\uparrow_i]_1$, for every $i \in [m-2], l \in [2, n+1]$;

- Rules for sending out the computed answer to the environment:

(g) $[\downarrow_{m-1,d} \rightarrow yes]_{b(l)}, \quad [\downarrow_{m,d} \rightarrow no]_{b(l)}$, for every $l \in [n+1]$ and $d \in \{L, R\}$;

(h) $[yes]_{b(l)} \rightarrow [\ ]_{b(l)} yes, \quad [no]_{b(l)} \rightarrow [\ ]_{b(l)} no$, for every $l \in [n+1]$;

(i) $[yes]_{skin} \rightarrow [\ ]_{skin} yes, \quad [no]_{skin} \rightarrow [\ ]_{skin} no$.

Next, we describe how $\Pi_M(n)$ simulates the work of M. We will see that $\Pi_M(n)$ can set up the initial configuration of M in $O(n)$ steps and that every configuration step of M can be simulated by the P system performing a constant number of steps. We distinguish the following three main stages of the simulation:

Stage 1: Setting up the initial configuration of M. Assume that M is provided with the input word $a_1 a_2 \ldots a_n$ ($a_i \in \Sigma, i \in [n]$). Then the input multiset of $\Pi_M(n)$ is $pos(w)$. During the first $2n$ steps, every object $a_{b(i)}$ in the input multiset finds its corresponding membrane with label $b(i)$. At the last step, $a_{b(i)}$ evolves to a, as the sub-index $b(i)$ is not needed any more. Meanwhile, in membrane 1 object d_0 evolves to object $d_{b(2n)}$ and $d_{b(2n)}$ evolves to $\uparrow_1$. After these steps, the lth tape-membrane of the system contains an object $X \in \Gamma$ if and only if the lth cell of the tape of M contains X. Moreover, the object $\uparrow_1$ occurring in the first tape-membrane represents that M's current state is s_1 (that is, the initial state) and that the head of M points to the first cell. Thus, after $2n$ steps the configuration of $\Pi_M(n)$ corresponds to the initial configuration of M.

Stage 2: Simulating a configuration step of M. Assume that M has the configuration appearing in Fig. 3 and that $\Pi_M(n)$ has the corresponding configuration appearing in Fig. 4 (for the sake of simplicity we assume that $l \in [n+1]$; the case when $l > l+1$ can be treated similarly). The simulation of the computation step of M starts as follows. Firstly, $\uparrow_i$ goes into a membrane with label s_i and then dissolves it using rules in (c). Meanwhile, $\uparrow_i$ evolves to ε. Let us remark that the system can always find a membrane with label s_i in the corresponding tape-membrane. Indeed, at the beginning of the computation, every tape-membrane contains $t(n)$ copies of a membrane with label s_i. Moreover, M can perform at most $t(n)$ steps and the simulation of one step dissolves exactly one membrane with label s_i.

Next, X_j goes into the membrane s'_i and then dissolves it. During the dissolution two new objects, X_r and $\downarrow_{t,d}$ are introduced according to the value

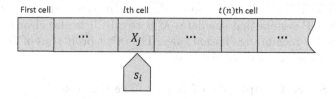

Fig. 3. A configuration of M

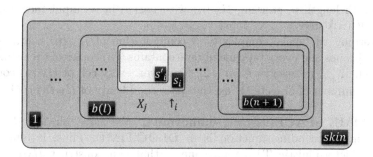

Fig. 4. The corresponding configuration of $\Pi_M(n)$

$\delta(s_i, X_j)$. Notice that in $\downarrow_{t,d}$, the index t corresponds to the index of the new state of M and d denotes the direction of the tape head. Now the simulation of the corresponding movement of the head is done as follows. According to the value of d we distinguish the following cases:

Case 1: $d = R$. In this case $\Pi_M(n)$ applies rules in (e): $\downarrow_{t,R}$ is sent into the next inner tape-membrane and, meanwhile, it evolves to $\uparrow_t$. This corresponds to the move of the tape head to the right.

Case 2: $d = L$. This case is similar to the previous one, but here $\Pi_M(n)$ applies rules in (f): $\downarrow_{t,L}$ is sent out of the current tape-membrane and it evolves to $\uparrow_t$. This corresponds to the move of the tape head to the left. Notice that if $l = 1$, then $\Pi_M(n)$ can apply only the second rule in (f) which means that in this case $\uparrow_t$ remains in the first tape-membrane. This still corresponds to the step of M, since in this case the head of M cannot move left.

Stage 3: Sending the correct answer to the environment. Whenever an object $\downarrow_{m-1,d}$ ($d \in \{L, R\}$) is introduced in a tape-membrane (i.e., when M enters its accepting state), the system introduces object *yes* using the first rule in (g). Then this object is sent out of the tape-membranes until it reaches the skin membrane using rules in (h). Finally, *yes* is sent out to the environment using the first rule in (i). $\Pi_M(n)$ performs a similar computation concerning object *no*.

It can be seen using the notes above that $\Pi_M(n)$ is a confluent polarization-less recognizer P system that simulates M correctly. It is also clear that $\Pi_M(n)$ does not employ membrane division rules. The other properties of $\Pi_M(n)$ mentioned in Theorem 1 are discussed next.

Time and Space Complexity of $\Pi_M(n)$. The time complexity of $\Pi_M(n)$ is measured as follows. As we already discussed, *Stage 1* takes $O(n)$ steps. It can be seen that the simulation of a step of M takes five steps. Thus, *Stage 2* takes $O(t(n))$ steps. Finally, *Stage 3* takes also $O(t(n))$ steps. Thus, for every word $x \in \Sigma^*$ with length n, starting $\Pi_M(n)$ with $pos(x)$ in its input membrane, it halts in $O(t(n))$ steps.

Concerning the space complexity, a configuration of $\Pi_M(n)$ contains $t(n)$ tape-membranes and every tape membrane contains $t(n)$ copies of the membrane structure $[[\ ]_{s'_i}]_{s_i}$, for every $i \in [m-2]$. Moreover, every cell of $\Pi_M(n)$ contains a constant number of objects. Thus, the space complexity of $\Pi_M(n)$ is $O(t^2(n))$.

(DLOGTIME, SPACE$(\log t(n))$)-uniformity. We have already discussed that our input encoding function is in **DLOGTIME**. Thus, it remains to describe a deterministic Turing machine F that can construct $\Pi_M(n)$ using $O(\log t(n))$ space. It is clear that the objects in Γ' and the rules of $\Pi_M(n)$ can be enumerated by F using $O(\log n)$ cells. Indeed, Γ' contains $O(mn)$ objects, but m here is a constant that depends only on M. Moreover, $\Pi_M(n)$ has $O(n)$ different rules.

Furthermore, as $\log t(n)$ is space constructible, F can construct $\log t(n)$ in unary form using $O(\log t(n))$ space. Using the unary representation of $\log t(n)$, the initial membrane structure of $\Pi_M(n)$ can be constructed by F as follows: when F constructs the lth tape-membrane, then it stores $b(l)$ on one of its tapes using at most $\log t(n)$ cells. Furthermore, when F constructs the kth membrane structure of the form $[[\ ]_{s'_i}]_{s_i}$ $(k \in [t(n)], i \in [m-2])$ in the lth tape-membrane, then it stores the words $b(k)$ and $b(i)$ on one of its tapes. This also needs $O(\log t(n))$ cells. Thus, the total number of cells used on the work tapes of F when it constructs $\Pi_M(n)$ is $O(\log t(n))$.

4   Conclusions

The simulation of the behaviour of a device of a computation model in a different model allows to see all problems from a new point of view. One of the frontiers of the current research in Membrane Computing corresponds to the computational power of P systems according to the power of the function that encodes the input and the function that constructs the family of P systems.

In this paper, we prove a general result in this line, since we show that every single-tape deterministic Turing machine working in $t(n)$ time can be simulated by a uniform family of recognizer polarizationless P systems with active membranes. Moreover, this is done without significant slowdown in the working time. Furthermore, if $\log t(n)$ is space constructible, then the members of the family can be constructed by a family machine that uses $O(\log t(n))$ space. As a particular case, this means that if $t(n)$ is a polynomial function, then the used family of P systems is (**DLOGTIME, L**)-uniform. Likewise, if $t(n)$ is an exponential function, then the used family is (**DLOGTIME, PSPACE**)-uniform.

As it is pointed out in [2], uniform families of polarizationless P systems with active membranes and without dissolution rules are at most as powerful as the used input encoding function (see Theorem 10 in [2]). This fact, together with the result of this paper, illustrates the importance of dissolution rules in P systems with active membranes when the polarizations of the membranes are not allowed.

It remains as an open question if (**DLOGTIME, SPACE**($\log t(n)$))-uniformity in Theorem 1 can be strengthened to (**DLOGTIME, L**)-uniformity (i.e., whether the construction of $\mathbf{\Pi}_M$ can be done using logarithmic space whatever the running time of M is). In our construction membrane division rules are not employed. Nevertheless, even if we used these rules, it is not clear how the tape-membranes or the membrane structures occurring in them could be constructed using logarithmic space. This might be a subject of further research.

Acknowledgements. Miguel A. Gutiérrez–Naranjo acknowledges the support of the project TIN2012-37434 of the Ministerio de Economía y Competitividad of Spain.

References

1. Alhazov, A., Leporati, A., Mauri, G., Porreca, A.E., Zandron, C.: Space complexity equivalence of P systems with active membranes and Turing machines. Theoretical Compuer Science **529**, 69–81 (2014)
2. Murphy, N., Woods, D.: The computational complexity of uniformity and semi-uniformity in membrane systems. In: Martínez-del-Amor, M.A., Orejuela-Pinedo, E.F., Păun, Gh., Pérez-Hurtado, I., Riscos-Núñez, A. (eds.) Seventh Brainstorming Week on Membrane Computing, vol. II, pp. 73–84. Fénix Editora, Sevilla (2009)
3. Pérez-Jiménez, M.J., Riscos-Núñez, A., Romero-Jiménez, A., Woods, D.: Complexity - membrane division, membrane creation. In: Păun et al. [10], pp. 302–336
4. Pérez-Jiménez, M.J., Romero-Jiménez, A., Sancho-Caparrini, F.: A polynomial complexity class in P systems using membrane division. In: Csuhaj-Varjú, E., Kintala, C., Wotschke, D., Vaszil, Gy. (eds.) Proceeding of the 5th Workshop on Descriptional Complexity of Formal Systems, DCFS 2003, pp. 284–294 (2003)
5. Pérez-Jiménez, M.J., Romero-Jiménez, Á., Sancho-Caparrini, F.: A polynomial complexity class in P systems using membrane division. Journal of Automata, Languages and Combinatorics **11**(4), 423–434 (2006)
6. Porreca, A., Leporati, A., Mauri, G., Zandron, C.: Introducing a space complexity measure for P systems. International Journal of Computers, Communications and Control **4**(3), 301–310 (2009)
7. Porreca, A.E.: Computational Complexity Classes for Membrane System. Master's thesis, Universitá di Milano-Bicocca, Italy (2008)
8. Porreca, A.E., Leporati, A., Mauri, G., Zandron, C.: Sublinear-space P systems with active membranes. In: Csuhaj-Varjú, E., Gheorghe, M., Rozenberg, G., Salomaa, A., Vaszil, Gy. (eds.) CMC 2012. LNCS, vol. 7762, pp. 342–357. Springer, Heidelberg (2013)

9. Păun, Gh.: P systems with active membranes: Attacking NP-complete problems. Journal of Automata, Languages and Combinatorics **6**(1), 75–90 (2001)
10. Păun, Gh., Rozenberg, G., Salomaa, A. (eds.): The Oxford Handbook of Membrane Computing. Oxford University Press, Oxford (2010)
11. Romero Jiménez, A., Pérez-Jiménez, M.J.: Simulating Turing machines by P systems with external output. Fundamenta Informaticae **49**(1–3), 273–278 (2002)
12. Sipser, M.: Introduction to the Theory of Computation. Cengage Learning (2012)
13. Valsecchi, A., Porreca, A.E., Leporati, A., Mauri, G., Zandron, C.: An efficient simulation of polynomial-space Turing machines by P systems with active membranes. In: Păun, Gh., Pérez-Jiménez, M.J., Riscos-Núñez, A., Rozenberg, G., Salomaa, A. (eds.) WMC 2009. LNCS, vol. 5957, pp. 461–478. Springer, Heidelberg (2010)

Categorised Counting Mediated by Blotting Membrane Systems for Particle-Based Data Mining and Numerical Algorithms

Thomas Hinze[1,2](✉), Konrad Grützmann[3], Benny Höckner[1],
Peter Sauer[1], and Sikander Hayat[4]

[1] Institute of Computer Science and Information and Media Technology,
Brandenburg University of Technology,
Postfach 10 13 44, 03013 Cottbus, Germany
{thomas.hinze,benny.hoeckner,peter.sauer}@tu-cottbus.de
[2] Friedrich Schiller University Jena, Ernst-Abbe-Platz 1–4, 07743 Jena, Germany
[3] Helmholtz Centre for Environmental Research – UFZ,
Permoserstr. 15, 04318 Leipzig, Germany
konrad.gruetzmann@ufz.de
[4] Harvard Medical School, 200 Longwood Avenue, Boston, MA 02115, USA
Sikander_Hayat@hms.harvard.edu

Abstract. Blotting turns out to be a rather common and effective approach in molecular information processing. An initial pool of molecules considered as sets of individual data becomes spatially separated according to the presence or absence of specific attributes like weight index or chemical groups and labels. In this connection, molecules with similar properties form a spot or blot. Finally, each blot can be visualised or analysed revealing a corresponding score index or count from the number of accumulated molecules. The entire variety of blots which emerge over time provides crucial and condensed information about the molecular system under study. Inspired by the idea to obtain significant data reduction while keeping the essential characteristics of the molecular system as output, we introduce blotting membrane systems as a modelling framework open for numerous applications in data mining. By means of three dedicated case studies, we demonstrate its descriptive capability from an explorative point of view. Our case studies address particle-based numerical integration, which suggests a model for the synchronised 17-year life cycle of *Magicicadas*. Furthermore, we exemplify electrophoresis as a way to carry out a variant of bucket sort.

1 Introduction and Background

From a technical point of view, biological information processing as well as molecular computing and particle-based algorithms commonly result in a huge amount of more or less raw data. Afterwards, an appropriate interpretation of these data sets from a holistic perspective towards evident conclusions turns out to be a challenging task [14]. In many cases, this is due to the partly diffuse nature of

© Springer International Publishing Switzerland 2014
M. Gheorghe et al. (Eds.): CMC 2014, LNCS 8961, pp. 241–257, 2014.
DOI: 10.1007/978-3-319-14370-5_15

molecular processes at a *mesoscale* level. By means of this term, we summarise a typical outcome of a measure or a direct observation obtained from an underlying experiment or system under study. Interestingly, the majority of visualisation techniques and analytical tools in biochemistry comprise a *spatial separation* of molecules or particles based on relevant attributes or properties. For instance, an electrophoresis spreads electrically charged molecules by their individual weights [15]. Other attempts to capture a molecular system employ fluorescence labels specifically attached to signalling molecules [4,16]. Here, the spatial distribution of these labels represents the overall behaviour of the system. In addition, high-resolution microscopy in many facets sheds light on the geometrical location of molecular clusters or even single molecules up to a nanometre scale [5].

All these techniques have in common that the number of molecules or particles present within predefined grid *regions* or accumulated towards distinguishable *clusters* gives the crucial information about the underlying system. Often, the number of molecules needs to overcome a certain *threshold* before taken into consideration for detectability. Finally, the number of molecules subject to a geometrical grid tends to be expressed by a kind of heatmap. Here, the range of potential molecular amounts becomes divided into several disjoint intervals while each of them is assigned to a corresponding colour or intensity value. Having a look at the grid mostly reveals a collection of spots or *blots* in different size and colour, sometimes partially overlapping, and almost certainly somehow blurry or frazzled.

A variety of dedicated blotting techniques have emerged during the last decades which produce two-dimensional blot diagrams, sometimes also called *blotting papers* [3,24]. The metaphor rather illustratively describes this form of data representation, especially in case of prevalent Southern, Western, and Northern blots [22]. These techniques allow among others a spatial separation of DNA (deoxyribonucleic acid), RNA (ribonucleic acid), or labelled proteins from an initial mixture according to their weights or according to the presence or absence of oligomeric subsequences. In application scenarios with a medical background, the resulting blot diagrams help to identify whether or not certain viral infections or gene mutations occurred. Both of these can imply the synthesis of malformed, functionally insufficient proteins [26]. From the percentage of malformed proteins in comparison to the total amount, a stage or degree of the damage can be hypothesised if there is enough empirical, statistical, or deducible significance.

The effect of spatial blotting can also be seen in nature. Control of cell differentiation and proliferation in the embryo of the fruit fly *Drosophila melanogaster* gives a fascinating example [25]. The underlying processes manage the formation of embryonic patterns from the fertilised egg [23]. Embryonic patterns mark an essential intermediate state in the morphogenesis of the organism which leads to its functional structures and appendages. In addition to the body proportions, during maturation the shape, positions and size of head and thorax, and at a more fine-grained level those of organs like eyes and wings, become mainly determined by embryonic patterns. In simple terms, the embryonic pattern quite precisely defines a geometrical grid throughout the longitudinal (anteroposterior) axis and

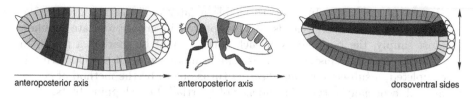

anteroposterior axis   anteroposterior axis   dorsoventral sides

Fig. 1. Schematic representation of an embryonic pattern in the fertilised egg of the fruit fly *Drosophila melanogaster*. The pattern forms a 7 × 4-grid whose 28 coordinated regions are characterised by individual presence of specific cytokine combinations. Along with cell differentiation and proliferation during maturation, functional structures and appendages of the organism emerge from corresponding initial regions of the embryonic pattern. It constitutes the anteroposterior axis together with its dorsoventral sides as well. Graphical respresentation inspired by fluorescence microscopy images (Hox coordinate gene expression states) in [25].

orthogonally along the so-called dorsoventral sides, see Figure 1. In the first developmental stage, the embryonic pattern separates seven dedicated regions anteroposterially and four regions dorsoventrally. Each of these regions is characterised by a specific mixture of a number of proteins called *cytokines* whose individual concentrations are spatially distributed according to the regions. Typically, within a region a total amount of one up to three different cytokines exhibit a high concentration while all other cytokines persist in low concentrations. The grid-like spatial distribution of cytokines results from an underlying expression scheme of so-called coordinate genes. The activation of these genes is controlled by a reaction cascade in several phases along a predefined time course. The activation cascade starts simultaneously from both opposite tips of the embryo triggered by the zygote (fertilised egg cell) in concert with environmental stimuli. In terms of a systemic understanding, the process of embryonic pattern formation reflects the functionality of *categorised counting*. Here, the categories symbolise all single regions of which the grid is composed, while the ratios of individual cytokine concentrations accumulated within each region indicate its spatial position inside the entire grid. In other words, each region can be identified by a specific index (count value) estimated from the involved cytokine concentration gradients. In subsequent phases of maturation, the initial embryonic pattern becomes more and more refined, with the cytokines acting as transcription factors specifically activating those parts of the genome whose resulting proteins lead to differentiated cells forming the variety of body structures.

All scenarios addressed here so far share a common essential principle consisting of three consecutive steps:

1. Particles or molecules which represent a pool of data create spatially distributed blots of diverse size or density. In a general term, this step is called *clustering*. Initiated by a more or less complex interplay of physical processes like transduction or diffusion mainly in conjunction with (bio)chemical reactions, clustering follows known principles of natural laws but can be enriched by stochastic effects. This stochasticity causes a certain bias inflating the

amount of raw data. In order to enable a later analysis, the geometrical location of each cluster needs to be captured in an appropriate manner. Most simply, the boundaries of each cluster might be marked a priori. In case the expected cluster positions remain unknown until the clustering is completed, a subsequent *classification* turns out to be the method of choice instead, especially if there is evidence of (partially) overlapping blots.

2. The number of relevant molecules within each cluster defines a dedicated qualitative score like a colour intensity or just an index for instance. This step can be covered by the term *counting*. The ability to carry out counting comes along with a previously finalised *categorisation*. To this end, a predefined setting of available categories becomes identified which in turn specifies the domain of potential and acceptable scores. A final set of distinct greyscales or a range of discrete measurement readings give typical examples for categories. Eventually, counting maps the molecular abundance into the corresponding category. Hence, we obtain a more or less tremendous data reduction. Afterwards, each cluster exhibits its count as essential information.

3. Based on the clusters and their corresponding counts, the final step comprises the generation of the system's *response*. Living organisms taken as natural systems like the fruit fly exhibit a special behavioural pattern like maturation for response. In contrast, man-made systems like electrophoresis chambers require external mathematical analysis instead, mostly involving statistics or deduction. In either case, a computation typically takes place having the response as output.

We say that a system operating in this manner performs *categorised counting*. Inspired by numerous further examples, the idea arises whether this common behavioural principle can be advantageously captured by a consistent dedicated description framework. Therefore, the notion of a *P system* [20] seems to be an ideal candidate due to its multiset-based nature. A *multiset* inherently supports the strategy of categorised counting: elements reflect the categories while their multiplicities stand for the corresponding count. Clustering is expressed by accumulation of elements into the underlying multiset. Putting all necessary descriptive ingredients together will lead us to the introduction of *blotting membrane systems*, a new class of P systems aimed at formalisation of categorised counting. The level of abstraction taken into consideration should be balanced in order to cope with the computational complexity of multiple particle systems entering the clustering process. The main focus is laid to facilitate explorative in-silico studies able to extract a condensed but sufficient description of the systems behaviour and/or possible conclusions from a (huge) set of slightly biased raw data. Having in mind that particularly the response stage in categorised counting might incorporate statistical techniques and deductive methods applied to an initial set of data, blotting membrane systems can open the field of *data mining* [8,10] for membrane computing. To the best of our knowledge, this is the first attempt at primarily addressing this line of research.

In Section 2, we familiarise the reader with the formal definition of blotting membrane systems together with all required prerequisites. Hereafter, three case studies selected from different facets of molecular information processing demonstrate their descriptive capability. We start with an initial example, particle-based numerical integration, presented in Section 3. This feature, in addition to a limiting threshold, is sufficient for a simple behavioural model of how insects of the species *Magicicada* can count a time span of rather exactly 17 years which comprises the synchronised life cycle of all individuals within the population. Section 4 is dedicated to electrophoresis, a commonly used technique to arrange electrically charged molecules by their weights. The resulting systems behaviour resembles the algorithmic strategy of bucket sort. A final discussion concludes benefits as well as open questions for future work.

2 Blotting Membrane Systems

Formal Prerequisites

Let A and B be arbitrary sets, $\emptyset$ the empty set, $\mathbb{N}$ the set of natural numbers including zero, $\mathbb{R}$ the set of real numbers, and $\mathbb{R}_+$ the set of non-negative real numbers. A and B are disjoint (share no common elements) iff $A \cap B = \emptyset$. The Cartesian product $A \times B = \{(a,b) \mid a \in A \wedge b \in B\}$ collects all tuples from A and B. For $A \times A$, we write A^2 for short. The term $\mathrm{card}(A)$, also written as $|A|$, denotes the number of elements in A (cardinality). A multiset over A is a mapping $F : A \longrightarrow \mathbb{N} \cup \{+\infty\}$. Multisets in general can be written as an elementwise enumeration of the form $\{(a_1, F(a_1)), (a_2, F(a_2)), \ldots\}$ since $\forall(a, b_1), (a, b_2) \in F : b_1 = b_2$. The support $\mathrm{supp}(F) \subseteq A$ of F is defined by $\mathrm{supp}(F) = \{a \in A \mid F(a) > 0\}$. A multiset F over A is said to be empty iff $\forall a \in A : F(a) = 0$. The cardinality $|F|$ of F over A is $|F| = \sum_{a \in A} F(a)$.

Definition of Systems Components

A *blotting membrane system* is a construct

$$\boxed{\Pi} = (P, L, C, B_1, \ldots, B_{|C|}, S, R, \mathrm{r}) \tag{1}$$

whose components mimic all ingredients of categorised counting, namely

- spatially distributed particles equipped with labels,
- resulting blots acting as categories,
- score values (counts) according to each category, and
- a response as follows:

We assume that the systems input consists of a final set of particles arbitrarily located at a two-dimensional, not necessarily bounded grid. Therefore, each particle carries its grid coordinates (Cartesian or by generic system) together with an individual label (like weight index or presence of a chemical fluorescence marker) beforehand responsible for processing the spatial separation.

L	arbitrary set of available labels
$P \subset \mathbb{R} \times \mathbb{R} \times L$	final set of particles, each of them specified by grid position and label

By means of the components C and $B_1, \ldots, B_{|C|}$, we capture the arrangement of particles into blots as well as the assignment of categories to the blots.

C	arbitrary set of available categories either defined explicitly or obtained implicitly as result of a classification over P
$B_1 \subseteq P$ $\vdots$ $B_{|C|} \subseteq P$	entirety of blots, each of them specified by the accumulated particles

In simple cases, the number of categories $|C|$ can be set explicitly, particularly in those studies which enable a precise prediction of the expected blots due to a sufficient knowledge of the systems behaviour. More elaboratively, the number of categories can result from a classification process taking into account spatial distances (or distance measures) between all or selected particles. To this end, a distance matrix of the incorporated particles is created first making each particle its own singleton category for the beginning. Out of the matrix, those two particles exhibiting the minimal distance to each other become identified. They are removed from the matrix by being merged into a common category. This new category is placed in the distance matrix again. This comes along with filling its distances to all other categories present in the matrix. There are different calculation schemes on how to obtain these distance updates originating a variety of classification approaches [6]. By iterating the merge of two nearest categories, the total number of categories decreases more and more. Usually, the merging process stops after a certain distance threshold is reached or a desired final number of categories emerged (*agglomerative hierarchical clustering*, [11]).

We denote the blots by the family of sets B_1 until $B_{|C|}$. If the condition $\bigcap_{i=1}^{|C|} B_i = \emptyset$ holds, the blots are said to be *non-overlapping*. Please note that the blots do not need to be necessarily disjoint. In general, a particle is allowed to be part of several (overlapping) blots.

$S : C \longrightarrow \mathbb{N}$	multiset subsuming the score values (counts) over all categories
R	arbitrary set specifying the response domain
$r : \mathbb{N}^{|C|} \longrightarrow R$	response function

The multiset S appears to represent the central part of the blotting membrane system since its core functionality of data reduction by categorised counting is expressed here. Typically, we choose $S(c) = |B_c|$ for all $c \in C$. In order to finalise the system's description, we still need to formalise its response. In this context, we initiate a response domain R capturing all of the system's potential outputs. Based on that, the response function r analyses the counts of all categories. Finally, it derives the corresponding response. This step might include statistical tests and/or some dedicated reasoning. Hence, the formal description of function r within application scenarios might become rather extensive.

A Toy Example: Particle-Based Approximation of Constant $\pi \approx 3.14$

Using a toy example, we illustrate the formalism of blotting membrane systems. To this end, we exemplify a simple particle-based rational approximation of the mathematical constant π. This application scenario utilises a square-shaped underlying grid equipped with Cartesian coordinates along with a centered point of origin. The grid inscribes a circle, for simplicity we choose a radius whose unit of length equals to 1. Now, a huge number of particles is randomly distributed on the underlying grid taking care that an equipartition of the particles is met. The equipartition ensures spatial homogeneity. Those particles placed within the circle form a blot

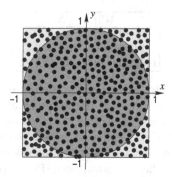

Fig. 2. Particles randomly distributed in spatial equipartition on an underlying square-shaped grid. The number of particles placed within the inscribed circle in comparison to the total number of particles provides a rational approximation of the constant π.

with a corresponding category on its own, see Figure 2. Beyond that, all particles in the whole grid are considered as a (partially overlapping) blot as well, substantiating a second category. Towards an approximation of $\pi = 3.14159265\ldots$, we only need to count the number of particles in both categories. Since the circle with radius 1 covers an area of π while the grid constitutes 4 surface units. As an approximation, we end in the responding relation:

$$\frac{\pi}{4} = \frac{\text{number of particles placed within the circle}}{\text{number of particles in total on the whole grid}}$$

Let us now formulate the dedicated blotting membrane system. To do so, we assume to have enough previously scattered particles P at hand whose coordinates come either from a numerical simulation based on a (pseudo) random number generator or from direct physical measurement. We employ a uniform label l for all particles. A resulting system might read:

$$\boxed{\Pi} = (P, L, C, B_1, \ldots, B_{|C|}, S, R, \mathrm{r}) \quad \text{with}$$
$$L = \{l\}$$
$$P = \{(0.70191, -0.21355, l), (0.02273, 0.91508, l), \ldots, (-0.45160, 0.52241, l)\}$$
$$C = \{\odot, \square\}$$
$$B_{\odot} = \{(x, y, l) \mid (x, y, l) \in P \wedge x^2 + y^2 \leq 1\}$$
$$B_{\square} = \{(x, y, l) \mid (x, y, l) \in P \wedge |x| \leq 1 \wedge |y| \leq 1\}$$
$$S(c) = |B_c| \ \forall c \in C$$
$$R = \mathbb{R}$$
$$\mathrm{r}(S) = 4 \cdot \frac{S(\odot)}{S(\square)}$$

A simulation case study discloses following numerical results for instance:

$|P|$	$S(\odot)$	$S(\square)$	rational approximation r of π	
10,000	7,928	10,000	3.1712...	(2 reliable digits)
1,000,000	785,502	1,000,000	3.1421...	(3 reliable digits)
100,000,000	78,542,447	100,000,000	3.1417...	(4 reliable digits)

Obviously, an ascending number of particles involved in the system leads to a higher accuracy of the approximation. Nevertheless, we are aware of the slow convergence behaviour. An additional decimal digit of π reliably figured out by the blotting membrane system requires a 100-fold increase of the total particle number due to the two-dimensional nature of the experimental setting. Of course, the numerical precision of particle coordinates needs to be adapted as well.

3   Particle-Based Numerical Integration

An evident application of categorised counting for molecular computation can be found in particle-based numerical integration. Enhancing the idea of a particle-based rational approximation of the constant π introduced in the previous section, we prepare a two-dimensional grid with the complete course of the desired real-valued function $f : \mathbb{R} \longrightarrow \mathbb{R}_+$ to be integrated numerically within a range $[a, b]$ of interest, see Figure 3. Subsequently, a huge number of particles becomes consistently scattered over the whole grid producing a spatially homogeneous particle distribution. Within a separate category, the number of particles placed below the function course of f is achieved by counting. Its amount in comparison with the total number of particles on the whole grid offers a rational approximation of the numerical integral to be calculated:

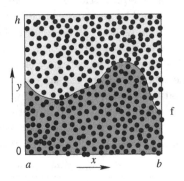

Fig. 3. Operating scheme of a particle-based numerical integrator

$$\frac{\int_a^b f(x)\,dx}{h \cdot (b - a)} = \frac{\text{number of particles placed below the function course of f}}{\text{number of particles in total on the whole grid}}$$

Written as a blotting membrane system, we obtain for instance (particle coordinates adjusted to $h = 10, a = 0, b = 10$):

$$\boxed{\varPi} = (P, L, C, B_1, \ldots, B_{|C|}, S, R, \mathrm{r}) \quad \text{with}$$
$$L = \{l\}$$
$$P = \{(3.46119, 1.83835, l), (0.92240, 2.70318, l), \ldots, (4.07919, 3.95624, l)\}$$
$$C = \{\int, \Box\}$$
$$B_{\int} = \{(x, y, l) \mid (x, y, l) \in P \wedge x \geq a \wedge x \leq b \wedge y \geq 0 \wedge y \leq \mathrm{f}(x)\}$$
$$B_{\Box} = \{(x, y, l) \mid (x, y, l) \in P \wedge x \geq a \wedge x \leq b \wedge y \geq 0 \wedge y \leq h\}$$
$$S(c) = |B_c| \; \forall c \in C$$
$$R = \mathbb{R}$$
$$\mathrm{r}(S) = h \cdot (b - a) \cdot \frac{S(\int)}{S(\Box)}$$

An impressive example for biological exploitation of numerical integration is inspired by cicadas, insects of the species *Magicicada*. Populations in northern America share a synchronous life cycle of 17 years while those in central America prefer 13 years [18]. Most of its existence is spent underground in a dormant state. Shortly before the end of the life cycle, all the adults of a brood emerge at roughly the same time to reproduce for several weeks. After laying their eggs, the adults die off and the cycle begins again. What stands out is that 17 and 13 are prime numbers, which suggests that the reproduction period does not coincide with the life cycles of potential predators. The simultaneous mass awakening of a brood also ensures that predators are overwhelmed by the number of cicadas so that a large number can survive. In order to guarantee a concerted awakening of all members of a brood, the species needs a precise molecular mechanism to measure the passage of the appropriate amount of time. Since it seems that there is no external stimulus with a natural period of 13 or 17 years, its exact estimation exclusively based on annual or even shorter cycles becomes a complicated task [28].

There is some evidence for a potential annual stimulus utilised by periodical cicadas: sap circulating through the root capillaries. Its intensity alters between high abundance during the growth period and almost absence during winter [7]. Cicada larvae could make use of the sap for nutrition while metabolic byproducts accumulate in terms of a numerical integration from its temporal course. Following this idea, the byproducts would persist within one or several vesicles whose outer membranes are going to burst after its content has reached a certain mass.

Up to now, we failed in retrieving detailed scientific publications on hypothesised or even verified mechanisms. A more or less speculative model aims at a combination of two processes, a slow growth on the one hand and a threshold on the other. Growth means a successive accumulation of a dedicated species. As soon as its concentration exceeds an inherently set threshold, the finalisation of the life cycle is initiated indicating the elapsed amount of 17 years. A successive accumulation organised for instance in annual cycles is useful for high precision. To this end, a core oscillator (like the periodical sap cycle) could provide an annually altering signal of the form $a + \sin(bt)$ subject to time t. A simple signal

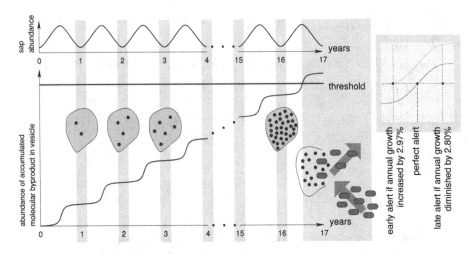

Fig. 4. Schematic representation of a molecular numerical integrator possibly residing in periodical 17-year cicadas for control and synchronisation of population life cycle

integration then produces a temporal course of the form $at - \frac{1}{b} \cdot \cos(bt) + C$ with successive, staircase-shaped growth, see Figure 4.

The molecular alert after reaching the threshold could initiate a signalling cascade which in turn releases trigger molecules into the environment. The trigger molecules on their own could interact by a special form of *quorum sensing* [2,19]: A cicada larva needs to perceive enough trigger molecules in conjunction with having met its inherent threshold in order to finalise its life cycle. This finetuning synchronisation strategy seems to be sufficiently robust but nevertheless, it is more prone to premature or late alert than a discretely operating n-ary counter which in contrast requires a large and complex reaction network [13]. In simulation studies, we empirically found out that annual variation of byproduct increase within a range of approx. $-2.80\% \ldots + 2.97\%$ can be tolerated by sinusoidal numerical integration keeping the point in time when the threshold is reached within the growth period of year 17 (Figure 4, right hand side). Furthermore, a numerical integrator in concert with a finetuning sensing mechanism for population-wide synchronisation is sufficient to toggle the life cycle between a variety of years by a low number of slight evolutionary changes. Having this feature at hand, it becomes plausible how a widespread range of life times could emerge where those forming prime numbers resist the evolutionary selection driven by predators.

Let us now formalise the speculative model using a blotting membrane system which is focused on alerting life cycle finalisation. Here, the categorised counting mechanism needs to distinguish the accumulated byproduct (A) on the one hand and the sensed trigger molecules (T) on the other. To this end, we employ two molecular labels A and T, respectively. The underlying grid is symbolised by a plan view into the soil (arbitrarily chosen: $0 \leq x \leq 8$ and $0 \leq y \leq 3$). A spatial cluster of byproducts A (maximum cluster inherent distance: 0.03) marks the position of a cicada larva. Within a local circular environment (maximal distance: 0.8), it detects trigger molecules. The system response comprises overall alerting on life cycle finalisation:

$$\boxed{\Pi} = (P, L, C, B_1, \ldots, B_{|C|}, S, R, \mathrm{r}) \quad \text{with}$$
$$L = \{A, T\}$$
$$P = \{(1.123, 1.992, A), (1.125, 2.001, A), \ldots, (4.338, 0.874, T)\}$$
$$C = \cup B_{(\overline{x}, \overline{y}, l)} \text{ with } l \in L$$
$$B_{(\overline{x}, \overline{y}, A)} = \{(x, y, A) \mid (x, y, A) \in P \wedge \forall (a, b, A) \in P : (x - a)^2 + (y - b)^2 \leq 0.03\}$$
$$\text{whereas}$$
$$\overline{x} = \frac{1}{|B_{(\overline{x}, \overline{y}, A)}|} \cdot \sum_{(x, y, l) \in B_{(\overline{x}, \overline{y}, A)}} x \quad \text{and} \quad \overline{y} = \frac{1}{|B_{(\overline{x}, \overline{y}, A)}|} \cdot \sum_{(x, y, l) \in B_{(\overline{x}, \overline{y}, A)}} y$$
$$B_{(\overline{x}, \overline{y}, T)} = \{(x, y, T) \mid (x, y, T) \in P \wedge (x - \overline{x})^2 + (y - \overline{y})^2 \leq 0.8\}$$
$$S(\overline{x}, \overline{y}, A) = |D| \text{ with}$$
$$D = \{B_{(\overline{x}, \overline{y}, A)} \mid |B_{(\overline{x}, \overline{y}, A)}| \geq \text{threshold}_A \wedge |B_{(\overline{x}, \overline{y}, T)}| \geq \text{threshold}_T\}$$
$$R = \mathbb{N}$$
$$\mathrm{r}(S) = |\text{supp}(S)|$$

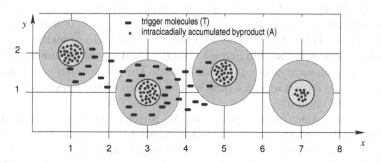

Fig. 5. Fictive cicada population given by a two-dimensional distribution of trigger molecules (T) released by three cicadas and individually accumulated byproduct (A). Central positions of cicadas were chosen randomly, molecules T and A also randomly placed within and around circular regions assigned to each cicada. Trigger molecules T reflect outcome of a potential quorum sensing process at a fixed point in time.

Figure 5 illustrates the formalism. P is composed of all dark dots, small ones and ellipsoidal ones. Small dots represent accumulated byproducts A arranged in four clusters while ellipsoidal dots exhibit trigger molecules T, all of them spatially distributed on a grid (soil). The classification identifies four byproduct categories corresponding to the clusters. They are named in accordance to their central coordinates: $B_{(1,2,A)}, B_{(3,1,A)}, B_{(5,1.5,A)}, B_{(7,1,A)}$. Each of them stands for a cicada larva surrounded by a circular environment which sensibilises for trigger molecules: $B_{(1,2,T)}, B_{(3,1,T)}, B_{(5,1.5,T)}, B_{(7,1,T)}$. For example, $B_{(7,1,T)} = \emptyset$ since there are no trigger molecules here. Let us require at least 20 byproduct molecules to form threshold$_A$ and at least 5 trigger molecules for threshold$_T$. Multiset S decides for each larva whether or not it exceeds both thresholds: $S = \{((1,2,A),1), ((3,1,A),1), ((5,1.5,A),0), ((7,1,A),0)\}$. The final response provides the number of larvae alerting finalisation of life cycle, here r$(S) = 2$.

4   Electrophoresis: A Molecular Bucket Sort

Electrophoresis subsumes a physical technique able to spatially separate electrically charged molecules by their weights [15]. Particularly, DNA (negatively charged) and many naturally originated proteins (twisted and folded chains of amino acids whose electrical charge is mainly determined by outer amino acid side chains) are beneficial candidates for widespread applications in molecular biology and chemical analysis [27].

Mostly, electrophoresis takes place within a special physical medium like a *gel* which carries and steers the molecules during the separation process. To do so, the gel is prepared in a way to be equipped with numerous *pores* forming woven channels or tunnels sufficiently sized to allow passage of charged sample molecules. For instance, *agarose* is commonly used to compose a gel suitable for electrophoresis of DNA. The fibre structure of agarose enables pores whose diameter usually varies between 150 and 500 nanometres while a DNA strand (in biologically prevalent B-DNA conformation) diametrally consumes merely 2 nanometres but its length can reach several hundred nanometres [9]. The ready-made gel, typically between 10 and 30 centimetres in length or width and up to 5 millimetres thick, is embedded in a gel *chamber* filled up with a buffer solution in order to adjust an appropriate pH environment. The gel chamber comes with two electrodes, a negative one and a positive one, placed at the opposite boundaries of the gel, see Figure 6.

Subsequently, the sample mixture of DNA strands to be separated is injected into the gel close to the negative electrode. Next, an electrical direct-current (DC) voltage, provided by an external power supply and mostly chosen between 80 and 120 volts, is applied to the electrodes. Driven by the electrical force, the negatively charged molecules begin to move towards the positive electrode along a lane through the pores of the gel. In order to mobilise, each molecule has to overcome its friction notable in both forms, with the gel on the one hand and inherently on the other. Interestingly, the resulting velocity of movement strongly depends on the mass (weight) of the individual molecules. Since small and light molecules induce low friction, they move faster than heavier exemplars. This distinction finally effects the resulting spatial separation according to the weights of the involved charged molecules. The process of electrophoresis is stopped by switching off the voltage shortly before the smallest molecules have reached the opposite end of the gel. For an easier visualisation of this process, the molecular mixture initially becomes enriched by a weakly binding dye whose velocity converges in compliance with the smallest sample molecules [27].

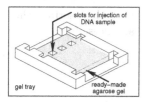 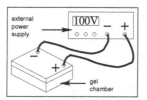 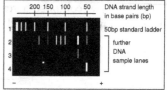

Fig. 6. Sketching technical instruments and outcome of agarose gel electrophoresis

In addition, the DNA sample molecules can be stained using a fluorescence marker like *ethidium bromide* [21]. This substance loosely binds to the hydrogen bonds of double-stranded DNA and persists there during the electrophoresis run. Ethidium bromide attached to DNA fluoresces under ultra violet (UV) light making the DNA visible inside the gel. Typically, the DNA after electrophoresis is arranged in so-called *bands* (sustained bar-shaped blots) along the underlying lane. Normally, these bands appear in light-grey up to white colours on a dark gel background. The colour intensities give a raw indication of the absolute number of molecules of almost the same mass accumulated within each band; see Figure 7, left hand side. To a first and mostly sufficient approximation, gel electrophoresis can be modelled by an obvious equation. The electrical force F_E needs to overcome the friction F_R. Movement of charged molecules starts up iff both forces are almost in parity to each other with slight (negligible) emphasis on F_E:

$$F_E \geq F_R, \text{ in good approximation } F_E = F_R$$

Now, we can resolve both forces by formulating their strength using a couple of dedicated parameters. The electrical force is defined as the product of the molecular electrical charge q with the electrical field E which in turn can be measurably expressed by the quotient of the voltage U and the distance h between the electrodes: $F_E = q \cdot E = q \cdot \frac{U}{h}$. In contrast, the friction in accordance with *Stokes' law* reads: $F_R = 6 \cdot \pi \cdot \eta \cdot r \cdot v$ assuming movement of a sphere where r denotes the radius, v symbolises its velocity, and η stands for the viscosity of the medium, mainly reflecting the average size of the pores. The velocity can be assumed to remain almost constant after a short acceleration phase in conjunction with switching on the electrical voltage. Putting everything together reveals:

$$v = \frac{q \cdot E}{6 \cdot \pi \cdot \eta \cdot r}$$

The only indeterminate parameter is the radius r of the anticipated sphere representing the moving charged molecule. In order to cope with that, we can imagine that the volume V_{molecule} of the charged molecule resembles the volume V_{sphere} of the anticipated sphere. Having this in mind, we can write $V_{\text{molecule}} = \frac{m}{\rho}$ with m denoting the mass (weight) of the molecule and ρ its density. Moreover, $V_{\text{sphere}} = \frac{4}{3} \cdot \pi \cdot r^3$. From that, we obtain:

$$r = \left(\frac{3}{4 \cdot \pi} \cdot \frac{m}{\rho} \right)^{\frac{1}{3}}$$

Let us now compose a resulting function $s : \mathbb{R}^2 \longrightarrow \mathbb{R}$ which describes the distance moved by a charged molecule with mass m after an elapsed time t:

$$s(m,t) = v \cdot t$$

$$= \frac{q \cdot E}{6 \cdot \pi \cdot \eta \left(\frac{3 \cdot m}{4 \cdot \pi \cdot \rho}\right)^{\frac{1}{3}}} \cdot t$$

$$= \underbrace{\frac{q}{6 \cdot \pi \cdot \left(\frac{3}{4 \cdot \pi \cdot \rho}\right)^{\frac{1}{3}}}}_{\text{taken as global parameter } G} \cdot \frac{E}{\eta} \cdot \frac{1}{m^{\frac{1}{3}}} \cdot t$$

$$= G \cdot \frac{E}{\eta} \cdot \frac{1}{m^{\frac{1}{3}}} \cdot t$$

For DNA agarose gel electrophoresis, the electrical field E frequently constitutes between $400 \frac{V}{m}$ and $500 \frac{V}{m}$ while the viscosity commonly differs from $0.001 \frac{kg}{m \cdot s}$ (consistency like water in large-pored gels) up to $0.02 \frac{kg}{m \cdot s}$ in small-meshed gels enhancing the friction along with producing heat. From empirical studies, we fitted a constant average value of approx. $6.794 \cdot 10^{-4} \frac{A \cdot s \cdot kg^{\frac{1}{3}}}{m}$ for G in agarose gel electrophoresis on double-stranded non-denaturing DNA. When employing the molecule mass m in kg along with elapsed time t in s and remembering that $1 VAs = 1 \frac{kg \cdot m^2}{s^3}$, the final value of the function is returned in metres.

By means of a complementary study, we face the mathematical model with corresponding experimental data captured within a blotting image. This study is dedicated to demonstrate that electrophoresis can be interpreted to execute a variant of *bucket sort* which ascendingly arranges the involved charged molecules by their masses. In concert with the notion of a blotting membrane system, we exploit the afore-derived function $s(m,t)$ for geometrical definition of the buckets, each of them representing a region on the gel assigned to a cluster. For the experiment, we utilise a predefined mixture of double-stranded DNA whose strand lengths reach from 100 base pairs (bp) up to 1000bp in steps of 100bp. Additionally, the sample contains strands with 1200bp and 1500bp. The whole sample acts as a so-called DNA ladder made from a cleaved plasmid (100bp standard ladder by New England BioLabs) composed of an almost uniform distribution of the nucleotides A, C, G, and T.

In order to disclose the relation between the mass of a DNA double strand and its length in base pairs, we need to consider the average mass of a nucleotide. Indeed, there are slight mass deviations between single nucleotides A (Adenine, $\approx 5.467 \cdot 10^{-25}$kg), C (Cytosine, $\approx 5.234 \cdot 10^{-25}$kg), G (Guanine, $\approx 5.732 \cdot 10^{-25}$kg), and T (Thymine, $\approx 5.301 \cdot 10^{-25}$kg). Each nucleotide mass comprises the chemical base together with its section of the sugar-phosphate backbone. On average, we obtain $\approx 5.4335 \cdot 10^{-25}$kg per nucleotide or $\approx 1.0867 \cdot 10^{-24}$kg per base pair. Marginal influences of dye and ethidium bromide are neglected.

The left hand side of Figure 7 depicts the agarose gel image under UV light making visible the individual DNA bands arranged within the lane after running

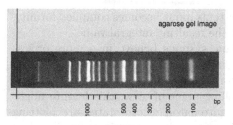 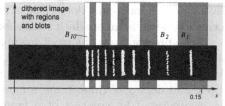

Fig. 7. Left: 100bp ladder with DNA bands visible in agarose gel. Bands at 500 and 1000bp emphasised by enhanced DNA concentration. **Right:** Dithered image taken from gel photo. Based on an underlying coordinate system in metre scale, altering background regions B_1 up to B_{10} define regions (buckets) in which the DNA molecules accumulate forming bands arranged as non-overlapping blots. DNA bands with more than 1000bp neglected in dithered image.

the electrophoresis for 2700 seconds (45 minutes). Each band corresponds to a predefined strand length. Using the gel image, a simple *dithering* (selectively applied to all bands between 100 and 1000 base pairs) generates a set of uniquely located dots from the bands; see right hand side of Figure 7. The dots are equipped with geometrical coordinates. At that stage, we have everything at hand to finally formulate the blotting membrane system from the experiment (running conditions $E = 400\frac{V}{m}, \eta = 0.001\frac{kg}{m \cdot s}$):

$$\boxed{\Pi} = (P, L, C, B_1, \dots, B_{|C|}, S, R, r) \quad \text{with}$$
$$L = \{l\}$$
$$P = \{(0.143, 0.082, l), (0.142, 0.077, l), \dots, (0.714, 0.079, l)\}$$
$$C = \{1, \dots, 10\}$$
$$B_i = \{(x, y, l) \mid (x, y, l) \in P \ \wedge$$
$$s\left((100 \cdot i - 50) \cdot 1.0867 \cdot 10^{-24}, 2700\right) \geq x \ \wedge$$
$$x \geq s\left((100 \cdot i + 50) \cdot 1.0867 \cdot 10^{-24}, 2700\right)\} \qquad \forall i \in C$$
$$S(c) = |B_c| \ \forall c \in C$$
$$R = \mathbb{N}^{|C|}$$
$$r(S) = (S(1), \dots, S(10))$$

5 Discussion and Conclusions

Along with a couple of case studies we demonstrated the descriptive practicability of blotting membrane systems. The main advantage of this formalism consists in its capability of tremendous data reduction. From a large number of geometrical dot coordinates together with some auxiliary data, a rather condensed systems output can be achieved retaining the crucial behaviour and characteristics of the system under study. For instance, in case of numerical integration, an amount of several million individual dots taken as systems input becomes compiled forming a single rational number which stands for the resulting integral value.

In its present form, blotting membrane systems behave in a more or less *static* manner. Currently, they lack any temporal or dynamical aspect [1,12,17]. A promising extension could take into account a possible *progression* of the blots, spots, and dots over time. From a modelling point of view, this feature might be incorporated by creation of a finite automaton whose states are blotting membrane systems. Using periodical trigger signals or by means of signalling events, a dedicated state transition from the previous system to its successor(s) could help to trace clusters together with their counts along a time line.

We believe that membrane computing as an innovative field of research sustainably benefits from a plethora of real-world applications making the underlying algebraic formalisms a powerful toolbox to cope with challenges in managing big data. Categorised counting can be seen as a technique of data mining which combines the possibility of massively parallel data processing promoted in membrane computing with the exploitation of statistical or deductive methods. Future studies will be intent upon strengthening this fruitful relationship.

References

1. Barbuti, R., Maggiolo-Schettini, A., Milazzo, P., Pardini, G., Tesei, L.: Spatial P Systems. Natural Computing **10**, 3–16 (2011)
2. Bernardini, F., Gheorghe, M., Krasnogor, N.: Quorum sensing P systems. Theoretical Computer Science **371**(1–2), 20–33 (2007)
3. Bowen, B., Steinberg, J., Laemmli, U.K., Weintraub, H.: The detection of DNA-binding proteins by protein blotting. Nucleic Acids Research **8**(1), 1–20 (1980)
4. Chalfie, M., Tu, Y., Euskirchen, G., Ward, W.W., Prasher, D.C.: Green fluorescent protein as a marker for gene expression. Science **263**(5148), 802–805 (1994)
5. Churchman, L.S., Ökten, Z., Rock, R.S., Dawson, J.F., Spudich, J.A.: Single molecule high-resolution colocalization of Cy3 and Cy5 attached to macromolecules measures intramolecular distances through time. PNAS **102**(5), 1419–1423 (2005)
6. Cohen, H., Lefebvre, C. (eds.): Handbook of Categorization in Cognitive Science. Elsevier (2005)
7. Dawson, T.E., Pate, J.S.: Seasonal water uptake and movement in root systems of plants of dimorphic root morphology: A stable isotope investigation. Oecologia **107**, 13–20 (1996)
8. Fayyad, U., Piatetsky-Shapiro, G., Smyth, P.: From Data Mining to Knowledge Discovery in Databases. American Assoc. for Artificial Intelligence **3**, 37–54 (1996)
9. Hames, D., Hooper, N.: Biochemistry, 3rd edn. Taylor & Francis (2005)
10. Han, J., Kamber, M., Pei, J.: Data Mining: Concepts and Techniques. Morgan Kaufmann (2011)
11. Hastie, T., Tibshirani, R., Friedman, J.: The Elements of Statistical Learning: Data Mining, Inference, and Prediction. Series in Statistics. Springer Verlag (2009)
12. Hinze, T., Fassler, R., Lenser, T., Dittrich, P.: Register Machine Computations on Binary Numbers by Oscillating and Catalytic Chemical Reactions Modelled using Mass-Action Kinetics. International Journal of Foundations of Computer Science **20**(3), 411–426 (2009)

13. Hinze, T., Schell, B., Schumann, M., Bodenstein, C.: Maintenance of Chronobiological Information by P System Mediated Assembly of Control Units for Oscillatory Waveforms and Frequency. In: Csuhaj-Varjú, E., Gheorghe, M., Rozenberg, G., Salomaa, A., Vaszil, Gy. (eds.) CMC 2012. LNCS, vol. 7762, pp. 208–227. Springer, Heidelberg (2013)

14. Hinze, T., Behre, J., Bodenstein, C., Escuela, G., Grünert, G., Hofstedt, P., Sauer, P., Hayat, S., Dittrich, P.: Membrane Systems and Tools Combining Dynamical Structures with Reaction Kinetics for Applications in Chronobiology. In: Frisco, P., Gheorghe, M., Perez-Jimenez, M.J. (eds.) Applications of Membrane Computing in Systems and Synthetic Biology. Series Emergence, Complexity, and Computation, vol. 7, pp. 133–173. Springer Verlag (2014)

15. Johannson, B.G.: Agarose Gel Electrophoresis. Scandinavian Journal of Clinical and Laboratory Investigation **29**(s124), 7–19 (1972)

16. Kremers, G.J., Gilbert, S.G., Cranfill, P.J., Davidson, M.W., Piston, D.W.: Fluorescent proteins at a glance. Journal of Cell Science **124**, 157–160 (2011)

17. Marchetti, L., Manca, V., Pagliarini, R., Bollig-Fischer, A.: MP Modelling for Systems Biology: Two Case Studies. In: Frisco, P., Gheorghe, M., Perez-Jimenez, M.J. (eds.) Applications of Membrane Computing in Systems and Synthetic Biology. Series Emergence, Complexity, and Computation, vol. 7, pp. 223–243. Springer Verlag (2014)

18. Marlatt, C.L.: The periodical cicada. Bull. U.S. Dept. Agri. Div. Entomol. Bull. **18**, 52 (1907)

19. Miller, M.B., Bassler, B.L.: Quorum Sensing in Bacteria. Annu. Rev. Microbiol. **55**, 165–199 (2001)

20. Păun, Gh.: Membrane Computing: An Introduction. Springer Verlag (2002)

21. Sabnis, R.W.: Handbook of biological dyes and stains: synthesis and industrial application. Wiley-VCH (2010)

22. Southern, E.M.: Detection of specific sequences among DNA fragments separated by gel electrophoresis. Journal of Molecular Biology **98**(3), 503–517 (1975)

23. Sparmann, A., van Lohuizen, M.: Polycomb silencers control cell fate, development and cancer. Nature Reviews Cancer **6**, 846–856 (2006)

24. Towbin, H., Staehelin, T., Gordon, J.: Electrophoretic transfer of proteins from polyacrylamide gels to nitrocellulose sheets: Procedure and some applications. PNAS **76**(9), 4350–4354 (1979)

25. Nüsslein-Volhard, C.: Determination of the embryonic axes of Drosophila. Development **113**, 1–10 (1991)

26. Lizotte-Waniewski, M., Tawe, W., Guiliano, D.B., Lu, W., Liu, J., Williams, S.A., Lustigman, S.: Identification of Potential Vaccine and Drug Target Candidates by Expressed Sequence Tag Analysis and Immunoscreening of Onchocerca volvulus Larval cDNA Libraries. Infection and Immunity **68**(6), 3491–3501 (2000)

27. Westermeier, R.: Electrophoresis in Practice. Wiley-VCH (2005)

28. Williams, K.S., Simon, C.: The ecology, behavior and evolution of periodical cicadas. Annual Review of Entomology **40**, 269–295 (1995)

Polymorphic P Systems with Non-cooperative Rules and No Ingredients

Sergiu Ivanov$^{(\boxtimes)}$

LACL, Université Paris Est – Créteil Val de Marne,
61, av. Général de Gaulle, 94010 Créteil, France
sergiu.ivanov@u-pec.fr

Abstract. Polymorphic P systems represent a variant of the bio-inspired computational model of P systems, in which the rules are not explicitly given in the description of the system, but are implicitly defined by the contents of certain membranes. In this paper we give a characterisation of the most basic class of such systems, in which only non-cooperative rules are allowed and no ingredients are included. We start by formulating two different formal definitions of non-cooperativity and then show that they have the same generative power. We also show that the generative power of polymorphic P systems is less than NRE and, finally, that the languages produced by such systems form a hierarchy related to the maximal allowed depth of the membrane structure.

1 Introduction

Membrane computing is a fast-growing research field opened by Gh. Păun in 1998. It presents a formal framework inspired from the structure and functioning of the living cells. In the paper [1], yet another relatively powerful extension to the model is defined, which allows the system to dynamically change its rules. The latter are thus not limited to some finite prescribed set of candidates. There were three main motives for this extension. Firstly, experience shows that "practical" problems need "more" computing potential than just computational completeness. Secondly, a very important computational ingredient was imported from computer science: the approach in which both the "program" and the "data" are represented in the same way. And finally, such an extension correlates with the biological idea that different actions are carried out by different objects which can, too, in their turn, be acted upon. The full motivation as well as references to related papers are given in the cited work [1].

In this paper we give a characterisation of the most basic class of polymorphic P systems, which only relies on non-cooperative rules and does not include any ingredients. We start by formulating two different formal definitions of non-cooperativity and then show that they have the same generative power. We also show that polymorphic P systems cannot generate all of NRE, and, finally, that the languages produced by such systems form a hierarchy related to the maximal allowed depth of the membrane structure.

© Springer International Publishing Switzerland 2014
M. Gheorghe et al. (Eds.): CMC 2014, LNCS 8961, pp. 258–273, 2014.
DOI: 10.1007/978-3-319-14370-5_16

The motivation for examining the class of polymorphic P systems with non-cooperative rules without any additional ingredients but polymorphism itself is twofold. On the one hand, this is the most restricted variant of polymorphic P systems, and so understanding its computing power is important for understanding the computing power of the general variant. On the other hand, polymorphic P systems without ingredients and with non-cooperative rules turn out to be more powerful than conventional transition P systems with non-cooperative rules, and the former may thus present interest from the practical viewpoint. In fact, polymorphism enables some otherwise very restricted models to generate rather "difficult" superexponential number languages. Given that an actual software implementation of polymorphic rules does not seem to require essentially more resources than that of invariant rules, restricted variants of polymorphic P systems may turn out useful in solving certain real-world problems. We would expect to find such applications in the domains in which massive parallelism is required, because non-cooperative rules which do not interact are intrinsically easy to parallelise.

2 Preliminaries

In this section we recall some of the basic notions of the formal language theory and membrane computing. For a more comprehensive overview of the mentioned topics we refer the reader to [2,3,7,8].

2.1 Finite Automata and Multisets

A (non-deterministic) *finite automaton* is the tuple

$$A = (Q, \Sigma, \delta, q_0, F),$$

where Q is a finite set of states, Σ is a finite set of input symbols, $\delta : Q \times \Sigma \to 2^Q$ is the transition function, q_0 is the initial state of the automaton and F is the set of final states. The automaton starts in the initial state q_0 and examines the input tape symbol by symbol. If it finds the symbol $a \in \Sigma$ in state $q_i \in Q$, it transitions in a non-deterministic way into one of the states from the set $\delta(q_i, a)$. If, at a certain step, the automaton is in state q_i and is reading a symbol a such that $\delta(q_i, a) = \varnothing$, it halts. The automaton A is said to *accept* (recognise) only those inputs for which it consumes the input entirely and halts in a final state.

We will refer to the families of sets which can be recognised by a finite automaton as *regular* families.

Let V be a finite set. A *finite multiset* w over V is a mapping $w : V \to \mathbb{N}$, which specifies the number of occurrences of each $a \in V$. The size of the multiset is defined as $|w| = \sum_{a \in V} w(a)$. A multiset w over V can be also represented by any string x such that it contains exactly $w(a)$ symbols a, for all $a \in V$. The *support* of w is the set of symbols which appear in it: $supp(w) = \{a \in V \mid w(a) > 0\}$.

2.2 Polymorphic P Systems

We will now define the notion of a polymorphic P system without ingredients. For the original definition we refer the reader to [1]. For a general introduction to P systems, the reader is referred to [4,6]. For a comprehensive overview of the domain, we recommend the handbook [7].

A *polymorphic P system* is defined as a tuple

$$\Pi = (O, T, \mu, w_s, w_{1L}, w_{1R}, \ldots, w_{mL}, w_{mR}, i_{out}),$$

where O is a finite alphabet and μ is a tree structure consisting of $2m + 1$ membranes, bijectively labelled by the elements of $H = \{s\} \cup \{iL, iR \mid 1 \leq i \leq m\}$. The label s is assigned to the skin membrane. We require that, for $1 \leq i \leq m$, $parent(iL) = parent(iR)$, where $parent(h)$ refers to the parent of the membrane h. Finally, the set $T \subseteq O$ describes the output objects, while $i_{out} \in H \cup \{0\}$ gives the output region, the symbol 0 standing for the environment.

The rules of a polymorphic P system are not explicitly given in its description. Essentially, such a system has m rules, and these rules change as the contents of the regions other than the skin change. Initially, for $1 \leq i \leq m$, the rule $i : w_{iL} \to w_{iR}$ belongs to the region defined by the parent membrane of iL and iR. If w_{iL} is empty, then the rule is considered *disabled*. For every step of the computation, each rule is defined in the same way, taking the current contents of iL and iR instead of the initial ones. We sometimes refer to the membranes iL and iR as to left-hand-side and right-hand-side membranes of the rule i, respectively.

For reasons of readability, we will often resort to *graphical presentation* of polymorphic P systems. In such figures, we will not draw the membranes corresponding to invariable rules, but will instead write the rules directly, as it is conventionally done for other P system models.

A polymorphic P system Π of degree $2m + 1$ is said to be *with strongly non-cooperative rules*, if, in any evolution, any of the membranes iL, $1 \leq i \leq m$, contains at most one symbol. A polymorphic P system Π of degree $2m + 1$ is said to be *with weakly non-cooperative rules*, if, in any evolution, all rules which are applied have exactly one symbol in the left-hand side.

Note that weak non-cooperativity allows left-hand sides of rules to contain more than one symbol and only requires that, whenever this happens, the rule be not applicable.

In our shorthand notation for classes of polymorphic P systems, we will write $ncoo_s$ and $ncoo_w$ to refer to the classes of polymorphic P systems with strongly and weakly non-cooperative rules respectively. We will also specify the number of membranes and whether disabling rules is allowed. Thus to refer to the family of polymorphic P systems with weakly non-cooperative rules, in which rule disabling is allowed, and which have at most k membranes, we will write the following expression:

$$OP_k(polym_{+d}(ncoo_w)).$$

If no bound on the number of membranes is specified, k is replaced by $*$ or is omitted. If disabling rules is not allowed, we write $-d$ in the subscript of *polym*.

For weakly non-cooperative polymorphic P systems, *not* allowing the disabling of rules would mean that all left-hand-side membranes are *not* empty at any step of the evolution. In the case of strong non-cooperativity, the same requirement would mean that no left-hand-side membrane iL contains an erasing rule (a rule of the form $a \to \lambda$).

We would like to remark that, due to the inherently dynamic nature of rules of a polymorphic P system, verifying whether the rules are weakly non-cooperative, or whether they can be disabled, are not straightforward tasks. Indeed, deciding if the rules are never disabled would mean checking if the languages generated in left-hand-side membranes contain the empty word. Proving weak non-cooperativity is even more complex: it would require showing that, whenever the contents of the left-hand-side membrane iL contain more than one symbol, this multiset is *not* a submultiset of the contents of the parent membrane of iL.

The *depth* of a polymorphic P system is defined as the height of the membrane structure μ seen as a tree. Thus, a polymorphic P system which has no rules has depth 1, a polymorphic P systems which has invariable rules is of depth 2, etc. To refer to a class of polymorphic P system of depth limited to d, we add the number d as a superscript to the notation we have introduced above:

$$OP_k^d(polym_{+d}(ncoo_w)).$$

A polymorphic P system is called *left-polymorphic* if only left-hand sides of the rules are allowed to vary. A polymorphic P system is called *right-polymorphic* if only right-hand sides of the rules are allowed to vary.

In the notation we have introduced in the previous paragraphs, we will use the symbols *lpolym* and *rpolym* to refer to the classes of left- and right-polymorphic P systems respectively.

Note that the effective implication of the definition of left-polymorphic P systems is that no right-hand side is allowed to contain any rules. The symmetric statement is true for right-polymorphic P systems.

3   Strong and Weak Non-cooperativity

In this section we are going to show that the notions of strong and weak non-cooperativity are equivalent in terms of generative power when no ingredients but disabling of rules are allowed.

We start by defining an instrument for analysing the evolution of a membrane in a (polymorphic) P system. Let O be a set of objects and $\bar{O} = \{\bar{a} \mid a \in O\}$. We abuse the symbol *supp* to define the mapping $supp : O \cup \bar{O} \to O$ in the following way: $supp(A) = \{a \mid a \in A \text{ or } \bar{a} \in A\}$. We also define the following *flattening* function $flt : (O \cup \bar{O})^* \to O \cup \bar{O}$:

$$flt(w) = \{\bar{a} \mid w(\bar{a}) \geq 0\} \cup \{a \mid w(a) \geq 0\} \cup \{a \mid w(\bar{a}) \geq 1\}.$$

We say that a multiset $w \in O$ *satisfies* a set $A \subseteq O \cup \bar{O}$ if $supp(w) = supp(A)$ and the following conditions hold:

$$a \in A \text{ and } \bar{a} \notin A \implies w(a) > 0,$$
$$a \notin A \text{ and } \bar{a} \in A \implies w(a) = 1,$$
$$a \in A \text{ and } \bar{a} \in A \implies w(a) > 1.$$

Consider a (polymorphic) P system with objects from O and pick a membrane h of it. We will refer to a family of sequences of sets $\mathcal{A} = \{A = (A_j)_{1 \leq j \leq m} \mid A_j \subseteq O \cup \bar{O}, m \in \mathbb{N}\}$ as to the *representation of evolution of h over $O \cup \bar{O}$* if the following conditions hold:

1. for any possible evolution $W = (w_j)_{1 \leq j \leq m}$ of the contents of h there exists a subfamily $\mathcal{A}_W \subseteq \mathcal{A}$ of sequences of length m such that, for any j, w_j satisfies $\bigcup_{A \in \mathcal{A}} A_j$, and

2. for any sequence $(A_j)_{1 \leq j \leq m} \in \mathcal{A}$, there exists an evolution $(w_j)_{1 \leq j \leq m}$ such that w_j satisfies A_j, for any $1 \leq j \leq m$.

When a membrane h admits a such a representation over $O \cup \bar{O}$ in which all sequences are regular, we will say that h is *REG-representable*.

The following lemma captures an important property of polymorphic P systems with regard to *REG-representability*.

Lemma 1. *Consider a polymorphic P system Π, pick a membrane h of it and consider the sets $L = \{jL \mid parent(jL) = h\}$ and $R = \{jR \mid parent(jR) = h\}$. If no membrane in L ever contains more than one symbol, the sequences of contents of all membranes in L are regular, and all membranes in R are REG-representable, then h is REG-representable.*

Proof. Because all right-hand sides in h are *REG*-representable, any (variable) rule j in h admits in its own turn a representation as a family of rules whose left-hand sides follow exactly the same evolution as the left-hand side of j, and whose right-hand sides come from the families of sequences of sets over $O \cup \bar{O}$ which represent the evolution of the right-hand side of rule j. We define the sequence $(R_j)_{1 \leq j \leq m}$ of *representations* of rules available in h as follows:

$$R_j = \{a \to U, \bar{a} \to U \mid a \in O, U \subseteq O \cup \bar{O}, a \to U \text{ represents a rule at step } j\}.$$

Suppose that w_0 is the initial contents of h and let

$$A_0 = \{\bar{a} \mid w(a) = 1\} \cup \{a\bar{a} \mid w(a) > 1\}.$$

We will now construct a family $\mathcal{A}$ of sequences over $O \cup \bar{O}$. The first element of each sequence $A = (A_j)_{1 \leq j \leq m}$ in $\mathcal{A}$ is A_0, while the element A_{j+1} is obtained from A_j by considering A_j as a multiset, non-deterministically applying the rules from R_j in a maximally parallel way, and then applying flt to the resulting multiset.

We claim that the family $\mathcal{A}$ is a regular representation of the evolution of h over $O \cup \bar{O}$. First off, the fact that all sequences in $\mathcal{A}$ are regular follows from the way this family is constructed. Next, the subfamily $\mathcal{A}_W$ for a fixed evolution W of h can be found by considering those sequences in which the rules applied at step j represent some of the rules applied in h at the same step. Indeed, suppose that condition (1) of representation holds for $\mathcal{A}$ up to the j-th step. Then, if rule r is applied at step j in h, $\mathcal{A}$ includes the sequences in which representations of r are applied. From the way we picked the sequences for $\mathcal{A}_W$ and how R_j is defined, it follows that the contents of h at step $j + 1$ will satisfy the union of $(j + 1)$-th elements of sequences in $\mathcal{A}_W$ as well. This implies that condition (1) of representation holds for $\mathcal{A}$.

Finally the evolution $(w_j)_{1 \leq j \leq m}$ of h corresponding, in the sense of condition (2), to a sequence $A = (A_j)_{1 \leq j \leq m} \in \mathcal{A}$, can be constructed in the following way. Whenever a representation $\bar{a} \to U$ of a rule $a \to u$ is applied to A_j, the rule $a \to u$ should be applied to an instance of a in w_j. If a representation $a \to Z$ of rule $a \to z$ is applied to A_j, the rule $a \to z$ should be applied to all the *remaining* instances of a in w_j.

The previous lemma can be immediately applied to draw the following important conclusion about the way in which the membranes in polymorphic P systems behave.

Theorem 1. *In a polymorphic P system Π with non-cooperative rules and no ingredients, every membrane is REG-representable.*

Proof. Invariable membranes are trivially REG-representable, while to show this property for the other membranes it suffices to inductively apply the statement of Lemma 1 starting with innermost membranes and going outwards.

The applicability of REG-representability in the context of polymorphic P systems is made clear by the following statement.

Lemma 2. *Consider a polymorphic P system Π and a weakly non-cooperative left-hand-side membrane iL of it. If iL is REG-representable, then it can be replaced with a strongly non-cooperative membrane iL' with invariable rules such that, in any computation, the evolution of the remaining membranes stays the same.*

Proof. Consider a left-hand-side membrane iL of Π and suppose that, at certain evolution steps, iL may contain more than one symbol. Consider a computation C of Π and two configurations C_k and C_m, $k < m$, such that in C_k the membrane iL contains the multiset x, in C_m it contains y or λ, while in all configurations C_j, $k < j < m$, iL contains more than one symbol. Since rule i is weakly *non-cooperative*, it is not applicable in any of these "intermediate" configurations. Therefore, we are interested in the *number* of steps during which the membrane iL may contain more than one symbol, rather than in the exact contents of iL during these steps.

Suppose iL contains the multiset y in C_m. According to our supposition, there exists a regular representation $\mathcal{A}$ of iL over $O \cup \bar{O}$. It follows from the definition of representation that $\mathcal{A}$ contains sequences whose k-th element is $\{\bar{x}\}$ and whose m-th element is $\{\bar{y}\}$ (condition (1)). Moreover, for *any* sequence $A \in \mathcal{A}$ whose k-th element is $\{\bar{x}\}$ and m-th element is $\{\bar{y}\}$, there exists an evolution of iL in which it contains the multiset x at the k-th step and y at the m-th step. This means that analysing the sequences from $\mathcal{A}$ suffices to generate the numbers of steps $m - k$. But, according to our supposition, $\mathcal{A}$ contains regular sequences only, so the distances in numbers of steps between configurations in which iL contains only one symbol form a regular set of numbers, too.

We can now construct the new membrane iL' in the following way. Consider the finite automaton recognising the sequences in $\mathcal{A}$ and replace the states corresponding to the situations in which the automaton has recognised a singleton $\{\bar{x}\}$ with the symbol x. Then, for each transition from state p to state q of the resulting automaton, add a rule $p \to q$ to iL'. Supposing that the set of states of the original automaton and the set of objects O are disjoint, the new membrane iL' accurately simulates the behaviour of the membrane iL.

The statements of Theorem 1 and Lemma 2 allow us to prove the desired result about the relationship between strongly and weakly non-cooperative rules.

Theorem 2. $NOP_*(polym_{+d}(ncoo_w)) = NOP_*(polym_{+d}(ncoo_s))$.

Proof. This statement is true because all weakly non-cooperative left-hand-side membranes can be successively replaced with strongly non-cooperative ones. Indeed, we know that all membranes of a polymorphic P system Π are *REG*-representable (Theorem 1), therefore all left-hand-side membranes are *REG*-representable. On the other hand, all *REG*-representable left-hand-side membranes can be replaced with strongly non-cooperative membranes with invariable rules (Lemma 2). Bringing these two observations together implies the statement of the theorem.

The proof of the previous theorem allows us to further conclude that having too deep left-hand-side membranes adds no power.

Corollary 1. *Given a polymorphic P system* $\Pi \in OP_*(polym_{+d}(ncoo))$, *it is possible to construct another polymorphic P system* Π' *such that* $N(\Pi') = N(\Pi)$ *and all left-hand-side membranes of* Π' *contain invariable rules.*

The practical implication of this corollary is that, in the case of polymorphic P systems with non-cooperative rules and no additional ingredients, the variability of left-hand sides of rules is only useful for slightly changing the scope of a rule and switching rules on and off.

We conclude this section by showing that, in the case of non-cooperative rules, explicitly disabling a rule by emptying its left-hand-side membrane can be simulated by replacing the empty multiset with a special symbol not belonging to the original alphabet.

Proposition 1. $NOP_*(polym_{-d}(ncoo)) = NOP_*(polym_{+d}(ncoo))$.

Proof. Take a polymorphic P system $\Pi \in OP_*(polym_{+d}(ncoo))$ and pick a left-hand-side membrane iL which becomes empty at a certain step of the computation. According to Corollary 1, we can consider that all the rules in iL are invariable, without losing generality. Now replace all the empty right-hand sides of rules in iL with the singleton multiset $\perp_{iL}$, where $\perp_{iL}$ does not belong to the alphabet of Π. Clearly, whenever $\perp_{iL}$ appears in iL, the rule i is effectively disabled and is blocked in this state forever. On the other hand, we avoid emptying the membrane iL, which proves the statement of the theorem.

Because it turns out that disabling of rules makes no real difference in terms of the number languages a (left-) polymorphic P system with non-cooperative rules can generate, we will sometimes avoid adding "$+d$" ("$-d$") to the shorthand notation for classes of polymorphic P systems with non-cooperative rules.

4   Left Polymorphism

In this section we will overview the computational power of left-polymorphic P systems. Remember that, in such P systems, the right-hand side of any rule is not allowed to embed any other rules. We start by showing that such polymorphic P systems are still more powerful than conventional transition P systems [7].

Proposition 2. $L_{2^n} = \{2^n \mid n \in \mathbb{N}\} \in NOP_*(lpolym(ncoo))$.

Proof. We construct the following left-polymorphic P system generating the number language L_{2^n}:

$$\Pi = (\{a\}, \{a\}, \mu, a, aa, a, a, a, \lambda, s), \text{ where}$$
$$\mu = [\,[\,[\,]_{2L}[\,]_{2R}[\,]_{3L}[\,]_{3R}]_{1L}[\,]_{1R}]_s.$$

The graphical representation of this P system is given in Figure 1.

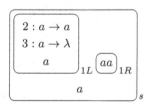

Fig. 1. A left-polymorphic P system generating $\{2^n \mid n \in \mathbb{N}\}$

Π works by repeatedly doubling the number of a's in the skin membrane, until the symbol a in $1L$ is rewritten into the empty multiset, which disables rule 1 and makes Π halt.

On the other hand, the following observation shows that left-polymorphic P systems cannot generate all recursively enumerable sets of numbers.

Proposition 3. $L_{n!} = \{n! \mid n \in \mathbb{N}\} \notin NOP_*(lpolym_{+d}(ncoo))$.

Proof. We will pick a left-polymorphic P system $\Pi \in NOP_*(lpolym(ncoo))$ and see what are the possible multiplicities of symbols in some of the multisets it generates. There exist derivations in which no more than one type of rule is applied per symbol type (e.g., only the rule $a \to bc$ is applied 5 times to all the 5 instances of a, even though there may be more rules consuming the same symbol). For such derivations, the multiplicities of all symbols in the halting configuration can be expressed as sums of products of the quantities of certain symbols in the initial contents of the skin by constant factors, which depend only on the (invariable) right-hand sides of the rules. Since generating the factorial would require multiplication by an *unbounded* set of factors, the preceding observation concludes the proof.

5   Right Polymorphism

In this section we will show that right-polymorphic P systems, just as their left-polymorphic counterparts, generate a wider class of languages than conventional transition P systems.

Proposition 4. $L'_{2^n} = \{2^n \mid n \in \mathbb{N}, n > 2\} \in NOP_*(rpolym(ncoo))$.

Proof. We will construct the following right-polymorphic P system generating the number language L'_{2^n}:

$$\Pi = (\{a, b\}, \{b\}, \mu, a, a, aa, a, a, a, a, a, b, s), \text{ where}$$
$$\mu = [\,[\,]_{1L}[\,[\,]_{2L}[\,[\,]_{3L}[\,]_{3R}[\,]_{4L}[\,]_{4R}]_{2R}]_{1R}]_s.$$

The graphical representation of this P system is given in Figure 2.

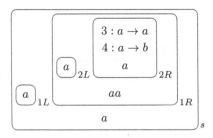

Fig. 2. A right-polymorphic P system generating $\{2^n \mid n \in \mathbb{N}, n > 2\}$

The principle behind the functioning of this polymorphic P system is essentially the same as the one used in the proof of Proposition 2: Π works by repeatedly doubling the number of a's in the skin. Having Π halt correctly is trickier, though, since we cannot disable rules and we cannot just rewrite the symbols in $1R$ to b, because then we could get rule 1 to have the form $a \to ab$, which would result in the production of the language $\{m \cdot 2^n \mid m, n \in \mathbb{N}\}$ (maybe without several shortest words) instead of L'_{2^n}. To work around this problem we allow *no choice* in membrane $1R$, that is, all instances of a are *always* rewritten into something, and it is the right-hand side of rule 2 that decides whether to reproduce the two instances of a and keep the exponentiation going, or transform them into b and stop the evolution. During the time b's take to propagate through the membrane structure, Π keeps multiplying the number in the skin by 2, which results in the fact that Π cannot generate the numbers 2 and 2^2 from $L_{2^n} \setminus L'_{2^n}$.

In the next section we will see that general polymorphic P systems (and thus right-polymorphic variants) cannot generate all number languages.

6   General Polymorphism

In this section we will show that there are languages which cannot be generated by polymorphic P systems with non-cooperative rules. The intuition for this observation comes from the fact that non-cooperative rules cannot *synchronise* separate processes running in the P system. Therefore, it suffices to pick a language which cannot be generated without such synchronisation. The following theorem formally captures this intuition.

Theorem 3. $L_{n!} = \{n! \mid n \in \mathbb{N}\} \notin NOP_*(polym(ncoo))$.

Proof. Suppose by contradiction that there exists a polymorphic P system $\Pi \in OP_*(polym(ncoo))$ over the set of objects O, which generates the factorial language. We will call those symbols which appear in the skin and whose descendants end up in the halting configuration of the skin *skin-useful*. A symbol a appearing in a right-hand-side membrane iR of the skin which becomes skin-useful after i is applied, or a symbol which can produce such a's, will be called *iR-useful*.

Remark first of all, that the skin must contain a rule with a variable right-hand side, which is applied an unbounded number of times. Indeed, if this were not the case, the polymorphic P system, just like a conventional transition P system, could not generate but a finite set of numbers.

According to Proposition 3, the skin of Π must include a rule with a variable right-hand-side membrane iR which may contain an unbounded number of iR-useful symbols. Nevertheless we may assume that the number of "growing" rules applied at each step, i.e. which consume a iR-useful symbol and produce more than one iR-useful symbol, should be bounded. Indeed, suppose that, for all right-hand-side membranes in the skin which may contain an unbounded number of such useful symbols, there exists derivations in which the number of growing rules applied at one step is unbounded. Remark now that, in a right-hand-side membrane iR, iR-useful symbols can be rewritten to useless symbols (or erased) in one of the following ways:

1. at some steps, for every iR-useful symbol a there exists a rule which rewrites it to some other iR-useful symbols, and another rule which rewrites it to useless symbols;
2. initially, all rules rewrite a to iR-useful symbols, but one of these rules r may later on change to rewriting a to useless symbols.

In both cases, rewriting an iR-useful a to useless symbols can be deferred however much desired, either by avoiding to apply the rules rewriting a to useless symbols, or by putting off the transformation of r to a rule rewriting a to useless symbols. We can therefore conclude that, in any case, the number of iR-useful symbols in a right-hand side can increase however much necessary. But then, the fact that the number of growing rules applied at a step in each right-hand-side membrane iR is unbounded means that there exist derivations in which the number of iR-useful symbols in iR grows exponentially. Given that the number of rules in the skin is fixed and finite, there exists such derivation $\mathcal{C}$ and a step number $j_0 \in \mathbb{N}$ after which, in $\mathcal{C}$, the total number of iR-useful symbols in the skin will increase by a non-contiguous series of factors, and thus Π will generate a number which does not belong to $L_{n!}$.

Since iR must be able to contain an unbounded number of iR-useful symbols, but the number of rules applied in iR at each step of the evolution should stay bounded, this membrane must always contain *two* groups of symbols: one of bounded size and the other one allowed to include an unbounded number of iR-useful symbols, with the property that the latter group is furnished by rules consuming symbols of the former group. But then, to properly halt, Π would need to have iR *both* rewrite its iR-useful symbols from the second group to useless symbols and stop the symbols of the first group from producing new useful symbols. However, since only non-cooperative rules are allowed in Π, it is always possible to inactivate the symbols of the first group *without* rewriting the useful symbols to useless ones, thus making the rule i multiply the quantities of some symbols in the skin by a constant factor, instead of a sequence of factors. We can therefore infer that, contrary to our initial hypothesis, Π cannot generate the factorial language, which concludes the proof.

The following statement concerning the computational power of *right-polymorphic* P systems is a direct consequence of the previous theorem.

Corollary 2. $L_{n!} = \{n! \mid n \in \mathbb{N}\} \notin NOP_*(rpolym(ncoo))$.

7   A Hierarchy of Polymorphic P Systems with Non-cooperative Rules

In this section we will show that the generative power of a polymorphic P system Π is essentially limited by its depth. The intuition for this remark comes from looking at the superexponentially growing P systems shown in [1] and from the observation that more nested rules means faster growth.

We briefly recall how superexponential growth can be achieved with polymorphic P systems.

Example 1. (cf. [1]) Consider the following (left-)polymorphic P system:

$$\Pi = (\{a\}, \{a\}, \mu, a, a, a, a, a, aa, s), \text{ where}$$
$$\mu = [\,[\,]_{1L}[\,[\,]_{2L}[\,]_{2R}]_{1R}]_s.$$

The graphical presentation of Π is given in Figure 3.

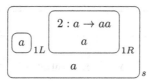

Fig. 3. A (left-)polymorphic P system with superexponential growth

After one step of evolution, the skin of Π will still contain the multiset a, and $1R$ will contain a^2. At the next step the skin will contain a^4 and $1R$ will contain a^4. It is easy to verify that, after k evolution steps, the skin of Π will contain $2^{\frac{k(k-1)}{2}}$ instances of a.

While the polymorphic P system from the previous paragraph does have superexponential growth, it never halts. Actually *generating* a superexponential number language requires somewhat more design effort. A possible approach using the technique we have shown in the proof of Proposition 4 is implemented in the following example.

Example 2. The following P system generates the superexponential number language $\{2^{\frac{n(n-1)}{2}} \mid n \in \mathbb{N}, n > 3\}$.

$$\Pi = (\{a, b\}, \{b\}, \mu, a, a, a, a, a, aa, a, a, a, a, a, b, s), \text{ where}$$
$$\mu = [\,[\,]_{1L}[\,[\,]_{2L}[\,[\,]_{3L}[\,[\,]_{4L}[\,]_{4R}]_{5L}[\,]_{5R}]_{3R}]_{2R}]_{1R}]_s.$$

The graphical representation of this P system is given in Figure 4.

Rules 1 and 2 of Π work exactly as the two rules of the P system shown in the previous example, while the other three rules are used to assure proper halting in the same way as it is done in the construction from Proposition 4.

By further nesting rule 2 of the previous example, one can easily see how a polymorphic P system of depth d can generate the language

$$L_d = \left\{2^{\frac{n \cdot (n-1) \cdot \ldots \cdot (n-(d-2)+1)}{1 \cdot 2 \cdot \ldots \cdot (d-2)}} \,\middle|\, n \in \mathbb{N}, n > d-1\right\} = \left\{2^{\binom{n}{d-2}} \,\middle|\, n \in \mathbb{N}, n > d-1\right\}.$$

It turns out that L_d is also essentially the hardest language a polymorphic P system of depth d can generate.

Theorem 4. $L_{d+1} = \left\{2^{\binom{n}{d-1}} \,\middle|\, n \in \mathbb{N}, n > d\right\} \notin NOP_*^d(polym(ncoo)), d > 1.$

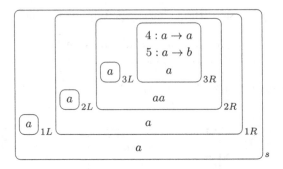

Fig. 4. A polymorphic P system generating $\{2^{\frac{n(n-1)}{2}} \mid n \in \mathbb{N}, n > 3\}$

Proof. For $d = 2$, the statement follows from the fact that transition P systems with invariable rules cannot generate non-semilinear languages [7].

Consider a polymorphic P system Π of depth d, a right-hand-side membrane iR, and the sequences of words that may appear in iR during an evolution of Π. Remark now that the speed at which the size of such words may grow depends directly on the depth of iR seen as a polymorphic P system (cf. Example 1). Thus the contents of iR cannot grow at a faster rate than $Ic^{p(n)}$, where I is the initial number of objects in the system, $c \in \mathbb{N}$ is the maximal size of a right-hand side of an invariable rule in Π, and $p(n)$ is a polynomial in n of degree $d - 2$, where $d - 1$ is the depth of membrane iR [1].

Suppose for the sake of contradiction that there exists a P system Π of depth d that generates L_{d+1} and focus on the ways in which Π could generate this language. We adopt the terminology from the proof of Theorem 3 and call the symbols whose descendants end up in the skin membrane in the halting configuration skin-useful. To produce an infinite language, Π should employ growing rules: rules which consume a skin-useful symbol and produce more than one skin-useful symbol. If the number of growing rules applied at each step is bounded, then the size of the contents of the skin at step j can be expressed as a finite sum of products of the form $If_1 \cdot \ldots \cdot f_{j-1}$, where f_k, $1 \leq j \leq j - 1$, is a factor given by the right-hand side of a rule available in the skin at step k, and c is the quantity of a symbol in the initial configuration of the skin. But then, the languages Π could generate are bounded from above by $kIc^{p(n)}$, where the constant k is the maximal number of growing rules which can be applied in the skin at a step, while $Ic^{p(n)}$ is the upper bound on the growth of all right-hand-side membranes. However, since $p(n)$ is a polynomial of degree $d - 1$, this means that Π cannot generate L_d.

Suppose now that the number of growing rules applied at each step of Π is unbounded; this also means that the number of useful symbols in the skin is unbounded. Consider the possible ways for Π to achieve halting:

1. the symbols in the skin are allowed to choose between the rules which lead to halting in a bounded number of steps and the rules which lead to further growth,
2. the rules are changed in such a way that the symbols added to the skin halt in a bounded number of steps.

If Π halts by the first scenario, we may consider a configuration in which the skin contains at least three skin-useful symbols which choose between continuing the growth or halting. Since these symbols appear in the same configuration, we may assume that, if more than one of them chooses to grow or halt, then they evolve in exactly the same way. Pick three derivations in which only one of these symbols chooses to halt, two of them choose to halt, and all three of them do. Then, the three numbers produced by Π will have the form n, $n+c$, and $n+2c$, and therefore $N(\Pi) \setminus L_{d+1} \neq \varnothing$.

Consequently, Π should halt by the second scenario. If the growing rules in the skin can produce useful symbols after their right-hand sides stop growing, then the number of useful symbols in the skin can be eventually multiplied by a constant factor, which means that Π will not generate L_{d+1}. Therefore, it should be that iR-useful symbols in any right-hand-side membrane iR are rewritten to useless symbols. The iR-useful symbols must not be allowed to choose between rules. Indeed, in that case there would exist derivations in which all iR-useful symbols but a bounded number of them choose to be rewritten to useless symbols, rule i would not achieve its maximal growing rate, and Π would not generate L_{d+1}. But then, the only way to rewrite iR-useful symbols to useless symbols would be, again, to modify the right-hand sides of the growing rules in iR.

By iteratively repeating this argument (and going deeper into the nested right-hand-side membranes), we conclude that, while the growth of the contents of the skin membrane of Π is bounded by $Ic^{q(n)}$, with $q(n)$ a polynomial of degree $d-1$, Π would need *one more* level of nesting in its deepest right-hand-side membrane to be able to halt and actually produce a language of the form $\{Ic^{q(n)} \mid n \in \mathbb{N}\}$. Therefore, no polymorphic P system of depth d can produce the language L_{d+1}.

The previous theorem provides the language L_{d+1} which separates the classes of number languages generated by polymorphic P systems of depth d and $d+1$. Combined with the obvious inclusion between of the former class into the latter, this observation yields the following conclusion.

Corollary 3. $NOP_*^d(polym(ncoo)) \subsetneq NOP_*^{d+1}(polym(ncoo))$.

Theorem 4 also gives the relationship between *left*-polymorphic and general polymorphic P systems. Indeed, Corollary 1 effectively states that the depth of any left-polymorphic P system is at most 3, and therefore the following assertion is true.

Corollary 4. $NOP_*(lpolym(ncoo)) \subsetneq NOP_*(polym(ncoo))$.

Establishing whether a similar inclusion is true for *right*-polymorphic P systems is an open problem.

8   Conclusion and Further Discussion

In this paper we have explored some of the fundamental properties of the most basic class of polymorphic P systems introduced in [1]: polymorphic P systems with non-cooperative rules and without any additional ingredients. We presented new special cases of such P systems (left- and right-polymorphic variants) and characterised the generative power of each of them, as well as of general polymorphic P systems. We have concluded the paper by bringing to light an *infinite* hierarchy of classes of polymorphic P systems with the base case being the usual non-polymorphic transition P systems.

The central conclusion of the paper is that, despite the apparent simplicity and restrictiveness of the definition, polymorphic P systems with non-cooperative rules and no additional ingredients are a very interesting object of study. We now directly proceed to formulating the questions which have been left unanswered in the paper.

The first question is concerned with the right-polymorphic variant of P systems. Just by looking at the definitions of left- and right-polymorphic P systems, it might seem that the generative power of both of them is strictly inferior to that of the most general version, and this is indeed the case for the left-polymorphic variant. The situation is different in the case of right-polymorphic P systems though. Indeed, various arguments detailed in the paper, and in particular the proof of Theorem 4, seem to imply that the actual power of polymorphism comes with varying right-hand-side membranes. Confirming or disproving the supposition that right-polymorphic P systems are as powerful as the general variant is a matter of further research.

A further question concerns actual upper bounds on the power of different variants of polymorphic P systems. While we showed that certain languages cannot be generated, showing inclusion into one of the known families of languages would be an interesting problem to attack.

Finally, we remind that we have only considered *the most restricted* version of polymorphic P systems in this paper. While adding ingredients to the model and/or allowing cooperative rules quickly renders the systems computationally complete [1] and thus (probably) less interesting for strictly theoretical research, applications of such models may present some interest. The fundamental feature of polymorphic P systems is that, in a way, they lie in between conventional models with static membrane structures, which require substantial design effort to attack practical problems, and the models with dynamic membrane structures, which often rely on *duplicating* computing units on the fly, together with their data [5]. This position, which we believe to be quite advantageous, may make polymorphic P systems a practical tool for solving certain real-world problems.

Acknowledgements. Sergiu Ivanov gratefully acknowledges Artiom Alhazov for fruitful discussions and valuable comments.

References

1. Alhazov, A., Ivanov, S., Rogozhin, Yu.: Polymorphic P systems. In: Gheorghe, M., Hinze, T., Păun, Gh., Rozenberg, G., Salomaa, A. (eds.) CMC 2010. LNCS, vol. 6501, pp. 81–94. Springer, Heidelberg (2010)
2. Freund, R., Verlan, S.: A formal framework for static (tissue) P systems. In: Eleftherakis, G., Kefalas, P., Păun, Gh., Rozenberg, G., Salomaa, A. (eds.) WMC 2007. LNCS, vol. 4860, pp. 271–284. Springer, Heidelberg (2007)
3. Hopcroft, J.E., Motwani, R., Ullman, J.D.: Introduction to automata theory, languages, and computation - international edition, 2nd edn. Addison-Wesley (2003)
4. Păun, Gh.: Membrane Computing: An Introduction, Natural Computing Series Natural Computing. Springer (2002)
5. Porreca, A.E., Leporati, A., Mauri, G., Zandron, C.: P systems with active membranes. Trading Time for Space 10(1), 167–182 (2011)
6. Păun, Gh.: Computing with membranes. Journal of Computer and System Sciences 61, 108–143 (1998)
7. Păun, Gh., Rozenberg, G., Salomaa, A.: The Oxford Handbook of Membrane Computing. Oxford University Press Inc, New York (2010)
8. Rozenberg, G., Salomaa, A. (eds.): Handbook of Formal Languages: Beyond Words, vol. 3. Springer-Verlag New York Inc, New York (1997)

Spiking Neural P Systems with Astrocytes Using the Rules in the Exhaustive Mode

Yuan Kong[1](✉) and Dongming Zhao[2](✉)

[1] Key Laboratory of Image Processing and Intelligent Control, School of Automation, Huazhong University of Science and Technology, Wuhan 430074, Hubei, China
kongyuan1122@126.com
[2] School of Automation, Wuhan University of Technology, Wuhan 430070, Hubei, China
dmzhao@whut.edu.cn

Abstract. Spiking neural P systems (SN P systems, for short) are a class of distributed parallel computing devices inspired by the way neurons communicate by means of electrical impulses or spikes. SN P systems with astrocytes are a new variant of SN P systems, where astrocytes are introduced to control the amount of spikes passing along synapses. In this work, we investigate the computation power of SN P systems with astrocytes with the rules in any neuron used in the exhaustive manner, that is, the enabled rule in any neuron should be used as many times as possible at any moment. Specifically, it is obtained that such SN P systems can compute/generate any set of Turing computable natural numbers.

Keywords: Membrane computing · Spiking neural P system · Astrocyte

1 Introduction

Spiking neural P systems (shortly named SN P systems) were introduced in [3] and investigated in [5,11,14], aiming to incorporate specific ideas from spiking neurons into membrane computing.

Generally, an SN P system can be represented as a directed graph, where neurons are placed in the nodes and arcs represent the synapses connecting neruons. Each neuron can contain a number of spikes and a set of spiking (also called firing) rules. With the application of the rules, a neuron can send information to other neurons in the form of spikes. One of the neurons is specified as output neuron, whose spikes are also sent to the environment. The result of a computation is associated with the number of steps between the first two spikes sent out by the output neuron to the environment.

In previous works, SN P systems have been proved to be powerful computing models. SN P systems were proved to be Turing universal as natural number acceptors and generators [3], that is, they can compute any set of Turing computable natural numbers. SN P systems were also investigated as language acceptors and generators [1,2], and as recursive function computing devices [9,15].

© Springer International Publishing Switzerland 2014
M. Gheorghe et al. (Eds.): CMC 2014, LNCS 8961, pp. 274–283, 2014.
DOI: 10.1007/978-3-319-14370-5_17

Several classes of SN P systems were considered: asynchronous SN P systems with local synchronization were proposed in [19], SN P systems with astrocyte-like control [13,16], homogenous SN P systems have been developed in [21]. In recent works, a lot of new candidates of SN P systems have been proposed, such as SN P systems with rules on synapses [20], SN P systems with anti-spikes [8,10,18]. Most of the variants of SN P systems are universal as number generating/accepting devices, language generating devices or function computing devices. SN P systems with neuron division and budding were also proposed. These systems can generate an exponential working space (new neurons) in linear computation steps time, thus solving computationally hard problems in a polynomial time, by a time-space trade-off strategy [6,12].

In the present work, we deal with a class of SN P systems with astrocytes from [13,16], but the application of rules in each neuron is done in the exhaustive manner (investigated in [22]). At any step of the computation, each neuron will use its rule in the exhaustive manner, that is, one of the enabled rules in the neuron will be used as many times as possible; meanwhile the astrocytes have excitatory or inhibitory influence on the spikes passing along a certain number of synapses. Specifically, (1) if the number of spikes passing along the synapses is less than a given threshold, then the astrocyte has an excitatory function, i.e., the spikes can "safely" arrive at the target neurons; (2) if the number of spikes passing along the synapses is larger than the threshold, then the astrocyte has an inhibitory function and no spike can arrive at the target neurons; (3) if the number of spikes passing along the synapses is equal to the value of the threshold, then the astrocyte non-deterministically chooses to pass or annihilate the passing spikes.

In this work, we investigate the computing power of SN P systems with astrocytes and the application of rules in the exhaustive manner. It is found that the systems can compute/generate any set of Turing computable natural numbers, thus can achieve Turing universality as number generators. In the universality proof, the feature of delay (defined in classic SN P systems) is not used.

2 Spiking Neural P Systems with Astrocytes

In this section, we introduce SN P systems with astrocytes. It is useful for readers to have some familiarity with basic elements of formal language theory, e.g., from [17].

A *spiking neural P system with astrocytes* (*SNPA system*, for short), of degree $m \geq 1$, $l \geq 1$, is a construct of the form

$$\Pi = (O, \sigma_1, \ldots, \sigma_m, syn, ast_1, \ldots, ast_l, \sigma_{out}, \sigma_{in}), \text{ where:}$$

- $O = \{a\}$ is the singleton alphabet (*a* is called *spike*);
- $\sigma_1, \ldots, \sigma_m$ are *neurons*, of the form $\sigma_i = (n_i, R_i)$, $1 \leq i \leq m$, where:
  (1) $n_i \geq 0$ is *the initial number of spikes* contained in σ_i;

(2) R_i is a finite set of *rules* of the following form: $E/a^c \to a^p$, where E is a regular expression over O, and $c \geq 1$, $p \geq 0$ with $c \geq p$.

- $syn \subseteq \{1, 2, ..., m\} \times \{1, 2, ..., m\}$ with $(i, i) \notin syn$ for $1 \leq i \leq m$ (*synapses between neurons*);
- $ast_1, \ldots, ast_l$ are *astrocytes*, of the form $ast_i = (syn_{ast_i}, t_i)$, where $1 \leq i \leq l$, $syn_{ast_i} \subseteq syn$ is the set of synapses controlled by astrocyte ast_i, $t_i \in \mathbb{N}$ is the *threshold* of astrocyte ast_i;
- $in, out \in \{1, 2, ..., m\}$ indicate the *input* and *output* neurons, respectively.

The rules $E/a^c \to a^p$ with $p \geq 1$ are called *firing* rules. If $p = 0$, then the rules are called *forgetting* rules.

In this work, we consider SNPA systems with exhaustive use of rules. A rule $E/a^c \to a^p$ is applied in an exhaustive way as follows. If neuron σ_i contains k spikes, and $a^k \in L(E)$, $k \geq c$, then the rule can be applied. Assume that $k = sc + r$, for some $s \geq 1$ (this means that we must have $k \geq c$) and $0 \leq r < c$. Then sc spikes are consumed, r spikes remain in the neuron σ_i, and sp spikes are produced immediately. As usual, the sp spikes are replicated and exactly sp spikes are sent to each of the neurons σ_j such that $(i, j) \in syn$. In the case of the output neuron, sp spikes are also sent to the environment. Of course, if neuron σ_i has no synapses leaving from it, then the produced spikes are lost.

In each time unit, if neuron σ_i can use one of its rules, then a rule from R_i must be used. If two or more rules can be applied in the neuron, only one of them is chosen non-deterministically. From the above description, the rules are used in the sequential manner in each neuron, but neurons function in parallel with each other.

In SNPA systems, astrocytes can sense the spikes traffic along the neighboring synapses. Assume that astrocyte ast_i has a given threshold t_i, and there are k spikes passing along the synapses contained in syn_{ast_i}. If $k > t_i$, then astrocyte ast_i has an inhibitory influence on the controlled synapses and the k spikes are suppressed (namely, the k spikes are lost from the system). If $k < t_i$, then astrocyte ast_i has an excitatory influence and the k spikes survive and reach their destination neurons. If $k = t_i$, then astrocyte ast_i non-deterministically chooses an inhibitory or excitatory influence on the controlled synapses.

The *configuration* of the system is of the form $\langle r_1, \cdots, r_m \rangle$, which means that neuron σ_i contains $r_i \geq 0$ spikes. With the above notation, the *initial configuration* can be expressed as $C_0 = \langle n_1, \cdots, n_m \rangle$. Using the application of the rules as described above, one can define *transitions* among configurations. Beginning with the initial configuration, we can get a sequence of transitions which is called a *computation*. A computation is successful if it reaches a configuration where no rule can be used. The *result of a computation* of the system is defined as the distance of the first two spikes sent out by the output neuron.

We denote by $N_2^{ex}(\Pi)$ the set of numbers generated in exhaustive way by an SNPA system Π (the subscript indicates that we only consider the distance between the first two spikes of any computation, the superscript indicates that the rules of the system Π works in an exhaustive way). By $N_2^{ex}SNPA$ we denote the family of such sets of numbers generated by SNPA systems with exhaustive use of rules.

3   Universality of SNPA Systems with Exhaustive Use of Rules

In this section, we prove that SNPA systems with exhaustive use of rules (without delay) can generate any set of Turing computable natural numbers.

The following proof is based on the simulation of register machines. A register machine is a construct $M = (m, H, l_0, l_h, I)$, where m is the number of registers, H is the set of instruction labels, l_0 is the start label (labeling an ADD instruction), l_h is the halt label(assigned to instruction HALT), and I is the set of instructions, labeled in a one-to-one manner by the labels from H, thus precisely identifying it. The instructions are of the following forms:

- $l_i : (\text{ADD}(r), l_j, l_k)$ (add 1 to register r and then go to one of the instruction with labels l_j, l_k non-deterministically chosen),
- $l_i : (\text{SUB}(r), l_j, l_k)$ (if register r is non-empty, then subtract 1 from it, and go to the instruction with label l_j; otherwise, go to the instruction with label l_k),
- $l_h : \text{HALT}$ (the halt instruction).

A register machine M computes (generates) a number in the following way: starting with all register empty (i.e., storing the number zero), the system applies the instruction with label l_0 and continues to apply instruction as indicated by the labels (and made possible by the contents of registers); if the system reaches the halt instruction, then the number n present in register 1 at that time is said to be generated by M. The set of all numbers generated by M is denoted by $N(M)$. It is known that register machines characterize NRE (the family of Turing computable sets of numbers), and this can be obtained even if we impose that the first register is never decremented during a computation [7].

Theorem 1. $N_2^{ex} SNPA = NRE$.

Proof. It is enough to prove the inclusion $NRE \subseteq N_2^{ex} SNPA$; the converse inclusion is straightforward (or we can invoke for it the Turing-Church thesis). To this aim, we us the characterization of NRE by means of register machines used in the generative mode. Let us consider a register machine $M = (m, H, l_0, l_h, I)$. Without any loss of generality, we assume that in the halting configuration, all registers different from register 1 are empty, and that output register is never decremented during a computation. In what follows, a specific SNPA system Π is constructed to simulate the register machine M.

The system Π consists of three of types of modules-ADD module, SUB module, and FIN module as shown in Figures 1, 2, 3, respectively. Each module is composed of neurons and astrocytes. ADD module and SUB module are used to simulate the ADD and SUB instructions of M, respectively; FIN module is used to output a computation result.

In general, for each register r of M, a neuron σ_r is associated. Specifically, if register r contains the number $n \geq 0$, then neuron σ_r contains 3^{n+1} spikes; if neuron σ_r contains 3 spikes, which means that register r is empty. The content of register r is increased by one, meaning the number of spikes in neuron σ_r is multiplied by 3; the content of register r is decreased by one (if the register is non-empty), meaning the number of spikes in neuron σ_r is divided by 3. For each label l_i of an instruction in M, a neuron σ_{l_i} is associated. Moreover, the additional neurons are considered in modules: for ADD module, the additional neurons are $\sigma_{l_{i,j}}$ $(j = 1, 2, \cdots, 7)$, $\sigma_{r(1)}$, $\sigma_{r(2)}$, $\sigma_{r(3)}$; for SUB module, the additional neurons are $\sigma_{l_{i,j}}$ $(j = 1, 2, \cdots, 4)$, $\sigma_{r(4)}$, $\sigma_{r(5)}$; for FIN module, the additional neurons are $\sigma_{l_h^j}$ $(j = 1, 2, \cdots, 4)$ and σ_{out}. In the initial configuration, all neurons are empty, with the single exception of neuron σ_{l_0} associated with the initial instruction l_0 of M, which contains exactly two spikes. During a computation, a neuron σ_{l_i} having two spikes inside will become active and start to simulate an instruction $l_i : (\mathsf{OP}(r), l_j, l_k)$ of M: starting with neuron σ_{l_i} activated, operating neuron σ_r as requested by OP, then introducing two spikes into neuron σ_{l_j} or neuron σ_{l_k}, which becomes in this way. When neuron σ_{l_h} (associated with the label l_h of the halting instruction of M) is activated, a computation in M is completely simulated in Π; after that the output neuron σ_{out} fires twice, at an interval of time that corresponds to the number stored in register 1 of M.

Module ADD (shown in Figure 1) - simulating an ADD instruction l_i : $(\mathsf{ADD}(r), l_j, l_k)$.

The initial instruction of M (the one with label l_0), is an ADD instruction. Assume that at step t, an instruction $l_i : (\mathsf{ADD}(r), l_j, l_k)$ has to be simulated, with two spikes present in neurons σ_{l_i} and no spike in any other neurons, except those neurons associated with the registers. Having two spikes inside, neuron σ_{l_i} is fired, sending a spike to neurons $\sigma_{l_{i,1}}$, $\sigma_{l_{i,2}}$, $\sigma_{l_{i,3}}$, $\sigma_{l_{i,4}}$, $\sigma_{l_{i,5}}$, σ_r, respectively. Without any astrocyte controlling synapses $(l_i, l_{i,4})$, $(l_i, l_{i,5})$ and (l_i, r), the spikes moving along these synapses can reach neurons $\sigma_{l_{i,4}}$, $\sigma_{l_{i,5}}$ and σ_r. At step $t + 1$, each of neurons $\sigma_{r(1)}$, $\sigma_{r(2)}$, $\sigma_{r(3)}$ receives the spikes both from neurons σ_r and $\sigma_{l_{i,5}}$, and each of them is fired by the rule $a(a^3)^+/a^3 \rightarrow a^3$. At step $t + 2$, neuron σ_r removes the remained spikes; neurons $\sigma_{r(1)}, \sigma_{r(2)}, \sigma_{r(3)}$ send spikes to neuron σ_r, and they forget the remained spike. In this way, the number of spikes in σ_r is tripled and returned to itself (that is, neuron σ_r contains 3^{n+1} spikes), simulating that the number stored in register r is increased by one.

In turn, there are three spikes passing along the synapses controlled by astrocyte ast_1 (that is, the three spikes pass along synapses $(l_i, l_{i,1}), (l_i, l_{i,2}), (l_i, l_{i,3})$) in step t. Thus, the number of spikes passing along the synapses controlled by astrocyte ast_1 equals its threshold, and ast_1 non-deterministically chooses an inhibitory or excitatory influence on its controlled synapses.

(1) If astrocyte ast_1 has an inhibitory influence on its controlled synapses, then the three spikes passing along synapses $(l_i, l_{i,1})$, $(l_i, l_{i,2})$, $(l_i, l_{i,3})$ are suppressed and cannot reach their target neurons. Neuron $\sigma_{l_{i,7}}$ is fired after receiving a spike from each of neurons $\sigma_{l_{i,4}}$ and $\sigma_{l_{i,5}}$. At step $t + 1$, neuron $\sigma_{l_{i,7}}$ sends two spikes to neuron σ_j, which becomes activated, starting to simulate the instruction l_j of M.

(2) If astrocyte ast_1 has an excitatory influence on its controlled synapses, then each of neurons $\sigma_{l_{i,1}}$, $\sigma_{l_{i,2}}$ and $\sigma_{l_{i,3}}$ receives a spike from neuron σ_{l_i}. So,

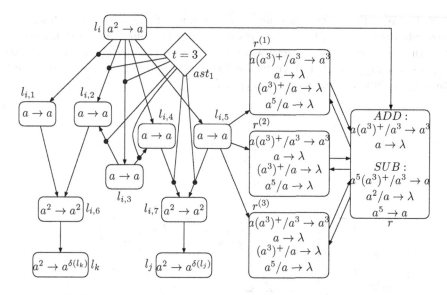

Fig. 1. Module ADD (simulating $l_i : (\texttt{ADD}(r), l_j, l_k)$)

neuron σ_{l_k} can receive two spikes from intermediate neuron $\sigma_{l_{i,6}}$ and becomes activated, starting to simulate the instruction l_k of M; neuron σ_{l_j} cannot receive any spike.

Therefore, from firing neuron σ_{l_i}, the system Π non-deterministically fires one of neurons σ_{l_j} and σ_{l_k}, which correctly simulates the ADD instruction $l_i :$ $(\texttt{ADD}(r), l_j, l_k)$.

Module SUB (shown in Figure 2) - simulating a SUB instruction $l_i :$ $(\texttt{SUB}(r), l_j, l_k)$.

A SUB instruction l_i is simulated by the system Π in the following way. Initially, neuron σ_{l_i} has two spikes, and other neurons are empty, except neurons associated with registers (if register r is non-empty, then it holds a number of spikes of the form 3^n $(n \geq 2)$; if register r is empty, then it has 3 spikes). Assume that at step t, with two spikes inside, neuron σ_{l_i} is fired by the rule $a^2 \rightarrow a$, sending two spikes to neurons $\sigma_{l_{i,1}}$, $\sigma_{l_{i,2}}$ and σ_r, respectively. For neuron σ_r, there are two cases.

(1) At step $t+1$, neuron σ_r has 3^n $(n \geq 2)$ spikes (corresponding to the fact that the number stored in register r is n). In this case, at step $t+1$, neuron σ_r sends a spike to each of neurons $\sigma_{r^{(4)}}$ and $\sigma_{r^{(5)}}$, meaning that the number of spikes in σ_r is divided by 3, and the two spikes remained in neuron σ_r will be forgotten by the rule $a^2/a \rightarrow \lambda$ in the next step. At step $t+2$, neuron $\sigma_{r^{(4)}}$ returns 3^{n-1} spikes to neuron σ_r, and the remained two spikes will be forgotten. In this way, the number of spikes in neuron σ_r becomes 3^{n-1}, which simulates that the number stored in register r is decreased by one.

Since neuron σ_r contains at least 3^2 spikes, there are at least 3 spikes passing along the synapse $(r, r^{(5)})$ controlled by astrocyte ast_2. However, neuron $r^{(5)}$

cannot receive the spikes from neuron σ_r because of the inhibitory influence of astrocyte ast_2. At step $t+2$, the spikes sent out by neuron $\sigma_{l_{i,3}}$ reach neurons $\sigma_{l_{i,4}}$ and σ_{l_j} because of the excitatory influence of astrocyte ast_3. In the next step, neuron $\sigma_{l_{i,4}}$ forgets the received spikes, while neuron σ_{l_j} becomes activated, starting to simulate the instruction l_j of M.

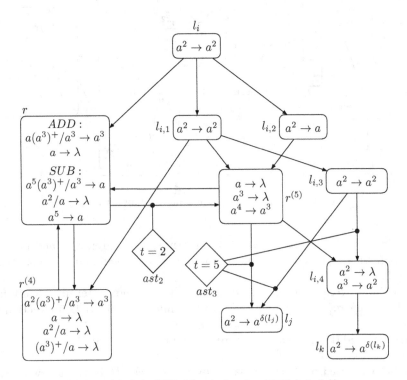

Fig. 2. Module SUB (simulating $l_i : (\mathtt{SUB}(r), l_j, l_k)$)

(2) At step $t+1$, neuron σ_r has 3 spikes (corresponding to the fact that the number stored in register r is zero). In this case, neuron $\sigma_{r^{(4)}}$ will forget the received spike from neuron σ_r, neuron $\sigma_{r^{(5)}}$ returns 3 spikes to neuron σ_r. At step $t+2$, astrocyte ast_3 has an inhibitory influence on its controlled synapses, because the number of spikes passing along the synapses controlled by astrocyte ast_3 is greater than the threshold of astrocyte ast_3. Thus, no spike reaches neuron σ_{l_j}, while neuron $\sigma_{l_{i,4}}$ receives three spikes from neuron $\sigma_{r^{(5)}}$ and sends two spikes to neuron σ_{l_k}. With two spikes inside, neuron σ_{l_k} becomes activated, starting to simulate the instruction l_j of M.

The simulation of SUB instruction is correct: the system Π starts from σ_{l_i} having two spikes inside, and it ends with sending two spikes to neuron σ_{l_j} (if the number stored in register r is greater than 0), or sending two spikes to neuron σ_{l_k} (if the number stored in register r is 0).

Since it is not sure l_j and l_k labels of ADD, SUB or halting instructions, the rules contained by neurons σ_{l_j} and σ_{l_k} (in ADD and SUB modules) are written in the form $a^2 \to a^{\delta(l_s)}$. The function $\delta : H \to \{1, 2\}$ is defined as follows:

$$\delta(l) = \begin{cases} 1, & \text{if } l \text{ is the label of an ADD instruction;} \\ 2, & \text{if } l \text{ otherwise.} \end{cases}$$

Note that it is possible to have interference between the ADD and SUB modules. Specifically, if the ADD and SUB instructions act on the same register r, then neuron σ_r sends spikes to all neurons $\sigma_{r(s)}$, $s = 1, 2, 3, 4, 5$, and simulates the ADD and SUB instructions, respectively. If an ADD instruction is simulated, then neuron σ_r sends 3^n $(n \geq 1)$ spikes to neurons $\sigma_{r(4)}$ and $\sigma_{r(5)}$. Neuron $\sigma_{r(4)}$ forgets the received spikes using the rule $(a^3)^+/a \to \lambda$, and neuron $\sigma_{r(5)}$ cannot receive any spikes because of the inhibitory influence of astrocyte ast_2 of SUB module. If a SUB instruction is simulated, then neuron σ_r sends 3^n $(n \geq 1)$(in the case of register r is non-empty) or zero (in the case of register r is empty) spikes to neurons $\sigma_{r(s)}$, $s = 1, 2, 3$. When 3^n $(n \geq 1)$ spikes are received by neurons $\sigma_{r(s)}$, $s = 1, 2, 3$, they will be forgotten by the rule $(a^3)^+/a \to \lambda$. When no spike is received by neurons $\sigma_{r(s)}$, $s = 1, 2, 3$, it never has interference between the ADD and SUB modules. Hence, there is no wrong interference between ADD and SUB instructions.

Module FIN (shown in Figure 3) - outputting the result of a computation.

Assume that the computation in M halts (that is, the halting instruction is reached), meaning that neuron σ_{l_h} has two spikes and is fired, sending two spikes to each of neurons $\sigma_{l_h^1}$ and $\sigma_{l_h^2}$. At that moment, neuron σ_1 contains 3^{n+1} spikes, for $n \geq 1$ being the contents of register 1 of M. In the third step after activating σ_{l_h}, neuron σ_{out} is fired by the rule $a^4 \to a$, sending a spike to the environment, which is the first spike sent out by the system Π to the environment. At the same time, neuron σ_1 is fired by the rule $a^5(a^3)^+/a^3 \to a$, sending 3^n spikes to neurons $\sigma_{l_h^4}$ and σ_{out}; neuron $\sigma_{l_h^3}$ sends two spikes to neurons $\sigma_{l_h^1}$, $\sigma_{l_h^4}$ and σ_{out}. The work of neurons $\sigma_{l_h^1}$ and $\sigma_{l_h^4}$ is similar to neurons σ_1 and $\sigma_{l_h^3}$ until one of neurons σ_1 and $\sigma_{l_h^4}$ contains $3^2 + 2$ spikes. Since two spikes are received alternately from neurons $\sigma_{l_h^1}$ and $\sigma_{l_h^3}$, neurons σ_1 and $\sigma_{l_h^4}$ can apply the rule $a^5(a^3)^+/a^3 \to a$, indicating that the number of spikes contained in neurons σ_1 and $\sigma_{l_h^4}$ can be divided repeatedly by 3.

Astrocytes ast_4 always has an inhibitory influence on its controlled synapses until one of neurons σ_1 and $\sigma_{l_h^4}$ sends out three spikes to neuron σ_{out} at the last step. Furthermore, neuron σ_{out} receive two spikes from one of neurons $\sigma_{l_h^1}$ and $\sigma_{l_h^3}$. Thus, neuron σ_{out} is fired again by the rule $a^5 \to a$, sending a spike to the environment (this is the second spike sent out by the system Π to the environment). Clearly, the distance between the two spikes sent out of the system Π is n.

From the above description of the modules and their work, we find that the register machine M is correctly simulated by the system Π. Therefore, $N_2^{ex}(\Pi) = N(M)$. This completes the proof. $\square$

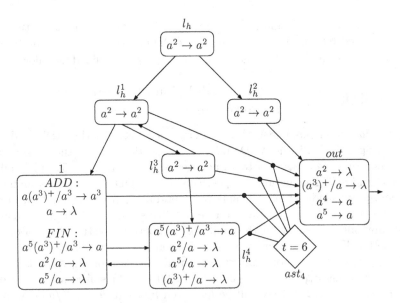

Fig. 3. Module FIN

Note that the use of astrocytes helps in what concerns the complexity of the systems used in the proof. For instance, the ADD modules do not use rules with delay, and the forgetting rules are only present in the neurons connected with neuron σ_r; the maximal number of spikes consumed by a rule and the number of neurons used in FIN module are smaller than the ones in Theorem 5.1 in [4].

4   Conclusions and Remarks

In this work, we discuss the computing power of SNPA systems with the exhaustive use of rules, where exhaustive means that when a rule is enabled, it is used as many times as possible in the respective neuron. By considering astrocytes, the universality of SN P systems with exhaustive use of rules can be obtained even if the feature of delay in firing rules is not used, while the delay should be used if no astrocyte is considered [4]. This suggests that the astrocytes are powerful ingredients for the computing power of SN P systems. There still remains some open problems, such as how can we remove the forgetting rules from our construction or to find small universal SN P systems with astrocytes, working in the exhaustive mode.

Acknowledgments. This work was supported by China Postdoctoral Science Foundation funded project (2014M550389).

References

1. Chen, H., Freund, R., Ionescu, M., Păun, Gh., Pérez-Jiménez, M.J.: On string languages generated by spiking neural P systems. Fund. Inform. **75**, 141–162 (2007)
2. Chen, H., Ionescu, M., Ishdorj, T.-O., Păun, A., Păun, Gh., Pérez-Jiménez, M.J.: Spiking neural P systems with extended rules: universality and languages. Natural Comput. **7**(2), 147–166 (2008)
3. Ionescu, M., Păun, Gh., Yokomori, T.: Spiking neural P systems. Fund. Inform. **71**(2–3), 279–308 (2006)
4. Ionescu, M., Păun, Gh., Yokomori, T.: Spiking neurla P systems with exhaustive use of rules. Int. J. Unconv. Comput. **3**(2), 135–154 (2007)
5. Ibarra, O.H., Păun, A., Păun, Gh., Rodríguez-Patón, A., Sosík, P., Woodworth, S.: Normal forms for spiking neural P systems. Theor. Comput. Sci. **372**(2), 196–217 (2007)
6. Leporati, A., Mauri, G., Zandron, C., Păun, Gh., Pérez-Jiménez, M.J.: Uniform solutions to SAT and Subset Sum by spiking neural P systems. Nat. Comput. **8**(4), 681–702 (2009)
7. Minsky, M.: Computation: finite and infinite machines. Prentice-Hall, Englewood Cliffs (1967)
8. Metta, V.P., Kelemenová, A.: Universality of spiking neural P systems with anti-spikes. In: Gopal, T.V., Agrawal, M., Li, A., Cooper, S.B. (eds.) TAMC 2014. LNCS, vol. 8402, pp. 352–365. Springer, Heidelberg (2014)
9. Neary, T.: A universal spiking neural P system with 11 neurons. In: Proceedings of the Eleventh International Conference on Membrane Computing (2010)
10. Pan, L., Păun, Gh.: Spiking Neural P Systems with Anti-Spikes. Int. J. of Computers, Communications & Control **4**(3), 273–282 (2009)
11. Pan, L., Păun, Gh.: Spiking neural P systems: An improved normal form. Theor. Comput. Sci. **411**(6), 906–918 (2010)
12. Pan, L., Păun, Gh., Pérez-Jiménez, M.J.: Spiking neural P systems with neuron division and budding. Sci. China Inform. Sci. **54**(8), 1596–1607 (2011)
13. Pan, L., Wang, J., Hoogeboom, H.J.: Spiking neural P systems with astrocytes. Neural Comput. **24**(3), 805–825 (2012)
14. Păun, Gh.: Membrane computing: An introduction. Springer-Verlag, Heidelberg (2002)
15. Păun, A., Păun, Gh.: Small universal spiking neural P systems. BioSystems **90**(1), 48–60 (2007)
16. Păun, Gh.: Spiking neural P systems with astrocyte-like control. J. Univers. Comput. Sci. **13**(11), 1707–1721 (2007)
17. Rozenberg, G., Salomaa, A. (eds.): Handbook of formal languages. Springer-Verlag, Berlin (1997)
18. Song, T., Pan, L., Wang, J., Venkat, I., Subramanian, K.G., Abdullah, R.: Normal forms of spiking neural P systems with anti-spikes. IEEE T. Nanobio. Sci. **11**(4), 352–359 (2012)
19. Song, T., Pan, L., Păun, Gh.: Asynchronous spiking neural P systems with local synchronization. Inform. Sci. **219**, 197–207 (2012)
20. Song, T., Pan, L., Păun, Gh.: Spiking neural P systems with rules on synapses. Theor. Comput. Sci. **529**(10), 82–95 (2014)
21. Zeng, X., Zhang, X., Pan, L.: Homogeneous spiking neural P systems. Fund. Inform. **97**(1), 275–294 (2009)
22. Zhang, X., Zeng, X., Pan, L.: On string languages generated by spiking neural P systems with exhaustive use of rules. Nat. Comput. **7**(4), 535–549 (2008)

Simulating Elementary Active Membranes with an Application to the P Conjecture

Alberto Leporati, Luca Manzoni, Giancarlo Mauri, Antonio E. Porreca[✉],
and Claudio Zandron

Dipartimento di Informatica, Sistemistica e Comunicazione,
Università degli Studi di Milano-Bicocca,
Viale Sarca 336/14, 20126 Milano, Italy
{leporati,luca.manzoni,mauri,porreca,zandron}@disco.unimib.it

Abstract. The decision problems solved in polynomial time by P systems with elementary active membranes are known to include the class $\mathbf{P}^{\#\mathbf{P}}$. This consists of all the problems solved by polynomial-time deterministic Turing machines with polynomial-time counting oracles. In this paper we prove the reverse inclusion by simulating P systems with this kind of machines: this proves that the two complexity classes coincide, finally solving an open problem by Păun on the power of elementary division. The equivalence holds for both uniform and semi-uniform families of P systems, with or without membrane dissolution rules. Furthermore, the inclusion in $\mathbf{P}^{\#\mathbf{P}}$ also holds for the P systems involved in the P conjecture (with elementary division and dissolution but no charges), which improves the previously known upper bound **PSPACE**.

1 Introduction

The computational power of P systems with elementary active membranes working in polynomial time was first investigated in [10]. The ability of P systems to exploit parallelism to perform multiple computations at the same time allows an efficient solution of **NP**-complete problems. This feature was further exploited [8] to show that P systems with elementary active membranes can solve all $\mathbf{P}^{\mathbf{PP}}$ problems (or $\mathbf{P}^{\#\mathbf{P}}$ problems, due to the equivalence of the two classes).

While all the previous results showed an ever increasing lower bound for the power of this class of P systems, the upper bound for their computational ability was proved to be **PSPACE** [9]. Therefore, until now it was only known that this class is located between $\mathbf{P}^{\#\mathbf{P}}$ and **PSPACE**. In this paper we show that the already known lower bound is, in fact, also an upper bound. This implies that non-elementary membrane division is necessary in order to solve **PSPACE**-complete problems (unless $\mathbf{P}^{\#\mathbf{P}} = \mathbf{PSPACE}$), as conjectured by Sosík and Pérez-Jiménez and formulated as Problem B by Păun in 2005 [5]. This bound

---

This work was partially supported by Università degli Studi di Milano-Bicocca, FA 2013: "Complessità computazionale in modelli di calcolo bioispirati: Sistemi a membrane e sistemi di reazioni".

M. Gheorghe et al. (Eds.): CMC 2014, LNCS 8961, pp. 284–299, 2014.
DOI: 10.1007/978-3-319-14370-5_18

has also an interesting implication for the *P conjecture* [5, Problem F], stating that P systems with elementary division and dissolution but no charges can solve only problems in **P**. The previously known upper bound for the computational power of that class of P systems was also **PSPACE** but, since those systems are a weaker version of the ones studied here, the $\mathbf{P}^{\#\mathbf{P}}$ bound also applies to them.

The main idea behind the simulation of P systems with elementary active membranes by Turing machines with $\#\mathbf{P}$ oracles is similar to one from [9]: we cannot store the entire configuration of the P system, since it can grow exponentially in time due to elementary membrane division. Therefore, instead of simulating directly the behaviour of the elementary membranes, we only simulate the interactions between them and their parent regions. Indeed, from the point of view of a non-elementary membrane, all the membranes it contains are just "black boxes" that absorb and release objects. We thus only store the configurations of non-elementary membranes and, when needed, we exploit a $\#\mathbf{P}$ oracle to determine how many instances of each type of object are exchanged between elementary membranes and their parent regions. As will be clear in the following, while doing so we also need to take special care for send-in rules, since they require, in some sense, a partial knowledge of the parent's multiset of objects, and conflicts between send-in rules competing for the same objects that can be applied to different membranes may be difficult to resolve. Thus, we have devised a way to provide a "centralised control" that allows to correctly apply the different send-in rules.

The paper is structured as follows. In Section 2 the basic definitions concerning P systems and the relevant complexity classes are briefly recalled. The simulation of P systems is described in Section 3; in particular, the three phases of the simulation algorithm requiring more computing power than a deterministic Turing machine working in polynomial time are detailed in Section 3.1 (movement of objects into elementary membranes), Section 3.2 (releasing objects from elementary membranes), and Section 3.3 (establishing if a membrane is elementary). The theorem stating the main result and the implications for the P conjecture are presented in Section 4. The paper is concluded with a summary of the results and some directions for future research in Section 5.

2   Basic Notions

We begin by recalling the basic definition of P systems with (elementary) active membranes [4].

Definition 1. *A P system with elementary active membranes of initial degree $d \geq 1$ is a tuple $\Pi = (\Gamma, \Lambda, \mu, w_{h_1}, \ldots, w_{h_d}, R)$, where:*

- *Γ is an alphabet, i.e., a finite non-empty set of symbols, usually called* objects;
- *Λ is a finite set of labels for the membranes;*
- *μ is a membrane structure (i.e., a rooted unordered tree, usually represented by nested brackets) consisting of d membranes labelled by elements of Λ in a one-to-one way;*

– $w_{h_1}, \ldots, w_{h_d}$, *with* $h_1, \ldots, h_d \in \Lambda$, *are strings over* Γ, *describing the initial*
multisets of objects placed in the d regions of μ;
– *R is a finite set of rules.*

Each membrane possesses, besides its label and position in μ, another
attribute called *electrical charge*, which can be either neutral (0), positive (+)
or negative (−) and is always neutral before the beginning of the computation.
The rules in R are of the following types[1]:

(a) *Object evolution rules*, of the form $[a \to w]_h^\alpha$
They can be applied inside a membrane labelled by h, having charge α and
containing an occurrence of the object a; the object a is rewritten into the
multiset w (i.e., a is removed from the multiset in h and replaced by w).

(b) *Send-in communication rules*, of the form $a\,[\,]_h^\alpha \to [b]_h^\beta$
They can be applied to a membrane labelled by h, having charge α and such
that the external region contains an occurrence of the object a; the object a
is sent into h becoming b and, simultaneously, the charge of h becomes β.

(c) *Send-out communication rules*, of the form $[a]_h^\alpha \to [\,]_h^\beta\, b$
They can be applied to a membrane labelled by h, having charge α and
containing an occurrence of the object a; the object a is sent out from h to the
outside region becoming b and, simultaneously, the charge of h becomes β.

(d) *Dissolution rules*, of the form $[a]_h^\alpha \to b$
They can be applied to a membrane labelled by h, having charge α and
containing an occurrence of the object a; the membrane is dissolved and
its contents are left in the surrounding region unaltered, except that an
occurrence of a becomes b.

(e) *Elementary division rules*, of the form $[a]_h^\alpha \to [b]_h^\beta\,[c]_h^\gamma$
They can be applied to a membrane labelled by h, having charge α, containing an occurrence of the object a but having no other membrane inside
(an *elementary membrane*); the membrane is divided into two membranes
having label h and charges β and γ; the object a is replaced, respectively,
by b and c, while the other objects of the multiset originally contained in
membrane h are replicated in both membranes.

Notice that "being an elementary membrane" is a *dynamic* property: even if a
membrane originally contained other membranes, the dissolution of all of them
makes the membrane elementary; if this happens, we also assume that any elementary division rules involving it become applicable, provided that its multiset
and charge match the left-hand sides of the rules[2]. Clearly, once a membrane is
elementary it can never become non-elementary.

Since it is an essential technical detail in this paper, we carefully distinguish the concepts of *membrane* and *membrane label*, since membrane division

---

[1] The general definition of P systems with active membranes [4] also includes *non-
elementary division rules* (type (f)), which are not used in this paper.

[2] The results of this paper, as well as the previous $\mathbf{P}^{\#\mathbf{P}}$ lower bound [8], continue
to hold even if we assume that R can only contain elementary division rules for
membranes that are *already* elementary in the initial configuration of the P system.

allows the creation of multiple membranes sharing the same label. In the rest of the paper, we use the expression "membrane h" (singular) only when a single membrane labelled by h is guaranteed to exist, and refer to "membranes (labelled by) h" (plural) otherwise.

Definition 2. *The instantaneous configuration of a membrane consists of its label h, its charge α, and the multiset w of objects it contains at a given time. It is denoted by $[w]_h^\alpha$. The (full) configuration $\mathcal{C}$ of a P system Π at a given time is a rooted, unordered tree. The root is a node corresponding to the external environment of Π, and has a single subtree corresponding to the current membrane structure of Π. Furthermore, the root is labelled by the multiset located in the environment, and the remaining nodes by the configurations $[w]_h^\alpha$ of the corresponding membranes.*

A computation step changes the current configuration according to the following set of principles:

- Each object and membrane can be subject to at most one rule per step, except for object evolution rules: inside each membrane, several evolution rules can be applied simultaneously.
- The application of rules is *maximally parallel*: each object appearing on the left-hand side of evolution, communication, dissolution or elementary division rules must be subject to exactly one of them (unless the current charge of the membrane prohibits it). Analogously, each membrane can only be subject to one communication, dissolution, or elementary division rule (types (b)–(e)) per computation step. In other words, the only objects and membranes that do not evolve are those associated with no rule, or only to rules that are not applicable due to the electrical charges.
- When several conflicting rules can be applied at the same time, a nondeterministic choice is performed; this implies that, in general, multiple possible configurations can be reached after a computation step.
- In each computation step, all the chosen rules are applied simultaneously (in an atomic way). However, in order to clarify the operational semantics, each computation step is conventionally described as a sequence of micro-steps as follows. First, all evolution rules are applied inside the elementary membranes, followed by all communication, dissolution and division rules involving the membranes themselves; this process is then repeated to the membranes containing them, and so on towards the root (outermost membrane). In other words, the membranes evolve only after their internal configuration has been updated. For instance, before a membrane division occurs, all chosen object evolution rules must be applied inside it; this way, the objects that are duplicated during the division are already the final ones.
- The outermost membrane cannot be divided or dissolved, and any object sent out from it cannot re-enter the system again.

A *halting computation* of the P system Π is a finite sequence $\mathcal{C} = (\mathcal{C}_0, \dots, \mathcal{C}_k)$ of configurations, where $\mathcal{C}_0$ is the initial configuration, every $\mathcal{C}_{i+1}$ is reachable from $\mathcal{C}_i$ via a single computation step, and no rules of Π are applicable in $\mathcal{C}_k$.

P systems can be used as language *recognisers* by employing two distinguished objects **yes** and **no**: we assume that all computations are halting, and that either object **yes** or object **no** (but not both) is sent out from the outermost membrane, and only in the last computation step, in order to signal acceptance or rejection, respectively. If all computations starting from the same initial configuration are accepting, or all are rejecting, the P system is said to be *confluent*. All P systems in this paper are assumed to be confluent.

In order to solve decision problems (i.e., decide languages), we use *families* of recogniser P systems $\boldsymbol{\Pi} = \{\Pi_x : x \in \Sigma^\star\}$. Each input x is associated with a P system Π_x that decides the membership of x in the language $L \subseteq \Sigma^\star$ by accepting or rejecting. The mapping $x \mapsto \Pi_x$ must be efficiently computable for inputs of any length, as discussed in detail in [2].

Definition 3. *A family of P systems $\boldsymbol{\Pi} = \{\Pi_x : x \in \Sigma^\star\}$ is said to be (polynomial-time) uniform if the mapping $x \mapsto \Pi_x$ can be computed by two polynomial-time deterministic Turing machines E and F as follows:*

- *$F(1^n) = \Pi_n$, where 1^n is the length of x in unary and Π_n is a P system with a distinguished input membrane working on all inputs of length n.*
- *$E(x) = w_x$, where w_x is a multiset encoding the specific input x.*
- *Finally, Π_x is simply Π_n with w_x added to its input membrane.*

The family $\boldsymbol{\Pi}$ is said to be (polynomial-time) semi-uniform if there exists a single deterministic polynomial-time Turing machine H such that $H(x) = \Pi_x$ for each $x \in \Sigma^\star$.

Any explicit encoding of Π_x is allowed as output of the construction, as long as the number of membranes and objects represented by it does not exceed the length of the whole description, and the rules are listed one by one. This restriction is enforced in order to mimic a (hypothetical) realistic process of construction of the P systems, where membranes and objects are presumably placed in a constant amount during each construction step, and require actual physical space proportional to their number; see also [2] for further details on the encoding of P systems.

Recall that the classes of decision problems solved by uniform and semi-uniform families of P systems working in polynomial time with evolution, communication, dissolution, and elementary division rules are denoted by $\mathbf{PMC}_{\mathcal{AM}(-n)}$ and $\mathbf{PMC}^\star_{\mathcal{AM}(-n)}$, respectively. When dissolution is not allowed, the two corresponding classes are denoted by $\mathbf{PMC}_{\mathcal{AM}(-d,-n)}$ and $\mathbf{PMC}^\star_{\mathcal{AM}(-d,-n)}$.

Finally, we recall the definitions of the complexity classes $\#\mathbf{P}$ and $\mathbf{P}^{\#\mathbf{P}}$ (the latter being equivalent to $\mathbf{P}^{\mathbf{PP}}$), and a notion of completeness for $\#\mathbf{P}$ [3].

Definition 4. *The complexity class $\#\mathbf{P}$ consists of all the functions $f \colon \Sigma^\star \to \mathbb{N}$, also called* counting problems, *with the following property: there exists a polynomial time nondeterministic Turing machine N such that, for each $x \in \Sigma^\star$, the number of accepting computations of N on input x is exactly $f(x)$.*

A function $f \in \#\mathbf{P}$ is said to be $\#\mathbf{P}$-complete under parsimonious reductions if and only if for each $g \in \#\mathbf{P}$ there exists a polynomial-time reduction $r \colon \Sigma^\star \to \Sigma^\star$ such that $g(x) = f(r(x))$ for each $x \in \Sigma^\star$.

Definition 5. *The complexity class $\mathbf{P}^{\#\mathbf{P}}$ consists of all decision problems (languages) recognisable in polynomial time by deterministic Turing machines with oracles for $\#\mathbf{P}$ functions. These are Turing machines M^f, with $f \in \#\mathbf{P}$, having a distinguished oracle tape and a query state such that, when M^f enters the query state, the string x on the oracle tape is immediately (i.e., at unitary time cost) replaced with the binary encoding of $f(x)$.*

3   The Simulation Algorithm

Let $L \in \mathbf{PMC}^{\star}_{\mathcal{AM}(-n)}$ be a language, and let $\Pi = \{\Pi_x : x \in \Sigma^{\star}\}$ be a semi-uniform family of confluent recogniser P systems with elementary active membranes deciding L in polynomial time. Let H be a polynomial-time deterministic Turing machine computing the mapping $x \mapsto \Pi_x$.

A straightforward deterministic simulation of Π, which stores the entire configuration of a P system and applies the rules in a step-by-step fashion, in general incurs an exponential slowdown, due to the exponential size of the configurations of the P systems, even when a binary encoding of the multisets is employed: indeed, by the "Milano Theorem" [10], the exponential space (and time) blowup of the simulation is due to the exponential number of elementary membranes created by division, and not to the number of objects itself. Here we simulate Π with a polynomial slowdown by means of a deterministic Turing machine with a $\#\mathbf{P}$ counting oracle.

We begin by observing that we do not need to *explicitly* store the configurations of the elementary membranes (either those that are elementary in the initial configuration, or those that become elementary during the computation), *as long as we can somehow keep track of the interactions between them and their parent regions.* Specifically, we need a way to track the objects that are released from the elementary membranes (via send-out or dissolution rules) and those that are absorbed by them (via send-in rules). We call *partial configuration* the portion of configuration of a P system that we store explicitly, in which we exclude the elementary membranes (unless, temporarily, in the very moment they become elementary and there is only a polynomial number of them) but include the environment surrounding the outermost membrane. An example of partial configuration is shown in Fig. 1.

Since the environment is where the result of any computation of a recogniser P system Π_x is ultimately decided, by the presence of an object **yes** or **no**, an up-to-date partial configuration is sufficient for a Turing machine to establish whether Π_x accepts or rejects. Furthermore, a partial configuration can be stored efficiently when the multisets are encoded in binary, since it consists of a polynomial number of regions containing an exponential number of objects [7].

The main technical result of this paper is a procedure for computing the final partial configuration of a P system in Π from the previous partial configurations and the initial full configuration, by using a counting oracle to reconstruct the interactions between the partial configuration and the elementary membranes. This simulation exploits the assumption of confluence of the P systems in Π

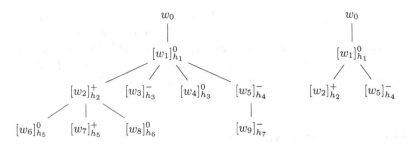

Fig. 1. A full configuration and a partial configuration for the same P system, where in the latter the configurations of all elementary membranes have been removed

when choosing the multiset of rules to apply at every time step. In principle, the simulation can be adapted to work with any deterministic way of choosing the rules but, in order to simplify the presentation, we give the following priorities:

> *Object evolution rules have the highest priority, followed by send-in rules, followed by the remaining types of rule. Inside these three classes, the priorities are given by any fixed total order.*

Algorithm 1 provides an overview of the simulation; the algorithm takes a string $x \in \Sigma^*$ as input. First of all, it simulates the machine H that provides the uniformity condition for Π on input x, thus obtaining a description of the P system Π_x (line 1). It also stores the initial configuration of Π as a suitable labelled tree data structure (line 2).

1 construct the P system Π_x by simulating H on x
2 let $\mathcal{C}$ be the initial (full) configuration of Π_x
3 **for** each time step t **do**
4   **for** each label h in $\mathcal{C}$ **do**
5   **if** h denotes an elementary membrane **then**
6   remove its configuration from $\mathcal{C}$
7   **else**
8   apply the rules to membrane h
9   remove from membrane h the objects sent into
                  elementary children membranes (see Algorithm 2)
10   **for** each label h' denoting elementary membranes **do**
11   add the output of all membranes
              labelled by h' to their parent multiset
12   **if yes** or **no** is found in the environment **then**
13   **accept** or **reject** accordingly

Algorithm 1. Simulation of a semi-uniform family Π of P systems with elementary active membranes on input x.

The main loop (lines 3–13) is repeated for each time step of Π_x, and consists of three main phases. First, the algorithm iterates (lines 4–9) through all membrane labels in the current partial configuration $\mathcal{C}$. The configurations of membranes that have become elementary during the previous computation step are removed from $\mathcal{C}$ (lines 5–6), as described in Section 3.3. Instead, the rules are applied normally [10] to non-elementary membranes (line 8), and the objects that are sent into their children elementary membranes are also removed from them (line 9); the latter operation will be detailed in Section 3.1. In the second phase the algorithm computes the output of the elementary membranes and adds it to their parent membranes (lines 10–11). This phase will be detailed in Section 3.2. Finally, in the third phase (lines 12–13) the algorithm checks whether the object **yes** (resp., **no**) was sent out from the outermost membrane in the current computation step of Π_x; if this is the case, the simulation halts by accepting (resp., rejecting) x.

3.1 Moving Objects *into* Elementary Membranes

Line 9 of the simulation algorithm requires the removal from a specific non-elementary membrane h of the objects sent into its elementary children membranes. While the current configuration of h is known, as it is stored in the partial configuration $\mathcal{C}$, the configuration of its children membranes is not stored.

We solve this problem by nondeterministically simulating each elementary children membrane of h having label h'; each computation keeps track of just a single membrane h' among those obtained by division, starting from the moment the initial (unique) membrane h' became elementary, up to the current time step. In order to do so, whenever a membrane becomes elementary (a fact discovered at line 5 of the simulation algorithm), before removing it from $\mathcal{C}$ the algorithm stores its label, its configuration, and the current time step t; this only requires polynomial space, since at most one configuration per label is stored.

We are only interested in simulating the *internal* configuration of elementary membranes (i.e., the multiset it contains and its charge), without keeping track of any objects released from them either by send-out or dissolution rules. Hence, the only problematic rules are those of type send-in, since multiple membranes sharing the same parent compete for the same objects, but cannot coordinate because each membrane is simulated by a different computation; recall that distinct computations of a nondeterministic Turing machine do not communicate. In order to solve the conflicts, a table $\mathsf{apply}[r, t]$ can be precomputed, associating each send-in rule $r = a\ [\ ]_h^\alpha \to [b]_h^\beta$ and time step t with the set of individual membranes with label h that must apply r at time t.

Computing the entries of the table apply first requires us to name each individual membrane among those sharing the same label. In order to do so, we exploit a solution already proposed by Sosík and Rodríguez-Patón [9], attaching to each elementary membrane an identifier computed as follows:

- When membrane h becomes elementary, its identifier is $id = 0$.
- If a membrane has identifier id at time τ and no division occurs at that time, its new identifier at time $\tau + 1$ is $2 \times id$.

– If a membrane has identifier id at time τ and a division occurs at that time, the new identifiers of the two resulting membranes at time $\tau + 1$ are $2 \times id$ and $2 \times id + 1$, respectively.

This ensures that, at time t, each membrane with label h has a unique identifier in the range $[0, 2^t - 1]$ (although not all identifiers in that range need to correspond to actual membranes).

Example 1. The procedure that assigns unique identifiers to elementary membranes sharing the same label can be represented graphically. On the left, we show a tree of membrane divisions (not to be confused with a configuration tree, as illustrated in Fig. 1): time goes downward, starting from the moment t_0 when the membrane became elementary, each level representing a time step; notice that not all membranes necessarily divide at each step. On the right, we show the identifiers assigned to the membranes:

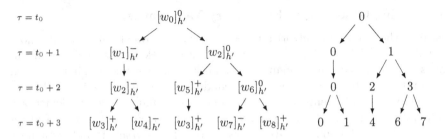

Notice how all identifiers differ, even for membranes having the same configuration: for example, the two copies of $[w_3]_{h'}^+$ at time $\tau = t_0 + 3$ have identifiers 0 and 4. Furthermore, not all identifiers between 0 and $2^t - 1$ correspond to a membrane: here 2, 3, and 5 do not correspond to any membrane.

Naively storing arbitrary subsets of $[0, 2^t - 1]$ as entries of the table apply requires an exponential amount of space with respect to t. We can, however, exploit the hypothesis of confluence of the family Π and choose, among all possible computations of the simulated P system, the computation where each send-in rule $r = a \,[\,]_h^\alpha \rightarrow [b]_h^\beta$ is applied, at each step t, to all (and only the) membranes h having charge α whose identifiers are included in an interval, to be computed as described below. Distinct intervals involving the same membrane label h may overlap only for rules r_1, r_2 having a different charge on the left-hand side, as shown in the following example.

Example 2. Consider the P system of Example 1 at time $t = 3$, and suppose the following rules (sorted by priority) are associated to the membrane label h':

$$r_1 = a \,[\,]_{h'}^- \rightarrow [c]_{h'}^+ \qquad r_2 = a \,[\,]_{h'}^+ \rightarrow [d]_{h'}^+ \qquad r_3 = b \,[\,]_{h'}^+ \rightarrow [e]_{h'}^0$$

Furthermore, suppose the parent membrane h of h' contains exactly 3 instances of object a and 4 instances of b. Then, one of the possible choices of intervals of identifiers, which is consistent with the previous discussion, is

$$\mathsf{apply}[r_1, t] = [0, 7] \qquad \mathsf{apply}[r_2, t] = [0, 3] \qquad \mathsf{apply}[r_3, t] = [4, 7]$$

The interval $\mathsf{apply}[r_1, t]$ contains exactly 2 identifiers of membranes h' having negative charge (the maximum number of instances of a that can be sent in by means of rule r_1); the interval $\mathsf{apply}[r_2, t]$ contains only 1 identifier of membranes h' with positive charge (since only one copy of a remains that is not used up by rule r_1); finally, the interval $\mathsf{apply}[r_3, t]$ contains the remaining 2 identifiers of membranes h' with positive charge, leaving two instances of b unused by send-in rules. Notice that the interval $\mathsf{apply}[r_1, t]$ overlaps with the others, since rule r_1 is applied to membranes h' having different charge than those where r_2 and r_3 may be applied, while $\mathsf{apply}[r_2, t]$ and $\mathsf{apply}[r_3, t]$ are necessarily disjoint.

e1	set $id := 0$
e2	**for** each time step $\tau \in \{t_0, \ldots, t - 1\}$ **do**
e3	set $newid := 2 \times id$
e4	**for** each applicable evolution rule $r \in R$ involving h' **do**
e5	apply r as many times as possible
e6	**for** each non-evolution rule r applicable to h' **do**
e7	**if** $r = [a]_{h'}^{\alpha} \to [\,]_{h'}^{\beta}\, b$ **then**
e8	remove an instance of a from the membrane
e9	change the charge of the membrane to β
e10	**else if** $r = [a]_{h'}^{\alpha} \to b$ **then**
e11	reject
e12	**else if** $r = [a]_{h'}^{\alpha} \to [b_0]_{h'}^{\beta_0}\, [b_1]_{h'}^{\beta_1}$ **then**
e13	nondeterministically guess a bit i
e14	set $newid := newid + i$
e15	rewrite an instance of a to b_i
e16	change the charge of the membrane to β_i
e17	**else if** $r = a\,[\,]_{h'}^{\alpha} \to [b]_{h'}^{\beta}$ and $\mathsf{left}[r, \tau] \le id \le \mathsf{right}[r, \tau]$ **then**
e18	add an instance of b to the membrane
e19	change the charge of the membrane to β
e20	set $id := newid$

Algorithm 2. Nondeterministic simulation of steps t_0 to $t - 1$ of an elementary membrane h'. Here t_0 is the time when membrane h' became elementary.

We can store each interval $\mathsf{apply}[r, t]$ as the pair of bounds $\mathsf{left}[r, t]$ and $\mathsf{right}[r, t]$. This only requires two binary numbers per each original entry $\mathsf{apply}[r, t]$; hence, the information contained in the table can now be stored in polynomial space.

The pseudocode for the nondeterministic simulation of the elementary membranes labelled by h', starting from the time t_0 when h' became elementary and up to time $t - 1$ (i.e., leaving out the last computation step), is shown as Algorithm 2. This is a straightforward simulation algorithm for P systems, as already described in the literature [7, 10], except for a few key differences:

- the simulation aborts by rejecting if the membrane dissolves within step $t-1$ (lines e10–e11);
- when simulating an elementary division (lines e12–e16) the algorithm performs a nondeterministic choice between the two membranes resulting from the division, and continues to simulate only one of them;
- before simulating a send-in rule (lines e17–e19), the algorithm checks whether the identifier of the membrane being simulated belongs to the range of identifiers of membranes applying that rule at time τ.

Notice that the loop of lines e6–e19 applies at most one non-evolution rule, as required by the semantics of P systems with active membranes.

Let $r = a \, [\,]_{h'}^{\alpha} \rightarrow [b]_{h'}^{\beta}$ be a send-in rule. We can simulate a further computation step of each membrane labelled by h', halting by accepting if rule r is actually applicable (i.e., the current membrane h' has charge α, and its identifier is in the correct range), and rejecting otherwise. As a consequence, Algorithm 2 with this additional step has as many accepting computations as the number of membranes having label h' where rule r is applied at time t. This proves the following:

Lemma 1. *Suppose we are given the configuration $[w]_{h'}^{\alpha}$ of an elementary membrane h', a set of rules, two time steps t_0 (corresponding to configuration $[w]_{h'}^{\alpha}$) and t expressed in unary notation[3], two tables* left *and* right *as described above, and a specific send-in communication rule $r = a \, [\,]_{h'}^{\alpha} \rightarrow [b]_{h'}^{\beta} \in R$. Then, counting the number of applications of rule r at time t is in $\#\mathbf{P}$.* □

Remark 1. Counting the number of satisfying assignments for a Boolean formula in 3CNF (a $\#\mathbf{P}$-complete problem) can be reduced in polynomial time to counting the number of send-in rules applied during the "counting" step by the P systems solving the THRESHOLD-3SAT problem described in [6]. This requires setting the threshold to 2^m, where m is the number of variables. Hence, the counting problem of Lemma 1 is actually $\#\mathbf{P}$-complete.

Line 9 of Algorithm 1 can thus be expanded as Algorithm 3, where the entries of left and right are also computed. The number of objects sent in from h to its children membranes h' by means of a rule $r = a \, [\,]_{h'}^{\alpha} \rightarrow [b]_{h'}^{\beta}$ can be computed (line 9.8) as the minimum k between the number of instances of a contained in h and the number m of membranes h' having charge α which have not yet been assigned a send-in rule. The initial value of m is thus the number of membranes h' having identifier at least left$[r, t]$ and charge α. The membranes h' having charge α and an identifier smaller than left$[r, t]$ have already been assigned to a different interval, and will apply a different send-in rule. The algorithm can then remove k copies of a from h (line 9.9). The value of right$[r, t]$ must then be updated, in order to ensure that exactly k membranes with label h' apply r at time t. A correct value for right$[r, t]$ can be determined by performing a binary search in the interval $\left[\text{left}[r, t], 2^t - 1 \right]$ while recomputing the value of m (line 9.12) as in Lemma 1.

---

[3] Expressing the number of time steps t in unary is necessary for the problem to be in $\#\mathbf{P}$, otherwise the value t might be exponentially larger than its representation, thus increasing the complexity of the problem.

9.1 **for** each elementary membrane label h' contained in h **do**
9.2   **for** each charge $\alpha \in \{+, 0, -\}$ **do**
9.3   set $\ell := 0$
9.4   **for** each rule $r = a\,[\ ]^{\alpha}_{h'} \rightarrow [b]^{\beta}_{h'}$ in R **do**
9.5   set $\mathsf{left}[r, t] := \ell$
9.6   set $\mathsf{right}[r, t] := 2^t - 1$
9.7   let m be the number of membranes with label h' and
                  $\mathsf{left}[r, t] \le id \le \mathsf{right}[r, t]$ where r is applicable at time t
9.8   set $k := \min\{m, \text{number of instances of } a \text{ in } h\}$
9.9   remove k instances of a from h
9.10   **while** $m \ne k$ **do**
9.11   update $\mathsf{right}[r, t]$ by binary search
9.12   recompute m
9.13   set $\ell := \mathsf{right}[r, t] + 1$

Algorithm 3. Removing from a non-elementary membrane h the objects sent into its elementary children membranes (Algorithm 1, line 9).

3.2 Moving Objects *from* Elementary Membranes

Line 11 of Algorithm 1 deals with communication in the opposite direction with respect to line 9, i.e., from the elementary membranes towards their parent.

For each label h' denoting an elementary membrane and for each object type a, the number of instances of a released from membranes with label h' at time t can be determined by first simulating these membranes up to time $t - 1$ by using Algorithm 2; the last time step is then simulated as follows:

- If a rule sending out a is applied, the computation accepts.
- If the membrane dissolves, the algorithm accepts as many times as the number k of instances of a in the simulated membrane. This requires "forking" k accepting computations, which in nondeterministic Turing machines corresponds to first nondeterministically guessing a number between 1 and k, and then accepting. This can be performed in polynomial time even if k is exponential, since the number of bits of k is polynomial.
- Otherwise, the computation rejects.

The number of accepting computations of the algorithm is the number of instances of a to be added to the parent of h'. This proves the following:

Lemma 2. *Suppose we are given the configuration $[w]^{\alpha}_{h'}$ of an elementary membrane h', a set of rules, two time steps t_0 (corresponding to configuration $[w]^{\alpha}_{h'}$) and t expressed in unary notation, two tables left and right as described above, and an object type a. Then, counting the number of instances of object a released (via send-out or dissolution rules) from membranes with label h' at time t is in #P.* □

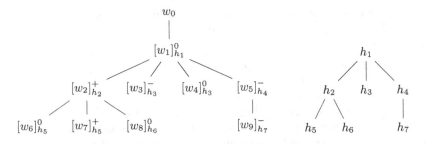

Fig. 2. A full configuration and the tree $\mathcal{T}$ containing the information about the inclusions among its membranes, expressed in terms of labels only

Remark 2. We can reduce the assignment counting problem of Remark 1 to counting the number of objects sent out by elementary membranes. Indeed, during the "checking" phase of the aforementioned algorithm for THRESHOLD-3SAT [6], all membranes containing a satisfying assignment simultaneously send out a specific object. Hence, the counting problem of Lemma 2 is also #**P**-complete.

3.3 Deciding if a Membrane is Elementary

In order to decide (line 5 of Algorithm 1) if a label h belongs to an elementary membrane at time t (recall that membranes sharing the same label are either all elementary and share the same parent, or there is only one of them) without keeping them in the partial configuration $\mathcal{C}$, we can use an auxiliary data structure. We employ a rooted, unordered tree $\mathcal{T}$ whose nodes are labels from Λ, i.e., no repeated labels appear in $\mathcal{T}$. This tree represents the inclusion relation between membranes before each simulated step, and it is initialised before entering the main loop of the simulation (lines 3–13). As an example, Fig. 2 shows a full configuration and the corresponding inclusion tree between membranes labels. This data structure is updated in two different steps of Algorithm 1: at line 8, when non-elementary membranes dissolve, and after the execution of line 5 (as described below).

Then, for each label h appearing in the partial configuration $\mathcal{C}$ (line 4), either it is associated to an internal node in $\mathcal{C}$, and in that case it is not elementary, or it is a leaf in $\mathcal{C}$, and then the node h has leaf children in $\mathcal{T}$. In that case, since we do not keep track of the elementary membranes in partial configurations, the algorithm needs to explicitly check, for each child membrane label h' of h, whether there does actually still exist at least one membrane with label h'.

Once again, we employ Algorithm 2 to simulate the elementary membranes with label h' up to time step $t - 1$; if the algorithm has not already rejected by then, this means that the simulated membrane still exists, and the computation must accept. In this case there is no need to count the number of accepting computations, but only to check whether there exists at least one. We can thus state the following:

Lemma 3. *Suppose we are given the configuration $[w]_{h'}^\alpha$ of an elementary membrane h', a set of rules, two time steps t_0 (corresponding to configuration $[w]_{h'}^\alpha$) and t expressed in unary notation, and two tables* left *and* right *as described above. Then, deciding whether there exists a membrane with label h' at time t is in* **NP**.   □

Remark 3. The most common solutions to **NP**-complete problems using P systems with elementary active membranes (such as [10]) first generate one membrane per candidate solution, then check all of them for validity. By dissolving all membranes containing invalid solutions, we can easily show that the decision problem of Lemma 3 is actually **NP**-complete by reduction from any other **NP**-complete problem.

4   A Characterisation of $P^{\#P}$

We are now able to analyse the complexity of the simulation algorithm.

Lemma 4. *Algorithm 1 runs in polynomial time on a deterministic Turing machine with access to an oracle for a $\#P$-complete function.*

Proof. Lines 1 and 2 can be executed in polynomial time due to the assumption of semi-uniformity of the family Π. The loop of line 3 simulates a polynomial number of time steps, and those of lines 4 and 10 iterate over sets of membrane labels. Hence, lines 5–9 and 11–13 are executed a polynomial number of times.

Line 6 simply consists in removing a node from a tree data structure, line 8 in the application of rules to a polynomial number of membranes, which can be performed in polynomial time [7,10], and lines 12–13 in a membership test.

Let $f \colon \Sigma^\star \to \mathbb{N}$ be $\#P$-complete under parsimonious reductions (e.g., #SAT). Then, the counting problems of Lemmata 1 and 2 and the decision problem of Lemma 3 can be reduced in polynomial time to evaluating f. Suppose we have access to an oracle for f.

The implementation of line 5 described in Section 3.3 employs the auxiliary tree data structure $\mathcal{T}$ (which can be scanned and updated in polynomial time), and can ascertain the existence of children membranes of h by performing a reduction and a query to the oracle for f at most once per label.

Moving objects into elementary membranes (line 9), as described in Section 3.1, executes Algorithm 3. This performs a polynomial number of iterations of lines 9.5–9.13. Lines 9.7 and 9.12 are reductions followed by an oracle query for f. The loop of lines 9.10–9.12 is executed a logarithmic number of times with respect to the exponential number of identifiers (i.e., a polynomial number).

Finally, line 11 of Algorithm 1, whose implementation is described in Section 3.2, computes the output of the elementary membranes. This also consists in performing a reduction and an oracle query to f for each elementary membrane label and each object type. The statement of the lemma follows.   □

As a consequence, we obtain the equivalence of several complexity classes for P systems with elementary active membranes to $\mathbf{P}^{\#\mathbf{P}}$.

Theorem 1. *The following equalities hold:*

$$\mathbf{PMC}^{[\star]}_{\mathcal{AM}(-d,-n)} = \mathbf{PMC}^{[\star]}_{\mathcal{AM}(-n)} = \mathbf{P}^{\#\mathbf{P}}$$

where $[\star]$ *denotes optional semi-uniformity instead of uniformity.*

Proof. The inclusions of the following diagram hold:

$$\mathbf{PMC}^{\star}_{\mathcal{AM}(-d,-n)}$$

$$\mathbf{P}^{\#\mathbf{P}} \subseteq \mathbf{PMC}_{\mathcal{AM}(-d,-n)} \qquad\qquad \mathbf{PMC}^{\star}_{\mathcal{AM}(-n)} \subseteq \mathbf{P}^{\#\mathbf{P}}$$

$$\mathbf{PMC}_{\mathcal{AM}(-n)}$$

Indeed, uniformity implies semi-uniformity, and adding dissolution rules does not decrease the power of P systems. Furthermore, P systems with restricted (without dissolution) elementary active membranes are able to efficiently simulate polynomial-time deterministic Turing machines with counting oracles [8]. The last inclusion $\mathbf{PMC}^{\star}_{\mathcal{AM}(-n)} \subseteq \mathbf{P}^{\#\mathbf{P}}$ follows from Lemma 4.   □

4.1   Consequences for the P Conjecture

In P systems without charges, the presence of dissolution rules possibly makes a difference. Without them, only problems in $\mathbf{P}$ may be solved in polynomial time [1], and the P conjecture [5, Problem F] claims that not even elementary division together with dissolution rules can break this barrier. However, the tightest known upper bound up to now was $\mathbf{PSPACE}$ [9].

P systems without charges are equivalent to P systems *with* charges where the membranes always remain neutral (i.e., no rule ever changes a membrane charge). Hence, the class of problems solved in polynomial time by the former model without non-elementary division rules, denoted by $\mathbf{PMC}_{\mathcal{AM}^0(-n)}$, is trivially included in $\mathbf{PMC}_{\mathcal{AM}(-n)}$. The corresponding inclusion also holds in the semi-uniform case. As a consequence, Theorem 1 implies the following improved upper bound for the P conjecture:

Corollary 1. $\mathbf{PMC}^{[\star]}_{\mathcal{AM}^0(-n)} \subseteq \mathbf{P}^{\#\mathbf{P}}$.   □

5   Conclusions

In this paper we have presented a simulation of polynomial-time semi-uniform families of P systems with elementary active membranes, characterising the complexity class $\mathbf{PMC}^{\star}_{\mathcal{AM}(-n)}$, by means of deterministic Turing machines working in polynomial time with access to a $\#\mathbf{P}$ oracle. This simulation and the previously known lower bound [8] complete the characterisation of this complexity class, as well as those obtained by requiring uniformity instead of semi-uniformity or disallowing dissolution rules: all these classes coincide with $\mathbf{P^{\#P}}$. This result is also interesting because it represents an improvement of the upper bound of the computational power for the class of P systems involved in the P conjecture. We hope that this step will help in the search for a solution to the conjecture.

In the future we plan to investigate the computational power of P systems with active membranes in which non-elementary division is allowed but limited to membranes of a certain depth. While unrestricted non-elementary division increases the computational power to **PSPACE**, we conjecture that limited division can generate a hierarchy of complexity classes. Furthermore, we plan to investigate the computational power of non-confluent P systems with active membranes using division rules. Currently, no upper bound tighter than **NEXP** is known for these classes of P systems.

References

1. Gutiérrez-Naranjo, M.A., Pérez-Jiménez, M.J., Riscos-Nuñez, A., Romero-Campero, F.J.: Computational efficiency of dissolution rules in membrane systems. International Journal of Computer Mathematics **83**(7), 593–611 (2006)
2. Murphy, N., Woods, D.: The computational power of membrane systems under tight uniformity conditions. Natural Computing **10**(1), 613–632 (2011)
3. Papadimitriou, C.H.: Computational Complexity. Addison-Wesley (1993)
4. Păun, Gh.: P systems with active membranes: Attacking NP-complete problems. Journal of Automata, Languages and Combinatorics **6**(1), 75–90 (2001)
5. Păun, Gh.: Further twenty six open problems in membrane computing. In: Gutiérrez-Naranjo, M.A., Riscos-Nuñez, A., Romero-Campero, F.J., Sburlan, D. (eds.) Proceedings of the Third Brainstorming Week on Membrane Computing, pp. 249–262. Fénix Editora (2005)
6. Porreca, A.E., Leporati, A., Mauri, G., Zandron, C.: Elementary active membranes have the power of counting. International Journal of Natural Computing Research **2**(3), 329–342 (2011)
7. Porreca, A.E., Leporati, A., Mauri, G., Zandron, C.: P systems with active membranes working in polynomial space. International Journal of Foundations of Computer Science **22**(1), 65–73 (2011)
8. Porreca, A.E., Leporati, A., Mauri, G., Zandron, C.: P systems simulating oracle computations. In: Gheorghe, M., Păun, Gh., Rozenberg, G., Salomaa, A., Verlan, S. (eds.) CMC 2011. LNCS, vol. 7184, pp. 346–358. Springer, Heidelberg (2012)
9. Sosík, P., Rodríguez-Patón, A.: Membrane computing and complexity theory: A characterization of PSPACE. Journal of Computer and System Sciences **73**(1), 137–152 (2007)
10. Zandron, C., Ferretti, C., Mauri, G.: Solving NP-complete problems using P systems with active membranes. In: Antoniou, I., Calude, C.S., Dinneen, M.J. (eds.) Proceedings of the Second International Conference on Unconventional Models of Computation, UMC'2K, pp. 289–301. Springer (2001)

Small Universal Spiking Neural P Systems with Cooperating Rules as Function Computing Devices

Venkata Padmavati Metta[1]([⊠]), Srinivasan Raghuraman[2],
and Kamala Krithivasan[2]

[1] Institute of Computer Science and Research Institute of the IT4Innovations
Centre of Excellence, Silesian University in Opava, Opava, Czech Republic
vmetta@gmail.com
[2] Indian Institute of Technology, Chennai, India
srini131293@gmail.com, kamala@iitm.ac.in

Abstract. The paper considers spiking neural P systems (SN P systems) with cooperating rules where each neuron has the same number of sets of rules, labelled identically. Each set is called a component (maybe empty). At each step only one of the components can be active for the whole system, and only the rules from the active component are enabled. Each neuron with enabled rules from this active component can fire. By using 59 neurons, a small universal SN P system with two components, working in the terminating mode, is constructed for computing functions.

1 Introduction

Cooperating distributed grammar systems (shortly called CD grammar systems) were introduced in [1] to model the blackboard type of problem solving architectures. A CD grammar system consists of several components (working as problem solving agents), which generate a common sentential form by taking turns in the rewriting process. The sentential form represents the blackboard which the agents might modify according to a certain protocol until a terminal string is generated. CD grammar systems with context-free components working in the cooperation protocol called terminal mode (or t-mode) are more powerful than context-free grammars; they characterize the class of ET0L languages, the languages generated by extended tabled interactionless Lindenmayer systems.

The concept of cooperation and distribution as known from the CD grammar systems was introduced to spiking neural P systems [5]. Spiking neural P systems [2] are parallel and distributed computing models inspired by the neurophysiological behaviour of neurons sending electrical pulses of identical voltages called spikes to the neighbouring neurons through synapses. An SN P system can be used as a computing device in various ways. Most of the previous research on SN P systems focused on three ways: as number generating/computing devices, as language generators, and as devices for computing functions.

A k-component SN P system with cooperating rules is represented as a directed graph where nodes correspond to the neurons; the input neuron has an incoming arrow and the output neuron has an outgoing arrow, suggesting

© Springer International Publishing Switzerland 2014
M. Gheorghe et al. (Eds.): CMC 2014, LNCS 8961, pp. 300–313, 2014.
DOI: 10.1007/978-3-319-14370-5_19

their communication with the environment. Each neuron has k sets of spiking or forgetting rules, called components (which can be empty) identified by the same labels in all neurons (here we use the labels 1, 2, ..., k). The arcs indicate the synapses between the neurons. Using spiking rules, the information in a certain neuron can be sent to its neighbouring neurons in form of spikes, which can be accumulated at the target neurons. When we use a forgetting rule in a certain neuron, a specified number of spikes will be removed from the neuron. In a computation step, one component from each neuron, with the label j, $1 \leq j \leq k$, is non-deterministically chosen and applied. This means, one rule from each component is used, as customary in SN P systems.

Generally, in an SN P system, a global clock is assumed to mark the time of the whole system. SN P systems work in a synchronous manner, that is, one rule must be applied for each neuron. Different neurons work in parallel. Using the rules in this way, the system passes from one configuration to another configuration; such a step is called a transition. A computation is a finite or infinite sequence of transitions starting from the initial configuration. A computation halts if it reaches a configuration where no rule can be used.

Spiking neural P systems with cooperating rules are based on cooperation among the components and passing of control between components in each neuron. Similar to the CD grammar systems, a series of cooperation protocols can been considered. For example, any component, once started, has to perform exactly k, at most k, at least k or an arbitrary number of transition steps. In the so-called t-mode, a component may stop working if and only if none of its rules is applicable. Selection of the next active component is non-deterministic and only one component generates the output at a step, other components wait for passing control. This paper considers the SN P systems with two components working in the t-mode.

In [5], the computational completeness has been proved both for asynchronous and for sequential cooperating SN P systems with two components using unbounded as well as general neurons working in the t-mode. In this paper, we take on one of the problems mentioned in [5].

Looking for small universal computing devices is a classical research topic in computer science, see, e.g., [3], and the references therein. This topic has been heavily investigated in the framework of SN P systems [11], where a universal SN P system with standard delayed rules was obtained by using 84 neurons for computing functions, and a system with 76 neurons can generate any set of Turing computable natural numbers. In [17], these results were improved: 67 neurons for standard delayed rules in the case of computing functions, and 63 neurons for standard rules in the case of generating sets of numbers. The number of neurons in universal SN P systems can be reduced to 3 with using infinite rules in neurons [7]; if we use a finite number of rules in each neuron, the number of neurons in universal SN P systems can be reduced to 10 [8]. Small universal systems were also constructed for certain variants of SN P systems, e.g., small universal SN P systems with anti-spikes are constructed in [4], small universal SN P systems with rules on synapses are constructed in [16], small universal sequential SN P Systems in [13], small universal spiking neural P systems working in the exhaustive mode in [9], and small universal asynchronous SN P systems in [10]. In this work, we investigate small universal SN P systems with two components (with standard rules, without delay) working in the t-mode. As devices of computing functions, we construct a universal SN P system with two components having 59 neurons. In [15], a small universal number generating SN P system with cooperating rules is constructed.

2   Universal Register Machines

We assume the reader to be familiar with formal language theory and membrane computing. The reader can find details about them in [14], [12] etc.

We pass now to introducing the universal register machines. Because the register machines used in the following sections are deterministic, we only recall the definition of this type of machines. A deterministic register machine is a construct $M = (m, H, l_0, l_h, I)$, where m is the number of registers, H is the set of instruction labels, l_0 is the start label (labelling an ADD instruction), l_h is the halt label (assigned to instruction HALT), and I is the set of instructions; each label from H labels only one instruction from I, thus precisely identifying it. When it is useful, a label can be seen as a state of the machine, l_0 being the initial state, l_h the final/accepting state.

The labelled instructions are of the following forms:

1. l_i: (ADD(r), l_j) (add 1 to register r and then go to the instruction with label l_j),
2. l_i: (SUB(r), l_j, l_k) (if register r is non-empty, then subtract 1 from it and go to the instruction with label l_j, otherwise go to the instruction with label l_k),
3. l_h : HALT (the halt instruction).

A register machine can compute any Turing computable function: we introduce the arguments $n_1, n_2, \ldots, n_k$ in specified registers $r_1, r_2, \ldots, r_k$ (without loss of the generality, we may assume that we use the first k registers), we start with the instruction with label l_0, and if we stop (with the instruction with label l_h), then the value of the function is placed in another specified register, r_t, with all registers different from r_t being empty. The partial function computed in this way is denoted by $M(n_1, n_2, \ldots, n_k)$. In the computing form, it is known (see e.g., [6]) that the deterministic register machines are equivalent with Turing machines.

In [3], universal computing register machines are defined as follows. Let $(\phi_0, \phi_1, \ldots)$ be a fixed admissible enumeration of the unary partial recursive functions. A register machine M_u is said to be universal if there is a recursive function g such that for all natural numbers x, y we have $\phi_x(y) = M_u(g(x), y)$. In [3], several universal register machines are constructed, with the input (the couple of numbers $g(x)$ and y introduced in registers 1 and 2, and the result

$$l_0 : (\text{SUB}(1), l_1, l_2), \qquad l_1 : (\text{ADD}(7), l_0), \qquad l_2 : (\text{ADD}(6), l_3),$$

$$l_3 : (\text{SUB}(5), l_2, l_4), \qquad l_4 : (\text{SUB}(6), l_5, l_3), \qquad l_5 : (\text{ADD}(5), l_6),$$

$$l_6 : (\text{SUB}(7), l_7, l_8), \qquad l_7 : (\text{ADD}(1), l_4), \qquad l_8 : (\text{SUB}(6), l_9, l_0),$$

$$l_9 : (\text{ADD}(6), l_{10}), \qquad l_{10} : (\text{SUB}(4), l_0, l_{11}), \qquad l_{11} : (\text{SUB}(5), l_{12}, l_{13}),$$

$$l_{12} : (\text{SUB}(5), l_{14}, l_{15}), \qquad l_{13} : (\text{SUB}(2), l_{18}, l_{19}), \qquad l_{14} : (\text{SUB}(5), l_{16}, l_{17}),$$

$$l_{15} : (\text{SUB}(3), l_{18}, l_{20}), \qquad l_{16} : (\text{ADD}(4), l_{11}), \qquad l_{17} : (\text{ADD}(2), l_{21}),$$

$$l_{18} : (\text{SUB}(4), l_0, l_h), \qquad l_{19} : (\text{SUB}(0), l_0, l_{18}), \qquad l_{20} : (\text{ADD}(0), l_0),$$

$$l_{21} : (\text{ADD}(3), l_{18}), \qquad l_h : \text{HALT}$$

Fig. 1. The universal register machine M_u from Korec [3]

obtained in register 0. In the following, we consider the specific universal register machine $M_u = (8, H, l_0, l_h, I)$, with the instructions (their labels constitute the set H) given in Fig. 1, which is also the one used in [11] (it has 8 registers numbered from 0 to 7 and 23 instructions).

3   Spiking Neural P Systems with Cooperating Rules

We pass on now to introducing SN P systems with cooperating rules investigated in [5].

Definition 1. An SN P system with cooperating rules is an SN P system of degree $m \geq 1$ with $p \geq 1$ components, of the form

$$\Pi = (O, \Sigma, \sigma_1, \sigma_2, \sigma_3, \ldots, \sigma_m, syn, in, out), \text{ where}$$

1. $O = \{a\}$ is the singleton alphabet (a is called *spike*);
2. $\Sigma = \{1, 2, \ldots, p\}$ is the label alphabet for components;
3. $\sigma_1, \sigma_2, \sigma_3, \ldots, \sigma_m$ are neurons, of the form

$$\sigma_i = (n_i, R_i), \ 1 \leq i \leq m;$$

where
   (a) $n_i \geq 0$ is the *initial number of spikes* contained in the neuron σ_i;
   (b) $R_i = \cup_{l \in \Sigma} R_{il}$, where each R_{il}, $1 \leq l \leq p$, is a set (can be empty) of rules representing a component l in σ_i having rules of the following two forms:
      i. $E/a^r \rightarrow a$, where E is a regular expression over O, $r \geq 1$ (if $L(E) = a^r$, then we write simply $a^r \rightarrow a$);
      ii. $a^s \rightarrow \lambda$, for some $s \geq 1$, with the restriction that $a^s \notin L(E)$ for any rule $E/a^r \rightarrow a$ of type i. from R_{il};
4. $syn \subseteq \{1, 2, 3, \ldots, m\} \times \{1, 2, 3, \ldots, m\}$ with $(i, i) \notin syn$ for $1 \leq i \leq m$ (the set of *synapses* among neurons);
5. $in, out \in \{1, 2, 3, \ldots, m\}$ indicate the *input* and *output* neuron, respectively.

The rules of the type $E/a^r \to a$ are spiking rules, and can be applied if the rule is contained in the active component and the neuron contains n spikes such that $a^n \in L(E)$ and $n \geq r$. When neuron σ_i spikes, its spike is replicated in such a way that one spike is sent immediately to all neurons σ_j such that $(i, j) \in syn$. The rules of type $a^s \to \lambda$ are forgetting rules; s spikes are simply removed ("forgotten") when applying. Like in the case of spiking rules, the left hand side of a forgetting rule must "cover" the contents of the neuron, that is, $a^s \to \lambda$ is applied only if the neuron contains exactly s spikes. For simplicity, in the graphical representation of the system, the rules in the component l of neuron σ_i are prefixed with l and the components inside the neuron are separated by lines. In a step, one component R_{ij} is chosen from each neuron σ_i, with the same l for each neuron.

As defined above, each component of the neurons can contain several rules. More precisely, it is allowed to have two spiking rules $E_1/a^{r_1} \to a$ and $E_2/a^{r_2} \to a$ with $L(E_1) \cap L(E_2) \neq \emptyset$ in the same component. This leads to a non–deterministic way of using the rules and we cannot avoid the non-determinism (deterministic systems will generate only singleton sets).

The *configuration* of an SN P system is described by the number of spikes in each neuron. Thus, the initial configuration of the system is described as $C_0 = \langle n_1, n_2, n_3, \ldots, n_m \rangle$.

The SN P system is synchronized by means of a global clock and works in a locally sequential and globally maximal manner with one component active at a step for the whole system. That is, the working is sequential at the level of each neuron. In each neuron, at each step, if there is more than one rule enabled from the active component, then only one of them (chosen non-deterministically) can fire. The system as a whole evolves in a parallel and synchronizes way, all the neurons (that have an enabled rule) choose a rule from the active component and all of them fire at once. Using the rules, the system passes from one configuration to another configuration; such a step is called a *transition*.

For two configurations C and C', we write $C \Longrightarrow_l^t C'$, if configuration C' can be reached from C by a sequence of transition steps using rules from lth component of each neuron, which cannot be continued.

A *computation* of Π is a finite or infinite sequence of transitions starting from the initial configuration, and every configuration appearing in such a sequence is called reachable. Therefore a finite (step) computation γ_t of Π in the t-mode is defined as $\gamma_t = C_0 \Longrightarrow_{j_1}^t C_1 \Longrightarrow_{j_2}^t \ldots \Longrightarrow_{j_y}^t C_y$ for some $y \geq 1$, $1 \leq j_y \leq p$, where C_0 is the initial configuration. A computation γ_t of Π halts when the system reaches a configuration where no rule can be used as per the t-mode cooperating protocol (i.e., the SN P system has halted).

With any computation, halting or not, we associate a spike train: a sequence of digits 0 and 1, with 1 appearing at positions corresponding to those steps when the output neuron sent a spike out of the system. With a spike train we can associate various numbers, which can be considered as generated by an SN P system. For instance, the distance in time between the first two spikes, between all consecutive spikes, the total number of spikes (in the case of halting computations), and so on.

It is clear that the standard SN P systems introduced in [2] are the special case of the cooperating SN P systems where the number of components is one. Similar to the standard SN P system, there are various ways of using this device. In the generative mode, one of the neurons is considered as the output neuron and the spikes of the output neuron are sent to the environment. An SN P system can also work in the accepting mode: a neuron is designated as the input neuron and two spikes are introduced in it at an interval of n steps; the number n is accepted if the computation halts.

When both an input and an output neuron are considered, the system can be used as a transducer, both for strings and infinite sequences, as well as for computing numerical functions. Like in the case considered in [11], in order to compute a function $f : N^k \rightarrow N$, where N is the set of all non-negative integers, k natural numbers $n_1, \ldots, n_k$ are introduced into the system by "reading" from the environment a binary sequence $z = 10^{n_1-1}10^{n_2-1}\ldots10^{n_k-1}1$. This means that the input neuron of Π receives a spike at each step corresponding to a digit 1 from string z and no spike otherwise. Note that $k + 1$ spikes are exactly inputted; that is, it is assumed that no further spike is coming to the input neuron after the last spike.

We start from the initial configuration and we define the result of a computation as the number of steps between the first two spikes sent out by the output neuron. The result is 0 if no spikes exit the output neuron and the computation halts. The computations and the result of computations are defined in the same way as for usual SN P systems - the time distance between the first two spikes emitted by the system with the restriction that the system outputs exactly two spikes and halts (immediately after the second spike), hence it produces a spike train of the form $0^b10^{r-1}1$, for some $b \geq 0$ and with $r = f(n_1, \ldots, n_k)$.

4   Small Universal Computing SN P Systems with Two Components Working in t-Mode

We proceed now to constructing a universal SN P system Π_u with cooperating rules, for computing functions. The system has two components and works in the t-mode. To construct a universal SN P system Π_u, we follow the way used in [11] to simulate a universal register machine M_u.

Before the construction, a modification should be made in M_u because subtraction operation on neurons corresponding to the registers where the result is placed is not allowed in the construction from [2], but the register 0 of M_u is a subject of such operations. That is why a further register has to be added– labelled with 8–and the halt instruction of M_u should be replaced by the following instructions:

l_h: (SUB(0), l_{22}, l'_h), l_{22}: (ADD(8), l_h), l'_h: HALT.

In this way, the obtained register machine M'_u has 9 registers, 24 ADD and SUB instructions and 25 labels.

The usual way of simulating a register machine M'_u by an SN P system is the construction of an SN P system with cooperating rules Π_u, where neurons are associated with each register and with each label of an instruction of the machine. For each register r of M_u, we associate a neuron σ_r. If a register r contains a number n, then the associated neuron σ_r will contain $2n$ spikes. Starting with neurons σ_1 and σ_2 already loaded with $2g(x)$ and $2y$ spikes, respectively, and introducing two spikes in neuron l_0, we can compute in our system Π_u in the same way as the universal register machine M_u from Fig. 1; if the computation halts, then neuron σ_8 will contain $2\phi_x(y)$ spikes.

With each label l_i of an instruction in M'_u, we associate a neuron σ_{l_i} and some auxiliary neurons $\sigma_{l_{i,q}}$, $q = 1, 2, \ldots$, thus precisely identified by label l_i. Specifically, modules ADD and SUB are constructed to simulate the instructions of M'_u. The modules are given in a graphical form in Figs. 3 and 4. In the initial configuration, all neurons of Π_u are empty. There are two additional tasks to solve: to introduce the mentioned spikes in the neurons σ_{l_0}, σ_1, σ_2, and to output the computed number.

The first task is covered by module INPUT presented in Fig. 2. After receiving the first spike from the environment, neuron σ_{in} starts in the second component and fires. Subsequently, neurons σ_{c_1} and σ_{c_2} send to neuron σ_1 as many pairs of spikes as one more than the number of steps between the first two input spikes, and after that they get "over flooded" by the second input spike and are blocked. In turn, neurons σ_{c_3} and σ_{c_4} start working only after collecting two spikes and stop working after receiving the third spike. No rule in the second component is applicable, so the systems switches to the first component and enables the firing of neuron σ_{c_5}. It sends two spikes to neuron σ_{l_0}, thus starting the simulation of M'_u. At that moment, neurons σ_1 and σ_2 are already loaded using spikes from the neurons σ_{c_1} through σ_{c_4}. Thus, at the end of the INPUT module, some of the neurons are still left with spikes, but this is not a cause for concern as those neurons will be nowhere reused.

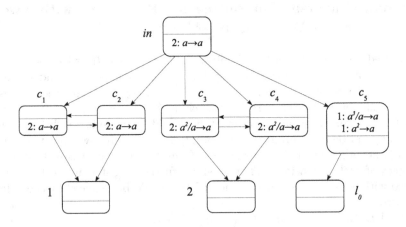

Fig. 2. INPUT module

In general, the simulation of an ADD or a SUB instruction starts by introducing two spikes in the neuron with the instruction label (we say that this neuron is activated).

Simulating l_i: (ADD(r), l_j) (module ADD in Fig. 3).

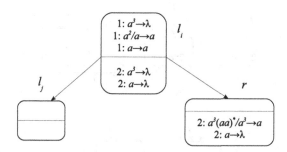

Fig. 3. Deterministic ADD module l_i: (ADD(r), l_j)

Assume that we are in a step t when we have to simulate an instruction l_i: (ADD(r), l_j), with two spikes present in neuron σ_{l_i} (like σ_{l_0} in the initial configuration) and no spikes in any other neuron, except in those associated with registers. Even if the system is in the second component at the time, it must switch over to the first component, since we are working in the t-mode and there are no rules in the second component which are currently applicable anywhere in the system. Having two spikes inside and now in the first component, neuron σ_{l_i} fires using the rule $a^2/a \rightarrow a$ producing a spike. This spike will simultaneously go to neurons σ_r and σ_{l_j}. In step $t + 1$, neuron σ_{l_i} fires again using the rule $a \rightarrow a$ and sends another spike to σ_r and σ_{l_j}. Note that there was no switch in the component as the first component still had a rule applicable. Therefore, from the firing of neuron σ_{l_i}, the system adds two spikes each to neuron σ_r and σ_{l_j} and activates the neuron σ_{l_j}. Consequently, the simulation of the ADD instruction is possible in Π_u.

Another important point to note is that if l_j is also the label for an ADD instruction, then σ_{l_j} will fire in step $t + 1$ itself using the rule $a \rightarrow a$. This does not hamper the correctness of the module since the second spike will also reach σ_{l_j} in the next step and another spike will be sent out by using the same rule. If it is a SUB instruction, σ_{l_j} will not fire in step $t+1$ as there is no rule applicable in the first component of the neuron corresponding to a SUB instruction, as we will see in the SUB module simulation.

Simulating l_i: (SUB(r), l_j, l_k) (module SUB in Fig. 4).

Assume that we are in a step t when we have to simulate an instruction l_i: (SUB(r), l_j, l_k), with two spikes present in neuron σ_{l_i} and no spikes in any other neurons, except in those associated with registers. Let us examine now Fig. 4, starting from the situation of having two spikes in neuron σ_{l_i} and neuron σ_r, which holds a certain number of spikes (this number is twice the value of the corresponding register r). Even if the system is in the first component at

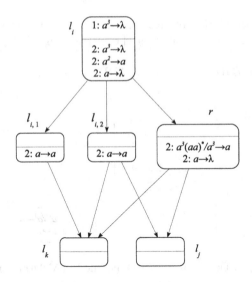

Fig. 4. SUB module: simulation of l_i: (SUB(r), l_j, l_k)

the time, it must switch over to the second component, since we are working in the t-mode and there are no rules in the first component which are currently applicable anywhere in the system. A spike from neuron σ_{l_i} goes immediately to neurons $\sigma_{l_{i,1}}$, $\sigma_{l_{i,2}}$ and σ_r. If σ_r does not contain any spikes to begin with (this corresponds to the case when register r is empty), then in the step $t + 1$, the spike sent by σ_{l_i} gets forgotten by virtue of the rule $a \to \lambda$ and σ_r is again left with no spikes, indicating that it is still zero. At the same time, neurons $\sigma_{l_{i,1}}$ and $\sigma_{l_{i,2}}$ send spikes using the rule $a \to a$. Thus, neurons σ_{l_j} and σ_{l_k} end with 1 and 2 spikes respectively. In the subsequent step $t + 2$, σ_{l_j} forgets the spike through the rule $a \to \lambda$. In the case of the neuron σ_{l_k}, if it corresponds to an ADD instruction, it will fire in the next step since the second component of the neuron corresponding to an ADD instruction has no rule applicable and the system cannot switch over to the first component as σ_{l_j} has an applicable rule. If it corresponds to a SUB instruction, it will fire in the same step and this does not create any issues as the operation is complete and the next one may begin. Thus the neuron σ_{l_k} gets activated, as required by simulating the SUB instruction.

If neuron σ_r has $2n$ spikes to begin with, where $n \geq 1$, then in the step $t + 1$, the rule $a^3(aa)^*/a^3 \to a$ is used in σ_r and $a \to a$ is used in neurons $\sigma_{l_{i,1}}$ and $\sigma_{l_{i,2}}$, and hence the neurons σ_{l_j} and σ_{l_k} receive 2 and 3 spikes respectively. The neuron σ_r now has 2 spikes lesser than when it started out and hence we have achieved the decrement of the register r by 1. In the subsequent step $t + 2$, σ_{l_k} forgets the spikes through the rule $a^3 \to \lambda$. In the case of the neuron σ_{l_j}, if it corresponds to an ADD instruction, it will fire in the next step since the second component of the neuron corresponding to an ADD instruction has no rule applicable and the system cannot switch over to the first component as σ_{l_k}

has an applicable rule. If it corresponds to a SUB instruction, it will fire in the step $t + 2$ and this does not create any problems as the operation is complete and the next one may begin. Thus the neuron σ_{l_j} gets activated, as required by simulating the SUB instruction.

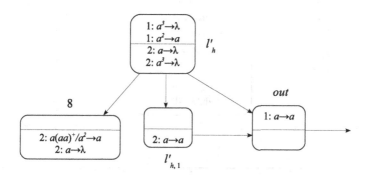

Fig. 5. Module OUTPUT

Another important point to note is that in our construction, the neuron σ_r is sending a spike. Note that there may be more than a single SUB instruction involving the same register r. In that case, when σ_r sends a spike, it would be sent to not just σ_{l_j} and σ_{l_k} but also to target neurons of all SUB instructions involving r. This is handled since the second components of both ADD and SUB modules have the forgetting rule $a \rightarrow \lambda$. So in the same step where σ_{l_k} forgets its three spikes, those target neurons which received a spike unnecessarily will also forget their spike received from σ_r. Since σ_r does not send spikes when it started out with a zero value, we do not have any problem in that case.

It is also important to note that the neurons σ_{l_i} associated with ADD instructions are different from those associated with SUB instructions: in the first case it starts firing after receiving either one spike or two spikes, in the latter case the neuron fires only after receiving two spikes.

Having the result of the computation in register 8, which is never decremented during the computation, we can output the result by means of the module OUTPUT from Fig. 5. When neuron l'_h receives two spikes, it fires and sends a spike to neurons σ_8, $\sigma_{l'_{h,1}}$ and σ_{out} with the system in the first component (it will switch to the first component even otherwise as only rules in the first component are enabled and we are working in the t-mode). Let t be the moment when neuron l'_u fires. Suppose the number stored in the register 8 of M'_u is n.

At step $t + 1$, neuron σ_{out} fires for the first time sending its spike to the environment. The number of steps from this spike to the next one is the function of the number computed by the system. Since no rules are enabled in the first component, the system switches to the second component. Now the two neurons σ_8 and $\sigma_{l'_{h,1}}$ spike during the next $n+1$ steps (σ_8 would fire $n+1$ times and $\sigma_{l'_{h,1}}$ would fire for one time). The neuron σ_{out} will become active only after $2n + 1$

spikes are removed from σ_8. So at time $t + n + 3$, the system again switches to the first component and the neuron σ_{out} fires for the second time. In this way, we get the spike train $..10^{n+1}1$, encoding the number $\phi_x(y)$ as the result of the computation. The overall design of the system is given in Fig. 6.

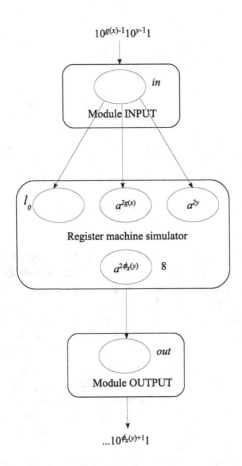

Fig. 6. The general design of the universal SN P system

Thus, the system Π_u has

- 9 neurons for the 9 registers,
- 25 neurons for the 25 labels,
- 28 neurons for 14 SUB instructions,
- 6 neurons in the INPUT module,
- 2 neurons in the OUTPUT module,

which comes to a total of 70 neurons. This number can be slightly decreased, by some "code optimization", exploiting some particularities of the register machine M'_u.

First, let us observe that the sequence of two consecutive ADD instructions l_{17}: (ADD(2), l_{21}), l_{21}: (ADD(3), l_{18}), without any other instruction addressing the label l_{21}, can be simulated by merging the modules for these two instructions and eliminating the neuron $\sigma_{l_{21}}$, and in this way we save the neuron associated with l_{21}.

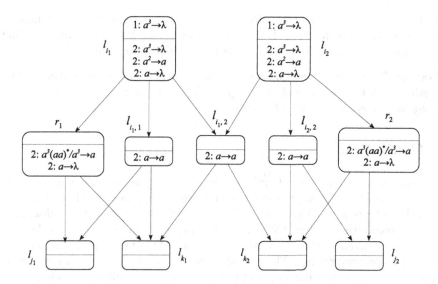

Fig. 7. A module simulating SUB-SUB instructions

If the two SUB instructions address different registers, then they can share one auxiliary neuron, as shown in Fig. 7. The working of any particular instruction is as described above. The only difference is that when one of the instructions executes, a spike is sent to the target neuron of another SUB instruction. Since the second components of both ADD and SUB modules have the forgetting rule $a \to \lambda$, those target neurons which received a spike will forget their spike received from $\sigma_{l_{i_1,2}}$.

By using the results as above, the 14 SUB instructions can be classified to four groups:

1. l_0: (SUB(1), l_1, l_2), l_3: (SUB(5), l_2, l_4), l_4: (SUB(6), l_5, l_3),
   l_6: (SUB(7), l_7, l_8), l_{10}: (SUB(4), l_0, l_{11}), l_{13}: (SUB(2), l_{18}, l_{19}),
   l_{15}: (SUB(3), l_{18}, l_{20}), l_{19}: (SUB(0), l_0, l_{18});
2. l_8: (SUB(6), l_9, l_0), l_{11}: (SUB(5), l_{12}, l_{13}), l_{18}: (SUB(4), l_0, l_h), l_h: (SUB(0), l_{22}, l'_h);
3. l_{12} : (SUB(5), l_{14}, l_{15});
4. l_{14} : (SUB(5), l_{16}, l_{17}).

All modules associated with the instructions in each group can share one auxiliary neuron. In this way, 7 neurons are saved from the first group, 3 neurons from the second group.

Overall 11 neurons are saved, thus an improvement is achieved from 70 to 59 neurons. We state this result in the form of a theorem in order to stress its importance.

Theorem 1. *There exists a universal computing spiking neural P system with two components working in the t-mode, having 59 neurons.*

This number can be reduced by using more components, for instance, the number of auxiliary neurons in the SUB module can be brought down to one by using four components. We state this result in the form of a theorem.

Theorem 2. *The number of neurons in the universal computing spiking neural P system with two components working in the t-mode can be further reduced by adding more components in the system.*

5   Conclusion

Starting from the definition of spiking neural P systems and following the idea of cooperating distributed grammar systems, we have proposed a class of spiking neural P systems with cooperating rules for which we have constructed a small universal computing system with two components working in the t-mode. The system constructed in this work has 59 neurons. This number can be reduced by using more components. Thus, further work could include smaller universal systems using more components and perhaps working in different modes.

Acknowledgements. The work was supported by EU project Development of Research Capacities of the Silesian University in Opava (CZ.1.07/2.3.00/30.0007) and European Regional Development Fund in the IT4Innovations Centre of Excellence project (CZ.1.05/1.1.00/02.0070).

References

1. Csuhaj-Varju, E., Dassow, J.: On cooperating/distributed grammar systems. Journal of Information Processing and Cybernetics (EIK) **26**, 49–63 (1990)
2. Ionescu, M., Păun, Gh., Yokomori, T.: Spiking neural P systems. Fundamenta Informaticae **71**, 279–308 (2006)
3. Korec, I.: Small universal register machines. Theoretical Computer Science **168**, 267–301 (1996)
4. Metta, V.P., Kelemenová, A.: Smaller universal spiking neural P systems with anti-spikes. Journal of Automata, Languages and Combinatorics **19**(1–4), 213–226 (2014)
5. Metta, V.P., Raghuraman, S., Krithivasan, K.: Spiking neural P systems with cooperating rules. In: Proc. of Conference on Membrane Computing (CMC 15), Prague, Czech Republic, pp. 267–282 (2014)
6. Minsky, M.: Computation – Finite and Infinite Machines. Prentice Hall, Englewood Cliffs (1967)

7. Neary, T.: A boundary between universality and non-universality in extended spiking neural P systems. In: Dediu, A.-H., Fernau, H., Martín-Vide, C. (eds.) LATA 2010. LNCS, vol. 6031, pp. 475–487. Springer, Heidelberg (2010)

8. Pan, L., Zeng, X.: A note on small universal spiking neural P systems. In: Păun, Gh., Pérez-Jiménez, M.J., Riscos-Núñez, A., Rozenberg, G., Salomaa, A. (eds.) WMC 2009. LNCS, vol. 5957, pp. 436–447. Springer, Heidelberg (2010)

9. Pan, L., Zeng, X.: Small universal spiking neural P systems working in exhaustive mode. IEEE Transactions on Nano-Bioscience **10**(2), 99–105 (2011)

10. Pan, L., Zeng, X., Zhang, X.: Small asynchronous universal spiking neural P systems. In: Proc. of IEEE Fifth International Conference on Bio-inspired Computing: Theories and Applications, pp. 622–630 (2010)

11. Păun, A., Păun, Gh.: Small universal spiking neural P systems. BioSystems **90**(1), 48–60 (2007)

12. Păun, Gh., Rozenberg, G., Salomaa, A. (eds.): Handbook of Membrane Computing. Oxford University Press, Oxford (2010)

13. Păun, A., Sidoroff, M.: Sequentiality induced by spike number in SN P systems: small universal machines. In: Gheorghe, M., Păun, Gh., Rozenberg, G., Salomaa, A., Verlan, S. (eds.) CMC 2011. LNCS, vol. 7184, pp. 333–345. Springer, Heidelberg (2012)

14. Rozenberg, G., Salomaa, A. (eds.): Handbook of Formal Languages, 3 vol. Springer, Berlin (1997)

15. Song, T., Pan, L.: A small universal spiking neural P system with cooperating rules as number generator. In: Proc. of Asian Conference on Membrane Computing (ACMC 2014), Coimbatore, India, pp. 33–44 (2014)

16. Song, T., Pan, L., Păun, Gh.: Spiking neural P systems with rules on synapses. Theoretical Computer Science **529**(10), 82–95 (2014)

17. Zhang, X., Zeng, X., Pan, L.: Smaller universal spiking neural P systems. Fundamenta Informaticae **87**, 117–136 (2008)

Spiking Neural P Systems
with Cooperating Rules

Venkata Padmavati Metta[1]($\boxtimes$), Srinivasan Raghuraman[2],
and Kamala Krithivasan[2]

[1] Institute of Computer Science and Research Institute of the IT4Innovations
Centre of Excellence, Silesian University in Opava, Opava, Czech Republic
vmetta@gmail.com
[2] Indian Institute of Technology, Chennai, India
srini131293@gmail.com, kamala@iitm.ac.in

Abstract. The concept of cooperation and distribution as known from
grammar systems is introduced to spiking neural P systems (in short,
SN P systems) in which each neuron has a finite number of sets (called
components) of rules. During computations, at each step only one of the
components can be active for the whole system and one of the enabled
rules from this active component of each neuron fires. The switching
between the components occurs under different cooperation strategies.
This paper considers the terminating mode, in which the switching occurs
when no rule is enabled in the active component of any neuron in the
system. By introducing this new mechanism, the computational power
of asynchronous and sequential SN P systems with standard rules is
investigated. The results are that asynchronous standard SN P systems
with two components and strongly sequential unbounded SN P systems
with two components are Turing complete.

1 Introduction

Cooperative grammar systems were introduced by Meersman and Rozenberg in
[6], in the context of two-level grammars. The systematic study of cooperating
distributed (for short, CD) grammar systems was initiated by Csuhaj-Varjú and
Dassow in [2], where productions are distributed over a finite number of sets,
called components. These components cooperate during the derivation process
by applying productions on a common sentential form; following some fixed
cooperation protocol.

The concept of cooperation and distribution as known from CD grammar
systems is introduced to spiking neural P systems. Spiking neural P systems [5]
are parallel and distributed computing models inspired by the neurophysiological
behaviour of neurons sending electrical pulses of identical voltages called spikes
to the neighbouring neurons through synapses. An SN P system is represented
as a directed graph where nodes correspond to the neurons having spiking rules
and forgetting rules. The rules involve the spikes present in the neuron in the
form of occurrences of a symbol a. The arcs indicate the synapses among the

M. Gheorghe et al. (Eds.): CMC 2014, LNCS 8961, pp. 314–329, 2014.
DOI: 10.1007/978-3-319-14370-5_20

neurons. The spiking rules are of the form $E \ / \ a^r \rightarrow a$ and are used only if the neuron contains n spikes such that $a^n \in L(E)$ and $n \geq r$, where $L(E)$ is the language represented by regular expression E. In this case a^r number of spikes are consumed and one spike is sent out. When neuron σ_i sends a spike, it is replicated in such a way that one spike is immediately sent to all neurons j such that $(i, j) \in syn$, where syn is the set of arcs between the neurons. The transmission of spikes takes no time, the spike will be available in neuron j in the next step. The forgetting rules are of the form $a^s \rightarrow \lambda$ and are applied only if the neuron contains exactly a^s spikes. The rule simply removes s spikes. For all forgetting rules, s must not be the member of $L(E)$ for any firing rule within the same neuron.

A rule is *bounded* if it is of the form $a^i/a^j \rightarrow a$, where $1 \leq j \leq i$, or of the form $a^k \rightarrow \lambda$, where $k \geq 1$. A neuron is bounded if it contains only bounded rules. A rule is called *unbounded* if is of the form $a^c(a^i)^*/a^j \rightarrow a$, where $c \geq 0$, $i \geq 1$, $j \geq 1$. A neuron is unbounded if it contains only unbounded rules. A neuron is *general* if it contains both bounded and unbounded rules. An SN P system is bounded if all the neurons in the system are bounded. It is unbounded if it has bounded and unbounded neurons. Finally, an SN P system is general if it has general neurons (i.e., it contains at least one neuron which has both bounded and unbounded rules).

The usual SN P systems are synchronous (a global clock is assumed) and work in a maximally parallel manner, in the sense that all neurons that are fireable must fire. However, in any neuron, at most one rule is allowed to fire. One neuron is designated as the output neuron of the system and its spikes can exit into the environment, thus producing a spike train. Two main kinds of outputs can be associated with a computation in an SN P system: a set of numbers, obtained by considering the number of steps elapsed between consecutive spikes which exit the output neuron, and a set of numbers, obtained by considering the total number of spikes emitted by the output neuron until the system halts. Two main types of results were obtained for synchronous SN P systems using standard rules (producing one spike): computational completeness in the case when no bound was imposed on the number of spikes present in the system, and a characterization of semi-linear sets of numbers in the case when a bound was imposed [5].

This paper introduces spiking neural P system with cooperating rules where each neuron has a finite number of sets of spiking and forgetting rules. Each set is called a component which can be empty. At any step or during a sequence of steps (depending on the mode of application) only one of the components is active for the whole system and only one of the enabled rules from this component of each neuron can fire during that step. After that another (not necessarily different) component of each neuron becomes active. The way of passing active control is called a protocol. Similar to CD grammar systems, series of cooperation protocols among the components in neurons of an SN P system can be considered, where for example any component, once started, has to perform exactly k, at most k, at least k, $k \geq 1$ or an arbitrary number of transition steps. In the so-called terminating mode, a component may stop working if and only if none of the rules in that component of any neuron is applicable. In any case, the selection of the next active component is non-deterministic and only one component generates the output at a step, other components wait for receiving control.

This paper considers asynchronous SN P systems [1], where in any step, a neuron can apply or not apply its rules which are enabled by the number of spikes it contains (further spikes can come, thus changing the rules enabled in the next step). Because the time between two firings of the output neuron is now irrelevant, the result of a computation is the number of spikes sent out by the system, not the distance between certain spikes leaving the system. It was proved that such asynchronous SN P systems with extended rules are equivalent to Turing machines (as generators of sets of natural numbers) but universality of such systems with standard rules is still an open problem. The additional non-determinism introduced in the functioning of the system by the non-synchronization has more computing power in the case of using two components. That is, two component SN P systems with standard rules working asynchronously are equivalent to the Turing machines (interpreted as generators of sets of (vectors of) numbers).

The paper also considers sequential SN P systems in which, at every step of the computation, if there is at least one neuron with at least one rule that is fireable, we only allow one such neuron and one such rule (both nondeterministically chosen) to be fired. Here, not every step has at least one neuron with a fireable rule. (Thus, the system might be dormant until a rule becomes fireable. However, the clock will keep on ticking.) The sequential unbounded as well as general SN P systems are proved to be universal [4]. A system is strongly sequential, if at every step, there is at least one neuron with a fireable rule. It is shown that strongly sequential general SN P systems are universal but strongly sequential unbounded SN P systems are not universal [4]. In this paper, we also prove that strongly sequential unbounded SN P systems with two components are universal.

The paper is organized as follows. In the next section, register machines are defined. SN P systems with cooperating rules are introduced in Section 3. The universality of asynchronous two component SN P systems with standard rules is proved in Section 4 and that of strongly sequential SN P systems with standard unbounded neurons is proved in Section 5.

2   Prerequisites

We assume the reader to be familiar with formal language theory, CD grammar systems and membrane computing. The reader can find details about them in [10], [3], [9] etc.

The family of Turing computable sets of natural numbers is denoted by NRE (the notation comes from the fact that these numbers are the length sets of recursively enumerable languages). The family of NRE is also the family of sets of numbers generated/recognized by register machines. For the universality proofs in this paper, we use the characterization of NRE by means of register machines [7]. Such a device - in the non-deterministic version - is a construct $M = (m, H, l_0, l_h, I)$, where m is the number of registers, H is the set of instruction labels, l_0 is the start label (labelling an ADD instruction), l_h is the halt label (assigned to instruction $HALT$), and I is the set of instructions; each label from H labels only one instruction from I, thus precisely identifying it.

The labelled instructions are of the following forms:

1. $l_i : (ADD(r), l_j, l_k)$ (add 1 to register r and then go to one of the instructions with labels l_j, l_k non-deterministically chosen),
2. $l_i : (SUB(r), l_j, l_k)$ (if register r is non-empty, then subtract 1 from it and go to the instruction with label l_j, otherwise go to the instruction with label l_k),
3. $l_h : HALT$ (the halt instruction).

A register machine M generates a set $N(M)$ of numbers in the following way: we start with all registers empty (i.e., storing the number zero), we apply the instruction with label l_0 and we continue to apply instructions as indicated by the labels (and made possible by the contents of registers). If we reach the halt instruction, then the number n present in register 1 (the registers are numbered from 1 to m) at that time is said to be generated by M. It is known (e.g., see, [7]) that register machines generate all sets of numbers which are Turing computable.

A register machine can also accept a set of numbers: a number n is accepted by M if, starting with n in register 1 and all other registers empty, the computation eventually halts (without loss of generality, we may assume that in the halting configuration all registers are empty). Deterministic register machines (i.e., with ADD instructions of the form $l_i : (ADD(r), l_j)$ working in the accepting mode are known to be equivalent to Turing machines.

It is also possible to consider register machines producing sets of vectors of natural numbers. In this case a distinguished set of v registers (for some $v \geq 1$) are designated as the output registers. A v-tuple $(l_1, l_2, \ldots, l_v) \in N^v$ is generated if M eventually halts and the contents of the output registers are $l_1, l_2, \ldots, l_v$ respectively.

Without loss of generality we may assume that in the halting configuration all the registers, except the output ones, are empty. We also assume (without loss of generality) that the output registers are non-decreasing and their contents is only incremented (i.e., the output registers are never the subject of SUB instructions, but only of ADD instructions).

We will refer to a register machine with v-output registers (the other registers are auxiliary registers) as a v-output register machine. It is well known that a set S of v-tuples of numbers is generated by a v-output register machine if and only if S is recursively enumerable. When dealing with vectors of numbers, hence with the Parikh images of languages (or with sets of vectors generated/recognized by register machines), we write $PsRE$.

3   Spiking Neural P Systems with Cooperating Rules

We pass on now to introducing SN P systems with cooperating rules investigated in this paper.

Definition 1. [SN P system with cooperating rules] An SN P system with cooperating rules is an SN P system of degree $m \geq 1$ with $p \geq 1$ components, of the form

$$\Pi = (O, \Sigma, \sigma_1, \sigma_2, \sigma_3, \dots, \sigma_m, syn, out), \text{ where}$$

1. $O = \{a\}$ is the singleton alphabet (a is called *spike*);
2. $\Sigma = \{1, 2, \dots, p\}$ is the label alphabet for components;
3. $\sigma_1, \sigma_2, \sigma_3, \dots, \sigma_m$ are neurons, of the form

$$\sigma_i = (n_i, R_i),\ 1 \leq i \leq m;$$

   where
   (a) $n_i \geq 0$ is the *initial number of spikes* contained in the neuron;
   (b) $R_i = \cup_{l \in \Sigma} R_{il}$, where each R_{il}, $1 \leq l \leq p$, is a set (can be empty) of rules representing a component l in σ_i having rules of the following two forms:
      i. $E/a^r \rightarrow a$, where E is a regular expression over O, $r \geq 1$ (if $L(E) = a^r$, then we simply write $a^r \rightarrow a$);
      ii. $a^s \rightarrow \lambda$, for some $s \geq 1$, with the restriction that $a^s \notin L(E)$ for any rule $E/a^r \rightarrow a$ of type i from R_{il};
4. $syn \subseteq \{1, 2, 3, \dots, m\} \times \{1, 2, 3, \dots, m\}$ with $(i, i) \notin syn$ for $1 \leq i \leq m$ (*synapses* among cells);
5. $out \in \{1, 2, 3, \dots, m\}$ indicates the *output* neuron.

Because we do not need the delay between firing and spiking (i.e., rules of the form $E/a^r \rightarrow a; d$, with $d \geq 1$) as well as extended rules (i.e., rules of the form $E/a^r \rightarrow a^q$, with $q \geq 1$) in the proofs below, we do not consider these features in the definition, but such rules can be introduced in the usual way.

The rules of the type $E/a^r \rightarrow a$ are spiking rules, and can be applied only if the neuron contains n spikes such that $a^n \in L(E)$ and $n \geq r$. When neuron σ_i spikes, its spike is replicated in such a way that one spike is sent immediately to all neurons σ_j such that $(i, j) \in syn$. The rules of type $a^s \rightarrow \lambda$ are forgetting rules; s spikes are simply removed ("forgotten") when applying such a rule. Like in the case of spiking rules, the left-hand side of a forgetting rule must "cover" the contents of the neuron, that is, $a^s \rightarrow \lambda$ is applied only if the neuron contains exactly s spikes. For simplicity, in the graphical representation of the system, the rules in the component l of neuron σ_i are prefixed with l and the components inside the neuron is separated by lines.

As defined above, each component of the neurons can contain several rules. More precisely, it is allowed to have two spiking rules $E_1/a^{r_1} \rightarrow a$ and $E_2/a^{r_2} \rightarrow a$ with $L(E_1) \cap L(E_2) \neq \emptyset$ in the same component. This leads to a non-deterministic way of using the rules and we cannot avoid the non-determinism (deterministic systems will compute only singleton sets).

The *configuration* of an SN P system is described by the number of spikes in each neuron. Thus, the initial configuration of the system is described as $C_0 = \langle n_1, n_2, n_3, \ldots, n_m \rangle$.

The SN P system is synchronized by means of a global clock and works in a locally sequential and globally maximal manner with one component active at a step for the whole system. That is, the working is sequential at the level of each neuron. In each neuron, at each step, if there is more than one rule enabled from the active component by its current contents, then only one of them (chosen non-deterministically) can fire. But still, the system as a whole evolves in a parallel and synchronising way, as in each step, all the neurons (that have an enabled rule) choose a rule from the active component and all of them fire at once. Using the rules, the system passes from one configuration to another configuration; such a step is called a *transition*.

In a component-l-restricted transition, we say that the symbol 1 is generated if at least one rule with label l is used and a spike is sent out to the environment by the output neuron and the symbol 0 is generated if no spike is sent out to the environment. Similar to CD grammar systems, several cooperation strategies among the components can be considered: we here consider only the five basic ones.

For two configurations C and C', we write $C \Longrightarrow_l^* C'$, $C \Longrightarrow_l^{=k} C'$, $C \Longrightarrow_l^{\leq k} C'$, $C \Longrightarrow_l^{\geq k} C'$, $C \Longrightarrow_l^t C'$, for some $k \geq 1$, if configuration C' can be reached from C as follows: (1) by any number of transitions, (2) by k transition steps, (3) by at most k transition steps, (4) by at least k transition steps, (5) by a sequence of transition steps using rules from lth component of each neuron, which cannot be continued, respectively.

A *computation* of Π is a finite or infinite sequence of transitions starting from the initial configuration, and every configuration appearing in such a sequence is called reachable. Therefore a finite (step) computation γ_α of Π in the mode $\alpha \in \{*, t\} \cup \{\leq k, = k, \geq k \mid k \geq 1\}$, is defined as $\gamma_\alpha = C_0 \Longrightarrow_{j_1}^\alpha C_1 \Longrightarrow_{j_2}^\alpha \ldots \Longrightarrow_{j_y}^\alpha C_y$ for some $y \geq 1$, $1 \leq j_y \leq p$, where C_0 is the initial configuration. A computation γ_α of Π halts when the system reaches a configuration where no rule can be used as per the cooperating protocol α (i.e., the SN P system has halted). This paper only works in the terminating mode, so for convenience the mode is not explicitly used in the definitions hereafter.

With any computation, halting or not, we associate a spike train: a sequence of digits 0 and 1, with 1 appearing at positions corresponding to those steps when the output neuron sent a spike out of the system. With a spike train we can associate various numbers, which can be considered as generated by an SN P system. For instance, the distance in time between the first two spikes, between all consecutive spikes, the total number of spikes (in the case of halting computations), and so on.

It is clear that the standard SN P system introduced in [5] is a special case of the cooperating SN P system where the number of components is one. Similar to the standard SN P system, there are various ways of using this device. In the generative mode, one of the neurons is considered as the output neuron and the spikes of the output neuron are sent to the environment. SN P systems can also be used for generating sets of vectors, by considering several output neurons, $\sigma_{i_1}, \sigma_{i_2}, \ldots, \sigma_{i_v}$. In this case, the system is called a v-output SN P system. Here a vector of numbers, $(n_1, n_2, \ldots, n_v)$, is said to be generated by the system if n_j is the number corresponding to the spike train from σ_{i_j}, where $1 \leq j \leq v$.

We denote by $C_p N_{gen}^{max}(\Pi)$ $[C_p Ps_{gen}^{max}(\Pi)]$ the set of numbers [of vectors, resp.] generated by a p-component SN P system Π in a maximally parallel manner, and by $NC_p Spik_2 P_m^{max}(\beta)$ $[Ps C_p Spik_2 P_m^{max}(\beta)]$, $\beta \in \{gene, unb, boun\}$, the family of such sets of numbers [sets of vectors of numbers, resp.] generated by cooperating SN P systems of type β (*gene* stands for general, *unb* for unbounded, *boun* for bounded), with at most m neurons and p components. When m is not bounded, it is replaced by $*$. The subscript 2 reminds us of the fact that we count the number of steps elapsed between the first two spikes.

An SN P system can also work in the accepting mode: a neuron is designated as the input neuron and two spikes are introduced in it at an interval of n steps; input n is encoded by $2n$ in the input register; the number n is accepted if the computation halts.

In the asynchronous case, in each time unit, any neuron is free to use a rule or not. Even if enabled, a rule is not necessarily applied, the neuron can remain still in spite of the fact that it contains rules which are enabled by its contents. If the contents of the neuron are not changed, a rule which was enabled in a step t can fire later. If new spikes are received, then it is possible that other rules will be enabled – and applied or not. This way of using the rules also applies to the output neuron, hence now the distance in time between the spikes sent out by the system is no longer relevant. That is why, for asynchronous SN P systems we take as the result of a computation the total number of spikes sent out; this, in turn, makes necessary considering only halting computations (the computations never halting are ignored, they provide no output). We denote by $C_p N_{gen}^{nsyn}(\Pi)$ $[C_p Ps_{gen}^{nsyn}(\Pi)]$ the set of numbers [of vectors, resp.] generated by an asynchronous cooperating SN P system Π with p components, and by $NC_p Spik_{tot} P_m^{nsyn}(\beta)$ $[Ps C_p Spik_{tot} P_m^{nsyn}(\beta)]$, $\beta \in \{gene, unb, boun\}$, the family of such sets of numbers [sets of vectors of numbers, resp.] generated by an asynchronous cooperating SN P systems of type β, with at most m neurons and p components. When m is not bounded, it is replaced by $*$. The subscript *tot* reminds us of the fact that we count all spikes sent to the environment.

In the strongly sequential case, in each neuron, in each time unit, at least one neuron contains a fireable rule and exactly one of them is chosen to fire non-deterministically. Here, the output can be interpreted in any of the earlier suggested ways. In this paper, we consider the distance in time between the first two spikes. We denote by $C_p N_{gen}^{sseq}(\Pi)$ $[C_p Ps_{gen}^{sseq}(\Pi)]$ the set of numbers [of vectors, resp.] generated by a strongly sequential cooperating SN P system Π, and by $NC_p Spik_2 P_m^{sseq}(\beta)$ $[Ps C_p Spik_2 P_m^{sseq}(\beta)]$, $\beta \in \{gene, unb, boun\}$, the family of such sets of numbers [sets of vectors of numbers, resp.] generated by strongly sequential cooperating SN P systems of type β, with at most m neurons and p components. When m is not bounded, it is replaced by $*$.

4   Computational Completeness of Asynchronous SN P Systems with Two Components Using Standard Rules

We pass now to prove that the power of two components in standard neurons (where standard rules, producing one spike at a time, are used) can compensate for the loss of power entailed by removing the synchronization.

Theorem 1. $NC_2Spik_{tot}P_*^{nsyn}(gene) = NRE.$

Proof. We only have to prove the inclusion $NRE \subseteq NC_2Spik_{tot}P_*^{nsyn}(gene)$, and to this aim, we use the characterization of NRE by means of register machines used in the generating mode.

Let $M = (m, H, l_0, l_h, I)$ be a register machine with m registers, having the properties specified above: the result of a computation is the number stored in register 1 at the end of the computation and this register is never decremented during the computation.

What we want is an asynchronous SN P system with two components Π which (1) simulates the register machine M, and (2) has its output neuron emitting the number of spikes equal to the number computed by M.

Instead of specifying all technical details of the construction, we present the three main types of modules of the system Π, with the neurons, their rules, and their synapses represented graphically. In turn, simulating M means to simulate the ADD instructions and the SUB instructions. Thus, we will have one type of module associated with ADD instructions, one associated with SUB instructions, and one dealing with the spiking of the output neuron (a FIN module). The modules of the three types are given in Figs. 1, 2 and 3 respectively.

For each register r of M, we consider a neuron σ_r in Π whose contents corresponds to the contents of the register. Specifically, if the register r holds the number $n > 0$, then the neuron σ_r will contain $2n$ spikes. With each label l_i of an instruction in M, we also associate a neuron σ_{l_i} with a single rule $a \to a$ in its first component and no rules in its second component. There are also some auxiliary neurons $\sigma_{l_{i,q}}$, $q = 1, 2, 3, \ldots$, thus precisely identified by label l_i. Initially, all these neurons are empty, with the exception of the neuron σ_{l_0} associated with the start label of M, which contains a single spike. This means that this neuron is activated. During the computation, the neuron σ_{l_i} which receives a spike will become active in its first component. Thus, simulating an instruction $l_i : (OP(r), l_j, l_k)$ of M means starting with neuron σ_{l_i} activated, operating the register r as requested by OP, then introducing a spike in one of the neurons σ_{l_j}, σ_{l_k} which becomes active in this way. When activating the neuron σ_{l_h}, associated with the halting label of M, the computation in M is completely simulated in Π; we will then send to the environment a number of spikes equal to the number stored in the register 1 of M. Neuron σ_1 is the output neuron of the system.

Simulating $l_i : (ADD(r), l_j, l_k)$ (module ADD in Fig. 1).

The initial instruction, that labelled l_0, is an ADD instruction. Assume that we are in a step when we have to simulate an instruction $l_i : (ADD(r), l_j, l_k)$,

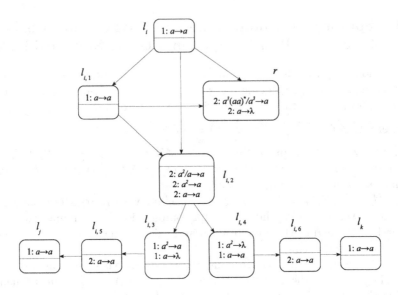

Fig. 1. ADD module: simulation of $l_i : (ADD(r), l_j, l_k)$

with a spike present in neuron σ_{l_i} (like σ_{l_0} in the initial configuration) and no spikes in any other neurons, except in those associated with registers. Even if the system is in the second component at the time, it must switch over to the first component, since we are working in the terminating mode and there are no rules in the second component which are currently applicable anywhere in the system.

Having a spike inside and now in the first component, neuron σ_{l_i} can fire, and at some time it will do it, producing a spike. This spike will simultaneously go to neurons σ_r, $\sigma_{l_{i,1}}$ and $\sigma_{l_{i,2}}$. The neurons σ_r and $\sigma_{l_{i,2}}$ cannot spike because the firing rules are present in their second components. The neuron $\sigma_{l_{i,1}}$ will spike at some time, then a spike will simultaneously go to the neurons σ_r and $\sigma_{l_{i,2}}$. Since no rules are enabled in the first component, the system switches to the second component. Before the system switches, the neuron σ_r receives two spikes from σ_{l_i} and $\sigma_{l_{i,1}}$, thus simulating the increase of the value of register r with 1. Now the system is in the second component. The neuron $\sigma_{l_{i,2}}$ has two spikes and it can fire by choosing one of its rules $a^2/a \rightarrow a$ or $a^2 \rightarrow a$ non-deterministically. If the neuron $\sigma_{l_{i,2}}$ uses its first rule $a^2/a \rightarrow a$, then it consumes one spike and sends a spike to each of the neurons $\sigma_{l_{i,3}}$ and $\sigma_{l_{i,4}}$. The neuron $\sigma_{l_{i,2}}$ is left with one spike and thus it has an enabled rule $a \rightarrow a$. The system switches to the first component only when no rules are enabled in the neuron $\sigma_{l_{i,2}}$. When the neuron $\sigma_{l_{i,2}}$ fires for the second time, neurons $\sigma_{l_{i,3}}$ and $\sigma_{l_{i,4}}$ receive another spike and the system switches to the first component. The neurons $\sigma_{l_{i,3}}$ and $\sigma_{l_{i,4}}$ have enabled rules and they can fire. The system will be in the first component as long as enabled rules are present in $\sigma_{l_{i,3}}$ and $\sigma_{l_{i,4}}$. After some time, the neuron $\sigma_{l_{i,3}}$ uses its spiking rule and sends a spike to $\sigma_{l_{i,5}}$ and the neuron $\sigma_{l_{i,4}}$ forgets its spikes. So eventually neuron $\sigma_{l_{i,5}}$ fires and sends a spike to σ_{l_j}, thus activating it.

If the neuron $\sigma_{l_{i,2}}$ uses its second rule $a^2 \to a$, then each of the neurons $\sigma_{l_{i,3}}$ and $\sigma_{l_{i,4}}$ receive one spike finally. After some time, the neuron $\sigma_{l_{i,4}}$ uses its spiking rule and sends a spike to $\sigma_{l_{i,6}}$ and the neuron $\sigma_{l_{i,5}}$ forgets its spikes. So after some time, neuron $\sigma_{l_{i,6}}$ fires and sends a spike to σ_{l_k}, thus activating it. Therefore, from the firing of neuron σ_{l_i}, the system adds two spikes to neuron σ_r and non-deterministically fires one of the neurons σ_{l_j} and σ_{l_k}. Consequently, the simulation of the ADD instruction is possible in Π.

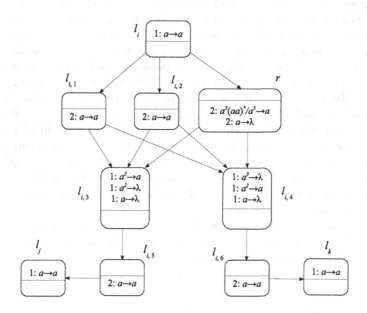

Fig. 2. SUB module: simulation of $l_i : (SUB(r), l_j, l_k)$

Simulating $l_i : (SUB(r), l_j, l_k)$ (module SUB in Fig. 2).

Let us now examine Fig. 2, starting from the situation of having a spike in neuron σ_{l_i} and no spike in other neurons, except neurons associated with registers; assume that neuron σ_r holds a number of spikes of the form $2n$, $n \geq 0$. Sometime, the neuron σ_{l_i} will fire and a spike goes immediately to each of the neurons $\sigma_{l_{i,1}}, \sigma_{l_{i,2}}$ and σ_r. The system must switch over to the second component, since we are working in the terminating mode and there are no rules in the first component which are currently applicable anywhere in the system.

If σ_r does not contain any spikes to begin with (this corresponds to the case when register r is empty), then eventually the spike sent by σ_{l_i} gets forgotten by virtue of the rule $a \to \lambda$ and σ_r is again left with no spikes, indicating that it is still zero. Eventually, neurons $\sigma_{l_{i,1}}$ and $\sigma_{l_{i,2}}$ also send spikes using their rule $a \to a$. Thus, neurons $\sigma_{l_{i,3}}$ and $\sigma_{l_{i,4}}$ end up with 2 spikes each and the system switches to the first component. After some steps, $\sigma_{l_{i,3}}$ forgets the two spikes through the rule $a^2 \to \lambda$ and the neuron $\sigma_{l_{i,4}}$ fires using its rule $a^2 \to a$. With no rules applicable in the first component, the system switches to the second component and eventually neuron $\sigma_{l_{i,6}}$ sends a spike to neuron σ_{l_k}, as required, thus finishing the simulation of the SUB instruction for the case when register r is empty.

If neuron σ_r has $2n$ spikes to begin with, where $n \geq 1$, then after some steps, the rule $a(aa)^+/a^3 \to a$ is used in σ_r. Hence, σ_r now has two spikes less than what it began indicating that r has been reduced by 1. Further, neurons $\sigma_{l_{i,3}}$ and $\sigma_{l_{i,4}}$ end up with 3 spikes each. After some steps, $\sigma_{l_{i,4}}$ forgets the three spikes through the rule $a^3 \to \lambda$ and the neuron $\sigma_{l_{i,3}}$ fires using its rule $a^3 \to a$. With no rules applicable in the first component, the system switches to the second component and eventually neuron $\sigma_{l_{i,5}}$ sends a spike to neuron σ_{l_j}, thus completing the simulation of the decrement case of the SUB instruction.

What remains to be examined is the possible interference between SUB modules. Note that there may be more than a single SUB instruction involving the same register r. Assume that we simulate the instruction $l_i : (SUB(r), l_j, l_k)$, hence neuron σ_r sends a spike to all neurons of the form $\sigma_{l_{i',3}}$ and $\sigma_{l_{i',4}}$ for which there is an instruction $l_i' : (SUB(r), l_j', l_k')$ in M. These spikes will be forgotten using the rule $a \to \lambda$ and this is the correct continuation of the computation. Note that the system will be in the first component as long as any spikes are present in the neurons of the form $\sigma_{l_{i',3}}$ and $\sigma_{l_{i',4}}$. Thus, the neurons $\sigma_{l_{i,5}}$ and $\sigma_{l_{i,6}}$ will become active only after the forgetting rule $a \to \lambda$ is applied in each neuron of the form $\sigma_{l_{i',3}}$ and $\sigma_{l_{i',4}}$.

This means that the simulation of the SUB instruction is correct, we started from l_i and ended in l_j if the register was non-empty (and we decreased it by one), and in l_k if the register was empty.

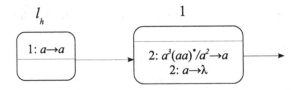

Fig. 3. FIN module: simulation of $l_h : HALT$

Simulating $l_h : (HALT)$ (module FIN in Fig. 3).

When the neuron σ_{l_h} is activated, it (eventually) sends one spike to neuron σ_1, corresponding to the register 1 of M. From now on, this neuron can fire, and it sends out one spike for each two spikes present in it, hence the system will emit a number of spikes which corresponds to the contents of the register 1 of M at the end of the computation (after reaching the instruction $l_h : HALT$).

Consequently, $C_2 N_{gen}^{nsyn}(\Pi) = N(M)$ and this completes the proof. $\square$

Clearly, the previous construction is the same for the accepting mode, and can be carried out for deterministic register machines (the ADD instructions are of the form $l_i : (ADD(r), l_j)$. Similarly, if the result of a computation is defined as the number of spikes present in a specified neuron in the halting configuration, then the previous construction is the same, we only have to add one further neuron which is designated as the output neuron and which collects all spikes emitted by neuron σ_1.

Theorem 1 can easily be extended by allowing more output neurons and then simulating a v-output register machine, producing in this way sets of vectors of natural numbers.

Theorem 2. $PsC_2Spik_{tot}P_*^{nsyn}(gene) = PsRE.$

5   Sequential Spiking Neural P Systems with Two Components

In this section, we restrict the model to operate in a sequential manner. Before considering the power of sequential SN P systems with two components, we first recall some results from [4] on the power of the sequential SN P systems with one component.

1. Sequential SN P systems with general neurons are universal.
2. Sequential SN P systems with unbounded neurons are universal.
3. Strongly sequential SN P systems with general neurons are universal.
4. Strongly sequential SN P systems with unbounded neurons are not universal.

The paper [4] makes use of delayed rules to achieve synchronization. Here the synchronization can be achieved by switching between the components and hence delayed rules are not required. Here we prove that two component strongly sequential SN P systems with standard unbounded neurons without any delay are computationally complete.

Theorem 3. $NC_2Spik_2P_*^{sseq}(unb) = NRE.$

Proof. Given some register machine M generating a set $N(M)$, we can simulate M with a strongly sequential unbounded SN P Π having two components which generates the set $C_2N_{gen}^{seq}(\Pi) = \{x \mid x \in N(M)\}$. The SN P Π's initial configuration will again start with the initial configuration for each module along with a single spike in neuron σ_{l_0}.

To create a strongly sequential unbounded SN P generating exactly $N(M)$ use the same ideas and methods given in Theorem 1. The ADD module is the same as the one shown in Fig. 1 but we remove the rule $2 : a \rightarrow \lambda$ from the neuron σ_r so that the subsystem becomes unbounded. Since no rules from σ_r are fired in the ADD module, the subsystem works correctly even in the sequential mode.

The new subtraction module is shown in Fig. 4. It is initiated with a single spike in neuron σ_{l_i} which immediately sends a spike to neurons σ_r, $\sigma_{l_{i,1}}$ and $\sigma_{l_{i,2}}$

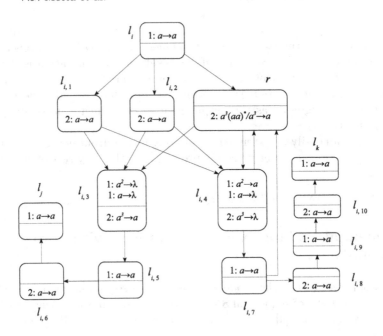

Fig. 4. Strongly sequential unbounded two component SN P SUB module

at time $t+1$ (where t is the time the initial spike is sent to neuron σ_{l_i}). If the value in the register r is not zero then the three neurons non-deterministically spike during the next three steps (time $t+2$, $t+3$, and $t+4$). This causes neuron $\sigma_{l_{i,3}}$ to spike and neuron $\sigma_{l_{i,4}}$ to forget sequentially during the following two time steps (time $t+5$ and $t+6$). Since no rules are enabled in the second component, the system switches to the first component. In the step $t+7$, neuron $\sigma_{l_{i,5}}$ fires and sends a spike to $\sigma_{l_{i,6}}$. Since neuron σ_r sends spikes to all neurons $\sigma_{l_{i',3}}$ and $\sigma_{l_{i',4}}$ where $l_{i'} : (SUB(r), l_{j'}, l_{k'})$, these neurons receive a single spike during the computation of instruction l_i. These spikes must be forgotten before the next instruction executes. Here, the system switches to the second component and fires the rule in the neuron $\sigma_{l_{i,6}}$ only after all spikes are removed from the neurons $\sigma_{l_{i',3}}$ and $\sigma_{l_{i',4}}$ using their forgetting rule $a \rightarrow \lambda$ present in their first components. When the neuron $\sigma_{l_{i,6}}$ fires, it initiates the instruction module l_j.

If σ_r does not contain any spikes to begin with (this corresponds to the case when register r is empty), then the neuron σ_r does not fire and the neurons $\sigma_{l_{i,3}}$ and $\sigma_{l_{i,4}}$ receive two spikes each. Since no rules are enabled in the second component, the system switches to the first component. This causes neurons $\sigma_{l_{i,3}}$ to forget and $\sigma_{l_{i,4}}$ to spike sequentially during the following two time steps (time $t+4$ and $t+5$). The spike from $\sigma_{l_{i,4}}$ goes simultaneously to neurons σ_r and $\sigma_{l_{i,7}}$ in time step $t+6$. Neuron $\sigma_{l_{i,7}}$ sends a spike to σ_r and $\sigma_{l_{i,8}}$ in time step $t+7$. Since no rules are enabled in the first component, the system switches to the second component. Now the neuron σ_r has three spikes. The neurons σ_r and

$\sigma_{l_{i,8}}$ fire sequentially in the next two steps $t + 8$ and $t + 9$. Thus the contents of σ_r is cleared indicating that r remains zero, as required. The spike from σ_r goes to $\sigma_{l_{i,3}}$, $\sigma_{l_{i,4}}$ and all neurons $\sigma_{l_{i',4}}$, where $l_{i'} : (SUB(r), l_{j'}, l_{k'})$. The neurons $\sigma_{l_{i,9}}$ and $\sigma_{l_{i,10}}$ with rules in different components ensures that the spikes in $\sigma_{l_{i,3}}$, $\sigma_{l_{i,4}}$ and all $\sigma_{l_{i',3}}$ and $\sigma_{l_{i',4}}$ are forgotten before enabling the instruction module l_k as the spike received by $\sigma_{l_{i,8}}$ (from $\sigma_{l_{i,7}}$) percolates through $\sigma_{l_{i,9}}$ and $\sigma_{l_{i,10}}$ to l_k.

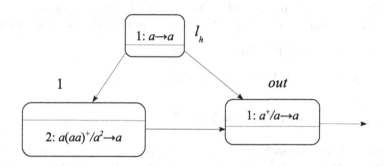

Fig. 5. Strongly sequential unbounded two component SN P output module

To simulate $l_h : (HALT)$, we create the module given in Fig. 5. When neuron l_h receives a spike, it fires and sends a spike to neurons σ_1 and σ_{out} with the system in the first component (it will switch to the first component even otherwise as only rules in the first component are enabled and we are working in the terminating mode). Let t be the moment when neuron l_h fires. Suppose the number stored in the register 1 of M is n.

At step $t + 1$, neuron σ_{out} fires for the first time sending its spike to the environment. The number of steps from this spike to the next one is the number computed by the system. Since no rule is enabled in the first component, the system switches to the second component. Now the neuron σ_1 spikes during the next n steps. The neuron σ_{out} will become active only after $2n$ spikes are removed from σ_1. So at time $t + n + 1$, the system again switches to the first component and the neuron σ_{out} fires for the second time. The interval between the two spikes emitted by σ_{out} is $(t + n + 1) - (t + 1) = n$, which is the number stored in the register 1 of M. The system halts after $n - 1$ steps with all neurons empty except neuron σ_1 which contains a spike.   □

Theorem 3 can easily be extended by allowing more output neurons and then simulating a v-output register machine, producing in this way sets of vectors of natural numbers.

Theorem 4. $PsC_2Spik_2P_*^{sseq}(unb) = PsRE$.

One more observation is that the module given in Fig. 4 works even if the system is asynchronous. It is now possible to construct a new system with ADD module shown in Fig. 1 without the rule $2 : a \rightarrow \lambda$ in the neuron σ_r, the SUB

module given in Fig. 4 and the FIN module given in Fig. 3 without the rule $2: a \rightarrow \lambda$ in the neuron σ_1 which would be unbounded and work correctly in the case of an asynchronous system. Hence, we have the following two theorems.

Theorem 5. $NC_2Spik_{tot}P_*^{nsyn}(unb) = NRE.$

Theorem 6. $PsC_2Spik_{tot}P_*^{nsyn}(unb) = PsRE.$

Finally, the system constructed in Section 4 with the FIN module in Fig. 5 would work for sequential systems. Hence, we have the following two theorems.

Theorem 7. $NC_2Spik_2P_*^{sseq}(gene) = NRE.$

Theorem 8. $PsC_2Spik_2P_*^{sseq}(gene) = PsRE.$

6   Conclusion and Discussion

The usual SN P systems operate in a maximally parallel manner. This model was shown to be computationally complete even with a variety of additional restrictions on the rule types [8,11]. In this paper, we introduced a spiking neural P system with cooperating rules. Computational completeness has been proved for asynchronous as well as sequential cooperating SN P systems with two components using unbounded as well as general neurons working in the terminating mode. This suggests that cooperating SN P systems are indeed more powerful by offering seamless synchronization without the use of any delays. Further work would include the construction of small universal systems. It would also be interesting to consider the languages generated by these systems using different number of components. Further, this paper considers only the terminating mode, which is known to be more powerful than others in the case of CD grammar systems. A discussion on if the same result holds for cooperating SN P systems working in other models would be worthwhile.

Acknowledgements. The work was supported by EU project Development of Research Capacities of the Silesian University in Opava (CZ.1.07/2.3.00/30.0007) and European Regional Development Fund in the IT4Innovations Centre of Excellence project (CZ.1.05/1.1.00/02.0070).

References

1. Cavaliere, M., Ibarra, O.H., Păun, Gh., Egecioglu, Ö., Ionescu, M., Woodworth, S.: Asynchronous spiking neural P systems. Theoretical Computer Science **410**(24–25), 2352–2364 (2009)
2. Csuhaj-Varjú, E., Dassow, J.: On cooperating/distributed grammar systems. Journal of Information Processing and Cybernetics (EIK) **26**, 49–63 (1990)
3. Csuhaj-Varjú, E., Dassow, J., Kelemen, J., Păun, Gh.: Grammar Systems. A Grammatical Approach to Distribution and Cooperation. Gordon and Breach, London (1994)

4. Ibarra, O.H., Woodworth, S., Yu, F., Păun, A.: On spiking neural P systems and partially blind counter machines. Natural Computing **7**(1), 3–19 (2008)
5. Ionescu, M., Păun, Gh., Yokomori, T.: Spiking neural P systems. Fundamenta Informaticae **71**, 279–308 (2006)
6. Meersman, R., Rozenberg, G.: Cooperating grammar systems. In: Winkowski, J. (ed.) MFCS 1978. LNCS, vol. 64, pp. 364–374. Springer, Heidelberg (1978)
7. Minsky, M.: Computation - Finite and Infinite Machines. Prentice Hall, Englewood Cliffs (1967)
8. Pan, L., Păun, Gh.: Spiking neural P systems: An improved normal form. Theoretical Computer Science **411**, 906–918 (2010)
9. Păun, Gh., Rozenberg, G., Salomaa, A. (eds.): Handbook of Membrane Computing. Oxford University Press, Oxford (2010)
10. Rozenberg, G., Salomaa, A. (eds.): Handbook of Formal Languages, vol. 3. Springer, Berlin (1997)
11. Zeng, X., Zhang, X., Pan, L.: Homogeneous spiking neural P systems. Fundamenta Informaticae **97**, 1–20 (2009)

Parallel Thinning
with Complex Objects and Actors

Radu Nicolescu[✉]

Department of Computer Science, University of Auckland, Private Bag 92019,
Auckland, New Zealand
r.nicolescu@auckland.ac.nz

Abstract. Based on our earlier complex objects proposal, we present
three novel concurrent membrane computing models for a fundamental
image processing task: the thinning (or skeletonisation) of binary images,
based on the classical Guo-Hall algorithm (A2). The first model is synchronous and uses one cell per pixel and relies on inter-cell parallelism;
the second model is an asynchronous version of the first; the third model
uses one single cell, with one sub-cellular object per pixel, and relies
on intra-cell parallelism. The static and dynamic qualities of our models validate our complex objects proposal: (i) the proposed models are
crisp (comparable to the best pseudocode); and (ii) complex objects concurrency and messaging can be efficiently emulated on a message-based
Actors framework (which opens a novel research path).

Keywords: Membrane computing · P systems · Inter-cell parallelism ·
Intra-cell parallelism · Prolog terms · Complex objects · Generic rules ·
Image processing · Guo-Hall algorithm · Parallel and concurrent mod-
els · Synchronous and asynchronous models · Termination detection ·
Message-based · Actor model

1 Introduction

We have previously used complex objects to successfully model problems in
a wide variety of domains: computer vision [8,9,14]; graph theory [6,18]; distributed algorithms [2,4,5,17,19,25]; high-level P systems programming [15,16];
numerical P systems [15,16]; NP-complete problems [15,16,19].

In this paper, we choose another test case, a fundamental image processing
task: thinning (or skeletonisation) of black-and-white images. Specifically, we
model Guo and Hall's algorithm A2 [10] and we assess the merits of our complex framework. We provide three closely related models, with a straightforward
translation between them:

- A *synchronous multi-cell* model, based on a 1 : 1 mapping between pixels
  and cells and essentially using the *inter-cell parallelism*;
- An *asynchronous multi-cell* model, based on a 1 : 1 mapping between pixels
  and cells and essentially using the *inter-cell parallelism*; and

© Springer International Publishing Switzerland 2014
M. Gheorghe et al. (Eds.): CMC 2014, LNCS 8961, pp. 330–354, 2014.
DOI: 10.1007/978-3-319-14370-5_21

- A (synchronous) *single-cell* model, based on a 1 : 1 mapping between pixels and sub-cellular complex objects and essentially using the *intra-cell parallelism*.

Further, although not detailed here (for lack of space), we provide a direct emulation of our three models in the *asynchronous* Actors framework [1,11], using F#'s mailbox processor library [24]. We conjecture that, given a good support for pattern matching, the translation from complex objects to Actors can be largely automatised, not only for similar image processing tasks, but for many other applications (such as we earlier studied), for both synchronous and asynchronous cases.

We are aware of only a few other quality studies proposing membrane computing models for thinning algorithms or other real-life complex image processing tasks. Reina-Molina et al. [23] propose a traditional tissue system, without mentioning any experimental mapping, and raise an *open question*: if other membrane computing versions can provide "better" (in a very loose sense) models. Reina-Molina and Díaz-Pernil [22] discuss a similar tissue based system. Peña-Cantillana et al. [20] discuss a related cellular model, mapped on the CUDA platform. Díaz-Pernil et al. [3] propose a spiking neural model also mapped on the CUDA platform.

We think that our study is a partial answer to the above open question: our complex objects seem to offfer crisper models, with fixed-sized rulesets, independent on the size of the image. Moreover, our approach seems to be the first offering multiple but closely related solutions for an image processing task, such as a pair of "twin" multi-cell/single-cell solutions, or a pair of "twin" synchronous/asynchronous solutions. Also, we are not aware of any other attempt that map membrane computing to an Actors based platform, so this is another novel path explored in this paper.

This study leads us to formulate a couple of open questions (not followed here), about a distributed termination detection of this algorithm or the merits of a partial asynchronous version of this algorithm. We are not aware of many membrane computing studies that could be related to these open problems. For example, Nicolescu and Wu [19] and Wu [26] have recently studied distributed termination detection for diffusing (single source) algorithms, but probably more studies are needed on non-diffusing (multiple source) algorithms, such as Guo-Hall's A2.

Because of space constraints, for the rest of the paper, we assume that the reader is already familiar with:

- basic definitions used in traditional *tissue-like transition P systems*, including state based rules, weak priority, promoters and inhibitors, e.g. as discussed in the membrane computing handbook [21];
- basic concepts of image processing and an understanding of Guo and Hall's *image thinning* algorithm A2 [10,20];
- basic concepts of *concurrent processing with functional programming*, using the message-based *Actor* model, e.g. as described in Syme's monograph [24].

However, to ensure some degree of self-containment, following Nicolescu et al. recent papers [15,16,19], we discuss two important extensions used: *complex objects* and *generic rules* (if our complex objects presentation is not enough, then we also suggest a quick recall of Prolog terms *unification*). Here we also extend the previously published format of complex objects and generic rules, by adding an optional *path* notation which enables efficient "micro-surgeries" on inner nested objects (without affecting their enclosing outer objects).

2   Background: Image Thinning

Thinning is the transformation of a digital binary image into a simplified, but topologically equivalent image, often called "skeleton". The image pixels are divided into two categories: (i) foreground, conventionally *black* or `true` (i.e. ordinal 1); and (ii) background, conventionally *white* or `false` (i.e. ordinal 0). Typically, the thinning process repeatedly turns *black* pixels to *white* (conceptually "deleting" them from the foreground), while trying (a) to keep the topological connectivity, and (b) to balance the whitening around the so called medial lines. The algorithm stops when no further changes can be made.

Intuitively, Figure 1 shows a thinning example: (1a) the original image, and (1b) a possible skeleton. For efficiency, many thinning algorithms make such changes solely based on the current pixel's 8-neighbourhood, where center pixel p_0 has the following neighbours (see also Figure 2a): p_1 at NW, p_2 at N, p_3 at NE, p_4 at E, p_5 at SE, p_6 at S, p_7 at SW, p_8 at W.

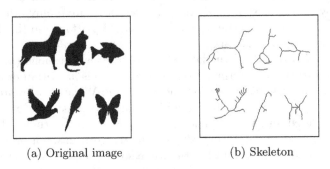

(a) Original image   (b) Skeleton

Fig. 1. Sample thinning (with Guo and Hall A2)

Because of paper size limits, we only outline the critical steps of Guo and Hall's algorithm A2 [10]; please see the original paper for more details on thinning and on this algorithm, including arguments for its correctness and efficiency.

Briefly, one partitions the pixels into an even/odd checkerboard pattern, where a pixel at (i, j) is even if $(i+j)\%2 = 0$, and odd otherwise. This algorithm makes alternative iterations, where at one step only even (or odd) black pixels are active and examined for possible changes. Figure 2b shows the essential pixel state changes of this algorithm: a white pixel remains white forever; a black pixel

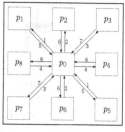

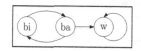

(b) Thinning statechart

- bi=black inactive
- ba=black active
- w=white

(a) The 8-neighbourhood

Fig. 2. The "standard" 8-neighbourhood and algorithm statechart

continuously alternates between an active and inactive state (determined by the checkerboard pattern and iteration number); and an active black pixel may turn white, under the specific conditions detailed below.

Besides being in the active state, the following three conditions[1] must be simultaneously true for properly changing the colour of a *black* pixel p_0 ("deleting" it from the foreground):

- $\beta = 1$, where

$$\beta = \mathbf{ord}(\neg((p_1 \wedge p_3 \wedge p_5 \wedge p_7) \vee (p_2 \wedge p_4 \wedge p_6 \wedge p_8)))$$

- $\gamma = 1$, where

$$\gamma = (\mathbf{ord}\,((\neg p_2) \wedge (p_3 \vee p_4))) + (\mathbf{ord}\,((\neg p_4) \wedge (p_5 \vee p_6))) + \\ (\mathbf{ord}\,((\neg p_6) \wedge (p_7 \vee p_8))) + (\mathbf{ord}\,((\neg p_8) \wedge (p_1 \vee p_2)))$$

- $\delta > 1$, where

$$\delta = (\mathbf{ord}\ p_1) + (\mathbf{ord}\ p_2) + (\mathbf{ord}\ p_3) + \\ (\mathbf{ord}\ p_8) + \qquad\qquad (\mathbf{ord}\ p_4) + \\ (\mathbf{ord}\ p_7) + (\mathbf{ord}\ p_6) + (\mathbf{ord}\ p_5)$$

These three values can be each time computed from scratch, according to the formulas, or precomputed and stored in three fast access tables, each one storing all values for all $2^8 = 256$ combinations of $p_1, p_2, \ldots p_8$. Or, even better, we can precompute all answers for the combined three conditions:

$$\psi = \mathbf{ord}((\beta = 1) \wedge (\gamma = 1) \wedge (\delta > 1)).$$

Also, to avoid special cases for pixels lying on the image borders, we assume that all border pixels are background (white). In this paper, we follow these two optimisations.

---

[1] Function $\mathbf{ord}(b)$ returns the ordinal value of boolean b, i.e. $\mathbf{ord}(\bot) = 0, \mathbf{ord}(\top) = 1$.

	$p_8, p_7, p_6, p_5, p_4, p_3, p_2, p_1$	β	γ	δ	ψ
0	0, 0, 0, 0, 0, 0, 0, 0	1	0	0	0
...	...	...	...	...	...
124	0, 1, 1, 1, 1, 1, 0, 0	1	1	5	1
125	0, 1, 1, 1, 1, 1, 0, 1	0	2	6	0
...	...	...	...	...	...
255	1, 1, 1, 1, 1, 1, 1, 1	0	0	8	0

(a) Excerpts of the β, γ, δ and ψ tables

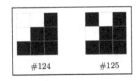

(b) Configurations of rows 124 (centre pixel can be "deleted") and 125 (centre pixel cannot be "deleted")

Fig. 3. Precomputed tables

Table 3a shows (in a compact way) a few rows of the β, γ, δ and ψ tables; the configurations of rows 124 and 125 are displayed in Figure 3b; the original article [10] explains the rationale of these three values (called $4 - connection$, $C(P)$, and $B(P)$, respectively).

This algorithm can be parallelised by allocating one distinct task for each pixel, provided that we have implicit or explicit *synchronisation barriers*, which ensure that the colour changes do not affect other pixels' evaluation of the "deletion" condition. This condition is implicit in *synchronous* settings; however, in *asynchronous* settings (as typical in parallel multi-cores applications), we need two explicit synchronisation barriers. Listing 1 shows a parallel pseudocode of the essential steps of Guo and Hall's algorithm A2 (using indentation to delimit blocks), assuming that colours are directly changed in the original pixels. We can safely use this approach, in a synchronous P system model, where all steps are implicitly synchronised.

Practically, to avoid excessive parallelisation overhead, one should reduce the number of tasks, by adequately partitioning the image and allocate a task to each subrange of pixels. Thus, the first line of Listing 1 should be replaced by the lines shown in Listing 2. This mixed approach is not further developed here, but is briefly mentioned again, as an open problem, in Section 5.

This algorithm raises an interesting *termination* issue, in the case of a distributed implementation over a cluster of computing nodes: how do all nodes learn that the algorithm has terminated, promptly and efficiently? Is there a master node that supervises the whole process, perhaps centralising the number of deleted pixels at each step (as we assume here), or do the nodes concurrently run an ad-hoc termination detection control layer?

Another interesting question is to find well-behaved *asynchronous* versions of this algorithm. While a full asynchronous version could arguably return bad results (e.g. far from the medial line), a restricted, globally asynchronous but locally synchronous (GALS) version may still give exact results. In Section 6, we propose an asynchronous Actors based version, where we precisely know the number of expected messages at each phase – this enables an ad-hoc local synchronisation, without the overhead of more general synchroniser [12].

Listing 1. Synchronous parallel pseudocode of Guo and Hall's algorithm A2

```
parallel for each pixel π[i,j] in image do
   if (π[i,j].colour = black) then
      π[i,j].active := ((i + j)%2 = 0)
      while (¬ terminated) do    // question: how do black cells know this?
         π[i,j].active := ¬ π[i,j].active
         if (π[i,j].active) then
            barrier              // phase synchronisation
            local ψ := ...       // needs the colours of its 8 neighbours
            barrier              // phase synchronisation
            if (ψ = 1) then      // i.e. (β = 1) ∧ (γ = 1) ∧ (δ > 1)
               π[i,j].colour := white
               break while
         else
            barrier              // phase synchronisation
            idle
            barrier              // phase synchronisation
```

Listing 2. Partitioning pseudocode for Guo and Hall's algorithm A2

```
Π = partition of input image    // question: what is the best partition?
parallel for each subrange in Π do
   coroutine for each pixel π[i,j] in subrange do
      ...    // the rest is identical
```

3   Background: Membrane Computing with Complex Objects

3.1   Complex Objects

Complex objects play the roles of cellular micro-compartments or substructures, such as organelles, vesicles or cytoophidium assemblies ("snakes"), which are embedded in cells or travel between cells, but without having the full processing power of a complete cell. In our proposal, complex objects represent structured data that have no own processing power: they are acted upon by the rules of their enclosing cells.

Technically, our *complex objects*, are Prolog-like *first-order terms*, recursively built from *multisets* of atoms and variables. *Atoms* are typically denoted by lower case letters, such as a, b, c. *Variables* are typically denoted by uppercase letters, such as X, Y, Z. For improved readability, we also consider *anonymous variables*, which are denoted by underscores ("_"). Each underscore occurrence represents a *new* unnamed variable and indicates that something, in which we are not interested, must fill that slot.

Terms are either (i) simple atoms, or (ii) *complex terms*, i.e. atoms (here called *functors*), followed by one or more parenthesized lists of comma-separated "arguments", which are *multisets/bags* of other objects (terms or variables). Functors that are followed by more than one list of arguments are called *curried* (by analogy to functional programming) and, as we see later, are useful to precisely described deep 'micro-surgical" changes which only affect inner nested objects, without directly touching their enclosing outer objects. Terms that do *not* contain variables are called *ground*, e.g.:

- Ground terms: a, $a(b)$, $a(\lambda)$, $a(b,c)$, $a(b,\lambda)$, $a(\lambda,c)$, $a(\lambda,\lambda)$, $a(b(c))$, $a(bc)$, $a(bc(\lambda))$, $a(b(c)d(e))$, $a(b(c),d(e))$, $a(b(c),d(e(\lambda)))$, $a(bc^2,d,eg)$; or, a curried form: $a(bc^2)(d,eg)$.
- Terms which are not ground: $a(b,X)$, $a(b(X))$, $a(Xc)$, $a(bY)$, $a(XY)$, $a(XX)$, $a(XdY)$, $a(Xc())$, $a(b(X)d(e))$, $a(b(c),d(Y))$, $a(b(X),d(e(Y)))$, $a(b(X), d(e(X)))$; or, a curried form: $a(b(c))(d(Y))$; also, using anonymous variables: $a(b\_)$, $a(X\_)$, $a(b(X),d(e(\_)))$.

Note that we may abbreviate the expression of complex objects by removing inner λ's as explicit references to the empty bag, e.g. $a(\lambda) = a()$, $a(b,\lambda) = a(b,)$. Complex objects can be formally defined by the following grammar:

```
<term>         ::= <atom> | <functor> ( '(' <arguments> ')' )+
<functor>      ::= <atom>
<arguments>    ::=  <bag-argument> ( ',' <bag-argument> )*
<bag-argument> ::= λ | ( <term-or-var> )+
<term-or-var>  ::= <term> | <variable>
```

Natural Numbers. Natural numbers can be represented via *bags* containing repeated occurrences of the *same* atom. For example, considering that l represents the unary digit, then the following complex objects can be used to describe the contents of a virtual integer *variable* a: $a() = a(\lambda)$ — the value of a is 0; $a(l^3)$ — the value of a is 3. Nicolescu et al. [15,16,19] show how arithmetic operations can be efficiently modelled by P systems with complex objects.

Indexed Symbols. Complex objects can sometimes be represented as *indexed symbols*, where lower-case indices stand for arguments, e.g. $a_k = a(k)$; this is especially convenient when indices represent numbers or cell IDs (which typically are numbers).

Unification. All terms (ground or not) can be (asymmetrically) *matched* against *ground* terms, using an ad-hoc version of *pattern matching*, more precisely, a *one-way first-order syntactic unification*, where an atom can only match another copy of itself, and a variable can match any bag of ground terms (including the empty bag, λ). This may create a combinatorial *non-determinism*, when a combination of two or more variables are matched against the same bag, in which case an arbitrary matching is chosen. For example:

- Matching $a(X,eY) = a(b(c),def)$ deterministically creates a single set of unifiers: $X,Y = b(c),df$.

- Matching $a(XY) = a(df)$ non-deterministically creates one of the following four sets of unifiers: $X, Y = \lambda, df$; $X, Y = df, \lambda$; $X, Y = d, f$; $X, Y = f, d$.
- However, matching $a(XY, Y) = a(def, e)$ deterministically creates a single set of unifiers: $X, Y = df, e$.

Performance Note. If the rules avoid any matching non-determinism, then this proposal should not affect the performance of P simulators running on existing machines. Assuming that bags are already taken care of, e.g. via hash-tables, our proposed unification probably adds an almost linear factor. Let us recall that, in similar contexts (no occurs check needed), Prolog unification algorithms can run in $O(ng(n))$ steps, where g is the inverse Ackermann function. Our conjecture must be proven though, as the novel presence of multisets may affect the performance.

Alternative Notations. Using Lisp terms instead Prolog terms, we could use an equivalent notation, where the functor becomes the first term in a parenthesised expression, instead of preceding it. For example, the Prolog-like term $a(bc^2, d, eg)$ could be rewritten as the Lisp-like term, (a, bc^2, d, eg), with additional commas to clearly separate items.

If there is no confusion with atomic symbols, simple complex terms with just one level of nesting can also be abbreviated by an indexed notation. For example, the term $a(i, j)$ could be rewritten as $a_{i,j}$.

3.2   Generic Rules

By default, rules are applied top-down, in the so-called *weak priority* order. *Rules* may contain *any* kind of terms, ground and not-ground; however, in this proposal, *cells* can only contain *ground* terms.

Pattern Matching. Rules are matched against cell contents using the above discussed *pattern matching*, which involves the rule's left-hand side, promoters and inhibitors. Moreover, the matching is *valid* only if, after substituting variables by their values, the rule's right-hand side contains ground terms only (so *no* free variables are injected in the cell or sent to its neighbours), as illustrated by the following sample scenario:

- The cell's *current content* includes the *ground term*:
  $n(l^{10}, n(l^{20}, f(l^{30}), f(l^{40})), f(l^{50}))$
- The following *rewriting rule* is considered:
  $n(X, n(Y, Y_1, Y_2), f(Z)) \rightarrow v(X)\, n(Y, Y_1, Y_2)\, v(Z)$
- Our pattern matching determines the following *unifiers*:
  $X = l^{10}, Y = l^{20}, Y_1 = l^{30}, Y_2 = l^{40}, Z = l^{50}$.
- This is a *valid* matching and, after *substitutions*, the rule's *right-hand* side gives the *new content*:
  $v(l^{10})\, n(l^{20}, f(l^{30}), f(l^{40}))\, v(l^{50})$

Generic Rules Format. More generally, we consider rules of the following *generic* format (we call this format generic, because it actually defines templates involving variables):

current-state objects... $\rightarrow_\alpha$ target-state [immediate-objects]...
$\qquad\qquad\qquad\quad$ (in-objects)... (out-objects)$_\delta$...
$\qquad\qquad\qquad\quad$ | promoters... ¬ inhibitors...

Where:

- *States* are complex objects (which can be *matched*, as previously described).
- All *objects*, *promoters* and *inhibitors* are *bags of terms*, possibly containing *variables* (which are *matched* as previously described).
- *Out-objects* are sent, at the end of the step, to the cell's structural neighbours. These objects are enclosed in round parentheses which further indicate their destinations, above abbreviated as δ; the most usual scenarios include: (a) $\downarrow_i$ indicates that a is sent to child i (unicast), (b) $\uparrow_i$ indicates that a is sent to parent i (unicast), (c) $\downarrow_\forall$ indicates that a is sent to all children (broadcast), (d) $\uparrow_\forall$ indicates that a is sent to all parents (broadcast), (e) $\updownarrow_\forall$ indicates that a is sent to all neighbours (broadcast).
- Both *immediate-objects* and *in-objects* remain in the current cell, but there is a subtle difference:
  - *in-objects* become available at the end of the current step only, as in traditional P systems (we can imagine that these are sent via an ad-hoc *loopback* channel);
  - *immediate-objects* become immediately available (i) to the current rule, if its uses the `max` instantiation mode, and (ii) to the succeeding rules (in weak priority order).
  Immediate objects can substantially improve the runtime performance, which could be required for two main reasons: (i) to achieve parity with best traditional algorithms, and (ii) to ensure correctness when proper timing is logically critical (often required in complex distributed algorithms). However, the systems presented in this paper do not use any immediate objects.
- Symbol $\alpha \in \{\texttt{min}, \texttt{max}\} \times \{\texttt{min}, \texttt{max}\}$, indicates a combined instantiation and rewriting mode, as further discussed below.

We often abbreviate the expression of rules by omitting the round parentheses around in-objects. This default conforms to the tradition and is convenient for rulesets (like here) which do not use immediate objects.

Example. To explain our combined instantiation and rewriting mode, let us consider a cell, σ, containing three counter-like complex objects, $c(c(a))$, $c(c(a))$, $c(c(c(a)))$, and the four possible instantiation⊗rewriting modes of the following "decrementing" rule:

$$(\rho_\alpha)\ S_1\ c(c(X)) \to_\alpha S_2\ c(X), \text{where } \alpha \in \{\text{min,max}\} \times \{\text{min,max}\}.$$

1. If $\alpha = \text{min} \otimes \text{min}$, rule $\rho_{\text{min} \otimes \text{min}}$ nondeterministically generates and applies (in the min mode) *one* of the following two rule instances:

$$(\rho_1')\ S_1\ c(c(a)) \to_{\text{min}} S_2\ c(a) \quad \text{or}$$
$$(\rho_1'')\ S_1\ c(c(c(a))) \to_{\text{min}} S_2\ c(c(a)).$$

Using (ρ_1'), cell σ ends with counters $c(a)$, $c(c(a))$, $c(c(c(a)))$. Using (ρ_1''), cell σ ends with counters $c(c(a))$, $c(c(a))$, $c(c(a))$.

2. If $\alpha = \text{max} \otimes \text{min}$, rule $\rho_{\text{max} \otimes \text{min}}$ first generates and then applies (in the min mode) the following *two* rule instances:

$$(\rho_2')\ S_1\ c(c(a)) \to_{\text{min}} S_2\ c(a) \quad \text{and}$$
$$(\rho_2'')\ S_1\ c(c(c(a))) \to_{\text{min}} S_2\ c(c(a)).$$

Using (ρ_2') and (ρ_2''), cell σ ends with counters $c(a)$, $c(c(a))$, $c(c(a))$.

3. If $\alpha = \text{min} \otimes \text{max}$, rule $\rho_{\text{min} \otimes \text{max}}$ nondeterministically generates and applies (in the max mode) *one* of the following rule instances:

$$(\rho_3')\ S_1\ c(c(a)) \to_{\text{max}} S_2\ c(a) \quad \text{or}$$
$$(\rho_3'')\ S_1\ c(c(c(a))) \to_{\text{max}} S_2\ c(c(a)).$$

Using (ρ_3'), cell σ ends with counters $c(a)$, $c(a)$, $c(c(c(a)))$. Using (ρ_3''), cell σ ends with counters $c(c(a))$, $c(c(a))$, $c(c(a))$.

4. If $\alpha = \text{max} \otimes \text{max}$, rule $\rho_{\text{min} \otimes \text{max}}$ first generates and then applies (in the max mode) the following *two* rule instances:

$$(\rho_4')\ S_1\ c(c(a)) \to_{\text{max}} S_2\ c(a) \quad \text{and}$$
$$(\rho_4'')\ S_1\ c(c(c(a))) \to_{\text{max}} S_2\ c(c(a)).$$

Using (ρ_4') and (ρ_4''), cell σ ends with counters $c(a)$, $c(a)$, $c(c(a))$.

The interpretation of $\text{min} \otimes \text{min}$, $\text{min} \otimes \text{max}$ and $\text{max} \otimes \text{max}$ modes is straightforward. While other interpretations could be considered, the mode $\text{max} \otimes \text{min}$ indicates that the generic rule is instantiated as *many* times as possible, without *superfluous* instances (i.e. without duplicates or instances which are not applicable) and each one of the instantiated rules is applied *once*, if possible.

If a rule does not contain any non-ground term, then it has one single possible instantiation: itself. Thus, in this case, the instantiation is an *idempotent* transformation, and the modes $\text{min} \otimes \text{min}$, $\text{min} \otimes \text{max}$, $\text{max} \otimes \text{min}$, $\text{max} \otimes \text{max}$ fall back onto traditional modes min, max, min, max, respectively.

Special Cases. Simple scenarios involving generic rules are sometimes semantically equivalent to loop-based sets of non-generic rules. For example, consider the rule

$$S_1\ a(I, J) \to_{\text{max} \otimes \text{min}} S_2\ b(I)\ c(J),$$

where I and J are guaranteed to only match integers in ranges $[1, n]$ and $[1, m]$, respectively. Under these assumptions, this rule is equivalent to the following set of non-generic rules:

$$S_1 \ a(i, j) \ \rightarrow_{\min} \ S_2 \ b(i) \ c(j), \ \forall i \in [1, n], j \in [1, m].$$

However, unification is a much more powerful concept, which cannot be generally reduced to simple loops.

Micro-surgery: Operations That Only Affect Inner Nested Objects.
Such operations improve both the crispness and the efficiency of the rules. Consider a cell that contains objects $o(abpq), r$ and a naïve rule which attempts to change the inner b to a d, if an inner p and a top–level r are also present:

$$S_1 \ o(bR) \ \rightarrow_{\min\otimes\min} \ S_2 \ o(dR) \ | \ o(p_-) \ r.$$

Unless we change the "standard" application rules, this rule fails, because an object locked as a promoter cannot be changed at the same time. We solve this problem without changing the standard application rules, by adding an access path to the inner objects needed. The *access path* is a slash delimited list of outer objects, in nesting order, which opens an inner bag for usual rewriting operations; the outer objects on the path are not themselves touched. For example, this modified rule will solve the problem:

$$S_1 \ o/b \ \rightarrow_{\min\otimes\min} \ S_2 \ o/d \ | \ o/p \ r.$$

This extension helps even more when we want to localise the changes to inner objects of a specific outer object. For example, consider a similar operation that needs to be applied on the innermost contents of object $o(i, j)(abpq)$, identified by its coordinates i, j.

$$S_1 \ o(i, j)/b \ \rightarrow_{\min\otimes\min} \ S_2 \ o(i, j)/d \ | \ o(i, j)/p \ r.$$

If all or most objects involved share the same path, than the path could qualify the whole rule; existing top-level objects could be qualified by usual path conventions, e.g. in our case, r could be explicitly qualified by either of $/$ or $../$:

$$o(i, j) :: S_1 \ b \ \rightarrow_{\min\otimes\min} \ S_2 \ d \ | \ p \ ../r.$$

Note that the usual rulesets are just a special case of this extension, when all rules are by default qualified with the root path $/$.

Note. For all modes, the instantiations are *conceptually* created when rules are tested for applicability and are also *ephemeral*, i.e. they disappear at the end of the step. P system implementations are encouraged to directly apply high-level generic rules, if this is more efficient (it usually is); they may, but need not, start by transforming high-level rules into low-level rules, by way of instantiations.

Benefits. This type of generic rules allow (i) a reasonably fast parsing and processing of subcomponents, and (ii) algorithm descriptions with *fixed size alphabets* and *fixed sized rulesets*, independent of the size of the problem and number of cells in the system (often impossible with only atomic symbols).

Synchronous vs Asynchronous. In our models, we do not make any *syntactic* difference between the synchronous and asynchronous scenarios; this is strictly a *runtime* assumption [13]. Any model is able to run in both the synchronous and asynchronous runtime "engines", albeit the results may differ.

As in traditional P systems, in the *synchronous* scenario, all rules in a step take exactly *one* time unit and then all message exchanges (including loopback messages for in-objects) are performed at the end of the step, in *zero* time (i.e. instantaneously). Alternatively, but logically equivalent, we can consider that rules in a step are performed in *zero* time (i.e. instantaneously) and then all message exchanges are performed in exactly *one* time unit. The second interpretation is useful, because it allows us to interpret synchronous runs as special cases of asynchronous runs.

In the *asynchronous* scenario, we still consider that rules in a step are performed in *zero* time (i.e. instantaneously), but then each message may take *any* finite real time to arrive at the destination. Additionally, unless otherwise specified, we also assume that messages traveling on the same directed arc follow a *FIFO* rule, i.e. no fast message can overtake a slow progressing one. This definition closely emulates the standard definition used for asynchronous distributed algorithms [12].

Obviously, any algorithm that works correctly in the asynchronous mode will also work correctly in the synchronous mode, but the converse is *not* generally true: extra care may be needed to transform a correct synchronous algorithm into a correct asynchronous one; there are also general control layers, such as *synchronisers*, that can attempt to run a synchronous algorithm on an existing asynchronous runtime, but this does not always work [12].

4   Multi-Cell P System (Synchronous)

This model is based on *inter-cell parallelism* and assumes that the image pixels are distributed over a rectangular grid of cells, one cell per pixel, linked into a graph corresponding to the "standard" 8-neighbourhood (we use the naïve grid topology). Figure 2a describes this layout, with arc labels, from center pixel to neighbours and from neighbours to center pixel.

Numeric complex cells contents are given as multisets over the unary base $\circ$, i.e. $\lambda = 0$, $\circ = 1$, $\circ\circ = \circ^2 = 2$, ...

Each cell starts in state S_0, with the following initial values:

- One (immutable) ID symbol, $\iota(I, J)$, which indicates its coordinates: $I =$ row number, $J =$ column number.
- One (mutable) symbol, $p(C)$, which indicates its current colour: $C = b =$ black, or $C = w =$ white. Intuitively, p_0 has colour C.
- A multiset of eight (immutable) symbols, $n(X, Y)$, representing a "table", which codifies the neighbourhood relation, from the current cell's point of view, e.g. my neighbour X (e.g. 1=NW) knows me as neighbour Y (e.g. 5=SE):

$$n(1,5) \qquad n(2,6) \qquad n(3,7)$$
$$n(8,4) \qquad\qquad\qquad n(4,8)$$
$$n(7,3) \qquad n(6,2) \qquad n(5,1)$$

- A multiset of 2^8 (immutable) symbols, $\psi(...)$, representing a "table", which completely defines the namesake table mentioned in Section 2, e.g.

$$\psi(0,0,0,0,0,0,0,0,0)\ldots$$
$$\psi(0,1,1,1,1,1,0,0,1)$$
$$\psi(0,1,1,1,1,1,0,1,0)\ldots$$
$$\psi(1,1,1,1,1,1,1,1,0)$$

- One (immutable) symbol, $a(H)$, where $H \in \{\lambda, \circ\} = \{0,1\}$, representing a target checkerboard marker, which is used to determine the current activity status:
  - If $H = \lambda = 0$, then cells $(0,0)$, $(1,1)$ are currently active, and cells $(1,0)$, $(0,1)$ are inactive.
  - If $H = \circ = 1$, then cells $(0,0)$, $(1,1)$ are currently inactive, and cells $(1,0)$, $(0,1)$ are active.
- A multiset of two (immutable) symbols, $\eta(X,Y)$, representing a "table", which codifies the checkerboard flip:

$$\eta(\lambda, \circ) \qquad \eta(\circ, \lambda)$$

Other used (mutable and temporary) symbols:

- Symbol $h(H)$ is the current cell's activity marker and flips at each iteration phase, using table η. The activity status is determined by testing $h(...)$ against the target activity marker, $a(...)$: if both markers have the same contents, i.e. $h(H) \wedge a(H)$, then the cell is currently active; otherwise, the cell is currently inactive.
- Symbol $p(X,C)$ indicates that my neighbour's X colour is C, or, intuitively $p_X = C$.

The ruleset given in Figure 4, which is also schematically represented in the flowchart of Figure 5, contains 8 states and 14 generic rules. This ruleset models the pseudocode of Listing 1, enhanced with details required by the multi-cell message-based distributed memory system.

Essentially, the synchronisation barriers are implicit and helped (as needed) by idempotent rules, which only advance the state, without any content change. The colours are exchanged by "properly timed" *push notification* messages, which ensure that no "contamination" is possible between "old" and "new" colours.

Initially, because they do not know any of their neighbours' colours, all cells (black and white) send their colour to all their neighbours. Later, only black cells that turn white send their new white colour to all their black neighbours (who might need this). This limits the number of exchanged messages to the minimum possible. The given ruleset does not include (i) the termination check, which could be done e.g. by using an extra master cell; nor does it include (ii) any post-termination cleaning (here all cells end with a full set of their final neighbours' colours).

$$S_0 \rightarrow_{\min \otimes \min} S_1 \mid p(w) \tag{1}$$

$$S_0 \rightarrow_{\min \otimes \min} S_{11} \, h(IJ) \mid \iota(I,J) \tag{2}$$

$$S_1 \rightarrow_{\max \otimes \min} S_2 \, (p(Y,w)) \updownarrow_X \mid n(X,Y) \tag{3}$$

$$S_2 \rightarrow_{\min \otimes \min} S_2 \tag{4}$$

$$S_{11} \, h/(\circ\circ) \rightarrow_{\min \otimes \max} S_{12} \, h/\lambda \tag{5}$$

$$S_{11} \rightarrow_{\max \otimes \min} S_{12} \, (p(Y,b)) \updownarrow_X \mid n(X,Y) \tag{6}$$

$$S_{12} \, p(X,w) \, p(X,b) \rightarrow_{\max \otimes \min} S_{13} \, p(X,w) \tag{7}$$

$$S_{12} \, h(H) \rightarrow_{\min \otimes \min} S_{13} \, h(\bar{H}) \mid \eta(H,\bar{H}) \tag{8}$$

$$S_{13} \rightarrow_{\min \otimes \min} S_{14} \mid h(H) \, a(H) \tag{9}$$

$$S_{13} \rightarrow_{\min \otimes \min} S_{34} \tag{10}$$

$$S_{14} \, p(b) \rightarrow_{\min \otimes \min} S_2 \, p(w) \mid \Psi \tag{11}$$

$$S_{14} \rightarrow_{\max \otimes \min} S_2 \, (p(Y,w)) \updownarrow_X \mid n(X,Y) \, \Psi \tag{12}$$

$$S_{14} \rightarrow_{\min \otimes \min} S_{12} \tag{13}$$

$$S_{34} \rightarrow_{\min \otimes \min} S_{12} \tag{14}$$

Fig. 4. Synchronous P ruleset for the multi-cell scenario

The Ψ rules 11 and 12 use a promoter designated (for brevity) by a meta-syntactic abbreviation, Ψ, which is detailed as follows:

$$\Psi = p(1,C_1) \, p(2,C_2) \, \ldots \, p(8,C_8)$$
$$\psi(C_1,C_2,\ldots,C_8,1)$$

These two rules check the "deletion" condition of Section 2, $\psi = 1$, using its namesake table and the colours received from the eight neighbours.

From the start state, S_0, cells follow two separate branches: (rule 1) white cells go to state S_1; while (rule 2) black cells go to state S_{11} and also start to compute their activity marker, h.

At state S_1, white cells: (rule 3) send white colour notifications to all their neighbours (all unknown at this stage); and then continue to state S_2, where (rule 4) they cycle indefinitely. This branch is missing in the high-level pseudocode of Listing 1, but required in our message-based distributed memory model.

At state S_{11}, black cells: (rule 5) collapse the content of their activity markers, h, to at most one single $\circ$; (rule 6) send their black colour notifications to all their neighbours (all unknown at this stage); and then continue to state S_{12}.

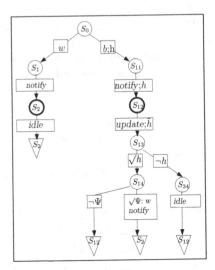

Fig. 5. Schematic flowchart for the multi-cell ruleset

State S_{12} is the start of the main black cell cycle, corresponding to the **while** line of Listing 1. Here, this cycle takes exactly *three* P steps and corresponds to *one* logical algorithm iteration. At state S_{12}, black cells: (rule 7) update their received colour notifications, in case previous neighbouring black cells have turned white; (rule 8) flip their activity indicator, h; and then continue to state S_{13}.

State S_{13} corresponds to the activity checking **if** line of Listing 1. Here, black cells follow two separate branches: (rule 9, **then** branch) active black cells continue to state S_{14}; while (rule 10, **else** branch) inactive black cells continue to state S_{34}.

At state S_{14}, active black cells take a decision based on the combined "deletion" condition, Ψ. Active black cells that validate Ψ (**if then** branch of Listing 1): (rule 11) turn white; (rule 12) send new (white) colour notifications to all their neighbours; and then *break* the cycle and continue to state S_2. Active black cells that remain black (rule 13) return to state S_{12} (to start a new iteration).

At state S_{34}, inactive black cells: (rule 14) take an idempotent "idle" step, required for proper synchronisation; and then go back to state S_{12} (to start a new iteration). Note that, at state S_{12}, black cells flip their activity indicator: thus, previously active black cells become inactive and vice-versa.

This analysis leads to the following proposition:

Theorem 1. *The multi-cell system, constructed and initialised as discussed above, correctly models Guo and Hall's parallel thinning algorithm A2.*

Remark 1. For clarity, this ruleset does not include rules to check the algorithm termination and then to change state to an idle final state. This can be done in several ways; perhaps the simplest practical way is to set up a dedicated master cell, which can centralize the number of changes of each logical iteration.

Unless such extra check is done, under the traditional termination rules, the cells will not know the termination and continue to run their cycles, but without changing their essential content, which is the colour.

One could investigate a more relaxed theoretical termination condition, which could say that a system terminates when it enters an endless cycle which exactly repeats the same cell states and contents.

Could the cells themselves detect this, running a control layer based on a combination of a distributed termination detection algorithm with a cycle detection algorithm, such as Floyd's "Tortoise and Hare" algorithm [7]? This seems to be an open question.

5   Single-Cell P System

The design is similar to the multi-cell synchronous model of Section 4. A single-cell system is automatically synchronous, so again there is no need for explicit synchronisation barriers.

The single-cell model uses one single cell and maps each pixel (i, j) to a sub-cellular structure (i.e. a new complex object), with a curried functor, $\sigma(i, j)(...)$. In the multi-cell model, each cell had its own state object, which controlled its lifeline. In the single-cell model, we simulate these states by local symbols in each sub-cell $\sigma(i, j)$: for consistency, we replace state S_i by symbol s_i and ensure that each sub-cell $\sigma(i, j)$ contains, at all times, exactly one such "state" symbol. Thus, this single-cell model is state-less.

The immutable target checkerboard symbol $a(H)$ and the immutable pre-computed tables, $n(X, Y)$, $\eta(H, \bar{H})$, $\psi(...)$, appear as top-level complex objects inside the single cell. Each $\sigma(i, j)(...)$ sub-cell contains a multiset which includes its own mutable colour symbol $p(C)$ and its own copies of the temporary mutable symbols used by the multi-cell model; the previous $\iota(i, j)$ ID is integrated as σ's first parameter list.

The ruleset, listed in Figure 6, is similar to the ruleset of the multi-cell model of Figure 4, but adapted to work in parallel on all $\sigma(i, j)(...)$ sub-cells.

Essential changes:

- All rules (except the "Ψ" rules 11 and 12, which are further discussed below) are qualified by an access path identifying the current sub-cell, $\sigma(I, J)$ ::, which also removes the need for $\iota(...)$ promoters
- Global items are qualified by the root access path: /
- All min instantiation modes are changed to max, which ensures that all $\sigma(I, J)$ sub-cells evolve in parallel
- States S_i are replaced by local symbols s_i, exactly one in each sub-cell $\sigma(I, J)$
- Rules for sending inter-cell colour notification messages are omitted (as we have now direct access to corresponding contents of the required "neighbouring" $\sigma(...)$ sub-cells).

For example, (multi-cell) rule 2 of Figure 4:

$$S_0 \rightarrow_{min \otimes min} S_{11} \; h(IJ) \mid \iota(I, J) \; p(b))$$

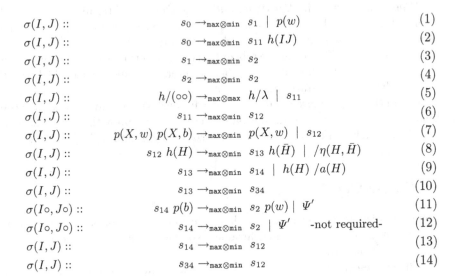

$$\sigma(I, J) :: \quad s_0 \rightarrow_{\text{max}\otimes\text{min}} s_1 \mid p(w) \tag{1}$$

$$\sigma(I, J) :: \quad s_0 \rightarrow_{\text{max}\otimes\text{min}} s_{11} \, h(IJ) \tag{2}$$

$$\sigma(I, J) :: \quad s_1 \rightarrow_{\text{max}\otimes\text{min}} s_2 \tag{3}$$

$$\sigma(I, J) :: \quad s_2 \rightarrow_{\text{max}\otimes\text{min}} s_2 \tag{4}$$

$$\sigma(I, J) :: \quad h/(\circ\circ) \rightarrow_{\text{max}\otimes\text{max}} h/\lambda \mid s_{11} \tag{5}$$

$$\sigma(I, J) :: \quad s_{11} \rightarrow_{\text{max}\otimes\text{min}} s_{12} \tag{6}$$

$$\sigma(I, J) :: \quad p(X, w) \, p(X, b) \rightarrow_{\text{max}\otimes\text{min}} p(X, w) \mid s_{12} \tag{7}$$

$$\sigma(I, J) :: \quad s_{12} \, h(H) \rightarrow_{\text{max}\otimes\text{min}} s_{13} \, h(\bar{H}) \mid /\eta(H, \bar{H}) \tag{8}$$

$$\sigma(I, J) :: \quad s_{13} \rightarrow_{\text{max}\otimes\text{min}} s_{14} \mid h(H) \, /a(H) \tag{9}$$

$$\sigma(I, J) :: \quad s_{13} \rightarrow_{\text{max}\otimes\text{min}} s_{34} \tag{10}$$

$$\sigma(I\circ, J\circ) :: \quad s_{14} \, p(b) \rightarrow_{\text{max}\otimes\text{min}} s_2 \, p(w) \mid \Psi' \tag{11}$$

$$\sigma(I\circ, J\circ) :: \quad s_{14} \rightarrow_{\text{max}\otimes\text{min}} s_2 \mid \Psi' \quad \text{-not required-} \tag{12}$$

$$\sigma(I, J) :: \quad s_{14} \rightarrow_{\text{max}\otimes\text{min}} s_{12} \tag{13}$$

$$\sigma(I, J) :: \quad s_{34} \rightarrow_{\text{max}\otimes\text{min}} s_{12} \tag{14}$$

Fig. 6. Synchronous P ruleset for the single-cell scenario

is changed to:

$$\sigma(I, J)/s_0 \rightarrow_{\text{max}\otimes\text{min}} \sigma(I, J)/s_{11} \, \sigma(I, J)/h(IJ) \mid \sigma(I, J)/p(b)$$

or, equivalently, to rule 2 of Figure 6:

$$\sigma(I, J) :: s_0 \rightarrow_{\text{max}\otimes\text{min}} s_{11} \, h(IJ) \mid p(b)$$

Note that this rule: (i) will be instantiated once for each sub-cell $\sigma(I, J)$ and all its instances will run in parallel; (ii) uses only local $\sigma(I, J)(...)$ objects, such as s_i, $h(...)$ and $p(...)$, and there is no need for the $\iota(I, J)$ promoter, which is directly subsumed by the sub-cell itself, $\sigma(I, J)$.

Multi-cell rules 3, 5, 6, 7 and 12 of Figure 4 need special consideration. Besides now redundant colour notifications, rule 3, 6 and 12 ensured proper state transfers. Examining the context, we conclude that we only need corresponding "state" transfer rules for rules 3 and 6, but not for rule 12 (which is left in the listing, but could safely be omitted).

Rules 5 and 7 can perform multiple operations on the same sub-cell $\sigma(I, J)$. Therefore, the corresponding singleton "state" symbols, s_{11} and s_{12}, are transformed as promoters; subsequent rules, 6 and 8, are enough to ensure the required "state" transfers.

The "Ψ'" transformations of the original rules 11 and 12 must offer fast access: (i) to "table" ψ, which is now global, and (ii) to the colours of "neighbouring" σ sub-cells, i.e. to all σ sub-cells which have coordinates in the range of plus/minus one from current coordinates. Therefore, these rules and all their objects (including all objects used in the Ψ' condition) use "custom" access paths, where I and

J represent now the coordinates of the NW neighbour (i.e. current coordinates minus 1). Under this arrangement, rules 11 and 12 are not applicable to border sub-cells: e.g. the "top-left" sub-cell, $\sigma(\lambda, \lambda)$, cannot match a $\sigma(I\circ, J\circ)$ term – intuitively, because it does not have any "neighbours" on its left or above. However, this is acceptable, under our initial simplifying assumption that all borders pixels are white from start.

Let us recall that (multi-cell) rules 11 and 12 of Figure 4 tested the following condition, Ψ:

$$\Psi = \; p(1, C_1) \; p(2, C_2) \; \ldots \; p(8, C_8)$$
$$\psi(C_1, C_2, \ldots, C_8, 1)$$

The colour notification rule 12 is not anymore needed, and (single-cell) rule 11 of Figure 6 tests now the following path qualified modified condition, Ψ':

$$\Psi' = \; /\sigma(I, J)/p(C_1) \qquad /\sigma(I\circ, J)/p(C_2) \qquad /\sigma(I\circ\circ, J)/p(C_3)$$
$$/\sigma(I, J\circ)/p(C_8) \qquad\qquad\qquad\qquad /\sigma(I\circ\circ, J\circ)/p(C_4)$$
$$/\sigma(I, J\circ\circ)/p(C_7) \;\; /\sigma(I\circ, J\circ\circ)/p(C_6) \;\; /\sigma(I\circ\circ, J\circ\circ)/p(C_5)$$
$$/\psi(C_1, C_2, \ldots, C_8, 1)$$

Theorem 2. *The single-cell system, constructed and initialised as discussed above, correctly models Guo and Hall's parallel thinning algorithm A2.*

6 Multi-cell P System (Asynchronous)

We first transform our *synchronous* multi-cell P system into a system that can also run in the *asynchronous* mode. Synchronous systems are easier to design, however, synchronous messages may slow down the evolution, may create deadlocks and may be difficult to map on Actors-based systems.

For this algorithm, we have a straightforward ad-hoc way to transform it into an asynchronous version. Essentially, we ensure that each black cell keeps adequate records about its black neighbours and it can cycle until all its due colour notifications are received.

Specifically, we require that all black cells *continue* to notify their neighbours at each logical iteration, even if they did not change colour or they are logically inactive. In principle, if I have received k black colour notifications from neighbours that were black at the previous logical step, than, at the next iteration, I wait until I see $k = k_b + k_w$ new colour notifications, where (i) k_b come from black cells that remained black (either they failed the Ψ test or they were logically inactive), and (ii) k_w come from active black cells that turned white. Additionally, I must be prepared to receive and safely keep ahead-of-round colour notifications, which some hurried black cells could send. There is a cost for this, of course, as the cells now exchange many more colour notifications; however, forcing a system to run synchronously would also involve a non-negligible synchronisation cost, esp. in a true distributed setting.

The ruleset of the asynchronous version, listed in Figure 7, is similar to the ruleset of the synchronous model of Figure 4. To enable a straightforward comparison, we kept the original rule numbers; rules that have been expanded have additional numbers with letter suffixes: e.g. the synchronous rule 2 was expanded into asynchronous rules 2a and 2b.

$$S_0 \rightarrow_{\min\otimes\min} S_1 \mid p(w) \tag{1}$$

$$S_0 \rightarrow_{\min\otimes\min} S_{11}\, h(IJ) \mid \iota(I,J) \qquad (2a) \tag{2}$$

$$S_0 \rightarrow_{\max\otimes\min} S_{11}\, q(X,b) \mid n(X,\_) \qquad (2b)$$

$$S_1 \rightarrow_{\max\otimes\min} S_2\, (p(Y,w))\, \updownarrow_X \mid n(X,Y) \tag{3}$$

$$S_2 \rightarrow_{\min\otimes\min} S_2 \tag{4}$$

$$S_{11}\, h/(\circ\circ) \rightarrow_{\min\otimes\max} S_{12}\, h/\lambda \tag{5}$$

$$S_{11} \rightarrow_{\max\otimes\min} S_{12}\, (p(Y,b))\, \updownarrow_X \mid n(X,Y) \tag{6}$$

$$S_{12}\, p(X,C)\, q(X,b) \rightarrow_{\max\otimes\min} S_{12}\, r(X,C) \qquad (7a) \tag{7}$$

$$S_{12} \rightarrow_{\min\otimes\min} S_{12} \mid q(\_,b) \qquad (7b)$$

$$S_{12}\, r(X,C) \rightarrow_{\max\otimes\min} S_{13}\, q(X,C) \qquad (7c)$$

$$S_{12}\, h(H) \rightarrow_{\min\otimes\min} S_{13}\, h(\bar{H}) \mid \eta(H,\bar{H}) \tag{8}$$

$$S_{13} \rightarrow_{\min\otimes\min} S_{14} \mid h(H)\, a(H) \tag{9}$$

$$S_{13} \rightarrow_{\min\otimes\min} S_{34} \tag{10}$$

$$S_{14}\, p(b) \rightarrow_{\min\otimes\min} S_2\, p(w) \mid \Psi'' \qquad (11a) \tag{11}$$

$$S_{14} \rightarrow_{\max\otimes\min} S_2\, (p(Y,w))\, \updownarrow_X \mid n(X,Y)\, \Psi'' \qquad (12a) \tag{12}$$

$$S_{14} \rightarrow_{\max\otimes\min} S_{12}\, (p(Y,b))\, \updownarrow_X \mid n(X,Y)\, q(X,b) \qquad (13a) \tag{13}$$

$$S_{14} \rightarrow_{\min\otimes\min} S_{12} \qquad (13b)$$

$$S_{34} \rightarrow_{\max\otimes\min} S_{12}\, (p(Y,b))\, \updownarrow_X \mid n(X,Y)\, q(X,b) \qquad (14a) \tag{14}$$

$$S_{34} \rightarrow_{\min\otimes\min} S_{12} \qquad (14b)$$

Fig. 7. Asynchronous P ruleset for the multi-cell scenario

We redefine the meaning of one symbol and we use two more, all indicating a colour C notified from neighbour X:

- $p(X,C)$: is now a *just-received*, but not yet *recorded* colour notification
- $q(X,C)$: is a *recorded* $p(X,C)$ colour notification
- $r(X,C)$: is a *temporary* stage of such a colour notification (between *just-received* and *recorded*)

Let us briefly discuss the new or enhanced rules of this asynchronous version, against corresponding "old" rules for the synchronous model. Rule 2a is identical to old rule 2 and is now complemented by rule 2b, which initialises each black cell with 8 *recorded* black notifications $q(X,b)$, $X \in [1,8]$. As we don't know anything yet about our neighbours, it is safe to initially assume that all our neighbours are black: all of them, black and white, will soon notify us their true colours.

In the synchronous setting, rule 7 updated our recordings, for neighbours that were recorded black and had just notified us of their changed colour; then, rule 7 went to state S_{13} – note that all colour notifications arrived synchronously (at the same time). Now, in an asynchronous setting, we cannot rush to state S_{13}, unless we have received all expected colour notifications, which may arrive with arbitrary delays. Therefore, rules 7a and 7b implement now a small loop, trapping us in state S_{12} until we have matched all *recorded* notifications, q, against newly *just-received* notifications, p. For proper recording, we first keep the updated *just-received* colours in *temporary* r objects; we further change these to *recorded* q objects, only after receiving all due notifications, when we break out of this small cycle and go to state S_{13}, by rule 7c. Any extra ahead-of-round notifications are safely kept for the next logical round, still as *just-received* notifications.

Rules 11a and 12a use a slightly new version of the meta-syntactic abbreviation, Ψ'', which is now defined in terms of recorded notifications, $q(...)$ (instead of $p(...)$):

$$\Psi = q(1, C_1)\, q(2, C_2)\, \ldots\, q(8, C_8)$$
$$\psi(C_1, C_2, \ldots, C_8, 1)$$

Rules 13a and 14a, the new versions of rules 13 and 14, ensure that now even black cells that are logically inactive or remain black still send black colour notifications to their recorded black neighbours – this is required for our local synchronisation. Rules 13b and 14b ensure that black cells still go to the loop state S_{12}, even if they have no black neighbours; obviously, these rules are not really required: these rules are here just to maintain full compatibility with the other versions and the idea that the system loops until it is properly terminated.

Example 1. Let us consider the first evolutionary steps of a cell, $\sigma(io, jo)$, corresponding to the centre pixel of configuration #125 of Figure 3b. Rule 2b initialises $\sigma(io, jo)$'s contents with 8 *just-received* colour notifications: $q(1, b)$, $q(2, b)$, $q(3, b)$, $q(4, b)$, $q(5, b)$, $q(6, b)$, $q(7, b)$, $q(8, b)$, which indicate that, at the next logical step, $\sigma(io, jo)$ expects 8 colour notifications (updates).

Next, all cells send their initial colours: white cells by rule 3 and black cells by rule 6. Cell $\sigma(io, jo)$ cycles on state S_{12} until it receives 8 distinct $p(X, C)$ notifications, for $X \in [1, 8]$. For example, assume that σ receives, in *order*, the following notifications (including one ahead of time, from its NE neighbour # 3, $\sigma(i \circ \circ, j))$: $p(3, b)$, $p(4, b)$, $p(1, b)$, $p(8, w)$, $p(2, w)$, $p(6, b)$, $p(7, b)$, $p(3, w)$, $p(5, b)$.

Note that the receiving FIFO order is important, as $\sigma(io, jo)$ first considers $p(3, b)$ and keeps $p(3, w)$ for the next logical iteration. Then, as all expected notifications have been received, and $\sigma(io, jo)$ will finally record the following colours: $q(1, b)$, $q(2, w)$, $q(3, b)$, $q(4, b)$, $q(5, b)$, $q(6, b)$, $q(7, b)$, $q(8, w)$, and will safely keep $p(3, w)$, for the next logical round.

Next, $\sigma(io, jo)$ will proceed to check its activity marker; if active, will test the Ψ'' condition on its received notifications, q, and decide to remain black; in any case (logically active or not), it will again send black colour notifications to all its neighbours, either by rule 13 or by rule 14; etc.

7   Actors Emulation

Traditional Actor systems can run efficiently on multi-cores, and there are novel extensions that extend Actors to heterogeneous platforms, involving clusters of nodes, with both CPU multi-core and GPU many-cores facilities. Therefore, mapping P systems to Actor based systems may prove to be a very promising emulation path.

Actor messaging is typically asynchronous, although some systems do also support some sort of synchronous messaging; for more details, please see Syme's monograph on F# [24].

A straightforward (but not the most efficient) Actors mapping of the asynchronous multi-cell model uses one actor for each cell (pixel) σ. All contents of σ become local variables in the corresponding actor. All P systems messaging, i.e. all colour notifications, is implemented as asynchronous messaging between actors. In F#, the lifetime of an actor is described by a sequence of mutually tail recursive async monad instances. A straightforward (but, again, not the most efficient) implementation of the ruleset maps each state to an async returning function. Leaving aside (as it would require too much additional space) part of the setup and a few other practical details, Figures 8 and 9 suggest the essential structure of such a cell actor.

```
type  Colour  =  |  White  =  0  |  Black  =  1  |  None  =  2

type  ReceivedColour  =  int  *  Colour

let  N =  [|  0;  5;  6;  7;  8;  1;  2;  3;  4  |]
let  DI  =  [|  0;  −1;  0;  1;  1;  1;  0;  −1;  −1  |]
let  DJ  =  [|  0;  −1;  −1;  −1;  0;  1;  1;  1;  0  |]

let  neighbour  (i:int,  j:int,  x:int)  =
    (i  +  DI.[x],  j  +  DJ.[x])

type  PixelActor  =  option<MailboxProcessor<ReceivedColour>>

let  N1  =  100
let  N2  =  100
```

Fig. 8. Simplified cell/pixel actor setup

```
let SetPixel (i:int, j:int, p:Colour) =
MailboxProcessor<ReceivedColour>.Start (fun inbox ->
        let h = ref 0
        let P = Array.create 8 Colour.None
        let Q = Array.create 8 Colour.Black

        let rec S0 () = async {
            match p with
            | Colour.White ->
                return! S1 ()
            | _ ->
                h := i + j
                return! S11 ()
        }

    and S11 () = async {
        while !h >= 2 do
            h := !h - 2
        for x = 1 to 8 do
            let n = neighbour(i, j, x)
            Pixels.[fst n, snd n].Value.Post (N.[x], p)
        return! S12 ()
        }

    and S12 () = async {
        let R = Array.create 8 Colour.None

        for x = 1 to 8 do
            if P.[x] <> Colour.None then
                Q.[x] <- Colour.None
                R.[x] <- P.[x]

        while Array.exists (fun c -> c = Colour.Black) Q do
            let! m = inbox.Receive()
            match m with
            | (x, c) when Q.[x] = Colour.Black ->
                Q.[x] <- Colour.None
                R.[x] <- c
            | (x, c) -> // Q.[x] = Colour.None
                P.[x] <- c

        for x = 1 to 8 do
            if R.[x] <> Colour.None then
                Q.[x] <- R.[x]

        return! S13 ()
        }

    // ...

    S0 () )
```

Fig. 9. Simplified cell/pixel actor body

A straightforward Actors mapping of the single-cell model uses one actor for each sub-cell (pixel) $\sigma(i, j)$. In this design, local contents of $\sigma(i, j)$ become local variables in the corresponding actor. All other top-level objects become global objects, accessible to all actors in the emulation. Because of these global shared objects, this is not a pure actor design, but, if properly designed, it can be both correct and efficient. Also, in this scenario, there need not be any messaging between actors, so actors can be replaced by more mundane tasks. However, if there are no messages that could be used for synchronisation, the system needs synchronisation barriers, as indicated in Section 2.

An interesting design (not developed yet) can combine these two designs, multi-cell and single-cell, for P system models and for their actor based implementations. One could partition the image in smaller rectangles and allocate sub-images to actors – potentially distributed on different nodes or using different computing devices, such as CPUs vs GPUs. Such a partitioned design could be efficient for processing very large images, when running on heterogeneous clusters or even on single multi-core nodes, by reducing the numbers of actors and thus eliminating some housekeeping overhead.

8   Conclusions

We present three membrane computing models for a complex image processing task – image skeletonisation: (i) a synchronous model using one cell per pixel and relying on inter-cell parallelism; (ii) an asynchronous model using one cell per pixel and relying on inter-cell parallelism; (ii) a (synchronous) model using one single cell, with one sub-cellular object per pixel, relying on intra-cell parallelism.

All three models are crisp, use reasonably small fixed-sized alphabets and rulesets, and are closely inter-related by way of almost mechanical translations. This experience has enabled us to further validate our complex objects proposal and enhance it with a "micro-surgery" facility, very useful for nested objects. The proposed models can be straightforwardly translated and implemented in a functional language with an Actors library.

Further work needs to be done to investigate the possible automation of these translations: (i) between multi-cell and single-cell P systems; (ii) from synchronous to asynchronous P systems; (iii) from P systems to Actors. Also, further work seems necessary to study heterogeneous designs, mixing ideas from multi-cell, single-cell, synchronous and asynchronous designs.

This study also suggests a couple of open questions: (i) to investigate partial asynchronous versions of similar algorithms and their merits (with respect to quality of results and runtime performance); (ii) to investigate an efficient distributed termination detection control layer, which is adequate for this algorithm (and other similar non-diffusing algorithms); possibly combining a distributed termination algorithm with a cycle detection algorithm.

Acknowledgments. Thanks to Zhengping Wang and to the anonymous reviewers for their most valuable comments and suggestions.

References

1. Agha, G., Thati, P.: An algebraic theory of actors and its application to a simple object-based language. In: Owe, O., Krogdahl, S., Lyche, T. (eds.) From OO to FM (Dahl Festschrift). LNCS, vol. 2635, pp. 26–57. Springer, Heidelberg (2004)

2. Bălănescu, T., Nicolescu, R., Wu, H.: Asynchronous P systems. International Journal of Natural Computing Research 2(2), 1–18 (2011)

3. Díaz-Pernil, D., Peña-Cantillana, F., Gutiérrez-Naranjo, M.A.: A parallel algorithm for skeletonizing images by using spiking neural P systems. Neurocomputing 115, 81–91 (2013)

4. Dinneen, M.J., Kim, Y.-B., Nicolescu, R.: A faster P solution for the Byzantine agreement problem. In: Gheorghe, M., Hinze, T., Păun, Gh., Rozenberg, G., Salomaa, A. (eds.) CMC 2010. LNCS, vol. 6501, pp. 175–197. Springer, Heidelberg (2010)

5. Dinneen, M.J., Kim, Y.B., Nicolescu, R.: P systems and the Byzantine agreement. Journal of Logic and Algebraic Programming 79(6), 334–349 (2010)

6. ElGindy, H., Nicolescu, R., Wu, H.: Fast distributed DFS solutions for edge-disjoint paths in digraphs. In: Csuhaj-Varjú, E., Gheorghe, M., Rozenberg, G., Salomaa, A., Vaszil, Gy. (eds.) CMC 2012. LNCS, vol. 7762, pp. 173–194. Springer, Heidelberg (2013). http://dx.doi.org/10.1007/978-3-642-36751-9_13

7. Floyd, R.W.: Nondeterministic algorithms. J. ACM 14(4), 636–644 (1967). http://doi.acm.org/10.1145/321420.321422

8. Gimelfarb, G., Nicolescu, R., Ragavan, S.: P systems in stereo matching. In: Real, P., Diaz-Pernil, D., Molina-Abril, H., Berciano, A., Kropatsch, W. (eds.) CAIP 2011, Part II. LNCS, vol. 6855, pp. 285–292. Springer, Heidelberg (2011). http://dx.doi.org/10.1007/978-3-642-23678-5_33

9. Gimelfarb, G., Nicolescu, R., Ragavan, S.: P system implementation of dynamic programming stereo. Journal of Mathematical Imaging and Vision 47(1–2), 13–26 (2013). http://dx.doi.org/10.1007/s10851-012-0367-6

10. Guo, Z., Hall, R.W.: Parallel thinning with two-subiteration algorithms. Commun. ACM 32(3), 359–373 (1989). http://doi.acm.org/10.1145/62065.62074

11. Hewitt, C.: Viewing control structures as patterns of passing messages. Artificial Intelligence 8(3), 323–364 (1977). http://www.sciencedirect.com/science/article/pii/0004370277900339

12. Lynch, N.A.: Distributed Algorithms. Morgan Kaufmann Publishers Inc., San Francisco (1996)

13. Nicolescu, R.: Parallel and distributed algorithms in P systems. In: Gheorghe, M., Păun, Gh., Rozenberg, G., Salomaa, A., Verlan, S. (eds.) CMC 2011. LNCS, vol. 7184, pp. 35–50. Springer, Heidelberg (2012)

14. Nicolescu, R., Gimelfarb, G., Morris, J., Gong, R., Delmas, P.: Regularising ill-posed discrete optimisation: Quests with P systems. Fundam. Inf. 131(3–4), 465–483 (2014)

15. Nicolescu, R., Ipate, F., Wu, H.: Programming P systems with complex objects. In: Alhazov, A., Cojocaru, S., Gheorghe, M., Rogozhin, Yu., Rozenberg, G., Salomaa, A. (eds.) CMC 2013. LNCS, vol. 8340, pp. 280–300. Springer, Heidelberg (2014)

16. Nicolescu, R., Ipate, F., Wu, H.: Towards high-level P systems programming using complex objects. In: Alhazov, A., Cojocaru, S., Gheorghe, M., Rogozhin, Yu. (eds.) 14th International Conference on Membrane Computing, CMC14, Chişinău, Moldova, August 20-23, 2013, Proceedings, pp. 255–276. Institute of Mathematics and Computer Science, Academy of Sciences of Moldova, Chişinău (2013)

17. Nicolescu, R., Wu, H.: BFS solution for disjoint paths in P systems. In: Calude, C.S., Kari, J., Petre, I., Rozenberg, G. (eds.) UC 2011. LNCS, vol. 6714, pp. 164–176. Springer, Heidelberg (2011). http://dx.doi.org/10.1007/978-3-642-21341-0_20
18. Nicolescu, R., Wu, H.: New solutions for disjoint paths in P systems. Natural Computing 11, 637–651 (2012). http://dx.doi.org/10.1007/s11047-012-9342-9
19. Nicolescu, R., Wu, H.: Complex objects for complex applications. Romanian Journal of Information Science and Technology (2014, to appear)
20. Peña-Cantillana, F., Berciano, A., Díaz-Pernil, D., Gutiérrez-Naranjo, M.A.: Parallel skeletonizing of digital images by using cellular automata. In: Ferri, M., Frosini, P., Landi, C., Cerri, A., Di Fabio, B. (eds.) CTIC 2012. LNCS, vol. 7309, pp. 39–48. Springer, Heidelberg (2012)
21. Păun, Gh., Rozenberg, G., Salomaa, A.: The Oxford Handbook of Membrane Computing. Oxford University Press Inc., New York (2010)
22. Reina-Molina, R., Díaz-Pernil, D.: Bioinspired parallel 2D or 3D skeletonization. IMAGEN-A 3(5), 41–44 (2013)
23. Reina-Molina, R., Díaz-Pernil, D., Gutiérrez-Naranjo, M.A.: Cell complexes and membrane computing for thinning 2D and 3D images. In: del Amor, M.A.M., Păun, Gh., Pérez-Hurtado, I., Romero-Campero, F.J. (eds.) Tenth Brainstorming Week on Membrane Computing. RGNC REPORT, vol. 1, pp. 91–110. Universidad de Sevilla (2012)
24. Syme, D., Granicz, A., Cisternino, A.: Expert F# 3.0, 3rd edn. Apress, Berkely (2012)
25. Wu, H.: Minimum spanning tree in P systems. In: Pan, L., Păun, Gh., Song, T. (eds.) Proceedings of the Asian Conference on Membrane Computing (ACMC2012), pp. 88–104. Huazhong University of Science and Technology, Wuhan (2012)
26. Wu, H.: Distributed Algorithms in P Systems. Ph.D. thesis, The University of Auckland, Auckland, New Zealand (2014)

Causal Nets for Geometrical Gandy–Păun–Rozenberg Machines

Adam Obtułowicz[(⊠)]

Institute of Mathematics, Polish Academy of Sciences,
Śniadeckich 8, 00-656 Warsaw, Poland
A.Obtulowicz@impan.pl

Abstract. An approach to the computational complexity beyond the known complexity measures of the consumed time and space of computation is proposed. The approach focuses on the chaotic behavior and randomness aspects of computational processes and is based on a representation of these processes by causal nets.

1 Introduction

A certain new approach to the investigations of the computational complexity of abstract systems allowing some unrestricted parallelism of computation is proposed, where the computational processes realized in a discrete time with a central clock by these systems are represented by causal nets similar to those in [4] and related to causal sets in [1].

The representation of computational processes by causal nets is aimed to provide an abstraction from those features of computational processes which do not have a spatial nature such that the abstraction could make visible some new aspects of the processes like an aspect of chaotic behavior or a fractal shape.

The aspects of a chaotic behavior and a fractal shape inspired by the research area of dynamics of nonlinear systems [20] regarding an unpredictability of the behavior of these systems[1] could suggest an answer to the following question formulated in [21]: *Is the concept of randomness, founded in the concept of absence of computable regularities, the only adequate and consistent one? In which direction, if any, should one look for alternatives?*

The answers may have an impact on designing pseudorandom number generators, cf. [23], [24], applied in statistics, cryptography, and Monte Carlo Method.

The proposed approach is aimed to provide a possibly uniform precise mathematical treatment of causal nets and related concepts which could serve for measuring of complexity of computational processes by using graph dimensions [13] and network fractal dimensions [19], [7], [8] in parallel to measuring complexity of random strings in [11] by Hausdorff dimension.

The proposed approach concerns the investigations of abstract computing devices which are geometrical Gandy–Păun–Rozenberg machines.

---

[1] Unpredictability due to sensitive dependence on initial conditions—an important feature of deterministic transient chaos [20] often having fractal shape.

© Springer International Publishing Switzerland 2014
M. Gheorghe et al. (Eds.): CMC 2014, LNCS 8961, pp. 355–372, 2014.
DOI: 10.1007/978-3-319-14370-5_22

The geometrical Gandy–Păun–Rozenberg machines are some modifications of the known Gandy–Păun–Rozenberg machines [14], [15].

The assumption that the sets of instantaneous descriptions of geometrical Gandy–Păun–Rozenberg machines are skeletal sets of finite directed graphs together with the features of machine local causation rewriting rules provides a natural construction of causal nets representing computational processes.

2   Geometrical Gandy–Păun–Rozenberg Machines

We refer the reader to Appendix A and Appendix B (quoting the main definitions of [14], [15]) for unexplained notions and notation concerning labelled directed graphs, Gandy–Păun–Rozenberg machines (briefly G–P–R machines), and generalized G–P–R machines.

We recall the main difference between G–P–R machines and generalized G–P–R machines:

– the auxiliary rules of the G–P–R machines are not specified and for every G–P–R machine $\mathcal{M}$ with its transition function $\mathcal{F}_\mathcal{M}$ and for every instantaneous description G of $\mathcal{M}$ the instantaneous description $\mathcal{F}_\mathcal{M}(G)$ is a colimit of the gluing diagram $\mathcal{D}^G$ determined by the set $\mathcal{P}\ell(G)$ of maximal applications of the machine rewriting rules to G.

– the generalized G–P–R machines are equipped with auxiliary rules besides the rewriting rules and for every generalized G–P–R machine $\mathcal{M}$ with its transition function $\mathcal{F}_\mathcal{M}$ and for every instantaneous description G of $\mathcal{M}$ the instantaneous description $\mathcal{F}_\mathcal{M}(G)$ is a colimit of the generalized gluing diagram $\mathcal{D}_G$ determined by both the machine rewriting rules and the auxiliary rules.

Definition 2.1. We define a *simple geometrical G–P–R machine* and a *strict geometrical G–P–R machine* to be the modifications of a G–P–R machine and a generalized G–P–R machine, respectively, such that

– in both cases of a simple and a strict machine we assume that
  • the set of labels of vertices of the directed graphs belonging to the set of instantaneous descriptions of a given machine is a one element set or equivalently these graphs are not labelled at all, an analogous assumption concerns the graphs appearing in the machine rewriting rules and auxiliary rules,
  • for every machine $\mathcal{M}$ there exists a natural number $n > 0$ such that for every graph G belonging to the set of instantaneous descriptions of $\mathcal{M}$ the set $V(G)$ of vertices of G is a set of ordered n-tuples of elements of $Q^\bullet$, where $Q^\bullet$ is the set of rational numbers, if necessary, extended to the recursive real numbers which are linear combinations of $\sqrt{2}$, $\sqrt{3}$, etc. with rational coefficients (hence we use the adjective 'geometrical'),

– in the case of a simple machine we impose a strenghtening that the graphs belonging to the set of instantaneous descriptions of the machine or appearing in the conclusions of the machine rewriting rules are not necessarily isomorphically perfect graphs.

Theorem. *For both cases of a simple and of a strict geometrical G–P–R machine if the set of its instantaneous description is a recursive set, then the transition function of the machine is a computable function.*

Proof. We prove the theorem for the case of a simple geometrical G–P–R machine $\mathcal{M}$ with its transition function $\mathcal{F}_{\mathcal{M}}$.

The following assignments are computable:

– the assignment to a finite gluing diagram its colimit constructed as in Appendix A in the domain of finite directed graphs,
– the assignment to an instantaneous description G of $\mathcal{M}$ the set $\mathcal{P}\ell(G)$ of maximal applications of the rewriting rules of $\mathcal{M}$,
– the assignment to an instantaneous description G of $\mathcal{M}$ the gluing diagram $\mathcal{D}^G$ which is determined by $\mathcal{P}\ell(G)$ in an effective way.

Hence the assignment to an instantaneous description G of $\mathcal{M}$ the result of the construction of a colimit of the gluing diagram $\mathcal{D}^G$ is also computable assignment. Therefore an effective search of that unique instantaneous description $G' = \mathcal{F}_{\mathcal{M}}(G)$ which is isomorphic to the above result of the construction of a colimit of the gluing diagram $\mathcal{D}^G$ suffices for reaching $\mathcal{F}_{\mathcal{M}}(G)$ in an effective way. This effective search is provided by the assumption that the set of instantaneous descriptions of the machine $\mathcal{M}$ is a recursive set. Thus the transition function $\mathcal{F}_{\mathcal{M}}$ is a computable function.

The proof of the theorem for the case of strict geometrical G–P–R machines is similar to the above proof.

Examples 2.1. (The simulation of cellular automata). The generalized G–P–R machine $\mathcal{M}^{SGL}$ in [15] is an example of a strict geometrical G–P–R machine, where $\mathcal{M}^{SGL}$ simulates the spatial and temporal behavior of a cellular automaton identified with the eastern expansion fragment of Conway's *Game of life*.

We show now an example of a simple geometrical G–P–R machine which is aimed to simulate the behavior of one-dimensional cellular automaton with two cell states $0, 1$ and with the rule 30 given by the formula

$$a_{i-1} \text{ xor } (a_i \text{ or } a_{i+1}),$$

cf. [23], [24], where xor is 'exclusive or'. This simple geometrical G–P–R machine, denoted by $\mathcal{M}^{30}$, is defined in the following way.

The instantaneous descriptions and the rewriting rules of $\mathcal{M}^{30}$ are defined by using the finite directed graphs cl_x^n (for an integer n and $x \in \{0, 1, !, \varnothing\}$) corresponding to the single cells for $x \in \{0, 1, !\}$, where cl_x^n are such that:

– the graph $\mathrm{cl}_\varnothing^n$ is the square

$$(n,1) \longrightarrow (n+1,1)$$

$$\uparrow \qquad\qquad \uparrow$$

$$(n,0) \longrightarrow (n+1,0)$$

together with the loop $((0,0),(0,0))$ in the case $n = 0$, and with the path from $(n+1,0)$ to $(n,1)$ containing three intermediate vertices $(n+1-\frac{i}{4},\frac{i}{4})$ with $\{1,2,3\}$,

– the graph cl_x^n for $x \in \{0,1,!\}$ consists of:
  • the graph $\mathrm{cl}_\varnothing^n$ as a subgraph,
  • the edge $((n,0),(n+1-\frac{x+1}{4},\frac{x+1}{4}))$ for $x \in \{0,1\}$, indicating that the graph cl_x^n corresponds to a cell in state x and called an *edge indicating a state of a cell,*
  • the edge $((n,0),(n+1-\frac{3}{4},\frac{3}{4}))$ for $x = !$.

An instantaneous description of $\mathcal{M}^{30}$ is that graph G which is the graph union (cf. Appendix A)

$$\mathrm{cl}_!^i \cup \left(\bigcup_{i<k<j} \mathrm{cl}_{x_k}^k \right) \cup \mathrm{cl}_!^j$$

for some integers $i < -1$, $j > 1$ and for some family $\mathrm{cl}_{x_k}^k$ $(i < k < j)$ with $x_k \in \{0,1\}$ for all integers k such that $i < k < j$.

The rewriting rules of $\mathcal{M}^{30}$ are given by

– $\mathrm{cl}_i^1 \cup \mathrm{cl}_j^2 \cup \mathrm{cl}_k^3 \vdash \mathrm{cl}_\varnothing^1 \cup \mathrm{cl}_{\rho(i,j,k)}^2 \cup \mathrm{cl}_\varnothing^3$ for $\{i,j,k\} \subseteq \{0,1\}$, where $\rho(i,j,k) = i \,\mathrm{xor}\, (j \,\mathrm{or}\, k)$,

– $\mathrm{cl}_!^2 \cup \mathrm{cl}_j^3 \cup \mathrm{cl}_k^4 \vdash \mathrm{cl}_!^1 \cup \mathrm{cl}_{\rho(0,0,j)}^2 \cup \mathrm{cl}_{\rho(0,j,k)}^3 \cup \mathrm{cl}_\varnothing^4$ for $\{j,k\} \subseteq \{0,1\}$,

– $\mathrm{cl}_i^1 \cup \mathrm{cl}_j^2 \cup \mathrm{cl}_!^3 \vdash \mathrm{cl}_\varnothing^1 \cup \mathrm{cl}_{\rho(i,j,0)}^2 \cup \mathrm{cl}_{\rho(j,0,0)}^3 \cup \mathrm{cl}_!^4$ for $\{i,j\} \subseteq \{0,1\}$,

– the identity rule 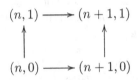 $\vdash$, where is the graph with single vertex 0 and with single edge which is a loop.

The graphs cl_j^2 and cl_j^3 appearing in the middle of the premises of the above rules are called the *centers* of these rules, respectively.

The one-dimensional cellular automata in [23], [24] and small Turing machines in [7], [8] can be simulated by simple G–P–R machines constructed in a similar way to the machine $\mathcal{M}^{30}$.

Example 2.2. (generation of the contours of the iterations of fractals). We show a simple geometrical G–P–R machine whose single rewriting rule serves for generating the contours of the iterations of Sierpiński gasket. This machine, denoted by $\mathcal{M}^{\mathrm{Sierp}}$ is defined in the following way.

Let Δ be a directed graph given by

$$V(\Delta) = \{(0,0),(\tfrac{1}{2},\tfrac{\sqrt{3}}{2}),(1,0)\},$$

$$E(\Delta) = \{((0,0),(1,0)),((0,0),(\tfrac{1}{2},\tfrac{\sqrt{3}}{2})),((1,0),(\tfrac{1}{2},\tfrac{\sqrt{3}}{2}))\}.$$

The graph Δ is a contour of an equilateral triangle.

The instantaneous descriptions of $\mathcal{M}^{\text{Sierp}}$ are graphs Δ_n (for a natural number $n \geq 0$) defined inductively by

$$\Delta_0 = \big(V(\Delta), E(\Delta) \cup \{((0,1),(0,1))\}\big),$$

$$\Delta_{n+1} = \bigcup_{i \in \{1,2,3\}} f_i(\Delta_n),$$

where f_1, f_2, f_3 are functions forming the iterated function system for Sierpiński gasket, cf. [18] and Appendix C, and for a directed graph G with $V(G) \subset Q^\bullet \times Q^\bullet$ $f_i(G)$ is a graph such that

$$V(f_i(G)) = \big\{ f_i(v) \,|\, v \in V(G) \big\},$$
$$E(f_i(G)) = \big\{ (f_i(v), f_i(v')) \,|\, (v, v') \in E(G) \big\}.$$

A unique rewriting rule of $\mathcal{M}^{\text{Sierp}}$ is of the form

$$\Delta_1 \vdash \Delta_2.$$

The graphs Δ_n $(n > 0)$ are the contours of the iterations of Sierpiński gasket.

The similar simple G–P–R machines can be constructed for some other fractals determined by iteration function system, e.g. 3D Sierpiński gasket.

3   Causal Nets of Geometrical G–P–R Machines

We propose some precise mathematical treatment of those concepts which express or explicate certain aspects and features of the computational processes realized by geometrical G–P–R machines and which can be investigated within 'experimental mathematics' by an analysis (sometimes heuristic) of the plots illustrating those concepts. The plots could be generated by computers like in [24].

Definitions 3.1. For both cases of a simple or of a strict geometrical G–P–R machine $\mathcal{M}$ and an initial instantaneous description G of $\mathcal{M}$ we define an *event with respect to G* to be an ordered pair (v, i) with $v \in V(\mathcal{F}_{\mathcal{M}}^i(G))$ for a natural number $i \geq 0$, where $\mathcal{F}_{\mathcal{M}}^0(G) = G$. Then we define a *full causal relation* $\prec_G$ *with respect to G* to be a binary relation defined on the set $Ev(G)$ of events with respect to G given by

$$(v, i) \prec_G (v', i') \quad \text{iff} \quad i' = i + 1 \text{ and there exists } h \in \mathcal{P}\ell(\mathcal{F}_{\mathcal{M}}^i(G))$$

such that $v \in V(\text{im}(h))$ and $v' \in V(\text{im}(q_h))$ for the h-th canonical injection $q_h : \mathcal{R}_{\mathcal{M}}(\text{dom}(h)) \to \mathcal{F}_{\mathcal{M}}^{i+1}(G)$ into the colimit of the gluing diagram $\mathcal{D}^{\mathcal{F}_{\mathcal{M}}^i(G)}$ in the simple case and of the generalized gluing diagram $\mathcal{D}_{\mathcal{F}_{\mathcal{M}}^i(G)}$ in the strict case, where $\mathcal{R}_{\mathcal{M}}(\text{dom}(h))$ is the conclusion of the rewriting rule with the premise $\text{dom}(h)$. Thus the ordered pair $\mathcal{N}_G = (Ev(G), \prec_G)$ is called a *full causal net of* $\mathcal{M}$ *with respect to G*.

The proper subnets of the full causal net $\mathcal{N}_G$ with respect to G correspond to various aspects and features of the computation of $\mathcal{M}$ starting with G.

For instance, in the case of Example 2.2 it is worth to consider a *causal net* $\mathcal{N}_G^{\mathrm{gr}}$ *of growth* with *causal growth relation* $\prec_G^{\mathrm{gr}}$ given by

$$(v, i) \prec_G^{\mathrm{gr}} (v', i') \quad \text{iff} \quad i' = i + 1 \text{ with } (v, i) \prec_G (v', i') \text{ and both } v \text{ and } v'$$

are new in $\mathcal{F}_{\mathcal{M}}^i(G)$ and in $\mathcal{F}_{\mathcal{M}}^{i+1}(G)$, respectively, whenever $i > 0$,

otherwise v' is new in $\mathcal{F}^{i+1}(G)$,

where a vertex x *is new in* $\mathcal{F}_{\mathcal{M}}^k(G)$ if $x \in V(\mathcal{F}_{\mathcal{M}}^k(G))$ and $x \notin V(\mathcal{F}_{\mathcal{M}}^{k-1}(G))$ for $k > 0$.

In the case of the machine in Example 2.2 the projection of $\mathcal{N}_{\Delta_0}^{\mathrm{gr}}$ into the phase space $Q^\bullet \times Q^\bullet$ yields Sierpiński gasket which is a fractal.

In the case of Examples 2.1 it is worth to consider a *causal net* $\mathcal{N}_G^{\mathrm{act}}$ *of activity* with *causal relation* $\prec_G^{\mathrm{act}}$ *of activity* given by

$$(v, i) \prec_G^{\mathrm{act}} (v', i') \quad \text{iff} \quad i' = i + 1 \text{ with } (v, i) \prec_G (v', i') \text{ and both } v \text{ and } v'$$

are the targets of the edges indicating the states

of the cells in $\mathcal{F}_{\mathcal{M}}^i(G)$ and in $\mathcal{F}_{\mathcal{M}}^{i+1}(G)$, respectively.

For the geometrical G–P–R machines simulating one-dimensional cellular automata like the machine $\mathcal{M}^{30}$ in Examples 2.1 one defines the *causal net* $\mathcal{N}_G^{\mathrm{stc}}$ *of strict changes* with the *causal relation* $\prec_G^{\mathrm{stc}}$ of *strict changes* given by

$$(v, i) \prec_G^{\mathrm{stc}} (v', i') \quad \text{iff} \quad i' = i + 1 \text{ and there exists } h \in \mathcal{P}\ell(\mathcal{F}_{\mathcal{M}}^i(G))$$

such that $h(v_1) = v$ and $q_h(v_2) = v'$ for those v_1, v_2 which are such that

v_1 is a vertex of the center of the rule $\mathrm{dom}(h) \vdash \mathcal{R}_{\mathcal{M}}(\mathrm{dom}(h))$

and both v_1, v_2 are the targets of the edges indicating the state

of a cell in the premise and in the conclusion of the rule, respectively.

Thus $\mathcal{N}_G^{\mathrm{stc}}$ is a subnet of $\mathcal{N}_G^{\mathrm{act}}$, moreover, in the case of $\mathcal{M}^{30}$ the plots for the one-dimensional cellular automaton with the rule 30 in [23], [24] illustrate appropriate nets $\mathcal{N}_G^{\mathrm{stc}}$.

The nets $\mathcal{N}_G^{\mathrm{stc}}$ $(G \in \mathcal{S}_{\mathcal{M}})$ coincide with space-time diagrams in [7], [8], where these diagrams are subject of the investigations of computational complexity by using fractal dimension.

The transitive closures $\prec_G^*$, $(\prec_G^x)^*$ $(x \in \{\mathrm{gr}, \mathrm{act}, \mathrm{stc}\})$ give rise to causal sets $\mathcal{C}_G = (Ev(G), \prec_G^*)$ and $\mathcal{C}_G^x = (Ev(G), (\prec_G^x)^*)$ $(x \in \{\mathrm{gr}, \mathrm{act}, \mathrm{stc}\})$ whose logical aspects can be approached like in physics [12] or like in concurrency theory [2].

The investigations of machine $\mathcal{M}^{\mathrm{Sierp}}$ defined in Example 2.2 suggest another approach to the idea of a causal net of a computation of a geometrical G–P–R machine which is introduced in the following definitions.

Definitions 3.2. For both cases of a simple or of a strict geometrical G–P–R machine $\mathcal{M}$ and an initial instantaneous description G of $\mathcal{M}$ we define a *rule application event with respect to G* to be an ordered pair (h, i) with $h \in \mathcal{P}\ell(\mathcal{F}_{\mathcal{M}}^i(G))$ for a natural number $i \geq 0$, where $\mathcal{F}_{\mathcal{M}}^0(G) = G$. Then we define a *rule application causal relation* $\succ_G^{\mathrm{app}}$ *with respect to G* to be a binary relation defined on the set $Ev^{\mathrm{app}}(G)$ of the rule application events with respect to G given by

$$(h, i) \succ_G^{\mathrm{app}} (h', i') \quad \text{iff} \quad i' = i + 1 \text{ and } \mathrm{im}(h) \text{ is a subgraph of } \mathrm{im}(q_{h'})$$

for the h'-th canonical injection $q_{h'} : \mathcal{R}_{\mathcal{M}}(\mathrm{dom}(h')) \to \mathcal{F}_{\mathcal{M}}^{i+1}(G)$ into the colimit of the gluing diagram $\mathcal{D}^{\mathcal{F}_{\mathcal{M}}^i(G)}$ in the simple case and of the generalized gluing diagram $\mathcal{D}_{\mathcal{F}_{\mathcal{M}}^i(G)}$ in the strict case. Thus the ordered pair $\mathcal{N}_G^{\mathrm{app}} = (Ev^{\mathrm{app}}(G), \succ_G^{\mathrm{app}})$ is called a *causal net of the rule application events with respect to G*.

For natural numbers $n > 0$ the *restrictions* of $\mathcal{N}_G^{\mathrm{app}}$ to n, denoted by $\mathcal{N}_G^{\mathrm{app}} \upharpoonright n$, are the ordered pairs $(Ev^{\mathrm{app}}(G) \upharpoonright n, \succ_G^{\mathrm{app}} \upharpoonright n)$ with $Ev^{\mathrm{app}}(G) \upharpoonright n = \{(h, i) \in Ev^{\mathrm{app}}(G) \mid i \leq n\}$, where $\succ_G^{\mathrm{app}} \upharpoonright n$ is the restriction of $\succ_G^{\mathrm{app}}$ to $Ev^{\mathrm{app}}(G) \upharpoonright n$.

Lemma 3.1. *Machine $\mathcal{M}^{\mathrm{Sierp}}$ is such that for every rule application event (h, i) with respect to Δ_0 with $i \geq 0$ there exists a unique ordered triple (h_1, h_2, h_3) of elements of $\mathcal{P}\ell(\mathcal{F}_{\mathcal{M}^{\mathrm{Sierp}}}^{i+1}(\Delta_0))$ such that the following condition holds:*

$$(\alpha) \qquad (h_j, i+1) \succ_{\Delta_0}^{\mathrm{app}} (h, i) \text{ and } h_j = f_j \circ h \text{ for all } j \in \{1, 2, 3\},$$

where f_1, f_2, f_3 form the iteration function system for Sierpiński gasket, cf. Appendix C, and $\circ$ denotes the composition of functions.

Proof. We prove the lemma by induction on i.

Corollary 3.1. *Causal net $\mathcal{N}_{\Delta_0}^{\mathrm{app}}$ of the rule application events with respect to Δ_0 for machine $\mathcal{M}^{\mathrm{Sierp}}$ is isomorphic to the (ternary) tree $\mathbb{T}$ whose vertices are finite strings (including empty string) of digits in $\{1, 2, 3\}$, the edges are ordered pairs $(\Gamma j, \Gamma)$ for a finite string Γ and a digit $j \in \{1, 2, 3\}$, where the graph isomorphism $\mathrm{iz} : \mathbb{T} \to \mathcal{N}_{\Delta_0}^{\mathrm{app}}$ is defined inductively by*

- $\mathrm{iz}(\text{empty string}) = (\mathrm{id}_{\Delta_0}, 0)$, *where id_{Δ_0} is the identity graph homomorphism on Δ_0,*
- $\mathrm{iz}(\Gamma j) = (h', \mathrm{length}(\Gamma) + 1)$ *for a unique h' which is the j-th element of a unique ordered triple which satisfies the condition (α) for that h for which $\mathrm{iz}(h) = (h, \mathrm{length}(\Gamma))$.*

Proof. The corollary is a consequence of Lemma 3.1.

Corollary 3.2. *Machine $\mathcal{M}^{\mathrm{Sierp}}$ is such that for every rule application event (h, i) with respect to Δ_0 for $i \geq 0$ the unique ordered triple (h_1, h_2, h_3) of elements of $\mathcal{P}\ell(\mathcal{F}_{\mathcal{M}^{\mathrm{Sierp}}}^{i+1}(\Delta_0))$ satisfying the condition (α) for h determines a directed multi-hypergraph $\mathcal{G}_{(h,i)}$ (see Appendix A) whose set of hyperedges is the set*

$\{(h_1, i+1), (h_2, i+1), (h_3, i+1)\}$, *the set of vertices is the union* $\bigcup_{1 \leq j \leq 3} V(\mathrm{im}(h_j))$ *and the source and target functions* s, t *are given by*

$$s((h_j, i+1)) = \{h_j((0,0)), h_j((1,0))\},$$
$$t((h_j, i+1)) = \{h_j((\tfrac{1}{2}, \tfrac{\sqrt{3}}{2}))\} \quad \text{for all } j \in \{1, 2, 3\}.$$

Moreover, for every rule application event (h, i) *with respect to* Δ_0 *for* $i \geq 0$ *the directed multi-hypergraph* $\mathcal{G}_{(h,i)}$ *is isomorphic to the directed multi-hypergraph* $\mathcal{G}_{(\mathrm{id}_{\Delta_0}, 0)}$.

Proof. The corollary is a consequence of Lemma 3.1.

Remark 3.1. The directed multi-hypergraph $\mathcal{G}_{(h,i)}$ in Corollary 3.2 could model some interaction between the rule application events in the computation process of $\mathcal{M}^{\mathrm{Sierp}}$ starting with Δ_0 and represented by $\mathcal{N}^{\mathrm{app}}_{\Delta_0}$. This interaction could be a gluing pattern understood as in the main theorem of [16].

Remark 3.2. Since the multi-hyperedge membrane systems $\mathcal{S}^{\mathrm{Sierp}}_n$ in [16] for $n \geq 0$ are aimed to display the self-similar structure of (the iterations of) Sierpiński gasket by using isomorphisms of directed multi-hypergraphs and net $\mathcal{N}^{\mathrm{app}}_{\Delta_0}$ represents the computation process of machine $\mathcal{M}^{\mathrm{Sierp}}$ starting with Δ_0, one can see (in the light of Corollaries 3.1 and 3.2) that the self-similar structure (or form) of the contours of the iterations of Sierpiński gasket coincides[2] with (or simply is) the process of their generation by machine $\mathcal{M}^{\mathrm{Sierp}}$. This coincidence is similar to the coincidence of *Nautilus* shell, illustrated in Fig. 1 in [22], with the process of its growth.

Final Remark 3.3. The author expects that the geometrical G–P–R machines and their extensions to higher dimensions could provide the mathematical foundations for *the atomic basis of biological symmetry and periodicity*[3] due to Antonio Lima-da-Faria [9]. These foundations could explicate the links of cellular automata approach to complexity in biology in S. Wolfram's *A New Kind of Science* with *Evolution without selection* [10] pointed out by B. Goertzel in his review of *A New Kind of Science* in [6].

Open Problem. One can define geometrical G–P–R machines whose instantaneous descriptions are finite graphs with vertices labelled by multisets and the machine rewriting rules contain multiset rewriting rules like in membrane computing [17].

How to extract in the case of these machines the counterparts of causal nets to be subject of measuring uncertainty via fractal dimension like e.g. in [7], [8].

---

[2] By Corollaries 3.1 and 3.2 the restrictions $\mathcal{N}^{\mathrm{app}}_{\Delta_0} \restriction n$ together with the directed hypergraphs $\mathcal{G}(h, i)$ provide a construction of multihyperedge membrane systems (with the restrictions $\mathcal{N}^{\mathrm{app}}_{\Delta_0} \restriction n$ as their underlying trees) isomorphic to $\mathcal{S}^{\mathrm{Sierp}}_n$.

[3] Selfsimilarity characterized in terms of geometrical G–P–R machines like in $\mathcal{M}^{\mathrm{Sierp}}$ case could be a counterpart of spatial periodicity with respect to both time and scale changes.

Appendix A. Graph-Theoretical and Category-Theoretical Preliminaries

A [*finite*] *labelled directed graph over* a set Σ of labels is defined as an ordered triple $\mathcal{G} = (V(\mathcal{G}), E(\mathcal{G}), \ell_{\mathcal{G}})$, where $V(\mathcal{G})$ is a [finite] *set of vertices* of $\mathcal{G}$, $E(\mathcal{G})$ is a subset of $V(\mathcal{G}) \times V(\mathcal{G})$ called the *set of edges* of $\mathcal{G}$, and $\ell_{\mathcal{G}}$ is a function from $V(\mathcal{G})$ into Σ called the *labelling function* of $\mathcal{G}$. We drop the adjective 'directed' if there is no risk of confusion.

A *homomorphism of a labelled directed graph* $\mathcal{G}$ *over* Σ *into a labelled directed graph* $\mathcal{G}'$ *over* Σ is an ordered triple $(\mathcal{G}, \mathrm{h} : V(\mathcal{G}) \to V(\mathcal{G}'), \mathcal{G}')$ such that h is a function from $V(\mathcal{G})$ into $V(\mathcal{G}')$ which satisfies the following conditions:

(H$_1$) $(v, v') \in E(\mathcal{G})$ implies $(\mathrm{h}(v), \mathrm{h}(v')) \in E(\mathcal{G}')$ for all $v, v' \in V(\mathcal{G})$,
(H$_2$) $\ell_{\mathcal{G}'}(\mathrm{h}(v)) = \ell_{\mathcal{G}}(v)$ for every $v \in V(\mathcal{G})$.

If a triple $h = (\mathcal{G}, \mathrm{h} : V(\mathcal{G}) \to V(\mathcal{G}'), \mathcal{G}')$ is a homomorphism of a labelled directed graph $\mathcal{G}$ over Σ into a labelled directed graph $\mathcal{G}'$ over Σ, we denote this triple by $h : \mathcal{G} \to \mathcal{G}'$, we write $\mathrm{dom}(h)$ and $\mathrm{cod}(h)$ for $\mathcal{G}$ and $\mathcal{G}'$, respectively, according to category theory convention, and we write $h(v)$ for the value $\mathrm{h}(v)$.

A homomorphism $h : \mathcal{G} \to \mathcal{G}'$ of labelled directed graphs over Σ is an *embedding of* $\mathcal{G}$ *into* $\mathcal{G}'$, denoted by $h : \mathcal{G} \rightarrowtail \mathcal{G}'$, if the following condition holds:

(E) $h(v) = h(v')$ implies $v = v'$ for all $v, v' \in V(\mathcal{G})$.

An embedding $h : \mathcal{G} \rightarrowtail \mathcal{G}'$ of labelled directed graphs $\mathcal{G}, \mathcal{G}'$ over Σ is an *inclusion of* $\mathcal{G}$ *into* $\mathcal{G}'$, denoted by $h : \mathcal{G} \hookrightarrow \mathcal{G}'$, if the following holds:

(I) $h(v) = v$ for every $v \in V(\mathcal{G})$.

We say that a labelled directed graph $\mathcal{G}$ over Σ is a *labelled subgraph* of a labelled directed graph $\mathcal{G}'$ over Σ if there exists an inclusion $h : \mathcal{G} \hookrightarrow \mathcal{G}'$ of labelled directed graphs $\mathcal{G}, \mathcal{G}'$ over Σ.

For an embedding $h : \mathcal{G} \rightarrowtail \mathcal{G}'$ of labelled directed graphs $\mathcal{G}, \mathcal{G}'$ over Σ we define the *image* of h, denoted by $\mathrm{im}(h)$, to be a labelled directed graph $\widehat{\mathcal{G}}$ over Σ such that $V(\widehat{\mathcal{G}}) = \{h(v) \mid v \in V(\mathcal{G})\}$, $E(\widehat{\mathcal{G}}) = \{(h(v), h(v')) \mid (v, v') \in E(\mathcal{G})\}$, and the labelling function $\ell_{\widehat{\mathcal{G}}}$ of $\widehat{\mathcal{G}}$ is the restriction of the labelling function $\ell_{\mathcal{G}'}$ of $V(\mathcal{G}')$ to the set $V(\widehat{\mathcal{G}})$, i.e., $\ell_{\widehat{\mathcal{G}}}(v) = \ell_{\mathcal{G}'}(v)$ for every $v \in V(\widehat{\mathcal{G}})$.

A homomorphism $h : \mathcal{G} \to \mathcal{G}'$ of labelled directed graphs over Σ is an *isomorphism* of $\mathcal{G}$ into $\mathcal{G}'$ if there exists a homomorphism $h^{-1} : \mathcal{G}' \to \mathcal{G}$ of labelled directed graphs over Σ, called the inverse of h, such that the following conditions hold:

(Iz$_1$) $h^{-1}(h(v)) = v$ for every $v \in V(\mathcal{G})$,
(Iz$_2$) $h(h^{-1}(v)) = v$ for every $v \in V(\mathcal{G}')$.

We say that a labelled directed graph $\mathcal{G}$ over Σ *is isomorphic* to a labelled directed graph $\mathcal{G}'$ over Σ if there exists an isomorphism $h : \mathcal{G} \to \mathcal{G}'$ of labelled graphs $\mathcal{G}, \mathcal{G}'$ over Σ.

For an embedding $h : \mathcal{G} \rightarrowtail \mathcal{G}'$ of labelled directed graphs $\mathcal{G}, \mathcal{G}'$ over Σ we define a homomorphism $\dot{h} : \mathcal{G} \rightarrow \mathrm{im}(h)$ by $\dot{h}(v) = h(v)$ for every $v \in V(\mathcal{G})$. This homomorphism $\dot{h}$ is an isomorphism of $\mathcal{G}$ into $\mathrm{im}(h)$, called an *isomorphism deduced by h*.

For a labelled directed graph $\mathcal{G}$ over Σ, the *identity homomorphism* (or simply, *identity of $\mathcal{G}$*), denoted by $\mathrm{id}_\mathcal{G}$, is the homomorphism $h : \mathcal{G} \rightarrow \mathcal{G}$ such that $h(v) = v$ for every $v \in V(\mathcal{G})$.

We say that a labelled directed graph $\mathcal{G}$ over Σ is an *isomorphically perfect labelled directed graph over Σ* if the identity homomorphism $\mathrm{id}_\mathcal{G}$ is a unique isomorphism of labelled directed graph $\mathcal{G}$ into $\mathcal{G}$.

Lemma A.1. *Let $\mathcal{G}$ be an isomorphically perfect labelled directed graph over Σ and let $h : \mathcal{G} \rightarrow \mathcal{G}'$, $h' : \mathcal{G} \rightarrow \mathcal{G}'$ be two isomorphisms of labelled graphs $\mathcal{G}, \mathcal{G}'$ over Σ. Then $h = h'$.*

We say that a set or a class $\mathcal{A}$ of labelled directed graphs over Σ is *skeletal* if for all labelled directed graphs $\mathcal{G}, \mathcal{G}'$ in $\mathcal{A}$ if they are isomorphic, then $\mathcal{G} = \mathcal{G}'$.

A *gluing diagram* $\mathcal{D}$ of labelled directed graphs over Σ is defined by:

- its *set $\mathcal{I}$ of indexes* with a distinguished index $\Delta \in \mathcal{I}$, called the *center* of $\mathcal{D}$,
- its *family $\mathcal{G}_i$ ($i \in \mathcal{I}$) of labelled directed graphs over Σ*,
- its *family gl_i ($i \in \mathcal{I} - \{\Delta\}$) of gluing conditions* which are sets of ordered pairs such that
  (i) $\mathrm{gl}_i \subseteq V(\mathcal{G}_\Delta) \times V(\mathcal{G}_i)$ for every $i \in \mathcal{I} - \{\Delta\}$,
  (ii) $(v, v') \in \mathrm{gl}_i$ implies $\ell_{\mathcal{G}_\Delta}(v) = \ell_{\mathcal{G}_i}(v')$ for all $v \in V(\mathcal{G}_\Delta)$, $v' \in V(\mathcal{G}_i)$, and for every $i \in \mathcal{I} - \{\Delta\}$,
  (iii) for every $i \in \mathcal{I} - \{\Delta\}$ if gl_i is non-empty, then there exists a bijection

$$b_i : L(\mathrm{gl}_i) \rightarrow R(\mathrm{gl}_i)$$

for $L(\mathrm{gl}_i) = \{v \,|\, (v, v') \in \mathrm{gl}_i \text{ for some } v'\}$ and $R(\mathrm{gl}_i) = \{v' \,|\, (v, v') \in \mathrm{gl}_i \text{ for some } v\}$ such that $\{(v, b_i(v)) \,|\, v \in L(\mathrm{gl}_i)\} = \mathrm{gl}_i$.

For a gluing diagram $\mathcal{D}$ of labelled directed graphs over Σ we define a *cocone* of $\mathcal{D}$ to be a family $h_i : \mathcal{G}_i \rightarrow \mathcal{G}$ ($i \in \mathcal{I}$) of homomorphisms of labelled directed graphs over Σ (here $\mathrm{cod}(h_i) = \mathcal{G}$ for every $i \in \mathcal{I}$) such that

$$h_\Delta(v) = h_i(v')$$

for every pair $(v, v') \in \mathrm{gl}_i$ and every $i \in \mathcal{I} - \{\Delta\}$.

A cocone $q_i : \mathcal{G}_i \rightarrow \tilde{\mathcal{G}}$ ($i \in \mathcal{I}$) of $\mathcal{D}$ is called a *colimiting cocone of $\mathcal{D}$* if for every cocone $h_i : \mathcal{G}_i \rightarrow \mathcal{G}$ ($i \in \mathcal{I}$) of $\mathcal{D}$ there exists a unique homomorphism $h : \tilde{\mathcal{G}} \rightarrow \mathcal{G}$ of labelled directed graphs $\tilde{\mathcal{G}}, \mathcal{G}$ over Σ such that $h(q_i(v)) = h_i(v)$ for every $v \in V(\mathcal{G}_i)$ and for every $i \in \mathcal{I}$. The labelled directed graph $\tilde{\mathcal{G}}$ is called a *colimit* of $\mathcal{D}$, the homomorphisms q_i ($i \in \mathcal{I}$) are called *canonical injections* and the unique homomorphism h is called the *mediating morphism* for $h_i : \mathcal{G}_i \rightarrow \mathcal{G}$ ($i \in \mathcal{I}$).

For a gluing diagram $\mathcal{D}$ one constructs its colimit $\widetilde{\mathcal{G}}$ in the following way:

- $V(\widetilde{\mathcal{G}}) = \bigcup_{i \in \mathcal{I}} (V_i \times \{i\})$, where

  $V_\Delta = V(\mathcal{G}_\Delta)$ for the center Δ of $\mathcal{D}$,

  $V_i = V(\mathcal{G}_i) - R(\mathrm{gl}_i)$ for every $i \in \mathcal{I} - \{\Delta\}$,

- $E(\widetilde{\mathcal{G}}) = \bigcup_{i \in \mathcal{I}} E_i$, where

  $E_\Delta = \{((v, \Delta), (v', \Delta)) \mid (v, v') \in E(\mathcal{G}_\Delta)\}$ for the center Δ of $\mathcal{D}$,

  $E_i = \{((v, i), (v', i)) \mid (v, v') \in E(\mathcal{G}_i) \text{ and } \{v, v'\} \subseteq V_i\}$

  $\qquad \cup \{((v, \Delta), (v', \Delta)) \mid (v, v'') \in \mathrm{gl}_i, \ (v', v''') \in \mathrm{gl}_i,$

  $\qquad\qquad \text{and } (v'', v''') \in E(\mathcal{G}_i) \text{ for some } v'', v'''\}$

  $\qquad \cup \{((v, \Delta), (v', i)) \mid v' \in V_i, \ (v, v'') \in \mathrm{gl}_i \text{ and } (v'', v') \in E(\mathcal{G}_i) \text{ for some } v''\}$

  $\qquad \cup \{((v, i), (v', \Delta)) \mid v \in V_i, \ (v', v'') \in \mathrm{gl}_i \text{ and } (v, v'') \in E(\mathcal{G}_i) \text{ for some } v''\}$

  for every $i \in \mathcal{I} - \{\Delta\}$,

- the labelling function $\ell_{\widetilde{\mathcal{G}}}$ is defined by $\ell_{\widetilde{\mathcal{G}}}((v, i)) = \ell_{\mathcal{G}_i}(v)$ for every $(v, i) \in V(\widetilde{\mathcal{G}})$.

The definition of a colimiting cocone of a gluing diagram $\mathcal{D}$ provides that any other colimit of $\mathcal{D}$ is isomorphic to the colimit of $\mathcal{D}$ constructed above. Hence one proves the following lemma.

Lemma A.2. *Let $\mathcal{D}$ be a gluing diagram of labelled graphs over Σ. Then for every colimiting cocone $q_i : \mathcal{G}_i \to \mathcal{G}$ $(i \in \mathcal{I})$ of $\mathcal{D}$ if $i' \neq i''$, then*

$$\big(V(\mathrm{im}(q_{i'})) - V(\mathrm{im}(q_\Delta))\big) \cap \big(V(\mathrm{im}(q_{i''})) - V(\mathrm{im}(q_\Delta))\big) = \varnothing$$

for all $i', i'' \in \mathcal{I} - \{\Delta\}$, where Δ is the center of $\mathcal{D}$ and the elements of nonempty $V(\mathrm{im}(q_i)) - V(\mathrm{im}(q_\Delta))$ with $i \neq \Delta$ are 'new' elements and the elements of $V(\mathrm{im}(q_\Delta))$ are 'old' elements.

A *generalized gluing diagram* $\mathcal{D}$ of labelled directed graphs over Σ is defined by:

- its *set $\mathcal{I}$ of indexes* with a distinguished index $\Delta \in \mathcal{I}$, called the *center* of $\mathcal{D}$,
- its *family $\mathcal{G}_i$ $(i \in \mathcal{I})$ of labelled directed graphs* over Σ,
- its *family* gl_j^i $((i, j)) \in \mathcal{I} \times (\mathcal{I} - \{\Delta\})$ and $i \neq j$) *of gluing conditions* which are such that
  - the set $\mathcal{I}^\Delta = \mathcal{I}$ with families $\mathcal{G}_i$ $(i \in \mathcal{I})$ and gl_i^Δ $(i \in \mathcal{I} - \{\Delta\})$ form a gluing diagram $\mathcal{D}^\Delta$ with Δ as the center of $\mathcal{D}^\Delta$,
  - for every $i \in \mathcal{I} - \{\Delta\}$ the set $I^i = \mathcal{I} - \{\Delta\}$ with families $\mathcal{G}_i$ $(i \in \mathcal{I} - \{\Delta\})$ and gl_j^i $(j \in \mathcal{I} - \{i, \Delta\})$ form a gluing diagram $\mathcal{D}^i$ with i as the center for $\mathcal{D}^i$,
  - the following conditions hold:

    (G_1) $R(\mathrm{gl}_i^\Delta) \cap L(\mathrm{gl}_j^i) = \varnothing$ for all i, j with $\{i, j\} \subset \mathcal{I} - \{\Delta\}$ and $i \neq j$,

(G_2) $(\mathrm{gl}_j^i)^{-1} = \mathrm{gl}_i^j$ for all i, j with $\{i, j\} \subset \mathcal{I} - \{\Delta\}$ and $i \neq j$, where for $Q \subset A \times B$

$$(Q)^{-1} = \{(x, y) \in B \times A \,|\, (y, x) \in A \times B\}.$$

For a generalized gluing diagram $\mathcal{D}$ of labelled directed graphs over Σ we define a *cocone* of $\mathcal{D}$ to be a family $h_i : \mathcal{G}_i \to \mathcal{G}$ ($i \in \mathcal{I}$) of homomorphisms of labelled directed graphs over Σ (here $\mathrm{cod}(h_i) = \mathcal{G}$ for every $i \in \mathcal{I}$) such that for every $i \in \mathcal{I}$ the sub-family $h_j : \mathcal{G}_j \to \mathcal{G}$ ($j \in \mathcal{I}^i$) is a cocone of the diagram $\mathcal{D}^i$.

For a generalized gluing diagram $\mathcal{D}$ a *colimiting cocone* of $\mathcal{D}$, a *colimit* of $\mathcal{D}$, the *canonical injections*, and the *mediating morphism* are defined in the same way as for a gluing diagram, e.g. a cocone $q_i : \mathcal{G}_i \to \widetilde{\mathcal{G}}$ ($i \in \mathcal{I}$) of $\mathcal{D}$ is called a *colimiting cocone of* $\mathcal{D}$ if for every cocone $h_i : \mathcal{G}_i \to \mathcal{G}$ ($i \in \mathcal{I}$) of $\mathcal{D}$ there exists a unique homomorphism $h : \widetilde{\mathcal{G}} \to \mathcal{G}$ of labelled directed graphs $\widetilde{\mathcal{G}}, \mathcal{G}$ over Σ such that $h(q_i(v)) = h_i(v)$ for every $v \in V(\mathcal{G}_i)$ and for every $i \in \mathcal{I}$.

Lemma A.3. *Let $\mathcal{D}$ be a generalized gluing diagram with finite set $\mathcal{I}$ of its indexes and with center Δ, such that the following condition holds:*
   (G_3) *for all $i, i', j \in \mathcal{I} - \{\Delta\}$ if $i \neq i'$, then $L(\mathrm{gl}_i^j) \cap L(\mathrm{gl}_{i'}^j) = \varnothing$.*

Then one constructs a colimit of $\mathcal{D}$ to be a labelled directed graph $\widetilde{\mathsf{G}}$ which is determined by an arbitrary nonrepetitive sequence $i_1, \ldots, i_{n_0}$ of elements of $\mathcal{I} - \{\Delta\} = \{i_1, \ldots, i_{n_0}\}$ and which is defined in the following way:

- $V(\widetilde{\mathsf{G}}) = \bigcup_{i \in \mathcal{I}} (V_i \times \{i\})$, *where* $V_\Delta = V(\mathcal{G}_\Delta)$, $V_{i_1} = V(\mathcal{G}_{i_1}) - R(\mathrm{gl}_{i_1}^\Delta)$, *for every k with $1 < k \leq n_0$*

$$V_{i_k} = V(\mathcal{G}_{i_k}) - \Big(R(\mathrm{gl}_{i_k}^\Delta) \cup \bigcup_{1 \leq m < k} L(\mathrm{gl}_{i_m}^{i_k})\Big),$$

- $E(\widetilde{\mathsf{G}}) = \bigcup_{i \in \mathcal{I}} E_i$, *where* $E_\Delta = \{((v, \Delta), (v', \Delta)) \,|\, (v, v') \in E(\mathcal{G}_\Delta)\}$,
   for every $i \in \mathcal{I} - \{\Delta\}$
   $E_i = E_i^1 \cup E_i^2 \cup E_i^3 \cup E_i^4$ *for*
   $E_i^1 = \{((v, i), (v', i)) \,|\, \{(v, i), (v', i)\} \subset V(\widetilde{\mathsf{G}}) \text{ and } (v, v') \in E(\mathcal{G}_i)\}$,
   $E_i^2 = \{((v, k), (v', j)) \,|\, \{(v, k), (v', j)\} \subset V(\widetilde{\mathsf{G}}), \ i \notin \{k, j\} \subset \mathcal{I},$
        $(v, v'') \in \mathrm{gl}_i^k, \ (v', v''') \in \mathrm{gl}_i^j, \text{ and } (v'', v''') \in E(\mathcal{G}_i) \text{ for some } v'', v'''\}$,
   $E_i^3 = \{((v, i), (v', j)) \,|\, \{(v, i), (v', j)\} \subset V(\widetilde{\mathsf{G}}), \ i \neq j \in \mathcal{I},$
        $(v', v'') \in \mathrm{gl}_i^j, \text{ and } (v, v'') \in E(\mathcal{G}_i) \text{ for some } v''\}$,
   $E_i^4 = \{((v, j), (v', i)) \,|\, \{(v, j), (v', i)\} \subset V(\widetilde{\mathsf{G}}), \ i \neq j \in \mathcal{I},$
        $(v, v'') \in \mathrm{gl}_i^j, \text{ and } (v'', v') \in E(\mathcal{G}_i) \text{ for some } v''\}$,
- *the labelling function $\ell_{\widetilde{\mathsf{G}}}$ is defined by $\ell_{\widetilde{\mathsf{G}}}((v, i)) = \ell_{\mathcal{G}_i}(v)$ for every $(v, i) \in V(\widetilde{\mathsf{G}})$.*

Proof. Since by (G_3) for all $i \in \mathcal{I} - \{\Delta\}$ and $v \in V(\mathcal{G}_i) - V_i$ there exists a unique ordered pair $(v^*, i^*) \in V(\widetilde{\mathsf{G}})$ such that $(v^*, v) \in \mathrm{gl}_i^{i^*}$, one defines the i-th component $q_i : \mathcal{G}_i \to \widetilde{\mathsf{G}}$ $(i \in \mathcal{I} - \{\Delta\})$ of colimiting cocone by

$$q_i(v) = \begin{cases} (v, i) & \text{if } v \in V_i, \\ (v^*, i^*) & \text{otherwise.} \end{cases} \qquad \square$$

Lemma A.4. *Let $\mathcal{D}$ be a generalized gluing diagram with finite set $\mathcal{I}$ of its indexes and with center Δ, such that the condition (G_3) holds and let $q_i : \mathcal{G}_i \to \mathcal{G}$ $(i \in \mathcal{I})$ be a colimiting cocone of $\mathcal{D}$. Then for every $H \subseteq \mathcal{I} - \{\Delta\}$ if*

$$\bigcap_{i \in H} (V(\mathrm{im}(q_i)) - V(\mathrm{im}(q_\Delta))) \neq \varnothing,$$

then H has at most two elements and if $H = \{i, i'\}$ with $i \neq i'$, then $\mathrm{gl}_{i'}^i$ is nonempty.

Proof. The lemma is a consequence of Lemma A.3 and the fact that two different colimits of a generalized gluing diagram are always isomorphic labelled graphs.

For two directed graphs $G_1 = (V(G_1), E(G_1))$, $G_2 = (V(G_2), E(G_2))$, we define their *union* by

$$G_1 \cup G_2 = (V(G_1) \cup V(G_2), E(G_1) \cup E(G_2)).$$

We introduce the following new concepts.

By a *directed multi-hypergraph* we mean a structure $\mathcal{G}$ given by its *set $E(\mathcal{G})$ of hyperedges*, its *set $V(\mathcal{G})$ of vertices* and the *source* and *target* mappings

$$s_{\mathcal{G}} : E(\mathcal{G}) \to \mathcal{P}(V(\mathcal{G})), \quad t_{\mathcal{G}} : E(\mathcal{G}) \to \mathcal{P}(V(\mathcal{G}))$$

such that $V(\mathcal{G})$ together with

$$\{(\mathcal{V}_1, \mathcal{V}_2) \mid s_{\mathcal{G}}(e) = \mathcal{V}_1 \text{ and } t_{\mathcal{G}}(e) = \mathcal{V}_2 \text{ for some } e \in E(\mathcal{G})\}$$

form a directed hypergraph as in [5], where $\mathcal{P}(X)$ denotes the set of all subsets of a set X.

We say that two directed multi-hypergraphs $\mathcal{G}, \mathcal{G}'$ are *isomorphic* if there exist two bijections $h : V(\mathcal{G}) \to V(\mathcal{G}')$, $h' : E(\mathcal{G}) \to E(\mathcal{G}')$ such that

$$s_{\mathcal{G}'}(h'(e)) = \{h(v) \mid v \in s_{\mathcal{G}}(e)\} \text{ and } t_{\mathcal{G}'}(h'(e)) = \{h(v) \mid v \in t_{\mathcal{G}}(e)\}$$

for all $e \in E(\mathcal{G})$.

Appendix B

We recall an idea of a Gandy–Păun–Rozenberg machine, briefly G–P–R machine, introduced in [14].

The core of a G–P–R machine is a finite set of rewriting rules for certain finite directed labelled graphs, where these graphs are instantaneous descriptions for the computation process realized by the machine.

The conflictless parallel (simultaneous) application of the rewriting rules of a G–P–R machine is realized in Gandy's machine mode (according to Local Causation Principle, cf. [3]), where (local) maximality of "causal neighbourhoods" replaces (global) maximality of, e.g. conflictless set of evolution rules applied simultaneously to a membrane structure which appears during the evolution process generated by a P system [17]. Therefore one can construct a Gandy's machine from a G–P–R machine in an immediate way, see [14].

For all unexplained terms and notation of category theory and graph theory we refer the reader to Appendix A.

Definition B.1. A G–P–R *machine* M is determined by the following data:

- a finite set Σ_M of labels or symbols of M,
- a skeletal set S_M of finite isomorphically perfect labelled directed graphs over Σ, which are called *instantaneous descriptions* of M,
- a function $\mathcal{F}_M : S_M \to S_M$ called the *transition function* of M,
- a function $\mathcal{R}_M : \text{PREM}_M \to \text{CONCL}_M$ from a finite skeletal set PREM_M of finite isomorphically perfect labelled directed graphs over Σ_M onto a finite skeletal set CONCL_M of finite isomorphically perfect labelled directed graphs over Σ_M such that $\mathcal{R}_M$ determines the *set*

$$\widetilde{\mathcal{R}}_M = \{P \vdash C \mid P \in \text{PREM}_M \text{ and } C = \mathcal{R}_M(P)\}$$

of rewriting rules of M which are identified with ordered pairs $r = (P_r, C_r)$, where the graph $P_r \in \text{PREM}_M$ is the *premise* of r and the graph $C_r = \mathcal{R}_M(P_r)$ is the *conclusion* of r,
- a subset $\mathcal{I}_M$ of S_M which is the set of *initial instantaneous descriptions of* M.

The above data are subject of the following conditions:

1) $V(\mathcal{G}) \subseteq V(\mathcal{F}_M(\mathcal{G}))$ for every $\mathcal{G} \in S_M$,
2) $V(\mathcal{G}) \subseteq V(\mathcal{R}_M(\mathcal{G}))$ for every $\mathcal{G} \in \text{PREM}_M$,
3) the rewriting rules of M are *applicable* to S_M which means that for every $\mathcal{G} \in S_M$ the set

$$\mathcal{P}\ell(\mathcal{G}) = \{h \mid h \text{ is an embedding of labelled graphs over } \Sigma$$
$$\text{with } \text{dom}(h) \in \text{PREM}_M \text{ and } \text{cod}(h) = \mathcal{G}$$
$$\text{such that for every embedding } h' \text{ of labelled graphs over } \Sigma$$
$$\text{with } \text{dom}(h') \in \text{PREM}_M \text{ and } \text{cod}(h') = \mathcal{G}$$
$$\text{if } \text{im}(h) \text{ is a labelled subgraph of } \text{im}(h'), \text{ then } h = h'\}$$

of *maximal applications*[4] h of the rules $\text{dom}(h) \vdash \mathcal{R}_M(\text{dom}(h))$ of M in places $\text{im}(h)$ is such that the following conditions hold:

---

[4] with respect to the relation of being a labelled subgraph which can be treated as a natural priority relation between the applications of the rewriting rules.

(i) $V(\mathcal{G}) = \bigcup\limits_{h \in \mathcal{P}\ell(\mathcal{G})} V(\mathrm{im}(h))$, $E(\mathcal{G}) = \bigcup\limits_{h \in \mathcal{P}\ell(\mathcal{G})} E(\mathrm{im}(h))$,

(ii) for all $h_1, h_2 \in \mathcal{P}\ell(\mathcal{G})$ the equation $\ell_{\mathcal{G}_{h_1}}(\dot{h}_1^{-1}(v)) = \ell_{\mathcal{G}_{h_2}}(\dot{h}_2^{-1}(v))$ holds for every $v \in V(\mathrm{im}(h_1)) \cap V(\mathrm{im}(h_2))$, where $\ell_{\mathcal{G}_{h_1}}$, $\ell_{\mathcal{G}_{h_2}}$ are the labelling functions of $\mathcal{G}_{h_1} = \mathcal{R}_\mathcal{M}(\mathrm{dom}(h_1))$, $\mathcal{G}_{h_2} = \mathcal{R}_\mathcal{M}(\mathrm{dom}(h_2))$, respectively, and $\dot{h}_1^{-1}$, $\dot{h}_2^{-1}$ are the inverses of isomorphisms induced by the embeddings h_1, h_2, respectively.

(iii) $\mathcal{F}_\mathcal{M}(\mathcal{G})$ is a colimit of a gluing diagram $\mathcal{D}^\mathcal{G}$ constructed in the following way (the construction of $\mathcal{D}^\mathcal{G}$ is provided by (ii)):

- the set $\mathcal{I}$ of indexes of $\mathcal{D}^\mathcal{G}$ is such that $\mathcal{I} = \mathcal{P}\ell(\mathcal{G}) \cup \{\Delta\}$, where $\Delta \notin \mathcal{P}\ell(\mathcal{G})$ is the center of $\mathcal{D}^\mathcal{G}$,
- the family $\mathcal{G}_i$ ($i \in \mathcal{I}$) of labelled graphs of $\mathcal{D}^\mathcal{G}$ is such that $\mathcal{G}_h = \mathcal{R}_\mathcal{M}(\mathrm{dom}(h))$ for every $h \in \mathcal{P}\ell(\mathcal{G})$, and $\mathcal{G}_\Delta$ is such that $V(\mathcal{G}_\Delta) = V(\mathcal{G})$, $E(\mathcal{G}_\Delta) = \varnothing$, and the labelling function $\ell_{\mathcal{G}_\Delta}$ is such that provided by (ii)

$$\ell_{\mathcal{G}_\Delta}(v) = \ell_{\mathcal{G}_h}(\dot{h}^{-1}(v))$$

for every $v \in V(\mathrm{im}(h))$ and every $h \in \mathcal{P}\ell(\mathcal{G})$, where $\dot{h}^{-1}$ is the inverse of the isomorphism $\dot{h}$ induced by the embedding h,
- the gluing conditions gl_h ($h \in \mathcal{P}\ell(\mathcal{G})$) of $\mathcal{D}^\mathcal{G}$ are defined by

$$\mathrm{gl}_h = \{(v, \dot{h}^{-1}(v)) \mid v \in V(\mathrm{im}(h))\}$$

for every $h \in \mathcal{P}\ell(\mathcal{G})$, where $\dot{h}^{-1}$ is the inverse of the isomorphism $\dot{h}$ induced by embedding h,

(iv) the following equations hold:

$$V(\mathcal{F}_\mathcal{M}(\mathcal{G})) = \bigcup_{i \in \mathcal{I}} V(\mathrm{im}(q_i))$$

and $$E(\mathcal{F}_\mathcal{M}(\mathcal{G})) = \bigcup_{i \in \mathcal{I}} E(\mathrm{im}(q_i))$$

for the canonical injections $q_i : \mathcal{G}_i \to \mathcal{F}_\mathcal{M}(\mathcal{G})$ ($i \in \mathcal{I}$) forming a colimiting cocone of the diagram $\mathcal{D}^\mathcal{G}$ defined in (iii),

(v) the canonical injection $q_\Delta : \mathcal{G}_\Delta \to \mathcal{F}_\mathcal{M}(\mathcal{G})$ is an inclusion of labelled graphs, where Δ is the center of $\mathcal{D}^\mathcal{G}$ and q_Δ is Δ-th element of the colimiting cocone in (iv).

Thus $\mathcal{F}_\mathcal{M}(\mathcal{G})$ is the result of simultaneous application of the rules $\mathrm{dom}(h) \vdash \mathcal{R}_\mathcal{M}(\mathrm{dom}(h))$ in the places $\mathrm{im}(h)$ for $h \in \mathcal{P}\ell(\mathcal{G})$, where one replaces simultaneously $\mathrm{im}(h)$ by $\mathrm{im}(q_h)$ in $\mathcal{G}$ for $h \in \mathcal{P}\ell(\mathcal{G})$, respectively.

A finite sequence $(\mathcal{F}_\mathcal{M}^i(\mathcal{G}))_{i=0}^n$ is called a *finite computation of* $\mathcal{M}$, the number n is called the *time* of this computation, and $\mathcal{F}_\mathcal{M}^n(\mathcal{G})$ is called the *final instantaneous description* for this computation if

$$\mathcal{F}_\mathcal{M}^0(\mathcal{G}) = \mathcal{G} \in \mathcal{I}_\mathcal{M}, \quad \mathcal{F}_\mathcal{M}^{n-1}(\mathcal{G}) \neq \mathcal{F}_\mathcal{M}^n(\mathcal{G}), \quad \text{and } \mathcal{F}_\mathcal{M}(\mathcal{F}_\mathcal{M}^n(\mathcal{G})) = \mathcal{F}_\mathcal{M}^n(\mathcal{G}),$$

where $\mathcal{F}^i_{\mathcal{M}}(\mathcal{G})$ is defined inductively: $\mathcal{F}^i_{\mathcal{M}}(\mathcal{G}) = \mathcal{F}_{\mathcal{M}}(\mathcal{F}^{i-1}_{\mathcal{M}}(\mathcal{G}))$.

For a computation $(\mathcal{F}^i_{\mathcal{M}}(\mathcal{G}))^n_{i=0}$ its *space* is defined by

$$\text{space}(\mathcal{M}, \mathcal{G}) = \max\{\text{the number of elements of } V(\mathcal{F}^i_{\mathcal{M}}(\mathcal{G})) \,|\, 0 \leq i \leq n\}$$

for $\mathcal{G} \in \mathcal{I}_{\mathcal{M}}$, where intuitively space$(\mathcal{M}, \mathcal{G})$ is understood as the size of hardware measured by the number of indecomposable processors used in the computations.

We recall the following definition from [15].

Definition B.2. A *generalized G–P–R machine* $\mathcal{M}$ is defined by the following data:

- the sets $\Sigma_{\mathcal{M}}$, $\mathcal{S}_{\mathcal{M}}$, $\mathcal{I}_{\mathcal{M}}$ and the functions $\mathcal{R}_{\mathcal{M}} : \text{PREM}_{\mathcal{M}} \to \text{CONCL}_{\mathcal{M}}$, $\mathcal{F}_{\mathcal{M}} : \mathcal{S}_{\mathcal{M}} \to \mathcal{S}_{\mathcal{M}}$, where $\mathcal{S}_{\mathcal{M}}$, $\text{PREM}_{\mathcal{M}}$, $\text{CONCL}_{\mathcal{M}}$ are skeletal sets of finite isomorphically perfect labelled directed graphs over $\Sigma_{\mathcal{M}}$, the sets $\Sigma_{\mathcal{M}}$, $\text{PREM}_{\mathcal{M}}$, $\text{CONCL}_{\mathcal{M}}$ are finite sets, the condition 2) holds for $\mathcal{R}_{\mathcal{M}}$, and $\mathcal{I}_{\mathcal{M}}$ is a subset of $\mathcal{S}_{\mathcal{M}}$;
- besides the function $\mathcal{R}_{\mathcal{M}}$ defining *rewriting rules* there is enclosed a new function $\mathcal{R}^a_{\mathcal{M}} : \text{PREM}^a_{\mathcal{M}} \to \text{CONCL}^a_{\mathcal{M}}$, where $\text{PREM}^a_{\mathcal{M}}$, $\text{CONCL}^a_{\mathcal{M}}$ are finite skeletal sets of finite isomorphically perfect labelled directed graphs over $\Sigma_{\mathcal{M}}$ and $\mathcal{R}^a_{\mathcal{M}}$ defines *auxiliary gluing rules* $P \overset{a}{\vdash} C$ ($P \in \text{PREM}^a_{\mathcal{M}}$, $C = \mathcal{R}^a_{\mathcal{M}}(P)$) for defining common parts of the boundaries of new compartments appearing in a step of an evolution process;
- the above data are subject of the following conditions:
  A) for every $\mathcal{G} \in \text{PREM}^a_{\mathcal{M}}$ we have $V(\mathcal{G}) \subseteq V(\mathcal{R}^a_{\mathcal{M}}(\mathcal{G}))$, the set $\mathcal{P}\ell(\mathcal{G})$ defined as in 3) satisfies 3)(ii), and there exists a generalized gluing diagram $\mathcal{D}_{\langle \mathcal{G} \rangle}$, called *gluing pattern determined by* $\mathcal{G}$, such that
     a_1) the set $\mathcal{I}_{\langle \mathcal{G} \rangle}$ of indexes of $\mathcal{D}_{\langle \mathcal{G} \rangle}$ is a set $\{\Delta\} \cup \dot{\mathcal{I}}_{\langle \mathcal{G} \rangle}$ with Δ being the center of $\mathcal{D}_{\langle G \rangle}$, $\dot{\mathcal{I}}_{\langle \mathcal{G} \rangle} \subseteq \mathcal{P}\ell(\mathcal{G})$, and $\Delta \notin \dot{\mathcal{I}}_{\langle \mathcal{G} \rangle}$;
     a_2) the family of graphs $\mathcal{G}_i$ ($i \in \mathcal{I}_{\langle \mathcal{G} \rangle}$) of $\mathcal{D}_{\langle \mathcal{G} \rangle}$ is such that $V(\mathcal{G}_\Delta) = V(\mathcal{G})$, $E(\mathcal{G}_\Delta) = \varnothing$, and $\mathcal{G}_h = \mathcal{R}_{\mathcal{M}}(\text{dom}(h))$ for $h \in \dot{\mathcal{I}}_{\langle \mathcal{G} \rangle}$;
     a_3) the gluing conditions gl^{Δ}_i ($i \in \dot{\mathcal{I}}_{\langle \mathcal{G} \rangle}$) are such that $\text{gl}^{\Delta}_i = \text{gl}_i$ for gl_i defined as in 3)(iii) for the gluing diagram $\mathcal{D}^{\mathcal{G}}$;
     a_4) $\mathcal{R}^a_{\mathcal{M}}(\mathcal{G})$ is a colimit of $\mathcal{D}_{\langle \mathcal{G} \rangle}$ with gluing conditions gl^i_j ($\{i, j\} \subseteq \dot{\mathcal{I}}_{\langle \mathcal{G} \rangle}$ and $i \neq j$) such that they are unique together with $\dot{\mathcal{I}}_{\langle \mathcal{G} \rangle}$ to make $\mathcal{R}^a_{\mathcal{M}}(\mathcal{G})$ a colimit of $\mathcal{D}_{\langle \mathcal{G} \rangle}$;
  B) for every $\mathcal{G} \in \mathcal{S}_{\mathcal{M}}$ the following conditions hold:
     b_1) for $\mathcal{P}\ell^a(\mathcal{G})$ defined as in 3) with $\text{PREM}_{\mathcal{M}}$ replaced by $\text{PREM}^a_{\mathcal{M}}$ and for every $h \in \mathcal{P}\ell^a(\mathcal{G})$ and gluing pattern $\mathcal{D}_{\langle \text{dom}(h) \rangle}$ determined by $\text{dom}(h)$ the set $\text{SCP}_h = \{h \circ h' \,|\, h' \in \dot{\mathcal{I}}_{\langle \text{dom}(h) \rangle}\}$, called the *scope of gluing pattern* $\mathcal{D}_{\langle \text{dom}(h) \rangle}$ *in place* h, is a subset of $\mathcal{P}\ell(\mathcal{G})$ defined as in 3) for $\mathcal{G}$ and $\text{PREM}_{\mathcal{M}}$, where $\circ$ denotes the composition of homomorphisms of graphs;
     b_2) the set $\mathcal{P}\ell(\mathcal{G})$ defined in 3) satisfies conditions 3)(i), (ii);
     b_3) the graph $\mathcal{F}_{\mathcal{M}}(\mathcal{G})$ is a colimit of a generalized gluing diagram $\mathcal{D}_{\mathcal{G}}$ such that

(β_1) the set $\mathcal{I}$ of indexes of $\mathcal{D}_\mathcal{G}$ is the same as the set of indexes of $\mathcal{D}^\mathcal{G}$ given in 3)(iii), i.e. $\mathcal{I} = \mathcal{P}\ell(\mathcal{G}) \cup \{\Delta\}$,

(β_2) the family of graphs $\mathcal{G}_i$ ($i \in \mathcal{I}$) of $\mathcal{D}_\mathcal{G}$ is the same as of $\mathcal{D}^\mathcal{G}$ defined in 3)(iii),

(β_3) the gluing condition gl_i^Δ is gl_i defined in 3)(iii) for every $i \in \mathcal{I} - \{\Delta\}$,

(β_4) for all h_1, h_2 with $\{h_1, h_2\} \subseteq \mathcal{I} - \{\Delta\}$ and $h_1 \neq h_2$ if there exists $h \in \mathcal{P}\ell^a(\mathcal{G})$ for which $\{h_1, h_2\} \subseteq \mathrm{SCP}_h$, then the gluing condition $\mathrm{gl}_{h_2}^{h_1}$ of $\mathcal{D}_\mathcal{G}$ is the gluing condition $\mathrm{gl}_{h_2'}^{h_1'}$ of the gluing pattern determined by $\mathrm{dom}(h)$ for h_1', h_2' such that $h \circ h_1' = h_1$ and $h \circ h_2' = h_2$,

(β_5) if there does not exist $h \in \mathcal{P}\ell^a(\mathcal{G})$ such that $\{h_1, h_2\} \subseteq \mathrm{SCP}_h$ for h_1, h_2 as in (β_4), then the gluing condition $\mathrm{gl}_{h_2}^{h_1}$ of $\mathcal{D}_\mathcal{G}$ is defined to be the empty set;

b_4) the colimiting cocone $q_i : \mathcal{G}_i \to \mathcal{F}_\mathcal{M}(\mathcal{G})$ ($i \in \mathcal{I}$) of $\mathcal{D}_\mathcal{G}$ is such that

(β_6) the conditions 3)(iv) and (v) hold with $\mathcal{D}^\mathcal{G}$ replaced by $\mathcal{D}_\mathcal{G}$,

(β_7) for every at least two element subset H of $\mathcal{I} - \{\Delta\}$ such that

$$\bigcap_{i \in H} \left(V(\mathrm{im}(q_i)) - V(\mathrm{im}(q_\Delta)) \right) \neq \varnothing$$

there exists $h \in \mathcal{P}\ell^a(\mathcal{G})$ such that H is a subset of SCP_h of gluing pattern determined by $\mathrm{dom}(h)$.

The gluing conditions gl_j^i of $\mathcal{D}_\mathcal{G}$ defined in (β_4), (β_5) determine common parts of the boundaries of new compartments appearing in a step of an evolution process.

Appendix C

Basing on [18] we present an iterated function system whose attractor is Sierpiński gasket. This iterated function system consists of the bijections from $\mathbb{R}^2$ onto $\mathbb{R}^2$ ($\mathbb{R}^2$ denotes the set of ordered pairs of real numbers) described in terms of matrices as follows:

$$f_1^{\mathrm{Sierp}}(\mathbf{x}) = \begin{bmatrix} 1/2 & 0 \\ 0 & 1/2 \end{bmatrix} \mathbf{x} \qquad\qquad \text{scale by } 1/2$$

$$f_2^{\mathrm{Sierp}}(\mathbf{x}) = \begin{bmatrix} 1/2 & 0 \\ 0 & 1/2 \end{bmatrix} \mathbf{x} + \begin{bmatrix} 1/2 \\ 0 \end{bmatrix} \qquad\qquad \text{scale by } 1/2$$

$$f_3^{\mathrm{Sierp}}(\mathbf{x}) = \begin{bmatrix} 1/2 & 0 \\ 0 & 1/2 \end{bmatrix} \mathbf{x} + \begin{bmatrix} 1/4 \\ \sqrt{3}/4 \end{bmatrix} \qquad\qquad \text{scale by } 1/2.$$

References

1. Bolognesi, T.: Causal sets from simple models of computation. Int. Journal of Unconventional Computing **6**, 489–524 (2010)
2. Diekert, V., Gastin, P.: From local to global temporal logic over Mazurkiewicz traces. Theoretical Computer Science **356**, 126–135 (2006)

3. Gandy R.: Church's thesis and principles for mechanisms. In: Barwise, J., et al. (eds.) The Kleene Symposium, pp. 123–148. North-Holland, Amsterdam (1980)

4. Gacs, P., Levin, L.A.: Causal nets or what is a deterministic computation. Information and Control **51**, 1–19 (1981)

5. Gallo, G., Longo, G., Pallottino, S., Nguyen, S.: Directed hypergraphs and applications. Discrete Appl. Math. **42**, 177–201 (1993)

6. Goertzel B.: Review of A New Kind of Science. http://www.goertzel.org/dynapsyc/2002/WolframReview.htm

7. Joosten, J.J., Soler-Toscano, F., Zenil, H.: Fractal dimension of space-time diagrams and the runtime complexity of small Turing machines. Electronic Proceedings of Theoretical Computer Science **128**, 29–30 (2013)

8. Joosten J.J., Soler-Toscano, F., Zenil, H.: Fractal dimension versus computational complexity. arXiv: 1309.1779v2 [cs.CC] (24 March 2014)

9. Lima-de-Faria, A.: Atomic basis of biological symmetry and periodicity. BioSystems **43**, 115–135 (1997)

10. Lima-de-Faria, A.: Evolution Without Selection. Form and Function by Autoevolution, Elsevier, Amsterdam (1988)

11. Lutz, J.H.: The dimensions of individual strings and sequences. Information and Computation **187**, 49–79 (2003)

12. Markopoulou, F.: The internal description of a causal set: what the universe looks like from inside. arXiv: gr-qc/9811053v2 (18 November 1999)

13. Nowotny, T., Requardt, M.: Dimension theory of graphs and networks. J. Phys. A Math. Gen. **31**, 2447–2463 (1998)

14. Obtułowicz, A.: Randomized Gandy-Păun-Rozenberg machines. In: Gheorghe, M., Hinze, T., Păun, Gh., Rozenberg, G., Salomaa, A. (eds.) CMC 2010. LNCS, vol. 6501, pp. 305–324. Springer, Heidelberg (2011)

15. Obtułowicz, A.: Generalized Gandy-Păun-Rozenberg machines for tile systems and cellular automata. In: Gheorghe, M., Păun, Gh., Rozenberg, G., Salomaa, A., Verlan, S. (eds.) CMC 2011. LNCS, vol. 7184, pp. 314–332. Springer, Heidelberg (2012)

16. Obtułowicz, A.: In search of a structure of fractals by using membranes as hyperedges. In: Alhazov, A., Cojocaru, S., Gheorghe, M., Rogozhin, Yu., Rozenberg, G., Salomaa, A. (eds.) CMC 2013. LNCS, vol. 8340, pp. 301–307. Springer, Heidelberg (2014)

17. Păun, Gh., Rozenberg, G., Salomaa, A. (eds.): The Oxford Handbook of Membrane Computing, Oxford (2009)

18. Riddle, L.: Classic iterated function system, Sierpiński gasket. http://ecademy.agnesscott.edu/~lriddle/ifs/siertri/siertri.htm

19. Rozenfeld, H.D., Gallos, L.K., Song, C., Makse, H.A.: Fractal and trans-fractal scale-free networks. Encyclopedia of Complexity and System Science, pp. 3924–3943. Springer (2009)

20. Strogatz, S.H.: Nonlinear Dynamics and Chaos. Perseus Books Publ., LLC (1994)

21. Volchan, S.B.: What is a random sequence. Amer. Math. Monthly **109**, 46–63 (2002)

22. Weibel, E.R.: Design of biological organisms and fractal geometry. In: Nonnenmacher, T.F. et al. (eds.) Fractals in Biology and Medicine, pp. 68–85. Springer, Basel (1994)

23. Wolfram, S.: Random sequence generated by cellular automata. Advances in Appl. Math. **7**, 123–169 (1986)

24. Wolfram, S.: A New Kind of Science. Wolfram Media (2002)

P System Computational Model as Framework for Hybrid (Membrane-Quantum) Computations

Yurii Rogozhin, Artiom Alhazov$^{(\boxtimes)}$, Lyudmila Burtseva, Svetlana Cojocaru, Alexandru Colesnicov, and Ludmila Malahov

Institute of Mathematics and Computer Science,
5 Academiei st., MD-2028 Chisinau, Republic of Moldova
{artiom,Svetlana.Cojocaru}@math.md,
acolesnicov@gmx.com, {luburtseva,lmalahov}@gmail.com

Abstract. This work presents a hybrid model of high performance computations, representing the P system framework with additional quantum functionalities. This model is supposed to take advantages of both biomolecular and quantum paradigms and to overcome some of their inherent limitations. We extend a recently proposed formal model of interface between a membrane system and quantum sub-systems. The problem of finding the longest common subsequence for a set of strings is exhibited as an example.

Keywords: Models of Computation · Parallelism and Concurrency · Quantum Computing · Biomolecular Computing · P Systems

1 Introduction

This research concerns the capability of the P system computational model[5] to provide a framework for hybrid computations, employing additional functionality from a quantum model.

The first hybrid computational model obtained by joining membrane- and quantum- approaches was proposed in the paper of A. Leporati [2] where QUREM (Quantum Unit Rules and Energy assigned to Membranes) P systems were introduced. Keeping the main frame of P systems, QUREM P systems change objects and rules: objects are represented as pure states of a quantum system, and rules are quantum operators. The result is a hybrid computation device, a membrane system with quantum operations, but computation itself is provided only by quantum formalism.

We propose our edition of hybrid computation model that keeps the entire expressivity of P systems. Classical P system formalism serves as the framework providing computations by elements of other models as well as communications between elements of different nature.

The authors acknowledge the project STCU 5384 awarded by the Scientific and Technology Center in Ukraine.

M. Gheorghe et al. (Eds.): CMC 2014, LNCS 8961, pp. 373–384, 2014.
DOI: 10.1007/978-3-319-14370-5_23

We introduced the first version of our hybrid computation model in [7]. There, two types of membranes coexist: classical membranes and quantum membranes, the latter containing a quantum device inside. During the further research this conception has been extended by adding capability to perform quantum computations to any membrane.

To formulate quantum functionality incorporated in the proposed hybrid model, we use the classical scheme of quantum device[8]. Particular methods of quantum computation, which form the quantum functionality of the hybrid model, are selected according to the requirements of each problem being solved.

Proposed hybrid computations have to support data passing from the P system (macro) level to quantum (micro) level and back. The communication process is heart of the hybrid computation model because it provides access to a different computational structure rather then just cloning existing ones. The communication is implemented by P system objects corresponding to the basis states of each initial and resulting qubit of the quantum device. The appearance of such objects in the membrane starts the quantum computation.

In [7], we presented hybrid solutions of two problems: SAT and image retrieval. In [6], the graph isomorphism problem was approached in the hybrid framework.

In this paper we will demonstrate the process of hybrid computation on the problem of finding the longest common subsequence for a set of strings. This problem was selected because of its hard computation class, and suitability to be decomposed to different computational levels.

2   Hybrid Computational Model

2.1   Membrane Level of the Hybrid Model

We use standard **membrane systems,** or **P systems,** which consist of a hierarchy of membranes. We do not restrict ourselves to one specific variant of P systems; instead, we select it in relation to the solved problem. For instance, two hybrid systems were presented in [7], one based on transitional non-cooperative P systems with atomic inhibitors, and the other based on tissue P systems with symport/antiport. In the present paper, we use **P systems with active membranes** as our membrane framework.

The **investigated model** will additionally suppose that, in any membrane, the apparition of some specific objects (quantum data, or quantum triggers) starts a quantum calculation. The said data are available as initial states of the quantum registers. After its termination the quantum calculation produces other specific objects (quantum results) inside the membrane. From the P system point of view, the quantum calculation lasts one step, or several steps, of the membrane calculation.

During quantum calculations in a membrane, application of P system rules to this membrane should be prohibited. Some aspects of this need more research. For example, division of a working quantum membrane would contradict the no-cloning theorem.

2.2   P Systems with Active Membranes

Definition 1. *P system with active membranes (without non-elementary membrane division) of initial degree $d \geq 1$ is a tuple $\Pi = (O, H, \mu, w_1, \cdots, w_d, R)$, where*

- *O is a non-empty finite alphabet of objects,*
- *H is a finite set of membrane labels;*
- *μ is a membrane structure (i.e., a rooted unordered tree, usually represented by a bracketed expression) consisting of d membranes labeled (not necessarily injectively) by elements of H;*
- *w_i, for every $i \in H$ mentioned in μ, are strings over O, describing the initial multisets of objects placed in the d regions of μ;*
- *R is a finite set of rules.*

Each membrane possesses, besides its label and position in μ, another attribute called polarization, which can be one of the elements of set E. For the purposes of the present paper, $E = \{0, 1, 2\}$.

The rules are of the following kinds:

(a) $[\, a \rightarrow u \,]_h^e$, $a \in O$, $u \in O^*$, $h \in H$, $e \in E$.
   Object evolution rules. They can be applied inside a membrane labeled h with polarization e and containing an occurrence of the object a; the object a is rewritten into the multiset w (i.e., a is removed from the multiset in h and replaced by all objects in u).

(b) $a[\, \,]_h^e \rightarrow [\, b \,]_h^{e'}$, $a, b \in O$, $h \in H$, $e, e' \in E$.
   Send-in communication rules. They can be applied to a membrane labeled h with polarization e and such that the external region contains an occurrence of the object a; the object a is sent into h becoming b and, simultaneously, the polarization of h is changed to e'.

(c) $[\, a \,]_h^e \rightarrow [\, \,]_h^{e'} b$, $a, b \in O$, $h \in H$, $e, e' \in E$.
   Send-out communication rules. They can be applied to a membrane labeled h with polarization e and containing an occurrence of the object a; the object a is sent out from h to the outside region becoming b and, simultaneously, the polarization of h is changed to e'.

(d) $[\, a \,]_h^e \rightarrow b$, $a, b \in O$, $h \in H$, $e \in E$.
   Dissolution rules. They can be applied to a membrane labeled h with polarization e and containing an occurrence of the object a; the membrane h is dissolved and its contents is released in the surrounding region, simultaneously changing an occurrence of a into b.

(e) $[\, a \,]_h^e \rightarrow [\, b \,]_h^{e'} [\, c \,]_h^{e''}$, $a, b, c \in O$, $h \in H$, $e, e', e'' \in E$.
   Elementary division rules. They can be applied to a membrane labeled h with polarization e, containing an occurrence of the object a, but having no other membrane inside (an elementary membrane); the membrane is divided into two membranes with the same label h and polarizations e' and e''; the object a is replaced, respectively, by b and c, while the other objects are copied to both membranes.

Each instantaneous configuration of a P system with active membranes is described by the current membrane structure, including the polarizations, together with the multisets located in the corresponding regions. A computation step changes the current configuration according to the following principles:

Each object and membrane can be subject to at most one rule per step, except for object evolution rules (inside each membrane any number of evolution rules can be applied simultaneously). no further rules can be applied to the idle objects and membranes. If not indicated otherwise, we assume the standard semantics of application of P system rules [5].

A computation halts when no rules are applicable at some step.

In this paper, we consider P systems with input. We include the input sub-alphabet $\Sigma \subseteq O$ and the input region i_0 in the tuple specifying the P system. The computation starts after some input multiset of objects from Σ is added to the input region. As the result of a halting computation, the contents of a dedicated region is usually taken; sometimes, only a specific sub-alphabet is considered, and sometimes multiple regions are considered.

2.3   Quantum Level of the Hybrid Model

We suppose a standard **quantum device** available for quantum calculations. The quantum device contains qubits organized in quantum registers. It works in three steps: non-quantum (classical) initialization of qubits when they are set in base states; quantum transformation when the qubits are not observed; non-quantum (classical) measurement that produces the observable result.

Several restrictions are imposed over the quantum device. After the initialization and after the measurement each qubit is in one of base states $|0\rangle$, or $|1\rangle$. During quantum calculation a qubit may be in the superposition of both states, or it may be entangled with other qubits. The initial data and the result are regarded as non-negative integers in binary notation. The quantum transformation is linear and reversible. The general rule is that arguments and results are kept in different quantum registers. Another general condition is that the ancillary qubits are not entangled with the argument and the result after the calculation [4, p. 36–37,46–47].

The construction of a quantum computer shown in Fig. 1 guarantees that all the above conditions are satisfied [4, p. 49]. Indices show the dimensionality: the device implements the calculation of integer function $f : [0, 2^N - 1] \rightarrow [0, 2^M - 1]$. We may omit the index when we do not focus on the dimensionality. V_f is a quantum implementation of function f, and $V_f^\dagger = V_f^{-1}$ is the inverse transformation. It uses R ancillary qubits $|w\rangle$. Register $|z\rangle$ is initialized by quantum data that appeared in the membrane and made the quantum calculation to start. In the hybrid scheme below, quantum registers are initialized through the input objects $I_{k,b}$, where $b = 0, 1$ is the binary value of the kth qubit in $|z\rangle$.

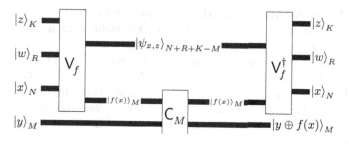

Fig. 1. Quantum calculation; initialization and measurement are not shown, indices denote the number of qubits in registers

2.4   Communication: Input/Output Signals and Triggering

We now focus on discussing the particularities of the hybrid model, namely, on the interaction between the bio-inspired sub-system and the quantum sub-system.

We now define the hybrid system as a tuple

$$\beta = (\Pi, T, T', H_Q, Q_N, Q_M, Inp, Outp, t, q_{h_1}, \cdots, q_{h_m}).$$

Here, Π is a P system, and $H_Q = \{h_1, \cdots, h_m\}$ is a subset of membrane labels in Π used for quantum calculations. T is a trigger and T' is the signal on obtaining the quantum result. Sub-systems $q_{h_1}, \cdots, q_{h_m}$ are the quantum sub-systems associated to the corresponding membranes from H_Q. The rest of the components of the tuple defining β specify the interaction between Π and q_{h_j}, $1 \leq j \leq m$.

For simplicity we assume that the running time of quantum sub-systems of the same type is always the same. To keep this time general, we include a timing function $t : H_Q \to \mathbb{N}$: the quantum computation in a sub-system of type q_{h_j} takes $t(h_j)$ membrane steps. It is an open general question how to calculate the timing of quantum calculation with respect to the timing of membrane calculation. We could use as the first rough estimation that quantum calculation takes three steps of membrane calculation (initialization, quantum transformation, measurement).

The input size (in qubits) for quantum systems is given by $Q_N : H_Q \to \mathbb{N}$. The output size (in bits) for quantum systems is given by $Q_M : H_Q \to \mathbb{N}$.

We would like to define the behavior of β in all possible situations, so we introduce the trigger $T \in O$, where O is the alphabet of Π. The work of a quantum sub-system starts whenever T appears inside the corresponding membrane. The initial state of a quantum sub-system of type q_{h_j} is produced from objects $Inp(h_j) = \{O_{k,h_j,b} \mid 1 \leq k \leq Q_N(h_j), \ b \in \{0,1\}\} \cup \{T\}$, so $Inp : H_Q \to 2^O$ is a function describing the input sub-alphabet for each type of quantum sub-system, the meaning of object $O_{k,h_j,b}$ being to initialize bit k of input by value b. We require that the set of rules satisfies the following condition: any object that may be sent into a membrane labeled h_j must be in $Inp(h_j)$.

If some bit k is not initialized, then the default value 0 is assumed. If multiple objects initialize bit k, it may be initialized to the first, the last, default, or random value, or we can propose the *extended initialization* described below in Subsection 2.5. If some objects are sent to a quantum membrane without the trigger, we assume they wait there until the trigger arrives.

The output of quantum sub-systems is returned to the membrane system in the form of objects from $Outp(h_j) = \{R_{k,h_j,b} \mid 1 \le k \le Q_M(h_j),\ b \in \{0,1\}\} \cup \{T'\}$, the meaning of object $R_{k,h_j,b}$ being that the output bit k has value b. In case of one-bit output, we often denote it **yes** and **no**.

The result of a quantum sub-system is produced in the membrane together with object T'.

There are two possibilities to synchronize quantum and membrane levels. We can use a timing function and wait for the quantum result by organizing the corresponding delay in membrane calculations, or we can wait for appearance of the resulting objects, or the trigger T'. For completeness, our model provides both possibilities. The topic needs further investigations.

The problem of some alternative evolution of the objects leading to the input into the quantum sub-system input can be always solved using a wrapper membrane (an extra membrane around the membrane used for quantum calculation), where the only rules applicable to the objects in it would be passing the input in, and passing the output out, if needed.

Another possible use of the wrapper membranes is to merge the input/output objects of the quantum sub-systems from objects of types $O_{k,h_j,b}$ and $R_{k,h_j,b}$ into objects of types $O_{k,b}$ and $R_{k,b}$, where the proper handling depending on h_j is done during their passage into/outside the wrapper membrane.

2.5   Initialization of the Quantum Device

We can give here only a very abstract description of quantum device because its physical implementation is unimportant. Before the quantum calculation starts, each qubit is to be set in one of basis states $|0\rangle$, or $|1\rangle$. The embedded measurement operation is used twice: before the quantum computation to set qubits to basis states, and after the quantum computation to obtain the result [4, p. 31].

As we use the measurement before the calculation, the qubits collapse in the basis states. Measurement is irreversible, therefore it is a classical operation.

Now we are to set qubits in initial states. For example, if we want to set them in the state $|0\rangle$, we are to check the state of each qubit and invert $|1\rangle$. This is not a quantum transformation.

Usually, all qubits are initially set to $|0\rangle_1$. (Several quantum algorithms use different initial values though.) In our case, we will use non-quantum tools to prepare the state $|z\rangle\,|w\rangle\,|x\rangle\,|y\rangle = |z_0\rangle_K\,|0\rangle_R\,|0\rangle_N\,|0\rangle_M$. Here z_0 is the number that entered the quantum membrane and initiated the process. z_0 is a parameter that somehow influences the performed quantum computation. Classical (non-quantum) initialization ends here.

As we parametrize our quantum device by $|z_0\rangle$, some preliminary quantum steps using this value may precede the main part of calculation. We can call this stage *the extended initialization*. Some authors call it *compilation*.

For example, if multiple objects initialize bit k, say, $(O_{k,h_j,0})^s(O_{k,h_j,1})^t$, then the k-th qubit can be set to the state $\frac{1}{\sqrt{s^2+t^2}}(s\,|0\rangle + t\,|1\rangle)$. This technique is restricted: we do not provide objects that encode entangled states. This is made by an appropriate one-qubit quantum transformation that should be performed before any other calculations.

Another example: many quantum algorithms suppose that all qubits from register $|x\rangle$ are at once transformed by one-qubit Hadamard transformation

$$\mathsf{H} = \frac{1}{\sqrt{2}}\begin{pmatrix} 1 & 1 \\ 1 & -1 \end{pmatrix}$$

If $|x\rangle$ was set to $|0\rangle$ then each qubit of $|x\rangle$ is set in the state $\frac{1}{\sqrt{2}}(|0\rangle + |1\rangle)$. As the result, register $|x\rangle$ gets the state

$$|x\rangle = \frac{1}{2^{N/2}}\sum_{0 \le i < 2^N} |i\rangle,$$

that corresponds to a uniform superposition of all possible values of argument x. Application of the transformation V_f will then produce all possible values of $f(x)$ (quantum parallelism).

Configuration of quantum device depends on the parameters of a specific problem. The implementation of such a dependence is sometimes called compilation. It is possible to delegate all such operation to membrane level, or to include them inside the quantum device. They can be performed even at preparatory stage for the membrane level. Another variant is to consider these operations as an intermediate level of the system between membrane and quantum levels. The initialization of quantum device will also be a part of this level. It is logical as the initialization should be performed at the appearance of trigger T. We aim these problems for further research.

3 Finding the Longest Common Subsequence

3.1 Problem Formulation and Approach

An instance of the problem is given by strings $u_1, \cdots, u_n \in V^*, V = \{a_1, \cdots, a_k\}$. We assume without restricting generality that the first string is not longer than any other. We should find a string u_0 with the following properties:
1. u_0 is a subsequence of each $u_i, 1 \le i \le n$;
2. u_0 is the longest string satisfying the previous property.

We consider the following way of solving the problem. Membrane division is used to consider the possible subsequences of the first string. The quantum sub-systems are used to verify if the candidate strings are subsequences of all other input strings. Delay is organized in order for the candidate strings to be considered in the longest-to-shortest order. If a solution is found in some membrane, then a signal goes to the skin, is replicated and sent into the membranes verifying the candidates to stop the process. The delay was chosen as a compromise in order not to slow down the overall system too much, while preventing most of unnecessary computations for shorter strings after a solution is found.

3.2 P System

In the construction of our membrane framework, we use numbers n and $n_i = |u_i|$, $1 \leq i \leq n$. The strings are represented by symbols from $\Sigma = \{a_{j,l,0,0} \mid 1 \leq j \leq n_1, 1 \leq l \leq k\} \cup \{b_{i,j,l,0} \mid 2 \leq i \leq n, 1 \leq j \leq n_i, 1 \leq l \leq k\}$ as follows: the string representing the input multiset is

$$w_{in} = \prod_{1 \leq j \leq n_1} (a_{j,l,0,0} \mid u_1[j] = a_l) \prod_{2 \leq i \leq n, \ 1 \leq j \leq n_i} (b_{i,j,l,0} \mid u_i[j] = a_l).$$

Let $K = \lceil \log_2 k \rceil$ be the number of bits needed to encode one symbol of V, and let $N = \lceil \log_2 (n_1 + 1) \rceil$ be the number of bits needed to represent a number between 0 and n_1, inclusive.

We construct the following **hybrid** system.

$$\beta = (\Pi, T, T', H_Q = \{2\}, Q_N, Q_M, Inp, Outp, t, q_2), \text{ where}$$

$$Q_N(2) = N + K \sum_{j=1}^{n} n_j, \ Q_M(2) = 1, \ Outp(2) = \{\text{yes}, \text{no}, T'\}, \ t(2) = 3,$$

$$Inp(2) = \{T\} \cup \{I_{k,b} \mid 0 \leq k \leq N + K \sum_{t=1}^{n} n_t, \ 0 \leq b \leq 1\},$$

q_2 is a quantum system checking whether the first string
     is a subsequence of the other strings, and

$$\Pi = (O, \Sigma, \mu = [\ [\ ]_2^0 [\ ]_3^0 \ ]_1^0, w_1, w_2, w_3, R, 2)$$

is a **P system** with active membranes, where Σ is defined above, and

$$O = \{d_j, s_j \mid 0 \leq j \leq n_1\} \cup \{\text{yes}, \text{yes}', \text{no}, o, p_1', p_0', T'\} \cup Inp(2)$$
$$\cup \{c_{j,t} \mid 0 \leq j \leq n_1 + 1, \ 0 \leq t \leq j\} \cup \{c_t, c_t' \mid 0 \leq t \leq n_1\} \cup \{p_t \mid -1 \leq t \leq 5n_1\}$$
$$\cup \{a_{j,l,s,t} \mid 1 \leq j \leq n_1, \ 1 \leq l \leq k, \ 0 \leq s \leq j, \ 0 \leq t \leq s\}$$
$$\cup \{b_{i,j,l,s}, e_{j,l} \mid 1 \leq i \leq n, \ 1 \leq j \leq n_i, \ 1 \leq l \leq k, \ 1 \leq s \leq n_1 + 1\},$$
$$w_1 = \lambda, \ w_2 = d_0 c_{0,0}, \ w_3 = s_0,$$

and the set R is the union of the following rule groups (presented together with their explanations): generation, counting, building subsequences, input for the quantum sub-systems, and stopping.

Generation
$G_1. \ [\ d_j \ ]_2^e \rightarrow [\ d_{j+1} \ ]_2^0 [\ d_{j+1} \ ]_2^1, \ 0 \leq j \leq n_1 - 1, \ 0 \leq e \leq 1.$
Membrane 2 is divided n_1 times, each division representing the choice whether the subsequent symbol of the first string is selected for the candidate common subsequence.

$G_2. \ [\ d_{n_1} \ ]_2^e \rightarrow [\ ]_2^0 o, \ 0 \leq e \leq 1.$
Then the polarization is set to 0. Object o is not used in the system, it is only given because it is required by the types of the rules of P systems with active membranes.

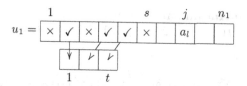

Fig. 2. Illustration of indices j, l, s, t appearing in objects $a_{j,l,s,t}$: string u_1 has symbol a_l in position j; position s is being considered, and t symbols have been chosen for the candidate subsequence. Indices j, l, s have similar meaning for symbols $b_{i,j,l,s}$, except j refers to a position in u_i, while s refers to a position in u_1.

Counting

C_1. $[\, c_{j,t} \to c_{j+1,t+e} \,]_2^e$, $0 \le j \le n_1$, $0 \le t \le j$, $0 \le e \le 1$.

Subscript t counts the number of selected (by setting the polarization to 1) symbols, out of j symbols of the first string considered.

C_2. $[\, c_{n_1+1,t} \to c_t p_{5(n_1-t)} \,]_2^0$, $0 \le t \le n_1$.

Remember the size of a chosen subsequence and initialize the delay counter.

C_3. $[\, p_t \to p_{t-1} \,]_2^0$, $1 \le t \le 5n_1$.

Delay the computation for the number of steps equal to 5 times the number of not selected symbols. In this way, the candidate strings are considered the longest to the shortest, until a common subsequence is found. These rules can be disabled if the polarization is switched to 2.

C_4. $[\, p_0 \to p_{-1} p_1' \,]_2^0$.

C_5. $[\, p_{-1} \,]_2^0 \to [\;]_2^1 o$.

Set the polarization to 1. In the next step, the input will be prepared for the quantum sub-system.

C_6. $[\, p_1' \to p_0' \,]_2^0$.

C_7. $[\, p_0' \,]_2^1 \to [\;]_2^0 o$.

The next step after having set the polarization to 1, it is again reset to 0 (simultaneously with initializing the quantum sub-system).

Building subsequences

B_1. $[\, a_{j,l,s,t} \to a_{j,l,s+1,t+e} \,]_2^e$,
$1 \le j \le n_1$, $1 \le l \le k$, $0 \le s \le j-1$, $0 \le t \le s$, $0 \le e \le 1$.

In the group $a_{j,l,s,t}$ of objects, the third subscript ranges over the positions of the first string, while the last subscript keeps track of the number of symbols chosen.

B_2. $[\, a_{j,l,j,t} \to b_{1,t+1,l,j+1} \,]_2^1$, $1 \le j \le n_1$, $1 \le l \le k$, $0 \le t \le s$.

The j-th symbol of the first string is chosen as the t-th symbol of the candidate subsequence.

B_3. $[\, a_{j,l,j,t} \to \lambda \,]_2^0$, $1 \le j \le n_1$, $1 \le l \le k$, $0 \le t \le s$.

The symbol is not chosen; the object representing it is erased.

B_4. $[\, b_{i,j,l,s} \to b_{i,j,l,s+1} \,]_2^e$, $1 \le i \le n$, $1 \le j \le n_i$, $1 \le l \le k$, $1 \le s \le n_1$.

Wait until the rest of the subsequence is chosen. These rules also apply to the input representing the other strings, synchronizing them.

Input for the quantum sub-systems

$I_1.$ [$b_{i,j,l,n_1+1} \rightarrow f(i,j,l)$]$_2^1$, $2 \le i \le n$, $1 \le j \le n_i$, $1 \le l \le k$, where

$$f(i,j,l) = I_{K(j-1+\sum\limits_{t=2}^{i-1} n_t)+1,g(l,0)} \cdots I_{K(j-1+\sum\limits_{t=2}^{i-1} n_t)+K,g(l,K-1)}, \quad 2 \le i \le n,$$

$$f(1,j,l) = e_{j,l} I_{K(j-1+\sum\limits_{t=2}^{n} n_t)+1,g(l,0)} \cdots I_{K(j-1+\sum\limits_{t=2}^{n} n_t)+K,g(l,K-1)},$$

where $g(l,b) = \lfloor (l-1)/2^b \rfloor \mathrm{mod} 2$ is the b-th bit of binary representation of number $l-1$.

$I_2.$ [$c_t \rightarrow c_t' T f(1,t+1,0) \cdots f(1,n_1,0) F(t)$]$_2^1$ where

$$F(t) = I_{K(\sum\limits_{t=1}^{n} n_t),g(t+1,0)} \cdots I_{K(\sum\limits_{t=1}^{n} n_t)+N-1,g(t+1,N-1)}.$$

The total number of input objects passed to a quantum sub-system (besides the trigger T) is $N + K \sum\limits_{t=1}^{n} n_t$.

Stopping

$S_1.$ [$s_j \rightarrow s_{j+1} s_{j+1}$]$_3^0$, $0 \le j \le n_1 - 1$.
2^{n_1} copies of object s_{n_1} are produced.

$S_2.$ [**yes** $\rightarrow$ **yes'**]$_2^0$.
We make sure that the computation is not stopped (a longer string not found yet). We do not use the trigger T' produced together with **yes**.

$S_3.$ [**yes'**]$_2^0 \rightarrow$ [ ]$_2^1$**yes**.
The polarization is set to 1.

$S_4.$ [c_t']$_2^1 \rightarrow$ [ ]$_2^1 c_t$.
The object is sent out storing the length of the found common string.

$S_5.$ c_t[ ]$_3^0 \rightarrow$ [c_t]$_3^1$.
One object c_t enters membrane labeled 3, switching its polarization to make sure this is done once.

$S_6.$ [c_t]$_3^1 \rightarrow c_t'$.
The object is primed again, dissolving membrane labeled 3, releasing objects s_{n_1} into the skin.

$S_7.$ s_{n_1}[ ]$_2^0 \rightarrow$ [o]$_2^2$.
Objects s_{n_1} enter all membranes labeled 2, with polarization 0, stopping the computations there by setting the polarization to 2.

$S_8.$ [c_t']$_1^0 \rightarrow$ [ ]$_1^1 c_t$.
Object c_t is sent out to the environment, representing the length of the longest common subsequence.

The system described above solves the longest common subsequence problem. The length of this subsequence is sent out, stored in one object, while all longest subsequences (there may be a large number of them) are represented in the elementary membranes with polarization 1.

It is worth noticing that, similarly to the approach used in [7], the construction is made in such a way that all input data for the quantum sub-system is produced simultaneously and all qubits are initialized, so the construction does not require a trigger to synchronize the input; we have included it in rule I_2 just to comply with the presented model.

3.3 Quantum Calculation

The quantum calculation needed to unveil if one string is a subsequence of other(s) is thoroughly described in [3]. The algorithm is a modification of well-known Grover search algorithm. It uses the techniques originally introduced by Grover: a query operator that marks the state encoding the element being searched by changing its phase, followed by an amplitude amplification of the marked state.

The paper [3] solves more general (and more complex) problem of approximate pattern matching. Nevertheless, the algorithm can be applied for exact pattern matching that is our case. The authors note that "The proof for the case where only exact matches exist, and the symbols in the pattern occur only in these matches, can be adapted straightforwardly, and will state that the probability of finding a solution using the algorithm above is at least $\frac{1}{4}$." Therefore, the state can be detected with probability very near to one by iterating this process four times. We do not focus on details in this paper.

4   Conclusion

This work continues the presentation of a hybrid computational model that combines in the framework of membrane computation elements of others (for today, only quantum) approaches. In current research, the detailing of P system framework construction and functionality is provided, and interaction of membrane and quantum levels are described.

To obtain true hybrid computation the proposed hybrid model has to provide mutual accepting of input/output by computation models of different nature and even different (macro/micro) levels. We presented, in the current paper, the communication scheme in detail. The technique includes both P system and quantum tools. P system formalism as the framework of hybrid model provides converting multisets to quantum registers contents and back procedure. Quantum computation ends with measurement, which prepare the registers content for uploading back in P system.

Since the main reason of proposing a hybrid computational model was practical needs of several domains delivering hard tasks, we develop our model interdependently with its application to solution of selected set of such type problems. One of them was used as illustrative example in this work.

Basing on implemented solutions of several problems, we extract the common feature that makes hybrid computation possible. Solving tasks of this type mostly supposes generating lists of candidates that then will be used for comparison to a pattern applying Grover search in the quantum device. In our further research, we plan to generalize these steps of solution both for P system and quantum devices.

The distribution of work between levels of hybrid system depends on the problem to be solved and may vary. In this paper we mostly use membrane replication to overpass the problem complexity while in [7] the power of quantum formalism was exploited. It would be interesting to combine both sources of computational power to aim, for example, the Σ_2^p computational complexity class.

References

1. Alhazov, A., Burtseva, L., Cojocaru, S., Colesnicov, A., Malahov, L.: An Approach to Implementation of Hybrid Computational Paradigm. In: The Third Conference of Mathematical Society of the Republic of Moldova, IMCS-50, pp. 437–440 (2014)
2. Leporati, A.: (UREM) P Systems with a Quantum-like Behavior: Background, Definition, and Computational Power. In: Eleftherakis, G., Kefalas, P., Păun, Gh., Rozenberg, G., Salomaa, A. (eds.) WMC 2007. LNCS, vol. 4860, pp. 32–53. Springer, Heidelberg (2007)
3. Mateus, P., Omar, Y.: Quantum Pattern Matching. arXiv:quant-ph/0508237v1
4. Mermin, N.D.: Quantum Computer Science: An Introduction. Cambridge University Press (2007)
5. Păun, Gh.: Membrane Computing: An Introduction. Springer (2002)
6. Rogozhin, Yu., Alhazov, A., Burtseva, L., Cojocaru, S., Colesnicov, A., Malahov, L.: Hybrid (Membrane-Quantum) Model of High Performance Computations in Solving Problems of Computer Algebra Domain (in preparation)
7. Rogozhin, Yu., Alhazov, A., Burtseva, L., Cojocaru, S., Colesnicov, A., Malahov, L.: Solving Problems in Various Domains by Hybrid Models of High Performance Computations. Computer Science Journal of Moldova 22(1(64)), 3–20 (2014)
8. Williams, C.P.: Explorations in Quantum Computing. Springer (2008)

Fault Diagnosis Models for Electric Locomotive Systems Based on Fuzzy Reasoning Spiking Neural P Systems

Tao Wang[1], Gexiang Zhang[1], and Mario J. Pérez-Jiménez[2]([✉])

[1] School of Electrical Engineering, Southwest Jiaotong University,
Chengdu 610031, People's Republic of China
wangtaocdu@gmail.com, zhgxdylan@126.com
[2] Department of Computer Science and Artificial Intelligence, Research Group
on Natural Computing, University of Sevilla, 41012 Sevilla, Spain
marper@us.es

Abstract. This paper discusses the application of fuzzy reasoning spiking neural P systems with real numbers (rFRSN P systems) to fault diagnosis of electric locomotive systems. Relationships among breakdown signals and faulty sections in subsystems of electric locomotive systems are described in the form of fuzzy production rules firstly and then fault diagnosis models based on rFRSN P systems for these subsystems are built according to these rules. Fuzzy production rules for diagnosing electric locomotive systems are abstracted from the fault diagnosis analysis of the subsystems and the causality among faulty sections, faulty subsystems and electric locomotive systems. Finally, a diagnosis model based on rFRSN P systems for electric locomotive systems is proposed.

Keywords: Fuzzy reasoning spiking neural P system · Fault diagnosis · Electric locomotive system · Real number · SS4 electric locomotive systems

1 Introduction

Spiking neural P systems (SN P systems), introduced in [2] in the framework of membrane computing, is a new class of computing devices which are inspired by the neurophysiological behavior of neurons sending electrical impulses (spikes) along axons to other neurons. Since then, SN P systems have become a hot topic in membrane computing [3]-[21], including investigations focusing on the use of SN P systems and their variants to solve engineering problems in power systems [18]-[21].

In [18], fuzzy reasoning spiking neural P systems with real numbers (rFRSN P systems) were introduced in order to capture the diagnosis knowledge representation and reasoning. The merits of rFRSN P systems lie in visually describing fuzzy production rules in a fuzzy diagnosis knowledge systems, where they effectively model the relationships among breakdown signals and faulty sections and represent and handle fuzzy knowledge/information. This paper discusses the

© Springer International Publishing Switzerland 2014
M. Gheorghe et al. (Eds.): CMC 2014, LNCS 8961, pp. 385–395, 2014.
DOI: 10.1007/978-3-319-14370-5_24

application of rFRSN P systems to the fault diagnosis of the Shaoshan4 (SS4) electric locomotive systems (always indicate SS4 electric locomotive systems).

Electric locomotive systems are composed of several subsystems with different functions; meanwhile, these subsystems consist of numerous sections. Thus, a locomotive system can be viewed as a hierarchical tree structure of sections and subsystems [22,23]. To build fault diagnosis models based on rFRSN P systems for different subsystems, relationships among breakdown signals and faulty sections in subsystems are abstracted and described in the form of fuzzy production rules firstly. Then, fault diagnosis models for these subsystems are built based on these rules. Fuzzy production rules for diagnosing electric locomotive systems are derived in accordance with causality rules among faulty sections, faulty subsystems and SS4 electric locomotive systems. It is worth pointing out that rFRSN P systems used in this paper contain three types of rule neurons, i.e., $GENERAL$, AND and OR, while the ones in [18] only contain two types: AND and OR.

This paper is structured as follows. Section 2 introduces preliminary definitions and concepts utilsed in this work. The fault diagnosis models for key subsystems and electric locomotive systems are presented in Section 3. Conclusions are drawn in Section 4.

2   Preliminaries

In this section, we briefly review the basic concepts of rFRSN P systems [18]. Here, only the necessary prerequisites are introduced.

Definition 1: An rFRSN P system of degree $m \geq 1$ is a tuple $\Pi = (O, \sigma_1, \ldots, \sigma_m, syn, in, out)$, where:

(1) $O = \{a\}$ is a singleton alphabet (a is called spike);
(2) $\sigma_1, \ldots, \sigma_m$ are neurons, of the form $\sigma_i = (\theta_i, c_i, r_i), 1 \leq i \leq m$, where:
    (a) θ_i is a real number in $[0, 1]$ representing the potential value of spikes (i.e. value of electrical impulses) contained in neuron σ_i;
    (b) c_i is a real number in $[0, 1]$ representing the fuzzy truth value corresponding to neuron σ_i;
    (c) r_i represents a firing (spiking) rule contained in neuron σ_i with the form $E/a^\theta \rightarrow a^\beta$, where E is the firing condition and its form will be specified below, θ and β are real numbers in $[0, 1]$;
(3) $syn \subseteq \{1, 2, \ldots, m\} \times \{1, 2, \ldots, m\}$ with $i \neq j$ for all $(i, j) \in syn, 1 \leq i, j \leq m$, is a directed graph of synapses between the linked neurons;
(4) $in, out \subseteq \{1, 2, \ldots, m\}$ indicate the input neuron set and the output neuron set of Π, respectively.

In rFRSN P systems, each neuron associates with either a fuzzy proposition or a fuzzy production rule, and $c_i \in [0, 1]$ is used to express a truth value of this fuzzy proposition or confidence factor (CF) of this fuzzy production rule. Each neuron σ_i contains only one firing (spiking) rule, of the form $E/a^\theta \rightarrow a^\beta$, where $E = a^n$ and n is the number of input synapses from other neurons to the neuron. It can be applied if and only if σ_i contains at least n spikes, otherwise, the rule cannot be enabled until n spikes are received. For neuron σ_i, if its firing rule is applied, then its pulse value θ_i is consumed and a new spike with value β is produced in σ_i. Once the spike with value β is emitted from σ_i, each neuron σ_j with $(i, j) \in syn$ immediately receives this spike.

In rFRSN P systems, the neurons are extended to four types (proposition neurons and three kinds of rule neurons: $GENERAL$, AND and OR) and the pulse value contained in each neuron is no longer the number of spikes represented by a real value, but a real number in $[0, 1]$ representing the potential value of spikes contained in neuron σ_i. For neuron σ_i, if $\theta_i > 0$, then the neuron contains a spike with pulse value θ_i; otherwise, it contains no spike and its pulse is 0. For different types of neurons, their definitions and the operations for pulse values are different. We only introduce the definition of GENERAL rule neurons. Details about the other three types of neurons can be found in [18].

Definition 2: A $GENERAL$ rule neuron is associated with a fuzzy production rule which has only one proposition in the antecedent part of the rule. Such a neuron is represented by a rectangle, as shown is Fig. 1.

A $GENERAL$ rule neuron has only one presynaptic proposition neuron and one or more postsynaptic proposition neurons. If a $GENERAL$ rule neuron receives a spike from its presynaptic proposition neuron and its firing condition is satisfied, then the neuron fires and produces a new spike with the potential value $\beta = \theta * c$, where β, θ and c are real numbers in $[0, 1]$.

Fig. 1. A $GENERAL$ rule neuron (a) and its simplified form (b)

3 Fault Diagnosis Models for Electric Locomotive Systems Based on rFRSN P Systems

In this section, fault diagnosis models based on rFRSN P systems for SS4 electric locomotive systems and their main subsystems, i.e., main circuit systems, power supply systems, traction and breaking systems, are proposed. Since an SS4 electric locomotive system can be viewed as a hierarchial tree structure of subsystems and sections shown in Fig. 2, we can build the diagnosis models from leaves to the top (that is, the root) of the tree. Thus, we firstly build the models for subsystems and then analyze these models and relationships among an electric locomotive system, its subsystems and faulty sections in these subsystems. Finally, a fault diagnosis model for SS4 electric locomotive systems is proposed.

3.1 A Fault Diagnosis Model for the Main Circuit Systems

Fuzzy production rules (*Rules* 1 to 16), describing the relationships between breakdown signals detected and candidate faulty sections, for main circuit

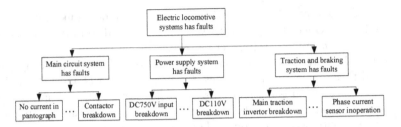

Fig. 2. A hierarchial tree structure of components in an SS4 electric locomotive system

systems of electric locomotives are described as follows, where CF represents the certainty (confidence) factor of a rule, $P_1, \ldots, P_{18}$ are propositions whose meanings are shown in Table 1. According to these fuzzy production rules, a fault diagnosis model based on rFRSN P systems for main circuit systems $\Pi_1 = (O, \sigma_1, \ldots, \sigma_{34}, syn, in, out)$ is built, as shown in Fig. 3, where:

(1) $O = \{a\}$ is the singleton alphabet (a is called spike);

(2) $\sigma_1, \ldots, \sigma_{18}$ are proposition neurons associated with propositions $P_1, \ldots, P_{18}$, respectively;

(3) $\sigma_{19}, \ldots, \sigma_{28}, \sigma_{30}, \ldots, \sigma_{34}$ are $GENERAL$ rule neurons associated with fuzzy production rules $R_1, \ldots, R_{10}, R_{12}, \ldots, R_{16}$, respectively; σ_{29} is an OR rule neuron associated with fuzzy production rule R_{11};

(4) $syn = \{(1, 19), (2, 20), (3, 21), (4, 22), (5, 23), (6, 24), (7, 25), (8, 26), (9, 27),$ $(10, 28), (11, 29), (12, 29), (13, 30), (14, 31), (15, 32), (16, 33), (17, 34), (19, 13),$ $(20, 13), (21, 13), (22, 14), (23, 14), (24, 14), (25, 15), (26, 15), (27, 16), (28, 16),$ $(29, 17), (30, 18), (30, 15), (31, 18), (31, 15), (32, 18), (33, 15), (34, 18)\};$

(5) $in = \{\sigma_1, \ldots, \sigma_{12}\}$, $out = \{\sigma_{18}\}$.

Rule 1: IF P_1 THEN P_{13} (CF=0.95); *Rule 9:* IF P_9 THEN P_{16} (CF=0.95)
Rule 2: IF P_2 THEN P_{13} (CF=0.85); *Rule 10:* IF P_{10} THEN P_{16} (CF=0.9)
Rule 3: IF P_3 THEN P_{13} (CF=0.9); *Rule 11:* IF P_{11} OR P_{12} THEN P_{17} (CF=0.9)
Rule 4: IF P_4 THEN P_{14} (CF=0.8); *Rule 12:* IF P_{13} THEN P_{15} AND P_{18}(CF=1.0)
Rule 5: IF P_5 THEN P_{14} (CF=0.85); *Rule 13:* IF P_{14} THEN P_{15} AND P_{18}(CF=0.9)
Rule 6: IF P_6 THEN P_{14} (CF=0.8); *Rule 14:* IF P_{15} THEN P_{18} (CF=0.9)
Rule 7: IF P_7 THEN P_{15} (CF=0.95); *Rule 15:* IF P_{16} THEN P_{15} (CF=0.85)
Rule 8: IF P_8 THEN P_{15} (CF=0.8); *Rule 16:* IF P_{17} THEN P_{18} (CF=0.85)

Table 1. Meaning of each proposition in fuzzy production rules for main circuit systems

P_1	pantograph bounce	P_{10}	nonlinear resistor sparkwear
P_2	mechanical part damaged	P_{11}	coil/main contact sparkwear
P_3	scratching of pantograph	P_{12}	contact in poor contact
P_4	insulating oil damp	P_{13}	no current in pantograph
P_5	cooling system breakdown	P_{14}	traction transformer breakdown
P_6	transformer internal breakdown	P_{15}	pulling motor inoperation
P_7	electrical strength reduction	P_{16}	circuit breaker inoperation
P_8	electromotor overload	P_{17}	contactor breakdown
P_9	isolating switch sparkwear	P_{18}	main circuit breakdown

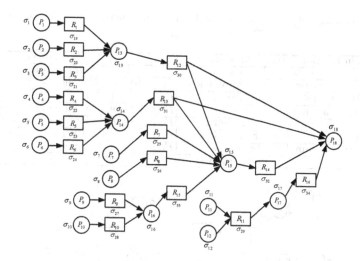

Fig. 3. A fault diagnosis model based on rFRSN P systems for the main circuit systems

3.2   A Fault Diagnosis Model for the Power Supply Systems

Fuzzy production rules (*Rules* 1 to 13), describing the relationships between breakdown signals detected and candidate faulty sections, for power supply systems of electric locomotives are described as follows, where CF represents the certainty (confidence) factor of a rule, $P_1, \ldots, P_{17}$ are propositions whose meanings are shown in Table 2. According to these fuzzy production rules, a fault diagnosis model based on rFRSN P systems for power supply systems $\Pi_2 = (O, \sigma_1, \ldots, \sigma_{30}, syn, in, out)$ is built, as shown in Fig. 4, where:

(1) $O = \{a\}$ is the singleton alphabet (a is called spike);
(2) $\sigma_1, \ldots, \sigma_{17}$ are proposition neurons associated with propositions $P_1, \ldots, P_{17}$, respectively;
(3) $\sigma_{18}, \ldots, \sigma_{21}, \sigma_{23}, \sigma_{24}, \sigma_{26}, \ldots, \sigma_{30}$ are *GENERAL* rule neurons associated with fuzzy production rules $R_1, \ldots, R_4, R_6, R_7, R_9, \ldots, R_{13}$, respectively; σ_{22} is an *OR* rule neuron associated with fuzzy production rule R_5; σ_{25} is an *AND* rule neuron associated with fuzzy production rule R_8;
(4) $syn = \{(1, 18), (2, 19), (3, 20), (4, 21), (5, 22), (6, 23), (7, 24), (8, 25), (9, 26),$ $(10, 27), (11, 22), (12, 28), (13, 25), (14, 29), (16, 30), (18, 17), (19, 10), (20, 10),$ $(21, 11), (22, 12), (23, 14), (23, 13), (24, 13), (25, 15), (26, 16), (27, 17), (27, 11),$ $(27, 13), (27, 14), (28, 14), (28, 17), (29, 16), (30, 17)\}$;
(5) $in = \{\sigma_1, \ldots, \sigma_9\}, out = \{\sigma_{15}, \sigma_{17}\}.$
    Rule 1: IF P_1 THEN P_{17} (CF=0.9)
    Rule 2: IF P_2 THEN P_{10} (CF=0.8)
    Rule 3: IF P_3 THEN P_{10} (CF=0.85)
    Rule 4: IF P_4 THEN P_{11} (CF=0.9)
    Rule 5: IF P_5 OR P_{11} THEN P_{12} (CF=0.85)
    Rule 6: IF P_6 THEN P_{13} AND P_{14} (CF=0.8)
    Rule 7: IF P_7 THEN P_{13} (CF=0.95)
    Rule 8: IF P_8 AND P_{13} THEN P_{15} (CF=0.85)
    Rule 9: IF P_9 THEN P_{16} (CF=0.9)

Table 2. Meaning of each proposition in fuzzy production rules for power supply systems

P_1	main traction invertor breakdown	P_9	fan breakdown
P_2	current collector breakdown	P_{10}	DC750V input breakdown
P_3	locomotive current collector breakdown	P_{11}	110V DC/DC chopper inoperation
P_4	110V DC/DC chopper breakdown	P_{12}	DC110V breakdown
P_5	110V accumulator breakdown	P_{13}	280V DC/DC chopper inoperation
P_6	auxiliary inverter breakdown	P_{14}	auxiliary inverter inoperation
P_7	280V DC/DC chopper breakdown	P_{15}	DC280V breakdown
P_8	280V accumulator breakdown	P_{16}	fan inoperation
P_{17}	main traction invertor inoperation		

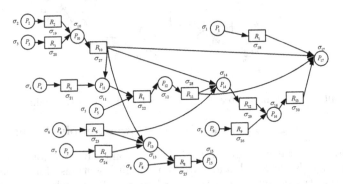

Fig. 4. A fault diagnosis model based on rFRSN P systems for the power supply systems

Rule 10: IF P_{10} THEN P_{11} AND P_{13} AND P_{14} AND P_{17} (CF=0.85)
Rule 11: IF P_{12} THEN P_{14} AND P_{17} (CF=0.8)
Rule 12: IF P_{14} THEN P_{16} (CF=0.95)
Rule 13: IF P_{16} THEN P_{17} (CF=0.9)

3.3 A Fault Diagnosis Model for the Traction and Braking Systems

Fuzzy production rules (*Rules* 1 to 10), describing the relationships between breakdown signals detected and candidate faulty sections, for traction and braking systems of electric locomotives are described as follows, where CF represents the certainty (confidence) factor of a rule, $P_1, \ldots, P_{16}$ are propositions whose meanings are shown in Table 3. According to these fuzzy production rules, a fault diagnosis model based on rFRSN P systems for traction and braking systems $\Pi_3 = (O, \sigma_1, \ldots, \sigma_{26}, syn, in, out)$ is built, as shown in Fig. 5, where:

(1) $O = \{a\}$ is the singleton alphabet (a is called spike);
(2) $\sigma_1, \ldots, \sigma_{16}$ are proposition neurons associated with propositions $P_1, \ldots, P_{16}$, respectively;
(3) $\sigma_{17}, \sigma_{18}, \sigma_{23}, \ldots, \sigma_{26}$ are *GENERAL* rule neurons associated with fuzzy production rules $R_1, R_2, R_7, \ldots, R_{10}$, respectively; $\sigma_{20}, \ldots, \sigma_{22}$ are *OR* rule neurons associated with fuzzy production rules $R_4, \ldots, R_6$, respectively;
(4) $syn = \{(1, 17), (2, 18), (3, 19), (4, 19), (5, 19), (6, 20), (7, 20), (8, 21), (9, 22),$ $(10, 23), (11, 22), (12, 24), (13, 25), (14, 26), (15, 21), (17, 16), (18, 16), (19, 13),$ $(20, 14), (21, 16), (22, 16), (23, 16), (24, 16), (25, 15), (26, 16)\}$;

(5) $in = \{\sigma_1, \ldots, \sigma_{12}\}$, $out = \{\sigma_{16}\}$.
   Rule 1: IF P_1 THEN P_{16} (CF=0.85)
   Rule 2: IF P_2 THEN P_{16} (CF=0.8)
   Rule 3: IF P_3 OR P_4 OR P_5 THEN P_{13} (CF=0.9)
   Rule 4: IF P_6 OR P_7 THEN P_{14} (CF=0.95)
   Rule 5: IF P_8 OR P_{15} THEN P_{16} (CF=0.9)
   Rule 6: IF P_9 OR P_{11} THEN P_{16} (CF=0.8)
   Rule 7: IF P_{10} THEN P_{16} (CF=0.7)
   Rule 8: IF P_{12} THEN P_{16} (CF=0.85)
   Rule 9: IF P_{13} THEN P_{15} (CF=0.95)
   Rule 10: IF P_{14} THEN P_{16} (CF=0.75)

Table 3. Meaning of each proposition in fuzzy production rules for traction and braking systems

P_1	DC110V breakdown	P_9	main protective relay breakdown
P_2	control source converter plate breakdown	P_{10}	traction power controller breakdown
P_3	U-phase current sensor breakdown	P_{11}	A/D breakdown
P_4	W-phase current sensor breakdown	P_{12}	25/5V breakdown
P_5	V-phase current sensor breakdown	P_{13}	more than one among P_3, P_4 and P_5 happen
P_6	first linear electromotor group breakdown	P_{14}	linear electromotor inoperation
P_7	second linear electromotor group breakdown	P_{15}	phase current sensor inoperation
P_8	main traction invertor breakdown	P_{16}	traction and braking system inoperation

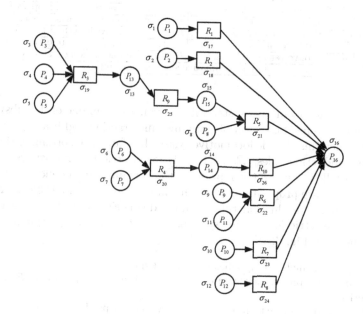

Fig. 5. A fault diagnosis model based on rFRSN P systems for the traction and braking systems

3.4   A Fault Diagnosis Model for the Electric Locomotive Systems

From Fig. 3 to Fig. 5, we know that if there is no current in pantograph or traction transformers breakdown or pulling motors inoperation or contactors breakdown, then the main circuit system of electric locomotive systems has faults; if DC750V input breakdown or fan inoperation or main traction invertor breakdown or DC110V breakdown, then the power supply system of electric locomotive systems has faults; if DC750V input breakdown or fan inoperation or main traction invertor breakdown or DC110V breakdown, then the power supply system of electric locomotive systems has faults; if the main traction invertor breakdown or DC110V breakdown or control source converter plate breakdown or main protective relay breakdown or traction power controller breakdown or A/D breakdown or 25/5V breakdown or linear electromotor inoperation or phase current sensor inoperation, then the traction and braking system of electric locomotive systems has faults.

Table 4. Meaning of each proposition in fuzzy production rules for electric locomotive systems

P_1	no current in pantograph	P_{10}	main protective relay breakdown
P_2	traction transformer breakdown	P_{11}	traction power controller breakdown
P_3	pulling motor inoperation	P_{12}	A/D breakdown
P_4	contactor breakdown	P_{13}	25/5V breakdown
P_5	DC750V input breakdown	P_{14}	linear electromotor inoperation
P_6	fan inoperation	P_{15}	phase current sensor inoperation
P_7	main traction invertor breakdown	P_{16}	main circuit system has faults
P_8	DC110V breakdown	P_{17}	power supply system has faults
P_9	control source converter plate breakdown	P_{18}	traction and braking system has faults
P_{19}	electric locomotive systems has faults		

For an electric locomotive system, if one or more than one of its subsystems (main circuit systems, power supply systems, and traction and braking systems) have faults, then this electric locomotive system has faults. According to the analysis, fuzzy production rules (*Rules* 1 to 4) for electric locomotive systems are described as follows, where CF represents the certainty (confidence) factor of a rule, $P_1, \ldots, P_{19}$ are propositions whose meanings are shown in Table 4. According to these fuzzy production rules, a fault diagnosis model based on rFRSN P systems for electric locomotive systems $\Pi_4 = (O, \sigma_1, \ldots, \sigma_{23}, syn, in, out)$ is built, as shown in Fig. 6, where:

(1) $O = \{a\}$ is the singleton alphabet (a is called spike);
(2) $\sigma_1, \ldots, \sigma_{19}$ are proposition neurons associated with propositions $P_1, \ldots, P_{19}$, respectively;
(3) $\sigma_{20}, \ldots, \sigma_{23}$ are OR rule neurons associated with fuzzy production rules $R_1, \ldots, R_4$, respectively;
(4) $syn = \{(1, 20), (2, 20), (3, 20), (4, 20), (5, 21), (6, 21), (7, 21), (7, 22), (8, 21), (8, 22),$ $(9, 22), (10, 22), (11, 22), (12, 22), (13, 22), (14, 22), (15, 22), (16, 23), (17, 23),$ $(18, 23), (20, 16), (21, 17), (22, 18), (23, 19)\}$;
(5) $in = \{\sigma_1, \ldots, \sigma_{15}\}$, $out = \{\sigma_{19}\}$.

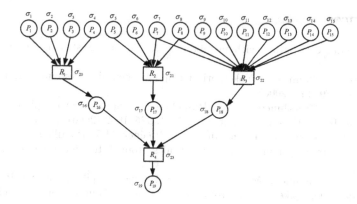

Fig. 6. A fault diagnosis model based on rFRSN P systems for the electric locomotive systems

Rule 1: IF P_1 OR P_2 OR P_3 OR P_4 THEN P_{16} (CF=0.95)
Rule 2: IF P_5 OR P_6 OR P_7 OR P_8 THEN P_{17} (CF=0.95)
Rule 3: IF P_7 OR P_8 OR P_9 OR P_{10} OR P_{11} OR P_{12} OR P_{13} OR P_{14} OR
        P_{15} THEN P_{18} (CF=0.95)
Rule 4: IF P_{16} OR P_{17} OR P_{18} THEN P_{19} (CF=0.98)

4   Conclusions

In this study, rFRSN P systems are applied in fault diagnosis of electric locomotive systems. This study focuses on describing relationships among breakdown signals, faulty sections, faulty subsystems and faulty electric locomotive systems in the form of fuzzy production rules by using syntactical ingredients provided by rFRSN P systems. It proposes fault diagnosis models based on rFRSN P systems for SS4 electric locomotive systems. These models can visually and formally describe relationships among breakdown signals detected and candidate faulty sections or faulty systems. This work is an important theoretical basis for proposing a novel bio-inspired method for fault diagnosis of electric locomotive systems by using rFRSN P systems. To test and verify the practical implementation and scalability of the proposed method, our future work includes the development of diagnosis algorithms for the models proposed in this paper and model reduction algorithms for the models used in specific cases. Experiments with a tool we aim to develop will prove the effectiveness of these algorithms and the approach presented in this paper.

Acknowledgments. This work is supported by the National Natural Science Foundation of China (61170016, 61373047, 61170030), the Program for New Century Excellent Talents in University (NCET-11-0715) and SWJTU supported project (SWJTU12CX008). The last author acknowledges the support of the project TIN 2012-3734 of the Ministerio de Economía y Competitividad of Spain.

References

1. Păun, Gh.: Computing with membranes. J. Comput. Syst. Sci. **61**(1), 108–143 (2000)
2. Ionescu, M., Păun, Gh., Yokomori, T.: Spiking neural P systems. Fund. Inform. **71**(2–3), 279–308 (2006)
3. Păun, Gh., Pérez-Jiménez, M.J., Rozenberg, G.: Spike train in spiking neural P systems. Int. J. Found. Comput. Sci. **17**(4), 975–1002 (2006)
4. Chen, H., Ishdorj, T.O., Păun, Gh., Pérez-Jiménez, M.J.: Handling languages with spiking neural P systems with extended rules. Rom. J. Inf. Sci. Tech. **9**(3), 151–162 (2006)
5. Freund, R., Ionescu, M., Oswald, M.: Extended spiking neural P systems with decaying spikes and/or total spiking. Int. J. Found. Comput. Sci. **19**(5), 1223–1234 (2008)
6. Cavaliere, M., Ibarra, O.H., Păun, Gh., Egecioglu, O., Ionescu, M., Woodworth, S.: Asynchronous spiking neural P systems. Theor. Comput. Sci. **410**(24–25), 2352–2364 (2009)
7. Pan, L.Q., Păun, Gh.: Spiking neural P systems: an improved normal form. Theor. Comput. Sci. **411**(6), 906–918 (2010)
8. Pan, L.Q., Zeng, X.X.: Small universal spiking neural P systems working in exhaustive mode. IEEE Trans. on Nanobiosci. **10**(2), 99–105 (2011)
9. Metta, V.P., Krithivasan, K., Garg, D.: Spiking neural P systems with anti-spikes as transducers. Rom. J. Inf. Sci. Tech. **14**(1), 20–30 (2011)
10. Ionescu, M., Păun, Gh., Pérez-Jiménez, M.J., Rodríguez-Patón, A.: Spiking neural P systems with several types of spikes. Int. J. Comput. Commun. **71**(2–3), 648–656 (2011)
11. Zhang, X.Y., Luo, B., Fang, X.Y., Pan, L.Q.: Sequential spiking neural P systems with exhaustive use of rules. BioSystems **108**, 52–62 (2012)
12. Cabarle, F.C., Adorna, H.N., Martínez-del-Amor, M.A., Pérez-Jiménez, M.J.: Improving GPU simulations of spiking neural P systems. Rom. J. Inf. Sci. Tech. **15**(1), 5–20 (2012)
13. Cabarle, F.G.C., Adorna, H.N.: On structures and behaviors of spiking neural P systems and Petri nets. In: Csuhaj-Varjú, E., Gheorghe, M., Rozenberg, G., Salomaa, A., Vaszil, Gy. (eds.) CMC 2012. LNCS, vol. 7762, pp. 145–160. Springer, Heidelberg (2013)
14. Song, T., Pan, L.Q., Păun, Gh.: Asynchronous spiking neural P systems with local synchronization. Inform. Sciences **219**, 197–207 (2013)
15. Jiang, K.Q., Song, T., Pan, L.Q.: Universality of sequential spiking neural P systems based on minimum spike number. Theor. Comput. Sci. **499**, 88–97 (2013)
16. Zhang, G.X., Rong, H.N., Neri, F., Pérez-Jiménez, M.J.: An optimization spiking neural P system for approximately solving combinatorial optimization problems. Int. J. Neural Syst. **24**(5), 1–15 (2014)
17. Wang, J., Shi, P., Peng, H., Pérez-Jiménez, M.J., Wang, T.: Weighted fuzzy spiking neural P system. IEEE Trans. Fuzzy Syst. **21**(2), 209–220 (2013)
18. Peng, H., Wang, J., Pérez-Jiménez, M.J., Wang, H., Shao, J., Wang, T.: Fuzzy reasoning spiking neural P system for fault diagnosis. Inform. Sciences **235**, 106–116 (2013)
19. Xiong, G.J., Shi, D.Y., Zhu, L., Duan, X.Z.: A new approach to fault diagnosis of power systems using fuzzy reasoning spiking neural P systems. Math. Probl. Eng. (2013). http://dx.doi.org/10.1155/2013/815352

20. Wang, T., Zhang, G.X., Rong, H.N., Pérez-Jiménez, M.J.: Application of fuzzy reasoning spiking neural P systems to fault diagnosis. Int. J. Comput. Commun. **9**(6), 786–799 (2014)
21. Tu, M., Wang, J., Peng, H., Shi, P.: Application of adaptive fuzzy spiking neural P systems in fault diagnosis of power systems. Chinese J. Electron. **23**(1), 87–92 (2014)
22. Zhang, C.Y.: Research on fault diagnosis method of electric locomotive systems based on Petri net (M.S Degree Thesis). Central South University, Changsha, China (2010)
23. Zhang, Y.S., Zhu, L.J.: Shaoshan4 Locomotive. Chinese Railway Publishing House, Beijing (2001)

Author Index

Printed in the United States
By Bookmasters

Printed in the United States
By Bookmasters